GENDER
Crossing Boundaries

Grace Galliano
Kennesaw State University

WADSWORTH
CENGAGE Learning™

Australia • Brazil • Japan • Korea • Mexico • Singapore • Spain • United Kingdom • United States

WADSWORTH
CENGAGE Learning

Gender: Crossing Boundaries
Grace Galliano

Psychology Editor: Marianne Taflinger

Assistant Editor: Dan Moneypenny

Editorial Assistant: Nicole Root

Marketing Manager: Lori Grebe

Marketing Assistant: Laurel Anderson

Project Manager, Editorial Production:
    Kirk Bomont

Print Buyer: Vena Dyer

Permissions Editor: Karyn Morrison

Production Service:
    Scratchgravel Publishing Services

Text Designer: Anne Draus, Scratchgravel
    Publishing Services

Photo Researcher: Robin Sterling

Copy Editor: Linda Purrington

Illustrator: Greg Draus,
    Scratchgravel Publishing Services

Cover Designer: Irene Morris

Cover Image: Bob Krist/Corbis

Compositor: Scratchgravel Publishing
    Services

For product information and technology assistance, contact us at
Cengage Learning Customer & Sales Support, 1-800-354-9706

For permission to use material from this text or product,
submit all requests online at **www.cengage.com/permissions**
Further permissions questions can be e-mailed to
permissionrequest@cengage.com

Library of Congress Control Number: 2002104236

ISBN-13: 978-0-534-39126-3

ISBN-10: 0-534-39126-5

Wadsworth Cengage Learning
20 Davis Drive
Belmont, CA 94002-3098
USA

Cengage Learning is a leading provider of customized learning solutions with office locations around the globe, including Singapore, the United Kingdom, Australia, Mexico, Brazil, and Japan. Locate your local office at **www.cengage.com/global**

Cengage Learning products are represented in Canada by Nelson Education, Ltd.

To learn more about Wadsworth, visit **www.cengage.com/wadsworth**

Purchase any of our products at your local college store or at our preferred online store **www.cengagebrain.com**

Printed in the United States of America
6 7 8 9 10   18 17 16 15 14

Brief Contents

Contents

PART II   A Life Span Approach to Understanding Gender

4
Gender and the Body   63
Hindsight, Oversights, and Insights

5
Life Span Gender Development   90
From Womb to Tomb

PART III   The Gendered Life

9
Gender and Education   187
Choices, Changes, and the Status Quo

10
Gender and Work   211
Segregation Now, Segregation Forever?

11
Gender and Physical Health   237
On Labor, Lifestyle, and Longevity

15
Gender and the Future   331
A Global View

Features

ABCs of GENDER (ATTITUDES, BEHAVIORS, AND CONCERNS)

ZOOM & ENLARGE

SLIDE SHOW

Preface

My primary goal in writing this book was to create an engaging, thought-provoking text that offers the most current thinking and findings on gender—all in a multicultural and cross-cultural context. After many years in the classroom at an institution devoted to instructional excellence, particularly in psychology, the excitement of learning and teaching remains alive within me. I hope to communicate some of that excitement and intrinsic pleasure to the student reader.

Why a Text on the Psychology of Gender?

Innovations in psychology (and other fields as well) traverse a predictable pathway. At first they represent a radical departure from the status quo. If valuable and productive, they are slowly integrated into the mainstream. These innovations change the mainstream and are in turn modified by their acceptance and integration. In the 1960s, a course on the psychology of women represented a true innovation, a needed challenge to the androcentric and ethnocentric traditions of psychology. Today, such courses are a respected and established part of the course offerings at most colleges and universities. The insights, perspectives, and research findings gleaned from the study of women's psychology are now well integrated into mainstream psychology. There will always be instructors who strongly believe in the need for a course that attends to the special issues and life experiences of women. There will also be instructors who see the need for a comparable course on the psychology of men. Both areas of study are worthwhile explorations of human diversity, but by their very nature the courses emphasize the *differences* between women and men. Yet the overwhelming conclusion is that women and men are more similar than different. Consideration of a psychology of gender allows equal play to both differences and similarities.

Forty years of transformation in both the real world and within psychology have convinced me that a psychology of *gender* is now a more useful approach. Women's struggle for equality continues all over the world, and that struggle is in relation to men. To understand the persistent personal and institutional barriers to equality, one must understand both men and women as equally gendered.

Every human society is organized on the basis of gender. That is, some roles, statuses, and behaviors are prescribed as appropriate for women and some are prescribed for men. Yet in postindustrial societies, there is greater and greater overlap in the roles, statuses, and behaviors of men and women. Thus it seems more practical and realistic to study both women and men in those shared roles, statuses, and behaviors. The 19th-century notion of "separate spheres" is indeed outmoded.

Perceived differences in the personalities and behaviors of women and men have been shown to be largely due to situational and contextual factors. Among the most powerful of those factors are the gender-related norms and expectations that men and women bring to all their social interactions. These norms and expectations become more visible in the presence of members of the other gender. Again, this social reality can be analyzed only by considering both women and men.

Guiding Principles in Preparing This Book

The psychology of gender is an evolving area of knowledge and understanding. Research findings continue to accumulate, and a theoretical synthesis of those findings is an ongoing process. It is exciting to delve into an area rich with innovative material. It is also humbling to realize how quickly new research findings, social changes, and world events can alter our thinking about gender.

The study of gender is a multidisciplinary endeavor. Gender is an intrapsychic, interpersonal, social, and cultural phenomenon, and therefore the insights of anthropologists and sociologists as well as psychologists are invaluable in reaching some understanding of the issues. The spirit of this text also seeks to honor the insights of selected philosophers, poets, theologians, and political thinkers.

Gender roles and gender relations are not static. Every society's current gender arrangements are powerful enough to create the illusion that they are somehow universal and immutable. However, historical and cross-cultural perspectives make it clear that constructions of gender have changed over the centuries and will continue to change in the future.

The world is too small to focus solely on the gender roles and gender relations of middle-class college students in the United States. The 21st-century student will be a citizen of the world. Thus, students must become exquisitely aware of the many forms that gender takes all over the world and be prepared to encounter and appreciate both gender universals and gender distinctions.

Gender is a lifelong process. From birth to death, gender affects both the experiences that life brings to us and the choices we make. A developmental perspective on gender roles is an enlightening one.

Attention to sound pedagogical principles can enhance both the teaching and learning experiences. I have tried to apply the experience gained in the undergraduate classroom in structuring this text.

Learners are the best teachers. By having this text classroom tested, I received invaluable information about what interested and perhaps moved the student reader. That feedback has been incorporated into the structure and content of the text.

Organization of the Text

The text is unevenly divided into four parts. The first part (*Foundations for a Psychology of Gender*) includes three chapters and establishes a solid philosophical and methodological base for the study of the psychology of gender.

The second part (*A Life Span Approach to Understanding Gender*) examines the varied facets of gender as they exist over the course of a lifetime. The section begins with a chapter about the physical markers that each society uses for gender assignment and for achieving gender ideals. Subsequent chapters cover the developmental and interpersonal aspects of gender.

The third part (*The Gendered Life*) is devoted to those aspects of life experience where gender constructions and gender relations play an important role. Sexuality, education, occupation, and health are explored here.

The last part of the text (*The Gendered Society*) moves to a more sociological level of analysis. An examination of how media both reflect and maintain current gender arrangements begins this section. Power differentials are a central component of traditional gender roles and relations, and thus a careful analysis of power on both the personal and political levels follows. The last chapter explores projections of gender roles and gender relations in the future.

Chapter Openers and Special Features

Every chapter begins with a thought-provoking quotation related to the material in the chapter. These quotations can easily serve as starting points for class activities, discussions, or lectures.

Also at the beginning of each chapter is a vignette entitled *Encounters with Gender*. Each vignette poses a problem or dilemma related to one or more facets of gender as discussed in that chapter. In the vignettes, gender-related issues are presented in a varied historical, cross-cultural, or multicultural context. Through a series of questions, the student is asked to reflect on what gender-related and/or culture-related factors may be at work in creating the scenario described in the vignette. In the body of each chapter reference is made to the *Encounter* to illustrate or exemplify an important point or concept.

Throughout each chapter *Critical Thinking Challenges* invite the reader to think more deeply and more critically about the material at hand. These challenges can also serve as fruitful foundations for group or whole-class discussions. For example, in Chapter 6 (on a life span view of gender and relationships), the reader is asked to reflect on traditional American wedding rituals. What is the symbolism involved in a father "giving the bride away" to her husband? Why does a bride's family traditionally pay for the wedding? In Chapter 11 (on gender and physical health) students are asked to reflect on gender differences in longevity and evaluate which of two competing explanations seems more valid to them.

The boxed feature entitled *ABC's of Gender (Attitude, Beliefs, and Concerns)* invites the student/reader to self-evaluate and self-report on an issue of gender-related behavior that is relevant to the chapter content. For example, in Chapter 1 (an overview of the psychology of gender) students are asked to explore their perceptions and beliefs regarding the behavior of men and women. They are also asked to note how their beliefs and observations can form the basis for stereotypes. In Chapter 10 (on gender and work) students investigate their own attitudes about gender and occupation. They are asked to create pie charts to illustrate their projections about how they will balance employment and family responsibilities in the future. They can then compare their ideal situation with what they believe is a more realistic expectation.

The *Zoom & Enlarge* boxes offer an expanded exploration of an interesting or unusual gender-related issue. For example, in Chapter 2 (on methods in gender research), this feature explores the controversy regarding whether psychologists should study gender differences at all. In Chapter 5 (on gender through the life span, the Zoom & Enlarge box examines cultural and gender-related differences in death rituals. Chapter 9 (on gender and education) includes a box on the Taliban's attempted destruction of the education, employment, and health of Afghani girls and women.

The *Slide Show* boxes offer a cross-cultural look into a gender-related issue. For example, in Chapter 8 (on gender and sexuality) the significance of same-sex sexual behavior is explored in societies as diverse as Mexico, Micronesia, southern Africa, early 20th-century China, Native American tribes, ancient Greece, modern India, and Zimbabwe. In Chapter 14 (on gender and power), the issue of domestic violence is examined in Russia, Brazil, Lebanon, Romania, Serbia, and Quebec, Canada.

Several cartoons throughout the book offer a more lighthearted and occasionally poignant look at various aspects of gender and gender relations.

Contributing to Successful Learning

I have attempted to create this text with equal attention to motivating student interest and facilitating student learning.

In terms of pedagogical aids, a complete outline is offered at the beginning of every chapter, followed by a set of learning objectives. Many instructors have strong feelings about the utility and benefit of learning objectives. Some instructors believe they move the student toward memorization and the empty parroting of concepts. They may believe that students lose sight of the bigger picture contained within a chapter. Other instructors believe learning objectives focus the student's attention on the organization and interrelationships of the important content of the chapter. For instructors and students who find learning objectives helpful, they lay out the criteria for mastery of the chapter's content.

An introductory overview of each chapter prepares the student for what is to come and prompts the reader regarding the organization and emphases of the chapter.

Every chapter includes a running glossary with new or unusual terms set in boldface and defined on the same page on which they appear. Students typically report that this is one of most helpful features for a text to have. The chapters end with a summary list, thereby providing another overview of the main points.

Wherever a large body of related knowledge is presented, a summary table offers the student an overview of the material. For example, Chapter 3 (on theories of gender) introduces a multitude of theoretical approaches to the development and maintenance of gender identity and gender-related behavior. A summary table names the various theoretical approaches, lists the central concerns of the theory, offers the names of the major proponents of those theories, and lists some of the major concepts associated with the theory.

Student reviewers were unequivocal about two textbook features that assist them in reading, comprehending, and retaining chapter content: (1) numerous practical examples for all concepts introduced and (2) intermittent review breaks in the flow of text. Every attempt has been made to respond to these suggestions for pedagogical improvement.

What's Distinctive About This Text?

◆ Chapter 1, *Thinking About Sex and Gender: Doing What Doesn't Come Naturally*. Whereas most gender texts begin with an exploration of the distinction between sex and gender, this first chapter offers a thorough multifaceted definition of gender. It presents gender as an intrapsychic, interpersonal, social, and cultural phenomenon. The chapter also sets the stage for a multicultural perspective on gender. The *Zoom & Enlarge* box called "Gender and the Beginning Student" is my personal favorite because it offers the voice of the beginning student in defining gender.

◆ Chapter 2, *Studying Gender: False Starts and Leaps into the Abyss*. In addition to an overview of the methods used to study gender, this chapter explores the history of the psychology of gender. A *Zoom & Enlarge* feature asks the question, "Should Psychologists Study Gender Differences?" A *Slide Show* box takes a novel approach to showing the application of research methods. It summarizes a series of gender-related studies carried out in several nations (China, the West Bank of Palestine, Peru, Finland, Spain, and the United States).

◆ Chapter 3, *Theories of Gender: On Fallacies and "Phallocies."* Beginning with a quick historical overview, the chapter looks across disciplines to explore various approaches to gender. One section of the chapter is devoted to an Eastern perspective on gender and the maintenance of harmony (*yin* and *yang*). An unusual *Zoom & Enlarge* box explores the understandings offered by a cross-species perspective.

◆ Chapter 4, *Gender and the Body: Hindsight, Oversights, and Insights*. This chapter explores the various bodily aspects of gender, including neuroanatomy and ostensible brain-based cognitive differences. One unusual feature of the chapter is an exploration of how various intersex conditions affect the development of gender. Another feature of the chapter that is likely to have strong interest for students is a historical and cross-cultural discussion about the modification of genitalia to mark cultural membership and/or gender ideals.

◆ Chapter 5, *Life Span Gender Development: From Womb to Tomb*. This chapter offers a life span developmental view of gender and gender roles. Of course, the process of gender role socialization is discussed, but some unique content covers the relationship between gender and the care-giver role across cultures. The gender-related aspects of both widowhood and death are also examined across selected cultures.

◆ Chapter 6, *Gender and Relationships: A Lifetime of Connected Lives*. Throughout life, gender is a major determinant of how we conduct our relationships. Some unique features of this chapter involve a discussion of gender and sibling relationships, cross-sex friendships, and romantic relationships among gay and lesbian couples. A discussion of the marital relationship takes a historical and cross-cultural perspective, with special attention to the impact of slavery and segregation on African-American marriages. There are two unusual boxed features. One involves the adaptation of American Valentine's Day rituals into Japanese corporate culture and the other looks at modern-day polygamy in the United States.

◆ Chapter 7, *Gender as Social Performance: A Worldview*. This chapter opens with an exploration of what are considered the *core essences* of the differences between women and men. This should engender an intense classroom discussion on students' views of the basic nature of men and women, masculinity and femininity. The gender-in-context perspective is applied in confronting strongly held beliefs on gender-related differences in emotional expressiveness, personality characteristics, and social behavior. A box discusses the origins of linguistic gender, with a cross-cultural perspective that helps the student see that gender isn't always the basis for language forms. Students are also challenged to come up with nonsexist versions of common words and concepts.

◆ Chapter 8, *Gender and Sexuality: Private Lives and Public Meanings*. This chapter offers a unique examination of how gender influences private sexuality as well as the public meanings attached to sexual expression. An in-depth examination of the gender-related aspects of same-sex sexual orientation follows, including a boxed feature on the varied meanings of same-sex sexual expression across several cultures. The gender-related aspects of both erotic and reproductive sexuality across selected cultures are discussed. A section on "problematic sexuality" explores the private problem of sexual dysfunction and the public problem of commercialized sex.

◆ Chapter 9, *Gender and Education: Choices, Changes, and the Status Quo*. Students believe they freely choose their educational pathways, often without realizing how powerfully gender influences their decision-making processes. The special relationships among gender, mathematics, the sciences, and information technology are discussed at length. A section on education across cultures contrasts the educational issues of industrial and postindustrial nations with those of achieving basic literacy in the developing world.

◆ Chapter 10, *Gender and Work: Segregation Now, Segregation Forever?* In keeping with the attempt to provide a sociocultural context for the text, this chapter presents a brief history of human work. The origins and current status of occupational segregation are analyzed. An unusual section on occupational barriers in management follows. The concepts of the sticky floor, the glass ceiling, and the high-speed escalator for some who cross traditional occupational boundaries will intrigue students. The balancing act between employment and family responsibilities is explored by comparing parental-leave and child-care policies of the United States, Canada, and Sweden. A student-contributed boxed essay offers a close-up view of what happens to men who take on jobs that are considered traditionally feminine. In a self-assessment exercise students evaluate their own attitudes about gender and work. They can then project their own future plans regarding the balance between occupational and family life responsibilities. This exercise should provide the fuel for a passionate discussion about gender, work, and family, especially in the current uncertain economic climate.

◆ Chapter 11, *Gender and Physical Health: On Labor, Lifestyle, and Longevity.* This chapter was written with the special expertise offered by Dr. Linda Travis, a clinical health and geropsychologist at the University of Rochester Medical Center, Department of Psychiatry. An unusual historical and cross-cultural analysis of gender roles, health, and illness begins the chapter. My own attraction to word play is evidenced in the contrast between occupational factors in health (production) and maternal health (reproduction). The various lifestyle aspects of traditional masculinity are associated with increased health risks. The chapter ends with a discussion of the central paradox of gender and physical health. Students can assess their own level of knowledge about gender and health through a self-administered questionnaire. In studying the material on gender and cross-cultural health, students will learn why even though less than 2% of South Korean women smoke, the rate of lung cancer deaths among them is rising sharply. They will also learn why more women than men are diagnosed with dementia.

◆ Chapter 12, *Gender and Mental Health: On Labels, Culture, and Boundary Violations.* The chapter begins with a vignette that illustrates how gender norms and culture can interact in influencing perceptions of mental health and psychopathology. Later in the chapter, gender-related factors in culture-bound syndromes are discussed. Eating disorders are discussed as a culture-bound syndrome. The areas of transgenderism and transvestism are presented with acknowledgment that these behaviors are considered disorders in Western society but may have varied meanings in other cultures. Five diagnostic categories of psychopathology are explored in terms of their gender-related features. In two, men predominate (substance use disorders and antisocial personality disorder). Women predominate in two others (affective disorders and anxiety disorders). A *Zoom & Enlarge* box on gender, culture, and psychopathology in modern Israel offers an interesting parallel with the United States. Students also have an opportunity to evaluate how their gender influences the way they cope with stressful and disturbing events.

◆ Chapter 13, *Gender and the Media: Tribal Tales for the 21st Century.* Standard topics for this area include how media influence gender socialization and how advertising both reflects and influences a society's gender norms and ideals. What is unusual in this chapter is the notion of television as a family life educator and an overview of changes in the presentation of gay men and lesbians in the mass media. The most unique aspect of the chapter involves a discussion of media that are relatively gender segregated, including pornography, media sports, soap operas, and talk shows. Magazines that cater more to one gender are also discussed. A boxed feature explores how gender issues have been depicted recently in films around the world. Two films that are considered the "best comedies ever made" both involve "gender-transgressive" themes.

◆ Chapter 14, *Gender and Power: The Personal and the Political.* This chapter begins with an analysis of power as a core component of the masculine gender role. Three examples of coercive power on the personal level are discussed (sexual harassment, domestic violence, and sexual assault). The chapter then moves to the societal level for an analysis of how masculine power is exerted through the legal, political, and military systems. Organized religion is also discussed as a source of gender-related power. The chapter looks at the ongoing process by which women are coming to share power in these social institutions. This transformation is exemplified in a boxed feature about two of the most powerful women in American foreign policy (*A Tale of Two Women: The Strongest Link*).

◆ Chapter 15, *Gender and the Future: A Global View.* The world changed on September 11, 2001. On that date, new spiritual, economic, and sociopolitical forces were set into motion all over the world. It is still too early to predict how they will influence the future of gender roles and gender relations. What is clear is that one of the tenets of the extremism that inspires terrorist acts is to attack and destroy symbols of social, economic, and political change. Some of the changes that are so threatening to these extremists exist in the worldwide movement toward greater gender equality.

Many futures are possible. This chapter makes few predictions about the future, but it raises many gender-related questions that will be answered during the reader's lifetime.

Acknowledgments

Marianne Taflinger has been a bountiful source of support, strategy, and creative inspiration. My heartfelt thanks go out to her. Anne Draus of Scratchgravel Publishing Services has been patient and persistent all through the complex process of transformation from manuscript to readable book. Bonnie Allen has truly been the most resourceful finder of lost and recalcitrant references to ever walk the earth. She helped me rest peacefully when I was not writing or revising the manuscript. Karyn Morrison has done an admirable job in securing permissions from innumerable sources. Robin Sterling shared her creative talents in securing the photographs that illustrate the text. My thanks also go to copy editor Linda Purrington. The flawless pages may be attributed to her carefulness, while any remaining errors or omissions can be safely attributed to me.

A special thanks to Lisa Crowe, a delightful and dedicated student, whom I am very proud to now consider a friend and colleague. As my research assistant, Lisa provided many hours of informative discussion and practical feedback. She consistently exceeded my expectations regarding every task I gave her. I predict a successful career in psychology for her. I couldn't have done it without her.

I also want to thank Dr. Linda Noble, Dean of Humanities and Social Sciences, and Dr. Valerie Whittlesey, chair of the Psychology Department at Kennesaw State University, for their practical and administrative support all through the creation of this text. Dr. Celia Reaves and Elaine Derrenbacher of Monroe Community College also deserve my thanks for their understanding and support during the last stages of creative frenzy.

Special and enormous thanks go to Dr. John Williams at Wake Forest University. His generosity of spirit and sage advice helped move this text to its present form. Michelle Tomarelli and her Psychology of Gender students at Texas A&M wrestled with this text when it was in a much more primitive form. Their views and reviews proved invaluable in making this book more student friendly and pedagogically sound. My thanks to Michelle and all her students.

A dedicated group of reviewers offered just the right balance of praise and criticism to help improve this text. The reviewers included Krianne Bursik at Suffolk University, Rose Cleary at Lewiston-Auburn College, Kathleen Crowley-Long at College of St. Rose, Janet Dizinno at St. Mary's University, Carie Forden at Clarion University of Pennsylvania, Beverly Goodwin at Indiana University of Pennsylvania, Suzy Horton at Mesa Community College, Barbara Ilardi at the University of Rochester, Robin Kowalski at Western Carolina University, Wendy Palmquist at Plymouth State College, Elizabeth Paul at the College of New Jersey, Anne Peplau at the University of California, Los Angeles, Cheryl Rickabaugh at the University of Redlands, William Russell at Graceland University, and Barbara Winstead at Old Dominion University.

Thanks also to my family, friends, and colleagues who patiently listened and listened and then listened some more as I labored over each chapter and feature. Thanks for your understanding and humor about it all.

Grace Galliano

1 Thinking About Sex and Gender
Doing What Doesn't Come Naturally

The great enemy of truth is often not the lie—deliberate, contrived and dishonest—but the myth—persistent, persuasive and unrealistic. Too often we hold fast to the clichés of our forebears. We subject all facts to a prefabricated set of interpretations. We enjoy the comfort of opinion without the discomfort of thought. ◆ J. F. Kennedy

Learning Objectives

After studying this chapter, you should be able to:

1. List and describe 10 components of the concept of gender.
2. Distinguish between the concepts of sex and gender, elaborating on the distinction between *sex differences* and *gender differences*.
3. Offer five reasons for studying the psychology of gender.
4. Explain why, in spite of a major methodological flaw, a cross-cultural perspective on gender is both theoretically useful and personally practical.
5. Compare the sources of gender-related knowledge for the layperson versus those of the gender scholar.
6. Explain the problematic aspects of the term *race* in describing groups and group differences.
7. Explain the problematic aspects of the term *difference* in describing the behaviors of women and men.
8. Explain the problematic aspects of relying on *individual experience* in attempting to understand gender.
9. List and describe eight themes that will characterize the presentation of the psychology of gender in this text.

Encounters with Gender

Melissa Smith, an African American, engages the legal services of attorney David Carlebach in a complex property dispute. She confers with him in his office many times, and they form a warm, professional relationship. In the course of her office visits, she notices that he always wears the small black skullcap (yarmulke) that signifies his identity as an Orthodox Jew. Mr. Carlebach is very successful in his legal representation, and Melissa is overjoyed at the outcome of the settlement. At their final meeting, Melissa steps toward David, reaches out to shake his hand, and moves closer to offer an appreciative, friendly hug. The attorney suddenly looks upset, and firmly twists his whole body away from Melissa so that she cannot come near him. He does not even shake hands with Melissa. Is this man just cold and distant? Is he deeply prejudiced against African Americans? Has Melissa violated professional boundaries? How do you view this encounter?

Overview

This first chapter begins with a far-ranging definition and explanation of the term *gender*. Be prepared for some surprises about this. I then mention some good reasons for embarking on a detailed study of gender and leave room for you to consider your own personal reasons for doing so. Some of the most commonly asked gender-related questions for members of North American society follow. The text takes a cross-cultural and multicultural perspective on gender. This approach examines gender as it exists across different societies and also in the different social and ethnic groups within North American society. There are crucial advantages to taking a cross-cultural and

multicultural perspective, as explained in this text. Most people rely on their own personal gender-related experiences to understand this complex phenomenon. In this text I rely on scientific studies and interdisciplinary insights to understand and explain gender.

Keep several issues in mind as you embark on your study of gender. These issues include the use of the term *race*, what we mean when we talk about gender differences, and whether our individual experiences are useful in understanding gender. A clear understanding of these issues will help clear your path of cognitive and ideological "junk." We then move to some important themes that will recur all through your reading of this book. You can spot them in the chapters ahead.

By the way, we'll get back to David and Melissa later on in the chapter. You will be seeing a comparable Encounter with Gender feature at the beginning of each chapter.

What Is Gender?

The study of gender is the study of human beings as women and men. People have been thinking and writing about men and women since the beginning of recorded history. In the past, most of those who recorded their thoughts on the subject were philosophers, physicians, writers, political leaders, religious leaders, artists, and song writers. And most were men, speaking from their own perspective. Psychologists too began thinking, writing, studying, and making pronouncements about women and men from the very earliest days of psychology. However, the systematic study of sex and gender really became a "hot item" in psychology and the other social sciences during the 1970s. It remains an area of lively research and debate, and it will continue to be so, well into the future. The psychology of gender is a controversial area of inquiry that is still "under construction," so this text can only offer you the latest word rather than the *last* word on the subject. We can begin by examining how some fairly typical beginning college students think about what gender is and is not (see Box 1.1). Compare their views with some more scholarly thinking about the meaning of gender (Deaux & LaFrance, 1998).

The term *gender* refers to the behaviors and cognitive processes that are more or less distinctive for women and men in a particular society. Another way of saying this is that gender is the sum of the observable differences between women and men. Of course, these behaviors and cognitive processes overlap greatly, yet defining gender in this way tends to emphasize the differences rather than the similarities among women and men.

Gender is a set of **stereotypes**. Here the emphasis is on *our beliefs* about the characteristics of men and women (see Box 1.2 to evaluate your beliefs about the typical, or perhaps stereotypical, characteristics of women and men). These beliefs may or may not be accurate, but they are incredibly powerful in influencing how we perceive women and men, how we interpret what they do and how we interact with members of both groups. These beliefs even influence how we perceive and evaluate ourselves. Gender stereotypes persist in at least five areas: personality traits, family roles, occupational roles, personal style, leisure activities, and appearances (Deaux, 1999).

Gender is a core aspect of internal self-identity. Here I am talking about the intrapsychic aspect of gender. The term *gender* refers to your inner sense of who you are. Being a woman or a man is a central aspect of who you experience yourself to be in the world. When asked to complete the statement "I am . . ." several times, most people are likely to refer to their gender within the first two or three responses. This demonstrates the centrality of gender to self-concept. Your sense of yourself as a gendered person operates at three levels. At the *cognitive* level, gender affects how you think about yourself, other people, and the world in general. At the *affective* (feeling) level, gender is related to how people respond emotionally, and how they evaluate those feelings. At the *behavioral* level, gender influences what people do in particular situations or environments (West & Fenstermaker, 1995).

For the vast majority of human beings, gender is an aspect of the self that is more profound, central, and stable than ethnicity, nationality, family role, age, religion, social status, or occupation. The depth of this core aspect of self-concept is seen by the confusion (and perhaps revulsion?) that many people feel at the idea of someone wanting to "pass" as a member of the other gender. It is very difficult for most of us to understand someone wanting to alter his or her body and lifestyle to fit that of the "other" gender.

Gender is a social category and social identity. Gender represents the first and most basic social learning about what people are ("he's a boy, a daddy, a man" and "she's a girl, a mommy, a woman"). This identity may be automatically given to someone by virtue of being born. For example, in many societies every woman physically capable of doing so will become a wife and mother. Or the identity may be achieved. In many societies, a boy becomes a man only after he has had a vision, has killed an antelope, or earns/produces enough to support himself and others (Clatterbaugh, 1997).

---

stereotype   **The belief (often unfounded) that all members of a group share the same traits or characteristics.**

Gender and the Beginning College Student

How does the typical college student think about gender? A large group of beginning students was asked to define or describe what is meant by the term *gender*. Accordingly, gender is . . .

. . . being male or female.

. . . the differences between women and men, sexually and psychologically.

. . . the male or female sexual orientation that we perceive ourselves to be.

. . . two categories, male and female. From these stem several man-made genders such as transvestites, homosexuals, bisexuals, heterosexuals, and post- and pre-op patients.

. . . the differences that make it hard for men and women to communicate and get along.

. . . the fine line between the sexes. Some people define themselves as a part of both sexes.

. . . the differences in how the sexes think and respond. Males are more analytical and withdrawn, and women are more emotional and open.

. . . a whole different outlook on life. Differences in reaction and actions in everyday life.

. . . inherited genetic characteristics of the two sexes, enforced by society's ideas of the roles of men and women.

. . . the biological and feministic types of people.

. . . the chemical and genetic things that distinguish male from female.

. . . the largest and most significant opposites in the universe, because without these particular differences, there would be nothing.

. . . the type of person you are: male, female, or homosexual.

. . . what makes a person act a certain way in a situation.

. . . the way society has established norms and values for the sexes. For example, men open car doors for women.

. . . the different characteristics that define each sex. Females are more passive, kind, soft, caring, nurturing. Men are more aggressive, brave, and domineering. This doesn't apply to everyone, though. It's a stereotype. But I've been taught this my whole life.

. . . the way you reproduce (eggs or fertilizers of eggs), but also your mind-set and how you view the world because of the chemicals in your head that produce gender.

. . . each person has their own idea of gender.

. . . is an outdated term.

These responses reveal how the average, intelligent person thinks about gender. They also reflect many of the issues to be examined by this text:

- The extent to which behaviors, traits, interests, preferences, and so forth are influenced by genes and hormones.
- An overlap and confusion among the concepts of sex, gender, and *sexual orientation* (that is, the sex of the person with whom one prefers to share sexual intimacies).
- An awareness that for some individuals, anatomy and an inner sense of who they are don't match.
- An awareness that sometimes perceived gender differences may be the product of deeply held stereotypes.

Write down your own definition or description of gender. Perhaps your instructor can collect these. At the end of the course, do this again to see if definitions have changed.

Gender is a set of male and female behavioral and mental potentials that are shaped and developed by particular societies. For example, an inborn potential for extremely fine motor control of the hands and fingers may be shaped to create someone skilled in exquisite embroidery or someone skilled in exquisite brain surgery. An inborn potential for great bodily strength might be shaped into that of the water car-

rier or the weightlifter. Thus every person's talents and abilities are channeled and shaped by a society's gender constructions.

The term *gender* refers to the various femininities and masculinities that characterize particular societies and subcultures. These concepts represent the constellation of behaviors, verbal and nonverbal communications, preferences, concerns, interests, styles,

ABCs of GENDER (ATTITUDES, BEHAVIORS, AND CONCERNS)   BOX 1.2

The Issue: Typicality versus Stereotypicality

Trait or Characteristic	More Typical of:		
	Women	Men	Equally So
1. Adventurous	_____	_____	_____
2. Considerate	_____	_____	_____
3. Ambitious	_____	_____	_____
4. Emotional	_____	_____	_____
5. Mathematical	_____	_____	_____
6. Sensitive	_____	_____	_____
7. Self-confident	_____	_____	_____
8. Kind	_____	_____	_____
9. Seeking approval	_____	_____	_____
10. Technology oriented	_____	_____	_____
11. Helpful	_____	_____	_____
12. Wise	_____	_____	_____

Which of these traits do you believe are more typical of women or men? Which do you believe characterize both genders equally? What is the basis for your responses? As you answer, consider the impact and validity of your personal experience and observations in forming your responses. At what point do such beliefs become stereotypes?

---

grooming, life goals, and a myriad of other things that make up a particular society's **prescriptions** and **proscriptions** for particular groups of females and males (Gilmore, 1990). For example, in North American society working-class masculinity involves physical skills and the ability to manipulate the physical environment. Upper-middle-class masculinity involves verbal skills and the ability to manipulate the economic, social, and political environment (Conway-Long, 1994).

Gender is a set of socially constructed roles. Roles are enactments of social relationships. Who is more likely to lead a group? Who typically attends to a group's emotional environment? Who is more likely to express anger directly? Who is supposed to protect whom? From whom does one need protection? Who is more likely to placate? Who is more likely to confront? Who is expected to initiate? Who is supposed to respond? Who defers more often? Who helps others, how? Of course, the public enactment of gender roles may be quite different from private behavior and interactions. However, people always act out gender roles in interactions with others. Thus gender is also a culturally prescribed and organized pattern of interactions for women and men (Eagly, 1987).

Gender is an ideal. It forms a template for what is attractive, desirable, notable, and valuable within oneself and others. People evaluate themselves and others based on their perceived distance from their socially created and internalized ideals for gendered individuals. These evaluative schemes may involve physical attributes. For example, in Western society a woman's sexual desirability may be evaluated in terms of her breast size. In another society (the Woodabe of Niger), a man's sexual desirability is evaluated in terms of his ability to roll and cross his eyes (see Figure 1.1). Or these gender ideals may involve specific abilities. For example, in Western society men's athletic ability is very highly valued. In another society (the Agta of the Philippines), women's hunting ability is very highly valued (Estioko-Griffin & Griffin, 1997).

Gender is a central organizing process of the psyche. The human mind tends to organize the world into dualities, that is, into two categories. The existence of two anatomically distinct categories of human beings is perfectly suited to that dualistic thinking. Gender theorists and people who study cognition have noted that people tend to apply the dualistic concepts of masculine and feminine to all kinds of things: deities, inanimate objects, and natural phe-

---

prescription   Those behaviors, attitudes, feelings, and so on that are considered desirable within a particular society.

proscription   Those behaviors, attitudes, feelings, and so on that are prohibited or considered taboo within a particular society.

FIGURE 1.1   Most of us socialized in Western societies consider breasts erotic. However, this reaction is not universal. In many cultures breasts are displayed publicly and stimulation of the breast is not a part of sexual "foreplay." In Woodabe society, face painting (we call it *makeup*) is used to accentuate the eyes and lips. Eye crossing and eye rolling is an erotic display among men. In Western society, which gender "dresses up" in elaborate face paint and impractical clothing to attract others?

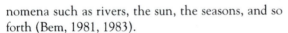

nomena such as rivers, the sun, the seasons, and so forth (Bem, 1981, 1983).

Gender is a system of power relationships in a society. It is an organized system of who leads, determines, controls, makes and changes rules, and who follows, obeys, and is affected by the rules and threats made by others. Power is concentrated in positions such as chief, shaman, monarch, warrior, property owner, lawmaker, law enforcer, possessor of wealth, developer of technology, and so forth. The gender system organizes who controls resources and who negotiates for resources. The system determines who is "seen" and who is "invisible" (Thompson & Pleck, 1995). It may involve who is "counted" or who is "named" (see Figure 1.2). Power is also related to the degree of *autonomy* a person has. In Iran, even the wealthiest woman may not purchase a ticket and sit inside a stadium to watch a men's soccer game. In the United States, a woman of even the highest status cannot safely walk the streets or roads alone at night.

Sex versus Gender

In the simplest terms, *sex* refers to the sex you are (male or female), not to the sex you do (as in making love). (You may recall that some of those beginning psychology students seemed confused about this.) Thus you may think of sex as a biological category: male or female. Categorization is usually determined at birth by visual inspection of the genitalia (is a penis or vulva visible?). In Chapter 5, you will learn about individuals whose biological sex may not be so easily determined. It may not be clear which gendered social prescriptions will best fit these individuals. Such people have taught psychologists a lot about the complex relationship between biological sex and psychosocial gender.

As noted earlier, within psychology and sociology the term *gender* is used to designate all those characteristics and behaviors that are considered appropriate, respectively, for the women and men who are members of a particular society (Unger & Crawford,

SMITHSONIAN NATIONAL BOARD

Hon. Frank A.Weil, *Chair* Hon. Max N. Berry, *Vice Chair*

Mrs. Laura Lee Blanton	Mr. Robert L. James	Mr. John Nelson
Mrs. Carolyn Blount	Mrs. Dona Kendall	Mrs. Joan Noto
Mrs. John M. Bradley	Mrs. James Kinnear	Mr. Heinz C. Prechter
Mr. Stephen F. Brauer	Mrs. Marie L. Knowles	Mrs. Charles H. Price
Hon. Henry E. Catto	Hon. Marc Leland	Baron Eric de Rothschild
Mr. Peter R. Coneway	Mr. Donald G. Lubin	Mr. A. R. Sanchez
Mr. Thomas E. Congdon	Ms. Elizabeth S. MacMillan	Mr. David M. Silfen
Mr. Frank Arthur Daniels, Jr.	Mr. John Macomber	Hon. Alan K. Simpson
Mr. Archie W. Dunham	Mrs. John W. Madigan	Ms. Kathy Daubert Smith
Dr. Sylvia Earle	Mr. Frank N. Magid	Mr. Kenneth L. Smith
Mrs. Jane Eisner	Mrs. Millicent Mailliard	Mr. C. D. Spangler
Mrs. Patricia Frost	Mrs. John F. Mars	Mr. Kelso F. Sutton
Ms. Nely Galan	Mr. Michael P. McBride	Mrs. Nancy Brown Wellin
Mr. Bert Getz	Mrs. Nan Tucker McEvoy	Mr. Anthony Welters
Mr. Stephen Hamblett	Mr. Kenneth B. Miller	Mr. Daniel W. Yohannes
Mr. Paul Hertelendy	Hon. Norman Y. Mineta	
Mr. Roger Horchow	Mr. Thomas D. Mullins	

HONORARY MEMBERS

Mr. Robert McC. Adams	Mr. Alfred C. Glassell, Jr.	Mr. Francis C. Rooney, Jr.
Mr. William S. Anderson	Mrs. Jean Bronson Mahoney	Mr. Wilbur L. Ross, Jr.
Mr. Richard P. Cooley	Hon. George C. McGhee	Mr. Lloyd G. Schermer
Mr. Joseph F. Cullman III	Justice Sandra D. O'Connor	Mrs. Gay F. Wray
Mr. Charles D. Dickey, Jr.	Mr. S. Dillon Ripley	

FIGURE 1.2 This listing of powerful people appeared in a recent issue of the *Smithsonian* magazine. Examine the list of names carefully. What does it tell you about gender, power, and names?

1998). Thus gender is a social construction that is related to a biological foundation.

How can one grasp the relationship between sex and gender? Perhaps it helps to think about a biological foundation with many potentials. That is, a building's foundation could be modified in various ways to eventually become a palace, a garage, an apartment house, or a platform for giving speeches or for launching rockets. The concept *gender* refers to what particular societies build onto that foundation. It includes what boys and men, girls and women, in a specific society are expected to be, do, prefer, and so on.

Remember two important points about this useful metaphor. First, understand that particular constructions can actually change the foundation on which they are built. Thus this biological foundation is not just *given*, nor is it unalterable. Environments and experiences can modify brains, whole bodies, nervous systems, and even hormonal systems to varying degrees. Second, there are limits to what experience and the environment can construct on this foundation. The biological foundation of gender is not infinitely modifiable. Thus biological potentialities and social development interact dynamically. This concept is very important in studying gender. As you continue your study of gender, you will see that the relationship between biological factors and social or experiential factors is a key dynamic that will resurface in several chapters of this book.

Exploring the behavioral factors associated with sex and with gender has led psychologists to distinguish between sex differences and gender differences (Unger, 1998). Although this distinction is generally useful, it remains strained. For example, under normal hormonal conditions the ability of female breast tissue to produce milk is clearly a sex difference. However, is the apparent differential in the incidence of major depression or **antisocial personality** a sex difference or a gender difference? Consider this question a "teaser" for what's to come later on in the text.

Why Study Gender?

Florence Denmark (1994), an eminent psychologist, called for "the engendering of psychology." That is, she wanted to see the development of a psychology

antisocial personality **A personality disorder characterized by the absence of conscience, remorse, or a sense of social responsibility.**

that is sensitive to gender and other kinds of human diversity. Noting that virtually all human behavior occurs in a gendered context, she called for the recognition of that reality throughout all areas of psychology. This text seeks to follow Denmark's suggestion.

On a more personal level, a few seconds after you were born someone glanced at your external genitals and pronounced, "Congratulations, you have a baby (girl, or boy)." With those words, a whole series of forces began to move, and these forces had a major influence on forming the person you are today. Of course, your genetic endowment regarding your physical characteristics and temperament were also extremely important in forming the ultimate you, as were your familial and physical environments. Peer influences, too, helped to shape you (Harris, 1998; Maccoby, 1998), but a great deal about you was shaped by how you yourself and others responded to your gender label. As a developing infant, were you surrounded by intense colors or by soft pastels? Were your toys hard and metallic, or soft and cuddly? Were gross motor movements (running, jumping, throwing) or fine motor movements (carrying, manipulating, arranging) encouraged? Did you elicit stroking and gentle handling, or did you ask for rough-housing? The list is endless. What is important here is that gender is a major formative factor in how you became you. Furthermore, your gender will continue to influence the path of your development for the rest of your life.

There are many good reasons for studying gender. First, if you want to understand more about who you are, how you are, and whom you are likely to become, then the study of gender is a great place to start. Second, for the student who is considering entering any field in which dealing with people is a major component (counseling, social work, management, law, health services, education, politics, consumer behavior, ministry, law enforcement, human resources, and so on) an understanding of gender and gender relations is crucial. The study of gender can be quite practical in that what you learn can be applied to your personal relationships, family life, and occupational endeavors. Third, gender roles and gender expectations are undergoing change all over the world. In some places, the rate of change may seem excruciatingly slow, whereas in others the rapidity of change creates both excitement and confusion (see

Figure 1.3). One thing is certain, though: These changes will have an impact on your private and occupational life. Fourth, issues of gender run all through every human society on an everyday basis. A look at a daily newspaper demonstrates how gender continues to be an area of strong and sometimes tragic contention in the world. We observe incidents of domestic violence, war, rape, the millions earned exclusively by male athletes, or poor women managing small business enterprises from Tuscaloosa, Alabama, to Harare, Zimbabwe (Todd, 1996). Why did the Taliban government of Afghanistan prefer to close desperately needed schools and clinics rather than allow women to continue *any* kind of paid work (Ellis, 2000)? Now that the Taliban are gone, will women have any real power in shaping the future of Afghanistan? Why are the orphanages of China filled only with baby girls? This list too is endless. Understanding gender can help you deal with the forces that shape the human endeavor both on a global level and in our community. Finally, understanding more about gender and gender roles can aid you in making better decisions as a citizen. Your understanding of gender issues may lead you to support or object to certain laws and public policies regarding family law, child care, education, public health, crime, or emphases in international policies and budgetary expenditures.

Thus gender is an important and multifaceted area of study and investigation within psychology. Gendered behavior is everywhere, so the possibilities for study and understanding are almost endless (Clatterbaugh, 1997).

Critical Thinking Challenge

Take a look at today's newspaper or online review of news. How many items have to do with gender, either directly or indirectly?

Commonly Asked Questions About Women and Men in Western Society

Most students who begin the study of the psychology of gender have great curiosity about those aspects of gender with which they have had personal encounters. Sometimes these interests take the form of questions, and the study of gender can help you answer some of those questions, even the very personal ones.

"You want only happiness, Douglas. I want wealth, power, fame, and happiness."

FIGURE 1.3 Here is a wry comment on recent changes in gender roles and expectations in our society.

Here are some of the most common questions that students ask about gender.

◆ Why are all women expected to have children and to then be their primary caretaker?
◆ Why is unpaid domestic work primarily a wife's responsibility even if she brings home more than half the income? Why are so many men unwilling to take on an equal share of child care and domestic responsibilities?
◆ Are women really paid less compared to men doing the same work?
◆ What does it mean to be a good father?
◆ Why do women and men seem to have such different attitudes about sexuality?
◆ Why are competitive sports so important to most men?
◆ Why are relatively few women in positions of leadership and authority in most societies?
◆ Why is gender inequality so difficult to reduce, let alone eradicate?
◆ Do men have more problems maintaining intimate relationships?

◆ Do women and men really think and communicate differently?
◆ Why are men and women often attracted to such different types of occupations?
◆ Can parents help their daughters and sons avoid the more negative aspects of traditional gender role socialization?
◆ How can men and women avoid or cope more effectively with the health problems that particularly affect each gender? As a group, why do men die so much earlier than women do?
◆ Why do many heterosexual men seem to dislike gay men so much?
◆ Is there a need for a men's movement, and if so, what form should that movement take?

Critical Thinking Challenge

What are your own question(s) about men, women, and gender? If you write them down, perhaps your instructor will collect them and your class can discuss how best to answer them.

Why Take a Global Perspective on Gender?

At this point in history, interest in the relationship between culture and human behavior is rising to a special prominence within psychology (Cooper & Denner, 1998; Miller, 1999). There is a general movement to incorporate culture as an important variable in the study of all human behaviors (Fowers & Richardson, 1996; Segall, Lonner, & Berry, 1998). Making this improved human psychology both truly cross-cultural (reflecting the study of behaviors across cultures) and multicultural (reflecting the study of the varying groups within a culture) remains an ongoing challenge.

This text takes a cross-cultural perspective and multicultural perspective on gender. Why? First, the process of seeking and inventing knowledge (a process called *science*) obliges scholars to question commonly accepted but untested statements regarding human behavior. For example, compared to women do all men (across cultures) prefer or require more novelty and variety in their sexual partners? A cross-cultural and multicultural perspective can help psychology become what it has always professed itself to be: the study of *human* behavior and mental processes (Landrine, Klonoff, Gibbs, Manning, & Lund, 1995).

Second, the world today is characterized by migration and immigration on an unprecedented scale. This worldwide mixing of people and cultures will be a critical factor in dealing effectively in the world of the 21st century. In the school, workplace, neighborhood, and community, cultural diversity will be the rule rather than the exception. Thus, understanding the differences and similarities among groups living within a society is very important.

Furthermore, most psychologists believe that gender is largely constructed by particular human groups. These groups may be as small as a family or as widespread as an entire nation. Variations on gender may be constructed by a clan, tribe, social class, ethnic group, or a religious group. Gender roles seem to emerge from human adaptations to particular environments, economic, political, or technological conditions (Reid & Hammersley, 2000). To understand the possibilities regarding gender, it is helpful to step outside one's own society's prescribed blueprint for women and men. By doing so, you can examine all the possibilities for those human blueprints. You can also discover the limits of those possibilities and potentialities.

Moreover, you can examine how prescribed blueprints are actually lived out. Anthropologists note that even in very traditional societies, violations of gender roles are relatively frequent. Few people conform absolutely to the gender prescriptions of their societies (Levant, 1995). However, too high a degree of violation may bring sanctions, ridicule, punishment, or even death in some societies. In North American culture, more severe punishments for gender role violations are likely to be levied against men. In other societies, women may experience more severe consequences for violations.

Critical Thinking Challenge

Do you accept the two preceding statements? Can you think of examples that would support or contradict these generalizations?

By taking a cross-cultural and multicultural perspective, you can marvel, compare, and enjoy the gender constructions of various societies, much as you might relish and celebrate the art, literature, cuisine, music, and architecture of those societies.

Studying gender across cultures also allows you both to appreciate and perhaps refute arguments about the *essential* differences between women and men. At the same time, such comparative studies allow you to identify and celebrate any true universals about men and women.

Also, remember that culture, like gender, affects virtually every aspect of life: food, clothing, housing, technology, economy, transportation, family activities, individual pursuits, community creation, government, religion, science, and sexuality. Culture influences how groups pass through the life cycle, from the reactions to a new birth, through the processes of child rearing, all the way to attitudes toward the elderly and the practices surrounding death (Berry, Dasen, & Saraswathi, 1997). Gender is an important aspect of all these cultural expressions. For example, family and community reactions may be very different in response to the birth of a boy or to that of a girl. Older adults may be revered and be granted the highest status, or be considered useless, according to their

---

SLIDE SHOW   **BOX 1.3**

Gender Relations Across Cultures: Some Everyday Encounters

Korea: In North America, women's smiles are expected, and even demanded by social norms. Warmth and friendliness are aspects of the gender ideal for feminine women in this society. In Korea, smiles are considered a sign of shallowness and thoughtlessness, especially among men. In the United States, Korean storeowners are often perceived as unfriendly and hostile because they almost never smile. Korean Americans may not smile when having their pictures taken for their drivers' licenses, and Korean-American children may not smile when having their pictures taken with Santa Claus because such occasions are considered too important for a smile.

Costa Rica: Teenage girls and young unmarried adult women from Costa Rica may easily go out for an evening with other female friends of similar age. However, among Ecuadorians a single woman in this age group may go out only if accompanied by a family member. To do otherwise would ruin the young woman's reputation. Despite similar language and other customs, Latin American societies are quite varied in terms of gender-related social norms.

Japan: In general, the Japanese do not approve of physical affection in public situations. Public touching between men

and women is particularly repugnant. Kissing in public, even between husbands and wives is strongly disapproved.

Saudi Arabia: In many Western societies, there are strong prohibitions against casual physical contact between men. However, it is not unusual to see Saudis and other Arab men walking hand in hand on public streets. Hand-holding is considered a sign of mutual trust and friendship among men.

Adapted from N. Dresser (1996), *Multicultural Manners* (New York: Wiley).

---

gender. Even in death, rites and mourning may be quite different for a deceased woman or man.

A last advantage of taking a cross-cultural perspective has to do with the practical benefits of knowing about differences and similarities in real-life interactions (Dresser, 1996). Do you recall the vignette at the beginning of the chapter? How did you interpret the attorney's behavior? Some knowledge of multicultural gender norms can come in very handy in such a situation. Among Orthodox Jews, physical contact between men and women who are not married is considered offensive and a serious interpersonal violation. No wonder David's reaction was so strong! Take a look at Box 1.3 to see some other interesting examples of cultural differences in gender-related behavior.

By the way, what is culture? Simply and basically, *culture* refers to the set of attitudes, values, beliefs, and behaviors that are shared by a group of people but that differ for every individual and that are communicated from one generation to another. In more psychological terms, culture involves "sharing the contents of minds" (Berry, Poortinga, Segall, & Dasen, 1992; Matsumoto, 1996).

Critical Thinking Challenge

Are you aware that normally we never see culture? It emerges or manifests only when we see or experience differences. Think about it.

One major organizational concept within cross-cultural psychology is the classification of societies along the dimension of individualism-collectivism (IC) (Kagitcibasi, 1997; Triandis, 1995). Members of individualistic cultures, such as Australia or Germany, tend to see themselves as separate and autonomous individuals. Their personal needs and goals take precedence. Members of collectivistic societies see themselves as fundamentally connected with others. In collectivistic cultures, such as India or China, personal needs and goals may be sacrificed to satisfy the group. Such categories are situation bound and interaction bound. Someone may display collectivistic tendencies at home or with close friends, but show individualistic tendencies with strangers or at work, or the reverse (Matsumoto, Weissman, Preston, Brown, & Kupperbusch, 1997). Such cultural differences are important when considering gender and gender roles across various societies.

TABLE 1.1   Journals Often Containing Reports of Gender-related Research

Journal Title	Journal Title	Journal Title
Archives of Sexual Behavior	Journal of Black Psychology	Men and Masculinities
Child Development	Journal of Comparative Family Studies	Psychology of Evolution and Gender
Cultural Diversity and Ethnic Minority Psychology	Journal of Cross-Cultural Psychology	Psychology of Women Quarterly
Feminism and Psychology	Journal of Family Psychology	Sex Roles
Feminist Studies	Journal of Gender, Culture and Health	Sexuality and Culture
Gender and Society	Journal of Marriage and the Family	Signs
Gender, Work and Organizations	Journal of Psychology and Human Sexuality	Women and Health
Hispanic Journal of the Behavioral Sciences	Journal of Social Issues	Women and Therapy

Also note that contemporary cross-cultural psychology has a weakness as formulated now. Most studies define a cross-cultural comparison in terms of a comparison between countries or societies. In reality, such comparisons are typically cross-city and, even more typically, cross-university. For example, researchers conducted a series of studies to validate a particular psychological measure. They used samples from the United States, Japan, South Korea, and Russia. However, all the participants in these studies were actually urban university students and therefore heavily influenced by Western values and attitudes (Matsumoto et al., 1997). Such individuals are hardly representative of the general population of their respective countries.

Resources for the Study of Gender

Almost every person born into every society masters the complexities of gender-appropriate behavior for his or her group. That leaves the question of *how* the typical person absorbs the gender prescriptions and proscriptions of her or his society. Chapter 4 discusses the details of this process, but you can probably already suggest a beginning answer to this question. You learned these norms from your parents, from your peers, from your religion, from the current media, and from the roles/activities you were encouraged to pursue or avoid. Because we live out the gender constructions of our society, we are, in one sense, already gender experts. However, that same immersion in the gender prescriptions of society prevents people from really *seeing* gender and all its manifestations. It's the

old and familiar story of the fish that has always lived in water and so cannot imagine a dry world. So, how does the gender scholar study gender?

The psychologist tends to use the tools and techniques of what is called the *scientific method*. This is discussed further in the next chapter. For right now, know that the most recent theories and findings about gender may be found in various scientific journals and books. Because gender is such a far-reaching phenomenon, these journals and books range across several disciplines. To get a sense of the many journals and books that were consulted to create this book, take a look at the References section at the back of the book. Table 1.1 also lists some current journals that are concerned with issues of gender. It might be interesting for members of your class to seek out a current issue of some of these journals and report about the various articles contained there.

Important Issues for the Study of Gender Across and Within Societies

As you begin your study of gender, there are three important issues for you to keep in mind: race and ethnicity, gender differences, and individual experience.

The Issue of Race and Ethnicity

Like gender, ethnicity is an important aspect of self-identity. Gender construction may vary considerably across ethnicities, so in taking a global approach to gender we must also deal with issues of ethnicity.

Most students are quite accustomed to seeing data arranged by race. The typical categories are white, black, Hispanic, Native American, and Asian. However, it has become clearer and clearer that there are serious problems with using such designations. Ostensibly, the purpose of this classification is to clarify and organize data, but such categories can often confuse and mislead consumers of information. They can also perpetuate stereotypes (Armstrong, 1995; Witzig, 1996; Wyatt, 1994). For example, what is your understanding of the designation *black* or *African American*? In North America, these terms usually refer to the descendents of Africans who were brought to North America against their will and held in slavery, which lasted for two centuries. Over those centuries, many "mixed" children were born, so that most so-called blacks have some European ancestors, and many so-called whites have African and Native American ancestors. For almost another hundred years, millions of African Americans were held in abject poverty and social isolation, and this continues to exert a negative social impact on the contemporary descendents of this group. However, a positive result has been the development of a lively and adaptive African-American subculture within the United States.

Should Secretary of State Colin Powell be classified as an African American? Some would argue no, because although some of his ancestors were brought as slaves to the Caribbean, West Indian culture is rather distinct from that of the North American continent. Moreover, his features reflect many European ancestors. What about someone who migrated to the United States last year from Mozambique? This person is clearly a black African, but (except for the discrimination both may encounter) has little in common, historically or culturally, with a person of partially African descent whose ancestors have lived in Canada or the United States for 250 years.

Critical Thinking Challenge

In my university is an instructor whose white, Jewish ancestors immigrated from eastern Europe to what is now South Africa over two hundred years ago. This instructor immigrated to the United States several years ago. Should he be classified as an African American? One could make a good argument that he should be. By the way, it wasn't very long ago that Jews were considered a nonwhite race (Sacks, 1998).

Why aren't individuals from Morocco, Algeria, or Libya who now live in the United States labeled as African Americans? What about dark-skinned Ethiopian Jews who migrate to Israel and then perhaps to the United States? Are they African Americans? Should the former president of Peru, Alberto Fujimori, be classified as Hispanic (his parents immigrated from Japan to Peru)? Are Hispanics those who speak Spanish? Are Portuguese-speaking Brazilians Hispanic? Are Spaniards Hispanic or white? What about a Bolivian or Mexican Indian who has never spoken Spanish? Are dark-skinned Puerto Ricans or Dominicans, African Americans, black, or Hispanic? Are Spanish-speaking Filipinos Asian or Hispanic? By the way, are Pakistanis, Indians, and Bangladeshis, Asians? You bet they are, but they are categorized as Caucasians (McKenzie & Crowcroft, 1994). What if they have very dark skin? Are they still Caucasians? Do you feel an ethnic headache coming on? You might want to invite an anthropologist to class to clarify all this.

Finally, researchers must deal with the issue of the rapidly increasing number of individuals whose parents are of more than one so-called race. This is a rapidly growing segment of the world's population. Even the U.S. Bureau of the Census has finally acknowledged this reality and has included such a category on the 2000 census forms.

Terms such as *race* constitute "a vague, unscientific term for a group of genetically related people who share *some* physical traits" (Glanze, Anderson, & Anderson, 1994, p. 657). More importantly, so-called racial differences in behavior are often really differences in socioeconomic status. For example, many medical studies classify participants by race and report racial differences in certain health-related behaviors. However, a study of breast cancer survival rates found that racial differences disappeared when socioeconomic status was controlled. That is, there was a substantially lower breast cancer survival rate among poor women, regardless of their skin color. Survival rates among middle- and upper-class women were similarly high, regardless of skin color or other so-called racial characteristics (Bassett & Krieger, 1986). The American Anthropological Association (1998) has called for an end to organizing social data by "race."

The term *ethnicity* incorporates social, psychological, religious, linguistic, dietary, and other cultural variables that may be useful in understanding particular behaviors or mental processes. Thus *ethnicity* refers to a group of people within a society or across societies who are seen as similar or as sharing a particular religion (such as Jews), culture (such as African Americans), language (such as Argentineans), or appearance (such as Scandinavians). As you can see, linguistic groups may run across ethnic groups, and ethnic groups may consist of virtually hundreds of subgroups (such as Native Americans).

Another reason for using the term *ethnicity* rather than *race* is that ethnicity is more clearly understood to be a social construction. *Race* is often erroneously seen as referring to a biological classification.

For all these reasons, this text will not use the term *race* in discussing multicultural issues. The term *ethnicity* or *ethnic group* is preferred. Although still imperfect, it seems to more accurately convey useful information.

The Issue of Gender Differences

A great deal of the classical psychological research about gender is devoted to the uncovering and explaining of differences between women and men. As discussed later, statements about such differences constitute a virtual battleground for researchers and other scholars with particular philosophical bents. For the moment, be aware of the controversy and take a quick, informed glance at this issue. Favreau (1993, 1997) has offered thoughtful overviews of the problem.

For example, it is typically reported, and generally believed, that boys play more roughly than girls do. In statistical terms, this may be translated as a significant gender difference in the average amount of rough-and-tumble play among children. Some researchers consider this a sex difference, because of the possible influence of male hormones. However, a more detailed look at this pattern of behavior reveals quite a different picture from what one might expect. In one fairly typical study, all the girls and most of the boys engaged in a low or medium level of rough-and-tumble play (DiPietro, 1981). Just a few boys engaged in a very high level of rough-and-tumble play. This pushed the average for boys way up, but the overall

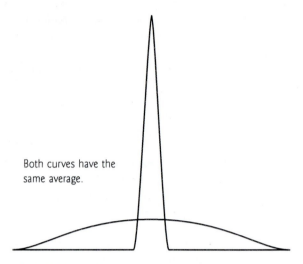

Both curves have the same average.

FIGURE 1.4   The reporting of "averages" can create a distorted picture of the gender-related behavior (Favreau, 1993, 1997).

pattern is missed when only the averages are reported (Kimball, 1995). Let's examine two more quick examples (see Figure 1.4).

Many psychology texts refer to gender differences in the depth and incidence of major depression. In large samples, the average level of depression is often found to be higher for women than for men. Yet a careful reconsideration of the scores often reveals that depression scores may not be normally distributed among women. A small group of women might be very depressed, and this affects the averages compared. Similarly, it is commonly reported that boys score higher on tests of mathematical abilities. This is typically interpreted to indicate superior mathematical abilities on the part of boys and men. It may be true that for boys, average scores on standardized tests are higher than those of girls, but often this is because a small group of boys scores exceptionally high. Thus a major challenge in studying gender is to determine when hypothesized or reported differences are real, rather than just statistical artifacts or the result of biased methods. Actually, there's much more to this mathematical mystification, but that too comes later in the text.

One last point about interpreting reports of sex or gender differences. Notice the language used in the preceding examples. Favreau (1993) cautions people about the way to describe differences. In interpreting the results of color-blindness tests, people may conclude that more men than women are color blind, but not that women see color better than men. We can say that more men than women commit crimes, but not that men are more criminal than women. Although it is accurate to say that more boys than girls have **dyslexia**, it is not fair or accurate to say that girls are superior readers compared to boys. In other words, when studying sex and gender be skeptical about sweeping, simplistic, and perhaps inaccurate statements about gender differences. Try to become aware of the biases embedded in what you read or see.

The Issue of Individual Experience

Let's return to the metaphor of you as a gendered person living in an ocean of gendered behaviors. As such, it is often difficult to see certain behaviors, preferences, interests, attitudes, and so on as *the* gender constructions of your particular society. In other words, because people are engulfed by the gender norms of their own upbringing, they find it difficult not to experience these norms as somehow natural, given, or universally human, even though they might not be. A cross-cultural and multicultural perspective should help in this regard, but it takes hard work and a clear, well-rested mind not to fall into this ethnocentric trap. (You may even catch me slipping on this one.)

A related issue concerns individual variations in experience. Recall that part of the definition of culture went like this: "the set of attitudes, values, beliefs, and behaviors shared by a group of people, *but that differ for every individual, . . .*" Zoom in on that last phrase, because it is important. All through this text you will encounter general statements about gendered behavior and cultural groups. Occasionally you may feel quite frustrated and want to e-mail me a fully capitalized message, "THAT DOES NOT APPLY TO ME, NOR TO THE PEOPLE I KNOW!" For example, you may read that patterns of male dominance in intimate relationships are maintained in American marriages because husbands are typically taller, older, wealthier, and better educated than their wives. You may want to protest that this is not true of your marriage nor that of your parents. Nonetheless, the arrangement described is the general pattern for North

American marriages. Make room for the fact that generalizations about women, men, ethnic groups, or whole societies do not apply to every member of each group. Nor does the fact that one's individual experience is very different from the majority negate the accuracy of more general statements.

One last point about individual experience: As human beings, we all rely on our personal experiences to understand the world, particularly other people. However, individual experiences may not be typical. For example, most women in your class will be seeking professional or semiprofessional jobs after graduation. Many will be managers or supervisors, or will work in other traditionally masculine occupations. Given these personal experiences and observations, one might assume there is now occupational equality in this society. But that is not true. For those who do not attend college (and most young people do not), there is still a tremendous level of gender segregation in the workplace. In general, women are still concentrated in the lowest-paid segments of the job market, and even when they have comparable jobs, women earn less (Institute for Women's Policy Research, 1999). For a quick snapshot of the problem, consider the gender of the servers at your local "Cheap Food Fast" emporium versus that of the servers at "The Best Place in Town." Consider who has the lowest-paid and the lowest-skilled jobs at the factories in your town. Who are the supervisors and managers at that factory? Why are women 80% of all lower-level clerical workers and 98% of all secretaries (U.S. Bureau of Labor Statistics, 2000)? Again, your individual experiences regarding gender and gender arrangements may be deceiving and not at all representative of the larger picture.

Recurrent Themes for Your Study of Gender

This chapter introduces the rest of the book. The following major themes will recur throughout this text.

Although sex is determined by biological factors, gender is mainly a social construction. That is, although biology offers a core set of behavioral and

---

dyslexia **A learning disorder characterized by impairment in dealing with written words.**

mental potentials for each individual, gender is largely a social phenomenon. Anatomy and physiology constrain certain reproduction-related behaviors. However, most of what makes up gender evolves from a human group's attempt to adapt to a particular ecological situation (Reid & Hammersley, 2000). This construction is then passed to the next generation of that human group through its child-rearing patterns and other socialization practices. Part of the challenge facing gender studies is uncovering the impact of biological potentials on behaviors and mental processes that are not related to reproduction. For example, is there a biology-based difference in the way women and men process and use spatial data? Is there a biology-based difference in the ways men and women aggress against others? The dynamic relationship between biological and psychosocial factors in the behavior of men and women will be a major theme in this text.

Gender is a lifelong process. We all manifest gender identity and perform socially prescribed gender roles literally from the moment of birth until our dying breath. During our lifetime, most of us will take a culturally prescribed position in the gender hierarchy of society. Thus another theme is the examination of individual construction and maintenance of a gendered existence throughout the lifetime.

The study of gender requires a multidisciplinary approach. Because gender is an individual, social, and cultural phenomenon, it is important to examine the findings and insights of many disciplines. Although most of what appears in this text emanates from the social sciences (primarily psychology, sociology, and anthropology), it also includes insights offered by biologists, physicians, historians, literary authors, theologians, and political leaders.

Gender is dynamic. The contents of a gender identity and of gender roles are not static. The gender prescriptions and proscriptions of a society, or even a family, change in response to economic, cultural, technological, and political forces. A look at the gender constructions of previous times reminds the observer of their adaptive nature. Your glimpse of gender as it exists in the world today should be tempered by the recognition that this glimpse is time bound (Deaux & LaFrance, 1998). On a global level, technological, ecological, economic, political, and social changes are occurring at a rapid pace. We can only guess how gender will be constructed in the future.

Gender is viewed as both a psychosocial phenomenon and a power arrangement. This text does not view gender and gender roles as being ordained or maintained by a supernatural deity nor by a biological imperative. Although it seriously considers and examines evolutionary perspectives on gender in depth, it views changes in gender roles and gender-typed expectations as aspects of social, political, and economic forces, not as violations of natural or spiritual laws.

More egalitarian gender arrangements are viewed in this text as more desirable and beneficial to both men and women. This viewpoint constitutes my bias, and it is important to be open about this. Some instructors and readers of the book may disagree with the values presented here. I and most students/readers of this text live in secular and democratic societies, in which equality of rights and opportunities for all citizens are major ideals. It is important to recognize that many societies and subcultures do not subscribe to these principles.

Gender roles both constrain and free individuals. The gender role prescriptions and proscriptions of a particular society offer a guide for appropriate and acceptable behavior. As such, they make social situations safer, more predictable, and more orderly. At the same time, gender roles can constrain the individual by limiting the development of that person's full potential. Consider the scientific discoveries and progress that may have been lost because women continue to be blocked from such pursuits. Consider the harm done to the children in a family in which a more patient, competent, and loving father leaves them each day to go off to paid employment, so that a frustrated, bored, and uneasy mother can fulfill the socially prescribed gender role as primary child-care giver.

Gender is enmeshed in various social institutions. Gender intertwines with many aspects of our lives as individuals and as members of our society. For example, gender influences our educational and occupational choices. Gender norms influence what we do romantically and sexually. They also influence our society's conception of how a family should be structured and maintained. Gender influences which kind of person has power over others and how that power is maintained and extended.

A Look Ahead

The first three chapters of this text build a firm foundation for your study of gender. In the next chapter, you'll be learning about the various ways that scholars have attempted to study gender (Chapter 2, "Studying Gender: False Starts and Leaps into the Abyss"). Then an overview of current theories of gender gives you some idea of how thinkers have tried to make sense out of all their varied observations about gender (Chapter 3, "Theories of Gender: On Fallacies and 'Phallocies'"). See which theories make the most sense to you.

The second group of chapters examine gender as an organizing force that operates across the life span. Chapter 4 ("Gender and the Body: Hindsight, Oversights, and Insights") examines the controversies surrounding the biological foundations of sex and gender. I also discuss what recent research has revealed about intersexed individuals and gender development. Chapter 5 ("Life Span Gender Development: From Womb to Tomb") explores the various manifestations of gender from birth until death. Finally, because gender is enacted with other people, I examine the influence of gender on how people conduct themselves in relationships (Chapter 6, "Gender and Relationships: A Lifetime of Connected Lives"). Continuing the theme of gender in a social context, Chapter 7 explores the impact of gender on all kinds of social situations ("Gender as Social Performance: A Worldview").

The following chapters organize our life experiences as gendered beings into particular segments. First I examine how gender influences sexual behavior (Chapter 8, "Gender and Sexuality: Private Lives and Public Meanings"). Then I take a good look at the gendered aspects of contemporary educational practices and choices (Chapter 9, "Gender and Education: Choices, Changes, and the Status Quo"). The workplace remains a major arena where gender issues are played out. In North American society, laws appear to provide equality of opportunity, yet gender-related problems persist (Chapter 10, "Gender and Work: Segregation Now, Segregation Forever?"). The gendered aspects of physical and mental health are reviewed in the next two chapters (Chapter 11, "Gender and Physical Health: On Labor, Lifestyle, and Longevity" and Chapter 12, "Gender and Mental Health: On Labels, Culture, and Boundary Violations").

The next chapters deal with the broader social aspects of gender. As soon as human beings evolved into conscious, language-using creatures, we began to want to hear "the story of our tribe" again and again. Early human groups may have huddled around a fire to hear an elder recount that story. In modern societies, the story is told and retold via sophisticated mass media, but the purposes and pleasures are still the same (Chapter 13, "Gender and the Mass Media: Tribal Tales for the 21st Century").

You may recall that one of the definitions of gender involved the power arrangements of particular societies. This book examines how personal, social, and political power continues to be concentrated in one gender in most societies. I discuss whether or not this arrangement can change, and consider whether it *should* change (Chapter 14, "Gender and Power: The Personal and the Political"). Finally, you have been born into a heavily gendered life and are going into a heavily gendered future (Chapter 15, "Gender and the Future: A Global View"). What can you expect in terms of gender and gender relations? The text makes some well-informed guesses, but they are only guesses. You and your classmates will be creating that future.

Summary

- Psychologists can identify and explain at least 10 components of gender.
- The term *sex* refers to a biological classification, superficially based on genital appearance. The term *gender* refers to those behaviors and characteristics considered appropriate for the women and men of a particular society.
- There is an important and dynamic relationship between certain biological factors determined by one's sex and the socially constructed phenomenon of gender.
- Psychologists and other social scientists often make a distinction between *sex differences* versus *gender differences*, but this is sometimes problematic.
- There are many good reasons for a formal study of gender, and these relate to commonly asked questions about men and women in our society.

◆ There are many advantages in taking a global perspective on gender. A rationale for a cross-cultural and multicultural perspective is the powerful influence of culture on so many aspects of social behavior. Cultural awareness is both enriching and of practical benefit.

◆ The most general definition of culture involves the sharing of minds. Cultures may be distinguished along the dimension of individualism/collectivism. Lack of representativeness is a major weakness of contemporary cross-cultural psychological research.

◆ Scientific books and journals relating to gender and cultural psychology are important resources for the gender scholar.

◆ Three important issues surround the study of gender. These include the issue of race and ethnicity, the issue of differences, and the issue of the validity of individual experience.

◆ In this text, eight themes will permeate the organization and presentation of the many facets of gender. These include gender as largely a social construction, gender as a lifelong process, a multidisciplinary approach to studying gender, gender as a dynamic process, gender as both a psychosocial phenomenon and as a power arrangement, gender roles as both freeing and constraining the individual, and gender as enmeshed in various social institutions (the family, religion, and so on).

InfoTrac College Edition

For more information, explore InfoTrac College Edition at

http://www.infotrac-college.com/Wadsworth

Enter search terms: gender identity, gender roles, gender stereotype.

2

Studying Gender
False Starts and Leaps into the Abyss

It is a truism of scientific research that the stance one takes affects the questions one asks and in turn, the answers that one's investigations yield. ◆ K. Deaux & M. LaFrance

Learning Objectives

After studying this chapter, you should be able to:

1. Describe the basic steps of the scientific method, and explain how they are related to three important philosophical assumptions regarding the nature of reality.
2. Referring to the earliest psychologists, explain the relationship among conceptualizations of group differences, evolutionary theory, gender, and ethnicity.
3. Summarize three conceptualizations of gender as envisioned by psychologists, emphasizing the strengths and weaknesses of the concept of androgyny.
4. Define the term *gender stereotype*, and summarize the findings relevant to understanding the importance of gender stereotypes.
5. Summarize the strengths and weaknesses of the case study, observation, and survey research, emphasizing the particular challenge presented by multicultural and cross-cultural surveys.
6. Summarize the strengths and weaknesses of the developmental, correlational, and experimental approaches, emphasizing the problems of causation and ex post facto studies.
7. Describe how meta-analyses are carried out, and explain why meta-analysis is a useful method for studying gender differences.
8. Contrast the qualitative approach with more traditional quantitative methods.
9. Explain the impact of the criticisms raised by feminist psychologists regarding the study of women and gender.
10. Contrast the current study of men as explicitly gendered with more traditional approaches, and then briefly summarize eight important issues in studying men and masculinity.
11. Explain why the issue of sexual orientation is important in studying gender.
12. Explain why cross-cultural and multicultural approaches are important in studying gender.
13. Summarize the main tenets of the social constructionist approach to gender.
14. Briefly describe two more important problems to consider in studying gender.

Encounters with Gender

The gaslight created a warm glow in the university auditorium. The audience of learned men puffed on their pipes and cigars, and eagerly awaited the eminent scientist, Dr. Edward H. Clarke, Harvard University's first professor of education. Great applause greeted Dr. Clarke, and all paid rapt attention as he presented his most recent findings on the problem of education for the fair sex. The audience members struggled to view the charts on the podium, but the conclusions were obvious. Responsible educators must take these incontrovertible scientific findings into consideration. The advancement of the human species was at stake! There was no doubt as to the facts: College-educated women had far fewer children than women who never attended college. Educational pursuits clearly caused damage to their reproductive capacities. Moreover, fully 42% of the women in Boston-area insane asylums had college degrees, compared to only 16% of the men inmates. Having women pursue university studies outside their natural spheres of child care, child welfare, and child education was harmful and dangerous both for women and for their offspring. Such unnatural pursuits could actually interfere with human evolution!

Can you counter Dr. Clarke's conclusions? How would you take issue with his data?

Overview

This chapter has three goals. First, to explain how past scholars have thought about and studied gender. Second, to offer you a critical evaluation of the current approaches and methods used to study gender. A third goal is to inspire you to ask and answer your own questions about gender. I begin by exploring what is meant by a "scientific study" of gender and then discuss some typical methodologies and research tools for the current study of gender. A discussion of some profound and contentious issues follows, and you will need to consider these issues throughout your study of gender. The ultimate purpose of this chapter is to help you make your own informed assessments about the quality and value of everything you encounter about gender, both in this text and in your everyday world.

Science and the Study of Gender

Most of the material in this text is the product of a singularly Western method of gaining knowledge and understanding the world, namely science. At the most basic level, science is nothing more than an agreed-on way of asking and answering certain kinds of questions. Not all questions can be answered by science, and science isn't the only way to answer questions, but the scientific method has certainly been a useful way to answer many questions. Science as a preferred method for the pursuit of knowledge developed during the 16th and 17th centuries (Richardson & Fowers, 1997; Riger, 1992). Two core ideas underlie all the sciences:

1. Laws govern all the processes of nature, including gender.
2. One can ultimately discover these laws and eventually understand nature, including gender.

How does one discover the laws by which nature (and gender) operate? There are three basic steps: Go out into the world and carefully collect data (measures) about some phenomenon, analyze that data, and then interpret what that data analysis means. These steps are based on important assumptions. One assumption is that the phenomenon of interest is directly observable (**empiricism**). For our purposes, this means that gender must be physically "out there," external to the observer. A second assumption is the concept of **materialism**, which means that everything can be physically described and therefore measured. Thus one should be able to measure and compare various aspects of gender. Third, there must be agreed-on methods for the collection of data (**logical positivism**). These are the philosophic bases for the natural sciences: biology, chemistry, astronomy, and more recently, the social science of psychology. These concepts constitute the philosophical toolbox that the psychological scientist brings to every question about gender. Inside the toolbox are the specific tools that the social scientist uses to answer questions. You may be wondering why we have gone on this little trek through the philosophy of science. It's because right now, these concepts and assumptions are being challenged by many (not all) who study gender (Marecek, 1995; Morawski, 1994; Unger, 1998). We will return to this important point toward the end of the chapter.

The 20th Century

Psychology had two main parents (and a very involved extended family). One parent was *philosophy*, particularly that branch of philosophy concerned with how people know what is out there in the world around them (*epistemology*). *Biology* was the second parent. You will be able to see these parental influences as I discuss the historical development of the psychology of gender.

Critical Thinking Challenge

Are you comfortable imagining two parents without giving either of them gender?

Early Psychology and the Study of Gender Differences

Psychology came into being as a discipline separate from philosophy toward the end of the 19th century. Wilhelm Wundt and his student Edward Titchener

---

empiricism **The pursuit of knowledge derived from the direct observation of nature.**

materialism **The idea that the facts of the universe can be explained in physical terms (and therefore can be measured).**

logical positivism **Facts or knowledge derived only through the methods of science.**

are considered the founders of modern scientific psychology, and they had two central concerns. Titchener's main interest was to reveal the structure and contents of the generalized adult mind. This generalized adult mind was assumed to be the white male or masculine mind and until fairly recently, virtually all the information about that mind was collected, analyzed, interpreted, and disseminated by white men. In contrast, Wundt's major interest was in *Volkerpsychologie* (folk psychology), that is, the study of the cultural aspects of behavior (Cole, 1996). Until recently, his 10 volumes about the influence of culture were largely ignored and psychology concentrated on the study of the individual.

Now, over a hundred years later, culture is regaining its rightful central place in the study of human behavior and mental processes (Miller, 1999; Pederson, 1999). Because Wundt's and Titchener's methodology was impractical, William James's *functionalism* came to the fore. Heavily influenced by Charles Darwin's (1859, 1879) new theory of biological evolution, functionalists became interested in how the characteristics of different groups helped them adapt and successfully reproduce in their environments. These differences in characteristics were called **variation**. Functionalists investigated how human groups and their members differed from each other on important psychological variables such as intelligence, personality, and physical abilities, and assumed the observed differences were rooted in biology (Schultz & Schultz, 1996).

These early psychologists observed that *men* did virtually all that was deemed important and valuable. Men ruled nations, conducted wars, controlled property and wealth, created new art, music, literature, and innovated new technology. In universities, men discovered or invented new knowledge. Other men led crude lives of ignorance, drudgery, and misery on farms or in mines and factories. Moreover, it was mainly men who filled the prisons and institutions for the feeble-minded. It was clear to these early scientists that men were truly very varied, and according to the new science of evolution, this social variation propelled the advancement of the species. This misapplication of evolutionary theory to human society became known as *social Darwinism* (Shields, 1975).

In contrast, women seemed so much more alike. No matter their social status, their lives were focused on the bearing and rearing of children. As a group,

women seemed so much less intelligent compared to men. Those few women who had an education produced or created little. Women seldom contributed new knowledge. Moreover, it was obvious that virtually all women were physically as well as mentally weaker than men. These early observers noted that these same less developed characteristics also seemed applicable to nonwhites. Thus, women and nonwhites (of both sexes) could be lumped together as inferior, and the basis for this inferiority was biological.

Critical Thinking Challenge

Although these sexist and ethnocentric conclusions may seem outrageous, be prepared to see more modern versions of these same ideas. Also, don't we all continue to base our beliefs about gender on our own observations and experiences in the environment that happens to surround us? What outrageous errors might *we* currently be making about gender?

These early psychologists and educators saw a natural order in nature, with educated white men of the upper classes as the highest examples of human evolution. In 1874, Dr. Edward Clarke (whom you met in the opening vignette) declared that a higher education for women resulted in "monstrous brains and puny bodies, abnormally active cerebration and abnormally weak digestion; flowing thought and constipated bowels" (quoted in Walsh, 1977, p. 126). During final examinations, many college students and faculty may indeed fit this description, but it seems to apply equally to both sexes!

The writings of Edward H. Clarke had a great impact on G. Stanley Hall, another influential psychologist and educator. Hall, too, believed that educating women damaged their reproductive organs, caused them to bear sickly children, and led to the loss of mammary function (Hall, 1903, 1904a, 1911). Both accurately observed that the well-educated women of their time were less likely to marry and that those who did marry tended to have far fewer children.

Hall concluded that these trends were caused by the physiological damage from excessive mental activity. He also concluded that those few women who

---

variation **The spontaneous appearance of changes in an organism. Some variations facilitated successful survival and were therefore naturally selected (passed on to offspring).**

had contributed intellectually constituted a third sex, or had no sex at all. Accordingly, he advised that appropriate education for women was for motherhood and other nurturing roles. Occupationally oriented education should be limited to women's natural spheres: social work, home economics, and elementary school teaching. Hall also believed that to continue the advancement of the species, adolescent boys needed male teachers to help them express their natural savage impulses. Hall suggested that floggings by these male teachers would help calm young men and teach them not to beat women later on in life. He also contended that only by separating young men and women could one guarantee their later attraction to each other (Diehl, 1997). Despite these views, Hall encouraged many women in their pursuit of graduate education and he took an active interest in the career success of his most promising women students. Interestingly, during the 1920s he wrote that the new "**flapper**" woman represented "a new and better womanhood" (Hall, 1922).

Critical Thinking Challenge

Note that Clarke and Hall were adhering to the rules of science: collecting data on observable phenomena, analyzing that data, and interpreting that data. Why do their conclusions seem so wrong?

An outstanding early woman psychologist, Leta Stetter Hollingworth, performed an incisive statistical analysis that demolished the notion that women were less variable and therefore inferior (Shields, 1975, 1982). Other early psychologists attempted to create a psychology in which the behavior of women and men was of equal interest, but despite their efforts, white male behavior, mental processes, and concerns became the norm against which other groups were compared and found lacking (O'Connell & Russo, 1983).

Over the following decades, psychologists ignored, omitted, or distorted the issues of gender and ethnicity in their research and theories. These ongoing traditions of sexism, racism, and ethnocentrism are well described in Robert Guthrie's *Even the Rat Was White* (1998), and in Naomi Weisstein's (1977) classic essay, "*Kinder, Kuche* and *Kirche* as Scientific Law: Psychology Constructs the Female.*" In case those German words are unfamiliar to you, they mean *children*, *kitchen*, and *church*.

When psychology temporarily abandoned research on the mind to concentrate on the observable aspects of learning (behaviorism), academic psychologists lost interest in gender differences and similarities. In contrast, the psychoanalysts had a great deal to say about the differences between women and men. As you will read in the next chapter, psychoanalysts interpreted any observed gender differences to indicate male superiority and female inferiority, and these were attributed to biology. The end result was the entrenchment of three major biases in psychology regarding gender, and the remnants of these biases persist today (Collins, 1998). First, male behavior was the norm against which the behavior of others was compared. Second, any revealed gender differences were quickly transformed into women's deficiencies. And third, rampant ethnocentrism prevailed regarding the universality of white, middle-class gender roles.

Modern Psychology and the Study of Gender

Up until the 1970s, masculinity and femininity were viewed as nonoverlapping concepts. An extreme version of this notion was that if women had a particular trait, then men had none of that trait, and vice versa (see Figure 2.1a). However, researchers could not identify *any* psychological traits that fit that pattern. Note how this idea continues in full flower in everyday language about men and women as the "*opposite sex.*"

Critical Thinking Challenge

Cognitive psychologists tell us that the way we talk about something influences how we think and feel about it. Do you think that using the term *opposite sex* increases our tendency to see women and men as very different from each other? Does this matter?

A second conceptualization was that masculinity and femininity were opposite poles of a single continuum (see Figure 2.1d). One's personality consisted of those characteristics considered either masculine or feminine (Burr, 1998). A person (a male) was either masculine, dominating, and logical to varying

flappers **Young women of the 1920s who disdained the conventional dress and behavior of their time.**

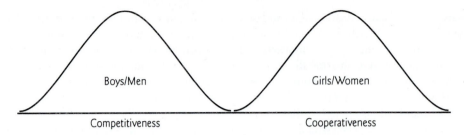

a. Nonoverlapping traits. Males and females have completely different characteristics. For example, all girls and women are cooperative to varying degrees; they are not at all competitive. All boys and men are competitive; they are not at all cooperative.

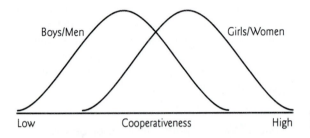

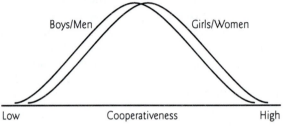

b. Overlapping trait. There is some overlap in the levels of any particular characteristic among both girls/women and boys/men. However, one gender manifests higher levels of a particular characteristic.

c. Overlapping trait. There is considerable overlap between the genders on any particular characteristics, but members of one gender are somewhat more likely to manifest extremely low or extremely high levels.

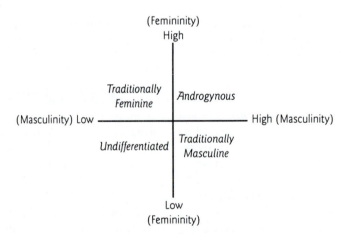

d. The Bem two-dimensional approach. The androgynous person scores high on *both* masculine and feminine traits. The undifferentiated person scores low on both masculine and feminine traits. The traditionally feminine person scores high on feminine traits and low on masculine traits. The traditionally masculine person scores high on masculine traits and low on feminine traits.

FIGURE 2.1   How do you visualize the differences between men and women? Which figure best reflects your beliefs regarding characteristics such as aggressiveness, helpfulness, and logical reasoning? Note that this perspective assumes that these characteristics are stable features that reside "within" the person. Later, you will see that this is a questionable assumption.

degrees, or a person (female) was feminine, submissive, and irrational to varying degrees. It was also assumed that men who were highly masculine and women who were very feminine would be considered psychologically healthier and thereby better adjusted (Lenny, 1991). However, empirical researchers found the world to be quite otherwise. A series of classic studies by Inge Broverman and her colleagues (1970, 1972) made clear how much more favorably traditionally masculine traits were valued. These researchers asked mental health professionals to indicate the psychological characteristics of a healthy man, a healthy woman, and a healthy *person*. The characteristics of the psychologically healthy man closely matched those of the healthy person, whereas the profile of a healthy woman was quite different from that of a psychologically healthy person. Can you see why? Take a look at the list of traits (Table 2.1). Which of the following people would strike you as more psychologically healthy? Person A is ambitious, competitive, direct, independent, self-confident, and not easily influenced. Person B is submissive, indirect, quiet, dependent, illogical, and has difficulty making decisions.

Thus the dilemma of middle-class femininity was revealed. Women who embodied traditional feminine traits were viewed as less psychologically unhealthy, and women who demonstrated more traditionally masculine characteristics were also viewed as maladjusted. The dilemma of psychology's traditional approach to gender was also revealed. The more psychologists went about measuring stereotypic gender traits, the more were these stereotypes maintained (Morawski, 1994). Although later researchers found significant methodological flaws in the Broverman studies, the differential valuing of traditional masculinity was clear (Phillips & Gilroy, 1985).

A newer conceptualization hypothesized femininity and masculinity as two separate and independent dimensions of the personality (Spence, Helmreich, & Stapp, 1974). In other words, one could measure and therefore compare "Jane's" or "Jack's" levels of both masculinity and femininity. In 1974, Sandra Bem published the Bem Sex-Role Inventory (BSRI), by which one could indeed measure these two separate dimensions (see Figure 2.1d). Regardless of a person's sex, high scores on the femininity scale and low scores on the masculinity scale suggested a very feminine-typed person. Regardless of sex, a highly masculine-typed person would score high on the masculinity scale and low on the femininity scale. Those individuals (regardless of sex) who scored high on both feminine and masculine traits were labeled as **androgynous**, and this was considered psychologically desirable. Those scoring low on both sets of characteristics were labeled *undifferentiated* and this suggested maladjustment.

Androgyny: A Critical Evaluation. The concept of *androgyny* generated a great deal of empirical research because it seemed a true breakthrough in scientific thinking about gender (Carlson & Videla-Sherman, 1990; Vonk & Ashmore, 1993). However, several shortcomings of the theory soon emerged. First, most studies merely **correlated** androgyny with a long list of other personality or behavioral traits. Therefore there was no way to demonstrate that femininity, masculinity, or androgyny *caused* these differences. A second issue had to do with what exactly the BSRI was measuring. Was it a personality trait, or was it a gender stereotype? Third, masculinity and femininity are surely more than traits. They include attitudes, preferences, physical features, social roles, interests, occupations, predispositions, and so on.

A fourth issue was the thorniest of all: Although intended to get psychology beyond the simplistic notions of dualistic thinking regarding gender, androgyny theory seemed ultimately to reinforce the very idea it sought to overcome (Bem, 1993). Consider the executive who brings his preschool children to the company day care center. He forgoes a promotion because the new job will require lots of overnight travel, misses work when his children are ill, and is equally willing to play basketball as paint his daughter's fingernails. Is it really more useful to evaluate him on a scale of masculinity, femininity, or even androgyny, when a more vital dimension seems to be that of responsive parent? Furthermore, does

---

androgyny   Having the psychological characteristics associated with both men and women. The term *androgyny* comes from the Greek words *andros*, man, and *gyne*, woman.

correlation   A relationship or association between two naturally occurring variables. The correlation coefficient *r* describes the strength and direction of that relationship ($r = -1.00$ to $+1.00$).

TABLE 2.1   Gender-Stereotypic Traits

Feminine	*Masculine*
Not at all aggressive	Very aggressive
Not at all independent	Very independent
Very emotional	Not at all emotional
Does not hide emotions at all	Almost always hides emotions
Very subjective	Very objective
Very easily influenced	Not at all easily influenced
Very submissive	Very dominant
Dislikes math and science very much	Likes math and science very much
Very excitable in a minor crisis	Not at all excitable in a minor crisis
Very passive	Very active
Not at all competitive	Very competitive
Very illogical	Very logical
Very home oriented	Very worldly
Not at all skilled in business	Very skilled in business
Very sneaky	Very direct
Does not know the way of the world	Knows the way of the world
Feelings easily hurt	Feelings not easily hurt
Not at all adventurous	Very adventurous
Has difficulty making decisions	Can make decisions easily
Cries very easily	Never cries
Almost never acts as a leader	Almost always acts as a leader
Not at all self-confident	Very self-confident
Very uncomfortable about being aggressive	Not at all uncomfortable about being aggressive
Not at all ambitious	Very ambitious
Unable to separate feelings from ideas	Easily able to separate feelings from ideas
Very dependent	Not at all dependent
Very conceited about appearance	Never conceited about appearance
Thinks women are always superior to men	Thinks men are always superior to women
Does not talk freely about sex with men	Talks freely about sex with men
Doesn't use harsh language at all	Uses very harsh language
Very talkative	Not at all talkative
Very tactful	Very blunt
Very gentle	Very rough
Very aware of feelings of others	Not at all aware of feelings of others
Very religious	Not at all religious
Very interested in own appearance	Not at all interested in own appearance
Very neat in habits	Very sloppy in habits
Very quiet	Very loud
Very strong need for security	Very little need for security
Enjoys art and literature	Does not enjoy art and literature at all
Easily expresses tender feelings	Does not express tender feelings at all easily

Note: These are the extreme poles of a seven-point rating scale.
Source: I. K. Broverman, S. R. Vogel, D. M. Broverman, F. E. Carlson, & P. S. Rosenkrantz (1972). Sex-role stereotypes: A current appraisal, *Journal of Social Issues, 28*(2), 59–78.

androgyny represent some sort of impossible ideal that ignores the requirements of culture? Even Sandra Bem herself has noted that the concept of androgyny continues the tradition of seeing gender typing as an internal and private characteristic. She concludes that such an approach to gender diverts attention away from the external structural and institutional forces that maintain the overvaluing of the masculine role, whatever its contents may be in a particular society (Bem, 1993).

Gender Stereotypes. Meanwhile, other researchers attempted to measure gender differences *not* as they might exist within those women and men who were being observed, but rather as they exist in the mind of the observer. That is, researchers began to tackle the content and impact of our gender stereotypes (Deaux, 1999).

The area of social psychology known as **social cognition** focuses on how we perceive and come to understand other people. What goes on within us as we observe another person, his or her behavior, a particular social interaction, or an entire complex social situation? We begin by organizing people into socially meaningful categories. This permits us to be more efficient about responding to and interacting with them appropriately. Different categories may be meaningful in different societies, but in most, categorization by gender is primary. Other major categorization schemes are age and ethnicity. In other words, apparent gender, ethnicity, and age are the first things we tend to notice about a person (Fiske & Neuberg, 1990; Fiske, 1993a). To understand the importance of classification by gender, note that most societies have elaborate rules about the constant announcing or display of one's gender (Goffman, 1979). Beginning at the very top of our bodies (hairstyle) and working down (level of grooming, clothing, fabrics worn, colors worn, bodily ornaments, facial paint, amount and placement of body hair, amount of skin exposed, accentuation of secondary sex characteristics, and finally foot coverings), all these announce our status as female or male, woman or man. Of course, in different societies the degree of differentiation in gender display may vary (see Figure 2.2). We also communicate gender via body language, voice depth and loudness, amount of space taken up, vocabulary used, and so on. If you still doubt that this is important to hu-

man beings, note how agitated people become when they cannot determine the gender of another person. They stare, squint, and whisper to others or smirk and laugh. They may threaten, injure, or even feel justified in killing someone who has violated this central social norm. Once we have applied the label *woman* or *man*, we then access a whole set of **schemas** to guide our interactions with that person (Bem, 1981, 1985). One type of schema is the **stereotype**. A stereotype includes beliefs about the target's personal traits, interests, occupation, values, goals, interactions, and competencies. These stereotypes determine what we notice, or remember about the person, how we interact with that person how we interpret any observed behavior. We even make predictions about others based on gender.

At the core of the masculine stereotype are notions of competency and doing things, whereas at the core of the feminine stereotype lie notions of warmth or expressiveness and relating to others (Spence & Buckner, 2000).

Although stereotypes are usually thought of negatively, they can be very helpful. They allow us to negotiate a very complex social world smoothly and astutely. They help us interact effectively with new individuals and new groups. However, whatever their positive value, stereotypes also serve as powerful social weapons, because they can destroy a target person's individuality. No matter what the target person is really like, he or she can be diminished and hammered into the same mental shape by stereotypes (Glick & Fiske, 1999). Gender stereotypes distort both people and reality itself. Take a look at Box 2.1 to see how stereotypes can distort the perceptions of both scientists and nonscientists.

Conclusion: Gender stereotypes wield enormous power. Most of us believe we are immune to such influences, but even very recent studies demonstrate that stereotypes are alive and well in all of us (Conway & Vartanian, 2000; Powlishta, 2000). The point here is that although we may all insist that gender and

---

social cognition   **An area of psychology that focuses on how we perceive and come to understand other people.**

schema   **A cognitive structure (mental concept) that guides our behavior and also how we process information.**

stereotype   **Culturally based belief that all members of particular human groups have the same characteristics.**

FIGURE 2.2 In some societies gender display is more differentiated than in others.

gender differences exist *out there* in the behavior of those we observe, the examples offered suggest that gender and gender differences *may exist primarily in our own perceptions and interpretations of behavior.*

Current Methods for Studying Gender: Potholes, Pitfalls, Caveats, and All Manner of Other Devilment

Most gender researchers assume that gender is something that is "out there" and can be observed, measured, studied, and explained with some degree of objectivity (a position known as *logical positivism*). Here

I evaluate the strengths and weaknesses of some of the specific tools researchers use to ask and answer questions about gender. I begin with those methods that seek to describe gender-related behavior.

Case Studies

A case study involves the collection of detailed information about one or more individuals. Although the case study approach lets the researcher delve into complex issues, it offers no protection against the researcher's personal and professional biases in selecting, organizing, and interpreting this information.

Revealing Gender Stereotypes in the Lab and in Life

The imagery and metaphors used to describe fertilization in biological and medical textbooks extend and reinforce many gender stereotypes. A medical anthropologist noted that female ova are often described as "passively awaiting" sperm. Sperm are described as "purposefully moving" through the reproductive tract "actively seeking" their target, which they then "aggressively assault." Sperm make a "perilous journey" to reach their prize. Sperm are described as "making a decision" (!) to penetrate an egg. Ova are described as in danger of death if not rescued by a fertilizing sperm. Most of us carry the stereotypic image of a single highly competitive sperm that is somehow "stronger" or "fitter" than the others (Darwinism strikes again!) and that is therefore able to penetrate the surface of the egg. A more accurate image seems to be that sperm *cooperate* so that several spermatozoa get closer to the surface of the egg. Actually, the release of certain chemicals allow the ovum to actively pull a sperm onto and into itself. Thus we see gender stereotypes applied and perpetuated even in descriptions of life on the cellular level, and the strength of those stereotypes distorts the accuracy of even scientific perception and description (Martin, 1987).

Research participants in one experiment all viewed the same videotape of two heavily snowsuited children playing in the snow. In the video, one child hit, threw snowballs at, and jumped on a second child. One group of participants was told that the children were two girls. Another group was told that the participants had seen a boy acting on a girl, a third was told a girl was acting on a boy, and the last was told a boy was acting on another boy. The "two boys" participants rated the behavior of the protagonist as being significantly *less* aggressive than in any of the other conditions. Here we see how stereotypic expectations influence our perception and interpretation of exactly the same behavior (Condry & Ross, 1985).

Gender stereotypes also have a strong relationship with perceptions of job prestige and salary levels. When research participants believed that a job required more stereotypically masculine traits, they rated the job higher in prestige and deserving of a higher salary. Here we see how stereotypic masculine traits continue to be differentially valued by members of our society (Glick, 1991; Glick, Wilk, & Perrault, 1995).

Traditionally, the case study has been the method of choice for clinical researchers to describe unusual behavior or mental states. For example, one might gain special insights into the behavior and mind-set of those who are initially distraught or seemingly confused about their biological sex and assigned gender (**transgendered** individuals) by interviewing such individuals at length about many aspects of their lives (Burke, 1996).

Observation

Observation involves collecting data about publicly observable behavior. The researcher carefully determines what specific behaviors to record, how to define these behaviors, and precisely how to measure them (**operational definitions**). The observation process should not influence the behavior studied. So far, that sounds rather clear-cut, but a classic study reminds us that when it comes to gender, all of us are so thoroughly immersed in a gendered universe that we cannot escape its influence. For example, participants observed a baby's tearful reaction to the unexpected popping up of a jack-in-the-box. When told that the baby was a girl, the observers reported that she cried because she was *frightened* by the experience. When told the baby was a boy, observers reported he cried because he was *angered* by the experience. These differences in interpretation were particularly strong for the male observers (Condry & Condry, 1976). Every observer is a gendered individual who lives in a heavily gendered world, and this affects how we perceive and interpret reality.

---

transgenderism **Continuum along which individuals engage in behaviors or mental processes associated with the other gender.**

operational definition **Defining something in terms of the operations required for its precise measurement (for example, defining your level of knowledge regarding gender by your average on several classroom tests).**

Surveys

Surveys usually involve structured self-report measures such as checklists and questionnaires that contain preset response options. Interviews use more open-ended questions. A strength of survey research is that it facilitates the collection of data from a great many individuals relatively quickly. A second advantage involves the opportunity to collect information about behaviors and mental processes that may not be public. But weaknesses also abound. Foremost is whether the respondents are truly representative of the population one wants to study. If a researcher wants to compare the child discipline styles of fathers versus mothers in Mexico, Zimbabwe, Saudi Arabia, and Japan, will a sample of parents who are college graduates from each of these societies be representative of each respective country's parents? That is extremely doubtful. Yet college students and graduates tend to be the most available survey participants. A second major problem has to do with the human tendency to present oneself in the best light possible. This inherent problem of all self-report data is called **social desirability**. Thus respondents' answers may not accurately reflect their actual gender-related attitudes and behaviors. Third, surveys provide *only correlational* data, and many gender researchers may be interested in *causative* factors. Fourth, the way questions are worded shapes the answers (Schwarz, 1999).

Surveys would seem to lend themselves easily to multicultural and cross-cultural gender research. However, the understanding and meaningfulness of survey items must be carefully considered. Across differing societies, this problem can be truly formidable (Gibbons, Hamby, & Dennis, 1997). Typical survey items ask respondents to indicate their level agreement with or acceptance of a statement. Take a look at the following three survey items:

A. It is okay for a woman to ask a man out on a date.
   1 = strongly disagree   2 = disagree
   3 = neither agree nor disagree   4 = agree
   5 = strongly agree
B. It is equally likely that a man or woman might have a lonely liver.
   1 = strongly disagree   2 = disagree
   3 = neither agree nor disagree   4 = agree
   5 = strongly agree

C. Sexual intercourse should be equally pleasurable for both the woman and the man.
   1 = strongly disagree   2 = disagree
   3 = neither agree nor disagree   4 = agree
   5 = strongly agree

The first item seems sensible to most members of Western societies, and it is the type of item that often appears on gender role attitude questionnaires, because most such questionnaires originate in Western societies. However, in societies where dating is unknown, or the idea of an unmarried man and woman spending time alone together before marriage is completely unacceptable, the item makes absolutely no sense. The second item may seem bizarre, but the concept of a lonely liver is quite familiar to the Hmong people of Laos (as well as to the Hmong who live in the United States and Canada). It refers to the sadness one feels when separated from loved ones (Dunnegin, McNall, & Mortimer, 1993). The third item may be offensive, obscene, or totally nonsensical in societies where sexual pleasure is simply not part of that society's gender construction of *woman*.

Developmental Approaches

How do the various aspects of gender change over a lifetime? One approach is to compare different age groups on some variable or factor of interest. Suppose you were interested in comparing how men and women conduct their friendships at different points in their lives. It might seem logical to study the friendship patterns of women and men in their 20s, those of another group in their 40s, another in their 60s, and still another in their 80s. This is called a *cross-sectional approach*. It is as if the researcher were taking a group photograph of behavior, attitudes, and feelings at a particular moment in the life span. Assuming one can identify comparable and representative groups, this sounds pretty easy. Actually, it's not that simple. You'll see why in a moment.

A more difficult approach is known as the *longitudinal study*. Here the same group of people born at

---

social desirability **The tendency of research participants to present themselves in the best possible way in terms of social norms.**

about the same time (a **cohort**) is followed for a length of time (from several months to several decades). For our example, friendship-related variables would be measured in a group of 20-year-olds and that same group would be reassessed when they were 40, 60, and 80 years old. Imagine the difficulties involved in locating a group of people every 10 years and in having them agree to be reevaluated! Then there's the problem of funding and passing down this research project to several generations of researchers. Such projects are expensive, and the final results might not be available for decades. Yet there are advantages to this approach, because the psychosocial environment influences each generational cohort. In North America, contemporary 80-year-olds formed their first friendships during the 1920s, a time of Prohibition laws and great change in social and sexual mores. Vast numbers of young men died in World War I, and women were emerging from those confining corsets and petticoats to bare their legs and cut their hair (recall G. Stanley Hall's reference to the new flappers of the 1920s). Sixty-year-olds in North America formed their first adult friendships in a cold war environment, under the threat of nuclear annihilation and with the energy of the second wave of the women's movement. These factors might have had a lifelong effect on the form and content of their friendships. Contemporary 20-year-olds in North America initiated their first friendships in a world of great gender role realignment, economic optimism, and a tidal wave of technological innovation. So, when comparing different age groups, concluding that the only difference between them is age is simplistic. Many developmentally oriented gender researchers try to conduct their studies with a combination of cross-sectional and longitudinal methods.

Correlational Studies

The specific methods just mentioned may all be used in correlational studies. By definition, a correlational study measures the strength and direction of a relationship between two or more naturally occurring variables (correlation). A mathematical formula is used to calculate the strength and direction of such a relationship (a correlation coefficient). Correlations describe relationships and can also be used to make predictions about groups (not individuals). For an example that may be close to home, your college or university admits only those students who achieved above a particular score on the SAT or ACT. This is because scores on these tests are strongly correlated with college GPAs. That is, they predict the likelihood that students can do college-level work. These scores are not fool-proof predictors, but they work fairly well. However, the greatest weakness of correlations is that they do not tell us what caused a behavior. For example, you might read that there is a strong correlation between being convicted of rape and the use of violent pornography. But you cannot conclude that looking at violent pornography caused some men to commit rape. Maybe internal impulses to rape caused them to seek out violent pornography. Or maybe a factor not even considered in the study (such as a history of childhood sexual abuse, or a brain lesion) led them to *both* seek out violent pornography *and* rape. Always be cognizant of this inherent limitation of all correlational studies.

Critical Thinking Challenge

Think back to E. H. Clarke's conclusions regarding causation in the relationships among childbearing, mental illness, and higher education. Are you now more able to refute his position? How?

Experimentation

Despite its many drawbacks (artificiality, lack of generalizability, and so forth), many traditional researchers consider the experiment the most powerful research technique available. The basic concept of experimentation is simple. A sample from a population of interest is randomly assigned to two or more conditions. Random assignment is very important, because it helps ensure that the groups in an experiment are equivalent on all relevant factors. Measure a variable of interest (the dependent variable, or DV) to demonstrate that the groups *are* equivalent on that variable. Then expose one of the groups to some variable (the usual term is "manipulate the independent

---

cohort   **Group of people born at about the same time and in the same society, thus implying similar social and historical influences.**

variable, or IV"), but do not expose the other group to the IV. Control group(s) may be left alone or given some placebo. Then remeasure the variable of interest (the DV) in both groups. Because the groups were equivalent on that variable before one group was exposed to the IV, one can infer that the newly found difference was *caused* by exposure to that variable.

Caveats. Many a budding gender researcher has fallen victim to a serious misunderstanding. Let's say a particular factor is measured in a group of men and women. Let's make up a factor called *ubiquitous plasticity,* and let's assume that all women research participants score higher on this factor than men do. The beginning researcher concludes that he or she has found a gender difference on that factor. That is, the difference found was caused by the gender of the participants. This is actually one type of *ex post facto* hypothesizing ("after the fact"). The factor, gender, existed *before* the researcher made the measurements. It is a subject variable that already differentiated the participants. Thus one cannot conclude that sex or gender *caused* the difference found (Babbie, 2001). However, many studies do compare groups of men and women on some factor. To ensure greater accuracy, any differences revealed should be referred to as *gender-related differences* (Unger & Crawford, 1998).

A misunderstanding of this basic concept also contributes to the overattribution of gender differences to biological causes. Suppose that researchers consistently find that girls develop language earlier than boys and have a significantly larger vocabulary by age 3. Can one conclude that being female or male caused this difference? That is, does possessing the chromosomal, hormonal, and neuroanatomical bases for classification as a female cause a person to have greater language ability? One might be tempted to conclude precisely that and to search for the biological basis for such a sex difference. So you can see how easy it is to jump to the conclusion of biological causation for such a difference. Would the tendency be the same if the variable measured were length of hair? That is doubtful. What about differences in athleticism? The important point here is that just because a sex or gender difference emerges in a study, or even in a thousand studies, it does *not* mean that biological factors are the cause of that difference (even

the eminent Edward Clarke made this error). Remember this important principle, because it will come up many times as you study gender.

Meta-Analysis

Meta-analysis is a statistical technique that combines the results of many studies in order to estimate the overall differences between groups (Hyde, 1994). Thus meta-analysis may be used to answer two questions: Is there a difference between groups on some variable of interest, and how large is that difference? This difference is called the *effect size* (Unger, 1990). The challenge in conducting a good meta-analysis is collecting *all* available research studies, including unpublished ones (Burn, 1996; Hyde & Linn, 1986). For example, one meta-analysis examined the stereotype that women self-disclose much more (reveal deeper feelings and thoughts) in relating to others. A meta-analysis of 205 studies revealed that women self-disclosed only slightly more than men did, and that for both sexes, having a woman as an interaction partner increased self-disclosure levels (Dindia & Allen, 1992). For many situations in which greater self-disclosure is desirable (counseling, psychotherapy, patient–physician communication, and so forth), having a woman in that professional role may facilitate better outcomes.

Qualitative Methods

The goal of the qualitative approach is to understand a behavior or mental process from the perspective of the person who is engaging in the behavior or mental process. The point is to hear and understand the meaning of particular experiences for different people. Most likely, a pregnancy would have a very different meaning for a newlywed of 20 than for a married woman of 50. Let's compare the traditional quantitative approach with the qualitative approach. Suppose a researcher wanted to understand the experiences and behavior of first-time fathers. The traditional researcher might hypothesize that such a man might be experiencing anxiety and mood changes. The researcher might also compare the amount of direct parent–infant contact by each parent. So the re-

---

caveat   **A warning, cautionary statement.**

searcher uses ostensibly objective measures of anxiety and mood change and then, perhaps, counts the seconds each parent or caretaker spends in direct eye contact, holding, rocking, feeding, and so on. The quantitative researcher ends up only with the pieces of behavior that he or she assumed were important. But all the other stuff that might be going on is completely lost! The qualitative researcher tries to take an open stance in seeking to understand the experience of the person studied. There is an emphasis on *process* rather than on static bits of behavior (Gubrium & Holstein, 1997). The qualitative researcher might interview first-time fathers at great length and try to elicit subjective descriptions of what the father is experiencing. ("At first, I was terrified of this tiny creature who took over our lives." "Sometimes I feel waves of gratitude to my wife." "That job stuff that had seemed so important, now seemed trivial.")

Critical Thinking Challenge

This would be a really good time to take another look at the quotation that opened this chapter. Is it now more meaningful? If so, why?

The difficulties surrounding qualitative approaches involve the requirement that the researcher have no preconceptions about the phenomenon to be studied. Think about how difficult this is. Moreover, the data collected are supposed to be sufficiently precise that two other researchers trained in the phenomenological method would interpret the material in the same way. Thus this method is similar to the case study method in that it involves collecting in-depth information, and it has the same weaknesses. There is a greater likelihood of individual bias. Also, the people studied may not be representative of any larger population. However, the qualitative researcher accepts this subjectivity as a reality in any human interaction and deals with it directly (Kidder & Fine, 1997).

Box 2.2 discusses how some of these research methods are used to study gender all over the world.

Critical Issues in the Study of Gender

Beyond the strengths and weaknesses of the specific methods used to study gender, there are several other issues you need to keep in mind.

Women and the Study of Gender

A minority of women and men have always spoken out on behalf of gender equality. Mary Wollstonecraft's *Vindication of the Rights of Women* (1792/1929), and John Stuart Mill's essay on *The Subjection of Women* (1869) are two important documents that set the stage for the first women's movement early in the 20th century. This first women's movement was centered mainly on the right to vote.

During the 1960s, the civil rights struggle of African Americans became a superb model for a social, economic, and political movement to change the social and legal norms of an entire society. The methods of the civil rights movement became the methods of a second wave of the women's movement that began in Canada, the United States, and Britain. Today, women and men all over the world are working toward increased rights and opportunities for women (Neft & Levine, 1997; Ray, 1999).

The early writers and thinkers of the second wave of the women's movement were mainly highly educated white women who spoke to the issues that concerned them (hooks, 1981, 1989, 1990). However, a much wider group of men and women contributed to the ultimate success of the movement. This second wave of the **feminist** movement has had an impact on virtually every aspect of life in industrialized nations: employment, education, business, law, politics, family relations, the media, and even our most intimate relationships. Within the field of psychology, feminist psychologists, whether researchers, educators, or practitioners examined every aspect of traditional psychology. They found evidence of deeply entrenched intellectual biases regarding gender, as well as systematic prejudice and discrimination against women and ethnic minorities. Even the ostensibly objective steps of the scientific method itself have come under intense scrutiny. Box 2.3 offers a feminist critique of the study of gender at each step of the scientific method.

Caveat. Research may be carried out by women, conducted with female participants, or focus on issues

---

feminist **One who believes in the social, economic, and political equality of the sexes.**

Using the Gender Researcher's Toolbox Around the World

China: A longitudinal approach was used to explore how parental warmth and indulgence affects children's social, emotional, and academic adjustment. Over the two years of the study, maternal warmth was associated with good emotional adjustment. Paternal warmth predicted later social and academic achievement in both girls and boys. Fatherly indulgence predicted later adjustment difficulties in both genders (Chen, Liu, & Li, 2000).

West Bank: Researchers used interviews and questionnaires to evaluate how living in a violent environment differentially affect the adjustment of girls and boys. One hundred Palestinian mothers and their children living on the West Bank during the Intifada (Palestinian uprising) were interviewed. Overall, Palestinian children displayed higher levels of behavior problems (anger, despair, psychic numbing, diminished competencies, posttraumatic stress disorder, and so on) and this increase was comparable to that of children in the United States who live in communities with chronic violence. For Palestinian children living in higher-violence communities, boys manifested significantly more total problems than did girls. In lower-violence conditions, there was no difference. However, an unexpected finding was that girls living in high-violence areas actually manifested fewer behavior problems than did girls in low-violence areas (Garbarino & Kostelny, 1996).

United States: An experiment demonstrated how the gender-typing of tasks influences cognitive abilities such as memory. Researchers asked participants to memorize identical shopping lists (for example, light bulbs, floor cleaner, and so on). Half the group was told the items might be found in a grocery store, and

half was told they might be found in a hardware store. Women participants demonstrated significantly better memory for the grocery list, whereas men demonstrated better memory for the hardware store items (Herrmann, Crawford, & Holdsworth, 1992).

Peru: Questionnaires and a qualitative approach were used to understand the experiences of women industrialists in Peru. Most of the women were of middle-class origins with college-age children. They found their endeavors liberating and empowering. They saw economic independence as a way of giving their children a better life. Many felt constrained by their belief that wives should not be more successful than their husbands (deBowman, 2000).

United States: A case study described the manifestation of gender identity disorder during childhood. A 7-year-old boy was evaluated because of his frequent intimations of "wanting to be a girl." A physical examination showed him to be physically well built and well coordinated, and to have normal genitalia. He refused to participate in rough play with other boys. His family and childhood history were unremarkable. In his imaginative play, the boy typically assumed female roles and imitated female fictional characters. He enjoyed doll play, kitchen toys, and drawing female figures. In spite of parental restrictions, he often attempted to cross-dress. When unhappy, he expressed the wish to be a girl (Spitzer, Gibbon, Skodol, Williams, & First, 1994).

Spain: A correlational approach was taken to study the relationship between gender and the importance of career aspirations in intimate relationships. In 148 dating couples, gender did not predict ca-

reer salience. More education and a more egalitarian gender ideology predicted greater career salience among married women, whereas more sexist gender ideology predicted greater career salience among married men. Having children and being dependent on a spouse was found to be related to lower career salience for married women, but not for men (Moya, Exposito, & Ruiz, 2000).

Finland: Researchers administered a survey instrument three times to evaluate men's and women's personal goals as they made the transition into parenthood (early in pregnancy, just before the birth, and three months postbirth). Women expressed fewer achievement goals and more family and health-related goals through this process. Men's goals changed in a parallel manner, but less intensely, compared to women (Salmela-Aro, Nurmi, Saistro, & Halmesmaki, 2000).

Across Cultures: A checklist survey instrument was used to answer the question "Do gender stereotypes vary across cultures?" College students in 30 countries over North America, South America, Europe, Asia, Africa, and Oceania rated 300 traits as to whether they were more frequently associated with women or with men. Of these, 100 were rated as being more typical of either men or women (see Table 2.2). Three traits were found to be universally identified with being female (sentimental, submissive, and superstitious). Six male-identified traits were also universal (adventurous, dominant, forceful, independent, masculine, and strong). Respondents in some societies rated the feminine stereotype more favorably (Italy, Peru, and Australia), whereas others (Japan, South Africa, and Nigeria) rated the masculine stereotype more favorably (Williams & Best, 1990).

A Feminist Critique of the Traditional Gender Research Process

The Collection of Data

- What data should be collected? There is an extensive body of research on aggression but comparatively little on nurturance.
- Gender matters in the actual face-to-face conduct of research. Researcher gender affects the responses of participants, and participant gender affects researchers. Good studies use participants and researchers of both genders.

Analysis of the Measures Collected

- Findings of sex and gender differences too easily became a chronicle of women's "deficiencies." Such differences were overly attributed to biological causes and were seldom analyzed regarding their practical significance (Hyde & Plant, 1995).
- It is important not to make men's standards and behavior the norm nor to consider women's behavior a deviation from those norms (Tavris, 1992).
- Scientific methods push researchers to search for differences between groups. A truckload of research studies that reveal no differences goes unpublished, whereas a few that show differences are published in scientific journals. This adds to the perception that men and women are very different (Favreau, 1997).

Interpreting the Data

- Gender bias influenced the evaluation and selection of research studies for publication (Swim, Borgida, Maruyama, & Myers, 1989; Top, 1991). The American Psychological Association now uses an anonymous system of review considering articles for possible publication.
- Interpretations of data collected may be androcentric and misogynistic. When introductory psychology students estimated their grades on an upcoming exam, men estimated their grades would be higher than the grades actually received. Women students tended to underestimate their grades. Analysts interpreted this to indicate that women students have lower self-esteem than their male counterparts. When researchers reexamined the data, it was clear that the women's estimates were, in fact, much closer to the actual grades received. A reinterpretation could emphasize the overly inflated self-concepts of the men (cited in Hyde, 1994).
- Feminist psychologists advocate for research carried out in the context of lives and realities other than that of the dominant majority group. For example, a growing research literature makes the African-American experience normative (Collins, 1998). There

is an increasing attempt to obtain a wider representation of research participants (Matsumoto et al., 1997; Saris & Johnston-Robledo, 2000).
- Sexist language has been virtually eliminated from psychological publications and instructional texts. (Has sexist language disappeared from your term papers?) But this linguistic gender neutrality can give rise to other problems. Such language can mask or mitigate certain realities. For example, in the vast majority of cases it is men who batter women. Referring to this phenomenon as *spouse abuse* or *domestic violence* clouds the central feature of this form of violence.
- The popular media and the general public seem to have insatiable appetites for notions of essential differences between men and women. Gender researchers should take responsibility for making sure that any differences found are not exaggerated or sensationalized.
- Many gender researchers have a more egalitarian society as an ultimate goal. Some critics contend that this goal can lead to researching only politically correct issues and the reporting of only those findings that are compatible with this goal (Halpern, 1996a, 1996b).

that are important to women. However, none of this guarantees that it is **nonsexist** research (Denmark, Russo, Frieze, & Sechzer, 1988).

Men and the Study of Gender

A complete psychology of gender must deal at length with the psychology of men. You may find that statement rather contradictory. Didn't you just learn that

traditional psychology was all about men and that the goal of feminist psychologists was to have women included and honored in all areas of psychology? Yes, two seemingly contradictory ideas can both be true. Traditional psychology developed with men, especially white Western men, as the generic human being

---

nonsexist Without bias or prejudice toward members of either gender (gender fair).

TABLE 2.2   The 100 Items of the Cross-Cultural Adjective Checklist

Male-Associated Traits		Female-Associated Traits	
Active	Loud	Affected	Modest
Adventurous	Obnoxious	Affectionate	Nervous
Aggressive	Opinionated	Appreciative	Patient
Arrogant	Opportunistic	Cautious	Pleasing
Autocratic	Pleasure-seeking	Changeable	Prudish
Bossy	Precise	Charming	Self-pitying
Capable	Progressive	Complaining	Sensitive
Coarse	Quick	Complicated	Sentimental
Conceited	Rational	Confused	Sexy
Confident	Realistic	Curious	Shy
Courageous	Reckless	Dependent	Softhearted
Cruel	Resourceful	Dreamy	Sophisticated
Cynical	Rigid	Emotional	Submissive
Determined	Robust	Excitable	Suggestive
Disorderly	Serious	Fault-finding	Superstitious
Enterprising	Sharp-witted	Fearful	Talkative
Greedy	Show-off	Fickle	Timid
Hardhearted	Steady	Foolish	Touchy
Humorous	Stern	Forgiving	Unambitious
Indifferent	Stingy	Frivolous	Understanding
Individualistic	Stolid	Fussy	Unintelligent
Initiative	Tough	Gentle	Unstable
Interests wide	Unfriendly	Imaginative	Warm
Inventive	Unscrupulous	Kind	Weak
Lazy	Witty	Mild	Worrying

Source: From J. E. Williams & D. L. Best (1994). Cross cultural views of women and men, in W. J. Lonner & R. Malpass (Eds.), *Psychology and culture* (Boston: Allyn and Bacon).

against which all others were compared. However, those currently involved in the psychology of gender are concerned with men as explicitly gendered individuals (Coltrane, 1998b). That is, gender researchers recognize that the male gender role and our conceptions of masculinity are also socially constructed, as is the feminine role. Like femininity, masculinity is a product of a particular time in a particular culture. The traditional masculine gender role may allow for varying degrees of power and privilege, but it can also distort and harm the individual, as can the traditional feminine gender role. What are some major gender-related issues that surround the study of men?

One of the most distinctive characteristics of masculinity or manliness is that something significant must be done to transform a male person into a man (Gilmore, 1990). In some societies, the transforma-

tion occurs by participation in a war or other life-threatening activity. In others, it may be sexual conquest, the acquisition of wealth, or some mortification of the body or mind (Bonvillain, 1998; Herdt, 1997). Because manhood is something that is acquired rather than merely developed, or automatically given at birth, manhood is always in danger of being lost. Losing one's masculinity is almost always accompanied by deep shame and humiliation (Kimmel, 1997).

A lifelong theme of traditional masculinity includes the active and ongoing eradication of anything even remotely feminine from a man's public presentation (Burn, 1996; Levant, 1995).

Scholars recognize that there are many masculinities. The concept of masculinity varies by culture, ethnicity, social status, and sexual orientation. Thus there is growing attention to masculinity and cultural diversity as well as to the experiences of gay men in a heterosexist society (Best & Williams, 1997; Hurwich & Tori, 2000; Lazur & Majors, 1995).

The first and second wave of the women's movement were focused on how external societal structures oppressed women. Early writers in the men's movement turned inward, emphasizing how gender socialization pushed men toward being competitive, unemotional (except for anger), tough, and seemingly independent. Popular books on the new masculinity divulged men's hurts about absent and rejecting fathers, the banishment of tenderness from their lives, and its substitution with casual sexual expression (Bly, 1990; Pleck, 1981a). However, such writings ignored the element of *power* in the relationship between the genders. More recent male-oriented gender research has explored the many aspects of masculine social power. One of the major paradoxes of masculinity is that whereas men, as a group, clearly have social, economic, and political power, each man typically feels uniquely without power (Johnson, 1997; Kaufman, 1993a).

Many students are familiar with the fact that in industrialized societies, women tend to outlive men by almost a decade. This difference in life span is almost always attributed to the extra stresses and strains that come with the traditional masculine gender role in such societies. It is interesting to note that this difference is seldom attributed to biological factors (Eisler, 1995).

Traditional masculinity promotes an emotional life that involves the constricted overdevelopment of anger and aggression, and the underdevelopment of the more tender emotions (Lynch & Kilmartin, 1999). This can result in the highly explosive masculine rage and violence that occurs in many societies and subcultures (Sattel, 1998).

Traditional masculinity prescribes an overemphasis on action to solve life's problems. This can result in a relative inability to cope with unsolvable or protracted problems or dilemmas (G. Smith, 1996). Thus men are more likely to find unbearable the stresses associated with a child or spouse who has a permanent disability or chronic lifelong illness.

One of the most exciting issues in the study of men relates to the changes in men's domestic roles as father and husband (Deutsch, 1999; NICHD, 2000). The realities of life within a dual-earner family mean such men spend more time caring for their children and doing household chores.

Critical Thinking Challenge

Studies of men's psychology are often subject to the same criticisms and suspicions that previously surrounded the psychology of women. How is the study of masculine gender issues regarded on your campus?

Sexual Orientation and the Study of Gender

Whatever else may go into our society's construction of women or men, femininity or masculinity, one of its central components has to do with **sexual orientation**. That is, a central aspect of establishing and maintaining the identity of an appropriate adult man or woman is one's attraction to, and sexual activity with, a person of the other gender. Therefore, it is not surprising that those who engage in erotic behavior with members of their own sex are seen as not being true members of their own gender. Women who engage in sexual activity with other women are derided with epithets that make reference to their pseudo-maleness. Men who prefer other men as sexual partners are ridiculed with names that evoke feminine traits of delicacy (*pansy*, or the British *poof*).

From the beginning of psychology's involvement in abnormal behavior and mental illness, same-sex sexual behavior was considered pathological and a clear-cut indication of mental illness. Although a few questioned this assumption (Hooker, 1957), mental health professionals concurred that a homosexual preference or orientation indicated personality disturbance, most particularly in gender identity. The lay public still tends to believe that there is a predictable relationship between one's sexual orientation and the degree to which someone adheres to traditional gender prescriptions in nonverbal behavior, mode of dress and grooming, occupational choice, recreational interests, and so on (Clatterbaugh, 1997; Simon, 1998). Conversely, those whose behavior or interests cross the gender line are considered likely to be homosexual, for example, the boy interested in ballet, or the woman who aspires to become a fighter pilot.

---

sexual orientation **An individual's socioerotic preference regarding the sex or gender of sexual partners.**

Moreover, homosexuality is presumed to imply a significant deviation from traditional gender roles. For example, lesbianism is typically considered incompatible with an interest in bearing and taking care of children. Male homosexuality is typically considered incompatible with traditionally masculine occupations such as warrior, truck driver, or professional football player. Male homosexuality is certainly considered incompatible with the father role. The real and imaginary relationships between sexuality and gender are discussed at length in Chapter 8.

Culture and the Study of Gender

Most students would find it unacceptable for geologists to say that they study only red rocks because red rocks predominated where they were born. If geologists implied that red rocks were superior or somehow more natural than other stones, even the most naïve student would be skeptical. For too long, psychology has focused on a very narrow slice of gendered behavior and mental processes: Researchers have concentrated on gender as it exists in the United States. Even more narrowly, they have focused on how it exists among white college students in the United States (Moghaddam & Studer, 1997). To understand the nature of gender, it is important to take a broader worldview. That's why this text includes studies of both cross-cultural and multicultural constructions of gender. We should take a moment here to distinguish between multicultural versus cross-cultural psychology. Multicultural psychology is concerned with group differences *within* a society. In the United States, these group differences typically focus on ethnicity: on African Americans, Native Americans, European Americans, and so forth (Goodstein & Gielen, 1998).

Critical Thinking Challenge

Do you recall the discussion in Chapter 1 regarding why it is inappropriate to refer to such groups as *races*? How would you explain this issue in your own words?

In Northern Ireland, religious preference is a factor in domestic cultural difference (Cairns & Darby, 1998). In Kuwait and Germany, large long-term populations of guest workers from other nations form the base for multicultural studies. In Canada, linguistic differences (speaking French or English) constitute a cultural delineator. Cross-cultural psychology is concerned with both human behavioral universals that transcend culture (for example, facial expressions of the basic emotions) versus those behaviors and mental processes that vary across cultures (for example, variations in **prosocial behavior** in societies oriented toward collectivism versus those oriented toward individualism (Kagitcibasi, 1997; Triandis, 1994, 1995). Thus cross-cultural and multicultural psychologists study the psychological similarities and differences of various cultural and ethnic groups.

Both multicultural and cross-cultural researchers, note that an important aspect of culture is the set of prescriptions and proscriptions (the "no-nos") for the way people should do things. We all have social positions relative to other social entities (a mother relative to a child, a student relative to a teacher). Most of us have learned to act out the prescribed role that goes with that position (such as how a friend is supposed to behave). A role is also subject to situation-specific norms (for example, in my role as professor, I would not discuss my personal health anxieties in class). Cultural psychologists hold that we have mastered certain norms for our behavior, including gender norms. In a particular setting, these norms *guide* how we behave. They do not *cause* us to behave that way. Thus in a gendered situation (and most situations are gendered to varying degrees), our behavior and mental processes are guided by our gender (and cultural) norms (Miller, 1999; Moghaddam & Studer, 1997).

The Social Constructionist Perspective

Positivists view human behavior as the result of identifiable *causes*. In the crudest terms, it is as if people were hit by a cause and therefore changed a particular aspect of their behavior (the effect). In reality, humans are interpreting creatures who try to make sense of and find meaning in whatever happens to them. How they respond or change after being affected by a variable is very difficult to predict.

prosocial behavior   Acts or behavior performed to help other people, done without expectation of reward or benefit to oneself.

Consider the offspring of alcoholic parents. Could a scientist predict the effect of such a complex experience? Growing up with two alcohol abusers, a child might decide it's best never to drink alcohol, or that a future life of alcohol abuse is unavoidable and inevitable—or something else entirely.

Gender scholars identified with the **social constructionist** perspective have taken issue with the basic assumptions of science. They note that although science claims to be value free and focused on objective facts, it is actually the enactment of certain Western cultural values (Burr, 1998; Marecek, 1995). As we have shown repeatedly, human beings are always engulfed in particular social and cultural processes (such as gender) and cannot easily step outside those processes. We are not detached knowers of an external universe. Positivistic approaches cannot deal adequately with the contradictions and complexities of human behavior. Social constructionists insist that gender is not "out there," away from the observer/researcher. Gender influences the construction of the very world that the person sees. This gendered construction is often based on linguistic forms. For example, imagine the world when your grandmother was a young woman. If her husband beat her, she was likely to believe she had experienced a personal and private tragedy that she had to overcome and that her problem had something to do with her failure as a woman and wife. The concept or phenomenon of battered woman simply did not exist. Today, that interaction between your young grandmother and her husband has a name and exists in the world as a labeled phenomenon called *wife abuse, battering,* or *domestic violence,* with its own dynamics, processes, recourses, and outcomes. Thus language creates what is real in the world (Wetherell, 1997). There were no battered women, date rapes, or mid-life crises until social scientists declared their existence.

Two More Problems in the Study of Gender

One of the most powerful devilments of gender and cultural research is the problem of **reification** or "thingification." Psychologists often proceed as if constructs such as *dependence* were real things, when actually they exist only in relation to others. One person is more dependent only relative to others, usually by comparison to members of dominant groups, that is, people with the resources to be independent (Hare-Mustin & Marecek, 1998).

A second aspect of reification has to do with causation. Suppose a researcher uncovers a reliable gender difference in our favorite fictitious variable, *ubiquitous plasticity.* We have explained nothing to say it is caused by differences in hormones, socialization, or culture unless we can pinpoint what specific aspect of hormonal action, socialization, or cultural practice brought this difference about. We must also seek to understand how this substance, practice, or experience brought it about. Insisting that it is caused by an interaction of biological and learned factors still does not satisfy the question as to what specifically caused that overall difference. At our present level of methodological sophistication, virtually all research on gender differences is merely descriptive.

The last problem involves the central paradox of all gender research. For those scholars interested in gender equality and social change, the ultimate goal is to *make* gender irrelevant as an organizing principle of modern society (Weber, 1998). But at the same time, gender researchers bring great attention to the issue of gender through their work. Can the factor of gender ever be made irrelevant in organizing access to power and privilege? Recall that traditional psychologists believed that sex or gender was irrelevant and that they were almost successful in making the behavior, mental processes, and life experiences of girls and women invisible. This position can result in the continued legitimization of male dominance. Take a look at Box 2.4 to see what some gender researchers have to say about this important controversy. This paradox will be an issue for the next generation of gender scholars. That's you.

---

social constructionism   **The philosophic view that there are no universal and objective truths about human behavior because people construct reality—often on the basis of language, culture, moment in history, and power arrangements.**

reification   **The tendency within the social sciences to treat abstract concepts as if they had a tangible form: to make an idea or concept into a "thing."**

Should Psychologists Study Gender Differences?

Is the study of gender differences a worthwhile pursuit? Here's what outstanding scholars in the field of gender research have to say about this question.

An Enthusiastic *Yes!*

Diane Halpern (1998b) reminds us that knowledge is power and that a lack of study produces only ignorance. To those who fear that research on gender differences perpetuates stereotypes, Halpern responds that gender stereotypes *predated* research and that stereotypes can change as a result of knowledge. Scientific research is the only way to dispel stereotypes and understand real differences. Speaking of stereotypes, she urges feminists not to live up to their own stereotype as rigid and conforming thinkers. After all, feminism is about open-minded and careful debate about what was assumed and taken for granted. Halpern believes strongly that even when findings do not appear to fit worthwhile social and political goals, we should not censor this knowledge. Halpern supports the idea that there are strong biology-based differences between the sexes in many areas. Moreover, she holds that the general public understands that findings of gender differences refer to average differences rather than specific individuals. Halpern is concerned that assuming there are no real gender differences can make males normative again. She notes that discussing the issue of sex and gender differences is a popular (and lucrative) pastime for the media and is of continuing interest to the general public. She concludes that sex differences sell!

A Cautious Yes!

Janet Shibley Hyde (1998) notes that study of gender differences dates back to the beginning of psychology and that since the 1970s it has become a growth industry. She believes it is here to stay because science, the media, and the public are intrigued with the question of how

women and men might differ. However, this pursuit has certain inherent problems. For example, only findings of significant difference) are published, whereas null findings (no differences found) are not. She notes that both the media and the public will leap on any reports of differences and neglect the fact that 10 subsequent researchers could not find any such differences. She also concludes that that a so-called difference is often so tiny it is virtually meaningless. Finally, Hyde reminds us that differences are invariably interpreted as female deficits and can be used in a way harmful to women. For example, reports of gender differences in mathematical ability were widely publicized (Benbow & Stanley, 1980). Years later, these reports were shown to adversely affect mothers' estimations of their daughters' math abilities (Jacobs & Eccles, 1992). Finally, Hyde concludes that differences are often interpreted as being caused by biological factors, even in the absence of any biological measures.

A Resounding *No!*

Robert Baumeister (1988), Rachel Hare-Mustin and Jeanne Marecek (1998), and Janice Yoder and Arnold Kahn (1993) all believe that the pursuit of gender differences has been full of conflict and mystification. They point out that the search for differences assumes that there is some stable, underlying essential difference between women and men and that it is located inside the person. Thus when a so-called difference emerges, it becomes a deficiency that the individual must "repair." Thus a lack of assertiveness supposedly explains why women are still rare in the corridors of power. Natural aggressiveness supposedly explains why men fill our prisons to overflowing. These descriptions tell us nothing about causation or origin, but *descriptions* quickly become *prescriptions*. If women are empathic, must a woman be empathic to be a real woman?

Looking for group differences can result in a bottomless whirlpool of ostensible differences. It clarifies nothing to search for the differences between the middle-class Latina lesbian with children versus the African-American working-class heterosexual woman without children. "What are the differences between women and men?" is simply the wrong question.

The Benefits Outweigh the Risks!

Alice Eagly (1998) believes that the continuing search for gender differences and similarities will ultimately produce a richer and more complete picture of gendered behavior. Eventually this research will reveal how contextual factors constrain and control gendered behavior. Eagly believes such research does not hide how constructed social roles and social hierarchies produce gender. Eagly also contends that social research provides an important balance for those who single-mindedly pursue biological causes for gendered behavior. She notes that when feminist psychologists embarked on their studies of gender differences in the 1970s, they hoped that harmful gender stereotypes would be dispelled and that rigorously scientific studies would show an absence of real gender differences in behavior, traits, and abilities (Morawski, 1994). However, the findings were considerably more complex than anticipated, and they continue to be so. Eagly predicts that with the continued accumulation of data about gender, such findings will eventually become redundant and of decreasing interest. Her vision is that gender will then cease to matter so much in psychological research and in everyday human behavior.

This material is adapted from several articles appearing in D. L. Anselmi & A. L. Law (Eds.), (1998). *Questions of Gender: Perspectives and Paradoxes* (New York: McGraw-Hill), pp. 89–107.

Summary

- The philosophical concepts of empiricism, materialism, and positivism are at the core of the scientific approach to studying gender. Basically, the scientific method involves collecting data according to particular rules, analyzing data, and then interpreting that data.

- The earliest psychologists were heavily influenced by misinterpretations of evolutionary theory in their approach to understanding human differences. This resulted in an androcentric and ethnocentric psychology. Feminist psychologists have confronted the sexism and ethnocentrism that permeated the concepts and methodology of traditional psychology.

- The study of gender stereotypes has been useful in understanding the distortions that surround the psychology of gender.

- The case study, observation, developmental approaches, and surveys are all methods for describing gender-related behavior and mental processes. Each method has its own strengths and weaknesses.

- Although studies of the correlations among variables permit the prediction of group behavior, they do not permit conclusions regarding causality. The experiment is a powerful research method that permits statements of causality. The dangers of *ex post facto* studies and overattribution to biological causes must be considered.

- Meta-analysis is a valuable method for the study of gender differences.

- Qualitative studies facilitate the understanding of gender-related processes and experiences, but certain weaknesses are inherent in this approach.

- Over the last several decades, important new research on men as explicitly gendered has gradually emerged.

- Beliefs about the relationship between sexual orientation and gender norms are important issues in the study of gender.

- Multicultural psychology focuses on group differences *within* a society. Cross-cultural psychology focuses on both similarities and differences *between* societies.

- Multicultural and cross-cultural perspectives are crucial for understanding and appreciating the social construction of gender in human groups. Cultural psychologists emphasize that social norms (such as gender and culture) *guide* but do not *cause* behavior.

- Social constructionists have offered strong critiques of positivistic approaches and have pointed out that social reality is often determined by language and power arrangements.

- Two additional problems in gender research are the problem of reification and the inherent paradox of gender studies.

InfoTrac College Edition

For more information, explore InfoTrac College Edition at

http://www.infotrac-college.com/Wadsworth

Enter search terms: gender and case study, gender and observation, gender and survey, gender and experiment, gender and qualitative, gender and meta-analysis, androgyny, masculinities, gender schema.

3 Theories of Gender

On Fallacies and "Phallocies"

My concern is that our field . . . may have developed something of an imbalance in the direction of theory and criticism. . . . I believe that feminist psychology, like traditional psychology has privileged theory over empirical data. . . . [I]f we want to be effective in creating social change . . . we have to have empirical data, and furthermore, it must be impressive data. ◆ J. S. Hyde

Learning Objectives

After studying this chapter, you should be able to:

1. Define the term *theory*, and describe the functions of theories, emphasizing the criteria for a good theory.
2. Briefly summarize how ancient Greek and later Christian philosophers viewed the basic nature of women and men.
3. Describe the central focus of the biological perspective on gender, explain the core concepts of the evolutionary approach, and evaluate the insights provided by cross-species comparisons.
4. Summarize the strengths and weaknesses of the biological approach to gender.
5. Explain the central concerns of the psychological perspective on gender, and briefly summarize some traditional psychoanalytic approaches to gender, and feminist reinterpretations of this perspective.
6. List and explain the core concepts of the social learning approach to gender acquisition, and contrast this with the cognitive-developmental and social-cognitive approaches, emphasizing Bem's gender schema theory.
7. Summarize feminist criticisms of traditional psychological theories of gender, and describe the two general approaches taken by feminist gender researchers.
8. Describe the rationale and core concepts of the gender-in-context perspective.
9. Summarize the strengths and weaknesses of the psychological perspective regarding gender.
10. Explain the central concerns of the traditional sociological perspective on gender, and contrast that with the more feminist approach of social role theory.
11. Summarize the strengths and weaknesses of the sociological perspective regarding gender.
12. Summarize the central concerns of the anthropological approach to gender, and evaluate its strengths and weaknesses.
13. Summarize the core concepts of one Eastern approach to nature (and gender).

Encounters with Gender

It was a beautiful summer day, and Urban Park was filled with people. In spite of the crowd, Teglot and Raldar spotted each other easily. Covered with sweat from their long runs, big smiles filled their faces as they embraced and kissed each other on the cheek. "Let's have lunch," said Teglot. "Let's catch up on everything. It's been way too long."

Two big mugs of beer accompanied their lunch. Raldar began: "So tell me what's been happening."

Teglot grinned and responded, "Business is really great. We're expanding and have doubled our workforce. There are bumps, of course, but our little company is doing well. What about you?"

Raldar sat up a little straighter and said, "I'm still on a big high from my promotion. I just love all this technical stuff I'm doing, and it's gonna make a difference in the world, but the overseas traveling is tough. Spouses tend to complain about managing the kids alone for two weeks at a time. I call the family every day, but all I get are complaints."

Teglot laughed and nodded, "Yeah, I know what you mean. Somebody just has to be there and figure out what to do when the kids get sick. We try to take turns, but it's never even." They reached out at almost the same moment to offer a supportive touch to the other. They both laughed out loud at that. That's the way it was with the two of them, almost always in synch.

As they finished and walked from the café, Raldar said, "Come take a look at my fancy new car. I just love it. It's safe and has great gas mileage."

Does this dyad consist of two men, two women or one of each? How did you decide? Did you change your mind at any point? Did the unusual names lead you to delay or suspend categorization by gender and attribute their behaviors to cultural influences?

Overview

This chapter defines *theory* and then explains the qualities of a good theory. It then takes a quick look back at some theoretical approaches to gender. Most of the chapter is devoted to contemporary perspectives on gender. Some of these approaches qualify as scientific mini-theories, whereas others are less formal conceptual frameworks. Still others offer just a perspective or framework for examining ideas and observations about men and women (Weis, 1998). A critical evaluation follows each perspective described.

The chapters ahead offer lots of ideas, facts, and unanswered questions. This chapter presents a variety of theories or frameworks with which to structure and organize those ideas, facts, and questions. That is, this chapter should help you organize the mountain of information to come. After all, that's what theories do best.

What Is a Theory, and Why Do We Need So Many of Them?

Typically, a chapter on theories of anything does not elicit great enthusiasm from students. The inevitable list of related and sometimes indistinguishable theories often seems far removed from the energized questions and experiences that students usually bring to a course about gender. However, theories are like the skeleton in your body. Without a skeleton, you would be a shapeless blob, unable to stand up and unable to move ahead. Your skeleton serves to connect and support everything in your body. It gives you shape and form and serves as the physical frame for your unique appearance. That's what theories do for bodies of knowledge and understanding.

For the nonscientist, a theory is a hunch about something (the gender of the characters in the opening vignette, for example). You may have a theory about why your neighbors are divorcing, or why most men seem so avid about sports. For the scientist, a theory is a set of concepts that attempts to connect all the bits and pieces of knowledge about something. Ideally, a theory can explain or account for all the findings regarding some phenomenon. Without a theory of gravity, we could not explain why rocks always fall, whereas birds and airliners rarely do. Theories are also used to generate new questions or hypotheses about that phenomenon. A good theory is judged by its usefulness in accurately predicting the outcome of these new investigations or studies.

Moreover, theories serve as the basis for how we interpret observations or data. For example, suppose you have been collecting SAT and ACT scores for 40 years. You observe that the average mathematics score for men is significantly higher than that of women. How would you interpret these data? If you hold to the theory that the brains of men and women are different, then you are likely to attribute that observation to differential brain structure. This could lead to studies that compare the brain anatomy or physiology of women and men in order to identify the specific source of this difference. But if you subscribe to the theory that women in North American society have formed a mental concept (a **schema**) of femininity that specifically excludes mathematics, then you might compare the mathematical performance of North American women with that of women in a society where interest and excellence in mathematics is considered very appropriately feminine, such as Hungary (Barinaga, 1994). In sum, theories organize observations and scientific findings, offer a sense of understanding about what is being studied, and guide future study of that subject.

A useful theory has certain specific qualities (Liebert & Spiegler, 1994):

---

schema **A cognitive structure or network of associations that guides and organizes one's perceptions and behaviors.**

◆ There is good empirical evidence to support the theory.

◆ The theory accounts for its phenomena as simply as it can (parsimony).

◆ The theory is as comprehensive as possible. That is, it covers as much of what is known about the phenomenon as possible.

◆ The theory does not contradict itself as new findings accumulate.

◆ The theory is testable. That is, it generates risky predictions that can be tested using scientific methods.

◆ The theory is useful in that it can be applied in practical situations (practical applicability).

◆ A good theory is taken seriously by knowledgeable others (acceptability).

Why are there so many gender-related theories? Gender is such a complex and far-ranging phenomenon that it has been very difficult to account for all its aspects with just one theoretical approach. After all, gender influences us on the intrapsychic level (how we think and feel inside ourselves) and on the interpersonal level (how we perceive, interact with, and are influenced by others). Gender also influences us socially (how groups, from dyads to whole societies, are organized and function) and culturally (through the values, beliefs, and arrangements that exist between and across societies).

A Quick Look Backward

It's hard to figure out where we are unless we know how we got there, so a look back to the beginnings of Western musings about women and men may be helpful. You may recall that philosophy is one of psychology's parents, and the ideas of certain ancient male Greek philosophers still influence modern thinking about gender. We must also consider the Bible as well as the writings of certain later Christian thinkers as a basis for Western thinking about gender.

Classical Greek philosophers dealt with four major questions regarding women and men (Agonito, 1977):

1. How are males and females opposite?
2. What is the relationship between females and males and the creation of new human beings? (A related question was how sex was determined before birth.)

3. Are women and men wise in the same ways?
4. Are men and women virtuous in the same ways?

Plato (428–348 BCE) devoted some of his writings to the nature of women and men. He concluded that men were generally active, whereas women were passive. He also concluded that before birth, new souls fell into male bodies, whereas the souls of cowardly and immoral men fell into female bodies. In terms of wisdom and virtue, men and women were equal and complementary. Although physical differences made it seem that they were very different, these differences were superficial rather than profound. Plato believed an ideal society would result when there was unity and equality between the sexes (Bluestone, 1987).

Aristotle (384–322 BCE) had a powerful influence on Western philosophical, and ultimately psychological, thinking about women and men. He challenged Plato's views regarding the complementarity and equality of the sexes. It was clear to him that in all the ways that mattered, women were inferior to men. He also made strong arguments against the existence of female seed and described women as infertile, imperfect, deformed, and as having a basic inability. Aristotle described the perfect child as a boy who resembled his father and offered a continuum of deviations from this perfection: a boy who resembled his mother, a girl who resembled her father, a girl who resembled her mother, and finally the absence of any offspring at all (Aristotle, translated 1912).

In terms of wisdom and virtue, Aristotle wrote that women were irrational and therefore unable to philosophize adequately. Women could have opinions, but not the authoritative knowledge of men. Further, women's virtue was in obedience, whereas men's virtue was in ruling others. Deep relationships (those with equality and reciprocity) were possible only between men (Aristotle, trans. 1912). Aristotelian philosophy was a major text of study for the earliest psychologists, and many of these same ideas reappeared in early psychology, fully attired in the cultural norms and conventions of 19th-century Europe and America (Allen, 1996).

St. Thomas Aquinas (1225–1274) was a very influential Christian philosopher and theologian who echoed the notion of great difference between the sexes. His writings too had a powerful impact on the early psychologists. In contrast, the mystic philosopher, composer, and poet Hildegard of Bingen (1098–1179) offered an alternative, but far less well known view-point. Educated in the gender-integrated Benedictine tradition, she articulated the first complete theory of sex complementarity. She believed that in contrast to our earthly existences, the souls of women and men would be completely equal in heaven. Hildegard believed that the ideal man developed the feminine side of his nature, whereas the ideal woman developed her masculine side (Allen, 1996).

Critical Thinking Challenge

What do you imagine this last idea meant in terms of the gender roles of men and women in 11th-century Germany? Consider asking a historian to speak to your class about gender roles under European feudalism.

Aristotelian philosophy had a major impact on later Islamic and Jewish philosophy. Early Islamic writers wrote only of men, and later adopted Aristotle's notion of the superiority of men over women. Jewish philosophers of the medieval period and Renaissance continued the biblical tradition of viewing women as parts of men and thus unable to exist apart from men (in the biblical account, God created the first woman, Eve, from a rib of the first man, Adam). Both these traditions concurred that women's contribution to the creation of offspring was not significant (Allen, 1996).

Psychology was born as a separate science late in the 19th century. As you read in the previous chapter, speculation regarding the nature of men and women began almost immediately and took some rather unusual turns over the first 12 decades of psychology's history. As you review some of the contemporary gender theories and approaches, evaluate them according to the seven criteria of a good theory that were described earlier.

The Biological Approach

There is a tendency to believe that what is biological is somehow a given, or some kind of bottom line. We tend to see psychological and cultural influences as built on that unchangeable foundation. Scholars in the field remind us, however, that such thinking is simplistic, because environmental factors clearly have an impact on how the brain and body develop and

function. Brain organization or hormonal processes may change in response to psychological or cultural influences. For example, neuropsychological texts state that although the verbal processes of language (sounds that have meaning) are located in the left hemisphere of the cortex, the emotional aspects of language (tone/inflection) are located in the right hemisphere (try saying "no" with different inflections or tones to see how many different emotional messages can be conveyed with the same word!). However, in Thai, Vietnamese, Chinese, and Norwegian the same word spoken with a different tone or inflection has a different meaning. Speakers of these languages have neurons that control tone and inflection in the left hemisphere (Moen, 1993). For a simpler example, consider how the age of **menarche** has dropped in developed nations, largely in response to better nutrition (Wheeler, 1991).

Genes, Genitalia, and Gender: A First Glimpse

What exactly are the connections among biological development, hormonal functioning, gender identity, and gender roles? The details of this fascinating controversy are told in Chapter 4, but for now we need only an overview.

Fertilization of an ovum (bearing only X-chromosomes) by an X-bearing sperm results in the conception of a genetic female (XX). If the sperm carries a Y-bearing chromosome, a genetic male (XY) results. Certain genes carried on these sex chromosomes can produce particular conditions and behaviors. For example, there are **sex-linked traits** such as hemophilia and color blindness. There are also **sex-limited traits**. To manifest, these genetically based conditions require a certain level of sex hormones in the bloodstream (for example, male-pattern baldness). As a fetus develops, sex chromosomes influence the development of gonads (ovaries or testes), which in turn secrete hormones (estrogens and androgens) that influence the development of the distinctive internal

---

menarche   **The first menstrual period of an individual.**

sex-linked traits   **Traits based on genes carried on X or Y chromosomes.**

sex-limited traits   **Traits based on genes carried on autosomes that do not determine sex and expressed when blood levels of sex hormones reach a critical level.**

reproductive structures and the external genitalia that characterize each sex. These hormones also influence certain aspects of brain development (specifically the **hypothalamus** and **pituitary gland**). In females, a cyclical relationship is established, so that beginning with puberty, levels of estrogens and progestins rise and fall over the course of approximately every 28 days. This hypothalamus-pituitary gland-ovary relationship results in the characteristically female repetitive menstrual and ovulatory cycles. In males, a negative feedback mechanism keeps the level of androgens in the body more or less constant. *Thus there is a clear sex difference in hypothalamic, pituitary, and gonadal functioning.* The important question for the gender scholar is whether any of the observed behavioral or cognitive differences between women and men are ultimately traceable to specific genetic or hormonal factors. In other words, are gender differences caused by differences in brain structure or in neural functioning?

For ethical reasons, most research in this area has been carried out with rats and monkeys. Both species tend to show significant behavioral differences when hormonal or brain development is manipulated, particularly in behaviors related to aggression, mating, and the care of offspring (Nadeau, 1996). However, things get much more complicated in human beings. For the moment, let's acknowledge that genetic, hormonal, and brain mechanisms have been hypothesized to underlie a myriad of personality traits, behaviors, and preferences (Collaer & Hines, 1995; Kimura, 1999). The five major areas where observable gender differences have been directly attributed to biological factors are viability, aggression, mood, cognitive abilities, and sexual orientation (see Table 3.1).

The Evolutionary Approach

Most college students are somewhat acquainted with the main concepts of Charles Darwin's theory of evolution (1859, 1879). According to Darwin, from time to time, individual organisms are born with spontaneous genetic changes or mutations. This is called **genetic variation**. If a change allows that individual to successfully reproduce (reproductive fitness) and therefore pass on that trait or feature to future generations, then it is said to be **adaptive.** Over many generations, adaptive characteristics come to permeate

TABLE 3.1   Where Biological Factors Are Believed to Have a Direct Influence

Area	General Description of Issues
Viability	Sex differences in rates of conception, spontaneous abortion, genetic abnormalities, vulnerability to birth defects, developmental disabilities, and learning disabilities (Stillion, 1995).
Aggression	Differences in rough-and-tumble play among young children. Differences in the commission of antisocial and violent acts (Dabbs & Hargrove, 1997; Sapolsky, 1997).
Mood	Mood changes correlated with stages of menstrual and ovulatory cycles. Differences in incidence of major depression (Cicchetti & Toth, 1998).
Cognitive abilities	Differences in mathematical ability, visual-spatial skills, verbal abilities, mental rotation, mechanical reasoning, nonverbal sensitivity, attitudes toward mathematics (Levy & Heller, 1998).
Sexual orientation	Controversial findings of differences in particular areas of the hypothalamus in homosexual men. Concordance rate of .50 homosexual men and their identical twin, and .24 for fraternal twins. Findings in lesbians are more equivocal (Pillard, 1998; Wickelgren, 1999).

all members of that species. That is how all species *evolve* or change. For example, perhaps walking upright contributed to human survival because it kept the hands free to handle a planting stick or a spear, or perhaps it facilitated the carrying of infants or larger

hypothalamus   A small structure located at the base of the brain that controls survival-related behaviors: fighting, reproduction, food and water intake, and so on.

pituitary gland   Gland connected directly to the hypothalamus; produces reproduction-related hormones and controls secretions in many other glands (called the "master gland").

genetic variations   Spontaneously appearing changes (genetic mutations) that accumulate among successful members of particular species; evolution is the result of this process.

adaptive   Having features that promote an organism's survival in its natural habitat.

quantities of food to a safer place. Thus genetically encoded physical traits are selected and passed on.

However, does the same principle apply to social behaviors as well as to physical traits? People who take an evolutionary perspective believe it does. They maintain that so-called traditional gender roles evolved because they were adaptive for our species (Burns, 2000; Geary, 1998). For example, David Buss (1995) believes that the human male tendency to prefer many sexual partners evolved because male sperm are plentiful and new sperm are produced all through a human male's life. A single male can impregnate many females with little investment of time and energy. Female ova are more rare (a female is born with all the eggs she will ever have), and a single pregnancy and birthing require a tremendous investment of biological energy. Thus the evolutionary argument goes, it is adaptive for human male genes to be spread around to many females (Bailey, Gaulin, Agyei, & Gladue, 1994). It is more adaptive for human females to refrain from copulation until they can locate the best genes, that is, those of a dominant male who is more likely to stay around, support, and protect offspring (Feingold, 1992). Accordingly, this explains why human females have to be courted, displayed to, and are more reluctant to copulate compared to human males. Investigators of evolutionary psychology hypothesize that only human females could breastfeed infants and therefore were not as mobile as were human males. Thus the feminine role of domestic caretaker evolved (Buss & Kenricks, 1998).

Critical Thinking Challenge

The evolutionary approach to gendered behavior has led to much controversy and bitter debate. How does it strike you at first reading?

Biological Approaches to Gender: A Critical Evaluation

The attribution of observed group differences to brain structure and hormonal functioning has a long and distressing history within psychology (Shields, 1975; Caplan & Caplan, 1997). It is important to note that the list of ostensibly physiologically based sex differences used to be much longer. Over the decades, the general trend has been for researchers to find that seemingly strong biological sex differences are more accurately attributed to social and other environmental origins (Feingold, 1994; Stumpf & Stanley, 1998). Yet many researchers are firmly convinced of gender differentials in neuroanatomy and physiology that go well beyond reproduction-related functions (Halpern, 1996b; Kimura, 1999).

The criticisms of evolution-based approaches have been fierce and frequent (Bem, 1993; Fausto-Sterling, 1992). First, there is no evidence that social behavior is linked to specific genes or combinations of genes. Second, the higher on the evolutionary scale, the more behavior is influenced by learning, rather than by genetic programming. Third, evolutionary psychologists tend to selectively discuss only those gendered behaviors that are in keeping with the theory just presented. Gendered behaviors that are not supportive of its central theses are ignored. That is, some gender-related behaviors are said to have evolutionary significance, whereas others are not. Fourth, it is poor science to deal with phenomena occurring at one level by explaining it at another level. For example, like all animals, human beings require food to sustain them, and our ancestors obviously foraged and scavenged rather successfully. But humans invented agriculture to provide a more stable and predictable source of food. It seems rather foolish to attribute the almost universal human activity of farming to genetic propensities (Bem, 1993). Fifth, there is a vast difference in the time scale involved in cultural gender arrangements versus evolution of a species. Sixth, just because a behavior is maintained over many generations is not proof that it is genetic. Generations of macaques (a species of monkey) have washed their food before eating it. However, this behavior can be traced to a particular macaque mother who innovated this technique when given cereal grains and sweet potatoes on a sandy beach. Each generation of macaques instructs the next about this behavior. Sixth, the gender differences in sexual behavior that are referred to in the theory can be explained in other, simpler ways. Last, the gender norms described in the theory are not human universals. In some human groups women pursue as many sexual partners as they have time for, and in others men's sexual pursuits are severely curtailed. Among other animals, there are species in which females demand sex, roam to hunt, and are more aggressive (such as lionesses), or in which males do most of the child care (penguins). Female chimps frequently run off for sex with nondominant males (Goodall, 1990). The study of other species, especially primates, can offer us some remarkable insights about the array of possibilities for male–female relationships. Take a look at Box 3.1 for a glimpse at some very different sociosexual arrangements.

Psychological Theories

Psychological theories about gender focus on four central questions:

1. How are physiological sex and the acquisition of gendered behavior and mental processes related?
2. How do gender identity and gender-typed behavior develop and manifest over the life span?
3. How can we account for both the similarities (universals) and differences in the behavior and mental processes of men and women?
4. Must one gender role (and the sex that occupies it) always be more valued than the other?

Critical Thinking Challenge

Each theory or approach discussed emphasizes one or more of these questions. Can you identify or pinpoint the emphasis in each theory presented?

Most psychological theorists emphasize gender as something internal to the individual. That is, gender is something that is either acquired from external sources (social learning theories) and internalized or that develops within the person (psychoanalytic and cognitive theories) and then displayed outwardly (externalized). These theorists refer to gender as the "expression" of this internalized personality trait or cognition. However, the gender-in-context perspective challenges this fundamental assumption by insisting that gender is not something we *have* but rather something we *do* West & Zimmerman, 1987; West & Fenstermaker, 1995). It may be helpful to keep this distinction in mind as you read about the various psychological approaches to gender.

Psychoanalytic Approaches

Although Freud's work is usually thought of as a psychological approach, an examination of it leads to two conclusions. First, Freudian theory is biologically

based, and second, it is not a scientific theory. The key determinant in Freud's theory is physical anatomy (Freud, 1924b). Furthermore, Freud's ideas do not meet most of the criteria for a good theory (Liebert & Spiegler, 1994). Yet I will discuss these ideas at length because they have influenced the thinking of many psychologists, educators, writers, and parents.

Core Freudian concepts such as the **oedipal conflict**, castration anxiety, and the phallic stage of psychosexual development make clear that most of Freud's writings about sex and gender focus on the male as normative (Freud, 1933). After all, females do not have a phallus. All the gender-related processes described by Freud take place at an unconscious level and center around **identification** with a parent of the same gender (Freud, 1965).

According to Freud, possessing a penis becomes an important issue for gender identity formation during the *phallic stage* of psychosexual development. During this period (age 3–6), the boy forms an intense attachment to his mother and desires to possess her exclusively. His father is a formidable rival, and the boy begins to fear castration from his father. This fear is further fueled by his discovery that girls have already "lost their penises." The oedipal conflict is resolved when the boy begins to identify with the father ("I cannot overpower him, so I will become like him: dominant, strong, and eventually I will possess my own woman"). He now begins to emulate the father's masculine characteristics. This resolution results in boys' forming a strong **superego**. That is, boys will develop a deep sense of conscience and strong moral ideals, which will give them a superior sense of justice and fairness. It also results in either fear of or contempt toward women (Freud, 1924a).

During the phallic stage, said Freud, girls come to resent their mothers. They blame their mothers for their anatomical deficit, and they envy boys

---

oedipal conflict Aspect of Freud's phallic stage (age 3 to 6) in which boy child wishes for exclusive possession of mother but fears castration at hands of powerful father; resolved by identification with father.

identification Psychological internalization and external adoption of characteristics of same-sex parent.

superego Moral aspect of Freud's model of personality structure; determines what is right or wrong and is the source of guilt after wrongdoing.

Cross-Species Comparisons

Every biology student soon learns that human beings are members of the primate order. Primates include monkeys, orangutans, gorillas, chimpanzees, bonobos, and human beings. All these groups evolved from a common ancestor about 6 million years ago. Researchers have found a 99% similarity between the DNA of bonobos and human beings (deWaal, 1998). They are indeed our closest cousins on the evolutionary scale (Figure 3.1). Perhaps we can learn something about gender by examining the relationships between males and females of those species most closely related to our own? Here are three gender-related vignettes from our extended family tree.

The image of life among the chimpanzees (*Pan troglodytes*) that has passed over from scientific research to the popular imagination is that of groups of chimps living together in a strict dominance hierarchy ruled by aggressive males. Adult male chimpanzees fight frequently to establish and maintain that hierarchy, and dominance means sexual access to as many females as the **alpha male** can control. Female chimps cradle their infants protectively, and show them off proudly to other females. Males aggressively defend sexual and territorial rights. Bands of agile, clever young male chimps go off to hunt the young of other primate species, and dominant males get the best parts of the kill (Goodall, 1990). Females and low-ranking males submissively approach powerful males to obtain whatever mor-

sels the males choose to give them, and they timidly take their turn at drinking water. These images reflect what some believe to be the essential nature of females and males when that nature is unencumbered by social norms, laws, and the other appurtenances of culture and civilization (Zihlman, 1996).

Contrast that scenario with the following picture of protogender relationships in another of our closest relatives. Bonobos (*Pan paniscus*) are an endangered species living in the forests of the Republic of the Congo (formerly Zaire). They have a very humanlike appearance, with distinctive red lips, black hair parted naturally down the middle, and a relatively upright posture when walking. Like humans, female bonobos can copulate at any time (in most animal species, females are sexual only during **estrus**). Females, though smaller than males, are clearly in charge of bonobo groups (deWaal, 1998). When they reach adulthood, females leave their birth groups, move into new bonobo troops, and bond with new females to find their place in the social hierarchy. A male's social ranking depends on that of his mother. Females control access to and distribution of choice foods, and males wait until they are offered a bite. Fighting is rare among bonobos, and although encounters with new groups may be loud, raucous, and nervous, there is no aggression. When two groups of bonobos meet, the females

of the two groups gradually approach each other and initiate sexual contact with each other. Speaking of sex, bonobos engage in kisslike behavior and typically copulate in a face-to-face position.

Observation of bonobo groups in the wild reveals that a great deal of time is devoted to male–female copulation, same-sex couplings, oral–genital activities, masturbation, and even group sex. One researcher calculated that the average bonobo initiates some sexual activity every 1½ hours. Why? Unlike the more common chimps (and perhaps more like humans?), sex is used to resolve power issues, reduce conflict, calm individuals, and signal friendliness. Compared to chimpanzee society, bonobo society suggests quite a different picture of the essential nature of relationships between and among the genders.

What about infant care in closely related species? In the wild, infant rhesus monkeys are almost constantly held or otherwise looked after by their mothers or other adult females. When a researcher placed individual adult rhesus monkeys in an enclosure with a solitary rhesus infant, both female and male adults showed equal behavioral interest in these "stranded" infants. However, when an adult female rhesus joined a male in the enclosure, adult males engaged in absolutely no parenting behavior (Gibber, 1981). Thus we begin to see the power of social situations, even among lower primates.

(**penis envy**). An unfulfilled longing for exclusive possession of the father becomes a longing for a baby. Later on in life it becomes a strong motivation to have children with a husband (a substitute for the father). Women's deep-seated wish for a penis is finally fulfilled with the birth of a son. Because girls do not have to resolve an oedipal conflict and subsequently identify with a strong parent, they lack strong super-egos. Therefore they lack a sense of justice or fair-

ness. According to Freud, adult femininity is characterized by passivity, longings for motherhood, plea-

---

alpha male   Male at the top of the dominance hierarchy, who thereby controls the behavior of those below him.

estrus   Hormonally determined period of sexual receptivity among females of other species.

penis envy   Experienced by girls after discovering their anatomical deficiency, according to Freud.

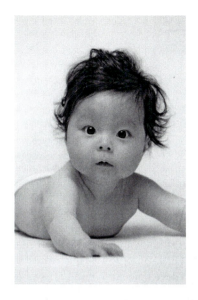

FIGURE 3.1 Can these snapshots from our extended family tree offer us additional insights into the origins of human gender relations?

sure in pain and suffering (masochism), self-love (narcissism), feelings of inferiority, a tendency toward jealousy, and a tenuous internalizing of social values regarding fairness and justice. A woman's ultimate goal is to be an attractive love/sex object for men. Her anatomically deficient body becomes her sole source of self-esteem (Freud, 1933). Note that there is no scientific evidence to support any of these ideas.

Continuing the Psychoanalytic Tradition. Later theorists in the psychoanalytic tradition include Carl Jung, Karen Horney, and Erik Erikson. Their respective theories varied considerably regarding the importance of gender in personality development. Here I will mention some aspects of their writings that speak directly to the issue of gender.

Karen Horney (1967) questioned many of Freud's assumptions regarding male superiority and female penis envy. She concluded that males envied women's power to create new life (womb envy). Horney believed that men overcompensated for their inability to produce infants by becoming driven to achieve and create in other areas of life. Womb envy also led men to defensively belittle the achievements of women. Horney stressed the importance of social and cultural forces in shaping personality. She concluded that the social valuing of boys over girls resulted in feelings of inferiority and greater neuroticism in girls. She saw women as adapted to an inferior status in society, which resulted in self-hatred, contempt for other women, and hostility toward men. Horney believed that women's feelings of inferiority were based on their acceptance of the social ideology of male superiority.

TABLE 3.2   Erik Erikson's Stages of Psychosocial Development

Psychosocial Crisis	Age of First Occurrence	Acquisition
Trust versus mistrust	Birth to 1½	Hope
Autonomy versus shame and doubt	1½ to 3	Will
Initiative versus guilt	3 to 5	Purpose
Industry versus inferiority	5 to 12	Competency
Ego integrity versus role conflict	12 to 18	Fidelity
Intimacy versus isolation	18 to 25	Love
Generativity versus stagnation	25 to 65	Care
Ego integrity versus despair	65+	Wisdom

Source: E. Erikson (1985). *The life cycle completed* (New York: Norton).

She hypothesized that this sense of inferiority could change if there were greater egalitarianism in society. Horney also articulated the concept of hypercompetitiveness, which she believed resulted in lower self-esteem, mistrust, neuroticism, and dogmatism in members of both genders (Horney, 1967).

Carl Jung described one aspect of an individual's personality as the *anima* or *animus* (Jung, 1959c). These Latin words refer to the idea of an unconscious feminine or masculine **archetype** that exists in each of us. These came about through the experiences of men and women living together throughout human history. Among women, the feminine anima predominates (is more visible), whereas among men the more masculine animus predominates. The anima in a man allows him to understand women, and the animus within a woman allows her to understand men. Disappointment results when a woman projects her ideal animus on a real man (all real men must fall short of this projected ideal), or a man projects his ideal anima on a real woman (all real women will necessarily fail the test). Jung viewed the positive aspects of a man's anima as being intuitive and feeling oriented. The more negative aspects include being moody and catty. For women, the positive aspects of the animus include logic and reason; on the negative side, it results in what Jung called *high-browism* and in exasperating ways of discussing something. The masculine animus includes reason, forceful argument, and social insensitivity. The feminine anima includes emotionality, social sensitivity, intuition, vanity, moodiness, and irrationality. However, to be a fully functioning human being every woman must acknowledge and allow expression of her animus, and every man must acknowledge and allow expression of his anima (Jung, 1959c).

Erik Erikson is best known for his theory of lifelong development (Erikson, 1985). In contrast to Freud, who described development in terms of psychosexual stages, Erikson described a series of lifelong psychosocial crises in which key developmental issues must be resolved (see Table 3.2). In terms of gender, the order of these developmental crises apply more to the socially prescribed order of life activities *for men*. For example, identity versus role confusion comes before intimacy versus isolation. For most men, our society prescribes establishing a firm identity (socially and occupationally) before settling into a stable relationship. For women, the reverse is still generally true. In fact, for many women social identity may still depend on that of her husband (is he a farmer or a physician?) and thus may be established *after* her involvement in a stable relationship (O'Connell, 1976). Also, men's identity is primarily centered around occupational attainment, whereas women's identity is more multifocused—around family roles, occupation, marriage, and child rearing.

Critical Thinking Challenge

The older, returning students in your class (both women and men) may want to comment on how issues of identity have shifted as they have matured.

Erikson did not entirely abandon Freud's emphasis on the importance of anatomy. Noting the apparent intrusive features of male genitalia and the apparent inclusive features of female genitalia, Erikson described

---

archetype An inherited idea or mode of thought that is derived from the experience of the human race and is present in the unconscious of each individual.

how boys are predisposed to *making* (initiating and conquering) and girls to *catching* (attracting and appealing). He also predicted that boys' play will consist of building towers and other intrusive features, whereas girls' sense of "inner space" will result in their preference for playing in enclosed places (Erikson, 1975).

Feminist Reinterpretations of Psychoanalytic Ideas About Gender. Nancy Chodorow is a feminist sociologist who focused on the mother–child relationship to account for observed differences in the personalities of men and women. She notes that in most societies women are the primary caretakers of children. Therefore, girls may remain closely attached and identified with their mothers all through life. However, most societies require that boys *not* behave like their mothers. To become masculine, boys must vigorously pursue becoming "not like a woman." Boys must actively reject all that is feminine and motherlike within themselves (Chodorow, 1978). Chodorow sees masculinity as the result of a complex and difficult process of separation, rejection, and lifelong ambivalence about women and femininity. This results in the devaluation of women and femininity. She concludes that the only way to overcome this devaluation is to change society so that women and men share parenting equally.

Feminist psychoanalyst Ellen Kaschak (1992) focuses on a key ingredient of the masculine gender role: power. Men have it, and women don't. Kaschak sees this as the core issue in explaining a number of gender-related problems in society. She believes boys are raised to believe that power is their right, which allows them to treat women as subordinate objects. This accounts for the prevalence of sexism, rape, incest, and so on. Women who fail to take power for themselves become passive, subordinate beings, and this explains the greater frequency of major depression among women. Also, such women may come to deny the existence or needs of even their physical bodies, and this may account for the greater incidence of eating disorders among women.

Social Learning and Cognitive Theories

According to classical learning theory, behaviors persist because they are reinforced (followed by a positive consequence), and others disappear because they are punished (followed by an **aversive consequence**).

A boy is rewarded for his interest in pointing guns and throwing balls, and punished for wearing jewelry. A girl is reinforced for her interest in dressing dolls and playing house, and punished for being loud.

Social learning theorists such as Walter Mischel (1966, 1993) and Albert Bandura (1977) maintain that direct reinforcement and punishment is not necessary. Children also observe and imitate models who are rewarded for certain behaviors (vicarious reinforcement). Boys learn that male models are highly valued and rewarded for athleticism and aggressive behavior. Girls learn that female models are highly valued and rewarded for an attractive appearance and taking care of others. Parents are the first models, and religious figures, legends, and other relatives may serve as models in traditional societies. In contemporary societies, movies, books, and television provide very powerful models (Burn, 1996).

Cognitive-Developmental and Social-Cognitive Theories. For most of us, social learning theories seem to make intuitive sense. We can see how years of reinforcement, punishment, modeling, and imitation might shape the gender-typed behavior of any individual. However, cognitive-developmental theory takes a counterintuitive approach, contending that gendered behavior follows from the cognition (understanding) that one is a girl or a boy (Kohlberg, 1966). In a male child, this cognition will later lead to a preference for and a valuing of *masculine* behaviors, interests, and attitudes. Understanding that "I am a girl" eventually leads to a preference for and valuing of whatever is socially prescribed as feminine behavior, interests. and attitudes.

Cognitive-developmental theorists take a stage approach to gender acquisition (Kohlberg, 1966). At the first stage of gender labeling, children merely distinguish between males and females. They classify others into one of these categories on the basis of observable features such as hair length, toys played with, and type of clothing worn (not genitalia). They come to believe that one can change into a girl or boy by changing one's hair length or clothing. Later, they achieve gender constancy; that is, they come to know that a person remains a girl or boy, regardless of their clothing, hair length, type of ornamentation (hair

---

aversive consequence Unpleasant, obnoxious, or unpleasant stimuli that elicit either escape or avoidance.

bows, bracelets, and so on), or toys played with. Once certain that he or she is permanently a boy or girl (gender identity), a child begins to strongly prefer what is perceived as appropriately boylike or girl-like. The social, emotional, and often moral boundaries around "girl things" and "boy things" often become very rigid. A boy may be mortified if only a pink bicycle is available for him to ride. A young girl may actively reject the opportunity to play basketball. As they grow up in our relatively gendered society, boys and girls also see that "boy stuff" is more valued than "girl stuff." A girl who can throw and catch a softball will gain status. But a boy who excels at jump-rope games loses status and is subject to ridicule (Kohlberg, 1966).

A more recent example of the cognitive approach is called *social-cognitive theory* (Bandura, 1986). This theoretical refinement also views the developing child as an active constructor of his or her gender identity. Accordingly, the child begins to form expectations about the response of others to her or his behavior and interests. The girl who really wants a microscope for her birthday may expect skepticism from her parents, and the boy who is intrigued by the strength and grace of ballet dancers may anticipate negative reactions if he makes his interest known to his peers.

Although Bandura (1986) did not emphasize biological factors in the development of gender typing, he did note that boys who are neither athletic nor have a masculine physique could not expect much reinforcement from peers. Physically unattractive girls will be in a similar position. In some societies a woman's slender, petite appearance would result in many rewards. In a society that values and expects physical strength and labor from women, such an appearance would result in aversive consequences.

The key difference between social-cognitive theory and traditional cognitive-developmental theory is that social-cognitive theory deals with the cognitions that we bring to new or future situations. It focuses on our anticipations and expectations in social situations.

Gender Schema Theory

Another cognitive approach to gender is offered by Sandra Bem's (1981, 1983, 1985, 1989) gender schema theory. A schema is a cognitive structure (mental con-

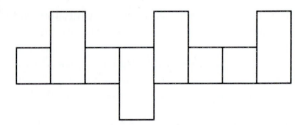

FIGURE 3.2   Schemas can direct your processing of data. Can you make out the word represented here? Clearly, you cannot. Suppose we tell you that it is a large zoo animal. Can you make it out now? Once you form a schema for interpreting these data, it quickly allows you organize and interpret the data into the word *elephant.*

cept) that guides our behavior and also how we process information. See Figure 3.2 to experience how acquiring a schema can direct your processing of visual data. We all possess a myriad of schemas to guide our behavior and mental processing. Your college schema guides you to take notes when an authority (your instructor) lectures. However, you do not take notes when an authority lectures during worship services (a sermon). Here, your religious ritual schema has been activated, to guide your perceptions and behavior.

Critical Thinking Challenge

My favorite way to explain schemas is to recount the story of a co-worker who asks another out for dinner. At the restaurant, the second inquires, "Is this a date, or are we just having dinner?" The person is asking what schema to apply, that is, how to interpret behaviors in that situation. Can you think of other examples of how schemas guide behavior and interpretations of reality?

Gender schema theory begins with the premise that if a society emphasizes the distinctions between women and men (that is, gender is believed to be very important), then members of that society will develop deeply embedded schemas about masculinity and femininity. They will apply these schemas to themselves, to other people, and to many other aspects of the world. Children who live in that society will organize new information and experiences according to gendered categories. Thus in a society where women and men wear very different clothing, groom and decorate themselves very distinctively, and are overtly restricted to certain activities or occupations (only women carry water or do secretarial work; only men beat drums or work with electricity), many things will be perceived in terms of gender. For the majority of white Americans, contact sports are masculine, and dancing is feminine.

Think back to the opening vignette. Most likely you tried to assign a gender to Teglot and Raldar. Did their strange names move you to employ an "other culture" schema that perhaps hindered applying a gender schema? On which cues, behaviors, emotional expressions, preferences, and so forth did you finally attend to make a gender categorization? Did your cognition change at various points in the story? Why? In the absence of visual cues, you probably used gender schemas to try to classify the characters.

Critical Thinking Challenge

Is dancing well part of the feminine schema for African Americans or for Latinos?

In our society, dogs are thought of as masculine, whereas cats are seen as feminine. Recently, at the zoo, I overheard a young man call out to a large breeding group of pink flamingos, "Good afternoon, ladies!" In a highly gender-schematic society many things are considered gendered. Boys and girls organize and regulate many aspects of their behavior, interests, attitudes, preferences, and so forth on the basis of their gender schemas. Children also learn that the masculine schema has greater power and prestige (Bem, 1993). We may extend this perspective to understanding individuals. Across cultures, highly gender-schematic individuals organize and remember many things on the basis of gender (Levy, 1994; Lobell, Bar-David, Gruber, Lau, & Bar-Tal, 2000). They tend to believe and behave as if women and men were very different from each other, and this view of the world can interfere with relating to members of the other sex. For example, men who are highly gender schematic are more likely to treat women as sex objects rather than as whole people (McKenzie-Mohr & Zanna, 1995).

Feminist Approaches to Gender

Many feminist psychologists believe that traditional psychology has contributed to the oppression of women through its gender-related theories (Weisstein,

1977). Feminists note that proclamations about supposed gender differences provide a feeding frenzy for the popular media. Best-sellers such as *Men Are From Mars and Women Are From Venus* (Gray, 1992) or *You Just Don't Understand Me: Women and Men in Conversation* (Tannen, 1990) and television programs with titles such as *Men, Women and the Sex Difference* contribute to the popular notion that men and women are very different.

In terms of a more scholarly approach to gender, **feminist empiricists** sought to correct the traditional biases of psychological research by restating and paying stricter attention to the rules of good research design and interpretation (Crawford, 1997; McHugh, Koeske, & Frieze, 1977). In general, they conclude that *sex and gender differences are few and relatively small* and that it is not clear whether the differences found even have any real importance (Hyde & Plant, 1995). Theorists who subscribe to this approach are described as **minimalists**. A second thread is referred to as the **feminist standpoint** approach. This perspective asserts that women are quite different from men because they have longstanding experience as a subjugated group and so they have a unique perspective on social relations. Two influential books that are representative of the feminist standpoint approach are *In a Different Voice* (Gilligan, 1982) and *Women's Way of Knowing* (Belenky, Clinchy, Goldberger, & Tarule, 1986). Proponents of this perspective may be described as **maximalists** (Eagly, 1996).

Critical Thinking Challenge

Earlier, you read about the work of Nancy Chodorow and Ellen Kaschak. Would you consider them minimalists or maximalists?

---

feminist empiricism   **Research conducted with traditional scientific methods but with the goal of eliminating sexist bias at all stages of the process.**

minimalism   **Theoretical emphasis on similarities between genders and de-emphasis on importance of any differences found.**

feminist standpoint   **Perspective that confronts traditional notions of scientific objectivity; places women's experiences at center of all study.**

maximalism   **Theoretical emphasis on differences between genders based on unique experiences of women as oppressed group.**

The Gender-in-Context Perspective

Whether the emphasis is on biological differences, acquired differences, or the ferreting out of real versus imagined differences (gender stereotypes), the issue of differences is at the core of the gender theories mentioned up until now. These theories imply that there are measurable and stable differences in personality traits, cognitive processes, personal preferences, characteristic ways of responding, and so forth. Such theories assume that both femininity and masculinity each has its own true essence and there is a real distinction or discontinuity between what is feminine and what is masculine. Masculinity and femininity have basically the same form today, and across cultures, as they have always had (DeLamater & Hyde, 1998).

Supporters of the gender-in-context approach see gender as arising from external and situational contexts (Gergen, 1994). That is, they view gender as existing in transactions between people in particular situations. They contend that certain ways of transacting are considered more appropriate to one sex or another (Davis & Gergen, 1997). By way of clarification, Bohan (1997) asks us to contrast what is meant by "a friendly person" versus "a friendly conversation." According to the gender-in-context perspective, competitiveness, dependence, or domination is a product of an interaction, not a person. Every person, regardless of sex, may behave aggressively, nurturantly, expressively, or rationally depending on the context and the social expectations brought to that interpersonal interaction or social situation. For example, women and men are much more likely to behave similarly in private than in public situations (Unger, 1998; Walkerdine, 1997), or when they don't know the sex of the person with whom they are interacting (Lightdale & Prentice, 1994). In other words, under the influence of certain cultural, interpersonal, and situational factors, we "do gender" (West & Zimmerman, 1987). The gender-in-context position illuminates many of the weaknesses of essentialist theories of gender. First, most theories of gender are based on research with middle-class, white college students—hardly representative of the human group. Whenever some statement is made or some conclusion drawn about gender differences, such as "men tend to . . ." or "women typically . . ." multiculturalists quickly ask, "*Which* men tend to . . .?" and "*Which*

women typically . . .?" (Parlee, 1997). Traditional gender theories quickly begin to break down when applied to a broader range of ethnic, national, class, or age groups (Marecek, 1995). Recall the question posed earlier about whether African Americans consider dancing well to be feminine? Are the qualities of independence, competitiveness, and athleticicism important aspects of the masculine gender role among Asian Americans? In mainstream North American society, the pursuit of casual sex is considered a highly masculine trait. As a group, gay men engage in more casual sex than do heterosexual men, but they are not perceived as more masculine because of this behavior. Second, many of the stereotypic traits or behaviors attributed to one gender or another appear to more accurately reflect power statuses or social contexts (Conway & Vartanian, 2000). When women are in superior status or in positions of power relative to other women or men, they begin to interact in ways that are more frequently observed in men (Cantor & Bernay, 1992). When men are placed in a social context that requires nurturance and emotional sensitivity (for example, as single fathers rearing young children), they begin to manifest the traits and behaviors required for that situation (Risman, 1989). Third, when scientific investigators seek stable and reliable gender differences in personality traits, behaviors, and mental processes, both in our society and others, these differences seem to appear and disappear depending on the situation (Bjorkqvist, 1994; White & Kowalski, 1994). This is true even for such highly gender-typed behaviors as aggressiveness (Burbank, 1994; Lightdale & Prentice, 1994), emotional attachment (Brehm, 1992), assertiveness (Crawford, 1994), influencibility (Eagly, 1987), and emotional expressiveness (Bromberger & Matthews, 1996). Chapter 7 explores more about how ephemeral gender differences in social behavior can be.

Many current social researchers have concluded that gender is an agreement that exists *in a social interchange*, not in a person (Deaux & LaFrance, 1998; Unger, 1998). Like social constructionists, they note the importance of language in conceptualizing gender (Hare-Mustin & Marecek, 2002). Consider the gender-related term "good father." The meaning of this term varies not by its inherent qualities, but by where and when it is used to describe behavior and cognition (Nazi Germany during the 1930s, North American

TABLE 3.3   Summary Table of Psychological Approaches to Gender

Theory or Approach	Central Concern	Major Exemplars	Major Concepts
Psychoanalytic	Gender identity formation	S. Freud K. Horney C. Jung E. Erikson	Identification Penis envy Womb envy Animus/anima Psychosocial crises
Feminist psychoanalytic reinterpretations	Devaluation of feminine Unequal power	N. Chodorow E. Kaschak	Boys' separation/rejection of mother Need for equally shared parenting Explanations for eating disorders and depression
Social learning	Gender acquisition and maintenance	W. Mischel A. Bandura	Vicarious reinforcement Modeling Imitation
Cognitive developmental	Gender identity formation	L. Kohlberg	Stage theory (labeling, constancy, differential valuing)
Social-cognitive	Gender identity formation and gender-related expectations	A. Bandura	Gender-related cognitions and expectations for future situations
Gender schema	Lifelong influence of gender schemas	S. Bem	Gender schema, variation in how gender-schematic an individual is
Feminist approaches	Psychology's contribution to devaluation of women	J. S. Hyde C. Gilligan M. Belenky et al.	Empiricism/minimalism Feminist standpoint/maximalism
Gender-in-context perspective	Contextual and situational effects on gender as performance	M. Gergen C. West R. Hare-Mustin	Gender performance, transaction, arises from external factors

suburbia during the 1950s, a Palestinian refugee camp in the year 2001). People act out or perform gender in particular contexts and situations, in accordance with the social conventions of a particular society at a particular time in history. Table 3.3 offers a summary of the theories and approaches described here, along with their major concepts and proponents.

The Psychological Approach: A Critical Evaluation

Psychoanalytic writings continue to fascinate. Freud's writings were a *reflection* of the social norms and gender roles of affluent Viennese society at the beginning of the 20th century, but they became a *prescription* for later generations of men and women. No matter how intriguing psychoanalytic ideas may be, they are not testable, they are not supported by scientific evidence, and they offer very complicated explanations for phenomena that can be more easily explained by simpler constructs.

There is generally good scientific support for the various social and cognitive theories (Bussey & Bandura, 1992), particularly their accounts of gender role acquisition (even when the theories contradict each other). The mechanisms they describe can account for many findings about gender and gender

ABCs of GENDER (ATTITUDES, BEHAVIORS, AND CONCERNS)   BOX 3.2

The Issue: Applying Theory to Explain Behavior

Below are some descriptions of behavior. How would the various theories discussed in this chapter (listed below) account for these behaviors?

Psychoanalytic theory

Biological theory

Social learning theory

Social-cognitive theory

Gender schema theory

Gender-in-context perspective

Nancy marries soon after high school. She enjoys caring for her four young children and earns a bit of income by providing occasional housekeeping services for other families. Over time, she develops her own house-cleaning business employing 10 workers.

Martha was raised in a religiously indifferent family. As a young adult, she becomes interested in religion and eventually joins the clergy. She rises to national leadership in her denomination.

Bob, a prison inmate, obtains extra luxuries (toiletries, cookies, and so on) by sewing and darning for other inmates. He eventually becomes a master embroiderer, and his work is sold as art in various galleries.

Lawrence is attractive and quite successful as a judge. Although he has occasional sexual relationships with women, he never marries nor does he father any children.

---

roles. However, they are weak in handling the instability of gender differences across social situations (Eagly, 1995).

Gender schema theory combines the strengths of social learning theory and cognitive-developmental theories. It considers the person as an active agent in his or her gender typing and also acknowledges the powerful influence of societal and cultural forces on the individual. Currently, it is considered a strong and influential approach to understanding gender (Lavale & Pelletier, 1992). It is a useful theory in cross-cultural application, because it can account for how any particular culture can impose its own content into the gender schema. Thus financial support of one's parents and children is part of the gender schema for Thai women (Gardiner & Gardiner, 1991). Graceful dancing and artistic creativity is part of the gender schema for Balinese men (Daniel, 1981).

The gender-in-context perspective has had a profound impact on current psychological thinking about gender. Recent research on gender has moved away from seeking gender within individuals to examining the social and situational factors that elicit gender-typed behaviors (Deaux & LaFrance, 1998). The result has been a new, robust approach that is sensitive to social setting, status, and cultural factors.

Can you apply the various psychological theories presented here to account for individual behavior?

Take a look at Box 3.2 for some unusual, but real-life pathways.

The Sociological Perspective

Sociologists focus on the behavior of groups within a society, in contrast with psychologists' emphasis on the behavior of individuals. Sociologists may, for example, compare the behavior of minority ethnic groups within a society, the relationship between socioeconomic status (class) and behavior, or the division of labor between the genders. Traditional sociologists viewed society as an orderly system based on the consensus of its members. They viewed gender roles as naturally emanating from the physical differences between women and men; specifically, from the greater size and strength of men and the childbearing and nursing capacities of women. Sociologists concluded three factors determined the development of gender roles: anatomical sex, the division of labor, and the regulation of sexuality. Anatomical sex determined social categorization. Physical strength and child-related responsibilities determined how survival tasks were distributed. Because men could never be absolutely certain that offspring were their own, they attempted to restrict and control women's sexuality. Family sociologists identified the central component of the masculine role as *instrumentality*. This core included an orientation toward action, accomplishment, and leadership. The core component of the feminine role was identified as *expressiveness* and included an orientation toward emotionality and relationships (Parsons & Bales, 1955).

Beginning in the 1960s, feminist perspectives began to influence sociological theory. Society was now "reconstructed" as an arrangement of power relationships. In most societies, men monopolized most of the available resources (money, property, political power, and so on), and attempted to dominate women (Baca-Zinn, Hondagneu-Sotelo, & Messner, 1997). Feminist sociologists had a major impact on the reformulation of sociological gender theories (Renzetti & Curran, 1995).

Sociologists assume that gender and gender roles are socially constructed and that they are transmitted to each generation by all the powerful agents of social learning (parents, social institutions, and so on). Let us examine one sociological theory that speaks directly to power-related gender arrangements and gender roles.

Social Role Theory

According to Alice Eagly (1987), a social role is a collection of prescriptions, prohibitions, requirements, and expectations for a person in a particular social category. Observable behavioral differences emerge from the social roles typically occupied by women and men. For example, it has been a consistent finding that compared to men, women are more accurate in interpreting nonverbal communications (Hall, 1984, 1998). What accounts for this? According to social role theory, individuals and groups who are subordinate will develop greater sensitivity to the moods and feelings of their superiors (Henley & LaFrance, 1997). For example, an employee must be more concerned about the mood and needs of a supervisor than the supervisor need be concerned about the mood, needs, or wishes of an employee. A fairly consistent finding has been that regardless of gender, individuals in subordinate roles demonstrate greater sensitivity to the nonverbal cues of those in superior roles (Hall, Halberstadt, & O'Brien, 1997; Snodgrass, 1985, 1992). In most societies, women are in subordinate positions relative to men. Therefore, more

women will develop this greater sensitivity to nonverbal cues. Similarly, because we more often observe men in leadership roles (president, legislators, CEOs, college presidents, orchestra conductors, religious leaders, and so on), we come to perceive that as a group, men possess leadership qualities.

Critical Thinking Challenge

Postindustrial society is characterized by an increasing overlap in women's and men's roles (more women entrepreneurs, more men with equal responsibility for children). What would social role theorists predict about changes among men and women in terms of gender-related qualities such as nurturance and ambition?

The Sociological Perspective: A Critical Evaluation

Although a sociological analysis offers useful insights into the functioning of complex societies, it does not allow for predicting or understanding individual behavior. Nor can sociological theory comfortably account for overlapping influences. For example, many behavioral differences commonly reported on the basis of ethnicity may be more accurately reflections of social class. Although teen pregnancy rates for African-American and Latina girls are reported as being higher than those for white teenage girls, the effect of social class is confounded. That is, when pregnancy rates for teens of the same social class within each ethnic group are compared, there is little difference among the groups (Gans, 1998).

Another problem is the issue of causation. Although sociological studies may point out important correlations between gender-related variables, they do not allow researchers to make statements about the causes of these variations in gendered behavior.

The Anthropological Perspective

Anthropologists study and compare whole societies or cultures. They attempt to describe and explain the origins and structures of those cultures (Gailey, 1987). Anthropology allows fascinating insights into the tremendous variability of human social forms by permitting comparisons among different societies. This is particularly useful in terms of gender roles, because anthropological studies constantly remind us how varied the content of gender roles can be among human groups. Older, classic **ethnographies** describe a world in which human groups could live in relative isolation from other groups and could develop social forms that contrasted mightily with each other. For example, the Sambia of Melanesia and the Etoro of New Guinea view same-sex sexual activity as the socially approved pathway to adult masculinity (Herdt, 1997; Kelly, 1976). Tibetan women could have two husbands, provided the men were brothers (Haviland, 1991). Today, human societies are much more interconnected. Videocassettes, television, and the Internet permeate even the most remote areas of the world.

Contemporary anthropological studies demonstrate that every human culture makes some distinction between women and men. These distinctions have to do with the roles or activities that men and women are to perform, the rights they have in relation to each other, and how their respective activities are to be valued by members of that society. Anthropologists generally agree that each culture socially constructs gender roles and that the content and requirements of these roles can vary widely. Anthropologists also note that societies differ by how distinct these gender roles are (the degree of overlap), how rigid the boundaries are between the roles approved for women and men, and how valued the tasks of each are (Bonvillain, 1998). For two examples of the differential valuing of activities according to gender, in certain areas of New Guinea men traditionally grew yams and women grew sweet potatoes. Yams were considered a more prestigious and valuable food (Rosaldo, 1974). In mainstream Western society, men may smoke cigarettes, pipes, and cigars. Women may smoke only cigarettes. Violators of this norm elicit comment, and perhaps negative consequences.

Critical Thinking Challenge

Can you think of any current examples in Western societies of men's activities being considered more valuable than similar women's activities?

Two dimensions emerge by which gender roles in different societies may be compared. The first has to do with the economic subsistence (or economic production) of a society. The second has to do with how the society is arranged politically, that is, how power

is distributed among the members of that society. Gender relations can be examined on the continuum from full equality to complete domination of one gender over the other. What is meant by equality? It relates to the level of autonomy among members of a particular gender. Gender inequality implies the denial of autonomy and rights for members of a particular gender. In small-scale foraging band societies, all individuals make important contributions and power hierarchies are minimal or even absent (Lepowsky, 1998; Miller, 1993). In general, there is more gender inequality in more complex societies. In developing or industrialized nation-states, economic specialization, and power hierarchies mean that different groups have differential access to resources and have different rights and privileges. In industrialized nations, the biggest gap is that of class, although gender cuts across class so that poor women have less power/status than poor men.

The Anthropological Perspective: A Critical Evaluation

Cultural anthropologists may study small-scale, relatively isolated human groups or complex contemporary nation-states. But just like psychologists and sociologists, anthropologists perceive and understand through their own culture-bound eyes. For example, when 19th-century British anthropologists studied the Igbo of midwestern Nigeria, they failed to "see" the autonomy and overt political power that women had in that indigenous society (VanAllen, 1997). These anthropologists brought the lens of gender relations in Victorian England with them and filtered their observations through that lens. How can we be certain that today's observations are not colored by some more recent ethnocentric lens?

An Eastern Perspective on Gender

Like other human groups, the Chinese have wondered about the inherent nature of men and women as well as their relationship with each other. In about 400 BCE, a school of philosophy arose in China that viewed everything in the cosmos to be related to and

---

ethnography   **Descriptive account of a culture or subculture.**

affected by everything else (naturalism). Our linear Western notion of cause and effect would have had little place in this perspective, because the Chinese saw everything in the universe as interconnected and striving toward balance or harmony. According to this approach, no distinction was necessary between what was physical and what was mental, or between what was human versus what was nature (Wu, 1986). Yet human consciousness has a tendency toward dualistic thinking, and Chinese consciousness is no exception (Creel, 1953). Thus the naturalists concluded that the entire cosmos can be characterized by two universal qualities that always exist in relation to each other. This duality is known as the principle of yin and yang. Everything in the universe may be considered either primarily yin or primarily yang: female and male, earth and heaven, moist and dry, interior of the body and exterior of the body, wood and fire, tranquil and active, inward-looking and outward-looking, moon and sun, and so on. The original sense of the terms *yin* and *yang* imply a gradual passing of one into the other, such as night passing into daylight. So, unlike Western notions of opposites, the inherent qualities of yin and yang are seen as contrasting but complementary and always in relation to each other (Allen, 1991; Hsi & Tsu-chien, 1967).

The Maintenance of Harmony

Everything stable in the cosmos was characterized by harmony between yin and yang. Although one aspect might be dominant, that was not its complete nature. Moreover, the balance was always relative. A man could be yin in relation to his ruler or father, but yang in relation to his wife. Although winter is yin, it gradually becomes the yang of summer and back again. Take a look at the symbol for the yin and yang principle (Figure 3.3). The dark area is yin, and the light area is yang. Note that the circle is not evenly divided, but rather each element carries over into the other, and *each contains the other at its core.*

Critical Thinking Challenge

What similarity does this last idea bear to those of Jung's concepts of anima and animus?

The concept of yin and yang was first applied to account for the nature of the universe, and then later

FIGURE 3.3   The yin-yang symbol represents the interpenetrability of opposites in nature.

applied to human conduct. A ruler who behaved badly disturbed the balance of yin and yang, and natural disasters would soon follow. Harmony was said to prevail if a husband led and a wife followed. Disharmony occurred if a man was ruled by his desires rather than by the pursuit of harmony. The pursuit of pleasure resulted in the loss of his strength of character. A woman accustomed to pleasure would lose her dutiful obedience. Misfortune inevitably followed both of these possibilities (Allen, 1991).

Proper balance between yin and yang became the central principle of Chinese philosophy. Virtually all aspects of life are considered in terms of yin and yang, including art, metallurgy, medicine, sexuality, cooking, marriage, and politics (Wu, 1986). In terms of sexuality, prolonged intercourse was recommended so that a man would not quickly lose too much yang and would instead absorb sufficient yin to reestablish harmony in his body.

An Eastern Perspective: A Critical Evaluation

These Chinese ideas of interrelationship and connection might have set a new pathway, very different from that set by Western ideas of linear causation, for discovering or inventing new knowledge. However, this never happened. For a variety of historical and cultural reasons, the emphasis in traditional Chinese scholarship became and remained the interpretation of classic writings (Allen, 1991).

Summary

♦ A scientific theory is a set of ideas or concepts that organizes knowledge about some phenomenon. The usefulness of a theory determines its quality. People can use theories to generate new questions and to interpret new data.

♦ Good (useful) theories are empirically based, parsimonious, comprehensive, noncontradictory, testable, practical, and acceptable to other experts.

♦ Biological approaches emphasize the influence of genes and hormones on the brain and nervous system. Evolutionary approaches emphasize gender as differential reproductive strategies for males and females. Cross-species comparisons reveal a wide array of male–female relationships.

♦ Psychological theories deal with issues of gender role acquisition, maintenance, and application in personality development and interpersonal interaction. Psychoanalytic theories emphasize anatomy and identification. Social learning theories emphasize reinforcement, punishment, vicarious reinforcement, observation, and modeling as the mechanisms for gender role acquisition and maintenance.

♦ Cognitive-developmental theorists take a counterintuitive, stage approach to gender identity formation and gender role acquisition. Gender schema theory emphasizes the formation of mental frameworks (schemas) that guide and direct behavior.

♦ Feminist approaches may be classified along the dimensions of empiricist/minimalist to feminist standpoint/maximalist.

♦ The gender-in-context perspective approaches gender as existing, not within a person, but within a socially constructed transaction between and among individuals.

♦ Social role theory is an example of a sociological approach to gender. So-called gender differences are viewed as emerging from the typical superior–subordinate roles enacted by women and men. Eventually men and women come to be seen as possessing the qualities their respective roles require.

♦ Anthropological approaches describe and compare whole societies regarding gendered behavior. Although all societies make some distinction between the roles of women and men, they differ regarding the contents of these roles, the rights and power of each gender, and the social and economic value placed on the activities of men and women.

♦ The Chinese principle of yin and yang emphasizes the maintenance of balance and harmony between related aspects of all things in the universe, including the relationships between women and men.

InfoTrac College Edition

For more information, explore InfoTrac College Edition at

http://www.infotrac-college.com/Wadsworth

Enter search terms: gender schema, gender-in-context, gender constancy, Carol Gilligan, social role theory, evolution and gender, feminist standpoint.

4 Gender and the Body
Hindsight, Oversights, and Insights

I have . . . learned about science and culture, about technology and language, about what the body could mean, does mean and perhaps should mean, to the life of the person. ◆ A. D. Dreger

Learning Objectives

After studying this chapter, you should be able to:

1. Summarize the findings, both conclusive and inconclusive, regarding sex differences in the hypothalamus and other brain structures.
2. List and explain four issues surrounding the influence of gonadal hormones on human behavior, especially in the area of cognitive abilities.
3. Evaluate the stereotype that males excel in math, emphasizing the relevant cross-cultural findings.
4. Summarize the strengths and weaknesses of the research on sex/gender differences in verbal abilities and visuospatial abilities.
5. Explain how Carroll's (1998) study of group differences in fingerprint patterns illustrates the inherent weaknesses of sex difference research.
6. Explain why understanding the findings on gender differences in brain structure, hormonal influences, and cognitive abilities is important.
7. List the components of sex and gender development from chromosomal sex to the roles of the fully gendered adult.
8. List two types of sex chromosome disorders and three gonadal hormone disorders, and then summarize how these conditions influence various components of gender development.
9. Explain how intersexuality can help us understand the relationship between the body and gender, and then summarize the controversies regarding the response to intersexuality in current Western society.
10. Offer several cross-cultural examples of how the body, particularly the genitals, serve to mark and express gender in various societies.

Encounters with Gender

In 1886, Sophie, age 42, a domestic servant, visited a local clinic in Belgium. One month into their first marriage, she and her husband were still unable to complete intercourse. An examination of Sophie's genital area showed her to have what appeared to be a "penis" of 5 centimeters without an opening at the tip. It was clearly capable of erection. Urine was excreted via an opening below this "penis." Her labia contained at least one testicle. However, Sophie had all the other bodily features of a typical woman. She felt like a woman, spoke, moved, dressed, and behaved like a woman, and was now married to a man who loved her as a wife. To the shocked and incredulous Sophie, the equally shocked and incredulous physician merely kept repeating, "But, my good woman, you are a man!" (adapted from Dreger, 1998b).

Overview

Our exploration of the complex relationship between gender and our biological characteristics will take us down three pathways, all equally controversial. First, we explore the question of whether the brains of women and men are different in terms of structure (anatomy) and functioning (physiology). This leads to the issue of whether neuroendocrine factors (hor-monal influences) offer the best explanation for the observed sex/gender differences in cognitive abilities. Our last stop within this section is an encounter with some of the problems involved in conducting research on human group differences. Our third path offers further insights into the relationship between gender and the body. For the vast majority of human beings, the physical markers of sex and gender are congruent. For some they are not. We can gain special insights from the **intersexed** about how genes, hormones, and genitalia-based gender assignment all contribute to the development of a gendered person. This chapter discusses what ultimately makes a person female or male, boy or girl. I also examine how North American society responds when a person does not neatly fit into a particular sex or gender category. Finally, the chapter looks at the relationship between gender and the body across cultures.

Sex, Gender, and the Brain: Are There Differences?

As you read in the previous chapter, chromosomal endowment (XX or XY) results in the prenatal development of particular gonads: ovaries or testes. During prenatal development, genetic influences diminish as the gonads begin to secrete particular sex hormones. These hormones affect the **hypothalamus** and the development of internal reproductive organs and external genitalia. Until the 6th week of development, it is impossible to tell the sex of an embryo by visual inspection. In genetic males, testicular hormones influence the formation of distinctively male internal and external structures over several weeks. By the 12th week, genital formation is complete. *No hormonal action is necessary for the formation of female internal structures.* This last point is an important principle in understanding prenatal sexual development (Fausto-Sterling, 2000). At birth, a look at the genitalia results in classification as male or female, and therefore assignment to a particular gender. At puberty, the hypothalamus stimulates the adjacent **pituitary gland** to initiate and regulate the menstrual and ovulatory cycles in women. In men, this system initiates and regulates a relatively steady level of androgens. These gonadal hormones are also responsible for the development and maintenance of the postpubertal secondary sexual characteristics. Thus we differentially come to have full breasts or full beards, soft skin or hard muscles, and broad hips or broad shoulders. These hormones also permit a wide variety of reproductive behaviors and functions such as conception, implantation, birthing, and lactation. When we go beyond these well-established facts, however, we step into a veritable minefield of contention. Sudden and unexpected eruptions of controversy and

social power may sometimes occur, and many of these eruptions have far-reaching social implications (MacIntyre, 1997). Critical thinking is often in short supply when questions of gender differences and the bodily self are the issue. First of all, what is the central question here? It's clear that biology and culture always interact, so it is more helpful to ask, *How much* does biology influence any *particular* feature of gendered behavior? and *How much* can socialization and culture account for *particular* differences? These questions lead to a host of others. How much do contextual factors influence these apparent differences in ability? Can differences in **cognitive ability** be modified by training, practice, or other interventions? How do these apparent differences in abilities manifest across cultures and ethnic groups? Why do some researchers report brain differences but subsequent studies fail to replicate such findings? Are other behavioral variations, such as sexual orientation and **handedness,** also based on brain differences?

That's just a sample of the questions that are running through the minds of scientists, practitioners, educators, policymakers, and sometimes even "the folks at the office." Perhaps you should put on a safety helmet (to protect your somewhat sexually differentiated brain), as we try to make our way through these controversies.

For some people, the notion of brain differences in areas other than reproduction-related processes is unacceptable (Hubbard, 1998; Springer & Deutsch, 1998). They see the heavy concentration (some say *segregation*) of one gender or another in certain educational, occupational, social, and interpersonal roles and statuses as *solely* the product of gender socialization and power arrangements. Others are equally adamant that evolutionary forces have brought about significant differences in brain anatomy and functioning

---

intersexed   **Having some of the physical characteristics of the other sex or sexually ambiguous characteristics.**

hypothalamus   **Part of the forebrain. It regulates body temperature, metabolic activity, and sexual behavior.**

pituitary gland   **Small, oval endocrine gland attached to hypothalamus. Controls other endocrine glands, and influences growth and maturation.**

cognitive abilities   **Abilities related to cognition or knowing. Includes awareness, perception, and reasoning.**

handedness   **A preference for using one hand or the other.**

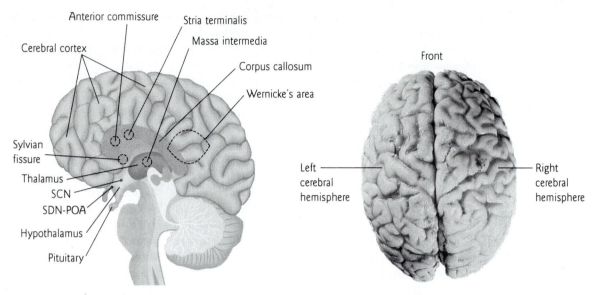

FIGURE 4.1   The parts of the brain labeled here are hypothesized to be distinctive in the two sexes.
Source: Adapted from R. Crooks & K. Baur (2002). *Our sexuality,* 8th ed. (Pacific Grove, CA: Wadsworth).

(Geary, 1999; Joseph, 2000; Mealy, 2000). Still others see hormonally differentiated brain functioning as the best explanation for the proficiencies and preferences of the two sexes (Kimura, 1999). Uh-oh! At this point you may need to transform that rigid safety helmet into a more flexible critical thinking cap. We will examine some basic, well-established findings and also try to make some sense out of often contradictory findings.

The Hypothalamus

The *anterior* hypothalamus is involved in certain mating behaviors in lower animals (male mounting and thrusting, and female **lordosis**). The *posterior* section is involved in releasing pituitary hormones, so that regular ovulation, menstruation, and sperm production occur (Figure 4.1 shows all the parts of the brain mentioned here). Some researchers claim that hypothalamic differentiation is the basis for gender identity formation, although this remains very uncertain (Grimshaw, Sitarenias, & Finegan, 1995). Others claim that adherence to prescribed gender role behaviors is also brain based, but the precise mechanism for this too remains elusive (Hines, 1993).

The sexually dimorphic nucleus of the preoptic area of the hypothalamus (SDN-POA) appears to

contain twice as many cells in young adult men than in women, but the significance of this is not clear (Swaab, Zhou, Fodos, & Hoffman, 1997). This differential changes over the life span. In men, large numbers of cells die after age 50, whereas among women this change occurs after age 70. Several studies have found differences in the SDN-POA in terms of cell count, cell volume, or both, between heterosexual and homosexual men (Allen & Gorski, 1992; LeVay, 1991; Swaab & Hofman, 1990), but cell volume is very susceptible to postmortem changes (these studies are carried out on brain tissue taken from cadavers). Attempts at replication for these findings have been very problematic. Meanwhile, other researchers debate about which areas of the hypothalamus even make up the SDN-POA (Swaab et al., 1997)!

Sex differences in the nuclei of the anterior hypothalamus have been associated with **sexual orientation** (McKnight, 1997). Examining a small sample of men's brain tissue, one researcher found the INAH-3 (third interstitial nucleus of the anterior hypothala-

---

lordosis   **A posture by which lower-mammal females signal readiness and willingness to mate.**

sexual orientation   **The direction of one's erotic interests: toward persons of one's own sex, of the other sex, or of both sexes.**

mus) to be larger among heterosexual men than among women and homosexual or bisexual men (LeVay, 1991). The work of Simon LeVay lingers in the popular media and mind, but more recent studies reveal no differences in the SDN-POA of men regardless of sexual orientation (Fausto-Sterling, 2000). Nor have earlier findings of genetic markers for homosexuality held up (Rice & Anderson, 1999; Wickelgren, 2000).

Other Brain Differences

Reports have emerged regarding sex differences in other parts of the brain; especially the corpus callosum, in the isthmus of the corpus callosum, and in the bulbous splenium of the corpus callosum (Fausto-Sterling, 2000). Other areas of interest include the bed nucleus of the stria terminalis (Zhou, Hofman, Gooren, & Swaab, 1995), the massa intermedia, and the anterior commissure (Allen & Gorski, 1992). Various groups of researchers have found sex differences in the percentage of cortical gray matter tissue, in the volume of the nuclei of the stria terminalis, in the shape of the sylvian fissure, in part of the thalamus, and in patterns of cerebral blood flow (Gur et al., 1995). Still others have found differences in the vasopressin-containing nucleus of the suprachiasmatic nucleus (SCN), with those of homosexual men being twice as large as those of heterosexual men (Swaab & Hofman, 1990). The SCN is the "clock" of the human brain in that it regulates **circadian** and other rhythms. No one knows how this might be related to gender or sexual orientation.

Again, replication of most of these findings has been problematic (Bailey, 1995). Critics point out that the use of certain laboratory chemicals and procedures in conducting this research can actually change brain tissue (Juraska, Nunez, Koss, & Christopher, 1998).

Several researchers have noted that sex differences in relative brain "size" are present from 2 years of age onward (Swaab & Hofman, 1995; Witelson, Glezor, & Kigor, 1995). However, "size" may be evaluated in very different ways: total space taken up, total number of neurons, density of the neurons, size of individual neurons, number of **dendritic synapses**, and so on (do you feel a headache coming on in your sexually differentiated brain?). These researchers suggest that the structural differences in the brain may be related to gender

TABLE 4.1 Sex Ratios for Selected Neurological and Psychiatric Disorders

Disease	Percent Female:Male
Anorexia nervosa	93%: 7%
Bulimia	75%:25%
Anxiety disorders	67%:33%
Depression	63%:37%
Multiple sclerosis	58%:42%
Severe mental retardation	38%:62%
Autism	29%:71%
Stuttering	29%:71%
Schizophrenia	27%:73%
Dyslexia	23%:77%
Sleep apnea	18%:82%
Tourette's syndrome	10%:90%

Source: Adapted from D. F. Swaab & M. A. Hofman (1995). Sexual differentiation of the human hypothalamus in relation to gender and sexual orientation. *Trends in Neuroscience, 18,* 265.

differences in the **epidemiology** of neurological and psychiatric diseases (see Table 4.1). Consider that about 75% of cases of **anorexia** and **bulimia** occur in women. In contrast, about 75% of cases of **dyslexia**, **sleep apnea**, and **Tourette's syndrome** occur in men. Men are almost three times as vulnerable to schizophrenia as are women. Researchers also note the powerful sex difference in the incidence of **transsexualism** (1 in 12,000 for men versus 1 in 30,000 for women;

circadian **Related to 24-hour biological rhythms, such as sleeping and waking.**

dendritic synapses **Spaces between the branches or extensions of individual nerve cells.**

epidemiology **Branch of medicine that deals with the causes, distribution, and control of diseases in populations.**

anorexia **Eating disorder characterized by fear of obesity, a distorted body image, aversion to food, and severe weight loss.**

bulimia **Eating disorder characterized by binge eating and purging.**

dyslexia **Neurological disorder characterized by reading, spelling, and writing difficulties.**

Sleep apnea **Sleep disorder characterized by temporary cessation of breathing.**

Tourette's syndrome **Neurological disorder characterized by body and facial tics accompanied by grunts, compulsive utterances, and obscenities.**

transsexualism **Gender identity disorder in which person experiences the self as a member of the other sex or gender.**

Bakker, van Kesteren, Gooren, & Bezemer, 1993). These researchers propose that transsexualism develops as a result of disturbed interaction between the developing brain and sex hormones. They note that 60% of male-to-female transsexuals are **androphilic** and 10% are **ambiphilic**. No less than 95% of female-to-male transsexuals are **gynecophilic** (Diamond, 1997). These findings suggest a relationship between gender identity development and sexual orientation, but again, the precise mechanism remains unknown.

There is evidence that language functions are more **asymmetric** among men's brains, with verbal functions more concentrated in the left hemisphere, and spatial skills more concentrated in the right hemisphere (Geschwind & Galaburda, 1987; Nyborg, 1994; Rugg, 1995). This greater **lateralization** in men's brains, the subsequent development of sex differences in the behavioral problems just listed, as well as differences in particular cognitive abilities have all been attributed to the effects of prenatal testosterone. Greater lateralization has also been associated with a greater incidence of left-handedness, stuttering, hyperactivity, and immune disorders among men. Men have higher incidence of **aphasia** after a stroke or other trauma to the left hemisphere, and they show larger discrepancies between measures of verbal and nonverbal intelligence after damage to either hemisphere (Levy & Heller, 1998).

In considering the issue of brain differences, we must evaluate the implicit assumption that brain differences *lead to* behavioral differences. However, consider the following findings regarding differences in brain structure and functioning. Japanese is written with both a phonetic alphabet (Kana), in which individual letters stand for particular sounds, and an ideographic orthography (Kanji) in which one pictogram stands for a whole word or idea. Different parts of the brain are involved in processing these two language forms (Yu-Huan et al., 1990). There is also a body of research that suggests that illiterates have somewhat different language organization in the brain compared to those who can read (Yu-Huan et al., 1992). These findings are helpful in reminding us that postnatal experience can have a lasting effect on brain structure and organization (Blonder, 1991; Laughlin, 1991). The human brain, particularly the cortex, may be too complex for simple stereotypic notions that too often have power arrangements embedded within them.

Often this hidden gender ideology becomes blatantly visible only with hindsight. See Box 4.1 for a historical perspective on the politics of brain research.

Gonadal Hormones and Behavior

In a review of studies involving the influence of gonadal hormones on behavior, Collaer and Hines (1995) concluded that the evidence is strongest for hormonal influences on childhood play patterns (rough-and-tumble play, toy preferences, playmate preferences). The evidence is much weaker regarding hormonal influences on sexual orientation and tendencies toward aggression. However, lines of research strongly suggest both short and long-term hormonal influences on a wide array of behaviors, especially cognitive abilities (Kimura, 1999; Saucier & Kimura, 1998). What can the beginning student of gender conclude from still another array of contradictory findings?

First, it is difficult to determine the relative contribution of factors such as genetics, brain structure or functioning, hormonal influences, life experiences, and socialization to behavioral sex differences (Halpern, 1996a). Second, although studies may describe atypical gender-typed behavior among patients with unusual gonadal hormone exposure, many individuals with similar exposure never come to the attention of practitioners (Bailey, 1995). You will read more about this later in the chapter. Third, even if gonadal hormones contribute to behavioral sex differences, that does not mean they are unalterable or that the differences are caused *only* by genetic or hormonal influences. As you have seen, environments can alter both brain structures *and* hormonal composition. Fourth, as you can see in Figure 4.2, differences invariably mean "an average disparity," so there is always great overlap in the distribution of a particular factor (Collaer & Hines, 1995). Although many gender

---

androphilia   **Erotic attraction to men.**

ambiphilia   **Erotic attraction to both men and women.**

gynecophilia   **Erotic attraction to women.**

asymmetry   **Increased concentration of development or function in one hemisphere.**

lateralization   **Localization of function to either the right or left hemisphere.**

aphasia   **Loss of ability to produce or comprehend language.**

A History of Sex and the Brain

In most societies, women and men occupied very different roles and statuses. Why were power, resources, and wealth so concentrated in the hands of men? Furthermore, why did even the brightest or wealthiest of women create, produce, or control so little? In days past, religion provided the answer to such questions: It was God's natural plan for an orderly universe. When religious doctrine ceased to have such power, people looked to science for explanations. Scientists began to search for brain differences that could account for white men's superior status and women's subordinate status. Phrenology was the first attempt to relate anatomy and physiology to specific behaviors. Phrenologists erroneously assumed that the physical features of the skull were related to the anatomical features of the brain beneath. In keeping with popular notions of the day, the study of the bumps and depressions on the skull found a less developed frontal lobe and generally softer brain tissue in women, thereby explaining women's gentler, more nurturant, and more compliant natures. Men's brains were harder and more developed for aggressiveness. Repeated public demonstrations of the nonsensical basis of this pseudoscience eventually led to its demise (Fancher, 1997).

Later researchers worked with actual brain tissue and found women's brains to be smaller. Thus, scientists proclaimed a physical basis for women's inferior reasoning ability. Numerous scientific papers noted the "missing five ounces" in the female brain. However, comparisons based on absolute size were problematic because big animals had brains larger than those of humans, but they were certainly intellectually inferior. The emphasis now shifted to notions of brain size relative to the size of the body. This too was problematic, because the brains of women are actually larger relative to their smaller body size. This led to a search for other measures to explain and support women's "naturally inferior" status (Shields, 1975). A panoply of variables such as overall brain surface area, the number of cortical convolutions (the "wrinkles" of the cortex), proportional weight, and the total number of cortical neurons each came to the forefront of explanation and justification, but each hypothesis died a scientific death. Until the end of the 19th century people believed that the frontal lobes of the cortex were the seat of intellect, and of course there was "proof" that men had more developed frontal lobes whereas

women had more developed parietal lobes. However, when new findings purported to show that parietal lobes were really the seat of intellect, numerous studies appeared showing men to have more developed parietal lobes (Shields, 1997).

The struggle for equality between the genders continues in every venue, including the neuroscientist's laboratory. Recently, new findings have come to the fore. Because more brain tissue must be damaged before women display severe disturbance, perhaps women's brains are more "efficient." Moreover, women's brains have a higher density of neurons in a smaller space. Women's less localized language functions appear to protect them from certain poststroke deficits. In contrast, hemispheric lateralization, and consequent superiority in visuospatial abilities, are often cited as the reasons for men's predominance in certain high-status occupations (engineering, architecture, aviation, and so on). Because supposedly objective findings sometimes seem to correlate with changes in social ideologies, it is sometimes difficult to achieve a balance between healthy skepticism and informed openness about sex, gender, the brain, and the body.

---

scholars like to cling to convenient notions regarding sex differences as rooted in biology, and gender differences as socially constructed, you can begin to see the continuing difficulty in such categorization. Box 4.2 offers more insight into this complex area of research.

Critical Thinking Challenge

How do genetics and the postnatal environment *interact* in determining height?

Sex, Gender, and Cognitive Abilities

The term *cognition* refers to the mental processes of perceiving, remembering, imagining, conceiving, judging, and reasoning. However, in terms of gender, three cognitive domains have received special attention (Caplan & Caplan, 1997). In their classic review of the research then available, Maccoby and Jacklin (1974) concluded that there was evidence of a predictable pattern of sex differences in mathematical

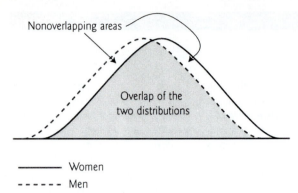

Nonoverlapping areas

Overlap of the
two distributions

——————— Women

- - - - - - Men

FIGURE 4.2   Remember that any discussion of sex or gender "differences" always implies tremendous overlap between women and men. A finding of difference predicts nothing about a single individual.

abilities, verbal abilities, and visuospatial abilities. Over the past 30 years, a mountain of research has accumulated to either extend and support, or narrow and contradict these conclusions (see Table 4.2).

Once the issue of differences in cognitive abilities was raised, the next question had to do with their origin. That is, to what degree are these differences based on genetic, hormonal, or neuroanatomic characteristics? To what degree do they result from socialization forces that may be more easily modified? You can apply what you've learned so far in appreciating and evaluating the findings described in Box 4.3.

In discussing findings of sex or gender differences in cognitive abilities, we must immediately deal with the file drawer phenomenon. As you learned in Chapter 2, the nature of most psychological research is the search for differences between groups. Findings of "no difference" are usually not publishable and end up in someone's file drawer. The result is an undue emphasis on sex and gender differences rather than on similarities. Any differences found are likely to be exaggerated. Moreover, this emphasis on differences increases the likelihood that spurious findings are likely to remain in the literature, even if not replicated (see Table 4.3 for an overview of some of these problems).

TABLE 4.2   Sex Differences on Cognitive Tests and Tasks

Areas in Which Women Usually Obtain Higher Average Scores	*Areas in Which Men Usually Obtain Higher Average Scores*
Tasks that require rapid access to and use of phonological, semantic and other information in long-term memory: verbal fluency, synonym generation, associative memory, spelling, anagrams, mathematical calculations, memory for spatial location	Transformations in visual working memory: mental rotation, waterlevel task
	Judgments about moving objects: dynamic spatiotemporal tasks
Knowledge areas: literature and foreign languages	Motor tasks that involve aiming: throwing balls or darts
Production and comprehension of complex prose: reading comprehension, writing	Knowledge areas: general knowledge, geography, math and science knowledge
Fine motor tasks: mirror tracing, pegboard tasks, matching and coding tasks	Fluid reasoning: proportional reasoning, SAT-M, GRE-Q, mechanical reasoning, verbal analogies, scientific reasoning
Perceptual speed: multiple-speed tasks, embedded letters	
Decoding nonverbal information: facial expressions	
Perceptual thresholds: lower for touch, taste, odor, hearing (over time)	
School grades: most subjects	
Speech articulation: tongue twisters	

Source: Adapted from D. Halpern (1996b). Public policy implications of sex differences in cognitive abilities. *Psychology, Public Policy and Law,* 2(3/4), 564.

The Neuroscientist, the Feminist, and the Critical Thinker: On Finding Differences

Michael Carroll (1998) notes that when researchers find evidence of sex or gender differences that *confirm* gender stereotypes, such findings are quickly assumed to have a biological basis. Such findings are challenged less frequently, subjected to less critical evaluation by other scientists, and more easily accepted by the public. He also believes that when findings of sex or gender differences emerge, researchers sometimes fail to consider alternative explanations for their findings. To illustrate this point, Carroll reviews the research literature on dermoglyphic asymmetry (DA), that is, the differences among fingerprint patterns. After all, most of us agree that fingerprints don't lie because they are easily and objectively observed. Fingerprints provide a useful arena for the discussion of sex or gender differences because they are not ideologically or emotionally charged. Most people know and are comfortable with the fact that except for identical twins, everyone has a unique set of fingerprints. Also, unlike math skills or verbal skills, no one assumes that some patterns of fingerprints are "superior" to others. Moreover, fingerprints are set during the fourth month of prenatal development, so if group differences in fingerprints correlate strongly with some other factor, this suggests a prenatal source for both factors. Some of what's to follow is complicated, and a lot of it may be unfamiliar, so we'll try to keep it as simple as possible.

There is an established body of research documenting ethnic differences in fingerprints, but there are only a few reports that describe gender differences in dermatoglyphic asymmetry (DA). Most

people have more ridges on the right hand (R>). Examining groups of self-identified heterosexual and homosexual men, Hall and Kimura (1994) found that although most of the men had the expected R> pattern of ridges, a pattern of L> (more ridges on the left hand) was more common among gay men. Thus L> might be considered a "marker" for male sexual orientation, and the finding implies that sexual orientation could be biologically based. In another study, using a sample of men and women believed to be overwhelmingly heterosexual, Kimura and Carson (1995) found that the L> pattern was more common among women. Thus we have evidence of a physical feature, not related to reproduction, that occurs differentially between women and men and between heterosexual and gay men. As in cognitive abilities, there is clearly much overlap, but there are also suggestions of an overall group difference. Note that such findings support the commonly held stereotypes that not only are women and men physically different but also that women and gay men are somehow similar. You may recall a similar idea from your reading on differentials in brain structure.

Now let's see if something as seemingly objective as fingerprint patterns *can* lie. Is the L> pattern really more common among women? Again, we return to the issue of *which* women? In the Kimura and Carson (1995) study, the L> pattern was more common among right-handed (dextral) women, but among left-handers, there was no sex difference. Consider also that a classic and well-accepted work in the field of fingerprint analysis (Holt,

1968) found more males to be L>. How could this be? The scientific detective would immediately suspect that perhaps sample differences were at the heart of the mystery. Holt's sample was British, whereas Kimura's were Canadian, so the groups probably differ more by ethnicity rather than by sex or sexual orientation. Furthermore, Hall and Kimura's (1994) heterosexual sample were Canadian college students, whereas their sample of gay men consisted of volunteer participants attending West Hollywood's Gay Pride Week celebrations in 1993. These two samples most certainly differed in terms of ethnicity. Carroll also notes the unusually high number of left-handed individuals in the gay sample, which also suggests that they were not a representative sample. Lastly, Carroll carefully examined other aspects of the methods used in both studies. He found that these researchers used an unusual finger-sampling technique. Without delving into the technical details, just know that this unusual technique increased the likelihood that a great gender difference in L> frequency would emerge. Thus these findings of ostensible biological and behavioral differences are most likely nothing more than artifacts of the methods and measurements used. Fingerprints *can* lie, especially when the lies confirm our most deeply held stereotypes. These biases in methods and measurements prompted one writer/researcher in the area of gender differences to conclude that when it comes to the biological bases of gender differences "believing is seeing" (Lorber, 1994).

ABCs of GENDER (ATTITUDES, BELIEFS, AND CONCERNS)   BOX 4.3

The Issue: Evaluating Scientific Findings

Can you apply what you have read in this chapter toward a critical evaluation of the following news items?

■ Researchers used magnetic resonance imaging to study brain activity while participants listened to excerpts from a novel. Among the women, there was brain activity in both temporal lobes; among the men, activity occurred mainly in the left temporal lobe. These findings were reported in the popular press and electronic media as confirming that "men listen half as well as women do" (Reuters Medical News, 2000d).

■ A recent brain-imaging study found that London cab drivers had a hippocampus (a structure in the limbic system of the forebrain) that was signifi-cantly larger compared to those of others. The hippocampus is involved in spatial relations, and this difference was attributed to the spatial chal-lenges presented by navigating such a complex city (Edidin, 2000).

■ Several reports were published the scarcity of left-handers among the elderly. It was hypothesized that dif-ferences in the brain organization of lefties was related to an earlier death. Subsequent researchers found that this "absence" was actually caused by historical social disapproval of left-handedness. Lefties were forced to use their right hands, and thus there were fewer left-handed individuals among older cohorts (Powell, 2001).

■ When baseball player Mark McGuire began using male hormone supple-ments to increase his muscularity, he soon began developing breasts. Al-though they were never discussed in public, testicular shrinkage and impo-tence were also likely side effects.

■ A study compared sleep patterns among gay men and lesbians with those of heterosexuals, and purported to find some differences. However, the heterosexuals were university stu-dents whereas the gay and lesbian sample were mainly patrons of British "public houses" (Rahman & Silber, 2000).

TABLE 4.3 Possible Biases in Gender Difference Research

Use of gender-biased models to generate questions
Likelihood of exaggerating differences
Likelihood of minimizing similarities
Experimenter expectations
File drawer phenomenon
Gender-biased interpretation of findings

Source: Adapted from T. MacIntyre (1997). Gender differences in cognition: A minefield of research issues, *Irish Journal of Psychology*, 18(4), 393.

Critical Thinking Challenge

In the recent past it was suggested that every relevant psychological study should include a statistical analysis to uncover any sex or gender differences in the behavior under study. How would you evaluate this suggestion?

Mathematical Abilities

"Boys excel in math." This stereotype is remarkably robust in some societies, particularly North American society. How can we check on the veracity of this well-established notion? First of all, what are "math-ematical abilities"? The term actually refers to a num-ber of skills and abilities: computation, mathematical problem solving, understanding and applying math-ematical concepts, performing arithmetic functions, applying algebraic formulas, solving geometric prob-lems, calculus, mathematical reasoning, and several more. Each of these processes requires somewhat dif-ferent abilities. Moreover, what should be the criteria for having *greater* mathematical ability? Should it be the rapidity of calculation or problem solving? Should it be accuracy? Should it be course grades? Should it be the ability to recognize which mathematical pro-cesses are appropriate to a problem? Should it be the efficiency of mathematical reasoning? Should it be standardized test scores?

Two of the most cited studies purporting to show "sex differences in mathematical reasoning ability," namely Benbow & Stanley (1980, 1983), were actually both studies of SAT scores for 50,000 high-ability students. Not only was the sample not representative, but it is well known that SAT scores are powerfully affected by the number of mathematics courses students have taken. A considerable body of research documents that boys are encouraged to complete more mathematics courses compared to girls (Caplan & Caplan, 1997; Catsambis, 1999).

Mathematical abilities are measured in two main ways: either via scores on standardized tests such as the SAT or via classroom test performance and course grades. Female students generally achieve higher scores on classroom tests and grades, whereas male students generally obtain higher scores on standardized tests (Duffy, Gunther, & Walters, 1997; Hyde & McKinley, 1997).

In evaluating the stereotype that boys excel in mathematics, we must ask, *"Which boys?"* A study involving mathematical performance in 19 nations found that gender differences in mathematical performance were directly related to educational and occupational opportunities (see Table 4.4). Boys do *not* do better in math everywhere. Gender differences in school mathematics performance have virtually disappeared in countries where women have equal opportunity (Baker & Jones, 1993; Feingold, 1994). Girls excel in classroom mathematics test performance in the United States, Canada, Sweden, Spain, England, and Wales (Kimball, 1995). No gender differences in mathematical computation or reasoning was found among Shanghai students (Huang, 1993). When the mathematical skills of European-American children were compared to those of Chinese-American and Taiwanese children, European-American children fared worst, regardless of gender (Huntsinger, Jose, Liaw, & Ching, 1997). Thus, cultural attitudes and classroom practices appear to be the keys to mathematics achievement.

A meta-analysis of gender differences in mathematics classroom performance examined 100 studies and revealed that female students outperformed males by a tiny amount (Hyde, Fennema, & Lamon, 1990). Girls showed a slight superiority in computation during elementary school and middle school. There were

TABLE 4.4 Mathematical Performance Around the World

Country	Effect Size
Superior Performance of Boys	
France	.37
Israel	.11
Luxembourg	.25
Netherlands	.17
New Zealand	.10
Ontario, Canada	.08
Swaziland	.21
Equal Performance	
British Columbia	.03
England–Wales	.04
Hong Kong	.05
Japan	.004
Nigeria	.07
Scotland	.01
Sweden	−.06
United States	−.01
Superior Performance of Girls	
French–Belgium	−.12
Finland	−.17
Hungary	−.13
Thailand	−.22

Source: Adapted from D. P. Baker & D. P. Jones (1993). Creating gender equality: Cross-national gender stratification and mathematical performance. *Sociology of Education, 66,* 91.

no apparent gender differences in understanding mathematical concepts. However, in high school and college men begin to excel in mathematical problem solving. These authors concluded that there was little support for the global conclusion that boys excel in math. Moreover, when SAT performance was analyzed according to ethnic group, Asian-American women scored best. Male superiority emerged only among white students in the United States. However, in examining the performance of mathematically precocious or gifted students, researchers found that male students consistently outperform female students (Robinson, Abbott, Berninger, & Busse, 1996). Among the most mathematically gifted, boys may outnumber girls as much as 13:1 (Hyde & McKinley, 1997).

Despite findings to the contrary, the stereotype of female inferiority in math remains robust in North

America, and mathematics continues to be perceived as more of a male domain. The stereotypic beliefs of parents, particularly mothers, influence their perceptions of their children's mathematical abilities according to the child's sex. This, in turn, influences the child's self-perceptions and motivation regarding ability in math (Terwilliger & Titus, 1995). These powerful stereotypes carry over to the classroom. Teachers generally agree that males do better in math. They are more likely to name male students as superior in math, and girls' better classroom performance is often perceived as a preference for the more routine aspects of mathematical computation (Brown & Joseph, 1999; Kimball, 1995).

Verbal Abilities

The term *verbal abilities* is as broad as it is vague. However, notions of female superiority in verbal facility seem firmly entrenched in the minds of parents, educators, students, and policymakers. In the research on sex/gender differences, verbal abilities include measures of activities as diverse as the speed of children's language acquisition, vocabulary, incidence of speech and language problems, anagram tasks, word analogies, grammatical judgments, spelling and punctuation, identifying synonyms and antonyms, reading comprehension, expressive vocabulary, and subtest scores on intelligence tests. In current usage, this term may actually refer to about 100 separate abilities or skills (Anselmi & Law, 1998), and the research literature in this area manifests several weaknesses. First, girls typically have higher scores than boys do on classroom tests and course grades all through elementary and middle school. However, the pattern is more uneven in high school and college (Savage & Gouvier, 1992). Boys typically outscore girls on the verbal section of the SAT. However, this may be because the verbal part of the SAT is heavily weighted with analogies, and this is the only verbal task on which boys outscore girls (Halpern, 1992). Moreover, boys with poorer verbal skills tend not to take the SAT, so that the sample is biased in favor of higher functioning boys. The populations typically tested (college students) are not representative of the general population in terms of age, social class, ethnicity, or educational experience (Halpern, 1996a). Meta-analyses estimate the average effect size for gender differences in verbal abilities to be only about 1% (Hyde & Linn, 1986). It bears repeating that even if there is an average difference, this does not necessarily mean that difference is evenly distributed (Feingold, 1995). For example, among those with language and speech problems gender differences are glaring. Boys with stuttering and reading problems outnumber girls about 3:1 (Halpern, 1996b), and boys diagnosed with dyslexia outnumber girls about 10:1 (Vandenberg, 1987).

Findings that girls have more extensive vocabularies, acquire vocabulary at an earlier age, and make more efficient use of language have been weakly consistent in the United States and China (Huang, 1993; Kramer, Delis, Kaplan, O'Donnell, & Prifitera, 1997; Mann, Sasanuma, Sakuma, & Masaki, 1990). However, Hyde and McKinley (1997) concluded that there are virtually no consistent gender differences in measures of verbal ability except that women perform better on tests of speech production, and Feingold (1994) found no consistent pattern of gender differences in verbal skills across several nations.

Visuospatial Abilities

The concept of visuospatial skills is also quite broad, and traditional measures typically involve map interpretation, locating the origin of sounds in a room, jigsaw puzzle performance, matching one shape to another, finding embedded shapes, mental rotation of a three-dimensional assembly of blocks, spatial perception, predicting how a sequence of gears will move, and spatiotemporal judgments (when a moving object will arrive at a destination) (Caplan & Caplan, 1997).

The Rod and Frame Test (RFT) developed by Herbert Witkin (Witkin et al., 1954) required participants to sit in a tilted chair, in a totally dark room with an unfamiliar male researcher, and assertively tell the experimenter when to stop moving a luminous rod suspended within a tilted frame. Men's more accurate performance on this task resulted in a very elaborate personality theory evaluating levels of *field dependence* and *field independence*. Such terminology elicited strongly held gender stereotypes (Haaken, 1988). Over the years that followed, men's superior RFT performance was clearly shown to be a function of the instructions given and of women's anxiety during the procedure, rather than of any inherent differences between women and men.

Substantial but inconsistent research findings have accumulated to suggest that men do in fact perform more accurately and efficiently on many of the visuospatial ability measures listed (Collins & Kimura, 1997). However, the pattern and magnitude of these differences varies by the particular test (Casey, 1996; Hyde & McKinley, 1997; James & Kimura, 1997). The debate continues over whether these performance differences originate from mainly genetic, neuroanatomical, or hormonal sources or from socialization (Geary, 1998; Hyde & McKinley, 1997).

Evolutionary psychologists offer a survival-based argument for differences in visuospatial performance. They insist that sexual selection factors among men resulted in greater development of "neurocognitive systems that support navigation in three-dimensional space" (Geary, 1996, p. 229). Ostensibly, successful hunting and exploration selected for the development of these abilities among men. Critics note that this ignores the equally likely scenario that women might select for spatial ability development based on their need to keep track of predators as well as children in dense forests or other unfamiliar territory. Their need for excellent spatial skills might actually be even more necessary for hunting small animals and for recalling the location of dependable food sources (Richardson, 1997a).

Studies attempting to relate visuospatial skills and hormonal influences are also quite problematic. Several studies have attempted to show variation in visuospatial performance in women at various times in the menstrual cycle, but replication has been inconsistent (Gordon & Lee, 1993; Kimura & Hampson, 1994). Attempts to correlate male testosterone levels with fluctuations in visuospatial performance have also been inconclusive (Moffat & Hampson, 1996).

Researchers who support a more sociocultural approach note the ethnic and cultural variations in cognitive skills performance, particularly when both genders have more equivalent educational opportunities (Bosacki, Innerd, & Towson, 1997). They point out that even relatively consistent findings may be artifacts of materials, methods, or measures that elicit stereotypical responses from participants. For example, when participants receive instructions that disguise or de-emphasize the spatial nature of a task, gender differences in performance disappear (Sharps, Welton, & Price, 1993). Women improve their visuospatial performance after practice (Okagaki & Frensch, 1994; Subrahmanyam & Greenfield, 1994; Vasta, Knott, & Gaze, 1996). However, these results too have been difficult to replicate.

Norwegian researchers compared visuospatial skills among technology and social science students, and found that women technology students scored lower than men majoring in the social sciences. They concluded that "females who enter education and occupations highly loaded with spatial abilities may, . . . set themselves in the same situation as if they were to compete with men in physical sports" (Nordvik & Amponsah, 1998, p. 1022). In other words, women were "naturally" less endowed with visuospatial abilities and therefore not suited for professions that required such skills to a high degree. Oops! One of those sudden sociopolitical explosions just occurred! When Norwegian adults significantly outscored Ghanaian adults on a series of spatial tests, *no one* suggested that Ghanaian adults were not suited to pursue education and occupations with a significant spatial component (Amponsah & Krekling, 1997)!

Conclusions Regarding Sex Differences in Cognitive Abilities

First and foremost, there is always great overlap between the sexes on cognitive abilities, so any differences found are very small, except in biased or highly selected populations (Crawford & Chafin, 1997; Hyde & McKinley, 1997). Second, findings of sex differences are inconsistent and vary by age, by ethnicity, and across societies (Amponsah & Krekling, 1997; Feingold, 1994). The concepts purported to show sex differences are often ill-defined clusters of concepts and may be gender biased. For example, why would visuospatial skills include map reading and engineering problems, but not clothes making, furniture arrangement, garden design problems, or organizing inadequate storage for a family of six? The inconsistencies in findings of sex differences in cognitive abilities seem directly related to weaknesses in the methods used (Sanders & Wright, 1997; Brown & Josephs, 1999). Contextual variables also affect performance. For example, when researchers replaced the "rod" in the Rod and Frame Test with a human figure and told participants it was a test of empathy, women outperformed men (Caplan & Caplan, 1997).

Practice and training affect performance on most cognitive skills (Vasta et al., 1996). For example, videogame practice improves women's performance on mental rotation problems (Subrahmanyam & Greenfield, 1994). The gradual decline in gender differences in cognitive abilities over the last 20 years, especially in more egalitarian societies, strongly suggests that psychosocial, environmental, and contextual forces exert a tremendous influence (Stumpf & Stanley, 1998; Basinger, 2000).

Critical Thinking Question

Can you think of typical childhood games and activities that might serve to train and provide practice in visuospatial skills for one gender, but not the other? If you do identify such games and activities, how could you design a study to demonstrate the impact of this differential training and practice later on in life?

For the beginning student of gender, these matters and controversies may seem rather remote and somewhat irrelevant. However, these issues have public policy implications (Halpern, 1996a). First of all, reports of sex differences in abilities, even if not replicated, always appear in popular print and electronic media. There seems to be a market for information that emphasizes or exaggerates differences between the sexes. Moreover, some individuals and organizations may find excuses to continue their discriminatory behavior and disempowering policies based on such notions.

In fact, only a few issues are clear. Every individual comes into the world with a particular genetic, hormonal, and neuroanatomical endowment. The social world then differentiates males from females. The brain is plastic all through life, so our biological propensities can be modified through experiences in that social world. Within the constraints set by particular societies, individuals select experiences that can enhance or diminish these propensities. Thus interaction between biological and environmental influences make it impossible to separate the two.

Stigmatized or disempowered groups (women, ethnic, and sexual minorities) are affected by beliefs about differences in abilities. For example, you have read that women students score higher on classroom mathematics tests and earn better grades in math, yet the stereotype persists that there is a "natural affinity" between mathematics and masculinity. Such notions have an impact on educational decisions, occupational choice, organizational hiring and promotion practices, salary levels, and so on. As you will read in Chapters 9 and 10, these notions about sex differences in cognitive abilities affect women's participation in mathematical, scientific, and technological realms in many societies. These are certainly areas of high status, power, and economic value in our society. They may also affect the level of men's participation in the more communicative, affective, and affiliative aspects of life. These are certainly the areas of greatest emotional and interpersonal satisfaction in most societies.

Critical Thinking Challenge

For the moment, assume that it is true that more women are prone to difficulties in mathematical and visuospatial abilities and that more men are prone to difficulties in verbal abilities. Why are so many resources dedicated to reading remediation (of benefit to boys) but essentially no resources dedicated to mathematics or visuospatial remediation (of benefit to girls)?

Genes, Gender, and Genitalia: New Insights

For the majority of human beings, there is a seamless developmental congruence among all the biological components of bodily sex and subsequent gender. These components include chromosomal sex, gonadal sex, hormonal sex, internal reproductive organs, and external genitalia (Fausto-Sterling, 2000). Because of this, newborns are easily assigned to one of two gender categories. Then gender identity development and rehearsal for adult gender role behavior begin. At puberty, secondary sex characteristics are also congruent. Thus the body is a primary marker for gender and adult gender roles. These include an approved interpersonal role, an occupational role, a social role, a reproductive and family role, and a public role involving levels of power.

Because these events typically occur so smoothly, sex and gender development seem sequential, unchangeable, dualistic, and deeply intertwined (Crouch, 1998). However, when someone is born

TABLE 4.5   The Components of Sex and Gender

Bodily Components	Psychosocial Components
Sex-determining genes	Gender identity
Sex chromosomes	Childhood gender role behavior
Gonads	Adult gender role behavior
Sexually dimorphic brain structures	Sexual orientation
Sex hormone levels or proportions	Approach to courtship and romance
Sex hormone receptors	Sexual functioning
External genitalia	Reproductive functioning and fertility
Internal genitalia	Psychological adjustment
Gender appropriate physical appearance (height, physique, muscularity, grooming, etc.)	Other?
Gender-appropriate nonverbal behavior (posture, gait, etc.)	
Secondary sex characteristics	

with, or later develops some incongruity in one or more of the bodily components of sex and therefore gender, we are suddenly confronted with profound questions of what exactly is a male or female, or what makes a person a girl or boy? Table 4.5 lists the components of sex and gender. Those with a disturbance or variation in one or more of the components of sex and gender, and particularly those who manifest one of the intersex conditions can be our best mentors and co-learners about sex and gender and about the meaning of the body in both of these. You met Sophie at the beginning of the chapter, so you have already had your first confrontation with the reality of intersexuality. One scholar wrote, "As I've learned from nearly eight years of study, intersexuality messes up just about every rule you have been led to believe about sex and gender" (Dreger, 1998a, p. 345). Let's begin at the beginning.

Sex Chromosome Disorders

Here are some basic chromosomal facts of life. First, for every 100,000 pregnancies, about 85,000 live births occur, and of these, about 550 babies have some unusual chromosomal endowment. Of these 550, about 150 involve the sex chromosomes (Money, 1994). Second, no person can survive without at least one X-chromosome, because this chromosome carries many genes that are essential to the establishment and maintenance of life (Jegalian & Lahn, 2001). Table 4.6 offers an overview of several sex chromosome variations. The important question for us is how any of these variations might affect the postnatal development of gender.

Turner Syndrome (45XO). The condition called Turner syndrome is estimated to occur in one of every 4,000 female births and involves having only one

TABLE 4.6   Selected Sex Chromosome Disorders

Chromosomes	Incidence	Gender Development
45XO (Turner syndrome)	1 in 4,000–5,000	Extremely short stature, strong interest in maternity
47XXX	1 in 1,000	Some retardation, fertile
47XXY (Klinefelter's syndrome)	1 in 1,000	Underdeveloped secondary characteristics, enlarged breasts, reduced sex drive, tall, some retardation
47XYY	1 in 1,000	Very tall, impulsive behavior, very reduced sperm production

X-chromosome (XO). There are three defining characteristics for Turner syndrome: (1) the presence of gonadal streaks rather than true ovaries; (2) an unusually short stature, seldom more than 5 feet; and (3) a wide array of bodily malformations (Kagan-Krieger, 1998). In terms of psychological development, self-esteem, self-concept, and body image are usually affected, and social isolation often results. Early research portrayed a passive, overcompliant, or nonassertive personality. Later studies described patterns of extroversion, talkativeness, and a low ability to postpone gratification. Recent studies report a higher incidence of hyperactivity. In general, Turner women have a strong feminine gender identity, and some studies described intensely stereotypic feminine behavior compared to sibling controls, particularly regarding maternalism. The educational and vocational achievements of Turner syndrome women are comparable to that of other unusually short individuals. In terms of reproductive role, hormones can induce a normal menstrual flow (a uterus is present). Many Turner syndrome women report that their infertility has a very negative psychological impact. Turner syndrome women can become pregnant with in vitro fertilization and deliver via cesarean section (El Abd et al., 1995).

One study involved 80 XO women. In 55 of the participants, the X was maternally derived (X_m) and in 25 it was paternally derived (X_p). The $45X_p$ group was better adjusted, with greater verbal and higher-order executive function skills. The $45X_m$ women were more vulnerable to disorders of language and social adjustment that are usually more common in males (Skuse et al., 1997). Although some studies of 45XO girls and women reported cognitive deficits in nonverbal intelligence, calculation, directional sense, motor coordination, and visuospatial abilities, others found a normal range of cognitive abilities (Pavlidis et al., 1993; Rohrbaugh & Ross, 1993; Swillen et al., 1993). Overall, the inconsistencies appear to be more the product of methodological weaknesses, rather than any discernible patterns among the women themselves (El Abd et al., 1995).

Supernumerary Chromosomal Endowment. What about extra chromosomal arrangements such as 47XXY (Klinefelter's syndrome), 47XYY, 47XXX, or 48XYYY? We won't go over each of these possibilities, because complex and varied patterns emerge. However, the following findings are relevant for our purposes. In general, the greater the number of extra chromosomes, the greater the number and severity of physical and mental anomalies (Harmon, Bender, Linden, & Robinson, 1998). Second, gonadal development in males is affected whenever an X chromosome is present. Male infertility is a common result, but females may be fertile. For example, 47XXY men typically have testicles that contain no sperm, and the penis is small. Postpubertal masculinization is slow and incomplete, so hormones are prescribed. There have been some reports of sexual, psychiatric, and neurological disorders. Other studies report difficulties with time-sequencing problems, but not with spatial perception. Still other studies describe problems in language and reading, but not in calculation. When eleven 47XXX girls were compared with their sisters, some adjustment and speech problems were evident, but most had no medical or mental symptoms. Mathematics was actually the strongest subject for some girls in this group. No differences were found regarding age at first sexual experience, number of marriages, pregnancies, or children (Harmon et al., 1998). Poorer adjustment seems more related to lower IQ as well as to lower socioeconomic status (Rovet, Netley, Bailey, Keenan, & Stewart, 1995). There is typically more antisocial behavior among XYY men. During the 1960s, researchers erroneously concluded that because a larger-than-predicted population of prison inmates had an extra Y, this chromosomal endowment was associated with a greater proclivity to violence. Later it became clear that such inmates tended to be imprisoned for nonviolent crimes. Also, many noncriminal men were identified as having supernumerary Y chromosomes as well. However, those with this syndrome do demonstrate a high level of impulsivity. The presence of an extra Y is correlated with average to high IQ, average to high achievement, and a decreased attention span (Money, 1994).

Conclusions. Turner syndrome women present no difficulty in manifesting a typical female gender identity. No differences in brain anatomy or functioning are apparent. Exceptionally short stature seems to be the main factor in their reported social and interpersonal difficulties. It is difficult to identify specific gender-related difficulties for those with extra sex chromosomes. Adjustment difficulties, including gender-related problems, seem more strongly related to the physical, cognitive, and intellectual deficits that accompany these chromosomal endowments (Money, 1997). The varied levels of functioning and life success suggest that environmental forces, particularly parental acceptance and involvement, have a tremendous impact on the deficits associated with sex chromosome disorders (Harmon et al., 1998).

Discordant Hormonal Influences

Gonadal hormones influence the development of the internal reproductive structures and the external genitalia. At birth, it is the appearance of the external genitals that determines gender assignment. Once announced, this assignment sets all the forces of family, society, and culture into action to form an appropriately gendered adult. Chromosomal and gonadal sex may sometimes be congruent, but hormonal difficulties result in varying levels of genital ambiguity. That is, the external genitals vary beyond the typical range of shapes and appearances. The internal structures may also differ to varying degrees. Again, the question for us is, what happens regarding gender identity and development when the external genitalia appear to be those of one sex but the person's other biological features are of the other sex? Or, much more often, what happens when the genitalia are ambiguous? That is, what happens when it is not

clear whether the genitalia are male or female? Can someone be assigned to either gender category and then successfully adapt? This idea certainly seems to be in keeping with the notion of gendered behavior as totally socialized by particular societies. Moreover, how important is it for genitalia to match the more typical genitalia of a particular gender? How much does genital appearance matter in successfully living out gender roles? See Table 4.7 for an overview of selected hormonal incongruities.

Androgen insensitivity syndrome (AIS) and congenital adrenal hypertrophy (CAH) are two additional common examples of discordant hormonal development. A third condition, 5a reductase deficiency, offers us a remarkable lesson of apparent sex and gender reassignment *at puberty*. Let's take a closer look at each of these and then focus on the insights they offer about the relationships among the physical body, hormonal influences, and gender-related behavior.

Androgen-Insensitivity Syndrome (AIS). Try to imagine the following situation: Even though she is 13 or 14, a young girl has yet to begin menstruating. A physical examination shows very typical female bodily features and genitalia. A psychological interview shows typical feminine gender identification and interests. An internal examination of the abdomen reveals that no ovaries, uterus, or fallopian tubes have developed, so the person is infertile. The gonads residing in the abdomen resemble testes, and

TABLE 4.7 Selected Hormonal Incongruities

Condition	Gonad	Internal Structures	External Genitalia	Gender Development
Androgen insensitivity syndrome (AIS)	Undescended testes	Neither male or female internal structures	Typical female with shallow vagina	Typically feminine
Congential adrenal hyperplasia (CAH)	Ovaries	Typical female	Ambiguous, enlarged clitoris with small vaginal pouch, scrotal fusion	Typically feminine with some "masculine" interests, frequently gynecophilic
5a reductase deficiency	Undescended testes at birth; descended at puberty	Partial male	Ambiguously female appearance at birth, masculinized at puberty	Childhood data not available, at puberty many assume masculine adult roles with difficult adjustment

they secrete a typical male level of testosterone. A chromosomal test reveals normal chromosomes, but they are XY. This girl may thus be categorized as an XY female.

Androgen-insensitivity syndrome is rare, about one in every 65,000 XY births, and it may recur within a family. A recessive gene on the X chromosome causes the body not to respond to testosterone. The insensitivity may be complete (CAIS) or partial (PAIS). Despite the presence of a normal level of testosterone, the body ignores it and develops along a female pathway. The external genitalia are unremarkably and unmistakably female. Because testes also secrete estrogen, breasts, and other typically female bodily contours develop. However, pubic hair and underarm hair are either absent or sparse.

In terms of the gender development of such individuals, the overwhelming majority of AIS individuals have a thoroughly feminine gender identity. They tend to follow the gendered behaviors, life patterns, and interests of other girls and women in their society. The incidence of other-sex and same-sex sexual orientations matches that of the general population. In the past, experts reassigned some AIS individuals as boys, contending that chromosomal and gonadal sex was the "true sex" of person. This usually led to severe maladjustment and sometimes to suicide, because secondary sex characteristics, gender identity, and gender roles were all clearly *feminine* (Dreger, 1998b; Money, 1997).

Congenital Adrenal Hyperplasia (CAH). Lying on top of the two kidneys are the adrenal glands. In both women and men, these glands produce a variety of hormones, including androgens. Occasionally, during prenatal development, a recessive gene causes these adrenal glands to produce unusually high levels of androgens. If the developing fetus is female, these hormones may cause the external genitals to become **virilized** to varying degrees. In extreme situations, the clitoris may enlarge into a true penis containing a urethral tube, and the labia majora (outer lips) may fuse into an empty scrotum. More often, the clitoris is merely enlarged but is capable of visible erection. The urethra and vagina may combine into a single opening. Inside the abdominal cavity are normal ovaries, fallopian tubes, and a uterus.

Among the Yupik of Alaska, CAH occurs about once in every 300 births. About half the affected infants are XX and half are XY. This condition is also found among French Reunion Islanders (1:2,000 births). Typical international statistics are 1:15,000 live births (Money, 1997). Most CAH infants are quite healthy, but there is a life-threatening, salt-losing type of CAH that must be treated with cortisol. For all CAH infants, cortisol stops further genital masculinization but does not reverse what has already taken place. Prenatal gonadal hormones have already influenced the hypothalamus. The gender assignment of the CAH infant may be problematic, because the genitals of the CAH girl are often very ambiguous.

Critical Thinking Challenge

Imagine yourself as the new parent of a CAH infant. What would be going through your mind and heart?

What about the gender development of individuals diagnosed with CAH? Regardless of sex assignment, CAH individuals tend to have a higher-than-average IQ and typically manifest high academic and career achievement. In other heavily gendered areas of life, complex patterns emerge. Among CAH girls, high energy and tomboyism are frequent. Postpubertal romantic/sexual interest is usually slow to develop. A unusually high number of CAH women are gynecophilic in their sexual orientation (Dittman, 1997). There have also been reports of gender dysphoria, less stereotypic toy preferences, less interest in infants, superior visuospatial skills, a somewhat higher incidence of learning disabilities, and deficits in quantitative abilities. According to parental reports, CAH girls and women tend to display more masculine activity levels, body postures, and movements. No differences in cognitive abilities have been documented. On aggression measures, CAH girls tend to score more like boys, but they fight no more than other girls do.

CAH boys enter puberty at a very young age, with marked penile development and the full complement of secondary sex characteristics. Testosterone levels remain very high, but such boys are gentle, not violent

---

virilized   **A more male-like appearance, e.g., an elongated clitoris or fused labia.**

or aggressive. CAH men are overwhelmingly gynecophilic in their sexual orientation (Dittman, 1997).

CAH infants suffering from salt-wasting problems show a much more dramatic pattern of behavioral differences than their peers, with many more seeking reassignment as males after puberty (Meyer-Bahlberg, 1998). However, it is very difficult to isolate the influence of chronic illness or treatments on the development of individuals with CAH. Try to imagine the psychological impact of repeated and intrusive childhood genital inspections by groups of anonymous medical experts, repeated surgeries, repeated painful childhood vaginal enlargements, and so forth (Collaer & Hines, 1995; Dittman, Kappes, & Kappes, 1992). In terms of reproductive role, CAH girls can maintain a pregnancy with hormonal support, but births must be by cesarean section.

Enzyme 5a Reductase Deficiency. Occasionally, during prenatal development, a 46XY male produces an insufficient amount of the 5a reductase enzyme. This enzyme is needed to transform testosterone into dihydrotestosterone (DHT). It is DHT that masculinizes external genitalia, so the genitalia of affected individuals appear ambiguously female at birth. However, at puberty a sudden masculinization begins, with voice deepening, muscular growth, and enlargement of what was taken to be a clitoris. Erection and sexual penetration can usually occur, but insemination is not usually possible, because of a misplaced urethra.

This condition has been found to be concentrated in several geographic areas in the Dominican Republic (Imperato-McGinley, 1974), Papua New Guinea (Imperato-McGinley, Miller, Peterson, Shackelton, & Gajdusek, 1991), Egypt (Essawi et al., 1997), and Oman, in the Middle East (Al-Attia, 1996). In the Dominican Republic those with this condition were known as *guevedoces* (testicles at 12). Ostensibly these adolescent girls changed to "feeling like men" at about age 16, even though their physical changes began at 12. They typically showed sexual interest in women, had their first intercourse between the ages 15 and 17, and later married women. They took roles as farmers and woodsmen, and their wives took on typical feminine roles. These studies were considered very important because they contradicted the well-accepted dictum that gender assignment had to be

accomplished by age 2½ (Money, Hampson, & Hampson, 1955, 1956; Money & Ehrhardt, 1972). Debate and controversy has continued over the Dominican research participants, and more recent reports suggest a much greater level of problematic new-gender adjustment (Fausto-Sterling, 2000).

Papuan society is characterized by very strict gender segregation. Traditionally, such "boys" were raised as girls and then reassigned at puberty, often with very difficult adjustment. More recently, they were reared as a third sex. Currently, because of increasing Western influences, they are assigned as boys who are considered to have a birth defect. In general, these individuals are less assertive and aggressive. They are usually described as more deferent and nurturant, erotically avoidant, and unusually timid (Imperato-McGinley et al., 1991).

Conclusions. Studies of intersexuals remain quite problematic, with small sample sizes (often less than 15) and spurious findings. There are also issues of biased selection factors. Although some individuals with ambiguous genitalia clearly have significant problems, many individuals with genetic, hormonal, and genital incongruities never seek treatment. Moreover, childhood experiences of parental shame, guilt, rejection, and repeated intrusive medical inspections and procedures, also contribute to problematic adjustment. Finally, there are serious problems regarding the biased gender-related measures used in such studies (Kessler, 1998; Money, 1997; Slijper, Drop, Molenaar, DeMuinck, & Sabine, 1998).

Gender and the Intersexed

Pick up any college text on human sexuality, and turn to the section or chapter on developmental sexology. You will soon come across grainy black-and-white photographs of intersexed individuals. They are usually naked and displayed along some measuring device so the observer can note their height. A black square often obscures their faces. More than anything, these photos resemble those taken at police line-ups. In police matters, it is the deviant criminal faces that matter. In the world of medical sexology, it is the deviant genitals that are the center of attention. Sometimes only the genitals are photographed, often with a latex-gloved hand assisting in the display. Thus the educated public meets intersexed human beings mainly as medical specimens. Television talk shows provide intersexuals for entertainment (Kessler, 1998). Genitals are never shown, but fantasies are encouraged, and the emphasis is usually on sexual behavior. Pornography also offers an intersex specialty, with unusual genitalia provided by special effects. For most of us, intersexuals function as a psychosocial boundary or limit from whom we can extract some comfort about our own normality. However, with their genitals covered and faces uncovered, we can experience intersexuals as full human beings with full lives. We can also gain a new appreciation for the bodily basis of sex and gender (see Figure 4.3).

In Western society, the birth of an infant with ambiguous genitals creates a psychosocial emergency (Crouch, 1998). Ambiguities of infant sex and therefore gender elicit responses of shame, guilt, secrecy, and ridicule in a way that other physical anomalies do not. This is because intersexuality violates certain deeply held cultural norms and beliefs about sex, gender, and the body (Kessler, 1998). First, people believe that genitals are naturally **dimorphic**. There is little recognition that genitals may in fact be quite varied and still very functional. Unusual genitals may also be quite acceptable to the person, their parents, and their future lovers (Kessler, 1998). Second, people believe that gender is also dimorphic. That is, there are *naturally* only two genders. Even those who adhere to the notion that gender is totally socially constructed may have difficulty with the notion of constructing more than two genders. Although more sophisticated members of our society may champion androgyny, most of us have fairly rigid limits, particularly when it comes to boys and men. Some societies construct a third or fourth gender (the "two-spirit people" of Native America or the *hijras* of India), but this is difficult for Westerners (L. E. Brown, 1997). Third, we view genitalia as the primary and essential markers of sex, gender, and gender identity (Preves, 1998). As a culture, North Americans believe that variant genitals threaten psychological health and lead to severe maladjustment and unhappiness. Lastly, North Americans assume that scientists, physicians, psychologists, and other experts have legitimate authority to define the relationship between gender and genitals (Dreger, 1998b).

Beginning in the 18th century, scientists and other experts became interested in intersexed individuals (see Box 4.4). Regardless of anatomical complexities, physiological uncertainties, and psychosocial roles, the presence of a particular gonad was the central factor in their determination of a person's *true sex* (Dreger, 1998b; Meyer-Bahlberg, 1998). That is, the emphasis was on reproductive role. Today, in many cities where large medical centers exist, a team of experts is typically assembled immediately after the birth of an intersexed infant (geneticists, pediatric endocrinologists, pediatric urologists, psychiatrists, psychologists, surgeons, and so on). This committee deals with any immediate threats to the infant's physical health, and after careful diagnostic tests and careful consultation, considers the infant's *optimal* gender. That is, in which gender category is the person most likely to satisfactorily function? This was the policy John Money and his associates originated during the 1950s and 1960s. Although this approach seems more humane and scientifically sounder than relying strictly on the presence of gonadal tissue, an examination of its application reveals the profound sociocultural biases and power considerations that govern the relationships among sex, gender, and the body (Diamond & Sigmundson, 1997a; Kessler, 1998).

The basic premises of this perspective were that all infants are psychosexually neutral at birth and that gender arises solely from psychosocial rearing. Therefore, chromosomal, hormonal, and neuroanatomical sex could be ignored or at least overridden by postnatal socialization. Third, children must have their gender identity fixed early in life. Gender identity development was viewed like language development: There was a critical period for its emergence; namely, from birth to about 2 years of age. Fourth, people assumed that the key component of gender identity was anatomy. From the earliest possible moment, a person's anatomy had to match the standard anatomy for his or her gender (Money et al., 1955). Intersexed individuals who refused to be assigned to a particular gender were labeled as severely disturbed, as were any reluctant parents (Money, 1994). Last, parents had to accept the experts' determination of the infant's "true sex." Experts were expected to communicate that the infant's sex was not ambiguous,

---

dimorphic   **Existing or occurring in two distinct forms.**

(a)

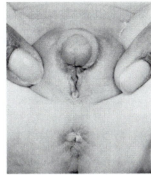

(c)

(b)

FIGURE 4.3   Images of intersexuality are influenced by cultural norms of sexuality and gender. (a) Photo from cover of a 1997 issue of *Chrysalis: The Journal of Transgressive Gender Identities*. (b) Martha Coventry, David Vandertie, Max Beck, Kristi Bruce, and Angela Moreno are intersex activists who seek medical and legislative reform regarding the treatment of intersex individuals. They recount their history of medically imposed secrecy, shame, and harmful sexual surgeries including clitorectomy. (c) Virilized female genitalia. (d) L.S., a Parisian fashion model. Because L.S. had testicles and was androphilic, she was considered "frankly homosexual."

Sources: (a) Courtesy of *Chrysalis: The Journal of Transgressive Gender Identities*, 2(5), 1997; (b) Photo courtesy of Intersex Society of North America; (c) R. Crooks & K. Baur (2002), *Our Sexuality*, 8th ed. (Pacific Grove, CA: Wadsworth), p. 55; (d) From the collections of the Wangensteen Historical Library of Biology and Medicine, Bio-medical Library, University of Minnesota.

(d)

ZOOM & ENLARGE   BOX 4.4

A History of Hermaphrodites

The Roman poet Ovid wrote of the god Hermes, the goddess Aphrodite, and their beautiful son Hermaphroditos. The nymph Salmacis saw Hermaphroditos bathing, and desired him so much that she begged the gods to join the two together so they would never be apart from each other. The gods granted her request literally and united their bodies into one, both fully man and fully woman. Thus we have the vision of the hermaphrodite as having the physical characteristics of both sexes. The idea of the hermaphrodite as an in-between sex began with Hippocratic writers in ancient Greece. They saw sex as a continuum from to-tally male to totally female, with her-maphrodites at the midpoint. Aristotelian thinkers conceived of individuals as hav-ing a true sex. Accordingly, some indi-viduals had *extra* sex organs, much as they might have an extra toe or finger. Great interest in hermaphrodites began in 16th- and 17th-century France. For ex-ample, Gottleib Gottlich earned a fortune exhibiting himself to medical men all over Europe. Some women of ambiguous sex tried to publicly change their sexual sta-tus because their earning potential would immediately increase. One Englishwoman fought to have her sex reassigned so she could become the rightful heir to a title and fortune based on her true sex. She landed in an asylum and medical men declared that her penislike organ had grown because of her delusions (Dreger, 1998b). By the 19th century, the study of *sexual monstrosities* (teratology) had de-veloped. True hermaphroditism, in which a person has one or more ovotestes, is extremely rare and poorly understood. In-tersexuality is more common, and up un-til recently was labeled *pseudohermaph-roditism*. Richard Goldschmidt first used the term *intersexuality,* in 1917, to refer to a wide range of sexual ambiguities (Dreger, 1998b).

---

only the genitals were. Surgeons and other experts would *correct* "unfinished" or "undeveloped" genitals. In contrast to 19th-century emphases on reproduc-tion, the newer emphasis was on ability to function in **copulation,** particularly for boys and men (see Fig-ure 4.4). For infants assigned as boys, the key require-ment was an "adequate" penis with no vagina. The major emphases were on penis size, "locker room" genital appearance, and the capacity for copulatory penetration. For example, micropenises were evalu-ated as "too small" if less than 2.5 centimeters (1 inch). Such infants were reassigned as girls; testes were removed so any reproductive potential was completely lost.

In addition to acceptable size, penises had to look adequate, be able to erect and become flaccid, expel urine and semen from the tip, and be acceptably shaped and colored. It is interesting to note that an early sample of untreated boys with micropenis were all heterosexually oriented, with satisfactory erec-tions and orgasms. A good number were sexually ac-tive. One had fathered a child. Penis size did not pre-clude a male role in terms of love-making. These men employed and had a positive attitude toward a variety of nonpenetrating sexual techniques (Reilly & Woodhouse, 1989). If boys with micropenis were assigned as girls, early surgery was strongly recom-mended because of concern about the boys perhaps feeling castrated if surgery was delayed. In contrast, there was no equivalent concern about trauma to girls if surgery (vaginal construction) was performed near puberty (Kessler, 1998).

For infants assigned as girls, the key requirement was an adequate vagina with no noticeable phallus. The emphases were on reproductive role and the con-struction of a vagina capable of accepting an erect pe-nis. There was little emphasis on erotic response. Cli-torises longer than 1 centimeter were considered too large and described as "cosmetically offensive" or "dis-figuring" and were removed or reduced (Kessler, 1998). There was little attention to how clitoral re-duction reduces the capacity for self-lubrication, erotic sensitivity, or change of vaginal shape during sexual arousal. For the CAH girl, years of painful dila-tion and stretching of a shortened vagina might be prescribed before reconstructive surgery was per-formed. It is interesting to note that in Asia, many parents of intersexed children resisted surgery and re-

---

copulation   **Engaging in sexual intercourse.**

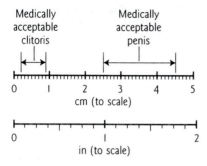

FIGURE 4.4 These are the medically acceptable clitoral and penile lengths.

assignment as girls because of the strong cultural preference for boys (Warne, Zajac, & MacLeon, 1998). Box 4.5 offers some cases of intersexuality in various societies.

These premises and policies were well accepted because of the prestige of theoreticians involved and their congruence with contemporary thought about gender (Kessler, 1998; Meyer-Bahlberg et al., 1996). However, an explosive uproar began with the now infamous John/Joan case. In the early 1960s, John was born a normal male twin who sustained an accidental destruction of his penis (*penis ablatio*). Consultation with a group of experts resulted in reassignment as a girl (Joan). This meant genital surgery to remove the testes, and ongoing hormonal treatments. Psychological counseling was employed to help Joan and her family make a good adjustment (Colapinto, 2000).

This case was often offered as evidence that gender was completely a social creation (Diamond & Sigmundson, 1997a, 1997b). Despite a lack of follow-up on Joan, the case was often cited in developmental psychology and biology texts, as well as feminist studies of gender socialization. However, the reports of Joan's "success" were erroneous. This person at age 14 had reverted to live as John. Diamond (1997) found that Joan had always protested feminine clothes, toys, and girl playmates. He/she had insisted on urinating standing up and refused to continue hormone treatments. At age 14, a suicidal John/Joan confronted his father, demanding to know the truth about his past. John then sought and obtained reassignment as a male. When contacted as an adult, he was married and was a father, via adoption. He functioned quite well in masculine life roles. Dia-

mond (1997) concluded that gender development was not infinitely pliable and that biology does matter. Such cases point out the critical need for ethical inquiry and follow-up in situations of intersexuality (Kipnis & Diamond, 1998).

The Intersexed Speak Up for Themselves. In 1992 Cheryl Chase founded ISNA (Intersex Society of North America), an organization dedicated to affirming a positive intersex identity and halting routine genital surgery on intersexed infants and children. There are now similar groups in Europe, Australia, and Asia (Warne et al., 1998). Activist members of this group continue to support genital surgery that is lifesaving or that improves the quality of life (for example, rerouting a urethra to pass urine safely out of the body). However, ISNA members insist that surgery for aesthetic or "cultural" reasons (for example, augmenting penis size or reducing clitoral size) should be delayed until the intersexed person can offer informed consent (Chase, 1998).

By 1997 ISNA had shifted its agenda to influencing the policies of the medical community. Today ISNA members are invited to meetings of medical and psychological professionals. The Internet has been crucial in uniting similarly affected individuals across the globe into support groups. Describing themselves as "Hermaphrodites with Attitude!" they openly challenge traditional medical thinking about immediate genital modification of ambiguous genitalia so that parents and society can be more comfortable. The members of ISNA see such interventions as genital mutilation. Their writings offer fascinating insights into some of the complex "genital politics" that underlie gender assignments for the intersexed. According to members of ISNA, immediate genital surgeries were prescribed to avoid psychological disturbance and feelings of freakishness, but they may actually contribute to such feelings. ISNA activists describe a cycle of shame and silence that produces more shame and silence. Many adult intersexuals complain that they were subjected to crisis surgeries without their consent. Further, many intersexuals feel they and their families were lied to about their physical conditions and anatomical histories. Members of ISNA advocate for complete and accurate information for the parents of intersexed children, as well as age-appropriate information for the children

SLIDE SHOW   **BOX 4.5**

Intersexuality Across Cultures: Three Case Histories

Oman (United Arab Emirates): This patient was the eldest of six children in the same family, all diagnosed with 5a reductase deficiency. Like her other siblings, she was assigned and reared as a girl in this extremely gender-segregated society. She was first seen as an 18-year-old student who had begun developing testicles and experiencing erections and emissions since the onset of puberty. She expressed great ambivalence about her gender. Her attractions were gynecophilic, but no sexual activity had taken place. At age 17, her parents had married her as a woman to a man who insisted on a divorce after a few days. The patient continued a feminine identity and expressed a strong determination to continue life as a woman. She underwent removal of the testicles, began estrogen therapy, and expressed considerable body satisfaction. She now expressed erotic interest in males and wished to remarry in another city where her history would not be public knowledge. Of her younger siblings, some retained their feminine gender identity and roles, whereas others did not (Al-Attia, 1996).

Germany: This 46XY infant was born with a scrotum but no penis. The baby was first given a female name, but then renamed and registered as a male. At 3½, he was hospitalized with repeated assessments, examinations, and presentations to groups of medical experts. They determined that without a penis, the child should be reassigned as girl and initial surgeries were performed. Various medi-

cal and postsurgical problems necessitated repeated hospitalizations. At age 7, a note was made regarding her adjustment and contentment with role as a girl. At age 12, she returned to the clinic with parental reports of increasingly masculine behavior and interests (refusal to wear girls' clothing and plans to be an automobile mechanic). Soon afterward, she began playing in an orchestra (as a girl) and became an accomplished musician. Although she recognized that a masculine gender would facilitate her success in this area, she stated her wish to continue as a girl. At age 14, the patient requested hormonal treatment to increase breast development. During puberty, her erotic attractions were gynecophilic. At age 15, she expressed interest in knowing more about her previous surgery. At age 16 she began an apprenticeship as an automobile mechanic but continued to wish for a musical career. At about age 17 the patient began working, living, and dressing as a young man. At age 20 the patient sought surgical reassignment as a male. Mastectomies were performed and androgen treatments begun. Reconstructive surgery was completed with testicular prostheses. By age 27 he had been married to a woman for several years and was discussing in vitro fertilization or adoption with his wife (Dittman, 1998).

United States (Asian-American): This person was Hmong, born in Laos, and came to the United States at age 5. She had a normal birth and childhood, and there were no questions regarding

sex and gender. During childhood, she preferred boy playmates and showed no typical house or doll play. At age 8, she began to feel something was wrong, but she could not pinpoint the problem. She became socially withdrawn, and at age 10 she stated that she was a boy. By age 11 she insisted on boys' clothing, a boyish haircut, and refused feminine roles in the household. She dropped out of school when assigned to girls' physical education and chorus. She finally confided her confusion to a school nurse, who was also Asian. Laboratory work showed a 46XY chromosomal arrangement and mixed internal and external genitalia. Surgical treatment to construct a male phallus began as well as androgen therapy. Masculine secondary sex characteristics appeared, and two additional surgeries were needed. When his psychological gender became unstable, he was hospitalized with a major depression but made rapid improvement. His parents were very cooperative at first but then quite resistant. They felt they had lost their only daughter. At age 16 he expressed an erotic interest in a Hmong-American girl. He requested counseling assistance in asking for dates and then for kissing and petting. At 18, he wanted to know if intercourse was possible with his small penis. He was counseled regarding intercourse and other nonpenetrative sexual techniques. He was also counseled for open communication with his partner (Reiner, 1996).

themselves. ISNA members believe that counseling and information about support groups should be part of the "treatment" for intersexed children and their families. They see this as a better way to assist individuals with whatever difficulties may arise all

through life. Childhood histories of frequent medical examinations, inspections, and interventions apparently lead many intersexuals toward phobic reactions to any medical assistance, and this creates health problems later in life.

Critical Thinking Challenge

How can one be certain that ISNA and similar groups truly represent the attitudes and preferences of most intersexuals?

The Relationship Between Transsexualism and Intersexuality. In many, if not all societies, there exists a small group of individuals who experience an inner psychological conflict regarding their bodily features (particularly their genitals and secondary sex characteristics) and their inner sense of who they "really are" in terms of their gender. That is, their bodily sex and gender identity are in conflict. In contrast to the intersexed, the genetic endowment, hormonal functioning, internal and external anatomy, and physiology of such individuals all appear typical and congruent according to the measures presently available. Most often there is nothing unusual about their familial or psychosocial environment. Nevertheless, these individuals have the psychological body image and gender ideal of the other sex and are fixed on that incongruence (Devor, 1997; Duden, 1991). Some begin in childhood to focus on changing their physical bodily appearance to agree with their psychological body image. They feel highly motivated to live out the behaviors and roles associated with the other gender in their society (clothing, grooming, occupations, social roles, and so on). This may mean cross-dressing and interpersonal interaction as a member of the other gender. Such concerns and behavior are viewed and valued differently in various societies. In most Western societies, this is considered a psychological disorder and labeled as **gender identity dysphoria (GID)** (American Psychological Association, 1994), and those who pursue surgical, hormonal, and psychosocial reassignment are called transsexuals. You will be reading more about such individuals in Chapter 12 ("Gender and Mental Health"). However, intersexuals who elect gender reassignment are specifically excluded from a diagnosis of gender identity dysphoria (Slipjer et al., 1998).

For the beginning gender student, all this can be very confusing. It may help to organize the issue as follows: Except for life-threatening, or quality-of-life issues, intersex activists want little or no surgical, hormonal, or medical intervention unless the person affected can give informed consent. They would like to preserve the reproductive and erotic capacity of intersexed people. Members of ISNA and similar groups seek a socially acceptable identity as intersexed individuals, and they wish each intersexed individual to live out the gender roles that feel most comfortable. In contrast, highly gender-dysphoric individuals actively pursue surgical, hormonal, and psychological interventions in order to be able to live successfully as a member of the sex and gender category other than the one they were born into. They are willing to lose reproductive and erotic capacity to have the genitalia and bodily appearance of the other sex. In other words, transsexuals want a particular anatomy and its accompanying social roles even at the expense of sexual functioning. Intersexuals want sexual functioning and less rigid notions of gender categorization, even in the absence of socially acceptable anatomy.

Genital Politics Around the World

Ritual marking or altering of the genitalia as a sign of gender or cultural membership is a phenomenon that exists across many cultures. Without these ritual markings, the person may not be considered a true or adequate woman or man in that society. Some of these alterations are familiar to us, but others seem strange. Try taking the perspective of an interplanetary anthropologist and merely observe the following uniquely human pursuits.

Ritual removal of the male foreskin (circumcision) has been documented from the ancient Egyptians to modern Australian aborigines, but the origins of this custom are unknown. Some hypothesize that circumcision affects the **somatic cortex** and makes circumcised men less sexually excitable and more sexually restrained. Ostensibly, early human groups learned that circumcision would make adult men more cooperative and tractable without impairing their fertility or aggressiveness (Immerman & Mackey, 1998). Today, circumcision is still obligatory for Jewish and Moslem men. In some places it is done during infancy, whereas in others circumcision or

---

gender identity dysphoria (GID)   Profound dissatisfaction and distress about one's gender identity and role. A preference for the identities and roles of the other sex.

somatic cortex   That section of the cortex (surface of the forebrain) that processes information about the body, such as location, orientation, and so on.

superincision (splitting of foreskin and folding it back) is a puberty rite. Australian aborigines practice penile subincision. The penis is slit from the tip to the base. The urinary opening is then in a more "female" position, and this has religious meaning.

In the United States, circumcision was rarely done before 1870. It was first popularized as a cure for male masturbation and later promoted as necessary for hygiene and disease prevention, even though the scientific evidence to support this policy was quite mixed (Van Howe, 1998). More recently some men's groups have begun to speak out against this practice as an example of genital mutilation. One such group is NOHARM (National Organization to Halt the Abuse and Routine Mutilation of Males). Some medical experts view circumcision as costly, painful, and unnecessary.

In Europe, talented boy singers were castrated in childhood so they could retain their high voices, and in ancient Byzantium boys were castrated to produce honest government officials (Bullough & Brundage, 1982). Ostensibly, castrated men would have no children for whom to amass goods or property. In 19th-century North America, castration was thought to cure insanity and homosexuality.

Many sub-Saharan societies, as well as Moslem Arab groups practice ritual female genital alteration. It is estimated that 130 million women have been subjected to this ritual and suffer its aftermath (Womankind News, 1999). A recent study found that Ethiopian Coptic Christians, and Ethiopian Jews also ritualized such modifications among girls (Grisaru, Lezer, & Belmaker, 1997). The level of modification ranges from sunna circumcision (removal of the clitoral prepuce) all the way to infibulation. This latter extreme involves removal of the entire clitoris, the labia minora, and about two thirds of the labia majora, followed by stitching together of the two sides of the vulva. A small opening is left for urination and menstrual discharge. Girls without these modifications are considered unfit for marriage and respectability. Girls are subjected to this dangerous and gruesome procedure at age 6, 7, or even later, and it often results in infection, chronic pain, permanent disability, infertility, and sometimes death. All such modifications are labeled as female genital mutilation (FGM) in North America, and a 1996 federal law outlawed the practice in the United States, even if the girls themselves request it. For both girls and boys, genital modification is done for the same purposes: genital conformity to promote and ensure gender conformity.

Critical Thinking Challenge

A bill has been introduced in the U.S. Congress to extend the ban on FGM to intersex surgery, as well as male circumcision. How would you evaluate this idea?

Affluence brings its own form of genital concerns. Articles in women's magazines sometimes suggest bodily modifications to move women's bodies closer to the current gender ideal (Havranek, 1998). Women whose inner labia are "too large" can have them surgically trimmed. Hymens can be reconstructed. Weak abdominal floor muscles (pubococcygeus, or PC, muscles) can be "corrected" to facilitate more and better orgasms (a simple exercise program can accomplish the same goal). Liposuction of the pubic mound has been touted as another means to better orgasms. Such articles often present testimonials from women who extol the sexual benefits derived from such surgery. In contrast, ISNA reports hearing from several women who underwent such surgery and offered testimonials of highly negative results that included chronic pain, disfigurements, and sexual dysfunction.

Critical Thinking Challenge

Which are more valid: enthusiastic testimonials or disgruntled complaints?

Men's bodies are no longer immune from the demands of gender ideals. Men's magazines and entertainment newspapers often contain ads for "penis extenders," but these are useless. However, surgical techniques do exist to increase penis length.

Conclusions

You have been on a long journey through the complexities of the relationship between the physical body and the social phenomenon of gender. As you can see, the debate about differences continues. Seemingly clear-cut differences have sometimes evaporated with changes in scientific methodology and social ideology. It will be up to the next generation of gender scholars and researchers (that might be you) to clarify the sources of the observed differences between women and men and also if those differences matter. You have also encountered a group of people who are no longer willing to hide and suffer with shame about their bodies and their gender. In telling us about their bodies and lives, they give us the gift of understanding our own gendered bodies and lives.

Summary

- ◆ Prenatal gonadal hormones organize the hypothalamus and the pituitary gland. At puberty, these structures activate and regulate the menstrual and ovulatory cycles in women. In men, they maintain a relative steady state for androgen levels.

- ◆ Methodological weaknesses and replication difficulties permeate the research on human sex differences in neuroanatomical and neuroendrocrine processes. The brain is plastic in response to postnatal experience. Nevertheless, observed differences in some cognitive abilities are attributed to brain and hormonal factors.

- ◆ The concepts of mathematical, verbal, and visuospatial abilities are vague as well as broad. Despite contradictory cross-cultural and multicultural evidence, the notion of male superiority in mathematics continues as a robust stereotype. A larger proportion of males are more vulnerable to problems in verbal abilities. Inconsistent findings regarding visuospatial abilities appear strongly related to weaknesses in the methodology and measures used in this research.

- ◆ The markers and transitions from chromosomal sex to gendered adult behavior are usually smooth and congruent. The impact of sex chromosome abnormalities (Turner syndrome and supernumerary chromosomes) as well as discordant hormonal functioning (AIS, CAH, and 5a reductase deficiency) on gender development varies considerably.

- ◆ Genital appearance is the major determinant of sex categorization and gender assignment in the vast majority of societies. Intersexuality offers insights into the various components of sex and gender development. In Western culture sex and gender are considered dimorphic. This results in attempts to quickly "correct" the ambiguous genitalia of intersexuals through surgery. ISNA and similar organizations have been fairly successful in achieving reconsideration of the medical policies regarding genital surgery for intersexed infants. Intersexuals challenge us to rethink our ideas about sex, gender, and genitalia.

- ◆ Bodily modifications, particularly genital modifications, are powerful markers of gender and gender ideals across many cultures.

InfoTrac College Edition

For more information, explore InfoTrac College Edition at

http://www.infotrac-college.com/Wadsworth

Enter search terms: gender and the brain, gender and math, intersex.

5 Life Span Gender Development

From Womb to Tomb

Social and cultural biases may have favored males; nature has been less kind.

◆ G. R. Lefrançois

Learning Objectives

After studying this chapter, you should be able to:

1. Describe the important features of the gendered context within which infants and toddlers develop, emphasizing how mothering and fathering influence gender development.
2. Describe the important gender-related features of childhood development.
3. Explain the concept of gender intensification during adolescence and summarize the gender-related findings in four areas of development.
4. Explain three important issues in understanding adult gender development, and then summarize the findings regarding gender and the three major roles of adulthood.
5. Evaluate the evidence regarding the concept of a midlife gender transition.
6. Explain how culture and gender influence the caregiver role in later adulthood.
7. Explain how demographic trends have changed the realities of old age for the elderly and their families.
8. Summarize the important features of widowhood as a gendered role around the world.
9. Summarize the gender-related features of the end of life.

Encounters with Gender

Your 7-year-old son Dennis has always been a loving, gentle boy. He takes pride in his grooming and appearance and has always been careful about caring for his toys and other belongings. Beth, a 7-year-old neighbor, and her girlfriends are his favorite playmates. At recess, he stays away from the rougher boys, and after school he likes to read and putter in a small garden. The neighborhood boys sometimes laugh at him and tease him about his awkwardness in running and throwing a ball. One has begun calling him "Denise." After watching a ballet performance on television, he often imitates the stylized movements of the dancers. How would you respond to Dennis, and would you attempt to intervene in any aspects of his development? How? When?

Overview

Gender is a lifelong process. In keeping with that idea, this chapter discusses gender issues across the life span, with examples selected from various societies. I examine gender development and expression during infancy, childhood, adolescence, adulthood, and the close of life. Various gender-related psychological concepts associated with these life stages are evaluated from a multicultural and cross-cultural perspective. As you read, see if you can identify the various definitions of gender that become more or less salient at each phase of the life span. You may want to begin with a short self-survey about your beliefs about gender and life roles (see Box 5.1).

Infancy and Toddlerhood Around the World

Every child is born into and develops in a particular sociocultural context or environment (Kagitçibasi, 1996). Within that context, the process of **socialization** will usually result in an appropriately gendered person (Martin & Ruble, 1997). That is, should boys *or* girls plant the seeds? Should women *or* men sell the harvest? As you know by now, the answers depend on the society in which a child grows up. Most psychologists see the family as the first and major

---

socialization Process of learning and adaptation to social and cultural norms.

ABCs of GENDER (ATTITUDES, BELIEFS, AND CONCERNS)   **BOX 5.1**

The Issue: Your Beliefs About Gender over the Life Span

Are the following statements true or false?

1. Fathers contribute more to traditional gender typing of children, especially boys.
2. Overall, girls are more fearful than boys.
3. Appropriate chores for 5-year-olds should include simple self-care tasks such as taking a dirty dish to the sink, self-bathing, and so on.
4. Single mothers always feel overly burdened because of the absence of a spouse or partner who shares in household tasks and child care.
5. Over the life span, the longest-lasting relationship is between a mother and a child.
6. In most traditional societies, the aged are honored and revered.
7. In most Western societies, wisdom is associated with advanced age, regardless of gender.

Answers:

1. Support for this idea is not consistent (Trehub, Unyk, Kamenetsky, & Hill, 1997). However, what does seem clear is that involved fathering results in less gender-stereotypic notions of masculinity among sons and the development of more socially desirable qualities such as empathy and sensitivity.

2. On the average, girls are slightly more fearful than boys at every age. However, researchers advise against stereotypical conclusions. Fearfulness and risk taking are *not* normally distributed. No gender differences are found at the risk-avoidant, low-risk-taking, or even moderate levels of risk-taking behavior. It is *only* at the most extreme levels of risk taking, particularly risks that involved potential self-harm, that strong sex differences emerge. These differences were strong enough to influence the averages at every age (Kagan, 1994; Kagan & Snidman, 1991).

3. All over the world and within many ethnic groups, both girls and boys as young as 5, are often assigned to caring for younger siblings (Weisner, 1989a, 1989b). Although Anglo-Australians tend to assign household chores to children as young as 5, Lebanese-Australians believed that this was too early an age for household chores. But they often assigned 5-year-olds of both sexes to look after younger siblings (Burns & Homel, 1989; Goodnow, 1996).

4. Contrary to popular stereotypes, many of the single mothers in one Canadian sample felt freer and less burdened because they did not have to look after a husband too (McMahon, 1995).

5. Most of us don't realize that over the life span, sibling relationships are the longest lasting. In old age, sisters have the closest relationships (Lee, Mancini, & Maxwell, 1990; Campbell, Connidis, & Davies, 1999).

6. This may be an oversimplification. For example, Kenya and Nigeria are at opposite ends of the African continent, and have little in common culturally. In both societies the elderly appear to be revered and socially powerful, but a closer examination reveals that it is not age alone that brings respect. The revered status of "elder" is achieved only by becoming a grandparent. Those with no grandchildren are considered rather defective and of questionable worth (Sangree, 1992).

7. Researchers studied the relationship among wisdom (exceptional understanding, judgment, and discretion), gender, and age in the United States. They found that college students rated older men and younger women wiser than older women and younger men (Hira & Faulkender, 1997).

---

representatives of that society. Thus, much attention regarding early gender socialization has focused on the influence of parenting adults and the physical and psychological environments they provide. That physical environment includes, but is not limited to food, clothing, toys, and approved activities. The psychological environment includes types of interactions, family configuration, emotional attachments, and types of instruction. Once beyond toddlerhood, interaction among peers must be added to the list of important factors influencing gender (Maccoby, 1998). Although many psychological theories attempt to account for the emergence of gender (see Chapter 3), it is clear that cognitive, intrapsychic, and social learning factors are *all* involved in the development of gender (Camilleri & Malewska-Peyre, 1997).

Gender and Infant Development

The family provides a heavily gendered environment for the new infant. One aspect of gender ideology that affects development is whether males or females are seen as more important (Hoyenga & Hoyenga, 1993). In most societies, male infants are more valued (China and Bangladesh, for example), but a few societies prefer females. These preferences influence the survival rate of boys and girls. For example, the Mukogodo people of Kenya developed extremely biased sex ratios in favor of girls over the five years previous to a study (Cronk, 1993). The Mukogodo are very poor relative to neighboring tribal groups, and their men are also stigmatized because they hunt (farming has higher status). Mukogodo men have great difficulty accumulating bride wealth, so most women marry outside their group. A daughter's birth means desperately needed future bride wealth. Mukogodo parents breastfeed their daughters longer and take them for medical care more often. In the past, there were similar findings among the Cheyenne of North America. Historians of the family tell us that in 19th-century rural America, boys were more valuable because of their potential for heavy farm work. Girls were more valued in urban areas because they could help support the family at an earlier age through factory work (Coltrane, 1998a).

In the United States, birth announcements speak volumes about the gendered sea in which the newest members of this society constantly swim. Bridges (1993) collected birth announcements from several diverse communities. Most boy announcements were illustrated with scenes of physical activity and action, such as throwing a ball or even driving a train (68%)! Scenes of immobility, such as sleeping or lying down, were more typical of girl announcements (54%). Descriptors such as "sweet" and "little" occurred more often in girl announcements. Boy cards mentioned feelings of "happiness" much more often.

Critical Thinking Challenge

What are these cards announcing about the gendered roles and expectations that will follow all through life?

Parents, Playtime, and Processing the World

Obviously, parents (or primary caretakers) are the most salient aspect of the setting in which children become gendered. Beyond toddlerhood, peer influences become equally if not more important (Maccoby, 1998). As you will see, those peer influ-

ences are maximized in gender-segregated groups during childhood (Harris, 1998).

Mothering. In about 90% of human cultures, women do virtually all child rearing. However, not all infants are cared for by their biological mothers, so here the term *mother* refers to the major caretaking role rather than to a biological relationship. What do mothers do? They provide physical care, emotional comfort and attachment, instruction in social behavior, instruction in self-care, and an environment for the development of gender. For example, in a study of French-speaking Canadian children, mothers were the major creators of gender-stereotypic environments, surrounding their children with gender-typed toys, clothing, colors, and room decorations (Pomerleau, Bolduc, Malcuit, & Cossette, 1990).

Mothers in India, Japan, and England were surveyed regarding the ages at which their children were expected to be able to accomplish certain developmental tasks. Both Japan and India are more collectivistic societies, so one would predict that expectations regarding child self-care, compliance, peer interaction, communication, emotional control, and environmental independence would be most similar in those two countries. However, English and Japanese mothers had the highest expectations and set a younger age for achieving almost all developmental goals. Much later ages were typical of India. Differing gender arrangements regarding parenting heavily influenced these findings. In Japan and England, a mother *alone* has primary responsibilities for both child care and household maintenance. These mothers need their children to become self-sufficient as soon as possible, so they impose more demanding expectations on their children, regardless of child gender. In India, mothering is shared with other female household members and servants. The Indian extended and **conjoint family** provides a much more indulgent context for child development (Joshi & MacLean, 1997).

In the industrialized West, poor women have always worked for wages to support their families. Beginning in the early 1960s, great numbers of middle-class mothers began entering the job market, and the

---

conjoint family   **Traditional Hindu household consisting of parents, several sons, their wives, and their children.**

research literature described the negative impact of paid maternal employment on children's development.

The early studies of middle-class maternal employment labeled the phenomenon under study as *mother absence*. How might such language affect the design, findings, and conclusions of these studies? This is what social-constructionists mean when they refer to the *discourse* surrounding a subject.

As maternal employment became normalized in middle-class North American society, a much more positive picture emerged from the research (Field, 1995). Today, about 70% of mothers with school-age children have paid employment outside the home (U.S. Bureau of the Census, 1998). In general, the impact of paid maternal employment is very complex because so many other variables are involved. These variables include the economic level of the family, other available adult caretakers, the age(s) and gender of the children, and the mother's attitudes toward her paid employment. Other influential variables include the amount of time spent with children, quality of child care, her beliefs about the effects of her paid work, and her marital status (Caruso, 1996; Gottfried, Gottfried, & Bathhurst, 1995).

Fathering. The paternal caretaking role takes many forms across societies. Fathers may provide protection, food, or other resources. A father's social status is the major determinant of his children's status, especially for male children. In the United States traditional gender ideology held that only the presence of a father ensured development of an individualistic and rugged masculine identity among sons. However, research suggests that father involvement is more likely to reduce gender stereotyping and increase both **empathy** and sensitivity among sons (Coltrane, 1996; Parke, 1996). A close relationship with a father appears to result in a more secure masculinity that does not require a rigid defense against the more "feminine" aspects of the self (Gerson, 1997; Pollack, 1998).

According to one overview, father–infant relationships were close in only 4% of human cultures, and in most cultures, the major father–child interaction was *play*. In industrial societies, fathers spend

about 14% of their time with children. In societies where both parents contribute to family support equally and where monogamy is the norm, fathers spend more time with their offspring. Beyond this, the nature and content of the father–child relationship varies greatly across cultures and subcultures. In general, compared to mothers, fathers interact less with children, take less responsibility for their actual care, do more playing, do less teaching of toddlers, and do more disciplining (Shulman & Seiffge-Krenke, 1997). Furthermore, fathers are more likely to take care of children in public settings and as a sole activity at the time. Mothers take care of children while doing multiple other tasks as well (Coltrane, 1998a).

A comparison of father roles in a Kenyan group (the Kipsigis) and in the United States (Cambridge, Massachusetts) revealed that U.S. American fathers were the primary caretakers of their young children significantly more often. Kipsigi infants were cared for by siblings as well as by mothers. Kipsigi fathers saw their roles largely as economic providers, whereas U.S. fathers saw their roles as providing emotional and cognitive stimulation, a close affective relationship, *and* economic support. The researchers concluded that these two communities represented distant points on the fathering continuum; one exemplified the extended family with a strong, distant, authority figure, whereas the other represented the small, more egalitarian, postindustrial family with relatively shared parenting (Harkness & Super, 1992). However, we should not assume that shared responsibility for child rearing comes only with industrialization. Among the Batek of Malaysia, mothers and fathers equally take care of children (Endicott, 1992). In any case, heavy paternal involvement and affective connection appear to have a positive effect on children's emotional development.

Recent research confirms men's increasing involvement with children in North American society, from pregnancy through all stages of infancy and childhood, as well as in overall parenting. The general trend of findings is that when fathers are more involved (a) children feel more in control of their lives, (b) there is greater cognitive stimulation, and (c) there are fewer stereotypical ideas about paternal

---

empathy   Identification with, and understanding of another's situation, feelings, and motives.

TABLE 5.1   The Development of Gender Understanding

Age	Development	Explanation
0–2	Gender awareness	Able to discriminate between male and female faces.
2–3	Gender labeling	Recognize others as girls or boys.
3–5	Gender consistency	One remains a boy or girl, even if superficial characteristics change.
3–6	Gender constancy	"I will be a girl or boy and will always be so." Provides motivation to become like others of their group, and master gender-appropriate behavior.
6+	Gender knowledge	"I am a girl or boy because of how my body (genitals) is made. Girls like to play with dolls and cook, while boys play rough and run around."

roles and characteristics (Cohen, 1998; LaRossa, 1997). Although all this has led to increased attention to fathering and the impact of fathers, the role of fathers continues to be poorly researched (Amato, 1998; Silverstein & Phares, 1996). Images of the nurturant and self-sacrificing *new father* have proliferated in postindustrial society and have become new gender ideals. At the same time, images of divorced fathers who disappear from their children's lives and the "deadbeat dad" who actively avoids economic and emotional responsibility for his children, also prevail (Hetherington, 1999a).

The Child's Developing Understanding of Gender. Infants between 9 and 12 months old appear able to discriminate between male and female faces even when hair length and clothing style are made similar (see Table 5.1). This suggests that the infant has already begun to process information about people along gender lines. Studies of gender labeling at later ages (2–3), indicates that children vary in terms of the age at which they recognize others as girls or boys. Earlier labelers were more gender typed in their later behaviors and had greater knowledge of gender stereotypes (Fagot & Leinbach, 1993, 1995). Later, toddlers learn attributes commonly associated with each group. For example, even 3-year-olds know that "boys hit people" and that "girls like babies" (Blakemore, 1998; Leaper & Gleason, 1996). Later on, children's gender knowledge includes awareness of gender-typed activities and interests, personal and social attributes, social relationships, stylistic and symbolic information, concepts, beliefs, as well as the enactment and adoption of gender roles. By age 3, children possess

scripts about everyday experiences, including gender scripts. Gender is irrelevant for some scripts (the "brushing teeth" script), whereas for others gender may become very salient (the "preparing dinner" or "fixing the bike" scripts). In general, boy scripts are better developed because from an early age boys are more concerned about violating gender role standards. Also, girls perform masculine scripts more often than boys perform feminine scripts. The important point here is that gendered behavior proliferates in early childhood and becomes much more obvious later on when interacting with peers, particularly with same-sex peers (Levy & Fivush, 1993).

Culture and the Gendered Childhood

For boys, the general themes of childhood gender socialization include (a) avoidance of femininity, (b) mastery of the physical competencies of boyhood, (c) importance of the peer group, (d) encouragement of aggression, (e) autonomy from adult supervision, and (f) rehearsal of the achievement and occupational roles of adulthood (Badinter, 1997; Messner, 1997). For girls, the general gender themes of childhood include (a) continued elaboration of and identification with the maternal role, (b) rehearsal of social and domestic roles, (c) awareness of the importance of physical appearance, (d) acquisition and acceptance of lower social status, (e) flexibility of gender-typed behavior and attitudes (Beal, 1994; C. L. Martin, 1995).

For both girls and boys, an important feature of childhood is the establishment of more rigid gender boundaries and a peak level of gender stereotyping. The general finding is that preschoolers are very flexible regarding gender roles, but as gender stereo-types are acquired this flexibility decreases (Katz & Kasanak, 1994). Stereotypes involve heavy gender typing for activities, occupations, and personality traits (Serbin, Powlishta, & Gulko, 1993). As children enter middle school, their gender role flexibility increases up until puberty, when increased rigidity returns, but girls have been found to be more flexible over all ages. However, levels of gender stereotyping and gender role inflexibility are influenced by many variables other than the child's gender. These include paternal absence, paid maternal employment outside the home, gender-typed parental roles, knowledge of gender-typed activities and occupations, and socio-economic level (Amato, 1998).

In the opening vignette, you met Dennis, a boy who failed to conform to the behavioral expectations for his gender. What was your reaction to Dennis? How would you feel if he were your son? How would you approach a discussion about your son with your spouse or partner? Would you protect Dennis from ridicule from other boys? What predictions would you make for Dennis as a teenager and adult regarding his occupational interests, interpersonal relationships, and sexual/romantic life?

Childhood gender socialization results in girls who are nurturant, caring, and kind. Gender-related goals for boys include autonomy, competitiveness, and emotional inexpressiveness. Boys are also socialized to feel entitled to privileges within the family and in society. Although social changes over the last 35 years have brought great change and choice to girls' socialization (academic achievement, athletic expression, and so on), broader choices for boys remain more uncertain (Coltrane, 1998b).

Play and Work During Childhood

As children grow, they encounter the gender-related expectations of childhood (see Table 5.2). In subsistence societies, a major component of children's daily lives involves work. In urban, industrialized societies, children's daily activities center on play (Nsamenang, 1992). Mothers have relatively more free time when their work is not directly tied to physical survival, and across most such societies mothers come to believe that children younger than 7 or 8 cannot do useful work (Hoyenga & Hoyenga, 1993).

For example, in rural West Africa children's work includes running small errands, household chores, and caring for small animals or younger siblings. By age 4, children of both sexes will care for younger siblings, but girls typically have more chores. Boys are generally allowed greater distances from home and are more often without adults. These differences eventuate in the gendered division of labor that exists in most societies (Block & Adler, 1994).

Highly **gender-schematic** white American preschoolers are much more likely to classify a group of toys by gender than by any other scheme (such as indoor versus outdoor toys). They also have greater recall for more gender-typed toys and events. Over time, girls' requests for and liking of gender-typed toys tends to decrease, but those of boys do not. Girls and boys given "masculine" toys are more likely to have masculine career aspirations, whereas girls given feminine chores and toys tend to have more traditionally "feminine" career aspirations (Levy, 1994; Welch-Ross & Schmidt, 1996). This is a good time to reiterate that there is nothing *inherently* masculine or feminine about toy choices. For example, in Western society knives are likely to be considered a masculine toy choice, but among the Yupik of Alaska, knives are strongly associated with young girls' play. However, Yupik girls sit together and use the knives to draw figures on expanses of mud as they tell each other stories (deMarais, Nelson, & Baker, 1994).

How do children respond to cross-gendered behavior? White preschool boys predicted a negative paternal response for play with cross-gender toys, but very few girls did (Raag & Rackliff, 1998). In a related study, children rated the performance of a masculine-behaving female as highest in competence, credibility, and "bossiness" (McAninch, Milch, Crumbo, & Funtowicz, 1996). In general, "tomboys" are much more acceptable than are "sissies," to both parents and peers (Rottnick, 1999). This is because "tomboys" constitute a lower-status person (girls) taking on the activities and attributes of a higher-status person (boys). Girls seem to be aware that boy-typed behaviors and activities are more valued, and many girls take pride in being able to perform them well (C. L. Martin, 1995).

---

gender-schematic behavior   Tendency to organize complex material or experiences in terms of gender.

TABLE 5.2   The Gendered Worlds of Childhood

Item	Girls	Boys
Chores	Generally more chores such as child care, household tasks, economic tasks	Generally fewer, but if similar, they try to devise distinct ways of doing them; may care for large animals.
Distance from home	Generally closer	Generally further away, especially for play.
Personality	Most cultures encourage greater nurturance, responsibility, and obedience. Greater flexibility and tolerance for gender deviance. Greater emphasis on social awareness and etiquette.	Most cultures encourage greater achievement and self-reliance. Also more anxiety about conforming to gender rules.
Aggressiveness/submissiveness	The greater the formal power of women, the more female aggressiveness is permitted. In rigidly stratified societies, obedience and submissiveness are encouraged because this increases the likelihood of "marrying up."	In polygynous societies, boys encouraged to be more aggressive and industrious.

Canadian college students were surveyed regarding their beliefs about cross-gender behavior in children. They evaluated such behavior in boys much more negatively. These students also believed that girls, but not boys, will outgrow cross-gender behavior. In general, they believed that cross-gender behavior was more likely to result in homosexuality, transsexualism, and mental pathology among boys, but not among girls. Women respondents were much more accepting of cross-gender behavior in all children (Martin, 1990).

Critical Thinking Challenge

Consider surveying your classmates regarding their response to Dennis, in the opening vignette. Do the men in your class feel differently about him than the women do? How would you explain any differences found?

Gender Segregation: Protection Against *Cooties*?

Across cultures and ethnicities an outstanding feature of middle and later childhood is gender segregation in play, friendships, and daily encounters. Even when children work in mixed-sex groups, their leisure activity preference is clearly to be with others of the same gender. Sex segregation begins at about 2 among girls and at 3 among boys, and extends to about age 11 for

both. By age 8, few children have cross-sex friends (Fagot, 1994; Gray & Feldman, 1997).

The differences in the play styles of these gender-segregated groups have been well studied by developmental researchers. Girls prefer dyads or small groups in private places. After age 5, boys prefer to play in rougher ways, in larger groups, and typically outdoors in public places (Alexander & Hines, 1994; Benenson, Del Bianco, Philippousis, & Apostoleris, 1997). Among both African-American and white children, boys rated the importance of companionship, loyalty, and common interests as their most important expectations for friends. In contrast, girls saw more individual distinctions among their friends, so their expectations differed according to the individual friends (Ray & Cohen, 1996). Both European-American and African-American girls tend to engage in more cooperative play that involves taking turns and shifting alliances, whereas boys engage in more rough-and-tumble play that involves fighting and other aggression. Boys also spend a great deal of energy in establishing, maintaining, and displaying dominance hierarchies (Alexander & Hines, 1994; Goodwin, 1994; Pollack, 1998).

Among boy groups, there is an emphasis on being better, stronger, and more powerful. This typically leads to a focus on fighting, guns, and superheroes. Girls arrange themselves according to "best friends": a relationship of equals, so they tend to avoid dominance contests. Although girl groups seek to solve conflicts by compromise, they challenge boys directly if the situation requires. Girl play may sound gentle and democratic, but high levels of interpersonal cruelty and verbal aggression may occur among girls who reject and betray each other (Grotpeter & Crick, 1996). In general, the presence of same-sex others leads to even more stringent segregation. Girls typically find interacting with boys unrewarding and unsatisfying. Boys usually find interacting with girls boring and understimulating. Girls often withdraw when boys attempt to dominate them and also when boys do not respond to girls' requests for change in the situation. Based on all this, a stereotype persists that boys and their dominating social style dampen girls' self-expression and interaction. However, girls' withdrawal behavior depends much more on situational factors (such as being outnumbered by boys) than on gender itself (Benenson et al., 1997).

Most of the developmental literature emphasizes gender separation and the differences between girls and boys during childhood, but in fact considerable intergender interaction does occur (Gray & Feldman, 1997; Thorne, 1993). At a summer camp for ethnically diverse poor children, there was moderate gender mixing, but stricter segregation was maintained during free-choice time. Children with history of attachment difficulties and who were unpopular with peers violated gender boundaries more often. These researchers concluded that gender segregation is an important sign of positive adjustment during middle childhood (Sroufe, Bennett, England, & Urban, 1993). However, other researchers suggest that sex-segregated play can exaggerate behavioral difficulties among highly gender-typed children. For such boys, high activity levels, rough physical play, and dominating behavior can become truly problematic. For girls, behaviors such as high levels of acquiescence, dependence, and passivity may become exaggerated in same-gender groups (Fabes, Shepard, Guthrie, & Martin, 1997).

Even though childhood gender segregation is universal, it does manifest differently in different cultures. In societies where men have much higher status, boys segregate earlier and more completely. The toys used in these segregated groups, and the kinds of interactions that gendered toys elicit, teach different things. Girls learn to follow rules and to keep in close

contact with others. Their games focus on rehearsal of social and life roles (the birthday party, being the mother). Boys tend to enact more fantasy and occupational roles (attacking aliens, being the police officer). Girls can more easily integrate adults into their play than can boys. Gender segregation appears to offer and reinforce gender-typed guidelines about appropriate behavior in adult social situations (Hibbard & Buhrmester, 1997; Maccoby, 1998). Many developmental psychologists believe that childhood gender segregation results in the development of somewhat different intellectual, emotional, and social competencies in the two genders. Segregation seems to establish rather distinct masculine and feminine "cultures" that continue to manifest in adult contexts such as occupational preferences, relationship expectations, personal habits, reasons for disputes and their method of resolution, and so on. Clearly, however, adult women and men come together smoothly and successfully in the world despite their somewhat segregated socialization experiences (Maccoby, 1998; Powlishta, 1995).

Conclusions

The development of gender seems best compared to "an intricate puzzle that the child pieces together in a rather idiosyncratic way" (Hort, Leinbach, & Fagot, 1991, p. 196). How any particular individual combines these elements is influenced by specific cultural and situational factors (Martin & Ruble, 1997). The behavioral pieces of the puzzle include toys, work and play activities, playmate preferences, communication styles, and interaction patterns. The cognitive components of childhood gender development include gender-related knowledge, gender stereotyping, and an array of evaluative processes related to gender. For example, is sports play more valued than doll play? Said differently, the question remains, Who actually *does* have the most cooties?

Puberty and Adolescence: The Intensification of Gender

Beginning in puberty, a truly gendered life begins. Physical changes accentuate the differences between the male and female body. Hormones cause the sexual system to become fully developed, and secondary sexual characteristics appear (Herold & Marshall, 1996). In most societies, clothing, ornamentation, and grooming styles accentuate and exaggerate these physical differences. In preindustrial societies, puberty rituals (especially for boys) mark a relatively abrupt transition from childhood to full adulthood. However, in industrial and postindustrial societies, there is a socially constructed time of life during which individuals have all the physical capacities of adults but may only gradually acquire the social and economic status of full adults (**adolescence**). The complex processes of sexual courtship and the establishment of long-term intimate relationship(s) begin. In industrialized societies, the sexual motivations that become urgent with physical maturity must be socially channeled, because having children early can become an obstacle to adequate preparation for social and economic independence. Relationships with family and friends must be renegotiated. Today, many more years of formal education and training are required for economic independence and success. Gender influences all these developmental issues in powerful ways. The wide array of gender-related changes that occur during this period of the life span has been summarized by the term **gender intensification** (Eccles & Bryan, 1994; Huston & Alvarez, 1990). This intensification involves increased pressures to conform to traditional notions of femininity and masculinity (Lobel & Bar, 1997; Ponton, 1997). A longitudinal study of the differential effects of gender intensification among young adolescents in the United States revealed that girls became increasingly involved with their mothers and boys with their fathers. This involvement was particularly strong when the family employed a traditional division of household chores and responsibilities (Crouter, Manke, & McHale, 1995). Increasingly distinctive masculinity and femininity among adolescents in Zimbabwe (Harrison, Stewart, Myambo, & Teureraishe, 1995), Turkey (Hortacsu, 1997), New Zealand (Chant & McIlwaine, 1998), and Croatia (Marusic & Bratko, 1998) suggest that *gender intensification is relatively universal.*

Many aspects of life may be subsumed under the rubric of gender intensification. The next sections consider four issues: (a) the emergence in a person of a gendered style of relating to others, (b) gender and moral development, (c) gender and the physical ideal, and (d) gender and self-esteem.

Gender and Relating to Others

A central dimension of adolescent development seems to be the degree to which individuals are concerned with a sense of connection to others, especially peers, rather than with psychological separateness. A study of **self-concept** was carried out among college students across five nations, namely Australia, mainland United States, Hawaii, Japan, and Korea. Findings confirmed that respondents from more collectivistic societies saw themselves as more interdependent. However, gender differences were best summarized by the extent to which people regard themselves as connected emotionally to others. Across all these societies, women saw themselves as much more emotionally connected to others (Kashima et al., 1995). Similarly, studies of adolescents in the United States confirmed that males developed their **identity** solely in *intrapersonal* terms, whereas girls focused more equally on both intrapersonal and *interpersonal* identity development (Lytle, Bakken, & Romig, 1997; Shulman & Seiffge-Krenke, 1997).

Gender also influences friendships and sibling relationships. In keeping with popular stereotypes, studies of gender and friendship generally find greater attachment, self-disclosure, and intimacy in women's friendships (Johnson, 1996; Veniegas & Peplau, 1997). Boys' friendships have a different tone. They rely on action to express connection (Pollack, 1998). There is an emphasis on "doing together" rather than "being together." The avoidance of open affection and emotional interchange appears related to fears about homosexuality. Boys often consciously reject any behavioral style that might be labeled as *feminine* (Kilmartin, 1994).

In cross-cultural studies of adolescent relationships, similarities within genders tend to override cultural differences. For example, one study compared perceptions of intimacy among Israeli Jewish, and

---

adolescence   **Transitional period between childhood and complete adulthood.**

gender intensification   **Magnification of gender differences in early adolescence; increased pressure to conform to traditional gender roles.**

self-concept   **Personal mental image or perception of one's own unique qualities.**

identity   **Self-definition; a conscious sense of who one is and how one is related to the rest of society.**

Israeli Bedouin adolescents. Girls in both ethnic groups reported higher levels of emotional closeness and relatedness than boys did. Although girls were more self-disclosing, no gender differences were found regarding respect for friends and conformity to social norms. The overall patterns of gender differences were almost identical. Female friendships involved more self-disclosure, whereas male friendships involved more joint activities (Elbedour, Shulman, & Kedem, 1997). A study of Turkish adolescents revealed similarly distinctive gender patterns (Yildirim, 1997).

Aggression. Psychologists and laypeople alike usually define "relating to others" in terms of behaviors that *women* tend to do. However, aggression and violence are also styles of relating to others. Moreover, researchers have defined aggression (hitting, fighting, and so on) in such a way that men's behavior is more likely to be perceived as aggressive. Researchers have emphasized physical rather than verbal aggression, and direct rather than indirect aggression (White & Kowalski, 1994). This is a good example of how even a seemingly gender-neutral term such as "relating to others" is actually heavily gendered. To compound the problem, social scientists have tended to study aggression only as an issue of gender difference and failed to examine the nature of aggression among girls and women. Researchers have also tended to rely on self-reports, thus invoking stereotypic self-concepts. A study tracing the development of aggression from infancy through adulthood revealed few gender differences during toddlerhood. Although parents sometimes reported more aggressive behavior by boys, these seemed more related to stereotypic parental expectations, because few differences were observed under controlled conditions. From ages 3 to 6, higher levels of male aggression emerged in segregated peer groups. Girls seem more adept at hiding aggression from adults, although both genders show equivalent levels of aggression toward their siblings (you and your classmates may want to swap some stories about this). Girls tend to use more verbal and relational aggression (withdrawal of friendship, exclusion, and so on), whereas boys use more physical aggression and personal insults. Most children decrease aggression and improve their interpersonal skills, but a sizable subgroup of boys does not decrease aggression over time. This seems sufficient to maintain the robust stereo-type that boys are more aggressive than girls (Crick, Bigbee, & Howes, 1996; Galen & Underwood, 1997; Loeber & Hay, 1997).

More recent cross-cultural studies and those employing a more balanced definition of aggression (intentional psychological or physical harm) have revealed remarkable variation in this highly gender-stereotypic factor (Burbank, 1994; Kopper & Emerson, 1996; Lepowsky, 1998). In a controlled laboratory environment, few sex differences in aggression emerged when anonymity was ensured, no retaliation was possible, there was equal provocation, and the gender of the target was unknown (Bettencourt & Miller, 1996; Lightdale & Prentice, 1994).

Critical Thinking Challenge

Regarding the findings just mentioned, how do situational influences affect the behavior of both women and men?

Aggression during adolescence appears related to young men's greater facility with weapons and to their greater susceptibility to collective aggression (gang membership) (Loeber & Hay, 1997). It is also during adolescence that cross-gender violence manifests, with girls reporting more physical and sexual aggression from boys. Fighting as a response to conflict begins as a masculine script during childhood, and in many societies it becomes more frequent and better defined during adolescence. One study examined Finnish adolescents' reactions to conflict situations. Rates of aggressive responses increased from preadolescence (age 11) to mid-adolescence (age 14) and then decreased (age 17). Boys' levels returned to the preadolescent level, whereas girls' aggression dropped to the very lowest levels possible (Lindeman, Harakka, & Kangas-Jarvinen, 1997).

Gender and Moral Development

The learned ability to judge right from wrong is termed *moral reasoning*. Lawrence Kohlberg devised a series of moral dilemmas and presented them to a sample of boys as they grew from elementary school age through young adulthood (Kohlberg, 1996, 1987). The best known of these dilemmas has to do with Heinz, whose wife will die without a particular drug. A druggist has the medicine, but demands a large amount of money, which Heinz cannot obtain. The dilemma posed involved whether Heinz is justified in stealing the drug. Kohlberg was less interested in the answers than he was in the reasoning process involved. Based on these longitudinal data, Kohlberg concluded that there were three general levels of moral reasoning (see Table 5.3).

Early research based on this model suggested that women, as a group, tended to fall into the lower stages of moral reasoning. This fueled popular and psychoanalytic stereotypes about the "moral inferiority" of women (Freud, 1924b). Carol Gilligan (1982) proposed an alternative view, namely that girls and women reasoned *differently* about moral issues. This feminine style of moral reasoning ostensibly originated from the unique experiences of girls as they grew up. Based on her own qualitative study of decision making when faced with an unwanted pregnancy, Gilligan concluded that women brought "a different voice" to moral decisions. Women's approach to moral dilemmas was based on connection with and concern for others, social harmony, and care. She contrasted this "care" perspective with the "justice and individual rights" perspective of men. This positive presentation of women's behavior was very appealing, and Gilligan's theory generated a great deal of interest and research (for example, Bolansky & Boggiano, 1994; Beutel & Marini, 1995). However, the theories of neither Kohlberg nor Gilligan have fared very well in terms of empirical support (Sochting, Skoe, & Marcia, 1994). Feminist and cross-cultural researchers were quick to point out the sexist bias, ethnocentrism, and methodological flaws in Kohlberg's work. For example, Walker (1984) examined 41 studies of moral reasoning among children and adolescents. Where there was a difference, girls and women used *higher* levels of moral reasoning. Gilligan's methodology has also been criticized (Gallotti, 1989). Findings in support of gender-specific moral reasoning styles have been very inconsistent. The generally well-supported conclusion is that women and men use both types of moral reasoning, depending on the situation (Clopton & Sorrell, 1993; Davis, 1994; Wark & Krebs, 1996). This finding has held up well across cultural groups (Brabeck, 1996; Stack, 1997). Once again, uproar about psychological gender differences seemed ultimately to be more about methods and measures than about essences and experiences (Martin, 1998).

TABLE 5.3 Kohlberg's Stages in the Development of Moral Reasoning

Level I	*Preconventional*
Stage 1	Based on avoidance of punishment
Stage 2	Based on rewards, benefits, and self-interest
Level II	*Conventional*
Stage 3	Based on standards of others: "good boy" or "good girl" orientation
Stage 4	Based on laws, maintenance of social order, etc.
Level III	*Postconventional*
Stage 5	Based on balance between individual rights and community values
Stage 6	Based on universal human rights

Gender and the Physical Ideal

"Body image lies at the heart of adolescence," according to one study comparing French and American adolescents' attitudes toward their bodies (Ferron, 1997, p. 736). Ideal body stereotypes generally divide along gender lines. Males prefer a medium build, and in the West the male body is valued for what it can do (strength, athleticism, and endurance). Adolescent men express more pride and satisfaction in body appearance and evaluate themselves on bodily efficiency, strength, size, and physical ability, particularly in sports (Graber, Brooks-Gunn, & Galen, 1998; Pope et al., 2000).

In Western society, the female body is valued for how it looks (beauty, youthfulness, and thinness) rather than for what it can do. This idealization of the thin body often results in many adolescent women responding negatively to the natural changes in their bodies. Girls' dissatisfaction with their looks is associated with lower self-esteem and is a risk factor for the development of eating disorders (Abell & Richards, 1996). Adolescent women in North America understand that their physical appearance is crucial for their life success. They evaluate themselves frequently regarding their physical attractiveness, and this may involve competing and conflicting gender ideals. Some researchers have concluded that white, heterosexual, middle-class women in the United States are overly identified with their physical appearance (Beren et al., 1996).

One cross-cultural researcher found that found that 75% of U.S. adolescents believed that they could achieve any body image they wanted through personal perseverance and willpower (diets and "training") and that a more perfect body would lead to greater popularity, acceptance, and love. Most French adolescents (75%) believed they were *predisposed* to a particular physical appearance (Ferron, 1997), as did most Mexican college students (Crandall & Martinez, 1996). A study of Canadian girls revealed a drop at puberty in both self-esteem and body image. A more positive body image was associated with both higher self-esteem and higher masculinity scores (Usmaniani & Daniluk, 1997).

Bogus positive feedback about appearance improved the body image of white women, whereas bogus negative feedback decreased it. However, such feedback had no impact on African-American women. This study supported previous findings regarding heavier ideal body weights, greater body satisfaction, and a lower incidence of eating disorders among black women (Henriques, Calhoun, & Cann, 1996). Moreover there appears to be a preference for larger body types among African-American men (Jackson & McGill, 1996).

Gender and Self-Esteem

Several well-regarded studies found a general decline in white girls' **self-esteem** through adolescence (American Association of University Women, 1991, 1992; Freiberg, 1991). This gender-related theme has been subsequently echoed in several popular works, as well as in some scientific studies (Abernathy et al., 1995; Chubb, Fertman, & Ross, 1997). These findings have been explained in terms of differing messages about women's adequacy, and achievement, differences in reinforcement, and an awareness of lower status.

One study of self-esteem among adolescents of varying ethnicity in the United States found that black and Latino males had the highest level of global self-esteem, and Native American and Asian-American women had lowest levels. In contrast, self-esteem among Taiwanese adolescents did not vary by gender. Researchers concluded that in the United States variables related to self-esteem include physical attractiveness and popularity. For Taiwanese youth, self-esteem is most strongly related to academic competence, because only 20% are able to

pass the examinations that allow them to go on to high school (Dukes & Martinez, 1994; Wu & Smith, 1997).

Three meta-analyses of self-esteem studies documented only slight gender differences in self-esteem, with men generally scoring higher on such measures (Feingold, 1994a; Kling, Hyde, Showers, & Buswell, 1999). Cross-cultural studies suggest that self-esteem is strongly related to the social and other environmental factors that surround the gendered person (Erkut et al., 1998).

Conclusions

Beginning in puberty several problematic methodological issues involved in studying gender rise to the fore. Studies of gender during childhood are focused on toy or activity preferences, whereas traditional studies about adolescents and adults are more focused on internal characteristics and traits. That is, they tend to revert to the concept of gender as something inside the person rather than as a situation-based factor (aggression, self-esteem, moral reasoning, and so on). Yet studies are remarkably inconsistent in demonstrating the existence of stable gender differences in traits and characteristics. Rhoda Unger (1990) has referred to these inconsistencies as the "now you see it, now you don't" phenomenon. Although the concept of postpubertal gender intensification has good support cross-culturally, the actual content of that intensification varies widely.

Adulthood

There are three important factors to consider in any discussion of adult gender issues. First, trying to capture the essence of gender in the adult, particularly on a global scale, is somewhat like trying to capture the wind in a box. As a fundamental aspect of human life and social organization, gender roles and gendered relationships are undergoing profound and rapid change all over the world (Chant & McIlwaine, 1998). Political upheaval, economic globalization, international media, technological innovation, and social realignments are all serving to reconstruct gender, in virtually all its manifestations.

---

self-esteem   **Pride in oneself; self-respect.**

Second, our psychological understanding of and approaches to studying gender are also changing rapidly (Anselmi & Law, 1998; Gergen & Davis, 1997; Lorber, 1994). As was mentioned earlier, psychologists, particularly personality psychologists, have traditionally seen gender as a collection of personal traits and characteristics that are relatively stable across time and across situations. The idea was that these traits somehow resided within the person and that a person had more or less of a particular trait based on his or her gender. A particular level or amount of this trait was believed to predict a wide range of actions, reactions, and choices (Deaux & Major, 1998). Thus women had "more" nurturance and empathy, so this made them appropriate for the caretaking of children. Men had "more" dominance, so this made them more appropriate for leadership and control of others. However, attempts to objectively observe and measure these traits led to a mass of inconsistent findings. As you read in earlier chapters, a more recent approach suggests that the roles that people carry out or the statuses they occupy *elicit* certain traits and behaviors. Men *or* women who are the sole caretakers of young children will, by necessity, display or perform more nurturing behaviors. Women *or* men in positions of leadership within corporations or the military will display or perform more dominating behaviors. Moreover, beyond mere roles, individuals behave in accordance with a socioculturally constructed "self-construal" ("the kind of person I am according to my gender") that guides their behavior in various situations (Cross & Madson, 1997; Wood, Christensen, Hebl, & Rothgerber, 1997). Thus, when it comes to gender, situational factors and contextual variables may be the best predictors of individual behavior. This approach is the "gender in context" perspective on gender.

Third, in considering constructions of gender in adults, we must return again to the issue of *whose gender?* Most gender-related research is carried out with young, white, middle-class university students in the United States, and many traditional gender-related concepts and descriptions no longer fit this population. Gender arrangements in other societies may vary greatly. Nor do traditional ideas of gender necessarily describe other North American ethnic minority groups, other age groups, or those involved in same-sex relationships. For example, the unique sociocultural degradation to which both Native Americans and Africans in North America were subjected have had a tremendous impact on adult gender roles in those two groups (Franklin, 1997). Until the middle of the 20th century, submissiveness, powerlessness, nonprotectiveness, and attributions of hypersexuality were major aspects of black masculine identity. Nevertheless, African-American fathers were crucial socialization agents for survival in this inhospitable environment (McAdoo, 1997a,b). Under slavery, whites regarded the African-American woman primarily as property and reproducer. Motherhood was often forced, and her children were considered a commodity to be sold for profit for others. Even after emancipation, most African-American women worked their whole lives as underpaid and often exploited employees in order to support their families (Collins, 1994). Segregation and racism precluded most African-American men from providing adequately for their families. These forces also necessitated that African-American women demonstrate many of the traits and behaviors that middle-class white society associated with men (assertiveness, ambition, protectiveness, and so on). Among Latinos and Latinas, gender roles continue to undergo rapid transformation because of the realities of migration, poverty, minority status, industrialization, and democratization (Ginorio, Guiterrez, Cauce, & Acosta, 1995; Hawkes & Taylor, 1999). Educated Native Americans seem to live in a biculturally gendered world. Tribal gender-related traditions are honored and lived out within the Native community, whereas mainstream white gender-related values and attitudes are maintained in the schoolroom and workplace (La Fromboise, Heyle, & Ozer, 1999; McNeil et al., 1999). Asian-American groups are so ethnically varied in terms of gender ideals that it is difficult to make any statements about the general characteristics of this complex group (Yee, Huang, & Lew, 1998). In our global overview of adult gender-related behaviors and characteristics, there is such variety that any but the most general statements soon dissolve into stereotypes. For even more complexity, across all these ethnic groups those in long-term same-sex relationships must renegotiate and redistribute social, household, and family roles in innovative ways. Formulating accurate and useful statements about adult gender for all these differing

Partnering, Parenting, and Making a Living Around the World

South Korea: The primary Confucian role expectation for Korean women is total devotion to the roles of wife and mother, with no participation in social activities. The second is obedience to her husband and never to surpass him economically or socially. The third expectation is filial piety to her parents-in-law through birthing a son and lifelong caretaking. However, over the last several decades middle-class women have entered the professions in large numbers. This has changed the configuration of their traditional roles. Researchers compared Korean women professors to full-time homemakers whose husbands were professors. Professional women experienced both greater role gratification and greater role strain. Income level, household assistance, overseas experience, and nontraditional gender role attitudes were strongly related to gratification. Younger age, birth order of husband, and husband's place of birth (rural rather than urban) were strongly related to strain. Researchers concluded that women were bearing the burden of social change in South Korea (Park & Liao, 2000).

Israel: In a study of attitudes and reactions to joblessness in Israel, there were no gender differences regarding perceptions of stigma concerning unemployment. But both men and women preferred unemployment to acceptance of a low-paying job. As in North America, more Israeli women postpone marriage and children to get advanced education. They are more likely to return to work shortly after childbirth, and they are working in previously all-male occupations. Unemployed men devote more time to job hunting. Women at all ages more likely to reject masculine-typed work than men were to reject feminine-typed work, but men's major reason for rejecting a job was that the work was feminine typed (Kulik, 2000).

Jamaica: Researchers studied fathering in a rural town. Traditional Jamaican fatherhood ideal roles are as heads of households, main breadwinners, and primary disciplinarians of children *and wives.* Several forces influence current fathering patterns. These include intense class tensions, violent political upheaval, fundamentalist religions, North American

popular culture, a tradition of multiple sex partners for both women and men, and a very unfavorable economic climate. Fatherhood often begins outside of a committed relationship, and by the time a couple settles to live together (often around 40 years of age) a woman may have children through several men. A man will have obligations of fatherhood to children in several households. Women head one third of the families in Jamaica, and some women reject marriage, believing it is "too much trouble." Many men travel regularly to England, Canada, and United States for months or years, and they send money home to families. This also contributes to father absenteeism. Most men aspire to be "good fathers," and are active with their children. Men who have traveled abroad return with more flexible ideas re household labor, and they will do domestic chores. Educated men often cannot find work, and alcoholism is a serious problem among men (Fox, 1999).

United States: Researchers conducted interviews on the maintenance of psycho-

---

groups is difficult. Having said all that, I will nonetheless now try to capture the wind in a box.

Up until the 1980s, being an adult was considered synonymous with being male, so two major studies of adult development—Levinson (1978) and Vaillant (1977)—focused on men's lives, or more specifically on white, middle-class American men's lives. Despite feminist criticisms and an array of works about women's lives, the ideas put forth about the development of this privileged group remain fixed in the popular imagination. Consider Vaillant's (1977) concept of the "midlife crisis." This term refers to the notion that sometime in middle adulthood some *men* begin to re-evaluate the choices and decisions they have made and experience an internal crisis, centered

on relinquished opportunities and unsatisfactory compromises. They may then radically restructure their lives, initiating divorce, changing occupations and lifestyles, and so on. The empirical evidence suggests that circumstances such as divorce, unanticipated health problems, job difficulties, and children's independence are what precipitate a re-evaluation of one's life choices and identity, rather than the other way around. Nevertheless, this colorful notion remains popular. Or consider the idea of the "empty nest syndrome." This originally referred to the difficulties faced by women whose children had grown and left home. The idea was that women had difficulty finding meaning and purpose in their lives because their children no longer needed them. Again, empirical re-

logical intimacy with 108 other-sex and same-sex couples that had been together for an average of 30 years. Sample was varied by ethnicity and by social class. Interviewees stated they experienced intimacy when they were able to share their inner thoughts and feelings, and when they felt these were accepted by their partners. This experience was associated with feelings of connection, peace, and contentment. Continued sexual involvement also promoted feelings of intimacy. Feelings of intimacy did not vary by gender, age, socioeconomic status, or education levels. Strong experiences of intimacy were also related to minimal relationship conflict, a confrontive conflict management style, mutual decision making, and a sense of relational equity. Heterosexual men mentioned positive observable qualities in their spouses. Both lesbian and heterosexual women mentioned these too and then mentioned their understanding of the underlying dynamics of that behavior. More lesbian couples had participated in couples therapy, and also reported higher levels of intimacy in more recent years (Mackey, Diemer, & O'Brien, 2000).

China: Researchers evaluated the impact of social pressure and social support on the distress levels of single parents in China. Fewer than 2.5% of all households in China consist of single parents. This very atypical group experiences bias and suspicion and is strongly stigmatized in this very familial culture. In this survey study, 67% were single mothers and 33% were single fathers. Virtually all were employed full time. Fifty-seven percent became single parents through divorce and 33% through death of a spouse. Education and family income had no impact on distress levels, nor did the ages or gender of children. Social pressure in the form of disapproval, stigma, and discrimination increased anxiety levels in this group. Instrumental (practical) social support was associated with reduced distress levels (Cheung & Liu, 1997).

Uzbekistan: This now independent republic was part of the former Soviet Union and represents a society in great transition. Old and new social values, democratic and communist ideals, Islamic and Western traditions all overlap in Uzbekistan. Most of the country is desert, but the fertile, green areas produce about one fourth of the world's cotton. Socially, the population is highly literate but in poor health due to the unrestrained use of agricultural chemicals. Under the Soviet system women could remain at home for 56 days with their new babies. Now they receive a year's pay and may stay at home for up to three years, but dire economic needs make this impossible. Education of girls is becoming shorter and viewed as less important. Islamic ideals regarding strict premarital chastity are again becoming prevalent. Control over family size is gradually returning to husbands. It is traditional for a son and his wife to remain with his parents and for the daughter-in-law to care for his elderly parents (Krengel & Greifeld, 2000).

search suggests that most women whose children have finally "flown the coop" are even happier than members of their cohort with children still at home. This reduction in parental responsibility is more accurately described as a feeling of being in the "prime of life," and such major changes in family structure affect everyone in the family, not just the mother (Mitchell & Helson, 1990).

Critical Thinking Challenge

Note that men's midlife crises were viewed as a normal developmental issue, whereas women's empty nest syndrome was considered a psychopathological condition, requiring treatment. Why do you think this was so?

Gender and the Major Roles of Adulthood

The most salient themes of young adult life may be said to be "partnering, parenting, and making a living" (see Box 5.2 for a global perspective). To say this a bit less rhythmically, the gender-related themes of young adulthood have to do with creating and maintaining a sexual/relational life, taking care of offspring, and managing one's occupational role (Goodnow, 1996; Vandewater & Stewart, 1998). All three dimensions are heavily gender laden, and each are explored at length in later chapters.

Partnering, Parenting, and Making a Living. Traditionally, it was part of the adult masculine role to initiate romantic and marital relationships. However, the social and emotional maintenance of such relationships was largely the domain of women. Although men might determine how many children a family might have, the primary parenting responsibilities were feminine concerns. Among the middle and upper class, the domain of occupation or career was primarily masculine. These notions date back to the 19th-century doctrine that white middle- and upper-class women and men naturally occupied *separate spheres*. Men dominated in the public and economic sphere, whereas women were confined to the domestic sphere (McCall & Yavacone, 1998). Currently, we see various attempts to redistribute and renegotiate these roles, across social class, ethnicity, and society. In the industrial and postindustrial world, flexibility, fluidity, and variability characterize all three major adult gender roles (Hogan, 1999; Welch-Ross & Schmidt, 1996). For example, in North America growing numbers of heterosexual women bear or adopt children without marriage. Many more lesbians and gay men are choosing to undertake the parenting role and are bearing or adopting children. Many more men co-parent and share household tasks equally. Men may depend on the earnings of a wife or partner while they seek further education or training. Women continue their paid employment even with very young children. They may obtain their education and vocational training years after the birth of their children. Occupations are becoming less gender typed: For example, the proportion of men in nursing is increasing steadily, whereas women are occupying more leadership roles in the military, and about one third of medical students are now women (Wear, 1997).

Critical Thinking Challenge

How are these recent gender-related trends represented in your class?

Researchers surveyed an ethnically representative sample of adult U.S. women regarding changes in gender role behaviors and ideologies. Labor force participation, more years of education, a younger age, and the respondents' own mothers' labor force participation were all associated with respondents' more egalitarian gender role attitudes. Higher-status jobs among women also predicted less traditional views. These relationships held equally among black, Latina, and white respondents. However, a stronger religious affiliation and being foreign born were associated with a more traditional gender role ideology. Daughters of immigrant mothers expressed more egalitarian views than did their mothers. These researchers concluded that ethnic women in the United States were becoming more similar in their attitudes (Harris & Firestone, 1998).

Two longitudinal studies offer some interesting insights into the relationship between gender roles and intimate relationships. Among married couples in the United States, the more husbands supported traditional masculine roles, the more dissatisfied their wives tended to be. Greater "femininity" in husbands was associated with more effective problem solving in the marriage (Bradbury, Campbell, & Fincham, 1995). Women college graduates who worked continuously over 25 years and also those who *began* careers at midlife were found to be more independent, autonomous, individualistic, resourceful, competitive, and rational compared to similar women who were never in paid employment. This last group was found to be more dependent and less ambitious, and self-reliant (Vandewater & Stewart, 1998).

Critical Thinking Challenge

Are the traits just listed stable personality characteristics, or are they merely the result of situational and contextual variables?

In most societies, including our own, having children is the central defining characteristic of "a real woman" (Michie & Cahn, 1997). The *motherhood mandate* still prevails (Russo, 1979). A study of Canadian mothers offers insights into the significance and experience of the mother role for adult women. Children were central to these women's self-concepts. A major proportion of their physical, cognitive, social, and emotional energy was given over to the well-being of their children. They had a positive attitude about the work involved in juggling family and paid work and in caring for and about their children. For these women, caring was both an activity and a treasured emotion. Their everyday experience of mothering involved a great deal of contingency planning: what to do if a child was ill, or needed comforting, instruction, discipline, and so forth. Moreover, these women actively maintained multiple identities, both occupationally and interpersonally. The author concluded that mothering qualities come neither from childhood socialization nor from physiological sources. Rather, they are a situational adjustment. That is, mothers behave the way they do because it is required by the situations in which they participate. The mothers studied also felt a personal commitment to these qualities and activities. These mothers worked (paid and unpaid) about 15 hours more per week than their male partners, and got substantially less sleep (McMahon, 1995).

In many nations, dual-earner couples are becoming the rule rather than the exception. A torrent of recent studies regarding this significant modification in gender roles provides fascinating insights into what happens to the characteristics of women and men when they share the domestic and occupational spheres more equally. In a large, ethnically diverse sample of young adults, there were no gender differences regarding work values, attitudes, and patterns. These similarities contrasted greatly with data from older samples (Cotton, Bynum, & Madhere, 1997; Ruhm, 1996). Second, although many couples do in fact distribute household, child care, and occupational roles more or less equally, many continue to self-report traditional gender role ideologies. Blue-collar men may approve of their partner's provider role, but they often insist that household duties should remain her domain (Alvesson & Billing, 1997; Deutsch & Saxon, 1998; Zuo, 1997). Third, women function quite effectively in their relatively new managerial, professional, and entrepreneurial roles. Any behavioral gender differences among those who occupy these positions seem firmly implanted in the stereotypic perceptions and thinking of the observers rather than in the actual behavior or characteristics of these women (Deal & Stevenson, 1998).

There is a serious lack of research on the adult development of gay men and lesbians (D'Augelli, 1994). The ways in which these groups maintain long-term marital-type relationships, how parenting roles are negotiated and maintained, and the relationship between occupational and couple roles remain relatively unexplored territory (Kimmel, 2000; Patterson, 2000; Stacey, 1996, 1998).

The Midlife Gender Transition: A Global View

Up through the early 20th century, many individuals never survived childhood diseases. Girls who survived childhood faced another great threat to a continued life, childbirth. Today, relatively few children in the industrialized West die in childhood. The vast majority of women in the West will survive past menopause, and this too is a relatively new phenomenon in the history of the genders (Mintz, 1998).

A traditional body of writing dating back to Carl Jung (1960) and David Guttman (1987) suggested some crossover in gender-related traits and characteristics in middle age. That is, among older cohorts men seemed to become kinder and gentler, whereas women became bolder. This crossover hypothesis found its way into "pop" psychology and gained acceptance (for example, see Borysenko, 1996). However, the empirical evidence was very mixed. The notion of gender crossover was very difficult to assess because enormous social changes were rapidly occurring in both work and family roles (James, Lewkowicz, Libhaber, & Lachman, 1995). Overall, researchers concluded that in older cohorts, it was the relatively rigid confinement of men to the occupational sphere and women to the child care and domestic spheres that elicited such differential behavior during the younger years. Psychologists referred to this as the parental emergency (Guttman, 1987). Current cohorts of young adults avoid this specialization by sharing more parental responsibilities, and the overall pattern of their gender-typed traits and behaviors is complex and unexplainable in terms of current theory. Contextual variables such as power differentials and economic status offer better explanations of any observed changes. In general, researchers seeking evidence of changes in gender typing at midlife concluded there was no support for these hypotheses. Satisfaction from family life was the most important determinant of life satisfaction for *both* women and men across all ages. Any changes appeared caused by modifications in life events such as fewer parenting responsibilities, or reaching maximum levels of occupational success (Carlson & Videla-Sherman, 1990). Similarly, studies examined an increase in women's perceived power with age in the United States, Kenya, and among both Arab and Jewish Israeli women. Findings revealed an increase in perceived power among middle-class women but not among lower-class women, thus contradicting theories that espouse a biological or intrapsychic basis for such changes. The researchers concluded that with increasing age and affluence, women are no longer required to present a meek public image (Friedman & Todd, 1991; Friedman & Pines, 1992).

The Grandparent Role. There are few formal norms regarding the grandparenting role in Western society, though it seems relatively well established that grandparents may be relied on in times of familial distress. Indeed, a national survey revealed that 1 in 10 grandparents have had primary care for grandchildren for at least six months. In general, grandfathers are less actively involved in child care than are grandmothers, and maternal grandmothers seem to be the most involved. The highest levels of grandmother involvement occur among Mexican-Americans (Fuller-Thompson et al., 1997). Approximately 30 percent of African-American households consist of extended families that include a grandmother. In a large proportion of African-American single-parent households, grandmothers provide child care, advice, and emotional support. A grandmother in the home typically reduces stress for economically disadvantaged families (Hunter, 1997). In the United States, grandchildren typically live closer to their maternal grandparents. Family social and communication activities are more typical of grandmothers, whereas outdoor, craft, and community activities are more typical of grandfathers. In general women function as kinkeepers, maintaining links among generations (Block, 2000).

Gender, Culture, and the Caregiver Role

One developmental marker of later adulthood is the reconfiguration of the family system, with adult children becoming caregivers of their aging parents. Gender and culture have a tremendous impact on this segment of the life span as well (Bookwala, Yee, & Schulz, 2000).

Critical Thinking Challenge

It has been said that all through the life span, men learn that women will care for them: mothers, lovers, wives, and daughters. Women learn they must take care of themselves or receive care from other women. Do you agree? Why or why not?

For the moment, the role and image of caregiver seems firmly ensconced within the feminine schema (Cancian & Oliker, 2000). Up until recently in American society, it was assumed that wives and daughters (particularly unmarried daughters) would care for ill and dying parents. In fact, a majority of studies reveal that across ethnic groups, women still provide most of the caregiving to parents (Ferguson, 2000; Kramer & Kipnis, 1995; Query & Flint, 1996). In order of frequency, caregivers are likely to be daughters, sisters, daughters-in-law, nieces, granddaughters, or female friends of the person needing care. Until recently, much of the work done to care for the ill or disabled has been taken for granted. In the United States, however, several recent gender-related demographic trends have changed these expectations. First, the proportion of old in society has been increasing dramatically, and the baby boom is quickly becoming the senior boom. Second, the old are living longer. These facts have resulted in an increased likelihood of disability or chronic illness in every family. Third, smaller families mean that there are fewer siblings to care for elderly parents. Fourth, women's increased participation in the labor force now means it cannot be taken for granted that an adult woman will be at home to care for elderly parents. These trends are global. All over the world, the proportion of older adults living with children has been decreasing. The Nordic countries have lowest rates of elderly parents living with their adult children; Japan has traditionally had the highest, but the rate is dropping there too (Hara & Minagawa, 1996; Sundstrom, 1994). In Nordic countries, caregiver needs are filled by the state. In the United States, only when women's free services are exhausted and financial resources spent do government services help with nursing home and limited community services.

In research studies, a thoroughly gendered definition of caregving has contributed to the "women are caregivers" stereotype. Thus men's active caregiving and involvement remained invisible. Women were estimated to more often serve as caretakers of elderly parents at a ratio of 3:1, but this has recently been revised to a 4:3 ratio (Marks, 1996). Recent studies of caregiving for parents have revealed the following gender-related realities (Cohler, 1998; Harris, 1998; Kramer & Kipnis, 1995):

◆ Women provide more frequent and more intensive types of care for their parents and later, their spouses.
◆ Women are more likely to be involved in activities of daily living (bathing, dressing, feeding, and so on).

◆ Women are burdened by more role conflicts, such as the competing demands of being a mother, spouse, and employee.

◆ Regardless of these demands, women feel more committed to the care of elderly parents.

◆ It is more difficult for women to find and afford help with caregiving.

◆ Men have the greatest difficulty with the emotional support aspects of caregiving.

◆ Men are more likely to give care by providing transportation, home and car repairs, and back-up help.

◆ Men are more likely to deal with finances, health workers, attorneys, and so on.

In families where there are sisters and brothers, sisters do most of the caretaking. In families where there are *only* brothers, they cooperate in doing *all* necessary caretaking.

For a somewhat different perspective on caregiving for elderly parents, consider Lee and Sung's (1998) comparison of caregiving among Korean-Americans and Anglo-Americans. The eldest son and his wife traditionally assume responsibility for a husband's parents' care. In this study, daughters-in-law cared for 55% of Korean elders, while daughters cared for only 28% of the elders. In the Anglo sample, 78% were cared for by daughters, and only 9% by daughters-in-law (all the elders had **dementia**).

Old Age

Until quite recently, the old have constituted a small minority of the world's population (Simic, 1978). At the turn of century in the United States, only 5% of white men and 7% of white women could expect to survive to 85 years. Now 18% of white men and 38% of white women can expect to reach 85. By 2035, one in four Americans will be over 65 and a great majority of this group will be women. As we consider older and older groups, the proportion of women increases. For example, in the 65- to 74-year-old range there are 83 men to 100 women, whereas among those 85 or older, there are only 39 men to 100 women. The major reasons for this are a declining birth rate and women's increasing longevity (see Table 5.4). The ethnic composition of the elderly in the United States is also changing. In the year 2020, 21% of the

elderly will be people of color, and by 2050, 33% of the elderly will be people of color (U.S. Bureau of the Census, 1996).

Images and Realities of Gendered Aging. During the 1960s and 1970s, the image of the aging population in the United States was that it was poor, infirm, frail, ill housed, isolated, and politically powerless. Today's popular image is that the old are affluent, politically powerful, and receive a high proportion of government benefits while not paying their share of taxes (Gonyea, 1994). Although many in industrialized societies cling to the myth that in the less developed world there is a happy intergenerational and extended family to care for the old, the reality is often widespread conflict and strife (Lee & Sung, 1998).

Retirement. The life stage known as *retirement* was invented/constructed in industrialized nations during the 20th century, and it has been strongly associated with the traditional masculine role. Women's retirement was ignored until the 1980s, and even today there is considerably less preretirement planning among women. For women who retire, decades of lower wages are transformed into a lower pension and a drastic reduction in income. Compared to retired men, retired women today are much more likely to be poor because of their longevity and chronic health problems. They are also more likely to be widowed and to live alone. Although the concept of "feminization of poverty" is well known, the particular form it takes among older women is not well recognized (Perkins, 1992).

A recent study of upcoming retirement among "boomer" women (born 1946-1964) demonstrates a somewhat different pattern. These women will have spent an average of 30 years in paid employment, and their earning patterns will resemble those of men. These baby boom women will be caring for their longer-lived parents for many more years after their retirement. There is no historical precedent for this phenomenon, and it creates quite a different reality for the retirement years (Dailey, 1998).

Traditional notions of masculinity can create difficulties for many men after retirement. The masculine

---

dementia Disorder characterized by loss of intellectual capacities and bodily functions, also personality disintegration.

TABLE 5.4   Gender and Life Expectancy: Demographic Trends

(a) The Declining Birth Rate (births per 1,000 women in each age group in United States)

Year	15–19	20–24	25–29	30–34	35–39	40–44
1960	89.1	258.1	197.4	112.7	56.2	15.5
1970	68.3	167.8	145.1	73.3	31.7	8.1
1980	53.0	115.1	112.9	61.9	19.8	3.9
1994	58.9	111.1	113.9	81.5	33.7	6.4

Sources: U.S. Bureau of the Census (1986, 1992, 1997).

(b) Increasing Life Expectancies in the United States (ethnic differences)

	1900–1902	1954[a]	1994
Women			
White	51.1	73.6	79.6
Black	35.0	65.8	73.9
Men			
White	48.2	67.4	73.3
Black	32.5	61.0	64.9

[a]Includes other nonwhite groups for 1954.
Source: U.S. Bureau of the Census (1997).

(c) Life Expectancies by Sex for Various Countries

Country	Men (at birth)	Women (at birth)
Austria	73.5	80.1
Canada	75.2	81.2
Czech Republic	69.7	76.7
Denmark	72.8	78.1
England/Wales	74.3	79.6
Finland	72.8	80.3
France	74.2	82.6
Germany	73.3	79.8
Hungary	65.3	74.6
Israel	75.3	79.3
Italy	74.4	80.8
Netherlands	74.6	80.4
Norway	74.9	80.7
Russian Federation	58.3	72.9
Sweden	76.2	81.6
United States	72.3	78.4

Source: World Health Organization (1998).

gender role emphasizes competency, activity, and productivity, mainly in the occupational sphere. Interpersonal independence and self-reliance are masculine gender ideals, and these may be difficult to maintain after retirement (Gradman, 1994). Ethnicity and social class also influence men's and women's adaptation to retirement. In general, blue-collar workers have a more positive attitude toward retirement. African

Americans are more likely to need to work after retirement and are generally less likely to see themselves as *retired* (Gibson, 1993).

Gender and Aging. Gender influences patterns of aging to a great degree. One study of the elderly revealed that a majority were women and that a high proportion were widowed, lived alone, were functionally impaired, and had reduced financial resources. More men in the group had spouses, were physically more independent, and had more control over their environment. These patterns emerge because women are more prone to chronic conditions, whereas men tend to die of acute conditions. Men who survive into old age tend to be healthier (Lowenthal & Haven, 1998).

Although elderly women tend to be poorer, their multiple life roles seem to better equip them to handle old age, particularly its accumulation of social and physical losses. Intimacy and emotional sharing with friends may continue regardless of age or physical condition. In contrast, men's preference for maintaining friendships through shared activities often becomes problematic in old age. Traditionally socialized women are more home and family oriented, thus enjoying greater role continuity into old age. Women tend to maintain more extensive social networks, and this too works to their advantage in old age. Women are more likely to receive support from multiple sources, and help seeking is more comfortable for women (Rawlins, 1992). To illustrate these patterns, consider a study of the social and support networks of the oldest-old (85+) in a relatively poor African-American community. Women received more help from relatives and friends, whereas men received more help from immediate family members. However, their children were not regular sources of support. Many women had developed fictive kin. These are long-term friends who take on family roles in times of need. Elderly women's participation as "church mothers" linked them to "church daughters" who cooked, did housekeeping, and provided transportation. Where family help was available, it was largely from biological daughters who typically had very limited resources themselves (Perry & Johnson, 1994).

An elderly group of Japanese-Americans (average age 72) was surveyed regarding their attitudes toward nursing homes versus home care. Given the strong family traditions of this ethnic group, the strong preference for nursing home care (if permanently disabled) was an unexpected finding. This preference was related to being unmarried/widowed, being female (the vast majority of respondents were both widowed and female), and a high level of acculturation to the United States. This unexpectedly positive attitude toward nursing home care was also strongly related to the existence of an ethnically appropriate nursing facility in that community (McCormick et al., 1996).

Widowhood: A Worldview

The term *widowhood* typically conjures up a mental image of an elderly woman, and this does reflect worldwide social and statistical realities. In some of the languages spoken in southern Africa, there is simply no word to describe a man whose wife has died (Owen, 1996). In developed countries, widows constitute from 8% to 13% of the adult female population. Many factors account for the relatively small number of widowers. These include traditions of polygamy, the age gap between marriage partners, the longer life expectancy of women, the high rate of widower remarriage, and men's higher risk of early death due to accidents, crimes, war, and AIDS.

Globally, virtually all widows lose status. In a few societies, widows have greater independence, a respected status, economic resources, and freedom from the restrictions of marriage, but most often the opposite is true (Dodge, 1995). In many developing nations, a widow often loses fundamental human rights, as do her children (Lopata, 1996). An extreme is the Hindu custom of *sati*, which required widows to immolate themselves on the dead husband's funeral pyre. Among the Hausa of Nigeria and the Hokkien of Taiwan, widows often must migrate because they lose the right to farm family land. Some are forced into prostitution to support themselves and their children. In the United States and England, isolation and economic deprivation are common (Owen, 1996).

The status of widows in Islamic societies varies greatly by nationality, class, ethnic group, number of children. and the historical era. The very first widow mentioned in Islamic scripture is Khadija. She was a wealthy caravan owner who actually employed the prophet Muhammed. She was 40 when she asked the

25-year-old Muhammed to marry her, and she contributed both financial and emotional support to the new religion. Under Islam, women lost the right to choose their own marriage partner, to manage their own property, and in some societies, the right to obtain divorce. However, the inheritance rights of widows and orphaned daughters were protected. In fundamentalist societies a widow is entitled to only one eighth of her husband's wealth and may be unable to secure even this (Jansen, 1997).

Recent studies of gender and widowhood in the Netherlands, Finland, and the United States revealed that widowers had clear advantages over widows regarding income resources, educational level, and health. However, widows had more emotional resources, such as close female friends, supportive neighbors, and available children. Despite women's disadvantages in income, education, and physical vitality, there was a remarkable lack of gender differences in life satisfaction. This finding was interpreted in terms of women's greater ability to adapt to multiple roles, their more multifaceted emotional relationships, their more numerous sources of support, and their role flexibility (wife, mother, worker, close friend, and so on). In contrast, men traditionally depend only on their wives for social and emotional support. There is a much higher rate of mortality for widowers than for widows within the first year after loss of a spouse (Martianen & Valkonen, 1996; Stevens, 1995).

Gender and the Grieving Process. Because women are more often the bereaved in our society, relevant studies are usually about widows. Our current understanding of bereavement is stereotyped in terms of woman's roles, status, and self-identity (Hockey, 1997). For example, there are endless cultural representations of women grieving (see Figure 5.1, for example), but virtually none of men. Thompson (1997) notes that grief involves the open expression of emotion, which is antithetical to Western society's notion of masculine inexpressiveness. This norm contributes to the idea that men do not need to grieve. However, this is not universal across cultures (Hortacsu, 1997). Furthermore, the traditional masculine role often elicits a preference for taking action in situations of bereavement. Psychological problems may result from the reluctance to undertake the emotional work of

FIGURE 5.1   The grieving process varies in different cultures.

grieving. This makes men more vulnerable to stress-related illnesses soon after a significant emotional loss (Barer, 1994).

Gender and Death

Death is viewed as the great leveler, but actually gender-related differences and inequalities persist even in death (Field, Hockey, & Small, 1997); see Box 5.3. Let's examine some gender-related differences regarding the end of life:

◆ Young men more likely to die from suicide, homicide, accidents, and from war.
◆ Young women are more likely to die and be injured from domestic violence.

ZOOM & ENLARGE   **BOX 5.3**

Gender and Death

Until the 18th century, in Europe and North America, the care of the dying was left to poor women. Even after death, poor women washed, dressed, and otherwise prepared the body for viewing and burial. However, all this changed with the medicalization and professionalization of death. Thereafter, men began to preside over most aspects of the experience of death (Field et al., 1997).

Among most Muslim groups, all public funeral rituals are carried out and attended only by men. Mothers, widows, and daughters, and other women friends and relatives gather together in a gender-segregated grief ritual. For example, when King Hussein of Jordan died in 1999 his American-born wife, Queen Noor, was

not allowed to attend the important public funeral. American Secretary of State Madeleine Allbright and First Lady Hillary Rodham Clinton were also segregated into a private women-only ritual. In an interview, Queen Noor indicated that she hid herself so she could attend her husband's burial (*Seattle Post-Intelligencer*, 1999).

Among both Turks and Greeks living in Berlin, men and women are separated during death rituals. Although of different faiths, they share Mediterranean culture. Women are expected to express loss, whereas men attend to the practical details of the death. In both home countries, only those of the same sex as the deceased wash and clothe the body. Tra-

ditionally, women held wakes, sang dirges, cooked special foods, and took care of the grave. Currently, however, almost 90% of these "guest worker" families send bodies back to the home country for burial. Traditionally, mourners gathered in the grieving family's home, but Berlin apartments are too small for this. Now women gather in the community center, whereas men gather in the prayer hall. Men used to carry out burials, but now they can only manage the transport of the body and deal with authorities. In mosques, women sit in separate rooms and follow funeral rituals on a monitor. In Greek Orthodox churches, women sit separately on the left side or upstairs (Jonker, 1997).

- Traditional gender norms expose men to more risks (work, chemical abuse, aggression, and so on), and these norms also restrict their use of medical services.
- Men are more likely to die relatively quickly from cardiovascular conditions, whereas women are more likely to die after an extended period of chronic illness (Crose, Leventhal, Haug, & Burns, 1997).
- Most people are aware that in general, females outlive males, even across species (Crose, 1997; Reuters Medical News, 2000c). However, class variables affect this. Upper-class men outlive lower-class women, regardless of ethnicity. This class difference is often misrepresented statistically as one of race or ethnicity.
- Because of the age norms surrounding marriage, women are much more likely to experience the death of a spouse or partner. They will also live for many more years beyond that loss. Furthermore, because women live longer, they are more likely to experience the death of siblings and friends (Zarit, Johansson, & Jarrott, 1998).
- In this society, men are more typically associated with the more public aspects of death: the physi-

cian, the funeral director, the clergyman, and so on. The masculine role involves giving public form to death, whereas the feminine role is to give emotional expression to death.

Summary

- Gender is a lifelong process. Infants and toddlers develop in the gendered environment provided by parents and society. Young children move from gender awareness to the complexities of full gender understanding and knowledge.
- Gender-differentiated work and play during childhood set the foundations for the gendered division of labor that characterizes traditional adulthood. Gender-segregated childhood peer groups have a powerful impact on later gender typing.
- Gender intensification marks the socially constructed period of life called *adolescence*. Gender similarities and differences in interpersonal relating, moral reasoning, body ideals, and self-esteem are some of the important gender themes of adolescence.
- Across all societies, the important tasks of adulthood involve the gendered roles of partnering,

parenting, and making a living. All three areas are undergoing transformation in today's world. Contextual and situational factors offer the best explanations for the inconsistencies regarding gender differences in behavior in these areas. Notions of midlife gender role crossover or convergence are not well supported, and they too seem related to contextual or situational variables.

◆ Later adulthood is characterized by caretaking for elderly parents, and this has been a heavily gendered role. The gendered meaning of retirement is undergoing change in the industrialized and postindustrial world.

◆ A growing segment of the world's population is made up of elderly women. Women's traditional gender role socialization better prepares them to cope with the physical decline and socioemotional losses associated with aging. Gender shapes the experiences of widowhood, grief, and even death.

InfoTrac College Edition

For more information, explore InfoTrac College Edition at

http://www.infotrac-college.com/Wadsworth

Enter search terms: gender and infancy, gender and toddler, gender and childhood, gender and adolescence, gender and young adulthood, gender and middle age, gender and old age.

6

Gender and Relationships
A Lifetime of Connected Lives

Relationships are the bread and the thread of life, they define existence and provide it with meaning. ◆ B. Laursen and W. M. Kukowski

Learning Objectives

After studying this chapter, you should be able to:

1. Briefly summarize the influence of gender in sibling relationships across the life span.
2. Summarize the important features of childhood and adolescent friendships for girls and boys, mentioning how these may be distinctive for those with a same-sex orientation.
3. Contrast the popular stereotype with the relevant research findings regarding how men and women conduct their friendships, mentioning cross-sex friendships.
4. Explain how dating facilitates partner selection in individualistic societies, contrasting this with romantic relationships among sexual minorities.
5. Evaluate the claims of evolutionary psychologists regarding human universals in partner preferences.
6. Contrast the central features of the arranged marriage versus the love marriage.
7. Summarize the historical and current marital patterns among African Americans as an example of the love-based marriage.
8. Explain how the nuclear family came to be normative, and summarize the important features of Peplau's classic marriage classification scheme.
9. List and describe the forces that precipitated ongoing changes in gender-related marital and family roles.
10. Summarize the important features of the current issues surrounding the distribution of child care, housework, and parenting roles in the postindustrial family.
11. Summarize the findings regarding parenting roles and the distribution of household tasks among gay and lesbian families.
12. Summarize the gender-related issues surrounding divorce and repartnering.

Encounters with Gender

Karen has always lived in a small, very homogenous midwestern community. Now she has graduated college and is very excited about her new job at an elementary school in the big city. Karen meets her new class and is enthralled by the ethnic diversity of her students. However, she is puzzled by a group of thoroughly enculturated East Asian girls, because their last names all suggest European origins (Schwartz, O'Leary, Polskaya, Romano, and so on). Karen has taken a special liking to Andrew Smith, an African-American boy with a great talent for science. All goes wonderfully well, but several incidents inform Karen that she has a great deal to learn about contemporary urban America. When Karen has the children create Father's Day gifts, she receives several phone calls from upset mothers. When Karen has occasion to call Andrew's Smith's home, a young child answers the phone and identifies herself as Saundra Johnson. Karen asks to speak to Mrs. Smith, but is told that no Mrs. Smith lives there. What is happening in Karen's class? What does Karen need to know about gender, ethnicity, and the family to work more effectively with her students and their families?

Overview

Relationships are a central feature of human life and society. This chapter examines the gender-related aspects of human relationships in various societies. We begin with a discussion of how gender influences sibling relationships. An exploration of same-sex and other-sex friendship follows. The gender-related aspects of courtship, marriage, parenting, and economic decisions are then reviewed, among both heterosexual and same-sex couples and families. In

North American society, *parenting* is virtually synonymous with *mothering*, and this bias has been reflected in the research literature. Recent changes and controversies surrounding the father role are examined. I also discuss the gender-related issues of divorce and repartnering.

A Lifetime of Gendered Relationships

A relationship exists when there are frequent, diverse, and enduring interactions between individuals (Laursen & Bukowski, 1997). Familial relationships provide the setting in which we learn gender and cultural norms and develop most of our affective, social, and cognitive abilities. In childhood and adolescence, same-sex friends continue the process of normative gender socialization. These gender norms are then embedded within our romantic, sexual, and marital relationships. For example, traditional parenting behaviors are distinguished on the basis of the parent's gender (Nock, 1998). For a second example, for the heterosexual majority relating to a gay or lesbian person may be confusing or even threatening because the normative boundary between friendship and erotic relationships may seem too weak.

Sibling Relationships

A majority of human beings grow up with siblings. A notable exception is modern China with its one-child family policy (Yang, Ollendick, Dong, Xia, & Zin, 1995). The sibling relationship is generally the longest-lasting life relationship, and gender plays a role in the overall quality of sibling relationships all through the life span. In middle-class Western society, the concept most associated with the sibling relationship is sibling rivalry. In other societies, older siblings, regardless of gender, are the primary caretakers of younger infants and toddlers, particularly when both parents are involved in agricultural work (Whiting & Edwards, 1988). Family sociologists note that in industrialized societies, sibling relationships are voluntary and based on personal preference, but in developing nations and also among many minority groups in North America, sibling relationships are obligatory and guarantee the well-being or even the survival of the family group (Ciccerelli, 1995; Yee, Huang, & Lew, 1998).

Sibling gender is a factor in several aspects of family relationships. For example, parents tend to make many more comparisons between same-sex siblings than between other-sex siblings. This sometimes provokes a lifetime of quarreling and antagonism among siblings (Bank & Kahn, 1997). Also, the presence of other-sex siblings tends to elicit more cross-gender play. Siblings may represent our first peer relationship with someone of the other gender (Rotundo, 1993). In adulthood and old age, sister–sister relationships tend to be the closest, especially in industrialized nations. In middle adulthood, brothers and sisters often develop a new closeness as they care for their elderly parents (Ciccerelli, 1995). In old age, siblings, especially sisters, are more likely to socialize and be the central source of mutual support (Campbell, Connidis, & Davies, 1999).

Gender and Friendship

In postindustrial society, friendship is a purely voluntary, preferential, and nonobligatory interdependent association or relationship that has no goals other than mutual enjoyment and continuation. Friendships are willingly undertaken and self-managed, and these qualities make friendship both very attractive and very vulnerable. The ability to form and maintain friendships is considered an important sign of good mental health and social adjustment (Salmela-Aro & Nurmi, 1996). Furthermore, individuals and couples often live far from their families of origin, so "friends" become an important source for sociability and support. Members of some groups (for example, gay men, lesbians, the disabled, or the elderly) may feel a lack of "place" in their families of origin. A circle of friends, bound by affection and shared lifestyle, often functions as a family (Nardi, 1992).

Friendships take many forms: close, committed, long term, or based solely on shared tasks or leisure activities. The best friendships are based on an appreciation of the uniqueness of the friend and a sincere wish for the other's well-being. Friendships are not considered "real" or sincere if they are based on personal gain. Friends tend to be similar in terms of sex, ethnicity, intelligence, economic status, and sexual orientation. These voluntary associations begin early in life. See Box 6.1 for a global perspective on culture and attitudes toward friendship.

SLIDE SHOW   BOX 6.1

Friendship: A Global Perspective

Cameroon, Africa: Among the Bangwa, parents arrange a lifelong friendship for newborns, and this friendship is considered more significant than a blood tie. The importance of friendship is emphasized in childhood, and Bangwa folktales and songs bemoan the loss of friendship. Bangwa children spend a great deal of time with their special same-sex friend, sharing confidences and walking hand in hand. This special friend typically helped negotiate marriages, and arranged healing ceremonies when illness occurred. When dying, the Bangwa often called for their friends rather than their kin (Brian, 1976).

Thailand: Up until quite recently in rural Thailand, it was common for pairs of young men to pledge a lifelong commitment of friendship in a public announcement of their relationship (Foster, 1976).

Guatemala: Among the Chinautleco, the *camaradia* of two teenage boys is treated with public recognition and respect. However, there is often possessiveness and jealousy in these relationships, and when the friends break up, they may use the intimate knowledge they have to hurt and embarrass each other (Reina, 1959).

Taiwan: In rural Taiwan, when a bride left for her wedding, the door to her father's house was symbolically slammed behind her. In her new husband's house, her only value was in bearing and nurturing a grandson. Married women spent much work time together (at the communal laundry, the marketplace, and so on). A woman had a warm and welcoming place among her women friends. If she complained of poor treatment, her husband's family would experience public pressure to change their ways. Men who behaved badly toward their wives also lost "face" in this court of public opinion (Wolf, 1972).

Childhood Friendships

Children develop preferences for particular playmates as early as 3 or 4 years of age. As children grow, their concepts of friendship become increasingly complex and focus on themes of satisfying interaction, acts of kindness, loyalty, and common interests. Cross-sex friendships are relatively uncommon. As you read in the previous chapter, most children prefer same-sex friends because of their similarity in level of activity, interaction style, and level of aggression (Moller & Serbin, 1996). In general, boys play in larger groups and describe their friendships in terms of loyalty, helping, shared activities, and awareness of each other's needs, but without overt affection (Pollack, 1998). In their more individual friendships, girls emphasize themes of closeness, verbal sharing, acceptance, and reciprocal emotional understanding. Gender is not the only matching variable in childhood friendships. Childhood friends also tend to be of the same age, ethnicity, social class, and level of academic achievement. Same-gender friends reinforce each other for gender-appropriate play, preferences, and communication style (Zucker, William-Smith, Kurita, & Stern, 1995).

Adolescent Friendships

The research literature suggests that friendships are the most important and satisfying relationships for adolescents in industrialized societies (Meeus & Dekovic, 1995; Richards, 1998). Adolescent friendships constitute a platform from which to explore and rehearse adult behaviors, roles, and identities. It is also clear that peer friendships have an important impact on adolescents' attitudes, behavior, and development in both negative and positive ways (Berndt & Keefe, 1995). For all adolescents, intimacy, trust, loyalty, generosity, and helpfulness become important aspects of friendships. Friends are often the source of advice, understanding, and self-acceptance for teenagers (Johnson, 1996). In general, girls' friendships are characterized more by verbal interaction *and* shared activities. Boys' friendships focus mainly on activities, particularly sports (Berndt & Keefe, 1992; Monsour, 1992).

Regardless of ethnicity, organized sports appear critical in developing mainstream masculinity in industrialized societies. Athletic pursuits with friends represent an entry into a virtually all-male world that is populated by important role models. For boys in

Western society, sports represent an approved way of connecting with others. However, the nature of sports leads boys to develop *positional identities*. That is, their position is based on being "better than" and/ or "beating" others (Messner, 1997). This is a theme that sometimes continues into adult male–male relationships.

Friendship and Sexual Orientation. For the majority of adolescents in industrialized societies, the expression of sexual/romantic interests begins during adolescence. Thus, most teenagers gradually expand their attention from same-sex friends to other-sex romantic/sexual partners. We will explore the complex relationships between gender and sexuality in the next chapter. Here I should mention the relationship issues that confront youth with a same-sex or bisexual orientation.

Gay and bisexual men often become aware their sexual orientation within the context of their childhood and adolescent friendships. They learn that very firm boundaries exist between boys in terms of physical affection and that violators are considered appropriate targets for ridicule, humiliation, and even physical injury (Corbett, 1998). Thus the gay male adolescent must learn to camouflage his developing sexual attractions (Hunter & Mallon, 2000).

For girls who become aware of erotic attractions toward friends and other girls during adolescence, life may not be as physically threatening as it is for boys, but it may be more confusing. The emotional intimacy and physical affection of women adolescents may sometimes blur the boundaries between friendship and erotic behavior. Although some teenage lesbians may be open, most have difficulties as they figure out how to cope with a stigmatized identity (L. M. Diamond, 1998).

Adult Friendships

It may be useful to begin this section with a popular contemporary stereotype and then follow with a bit of relevant history. First the stereotype: "When it comes to friendship, women talk and men do." Are the friendships of women and men really so very different? Some history reminds us how gender constructions can change over time.

Historically, writings on friendship have been devoted to men's friendships. These were described in terms of bravery, loyalty, duty, and heroism. In past times, masculine friendship was a moral and civic virtue. Through the 19th century, "manly love" was part of the definition of masculinity (Nardi, 1992). One study of letters exchanged among 19th-century male factory workers revealed an intimacy and tenderness that many contemporary men might find disconcerting (Hansen, 1992). In contrast, women were seen as incapable of true friendship. Historically, women were portrayed as unable to bond with other women and unable to commit to each other. The common understanding was that women's friendships were easily abandoned for male companionship (Rose, 1995). Folk wisdom suggested intense female jealousy and fierce competition for men. In contrast to the more public and "collegial" friendships of men, the situating of women's friendships in the private sphere also led to their dismissal as less important (Johnson, 1996).

Writings and research on friendship began to change in the 1970s. Today, "true" or "real" friendships are described in terms of intimacy, trust, caring, and nurturing; all characteristics that are highly associated with women and femininity (O'Connor, 1992). Friendships have come to be redefined in feminine terms, and now *men's* friendships often fail the test of the newly gendered criteria. Men are now often perceived to have difficulty forming and maintaining *real* friendships (Inman, 1996).

Just how different are the adult friendships of women and men? Although some researchers have concluded that there are large and pervasive gender differences in friendship patterns (Fehr, 1996), others tend to emphasize similarities. For example, both genders equally value trust and authenticity in friendships. Also, women and men appear to have similar friendship ideals. These include communication, intimacy, trust, and interpersonal sensitivity. In deeper, long-standing friendships, any differences between the genders substantially decline (Wright, 1998). Nevertheless, writers continue to describe men's preference for "side by side" relationships and to contrast that with women's preferences for "face to face" friendships (Wright, 1982). Women's friendships tend to emphasize reciprocity, whereas men's emphasize agreement and similarity. Men's friendships tend to be associative rather than reciprocal. Whereas women more often have complex and holistic friendships, men more typically have focused and circumscribed friendships with special-purpose partners, a "fishing buddy," or a "work buddy," and so on (Wright, 1998). Could adult friendships really constitute a case of stereotype accuracy? An interview study revealed that when women and men describe the general qualities of their friendships, their responses reflected the popular gender-related stereotypes described here. However, when they were asked what went on within their actual friendships, a different picture emerged. Men often self-disclosed and shared intimately, whereas women often pursued specific activities with specific friends (Walker, 1998). Thus there may be few differences in the actual friendships of women and men.

Other Gender-Related Characteristics of Adult Friendships. Friendship patterns change over the life span. Newlyweds have the largest number of friends. Among young adults, friendships overlap with work and parenting. Younger women have more friends than do women in their 40s. Women in their 50s tend to have a smaller but much closer group of friends. As they grow older, men have fewer friends. In old age, 12% of women and 24% of men report having no close friends (Hartup & Stevens, 1999).

Poorer individuals are more likely to mix friendship and kin relationships. Among working-class African-Americans, friendships are part of the extended family (O'Connor, 1992). In contrast to Anglos, Chicanas depend more on their families and less on friends for social support. Women's friendships are much less likely to cross language and ethnic boundaries than do those of men (Houston, 1994).

Over time, the intimacy level of men's long-term friendships comes to resemble those of women. However, there is comparatively little research on men's friendships, and even less on friendships among minority group men. The few studies of African-American male friendship tend to emphasize negative and antisocial behavior (for example, see Majors & Billson, 1992; Oliver, 1994).

Lesbian friendships are distinctive because deep and long-lasting friendships are often maintained with former sexual/romantic partners. Lesbians place a very high value on friendships, and the friendship aspect of romantic relationships is especially valued (Rose, Zand, & Cini, 1994). Friendship groups are also important in the gay male community (Nardi, 1992).

Cross-Sex Friendships

Recent social changes have led to more instances of women and men meeting as equals in more situations. There is evidence that this has resulted in an increase in cross-sex friendships. One hundred percent of male undergraduates and 70% of female undergraduates recently claimed one cross-sex relationship (Werking, 1997). Until recently, such friendships were considered trivial and anomalous because they tended to be fluid and undefined. This society continues to devalue cross-sex friendships and to emphasize same-sex friendship, heterosexual love, and sexual relationships (Werking, 1997). Often cross-sex friendships happen by default, such as when a romantic relationship fails or sexual attraction is unreciprocated (Rose, 1995). The cross-sex relationship mixes the elements of same-sex friendships (voluntary association without a sexual relationship) with those of heterosexual relationships. Cross-sex friends often have the role of tutor or informant who translates one gender's perspective to the other (Parker & deVries, 1993).

For women, the benefits of cross-sex friendships include knowing how men think; enjoyment of the less intense, activity orientation of men; and access to men's greater resources and status. Compared to men, women appear to have a more ambivalent view of their cross-sex relationships and are less likely to name a man as close friend (Rose, 1995).

For men, the benefits of cross-sex friendships include the relief from the hierarchy and rivalry of male friendships, along with more nurturing and emotional support (McWilliams & Howard, 1993). Cross-sex friendships appear more emotionally satisfying for men than for women (Werking, 1997). Unconventional men are more at ease in cross-sex friendships (Rose, 1995). Take a look at Box 6.2 to learn about an interesting Japanese custom that recognizes cross-sex relationships in quite another context.

ZOOM & ENLARGE   **BOX 6.2**

Gender, Global Capitalism, and the Meaning of Chocolate

In the United States, the public recognition of many relationships serves primarily to sell products. Mother's Day, Father's Day, Secretary's Day, Boss's Day, and so on all require cards and gifts. Valentine's Day represents a commercialization of romantic and marital relationships. The social prescription is for men to give gifts and cards to their romantic and marital partners. The cost of the gifts and what is written in the cards is interpreted as a sign of the importance of the relationship to the giver.

Japan has imported the thoroughly American notion of Valentine's Day along with its rampant commercialism. However, the Japanese have adapted Valen-tine's Day to express their own cultural messages about gender and important relationships.

For the Japanese, only chocolate is appropriate on Valentine's Day. Moreover, *only women may give chocolates to men,* and romance has nothing to do with it. These gifts of chocolate are given within offices, usually from women subordinates to male co-workers and supervisors. It is unclear how the American custom was transformed into women giving their male office mates and supervisors heart-shaped chocolates.

Valentine's Day is a touchy subject for Japanese men. It is not a joyous occasion, because it makes men vulnerable to women's evaluations. The number of chocolates a man receives is a measure of his popularity and worthiness, and this becomes public on Valentine's Day. Some men are demeaned by receiving only a few "obligatory" chocolates, whereas other men are exalted by receiving chocolates from large numbers of women. Accompanying messages such as "I admire you" or "I feel grateful to you" are especially treasured.

Source: Y. Ogasawara (1996). Meanings of chocolate: Power and gender in Valentine's gift giving, *International Journal of Japanese Sociology, 5,* 41–61.

Gender, Culture, and Courtship

The distinctions between more **collectivistic** versus more **individualistic** societies becomes very salient when it comes to marriage partner selection (Dion & Dion, 1993a). In collectivistic societies, a potential marriage represents the continuation of a family. Thus marriages must be carefully arranged to satisfy the needs and wishes of ancestors, parents, relatives, and the community. In more individualistic societies, we think of two individuals joining together to form a new family. In individualistic societies, the prescribed sequence is characterized by varying degrees of public announcement and ritual as the pair moves from a voluntary and impermanent relationship to one of obligation and permanence (at least, ideally). That is, the heterosexual pair goes from dating, to going steady (among adolescents), to going together (usually implying monogamy), to engagement, to marriage or cohabitation, to reproduction, and to "live happily ever after" (again, ideally). The masculine role requires men to formally initiate these various transitions. These social forms are based on masculine power, but in modern societies this power differential erodes over time. However, men continue to perceive themselves as generally having more power in heterosexual relationships (Sprecher & Felmlee, 1997).

Only in individualistic societies are the needs and desires of the members of a potential couple considered paramount in courtship. Romantic love is often characterized by intense feelings, disregard of others' views of the chosen one, and a relatively complete mutual absorption. In collectivistic societies, this would be disruptive. However, Western notions of individual choice and romantic love as the basis for marriage seem to be growing in popularity and acceptance around the world. In general, love marriages seem to result in greater marital satisfaction among women but not for men (Imamoglu & Yasak, 1997; Xiaohe & Whyte, 1990).

Dating and Romantic Relationships

Where mate selection is voluntary and based on personal preference, the courtship process is called *dating.*

---

collectivistic society   Society in which individual goals and needs are subordinated to those of others.

individualistic society   Society in which collective needs and goals are subordinated to those of the individual.

TABLE 6.1   The Dating Ritual: Actual Gendered Dating Scripts for First Date

Women's Script	Men's Script
Groomed and dressed	PICKED UP DATE
Was nervous	Met parents/roommate
Was picked up	TOOK DATE AWAY
INTRODUCED TO PARENTS, ETC.	Confirmed plans
Experienced courtly behavior (open doors, etc.)	Talked, joked, laughed
Taken away by date	Went to movies, show, or party
Confirmed plans	ATE AND PAID FOR MEAL
Got to know and evaluate date	OFFERED AND DRANK ALCOHOL
Talked, joked, and laughed	INITIATED SEXUAL CONTACT
Enjoyed date	Made out
Went to movies, show, or party selected by date	TOOK DATE HOME
Ate (Date paid)	ASKED FOR ANOTHER DATE
Drank alcohol	KISSED GOODNIGHT
Was asked for another date	Went home
Was told date will call again	
Accepted goodnight kiss	

Note: Italicized items refer to passive responses. Capital letters refer to active or initiating activities.
Source: Adapted from S. Rose & I. H. Frieze (1993). Young singles' contemporary dating scripts, *Sex Roles, 28,* 499–509.

However, contemporary dating has many purposes other than mate selection. These purposes include recreation, sociability, companionship, sexual activity, and status. Men are much more likely to date and to have multiple dating partners than are women. Although there is a tendency to believe that our choices in selecting dating partners or potential mates are limitless, in actuality the overriding principle remains **homogamy.**

Dating constitutes a highly gendered ritual. An examination of **dating scripts** among mainly white undergraduates in the United States revealed rather gender-typed scripts, with masculine scripts being proactive and feminine scripts being reactive (Rose & Frieze, 1993). Men have more power in initial dating situation, and women see their actions as very dependent on men's actions (see Table 6.1). Interactions, particularly first and early dates, are based on well-learned gender rituals (Alksnis, Desmarais, & Wood, 1996). Many college students are aware of the gender rituals associated with dating and may consciously seek to reject them. In one study of actual dating conversations, college men emphasized their cooking abilities, whereas women emphasized their achievement orientation (deWeerth & Kalma, 1995).

Regardless of gender, the criteria for a good date are the same (see Table 6.2). A good date is fun, easy to talk with, humorous, and not too serious. Early on, physical attractiveness is important for both participants. However, over time, the **matching principle** prevails.

When a dating relationship becomes a potential mate selection process, both women and men want a mate who is a good companion, affectionate, kind, considerate, loving, dependable, understanding, loyal, interesting to talk with, and honest, and who has a good sense of humor (Sedikides, Oliver, & Campbell, 1994). Women tend to be more practical about love, whereas men are generally more idealistic and romantic (Bierhoff, 1996). In general, people who display

homogamy   Partner similarity regarding age, ethnicity, religion, socioeconomic status (SES), appearance, intelligence, political attitudes, and so on.

dating script   A cognitive model used to guide and evaluate social interactions in dating events. Scripts are comprised of a coherent and expected sequence of events.

matching principle   The rule that lasting dyads (friends, spouses, and so on) tend to be at similar levels for factors such as physical attractiveness, personality traits, and social assets.

TABLE 6.2   Date Events or Components Rated Good, Bad, or Typical

Item	Good		Bad		Typical	
	M	**F**	**M**	**F**	**M**	**F**
Date makes sexual advances too early.				●		
Date repeatedly tells you how sexy you look.	●	●		●	●	
Date kisses you.	●	●			●	●
Date rejects your sexual advances.			●	●		
Date stares at you.	●	●		●	●	●
Date makes an effort to sit close to you.	●	●			●	●
Date leans in close to you whenever you are sitting together.	●	●		●	●	●
Date repeatedly touches you.	●	●		●	●	●
Date and you each pay for yourself.		●	●	●	●	●
Date pays for everything.		●				●
Date and you have similar interests.	●	●			●	●
Date smiles at you a lot.	●	●			●	●
Date holds your hand.	●	●			●	●
Date hugs you.	●	●			●	●
Date makes you laugh.	●	●			●	●
Date compliments you.	●	●			●	●
Date talks about his/her previous girl/boyfriend.			●	●		
Date does not talk very much.			●	●		
Date listens when you talk about yourself.	●	●			●	●

Note: Date events evaluated as good, bad, and typical by more than 25% of a sample of white college students. *Source:* Adapted from C. Alksnis, S. Desmarais, & E. Wood (1996). Gender differences in scripts for different types of dates. *Sex Roles, 34*(5/6), 332.

traditional masculinity and femininity are seen as very attractive dating partners. However, marital matches between such individuals tend to be low in interpersonal satisfaction, particularly for women. Androgynous individuals and more feminine-typed individuals are better romantic partners. One researcher concluded that "happiness is a feminine marriage partner" (Ickes, 1993, p. 74).

Critical Thinking Challenge

Why does it make sense that those who "possess" or who are more able to "do" traditional femininity would be better marriage partners?

Cohabitation. Living together before, or without marriage represents another level of commitment in heterosexual relationships. Decision making, communication, and satisfaction do not seem to vary from that of married couples. However, compared to married couples, a more egalitarian sharing of household chores seems to prevail.

Among lesbian couples, living together is more likely to have a marital meaning. This is less true among gay men (Murphy, 1997). Same-sex marriages remain quite controversial in our society. Except for the state of Vermont, which now recognizes domestic partnerships, cohabitation is the only option available to committed gay and lesbian couples. Since 1995, 36 states have passed laws prohibiting same-sex marriages (Lambda Legal Defense and Education Fund, 2001). However, Holland and some Scandinavian countries recognize registered partnerships (Deutsch, 2001a). Australia is also considering this possibility (Kendall, Leishman, Rogerson, & Walker, 2000).

Romantic Relationships Among Sexual Minorities

Contrary to popular stereotypes, lesbians and gay men are just as likely as heterosexuals to be coupled (Laird, 1993). Whatever the difficulties for heterosexual couples in establishing and maintaining a lasting love relationship, gay men and lesbians must do so without recognizable or socially acceptable models (Murphy, 1997). In Western society, those with a same-sex orientation are usually defined solely in terms of their sexual behavior, but it is important to recognize that all people go through the same human process of initial attraction, mutual selection, and interpersonal negotiation to establish and maintain more long-term relationships. Because they are socialized within the same society as heterosexual individuals, gay men and lesbians also value and idealize romantic love as a basis for more long-term partnering. However, gay men and lesbians cannot rely on traditional gender role prescriptions or expectations to guide them (Rutter & Schwartz, 1996).

Most lesbians meet each other within their wider social acquaintances. In contrast to gay men, lesbians are more likely to have a short period of more or less conventional dating before sexualizing their relationship. Gay men are more likely to meet in public situations such as organizations or bars. Although the AIDS epidemic has changed attitudes regarding casual sex considerably, a date between gay men is more likely to include sex. The level of commitment is developed later, over time (Scrivner, 1997).

A Global Perspective on Partner Selection. Across societies, some factors seem more or less universal in mate selection. Men consider youth and physical attractiveness in women very important. Women seem to prefer men who are physically adept, intelligent, and ambitious, and who have the potential to acquire resources. Such preferences have been documented across societies as distinct as the United States, Japan, and Russia (Hatfield & Sprecher, 1995). Some researchers offer an evolution-based explanation for this phenomenon, claiming that men seek those features in women that are associated with reproductive success (youth, health, symmetric faces, and so on). Women place greater importance on characteristics that predict greater well-being for her offspring, namely male wealth and status (Buss, 1994). A more sociocultural explanation would emphasize that an attractive partner gains a man status among other men. Accordingly, women's preferences are also understandable because they usually cannot obtain resources through their own efforts and abilities. Marriage to a wealthier man was the only hope for their children. A recent archival study across 37 cultures found that women strongly prefer mates who can acquire resources *only* when they live in societies with little or no educational or reproductive freedom for women (Kasser & Sharma, 1999).

The Marital Relationship

The idea of a man and a woman meeting, falling in love and then choosing to combine their lives permanently via a public ceremony is a powerful image in Western society. This idealized image is endlessly repeated in the media, literature, folktales, and art. Let's begin exploring gender and marriage by noting that in the two most populated nations of the world (India and China), arranged marriages are still the rule, rather than the exception.

The Arranged Marriage

Among most Asian groups, a potential marriage implies the continuation of the man's family line (Conway-Turner & Cherrin, 1998; Yee et al., 1998). Thus Chinese and Nepalese girls are raised with the knowledge that they will eventually leave their families of origin. In childhood, she must prepare herself for her future status as a lowly household member and eternal "outsider" in her future husband's family. The daughter-in-law role takes lifelong precedence over that of wife, and these traditions continue in some Chinese-American families (Hamilton, 1996). To learn more about diversity among Asian-American families, take a look at Box 6.3.

Even today in rural north India, girls are raised as temporary residents in their parents' homes and are prepared for lifelong residence elsewhere. Girls are trained to be demure, undemanding, and respectful of the decisions made for them. Such socialization helps to ensure a better fit into her in-laws' household. Formal education for girls is viewed as a way to attract a more educated husband rather than as preparation for employment. Among Indian Muslims, a boy's parents arrange marriages, whereas among Hindus a girl's parents do so. Brides are under the control and tutelage of the mother-in-law. A daughter-in-law's status in the family rises if she has sons. She can then look forward to someday being a powerful mother-in-law herself. Although it is easy to assume that complete passivity and acceptance characterize these young women, they actually have a long tradition of resistance and refusal, as well as a large repertoire of well-known obscene songs about in-laws (Jeffrey & Jeffrey, 1996).

The Love Marriage

Beginning in the 18th century, physical attraction and romantic love became the idealized basis for marriage in the West (Coltrane, 1998a; Mintz, 1998). In white, middle-class marriages, a gender-based social *asymmetry* is also prescribed. That is, a husband is typically older, taller, more well educated, and wealthier (at least potentially). African Americans traditionally based marriages almost solely on attraction and affection, because masculine resource acquisition was very difficult. Both women and men were forced to support a family by lifelong physical drudgery.

The African-American Marriage: Past and Present

It is impossible to understand contemporary marital patterns in the African-American community without understanding the history of Africans in the Western Hemisphere. Most Africans abducted into slavery were taken from West African societies in which women had a tradition of relative economic independence. However, a woman's *brother* had the greatest authority over her life. Marriage was utilitarian, driven by economics, and designed to continue family traditions and wealth.

Under American slavery, slaves could pick their own mates but had to ask "massah's" permission to marry. A typical slave marriage ceremony consisted of the couple jumping over a broom three times. Such marriages had absolutely no social or legal standing and a slaveholder could sell off any adult or child as he wished. Thus a slave family was defined by blood ties, not by marriage (Sudarkasa, 1999). Adult men were known in terms of their mates, for example, "Mary's Jim." Large numbers of children were born from the rape of slave women. For example, in Virginia in the early 1800s 20% of the children born outside of partnerships were classified as *mulatto* (D'Emilio & Freedman, 1988). Slave couples understood that their remaining together depended totally on a master's economic success and goodwill. When the overseas slave trade was outlawed in 1807, some

slave women were designated as "breeders" to increase their masters' wealth (Gutman, 1976). Under slavery, the father role was completely obliterated. He was neither "patriarch, provider, nor protector." He remained a "boy" in adulthood and became an "uncle" in old age (Staples & Johnson, 1993).

Immediately after emancipation, large numbers of African Americans combed the nation, searching for their spouses and children. Impoverished couples struggled to come up with the fees needed to legalize their marriages (Franklin, 1998). Because few black men could support a wife and children, marital relationships continued to be based on personal preference and affection rather than on economic hierarchy. African-American women were *always* in the dual role of full-time worker and mother. Basically, only three jobs were available for the African-American woman: domestic worker, laundress, and field-worker. As a domestic worker, she typically cared for two entire households and families. As laundress or field hand, she engaged in the same physical labor as her husband. Early in the 20th century, there was large-scale black migration from rural areas to cities in order to secure jobs. Whereas many black men had family traditions of skilled trade work (bricklaying, carpentry, and so on), white unionization forced black men out of these skilled trades. African-American families were crowded into decaying urban ghettoes, with rampant crime, unemployment, and poverty. Segregation and other forms of overt racism deprived African Americans of education, health, and economic opportunity. Low-paid work was available for women, and many became the primary providers for their families. Nonetheless, male-present, dual-worker families were the African-American norm until about 1925. Up until the 1960s, 75% of African-American households included both husband and wife (Franklin, 1998).

Mainstream white notions of female subordination and male domination have never applied to African-American families. Today most black marriages involve greater female autonomy, economic parity, individualism, role sharing, and mutual decision making (McAdoo, 1997a). This group marries less than other ethnic groups in the United States (Farrell, 1999). The lack of available men is a central factor. Among poor African Americans, large numbers of young men are the victims of violence. Many are incarcerated,

SLIDE SHOW   **BOX 6.3**

The Asian-American Family

During the 19th century, large numbers of Chinese men and smaller numbers of Japanese men were brought to the United States for mining and railroad work. A small number of Chinese women were allowed into the country to serve as prostitutes for those laborers. Discriminatory laws then essentially cut off Asian immigration. The Immigration Acts of 1965 and 1990 abolished these discriminatory policies. In 1960, Asians constituted only 9% of all immigrants, but this had increased to 44% by 1980 (Min, 1995a). There are now approximately 12 million Asian-Americans, and 66% are foreign born (U.S. Bureau of the Census, 1996). The children of Asian immigrants demonstrate the highest interethnic marriage rates (Mok, 1999). About 34% of Asian men and 40% of Asian women marry interethnically in North America (Lott, 1997; Root, 1998). In Hawaii, about 75% of Chinese immigrants marry interethnically. In dealing with issues of gender among Asian-Americans, we must recognize the great diversity of Asian societies. Thus we can here only glimpse marital and family relationships within these groups.

Native Hawaiians: The oldest woman presided over the traditional Hawaiian extended family, and she had great authority in maintaining harmony within it. A long-held tradition was to give one child to grandparents or to a childless female relative. It was believed that grandparents' lives would be incomplete without a child to rear. The most important goals in child rearing were affiliation, cooperation, and interdependence. A person was considered mature only when he or she could accurately perceive and attend to another's needs (Yee et al., 1998).

Japanese-Americans: Most Japanese-Americans have been born in the United States. The desire to escape patriarchal traditions and overbearing mothers-in-law are often given as reasons for the high interethnic marriage rate among *Nisei* and *Sansei* women (second- and third/fourth-generation Japanese-Americans) (Fong & Yung, 1995/1996). In traditional Japanese society, a woman is a full person only after birthing a child (Hara & Minagawa, 1996). Many Japanese-American families continue to feel conflict about American dating rituals (Elliot, 1996).

Filipino-Americans: Filipino-American families often offer a startling contrast to the Asian stereotype of patriarchy and female subordination. Filipino culture represents a blending of Asian, Spanish, and American traditions. Family ties and support are extremely important, and lineage is traced through the mother's line (a Spanish tradition), although property and wealth pass through the father's line. Love marriages are preceded by a formal courtship period, and households are often comprised of bilateral extended families. A majority of Filipino-American women have always been employed for pay, and they have central responsibility for family finances. Gender roles are quite egalitarian within the privacy of the home, but **machismo** and **marianismo** sometimes characterize public presentations (Dube, 1997). About 27% of Filipino-American women have college degrees. Intermarriages with non-Filipinos are very common. There is a visible Filipino-American gay and lesbian community (Manalansan, 1997).

Korean-Americans: More than 80% of Korean-American women are employed full time, yet there is low acceptance of this role. All housework and child care remain a wife's responsibility (Kim & Kim, 1995). A shortage of men has led many women to seek husbands in Korea, and this has contributed to gender role-related conflicts and family disharmony. Divorce rates are rising among Korean-American families. There is great pressure for sons to marry Korean women because

---

unemployed, or involved in chemical abuse (Chapman, 1997). Among middle-class black families, the rate of college-educated women to college-educated men is 2:1, and that too reduces the pool of marriageable men (Staples & Johnson, 1993). Moreover, black marriages are more likely to end in divorce than those of whites or Latinos. This helps us understand why some African-American women may have children with different fathers. Do you recall this chapter's opening vignette? The mystery surrounding Andrew Smith, his mother, and his sister, Saundra Johnson is easily solved. Andrew Smith's mother may have a different last name from any of her children (Staples & Johnson, 1993). For a teacher in an urban African-American community, it's wise not to presume the

---

machismo **Cultural tradition of male dominance, particularly in matters of sexuality and family. Men seen as entitled to authority and privilege. Associated with Latino culture.**

marianismo **Cultural tradition of female spiritual superiority and ability to endure suffering and self-sacrifice (Comas-Diaz, 1987). Associated with Latino culture.**

they must continue the family lineage. There is less concern about out-marriages for daughters (Min, 1995b).

Chinese Americans: The traditional Chinese household is organized according to Confucian principles, with father as undisputed head who deserves respect and loyalty, and women at the bottom of the hierarchy. The parent–child bond is more important than the marital bond. Traditional Chinese fathers are distant, aloof, and uninvolved with children. Mothers serve the father and intercede with him for the children. The first son is the most valued child, and his sense of filial piety is the most important goal of childhood socialization. A woman's role as daughter-in-law takes precedence over that of wife or mother (Hamilton, 1996). Fathering a first grandson raises the status of a son. Divorce rates among Chinese Americans are low but rising (Wong, 1995). The vast majority of Chinese-American women are employed, and often their superior earnings disrupt the traditional hierarchy, making conflict common. In a culture that emphasizes indirect communication and proscribes emotional expression, open discussion and renegotiation of roles can be problematic (Gao & Ting-Toomey, 1998).

Among Hong Kong Chinese immigrants, wives and children often remain in the United States, whereas husbands travel for long periods of time. Such husbands are called *astronauts*. Wives adapt as heads of households and become thoroughly acculturated to American life. They become accustomed to making unilateral decisions and disciplining their children. When their husbands return, there is often difficulty in shifting to more traditional, patriarchal ways of relating (Root, 1998).

Vietnamese Americans: At the end of the Vietnamese War, half a million South Vietnamese were abruptly evacuated from their native homeland and flown to the United States. They were followed by thousands of refugees who survived incredible hardships in their journey to North America. These traumatic circumstances have had a tremendous impact on marriage and family arrangements. Traditionally, a father's power was absolute, and a wife's status was below that of pets. Physical punishment for children and wives was common. Such authoritarian parenting has led to rebellion among Vietnamese-American youth (Dinh, Sarason, & Sarason, 1994). Among the first wave of evacuees, men were typically educated and had middle-class status. Once in the United States, the cultural shock was overwhelming. Men accustomed to power were now powerless and reduced to doing low-level menial labor at minimum wage. In contrast, their formerly home-bound and field-bound wives were now employed, and they experienced a substantial rise in status and resources. The uneven sex ratio (more men) also increased women's power. Friendship ties among Vietnamese-American women are formidable (Kibria, 1993).

Hmong-Americans: The Hmong were a tribal group living in the remote mountains of Laos. They offered vital assistance to the American military during the Vietnam War. With American loss and withdrawal, promises of land and other resources could not be kept, and over 100,000 Hmong were abruptly airlifted to California, Texas, Wisconsin, and Minnesota. Traditions of large families and early marriage continue, so that half of Hmong high school women in St. Paul, Minnesota, are usually married by their senior year. However, most remain in school. There is significant generational and cultural conflict among the Hmong-American families (Hutchinson & McNall, 1994).

white middle-class norm of a woman and her children all having one man's last name.

In the 1960s, writings regarding black mothers were quite negative. African-American mothers were blamed for encouraging docility *and* aggression, low achievement *and* unrealistic ambition in their sons, and for overfavoring their daughters. However, African-American parents did their very best to prepare their children for life in a racist society. Although white middle-class parents had the privilege of stressing self-direction and individuality in their children, poor black mothers knew that obedience, conformity, and respect for authority would help their children survive. For example, these values work well in a structured military setting, and military service has been a major avenue out of poverty and unemployment for African Americans (Staples & Johnson, 1993). The social, educational, and economic status of African Americans has improved considerably over the last two decades, but racism still limits opportunities. Racism also increases distress levels (Cose, 1999; Sellers, 2001).

The Nation of Islam holds that men have a natural right to act as overseers of women. Husbands must have "something above and beyond" a wife for her to look to him for psychological security. Yet Malcolm X had a close, mutually dependent relationship with his wife. After breaking with the Black Muslims, Malcolm X advocated for equal rights for Muslim women (Cone, 1991).

The Mainstream North American Marriage

Marriage in North American white mainstream culture was originally an economic and social arrangement based on a gendered division of the labor needed for survival. Legally and economically, a woman moved from being her father's property to that of being her husband's property. She had no legal rights, could not make contracts, inherit property, manage her own finances, or even have custody of her children if a divorce occurred.

Critical Thinking Challenge

In the traditional marriage ceremony, a father "gives the bride away" to another man. Her father's name is exchanged for that of her husband. The bride's family typically pays for the wedding celebration (should this be considered a bride price?). What other elements of the marriage ceremony are remnants of former gender statuses?

Instead of arranged marriages, Europeans and Americans fell in love and voluntarily bound themselves to each other (Stacey, 1996). Although romantic love is recognized in most human societies, it was not typically considered a suitable basis for marriage (Jankowiak & Fischer, 1999). During the 19th century, the Industrial Revolution forced families from farms to cities, so the network of kin was left behind. Men and older children (regardless of gender) left home each morning for a long day of backbreaking factory labor. Married women stayed at home to care for their several surviving children. Thus industrialization created the nuclear family among whites, with father as primary breadwinner and mother as economically dependent homemaker with children. Among middle-class families the "cult of true womanhood" celebrated domesticity, morality, and maternity. The doctrine of the "self-made man" encouraged

men to total devotion to work and material acquisition (Kimmel, 1996a). These two became complementary, and thus the doctrine of "separate spheres" became dominant among the middle and upper classes (Welter, 1978). Ideally, wives were confined at home, and husbands confined at the workplace. Although the remnants of these 19th-century notions linger today, massive socioeconomic and cultural upheaval has changed many of the central features of marriage and families (Staggenborg, 1998). Some call for more change, whereas others are frightened by the changes.

Letitia Peplau's classic classification of types of marriages based on gender roles still resounds today (Peplau & Campbell, 1989). In the traditional marriage, the husband is dominant because he controls resources. A wife and children are completely economically and socially dependent on a husband. She is responsible for all housework and child care. She makes decisions regarding housework and children, but he has ultimate authority in all matters. Thus all power, authority, and decision making on important issues flow from husband *down* to wife and children. Members of such couples typically have separate interests and leisure activities. These marriages are increasingly rare today.

In the modern marriage, a husband is less dominant. Although both idealize the notion of equal power, the husband has more power. His job and career decisions are central considerations. A husband encourages his wife's employment or education, but it is of secondary importance. Housework is divided into masculine and feminine tasks. He "helps" with child care, particularly by playing with the children. There is a strong emphasis on compatibility and shared leisure activities.

In the egalitarian marriage, there is equal power with minimal gender-typed roles. There is essentially equal income, housekeeping, child care, financial power, and decision making. A strong emphasis on companionship and sharing prevails. Such marriages thrive when the partners have similar attitudes regarding sex, child rearing, and lifestyle choices. Similar values regarding money, religious participation, and political views also help reduce conflicts. However, in the egalitarian marriage, all choices must be negotiated, so conflicts are inevitable. Gender is even a salient factor in how conflicts are processed. In keeping with gender roles and expectations, women are typically the emotional monitors of marital relationships. Wives are usually the ones to "bring up problems." Men are more likely to deny or avoid such discussions. When conflicts arise, men are more likely to avoid or withdraw. Women tend to defer in public but confront in private (Gottman & Carriere, 1994).

Critical Thinking Challenge

With all this discussion of marriage, we should take a moment to acknowledge the differential evaluations placed on those who do not marry. What are the stereotypes associated with the bachelor versus the spinster?

Forces for Gender Role Change

After World War II, several interacting forces led to the massive social changes continuing today. During wartime, large numbers of men were killed, separated from their families, and traumatized by the death and destruction they experienced. During that same war, large numbers of women in North America, of all ethnicities, held well-paying skilled jobs in the workforce. Other women were separated from their families as they too took on a variety of military roles. After the war, family relationships took on a new meaning. Women were forced to leave their wartime jobs. Family life became compelling for men, and middle-class women derived self-esteem from their roles as full-time homemakers and mothers (Weiss, 1998). The isolation that accompanied white flight to the suburbs and the new emphasis on *togetherness* further amplified these trends. At the same time, there was a growing tension between these domestic ideals and societal values of individuality and personal achievement. Waves of social change ensued, and these are now of global proportions. These forces cannot be ranked in order of influence or importance, so I will just list them and comment briefly about their impact on gender and family relationships.

◆ Increasing industrialization and urbanization meant that the large families required for farm labor were no longer practical. The birth rate declined, and two children became the norm in industrialized nations. It is interesting to note that Italy and Spain, both strongly family-oriented so-

cieties, now have Europe's lowest birth rates (Conway-Turner & Cherrin, 1998).

◆ Men became sole breadwinners but long hours and long commutes meant they had much less time at home with families (Stacey, 1996). In modern Japan, the normative middle-class "professional housewife" has little time with her "salaryman" husband who works long hours far from home (Dion & Dion, 1993b).

◆ New kinds of better-paying jobs demanded more years of education and more training, and so the trend toward later marriage became normalized.

◆ With the development of effective oral contraceptives women for the *first time in human history* could have intercourse without the constant fear of pregnancy. Thus, a basic feature of the heterosexual relationship was changed forever, and women's dependency on men was even further weakened.

◆ The social meaning that was attached to middle-class women's employment changed. A wife's employment moved from signifying a husband's financial inadequacy to symbolizing the pursuit of a better life for their children. Pressure increased to expand the limited employment options (teaching and nursing) for the growing numbers of educated women. It became clear that women enjoyed well-paying jobs and their children benefited from the enrichment that greater affluence permitted (Staggenborg, 1998). Today, full-time employment for married women ranges from about 70% in the United States to 86% in Sweden (Hirdman, 1998). All over the world, the gender gap in wage levels persists.

◆ A new ideal of companionate marriage emerged, and this also encouraged men's involvement in housework and child rearing (Pleck, 1981a).

◆ Of course, many new social problems emerged, too. In keeping with a long sociological and psychological tradition of mother-blaming, the cause of these problems was laid squarely on all those working mothers (Ladd-Taylor & Umanski, 1998). Employed mothers are blamed for crime, violence, declining educational standards, poverty, drug abuse, and STDs. Only recently have traditional patterns of *paternal* noninvolvement and absence come under scrutiny. Focus has shifted from the negative effects of mother absence to concerns about father absence.

SLIDE SHOW   BOX 6.4

Some Graphic Demographics

Here are some intriguing samples of information about the state of love and family relationships in the United States.

- Compared to 1970, eight times as many couples cohabited in 1997. About 36% of those couples have children younger than 15 living with them. This figure does not include gay and lesbian couples (U.S. Bureau of the Census, 1998).
- The median age at first marriage continues to rise.

	1970	1997
Women	20.8	25.0
Men	23.2	26.8

- Nearly 35% of adults between ages 25 and 34 in the United States have never been married. Among African Americans, the number is 54%.
- Almost 28% of children below age 18 are living with one parent. About 85% of such children live with their mothers.
- Forty percent of these children live with a mother who was never married (Vobejda, 1998).
- More than 50% of mothers with a child younger than 1 was working at least part time in 1990 (Cowan & Cowan, 1998).
- Each year, telephone companies report that the greatest number of calls on a single day are made on Mother's Day. The volume of telephone calls on Father's Day is indistinguishable from any other Sunday. However, the greatest number of *collect* calls are made on Father's Day (Mintz, 1998).

Gender, Culture, and the Postindustrial Family

Some proclaim that the family is close to total destruction in our postindustrial society. It seems more accurate to say that family roles are in a *state of transformation*. Although many still find it difficult to visualize a family as being other than the nuclear family of the 1950s, it is clear that at the moment, no single family pattern is statistically dominant. Box 6.4 offers some statistical images of today's family demographics. Moreover, domestic arrangements are increasingly diverse, particularly in Scandinavia and North America (Cowan & Cowan, 1998). For example, in Sweden and Denmark about 50% of children are born to unmarried women or couples (Jandt, 1998). These Nordic societies have responded to changes in familial gender roles in rather different ways. In Norway and Sweden, *both* parents are entitled to one year's leave at 90% of salary (although few fathers take advantage of this). Scandinavian workers get health care, reproductive services, subsidized day care, and paid sick leave to care for children (Hojgaard, 1998). Only 2% of Swedish single-parent families live below the poverty level compared to more than 50% in the United States. Among the top 18 industrialized nations, the

United States is alone in not offering universal health coverage, family allowances, or paid parental leave. The Family Leave Act of 1993 permits unpaid three-month maternity leave, but few families can afford it, and the policy applies only to firms with 50+ employees. In Canada, a parent may receive 57% of regular salary for 15 weeks (England, 1996). Although the Scandinavian model may not fit American society, it is important to see that there are other ways of thinking about gender roles and family responsibilities.

Child Care and Housework

The two main areas of family work are child care and housework, and these are the traditional domains of women (Blair & Lichter, 1991). No matter the technique of measurement, wives do most or all of the unpaid family work (see Figure 6.1). For employed women, this necessitates a second shift or double work day and this often produces the "drudge wife" (Brush, 1999). Only about 20% of men in dual-worker families in the United States share equally in household and child care responsibilities. Some researchers insist that our society is in the midst of a stalled revolution in that there is a clear and irreversible change in

FIGURE 6.1   This cartoonist makes a humorous but telling comment on contemporary family roles and patterns.

women's roles, but little change in men's roles (Walzer, 1998). The happiest of today's co-provider families are those in which men share equally in family tasks and feel positively about this (F. M. Deutsch, 2001). Men are more likely to participate fully in these tasks if their own mothers were employed or if they did household chores as children. For men, truly shared parenting provides self-esteem, emotional sustenance, and marital peace (Gerson, 1997).

Infant care is still primarily a mother's job, even in egalitarian marriages. In most dual-career marriages fathers still merely assist and participate rather than share in child care responsibilities (Walzer, 1998). A father's caretaking is often limited to recreational activities, such as reading to children, playing with them, or teaching them specific skills (Shulman & Seiffge-Krenke, 1997). Lest we form images of martyrlike women and indifferent men, we should note that often the mother role is such a central part of feminine identity that some women may have considerable difficulty in truly sharing that role with a spouse. The research suggests that a man will participate more fully in child care and housework when incomes are about equal, when there is a clear need for him to do so, and when both parents have more egalitarian gender role attitudes (F. M. Deutsch, 1999, 2001; Gilbert, 1998).

The Father Role

Traditional psychological and sociological research, theory and practice have both reflected and reinforced the assumption that parenting is mother's work (Endicott, 1992). Fathers were typically portrayed as minor figures: ineffective, incompetent, and perhaps biologically unsuited for child rearing. After decades of neglect and omission, the contemporary understanding of fatherhood is being informed by several new ideas.

First, the social construction of fatherhood varies by historical period and by culture. No universal aspect of fathering has yet been demonstrated. Although no father can bear or breastfeed an infant, father roles in various societies reveal a range of possibilities. Some fathers go through a painful symbolic childbirth with their mates, and others may have almost constant care of infants. In some societies, men are merely occasional playmates and mentors. In still others, fathers are distant and punishing patriarchal authorities (Lupton & Barclay, 1997; Queen & Haberstein, 1967).

Second, in North American society fathers play complex, multidimensional roles. These roles include that of companion, care provider, spouse, protector, moral guide, teacher, and breadwinner. Nonetheless, it still remains that parental roles totally transform a woman's life, but not a man's. In two-parent, dual-earner families, father–child involvement is higher, yet major caretaking responsibility remains with the mother (Walzer, 1998). As parental roles continue to blur, it appears that what is now unique about fathering is a positive emotional relationship that facilitates a child's sense of security, safety, and belonging. This appears much more beneficial than any modeling of traditional masculine skills, traits, or roles (Lamb, 1997a; Rohner, 1998).

Third, it appears that the women's movement and media attention have contributed to a new cultural construction regarding what it is to be a good father. Men in postindustrial societies appear to be gradually incorporating this reconstructed father role into their self-concepts (Dienhart, 1998; Strauss & Goldberg, 1999). However, serious institutional obstacles remain that prevent the new father, from *doing* this reconstructed gender role. Other than personal motivation, the most serious obstacle appears to be work demands that are predicated on the assumption that there is a full-time other to care for children and home. Also, some couples find egalitarian roles threatening. For example, when a sample of blue-collar couples who earned approximately equal incomes on shift work were interviewed, it was clear that they essentially shared equally in both household tasks and child care. Yet they reconciled their nontraditional lives with traditional gender ideology by insisting that, despite overwhelming evidence to the contrary, wives were *helping* with income, whereas husbands were *helping* with housework and child care (Deutsch & Saxon, 1998).

Fourth, the evidence is weak regarding traditional notions that father love predicts specific outcomes in children such as appropriate gender role development, negative behaviors (such as delinquency or substance abuse), or positive behaviors (such as high achievement) (Rohner, 1998).

Recently, attention has shifted from concern about the impact of maternal employment to the negative effects of fatherlessness. Few people would deny the benefits to children of having *at least* two loving adults as caretakers. However, does good parenting involve some essential quality that requires a male, especially a male who is biologically related? Is it true that adoptive parents, single parents, and step-families simply cannot provide an optimal environment for children? Take a look at Box 6.5 to explore the controversies surrounding the biological basis of the father role.

Critical Thinking Challenge

How do the "new biological" arguments about the importance of fathering compare with the "old biological" arguments of the evolutionary psychologists? You may recall that the evolutionary approach emphasizes a father's minimal investment in producing and rearing offspring (Bjorklund & Shackelford, 1999).

The Mother Role

In many cultures, the mother role offers a good illustration of a gender ideal: the idealized image of a mother and child gazing adoringly at each other. Motherhood is a unique experience for women. Continuous infant and child care demand commitment, consistency, patience, empathy, and responsibility, and therefore these characteristics usually come to the fore. The sheer physical work of mothering is often underestimated and unexpected (Kitzinger, 1995). The early months of infant care may involve sleep deprivation, repetitive drudgery, and relative social isolation. There may also be tension between a new mother and a neglected partner, as well as difficulties with other siblings. However, when a child is wanted, women of all ethnicities report the pleasures of connection with this new and amazing creature who was once part of the woman's own body (Bergum, 1997). Women believe their children's daily well-being depends on a mother's caring and concern. Thus, many mothers exist with a constant and special consciousness or awareness of their children. Artists, writers, psychologists, physicians, and many others (traditionally, men) have attempted to describe the experience of mothering. Descriptions of the real experiences of real mothers have only recently come to be valued (see Table 6.3) (Hays, 1996; McMahon, 1995).

In Western societies, the mothering and parenting roles are inextricably bound together, and it is difficult for most of us to separate them. However, this too varies across cultures. For example, in some Asian societies, a broader range of adults is responsible for parenting, particularly grandparents and close family friends (Yee et al., 1998). In mainstream North American society, the mother role is a *choice* among others, including childlessness. Other contemporary choices surrounding voluntary motherhood include fewer children, children at a later time in life, single parenthood, and children with a same-sex partner. However, we should remember that for many women in the world, the time, frequency, and context for motherhood are not matters of choice (McMahon, 1995). We should also recognize that motherhood is not always a revered identity. Terms such as *bastard* and *illegitimate* inform us that the mother role may be valued only in relation to the masculine social identities of father and husband.

BOX 6.5

The Postindustrial Father Role: Controversies and Contentions

In postindustrial societies, widespread social changes such as the economic independence of women, the postponement and overall decline in marriage rates, the rise in voluntary single parenthood, widespread divorce and redivorce, the growing acceptance of gay and lesbian families, and technological innovations such as donor insemination have all brought traditional conceptions of the father role under close re-examination. Some scholars contend these forces have brought about the near-destruction of the father role in the postindustrial family (Biller & Kimpton, 1997; Blankenhorn, 1995; Popenoe, 1996). According to this perspective, both marriage and fatherhood are indispensable for the good of society and children. These writers condemn the emergence of a "culture of nonmarriage" in which the purpose of marriage has shifted from "commitment and obligation to others, especially children, (to) mainly a vehicle for the emotional fulfillment of the adult partners" (Popenoe, 1996, p. 24). Advocates of this viewpoint believe that human males are biologically endowed to be social fathers and to provide resources and protection to mates and offspring. They contend that it is a human universal that biological fathers be identified and

that "fathering is a fundamental part of men's nature" (Popenoe, 1996, p. 165). At the same time, Popenoe notes that men "are not ideally suited biologically to be being the kinds of fathers that societies want them to be," so societies invented marriage to bind fathers to their mates for the care of offspring. Popenoe (1996) believes that optimal fathering can occur only within the structure of a marriage and only with biological offspring. He believes that second-adult households (where a spouse or partner is not biologically related to offspring) cannot provide adequately for children. Popenoe admits that this genetically powered push to father probably lasts only for the first four years of an offspring's life.

Louise Silverstein and Carl Auerbach (1999) offer a rebuttal to what they term a "neoconservative" and "essentialist" perspective on the father role. They fear that idealizing the two-parent heterosexual ideal demeans alternative family forms. Based on their study of 200 men from a variety of subcultures within the United States, these researchers concluded that children need at least one responsible and responsive adult as a consistent caretaker.

A household with more than one such adult provides an even more enriching environment for offspring. However, these authors contend that neither the sex of these adults, nor any biological relationship is a significant predictor of children's optimal development. They agree with Popenoe and others that active involvement with children is preferable and that many men feel disconnected and uninvolved with their children. However, they object to essentialist notions that men are biologically driven to nurture children. Further, they disagree that men will neglect their children unless they are legally and socially bound to a woman and their offspring. Silverstein and Auerbach (1999) believe the problem of paternal neglect will not be solved by forcing women back into traditional patriarchal relationships. They argue it will be better solved by social policies that help both men and women integrate their family and work roles. It can also be solved by a true sharing of household and child care responsibilities. They conclude that this next level of social change can begin with the socialization of sons and brothers to care for children adequately. What do you think?

The traditional psychological literature presents mothers as technical experts who work to produce an independent, achieving, and well-adjusted child (Gerson, Alpert, & Richardson, 1997). Explanations for how mothers do this have ranged from hypothesized natural instincts all the way to a deficit model of mothering that requires the intervention of male experts such as Dr. Benjamin Spock or Dr. T. Berry Brazelton (Thurer, 1994). The myth of the bad mother also persists in traditional psychology. Mother blaming was a central occupation of the traditional literature on developmental psychopathology (Caplan, 1989). For example, "**refrigerator mothers**" were said to cause

autism. Mothers who put their children in emotional **double binds** "caused" schizophrenia. Seductive

---

refrigerator mothers Term for cold mothers, from the since-discredited notion that autism was caused by maternal coldness and indifference.

autism A mental disorder characterized by self-absorption, inability to interact socially, repetitive behavior, and language dysfunction.

double bind According to a since-discredited theory, dysfunctional maternal communications that placed the child in an emotional double bind caused schizophrenia; for example, "A decent human being would never act like that around his loving mother."

TABLE 6.3   Real Mothers and Their Life Experience

Women's Perceptions of the Rewards of Motherhood

Item	Middle Class	Working Class
Watching their children learn and grow	65%	64%
Feeling special connectedness or special relationship with children	65%	54%
Fun or enjoyment being with children	52%	43%
Rediscovering/re-experiencing the world through their children's eyes	35%	11%
Strengthening of other social bonds	23%	12%

Women's Perceptions of the Disadvantages of Motherhood

Item	Middle Class	Working Class
No "worst things"/cannot articulate any	3%	25%
Work or practical demands involved	52%	29%
Problems of time/time pressures	52%	18%
Feelings of responsibility/concerns regarding parenting behavior	45%	46%
Changed pattern of life/constant need for planning and scheduling	35%	43%

Women's Descriptions of the Domestic Division of Child Care in Two-Parent Households

Item	Middle Class	Working Class
Mothers did less than half	4%	0%
Partners shared equally	30%	0%
Mothers did 51% to 60%	26%	18%
Mothers did 61% to 70%	15%	35%
Mothers did 71% to 80%	22%	23%
Mothers did 81% to 90%	3%	18%
Mothers did 91% to 100%	0%	6%

Note: Social class is another "situational and cultural" variable that influences the experience of the mother role. Participants were white mothers residing in Toronto, Canada.

Source: Adapted from M. McMahon (1995), *Engendering motherhood: Identity and self-transformation in women's lives* (New York: Guilford), pp. 197, 207.

mothers "caused" homosexuality in their sons. Mothers were at fault when fathers sexually abused their children. The stereotype proclaimed that the welfare mother had children only to increase her monthly benefits. African-American mothers were good when they reared white children as domestic workers, but bad when they reared their own children (Collins, 1994). According to Sigmund Freud, the mother was responsible for all manner of neuroses in her children (Thurer, 1994). The employed mother caused her children to become delinquent.

Feminists view the uneven distribution of child care and household work as a foundation for gender inequality. Such arrangements create and maintain gender inequalities outside the family in terms of more limited employment participation (Major, 1993). A more balanced view is that the mother role varies according to how reproduction and child care are institutionalized within a society. Today, the role of mother is simply no longer linked to that of homemaker in middle-class America. As you have seen, they were never linked for poor and minority group families. Mothering means different things among various cultural groups. For slaves, motherhood may have been the result of rape. A cultural preference for boys, and a survival-oriented one-child policy may mean grief and loss for today's Chinese mother as she places her infant daughter in an orphanage. Mothering is not a predetermined set of feelings and behaviors. Mothering exists in a situational and cultural context (Walzer, 1998).

Lesbian and Gay Families

For many, consideration of gay and lesbian families pushes the boundaries of fully gendered notions of marital and parenting relationships. The idea of homosexual couples committed to parenting may seem exotic, or even impossible. Of course, there have always been individuals with a same-sex erotic orientation who have been parents, but until recently they were invisible in mainstream society. Over the last 30 years, openly gay and lesbian families have become much more visible, and researchers estimate that 14 million children in the United States reside in such families (Stacey, 1998). How do same-gender couples deal with typically heavily gendered relationship issues? Although less informed individuals continue to view lesbians and gays as somehow confused regarding their gender identity, the guiding principle in understanding the reality of same-sex marital-type relationships is that they consist of two people who are the products of traditional gender-role socialization. As women, lesbians generally tend to focus more on their relationships. In general, gay men are more likely to emphasize independence and work success (Rutter & Schwartz, 1996).

Compared to heterosexual couples, gay and lesbian couples tend to distribute household chores on the basis of skill, interest, and work schedules. Lesbian couples tend to do more tasks together. Nor is the distribution of household chores related to relationship satisfaction. Thus, although gender is the strongest determinant of how household labor is distributed in heterosexual couples, no variable predicts the arrangement in same-sex couples (Patterson, 2000).

Most lesbians grow up with more or less traditional notions of gender and what it means to be a woman. Thus, it should come as no surprise that caretaking, nurturance, and family connection have the same value and interest for lesbians as they do for their heterosexual sisters. It has been estimated that about 25% of lesbians have children from previous heterosexual relationships or marriages. However, since the 1980s there has been a great upsurge in the number of single lesbians and lesbian couples who have elected to become mothers. Researchers sometimes refer to the "lesbian baby boom" (Patterson, Hurt, & Mason, 1998). Donor insemination and adoption are the major routes to forming families. However, custody and adoption laws have been biased against gays and lesbians, and some states have outlawed gay adoption (Lambda Legal Defense and Education Fund, 2001). Although most adoptions involve heterosexual couples, a considerable number of single women, as well as gay and lesbian couples, have been able to adopt children from eastern Europe, Latin America, and Asia. Do you recall this chapter's opening vignette and the group of highly acculturated East Asian children in Karen's urban classroom? Although most are probably the adopted children of heterosexual couples, many are likely to be the adopted children of single mothers and lesbian or gay couples. It's no surprise that some parents protested highly gendered institutions such as Father's Day or Mother's Day. Such traditions are easily transformed into Parent's Day.

Although the addition of children changes any couple relationship, lesbian couples with children from a previous heterosexual marriage tend to report greater relationship and sexual satisfaction compared to childless lesbian couples (Koepke, Hare, & Moran, 1992). Children of lesbian parents demonstrate the typical pattern of scores on tests of cognitive functioning, gender identity, and socioemotional adjustment. Nor can the general relationship quality of lesbians be distinguished from that of heterosexual couples with children. However, lesbian couples typically demonstrate more parenting awareness compared to heterosexual couples (Tasker & Golombok, 1997). Some researchers have found a slight tendency for the biological mothers in lesbian couples to do more of the daily caretaking of children (Patterson, 2000; Sullivan, 1996). There is no evidence that the sexual orientation of parents affects a child's sexual orientation (Golombok & Tasker, 1996). Nor are the children of lesbian couples more isolated from their grandparents or other relatives (Patterson et al., 1998). The most formidable problems for gay and lesbian parents emanate from the social stigma and legal problems that can haunt such families (Parks, 1998).

Does parental sexual orientation influence children's sexual orientation? Remember that about 98% of gays and lesbians have heterosexual parents.

Estimates of gay fathers range from 1 to 3 million, and they are demographically diverse in terms of age, ethnicity, class, education level, and occupation. Most are divorced, nonresidential parents who fathered children in earlier marriages. Gay fathers who are primary caregivers have typically established an openly gay lifestyle and then became parents through insemination agreements or through adoption. Adoption restrictions sometimes limit gay men to "difficult to place" children (disabled, mixed ethnicity, and so on). Some gay men co-parent with lesbian mothers. All these arrangements contribute to the current debate about what fathering really means. Earlier studies found gay men to be less traditional fathers, emphasizing nurturing more. Gay fathers are less likely to sexually abuse children. No differences were found in their children's cognitive abilities or autonomy (Silverstein, 1996b; Stacey, 1998). When gay fathers were compared with gay men without children, gay fathers reported greater self-esteem and fewer negative attitudes about homosexuality (Patterson & Chan, 1997). The adolescent children of gay fathers tend to be closed about their father's sexual orientation. Thus, the children of openly gay fathers must engage in more boundary control regarding information about their fathers (Patterson & Chan, 1997). Undergraduates tend to have the most negative attitudes toward gay fathers and their children than toward any other nontraditional family configuration (McLeod, Crawford, & Zechmeister, 1999). For another type of diversity in family makeup, take a look at Box 6.6.

Divorce and Repartnering

"The extended family is in our lives again. . . . Your basic extended family today includes your ex-husband or -wife, your ex's new mate, your new mate, possibly your new mate's ex-, and any new mate that your new mate's ex has acquired." ◆ Delia Ephron

We can no longer assume that children will grow up in a nuclear family with two biological parents. Nor can

our school schedules, work policies, and the emotional expectations of family life continue to presume that every household has a husband to earn income full time and a wife to take care of family needs full time.

Changes in family gender roles may make for more honest and satisfying relationships between women and men, as well as for children and parents. Divorce can rescue adults and children from unbearable situations, but it can also throw families into economic and psychological turmoil (Emery, Kitzman, & Waldron, 1999). We do not celebrate divorce. Ending a marriage is typically an agonizing process. Divorce can interfere with effective parenting and deprive children of needed resources (both emotional and material). Repartnering may solve some of the personal and economic problems associated with divorce, but it also introduces new tensions that can make things more difficult (Wallerstein, 1998).

In terms of gender, one may speak of his and of her reasons for divorce. Women complain of the lack of communication, affection, and shared interests. Men complain of nagging, whining, fault-finding, immaturity, and irresponsibility. Less common are economic factors, infidelity, alcoholism, and abuse. About one third who divorce also complain about their sexual relationships. Men tend to complain about inadequate quantity, whereas women complain about inadequate quality (Gottman & Carriere, 1994).

Several factors help explain the high rate of divorce in postindustrial society. First, our increased longevity has added a potential 20 to 30 more years together. Few emotions, even love, can usually last that long. Second, because less than half of one's life is now devoted to parenting, there is a more intense focus on the *quality* of married life. Third, marriage and family now have a different meaning and place in the life space. For middle-class women, marriage and motherhood were traditionally the *only* life paths. Marriage was the solution to the problems of living. Women were not encouraged (or even allowed) to develop or identify other life goals. Disillusionment and depression are predictable outcomes when marriage fails to live up to these high expectations. However, most women stayed married because they simply could not provide adequate support for their children. Women now have other choices.

For men, marriage was just a portion of their lives. Career and family goals were traditionally indepen-

ZOOM & ENLARGE   **BOX 6.6**

Gender in the Polygamous Family

The Church of Jesus Christ of Latter Day Saints (the Mormon Church)—one of the fastest growing religions within the United States—has its spiritual center in Salt Lake City, Utah. Although "The Principle" of plural marriage was an important aspect of the faith, polygamy (more correctly, polygyny, meaning multiple wives) was officially prohibited when Utah became a state in 1896. Those who engage in polygamy are officially excommunicated from the church. However, various fundamentalist sects have broken from the church and practice plural marriage. It is estimated that approximately 40,000 people now live in polygamous families. Only the first marriage is officially recorded. Later wives exist legally as single women with children. Some polygamous families are large, affluent, well-organized, and contributing members of their communities. For example, one well-known family consisted of five wives, 65 children, and more than 300 grandchildren. Adult sons operated numerous successful businesses. However, poverty is much more typical. Multiple wives and children live on welfare and depend on other federal programs. Husbands are employed intermittently.

Patriarchy, a unified and cohesive family, and very strict gender roles characterized all of the polygamous families that Altman and Ginat (1996) studied. The family patriarch saw himself as the hub of the family. He was usually described as distant, detached, and authori-

tarian. Patriarchs are expected to be active in the church and to be a source of religious wisdom and righteousness. He marries "good" women to mother his children. He must teach his wives and children important religious values and resolve conflicts within the family. He is "teacher, counselor, facilitator, arbiter, and decision maker" (Altman & Ginat, 1996, p. 388).

Wives manage the affairs of the home, care for children, and support the patriarch's leadership. Wives must encourage the patriarch to meet religious obligations, manage day-to-day life in the homes, have as many children as possible, and be responsible teachers and caregivers. The ideal is for families to be harmonious and well integrated. All daughters are expected to become homemakers and to raise their children to accept religious and patriarchal beliefs. All meals are prepared, served, and cleared by girls. Girls are the caretakers for all younger children. Sons are socialized to deal with any problem or discomfort in a "manly" way.

Husbands usually have a schedule for sleeping with wives. Ideally, resources are divided evenly among all wives, but in fact favorites frequently emerge. Women develop strong ties among themselves, particularly in families where husbands work far from home. They cooperate in all family tasks. Some actively court a prospective new wife for the family. Comothering is common and young chil-

dren may not distinguish their "real" mothers.

In one family, the patriarch was referred to as "Father." He declared that they would no longer celebrate Christmas, as the holiday had become too commercial. By his declaration, the new major family holiday became "Father's Birthday." All sons in the family had the father's first name as their middle name. The first-born son had Father's name as his first name and was called Junior. Conjoint dinners were presided over and controlled by Father, with no one speaking unless spoken to.

Some women have formed Tapestry of Polygamy, a self-help group that seeks to "free" women and children from polygamy. Other women, content with polygamous family life, have formed the Women's Religious Liberties Union and seek to legalize plural marriage. The state of Utah has become increasingly tolerant regarding such families. In 1991, Utah courts ruled that polygamous families could adopt. The governor of Utah first stated he saw polygamy as an issue of religious freedom, but later condemned the practice as wrong and as having no place in modern society. Utah's deputy attorney general sees this as an issue of sexual behavior between consenting adults. Several recent court cases involving statutory rape, child abuse, welfare fraud, and incest have brought polygamous groups into glaring headlines (Brooke, 1998; Murr, 1998).

---

dent, parallel, and nonconflicting. Ostensibly, men's marriages and families required little attention because these were a wife's responsibilities. This too has changed radically (Carter, 1987). Currently, about half of all marriages in the United States end in divorce, and about 60% of second marriages do as well. Some scholars suggest that divorce may soon come to

be normalized as one stage in the family life cycle (Hetherington & Stanley-Hagen, 1997).

Divorce affects a wife's life more drastically than a husband's. Ninety-two percent of children are in mothers' custody after divorce, and about half of child support payments are not fully paid. About 20% of noncustodial parents pay nothing at all. Virtually all poor families in the United States are women with dependent children. Court monetary awards are often based on the premise that a divorced mother will be able to get a decent paying job, find affordable child care, and soon remarry. About 35% of divorced women do not remarry, and their families will stabilize as single-parent families. In the year after divorce, a man's income typically continues to rise, whereas women's incomes drop drastically.

The heart of the emotional process of divorce is to retrieve one's self from the marriage. This means giving up all the hopes, dreams, and expectations previously invested in that marriage. This degree of self-direction sometimes goes against a major aspect of traditional gender role socialization for women. Many women invest their entire identity in marriage and believe they have the major responsibility for the success of that marriage. Throughout the entire cycle of marriage, divorce, single parenting, and remarriage, women are taught to bear major responsibility for seeing that it all works out happily for all others. Nevertheless, in North American society women more often initiate divorce (Hetherington, 1999b).

Traditional masculine socialization does not encourage men to examine and understand their part in the dissolution of their marriages. Acceptable and therefore predictable emotions for men are anger, outrage, and the desire for revenge. Because men often do not have a social support network, they may quickly get involved in another marriage or relationship. This tendency often leaves a man without the time or space to work on improving his relationship with his children, parents, or other family members (Seltzer & Brandreth, 1994).

Unless divorcing men take concrete steps, loss of their children is highly likely. The level of contact with children is strongly correlated with a father's willingness to continue financial support. Decreased contact also predicts an increase in the emotional distance between men and their children. Divorced Latino fathers are the least likely to retain contact with their children (McLanahan & Sandefur, 1994). The devoted postdivorce father must often learn how to conduct total relationships with their children. New living quarters must have adequate space for visiting children, and these fathers must master relating to children of various ages in new ways. They must also figure out how to manage these relationships

without relying on other women relatives or girlfriends.

Both genders find divorce stressful, but the "patterns and peaks" of distress differ by gender (Hetherington & Stanley-Hagen, 1997). Women find the period *before* deciding to end the marriage most difficult, as well as the actual process of separation and divorce. Men tend to feel the loss more strongly afterward, and they are more likely to harbor fantasies of reconciliation. Generally men are much less accepting of the end of their marriages. Distress and psychological and health problems often increase after divorce (Emery et al., 1999). A second peak of distress often occurs about 12 to 18 months later, with both parents and children exhibiting more psychological symptoms. Most families re-establish equilibrium within two years (Ahrons & Miller, 1993). Traditionally, most postdivorce research has centered on mother–child relationships and ignored the paternal bond. Although the general assumption is that children fare better if both parents are involved post divorce, the findings have been mixed on this (King, 1994). Continuing parental conflict makes for continuing difficulties among the children. The quality of postdivorce child contact is more vital than quantity. Noncustodial mothers generally do better with children than do noncustodial fathers. Noncustodial fathers are more permissive and tend to take on a more recreational and companionate role rather than that of teacher or disciplinarian. Relatively little is known about custodial fathers and their relationship with their children. Findings are mixed regarding whether children are better off with a same-sex parent. The quality of the parent–child relationship seems more important than the gender of custodial parent (Hetherington, 1999b).

Gender and Repartnering. The origins of second marriages changed in the 20th century. Previously, the most frequent precipitator of remarriage was widowhood. It is now divorce. Second marriages tend to be less homogamous than first marriages, and gender roles tend to be more egalitarian in terms of household responsibilities. On repartnering, relationships with previous spouses must be renegotiated, as must previous parenting roles. Residual hostilities must be tolerated or resolved. A complex matrix of relationships must be renegotiated and rearranged in blended families or step-families. There are few norms governing these new blended families (Buunk & Mutsaers, 1999; Fine, Coleman, & Ganong, 1999).

Summary

◆ Relationships give our lives meaning and purpose. Sibling relationships last the longest, and gender influences sibling relationships all through the life span.

◆ Childhood friendships reinforce gender-typed behavior and preferences. Adolescent friendships are very important and influential. The masculine emphasis on sports facilitates the development of positional identities and activity-oriented relating among men. The behavioral norms for same-sex friends may be problematic for adolescents with a same-sex or bisexual orientation, especially boys. Friendship norms in other societies may vary considerably.

◆ Historically, men's friendships were more valued. Since the 1970s, women's friendships have become the idealized norm. Although there are gender differences in friendships, these moderate over time. Adult friendship patterns vary over the life span and among various social groups. Cross-sex friendships are becoming more common, but continue to be devalued.

◆ In more collectivistic societies, arranged marriages prevail, but love marriages are becoming the global norm. Historical events shaped marital norms and patterns in the African-American community. Marital norms for the mainstream North American marriage evolved from the realities of the Industrial Revolution. Peplau described traditional, modern, and egalitarian marriages. Many factors precipitated the recent, massive, and ongoing changes in gender roles.

◆ In more individualistic societies, love and romance are the basis for marriage. Dating scripts are ritualized interactions based on gender. Cohabitation is increasingly common, and may precede or substitute for a traditional marriage. Gay men and lesbians also idealize romantic love as a basis for long-term relationships, but must construct these relationships without socially approved models. Recent research suggests that cross-cultural similarities in partner preferences are socioculturally, rather than biologically based.

◆ The postindustrial family is varied and complex in composition. Child care and housework remain the major arenas of gender-related contention in such families. The father role has undergone considerable scrutiny and reconstruction over the last two decades. The mother role has been synonymous with *parenting*, and this too is in the process of reconstruction. Lesbian and gay families are increasingly visible and offer an instructive alternative to gender-based division of family roles. Asian-American families are quite varied in terms of gender roles. Polygamous families demonstrate another form of family diversity.

◆ Divorce and repartnering are increasingly normative in postindustrial societies. One's gender influences the experience and meaning of divorce. The blended-family or step-family must renegotiate very complex family relationships without well-established norms or models.

InfoTrac College Edition

For more information, explore InfoTrac College Edition at

http://www.infotrac-college.com/Wadsworth

Enter search terms: gender and friendship, gender and marriage, gender and housework, father, mother, gay family.

7

Gender as Social Performance
A Worldview

People say, believe half of what you see, son, and none of what you hear. ◆ "I Heard It Through the Grapevine" (lyrics by Norman Whitfield and Barrett Strong)

Learning Objectives

After studying this chapter, you should be able to:

1. List and describe seven essential qualities by which women and men have been traditionally differentiated.
2. Summarize the central features of the agentic/instrumental and communal/expressive styles.
3. List the three components of emotion, and summarize the evidence supporting the notion that emotions are, in part, social constructions.
4. Explain the relationship between traditional femininity and the expression of positive emotions and the relationship between masculinity and lack of emotionality.
5. Offer a brief critique of the essentialist perspective on gender and emotions, and contrast this with the insights offered by the gender in context perspective.
6. Summarize the gender-related factors involved in the nonverbal channels of touch and facial display.
7. Evaluate the current stereotype regarding gender differences in communication, and then summarize the findings regarding contextual factors in gender-typed communication.
8. Explain why eliminating sexist language is desirable, and offer some examples of nonsexist terminology.
9. Summarize the current findings regarding the ostensible gender differences in seven important personality-related social behaviors, emphasizing the cultural and contextual factors that influence these behaviors.
10. Summarize the cross-cultural findings regarding how sociocultural change influences the performance of gender.

Encounters with Gender

Jason is completing his graduate studies in Manila, in the Philippines. He is invited to a university gathering, and soon strikes up a conversation with Ramona, a Filipino woman, who is related to the hosts. Ramona is very animated, frequently looks Jason in the eye, and is extremely attentive to all that Jason says. When Jason reveals something about his family life, she discloses something even more personal about her own. As the conversation continues, Ramona stands a little closer to Jason, smiling sweetly and occasionally touching him. Jason feels her interest and soon suggests they leave the party together to go to a nearby secluded nightspot. Ramona again smiles sweetly, but soon excuses herself politely and moves off to chat with friends elsewhere in the room. Jason is both perplexed and embarrassed. Was he inappropriate and crude? Was Ramona flirting and inviting a romantic/sexual overture? Was she waiting for Jason to take a risk, so she could reject and therefore demean him? How can we understand what happened here?

Source: Adapted from R. Brislin, K. Cushner, C. Cherrie, & M. Yong (1986), *Intercultural interactions: A practical guide* (Newbury Park, CA: Sage).

Overview

This chapter begins with some philosophical reflections on the essential differences between women and men. However, most of the chapter is devoted to everyday experience of gender as it exists in the people around us. It is about how we publicly perform our gender roles and how we interpret the gender performances of others. It is also about the public performances and interpretations of that performance in other societies. This may be a troublesome chapter because it challenges some very basic assumptions and understandings about gender and perhaps interpersonal reality. Many students/readers will find it difficult to accept that many of the phenomena they experience as profoundly "real" seem to disappear under closer scrutiny. You will see how stereotypes, expectations as well as interpersonal and cultural norms shape your own behavior (performances) and your understanding of the behavior of others. I examine ideas about the emotional lives of women and men, and then review what is known about how men and women communicate (and sometimes miscommunicate). Then I evaluate some deeply held notions about the distinctive personality characteristics and social behaviors of women and men.

Capturing the Elusive Essences

According to Sandra Bem (1993), we view and experience many aspects of life through a *gendered lens*. This lens may distort what is "out there" in many ways, yet it is so omnipresent and powerful we often mistake its distortions for reality. That is, we seldom observe a person, interact with someone, or describe an inner subjective experience that does not pass through this gendered lens or filter. This gendered lens is constructed from the influences of culture, socialization, stereotypes, expectations, and other social norms.

As we move through the world, we experience men and women as quite distinct from each other. What is the nature of that distinctiveness? Over the centuries, philosophers, theologians, and later, psychologists have attempted to capture some core essence that differentiates adult women and men. Traditional conceptions of adult women and men, both psychological and nonpsychological, have emphasized contrasting and **asymmetric** qualities (Deaux & Major, 1998; G. Smith, 1996). For example,

◆ There is the "rational man" versus the "emotional woman." Rationality was what distinguished humans from animals, and this quality was the province of men. The province of women was uncontrolled emotion and therefore irrationality. However, we should note that in 16th-century Europe, it was men who were generally considered "emotionally incontinent" (Shields, 1991).
◆ The mind was considered representative of man, whereas the body was representative of woman

(Mishkind, Rodin, Silberstein, & Striegel-Moore, 1987).
◆ There was man, the "higher" form, versus woman, the "lower" form. Man was closer to God. This was the hierarchy suggested by the Judeo-Christian creation myth, and it has been maintained throughout most (but not all) Western and Eastern religious traditions (King, 1993).
◆ There was the "achievement and autonomy oriented" man versus the "socioemotionally and relationally oriented" woman (Fischer, 1993; Gilligan, 1982).
◆ There was the "unique separateness" of the individual man versus the more amorphous "sameness and connectedness" of all women (Krugman, 1995; G. Smith, 1996).
◆ There was the "deficient and inadequate" female versus the "ideal and developed" male (Badinter, 1997; Michael, 1996).

More recently, social scientists, particularly psychologists, have attempted to describe (and quantify) the essential features that differentiate adult women and men with the terms *femininity* and *masculinity*. As you have learned, the contents of femininity and masculinity may vary greatly from society to society, and among the subcultures within a society. For example, the men of Bali dance gracefully, and the women of a certain South Korean ethnic group are expert divers. However, as Table 7.1 shows there are some pancultural universals (Williams & Best, 1990).

The terms **agentic/instrumental** have been used to describe the core features of the masculine style, whereas the terms **communal/expressive** serve to describe the core features of the more feminine style (Jung, 1959a; Bakan, 1966; Spence, 1985).

The more masculine style is viewed as status oriented and focused on dominance, instrumental rewards, and asymmetry. It is labeled as *restrictive* because it interrupts interaction, uses assertions, com-

---

asymmetric   **Not having equal balance.**

agentic/instrumental   **Essence of the masculine stereotype, concern with self-protection, self-assertion, self-preservation, and competency.**

communal/expressive   **Essence of the feminine stereotype, concern with harmony, participation, and cooperation.**

TABLE 7.1   The 100 Items of the Pancultural Adjective Checklist

Female-Associated			*Male-Associated*		
Affected	Foolish	Shy	Active	Humorous	Realistic
Affectionate	Forgiving	Softhearted	Adventurous	Indifferent	Reckless
Appreciative	Frivolous	Sophisticated	Aggressive	Individualistic	Resourceful
Cautious	Fussy	Submissive	Arrogant	Initiative	Rigid
Changeable	Gentle	Suggestible	Autocratic	Interests	Robust
Charming	Imaginative	Superstitious	Bossy	wide	Serious
Complaining	Kind	Talkative	Capable	Inventive	Sharp-witted
Confused	Mild	Timid	Conceited	Lazy	Showoff
Curious	Modest	Touchy	Confident	Loud	Steady
Dependent	Nervous	Unambitious	Courageous	Obnoxious	Stern
Dreamy	Patient	Understanding	Cruel	Opinionated	Stingy
Emotional	Pleasant	Unintelligent	Cynical	Opportunistic	Stolid
Excitable	Prudish	Unstable	Determined	Pleasure-seeking	Tough
Fault-finding	Self-pitying	Warm	Disorderly	Precise	Unfriendly
Fearful	Sensitive	Weak	Enterprising	Progressive	Unscrupulous
Fickle	Sexy	Worrying	Greedy	Rational	Witty
			Hardhearted		

Source: Adapted from J. E. Williams and D. L. Best (1990). *Measuring sex stereotypes: A multination study* (Beverly Hills, CA: Sage).

mands, threats, and boasts. The more feminine style is viewed as connection oriented and focuses on maintaining interpersonal relationships, harmony, cooperation, and support. It is labeled as *enabling* because it involves agreeing, acknowledging, and being more supportive in interactions (Nohara, 1996).

During adulthood the contrast between this communal/expressive feminine personality style and the agentic/instrumental masculine personality style seemingly becomes more delineated. A firmer pattern of gender-typed interests, behaviors, preferences, and attitudes emerges during adulthood, and most women and men tend to conform to them, no matter how these may vary across societies. The degree to which individuals adhere to these gender prescriptions is described as their level of gender role identification. So what's the problem with men and women being seen as "different" from each other in everyday behavior and interaction? The problem is that in many societies, those who demonstrate agentic/instrumental behaviors are considered better adjusted and tend to enjoy all sorts of personal, social, and economic privileges. In North American society, many more positive attributions and consequences are associated with the agentic/instrumental style (McCreary, Newcomb, & Sadava, 1998; Wetherell, 1997).

The agentic/instrumental essence is associated with activities such as mastering, controlling, overcoming, creating, producing, exploring, persuading, analyzing, understanding, and winning. The agentic/instrumental style is associated with descriptors such as aggressive, ambitious, adventurous, assertive, autonomous, clever, courageous, daring, dominant, enterprising, forceful, independent, resourceful, restless, sophisticated, stubborn, and wise. The communal/expressive essence implies an orientation toward loving and being intimate, nurturing, cooperating, encouraging, communicating, and sharing with others. The communal/expressive is associated with descriptors such as affectionate, charming, altruistic, enticing, gentle, kind, loyal, sensitive, sociable, sympathetic, and warm (McAdams, 1993).

So far, I've given an overview of the issue of gender as a basic differentiating essence among human beings (Bohan, 1997). Next I examine some of the key ingredients in the recipe that results in the experiential phenomena we label *femininity* or *masculinity*.

Gender and Emotion

Ask just about anyone about the obvious differences between women and men, and rather quickly someone will mention emotions or feelings. The unshakable social truism is that "women are more emotional than men." If you persist and ask them what they mean by this, they are very likely to say something like "You know, women cry more." Well, that's an everyday understanding of gender and emotion, and few would dispute this particular truism. However, our challenge is to look more deeply into this gendered performance of emotionality.

Everyone knows what feelings or emotions are. After all, we've been "having" them for decades. Actually, feelings or emotions are quite complex phenomena, and our knowledge and understanding of emotions is rather incomplete. There seem to be three overlapping components of emotion:

◆ *An inner, subjective, experiential component that is related to a verbal description of that experience.* "I felt really sad when my dog died." "I was furious when I saw what that drunken driver had done."

◆ *An overt behavioral or expressive component that is observable via an action or reaction.* Your nose wrinkles in disgust at the sudden sight of maggots, or your face flashes a happy smile when you receive an excellent grade on a term paper.

◆ *A physiological component that may or may not be overtly experienced* (Plutchik, 1993). Your face flushes as that attractive person finally talks to you. Your heart beats wildly, and your skin feels clammy as you investigate those strange sounds coming from your basement.

Culture and Context in Emotional Expression

The idea that emotions are a human universal goes all the way back to Charles Darwin (1872). This idea implies that all human beings experience the same emotions and express them the same way, and there is evidence to support this (Ekman & Friesen, 1975). However, emotions are also subject to a great degree of "social construction" (Griffiths, 1997; Russell, 1994). Language that describes emotions in particular cultures offers a guide to identifying and understanding the emotions of that culture. For example, over the last 300 years the words in English that describe emotions have shifted. In 17th-century Europe, only *overt behavior* or *public displays* were emotions. For contemporary Brits and Americans, internal private feelings are emotions (Harre, 1997). Culture also

guides which feelings will be experienced. For example, what would a woman feel when her husband takes a second wife? What would a husband feel when his wife sleeps with his brother? In both situations, a spouse's response might be pride, relief, joy, jealousy, or homicidal rage, just to name a few possibilities—all depending on culture. Furthermore, societies vary in terms of display rules for emotion (Matsumoto, 1996). In some societies no funeral is complete without loud weeping and wailing, whereas in others only a trembling but "stiff upper lip" is acceptable. A European woman's broad, toothy smile would be considered an excessive display in some societies. Members of many societies experience emotions that are unknown to others. Among the Maori of New Zealand and the Hmong of Laos and now of North America, emotions are derived from certain qualities of the internal organs such as stomach, heart, and so on. You may recall that in Chapter 2, I mentioned that the Hmong may experience a "lonely liver" when missing a loved one (Dunnegin et al., 1993). Spaniards may experience *verguenza ajena* when a stranger is making a fool of him- or herself. The Japanese experience *amae*, a positive feeling experienced when one is dependent on another (Doi, 1973, 1986). The point here is that our emotional experiences and the expression of emotions are guided by gender and cultural norms. Being a Spaniard, a man, a Hmong, or a woman does not *cause* these phenomena, but gender norms within a particular society guide our emotional experiences and behavior in powerful ways.

When it comes to emotion, the stereotype is "women have it and men don't." The idea that women simply express more emotions, are more sensitive to the emotions of others, more excitable, and more easily hurt compared to men, is a powerful social norm in our society (Plant, Hyde, Keltner, & Devine, 2000). Therefore, it seems only logical (and verifiable) that regardless of sex, individuals with a strong feminine gender identity are more likely to have greater knowledge about emotions, be able to label role-consistent emotions more accurately, and have a superior memory for emotional events (Davis, 1999; Seidlitz & Diener, 1998). Some additional correlates of the relationship between gender and emotionality may be summarized as follows. First, women should not display socially negative affect, such as anger (Fabes & Martin, 1991). However, this may differ across societies. German women reported no need to conceal rage, whereas women in the United States strongly believed that rage should be concealed (Kosmitski, 1988). In contrast, men should display minimal affect (Clatterbaugh, 1997). Positive affect in particular should be repressed, except in socially approved masculine pursuits such as athletic competition (Pollack, 1998). This lack of emotional expression ostensibly serves to demonstrate power and control (Timmers, Fischer, & Manstead, 1998). There is considerable social acceptance and approval for men's nonemotional relating to others (Beneke, 1997).

Second, it is generally assumed that emotional expressiveness is somehow related to relationality and communality. Although relating to others certainly requires the expression of emotion, the reverse is not true. One might express lots of emotion and yet still be unable to relate successfully (Fischer, 1993).

Third, beginning in the 19th century emotionality became a negatively valued characteristic that was antithetical to the more highly valued rationality. The feminist contribution was to reject the idea that emotionality could not exist alongside intellect or competence. Women's emotionality was declared a valued characteristic. However, emotionality was still seen as something women possessed and men did not.

Fourth, both women and men in mainstream North American society tend to believe their responses to anger, sadness, and jealousy are quite similar. However, women report seeking social support when sad, whereas men report engaging in more dangerous behavior when sad. When faced with jealous feelings, women report they would express their feelings nonverbally, seek a discussion with their partner, and enhance their physical appearance. Men report they would focus on the rival and buy gifts or spend money on a partner (Guerrero & Reiter, 1998; Watson, Biderman, & Sawyer, 1994).

Finally, socialization for differential emotional expressiveness begins early. Among children as young as 3½, both parents use more emotion words when discussing sad events with daughters (Fivush, Brotman, Buckner, & Goodman, 2000). In an examination of how young children master the art of suppressing a negative facial expression when they receive a disliked or disappointing gift, motivational variables and expectations, rather than some essential gender difference, were crucial. Boys expected more disapproval

for showing sadness, whereas girls expected more disapproval for showing anger (Davis, 1995). Regardless of gender, older adults generally report greater control over their emotions, greater stability of mood, less psychophysiological agitation, and greater ability to control the internal and external expression of emotions. In general, this emotional wellbeing declines only at the end of life. This trend was found among Catholic nuns, African Americans, Chinese Americans, and European Americans, as well as Norwegians (Carstensen & Charles, 1998; Gross et al., 1997).

Implicit in North American society's assumption that men and women are essentially different in terms of emotionality is that emotionality is a stable, internal personality trait that is independent of the situation, context, past experience, or sociocultural norms (Carroll & Russell, 1996). This unexamined assumption led researchers to an "unproductive" search for gender differences in emotionality (Shields, 1998). The resulting contradictory morass of findings appears to be another example of the "now you see it/now you don't" phenomenon of ostensible gender differences (Unger, 1981). There are other serious problems with this traditional culture-bound approach to understanding the relationship between gender and emotions. For example, the concept of "emotionality" is too gross and fails to distinguish among the emotions. There simply is no generalized "emotionality." There are only experiences and behavioral expressions of awe, contempt, love, suspiciousness, curiosity, and so on (Griffiths, 1997). Also, studies of emotion typically depend on self-reports. Therefore, when research participants are informed they are involved in a study of emotions or feelings, a whole set of gender-related biases and preconceptions are likely to be evoked, and these will influence the results of any study (Russell, 1994). Just the word *emotion* tends to activate a feminine schema (Bem, 1993).

The everyday notion of emotionality is intertwined with the feminine stereotype. That is, in everyday understanding, *emotionality* seems to refer only to the emotions that women may express: tearful happiness, sadness, or various levels of fear. Yet news accounts are full of reports of emotional expression by men: hostility, anger, and violent rage (Wilson, Daly, & Daniele, 1995). Expression of these more normatively "masculine" feelings is not usually labeled as emotionality. Moreover, why is crying "emotional," but not laughing? In other words, emotional expression is imbued with cultural meaning. In our society, one is considered to be behaving "emotionally" when one does what women are more likely to do. This is precisely what Sandra Bem means when she talks about seeing behavior through the lens of gender.

Critical Thinking Challenge

What are your predictions about the findings if a large sample of men and women were asked to report how frequently and how intensely they experienced fear over the previous month? What about anger?

Insights from the Gender-in-Context Perspective

Current research findings suggest that women and men are probably equivalent in their physiological arousal and subjective experience of emotion, but reports of the frequency, intensity, and certainly the overt expression of emotion are all subject to powerful gender norms and culture norms. In studying the relationship between gender and emotions, Shields (1991, 1998) recommends that the question needs to shift from "Are there gender differences in emotionality?" to "What variables exaggerate or attenuate emotional behavior along gender lines?" In gender-laden concepts such as emotion, it may be more productive to see gender as emerging from an interaction among actor, observer, and situational variables. As you know, this approach is referred to as the gender-in-context perspective (Kring & Gordon, 1998).

The gender-in-context perspective implies that emotionality will vary predictably across situations depending on its cultural meaning along gendered lines. For example, several reviews by Judith Hall (1978, 1984, 1987) demonstrated that women are more accurate in emotional decoding and expressing emotions via nonverbal communications. However, she also notes that virtually all these differences emerge only in settings that have **demand characteristics** for gender-appropriate behavior (young college students in a lab, minimally invested in interacting with strangers in front of an unfamiliar experimenter). Powerful culture-based public norms for gendered behavior such as "be nice," "be warm," "be attentive to what others are feeling," and so on are in effect for women in those settings, so more gender-typed interactions occur (Aukett, Ritchie, & Mill,

1988). It is interesting to note that this supposed female superiority in **decoding** emotion-related cues virtually disappears when female participants have to decode anger messages (Shields, 1995).

Critical Thinking Challenge

What gender norms might guide college men's behavior in a scientific laboratory, where they are interacting with strangers and being evaluated by an experimenter?

A study of anger and fear among Canadian and U.S. preadolescents, teenagers, and adults revealed that the social context was critical in eliciting any gender differences in emotionality. Interestingly, girls and women expressed the most fear when the frightening stimulus was a male engaging in stereotypically masculine behavior (Brody, Lovas, & Hay, 1995). In studies of anger expression among ethnically varied elementary school children and adolescents in the United States, no gender or differences were found. Although boys might respond with physical aggression, girls demonstrated essentially equivalent levels of more indirect aggression (Buntaine & Costenbader, 1997; Deffenbacher & Swaim, 1999). In a study of anger in close heterosexual relationships, the only gender difference that emerged was in anger expression: women were four times more likely to cry when angry (Fehr, Baldwin, Collins, & Patterson, 1999).

Several studies have revealed that levels of subjective emotional intensity, level of emotional expressiveness, and even the level of physiological response vary more by **gender role identification** than by sex. Thus, "masculine" and "androgynous" individuals are more likely to express anger directly and to be more easily distracted from sadness, regardless of sex (Kopper & Emerson, 1991; Kring & Gordon, 1998).

---

demand characteristics Confounding environmental factors present in a laboratory study that unintentionally affect participants' behavior.

decoding Converting from one form to another; in this case from a facial expression to an inference about the emotion it portrays.

gender role identification The extent to which an individual identifies with the gender stereotypes of her or his culture.

Gender and Communication

Much has been written, researched, and even sung about gender and communication (as well as miscommunication). Stereotypes are rampant, so let's see if current research can shed some scientific light on this lively area of gender relations.

Nonverbal Communication

Nonverbal communication is the link between our inner emotions and our interpersonal communication. When we encounter others, we use nonverbal cues to assess their immediate emotional state. We also transmit nonverbal information about our own emotional status. These nonverbal interactions will set the stage for how we will interact with someone verbally. I'll discuss two channels of nonverbal interaction: touch and facial display (smiling).

Touch. Touching constitutes the earliest and most basic interactive communication channel among human beings. Developmental studies looked at touch in terms of mother–infant warmth, nurturance, and emotional attachment (Field, 1994; Hamelin & Ramachandran, 1993). More recent social psychological studies examined touch in the communication of power and status (Henley, 1997). Touching was revealed to be a *privilege* of higher status (Henley & Freeman, 1995). For example, a teacher may touch students, but students may not touch a teacher. Gender patterns in social touch vary by age and social setting. Men are more likely to touch women than vice versa, but the pattern reverses among children. Cross-sex touch is more prevalent among adults, but same-sex touch is more prevalent when a child was involved. In public, nonintimate settings, men touch women more. However, this asymmetry disappears during moments of greeting or leaving (Major, Schmidlin, & Williams, 1990). So, are men or women more "touchy"? The most reasonable conclusion is that there is no gender difference in touching behavior. The frequency, direction, duration, and meaning of touch depend on the situation or context. Touching behavior is also regulated by cultural norms. In some Buddhist countries, women may not touch or even hand objects to Buddhist priests. The latter problem may be overcome by handing the object to a male intermediary, who will then pass it on (Axtel,

1993). You may recall that in an earlier chapter, I mentioned that Orthodox Jews may not touch someone of the other gender to whom they are not related.

Facial Display. In the United States, Canada, and many other Western societies, smiling is a central and often "required" component of feminine *gender display*. However, in other societies, smiling by persons of either gender may have quite different meanings. Regardless of gender, the Japanese will not smile for a driver's license photograph or even for a wedding photograph. Smiles would imply the person is not taking the occasion seriously. However, the Japanese are likely to smile when sad, apologetic, or angry. A smiling Korean is considered foolish and shallow, and a smiling Korean man is viewed as unmanly (Dresser, 1996). By the way, even in the United States, recent studies have shown that when politicians smile, observers pay less attention to the content of their messages (Krull & Dill, 1998; Ottati, Terkidsen, & Hubbard, 1997). This may make for an interesting dilemma of gender for the woman who is seeking public office. A study involving Dutch college students of both sexes demonstrated that both the occurrence and duration of smiling is guided more by culture-related situational norms (and demands), rather than by internal emotional states or by some essential gender factor (Jakobs, Manstead, & Fischer, 1999).

Language and Verbal Communication

Two other commonly held gender truisms are that men and women communicate differently and that women are somehow superior verbal communicators. Popular writings emphasizing the differences or problems in intergender communication constitute a veritable growth industry (Gray, 1992; Wood, 1994, 1996). These widely held beliefs have also spurred a considerable amount of research (Crawford, 1995).

In her best-selling book, *You Just Don't Understand: Women and Men in Conversation*, Deborah Tannen (1990) considers male–female conversation to be cross-cultural communication. Men and women are said to speak *genderlects* or gender-dialects (see

---

nonverbal communication **Communication without spoken words. Communication via facial expression, eye contact, body postures, and gestures.**

"That was a fine report, Barbara. But since the sexes speak different languages, I probably didn't understand a word of it."

FIGURE 7.1   Notions about gender differences in language are very popular and may be applied in a variety of situations.

Figure 7.1). These separate gendered societies take form in those gender-segregated childhood playgroups that were described in Chapter 5. Boy groups are inevitably hierarchical, with one boy giving orders and working to make them stick. Other boys know their place or challenge the **alpha** boy. Boy games have winners and losers and also elaborate rules that are the basis for arguments. Boys boast and argue about who is best. Meanwhile, girls are in pairs or small groups, with a best friend at the center of their social life. Their games involve intimacy, closeness, and turn-taking, and the games often do not have winners and losers. There are usually no orders, only wishes or preferences. Tannen (1990) concludes that among girls, there is more concern about being liked than about status. These childhood experiences then develop into distinct adult modes of interaction and communication.

Tannen believes that adult men often inhabit a subjective, experiential world in which each man is an "individual in a hierarchical social order in which he was either one-up or one-down" (Tannen, 1990, p.

24). For that man, conversations are negotiations in which individuals try to achieve and maintain the upper hand, and people must resist attempts to cut them down or push them around. In contrast, women live in a subjective, experiential world of connectedness. Conversations are negotiations for closeness, an exchange of confirmation and support. Reaching consensus is the goal. Conversations are a means to preserve intimacy and avoid isolation. Women may also try to achieve status and avoid failure, but these are not their central concerns. Men may also try to achieve involvement and avoid isolation, but these are not their central concerns. Tannen offers some illustrative examples. Many women feel it is "natural" to consult with their partners about decisions (such as an invitation to a weekend houseguest, a significant purchase, and so on), because it signifies involvement. Men may resist doing this because it feels like

---

alpha   In a social hierarchy, the "top member" or leader is the "alpha." This member has the most influence over the other members.

asking permission. Women may initiate a discussion by asking, "What do you think?" Men may hear this as their being asked to decide something.

Critical Thinking Challenge

A great deal of the popular literature about gender-related miscommunication is based on the experiences of counselors and therapists working with unhappily married couples. Happily married couples generally communicate well. Moreover, some unhappy partners seem to communicate very well with other-gender people with whom they are not legally coupled. Hmm!

Tannen was not the first to emphasize gender differences in language and communication. Almost 20 years earlier, Robin Lakoff (1973, 1975, 1978) declared the existence of a distinct women's language. This special language contained more meaningless phrases ("Oh dear!") and fewer strong expressions or expletives. Women used more empty adjectives that expressed emotion rather than intellectual evaluation ("It was lovely!"). Women also used more tag questions, and this was interpreted as expressing uncertainty ("It's cold in here, isn't it?"). Women's speech was characterized by more hedges and qualifiers ("It was kind of sweet"), and greater politeness, indirectness, and imprecision in declarative statements. In contrast, men generally talked more often and for longer periods of time in interactions. Men also interrupted more often and used more task-oriented language. Men used more direct techniques to influence the flow of conversation and were more likely to use directives (orders, commands) in their speech (Anderson & Leaper, 1998; West & Zimmerman, 1983, 1985, 1987).

These differences in communication were interpreted as reflecting women's more negative self-image and an adaptation to a lower status and lack of power. However these maximalist and essentialist notions about gender and communication have produced very inconsistent findings (DeLameter & Hyde, 1998). The research literature on gender and communication is now about 30 years old, and a considerable body of interdisciplinary literature has accumulated (Aries, 1996). However, controversy still continues about whether findings of difference are caused mainly by stereotypes and expectations or by actual

speech differences (Molm & Hedley, 1992). Additional controversies surround the interpretation of the data collected (Aries, 1996). Let's look at some more current understandings of gender and communication. (By the way, the very term *gender* comes from the study of linguistic communication. See Box 7.1 to learn more.)

The use of tag questions, hedges, and qualifiers varies more by age than by gender. Such usage also depends on the nature of conversation and the gender composition of group (Aries, 1996). However, it is true that women use more **back-channel** ("hmmm," "yes," "right") responses compared to men. The linguistic forms that make up so-called women's language appear to be more prevalent among white, middle-class women (and only in some contexts). They do not generally appear in the speech of ethnic minority women and are not observed across societies or in other languages. Gender differences in interruptions were more likely to occur when participants were interacting in larger groups rather than dyads. Men do tend to use less polite forms in their speech (threats, directives, commands). Women's greater politeness results in others feeling more liked, respected, and so on. It also makes women speakers more likeable (Carli, LaFleur, & Loeber, 1995). Gender differences in communication patterns are greater in groups of strangers than in groups where people know each other. For example, in a study that compared interaction patterns among undergraduate couples, the greatest gender differences occurred among casual daters, but researchers observed no such differences among serious daters or engaged couples (Heiss, 1992). In a study of married couples, researchers found no specialization in dyadic interaction roles (Levinger, 1994). Most importantly, communication patterns that initially appeared to be gender related may actually be status related (Ridgeway & Diekema, 1992). When interaction patterns are studied among other groups characterized by power disparities (prisoners and guards, children and parents, workplace subordinates and superiors), the familiar pattern of asymmetry emerges. That is, members of all less powerful groups seem to

---

back-channel Conversational fillers that communicate connection or listening, such as "uh-uh," "hmmm," "yes," "yeah," and so on.

ZOOM & ENLARGE   **BOX 7.1**

The Origins of Linguistic Gender

Psychologists and sociologists borrowed the term *gender* from the field of linguistics. Anyone who has studied a foreign language knows that some languages have masculine and feminine words. For example, in Spanish *el nariz* (the nose) is classified as masculine, whereas *la oreja*, (the ear) is feminine. How did grammatical gender originate?

Originally, Indo-European nouns were classified based on similarities of sound. The grammatical term *gender* is derived from the Latin *genus*, which meant "kind," or "type," or "class" and had absolutely nothing to do with sex. In the 5th century B.C.E., the philosopher Protagoras noted three noun classes in Greek. He termed them *masculine, feminine,* and *neuter* because he was convinced that sex was inherent in the classification of things (think back to Chapter 1). So he argued that even though the Greek word *peleks* (helmet) has an ending that would classify it as feminine, it should be changed to masculine. This is

how sex and gender began to enter discussions of normally sexless grammar.

In the 19th century, German grammarian Jakob Grimm saw the gender classification of words as a metaphorical extension of sex to the rest of the world. He saw grammatical gender as a "natural" order (now think back to those "elusive essences" at the beginning of the chapter). In Grimm's opinion, things named by masculine nouns were earlier, larger, firmer, more inflexible, quicker, active, mobile, and creative. Those that were feminine were later, smaller, softer, quieter, suffering/passive, and receptive. Another German scholar believed that only the most civilized races and "leading nations" used gender in their languages. Languages without gender distinctions were declared "in decline."

However, not all languages classify by "gender." For example, the Native American language of the Ojibwa uses the notion of **animacy** in its linguistic classification scheme. But what is animate to

the Ojibwa, might not be considered as such by others. The Ojibwa words for snow, snowshoe, and cooking pot suggest that these objects are alive, because they are powerful in traditional Ojibwa life. In Tamil, a language of South India, nouns are classified by whether they are high caste or low caste. In Dyirbal (Aborigine language spoken in Queensland, Australia) every noun must be preceded by a classifier telling to which category it belongs. But what are these categories? The *bayi* category includes men, kangaroos, possums, bats, most (but not all) snakes, and the moon. The *balan* category includes women, bandicoots, dogs, and anything connected with fire, water, sun, and the stars. The *balam* category includes all edible fruits and their plants, ferns, honey, and cigarettes. Among African languages, Swahili has seven classifications for nouns, whereas Bantu has between 10 and 20 such classifications, none of which have anything to do with sex or gender.

---

learn to interpret subtle nonverbal behaviors, to defer, to please, to notice, to attend to others' needs, speak tentatively and indirectly, be nonthreatening, and make others comfortable (Murphy & Zorri, 1996; Wood et al., 1997).

Gender-stereotypic communication patterns are likely to emerge in more socially ambiguous situations (Deaux & Major, 1998). For example, researchers examined the relationship among sex, gender-typed occupational familiarity, and role behavior. When participants were secure in their occupational role playing (women as kindergarten teachers and men as airline pilots), participants of both sexes produced more task-oriented communications. However, when participants of both sexes were insecure in their occu-

pational role playing (men as nurses and women as mathematicians), both sexes produced more socioemotional communications (Yamada, Tjosvold, & Draguns, 1987).

Women and men are most likely to use language differently when gender is a salient factor in the interaction. That's a complicated way of saying that one is more likely to see more gender-typed communication patterns when a woman and a man are trying to initiate conversation or flirt at a social gathering. Few, if any such differences will be apparent when purchasing an airline ticket or when stuck in a traffic jam

---

animacy   **Belonging to the class of things that are alive.**

FIGURE 7.2 The humor of this Stone Soup cartoon relies on knowledge of the masculine stereotypes of poor communication skills and lack of emotional expression.

(Howard & Hollander, 1997)! Also more stereotypical communication patterns will emerge in situations where there are concerns about self-presentation as an acceptably masculine or feminine person (Romaine, 1999). Think about what you might want to communicate about yourself at your first meeting with the parents of someone with whom you were romantically involved. Figure 7.2 captures many of the themes discussed here regarding emotional expression, communication skills, and self-presentation.

Gender-related communication expectations and stereotypes may reverse dramatically in some situations. For example, observational studies indicate that during interpersonal conflicts women will be more direct, confrontational, and hostile. Men are much more likely to avoid conflict and be cooperative in situations of interpersonal strife (Gottman, 1994; Wood, 1994).

Gender differences will also be more prominent when women believe there will be retaliation or other negative consequences for violations of gender-related expectations. They will also occur when members of one gender are in the minority (Brody et al., 1995).

Conclusions. An interactionist model of gender-related behavior seems the most helpful in understanding all these findings (Deaux & Major, 1998). Three factors interact to predict gendered patterns in communication:

1. Every person brings gender-related expectancies to interpersonal communications. Once activated, these expectations influence our behavior, and they in turn will help shape the behavior of our interaction partners.

2. At the same time, our self-conceptions as masculine or feminine persons within a particular society lead us to conform to the gender-related demands of the situation. This last item offers us a clue as to what may have transpired when (recall the vignette at the beginning of this chapter) Jason encountered Ramona in the context of Filipino cultural and gender norms. In the next section of this chapter we will solve the mystery why their encounter went awry.

3. Various situations exert strong or weak pressures for the display of gender-typed and gender-stereotyped behavior. The weakest pressures are exerted when women and men have equivalent statuses, resources, and competencies. Somewhat stronger pressures are exerted in initial, public, short-term, ambiguous, or unfamiliar situations. Pressures are strongest in situations where there are no clear role prescriptions or when gender is highly salient. The contextual model can account for the relevant findings rather well. Most contemporary communication researchers have concluded that gender factors are situationally variable (depend on setting, topic, role, status,

gender mix, and so on). Few reliable gender differences in communication occur across situations and contexts.

Gender and the Content of Conversations. Over 25 years ago, researchers surveyed college students regarding their beliefs about gender and conversational content. Respondents of both sexes associated gossip and trivial topics with women speakers. The tendency was to devalue the content of women's talk (Kramer, 1977). In subsequent studies, researchers concluded that in same-sex friendship groups, men were more likely to discuss topics such as sports, careers, and politics, whereas women were more likely to self-disclose feelings, motivations, relationships, and personal problems (Bischoping, 1993). However, although this might be true in some contexts, *in same-sex friend dyads*, men actually self-disclosed *more* (Leaper, Carson, Baker, Holiday, & Myers, 1995). The Situational Alarm sounds again! Even more recently, Clark (1998) compared the topics and objectives of everyday conversations among young undergraduate women and men in the United States. She noted that stereotypes regarding conversational content still prevailed. People believed that women typically discussed men and appearances. Men were believed to talk more about work and leisure activities. This researcher collected relevant self-report data both from pairs of friends and from pairs of casual acquaintances. There were striking gender similarities in both types of dyads. The most common topics for both men and women were a person of the other sex, a person of same sex, the dyad's immediate surroundings, other leisure activities, and academics. The most significant difference was the frequency of conversations about sports (men = 53%, women = 19%). In terms of the most common objectives of the interactors, again gender similarities prevailed in both types of dyads. These objectives included showing interest in what the other person says, communicating friendliness, and talking about topics of interest to the other person. Among friend dyads, "offering helpful advice" was the most common objective.

Sexist Communication

So far, we have been looking at gender similarities and differences in language and communication. It seems important to stop and consider the issue of gender bias in language. Gender-biased language is called *sexist language.* It is language that excludes, derogates, or demeans one gender or the other. Most often, sexist language has negative implications regarding girls and women.

Language is the primary means through which we understand the world and our place in it. Psycholinguists have been able to clearly and repeatedly demonstrate that our language influences the way we think and feel about the world and our place in it (Henley, 1989; Hyde, 1984). For example, is a couple without children *childless* or *child free?* Are the women or men who have experienced the trauma of a sexual assault, rape *victims* or rape *survivors?* Is one dealing with an *unborn baby* or a *fetus?* Is that attractive classmate a member of the *opposite sex* or a member of the *other sex?* Of the person who chooses to spend years or even decades caring for several children and a home, not to mention facilitating a partner's career, it is often said, "(so and so) doesn't work." When Margaret Thatcher became prime minister of England, newspaper accounts repeatedly identified her as a *housewife.* Actually she had just distinguished herself during a term as cabinet minister (Romaine, 1999). Why was it that in the recent past, a sexually unresponsive man was labeled as *impotent* (without power), whereas a sexually unresponsive woman was labeled as *frigid?* Therapists (and marketing executives) prefer the terms *erectile dysfunction* and *anorgasmic* (without orgasm), respectively. One sex therapist believes the term *preorgasmic* is much more helpful for women who are troubled by this issue (Barbach, 1982). As you have now experienced, words may not be magical, but they are certainly powerful in how we think and respond to almost everything in the world.

Critical Thinking Challenge

What do you think feminist activists of the 1970s meant when they said that among the goals of the second women's movement was the elimination of women's impotence and men's frigidity?

Traditions of sexist language tend to demean, infantilize, trivialize, and sexualize women (Adams & Ware, 1995). Take a look at Box 7.2 to see some examples of this tendency. One of the most recalcitrant

ABCs of GENDER (ATTITUDES, BELIEFS, AND CONCERNS)   BOX 7.2

The Issue: Dealing with Sexist Language

The following terms originally had equivalent meanings. Note how terms that refer to women have become both sexualized and derogatory.

Sir	Madam
Master	Mistress
Bachelor	Spinster (a woman who earned an independent living by spinning thread)
Wizard	Witch
Patron	Matron

Can you suggest nonsexist alternatives for the following?

Policeman
Waitress/waiter
Fireman
Salesman
Mailman
Airline steward/airline stewardess
Chairman
Foreman
Congressman
Mankind
Spokesman
Flagman
Military men

Bondsman
Draftsman
"Who will be manning the information booth today?"
Workman's compensation
"I borrowed the assignment sheet from a girl in my class."
Wanted: "Girl-Friday"
"Men at Work"
Mr./Mrs.
"All men are created equal"
"Our father, who art in heaven."
First Lady
Brotherhood Day
Brotherhood of Electrical Workers

---

remnants of sexist language is the *generic masculine*. Researchers have repeatedly demonstrated that when girls (and college women) read vocational material using the generic masculine, they experience lower self-confidence in their ability to participate or succeed in that profession (Hamilton, 1991). What images does your mind produce when you read the following sentences?

♦ "The astronaut must carefully check his equipment before leaving the safety of the space station."

♦ "In a testing situation, the neuropsychologist should pay close attention to the quality of his nonverbal interactions with the client."

Such language tends to discourage girls and women from imagining themselves in these roles and professions (Beal, 1994; Miller & Swift, 1991). Do you know anyone who needs to do a "sexist language check" on his or her communications?

Critical Thinking Challenge

Aside from avoiding penalties on APA-style papers, what personal and professional benefits might be gained from dropping sexist language habits from speech and writing?

The Rise and Fall of the Gendered Personality

In psychology, the term *personality* is usually defined as "an individual's psychological uniqueness or distinctiveness." Just as your body is unique (unless you are an identical twin), your personality is also unique. Where can one "see" another person's unique personality? Although there may be characteristic, internal ways of thinking or feeling, it is only when the person behaves, interacts, or responds that personality becomes evident to others. Thus, even for those theorists who see personality as a collection of individual traits, the traits are only evident when the person is doing something, especially in regard to others. So any discussion of "gender and personality" soon melts into a discussion of "gender and social behavior."

You may recall from an earlier chapter that one of the first steps in gender development is the establishment of a stable gender identity. Once gender identity is established, the person begins to both value and manifest the preferences, interests, traits, and behaviors prescribed for that identity within a particular society. Thus certain personality characteristics are associated with a particular gender within a particular society (Best & Williams, 1997). Infants may bring their individual temperaments into the

ZOOM & ENLARGE   **BOX 7.3**

Communicating Mainstream Masculinity and Femininity

Consider this list of mainstream, Western, middle-class, gender-related behavioral prescriptions (Doyle, 1989). How free are we to accept them or reject them as we choose? Generate a list of contexts or situations in which you experienced stronger pressures to "perform" these prescriptions.

Communicating masculinity

Actively avoid anything female or feminine

Be successful

Be aggressive or at least dominating

Be sexual

Be self-reliant and act as if you have few emotional needs

Communicating femininity

Appearance still counts the most

Be sensitive, caring, or at least attentive

Accept the fact that you will be treated negatively by others

Be superwoman

---

world, but the cultural environment shapes these qualities. A stable gender identity includes these gender-related qualities, and individuals hold them as personal ideals that guide their behavior. Individuals believe they possess these gender-related personal ideals and will perform them to varying degrees in particular situations (Walkerdine, 1997). Some of these ideals are listed in Box 7.3. People believe gendered others possess them too, and expect to observe them in others (stereotypes). They then treat others in ways that are likely to produce these very qualities. Thus notions of persistent and consistent gender-typed personality characteristics continue (see Table 7.2). To make it even more complicated, these gender-related personality qualities interact with the behavioral norms for age, ethnicity, and social class (Frable, 1997).

Feingold (1994a) conducted four meta-analyses of gender differences in personality as they were described in the psychological literature from 1958 to 1992. The general patterns were that men were more assertive and had slightly higher self-esteem than did women. Women scored higher on measures of extraversion, anxiety, trust, and nurturance. No differences were found in social anxiety, impulsiveness, activity, **locus of control**, or orderliness. These differences and similarities persisted across age, years of data collection, educational level, and nationality (Canada, China, Finland, Germany, Poland, Russia, and the United States). Now, let's take a look at some personality characteristics and related social behaviors that are commonly believed to be gender related.

Achievement

Many adults believe that girls and women still devalue their true capabilities and see themselves as less competent. Early researchers hypothesized that although boys and men were driven by either a motive to approach success, or a motive to avoid failure, a substantial proportion of girls and women were driven by a motive to avoid success (Atkinson, 1964; Horner, 1978). These internal personality traits ostensibly explained why women were concentrated in low-status roles and occupations and why men were concentrated at the highest levels of the socioeconomic pyramid. There was little attention to the external, environmental constraints that limited women's access to high-status occupations and positions, such as gender discrimination in education and hiring, or the "glass ceiling" (Kanter, 1993). Studies attempting to document gender differences in achievement strivings have been largely inconclusive and contradictory (Eccles, Barber, & Jozefowicz, 1999; Huguet & Monteil, 1995). Yet some differences have persisted.

Critical Thinking Challenge

Do you see how attributing gender differences in achievement striving to internal personality traits (rather than external, situational constraints such as discrimination) can become a form of "blaming the victim"?

---

locus of control   **Degree to which individuals believe they control their own destiny (internal), versus those who believe external factors determine what happens in their lives.**

TABLE 7.2   Gender Stereotypes in U.S. Society

Feminine Stereotype		Masculine Stereotype	
Affectionate	Loyal	Acts like a leader	Has leadership qualities
Cheerful	Sensitive to the needs of	Aggressive	Independent
Childlike	others	Ambitious	Individualistic
Compassionate	Shy	Analytical	Make decisions easily
Does not use harsh language	Soft-spoken	Assertive	Masculine
Eager to smooth hurt feelings	Sympathetic	Athletic	Self-reliant
Feminine	Tender	Competitive	Self-sufficient
Flatterable	Understanding	Defends own beliefs	Strong personality
Gentle	Warm	Dominant	Willing to take a stand
Gullible	Yielding	Forceful	Willing to take risks
Loves children			

Source: Adapted from Bem Sex Role Inventory (BSRI), in S. L. Bem (1974). The measure of psychological androgyny. Journal of Consulting and Clinical Psychology. 42. 155–162.

Gender socialization practices clearly influence achievement strivings. For example, middle-class mothers in the United States are more likely to engage in achievement-theme conversations with their sons and social-theme conversations with their daughters (Flanagan, Baker-Ward, & Graham, 1995). However, among working-class, minority group families in the United States, parents tend to have higher educational aspirations for their daughters than for their sons. This may help explain why the educational accomplishments of women tend to surpass those of men among African-Americans and other ethnic minority groups. For poor Chicano families, parents' achievement aspirations for their daughters are more ambivalent (Beal, 1994). Chicana daughters who leave home while unmarried to seek a college education and career may be labeled as *chicana falsa* (Leland & Chambers, 1999).

Parental beliefs regarding achievement were compared in Taiwan, Japan, and the United States. As early as the first grade, across all three societies, parents believed that boys are better at math, whereas girls are better at reading. Across all three cultures, children were aware of their parents' beliefs. In the Japanese families, mothers were intensely involved in their sons' education but much more relaxed about their daughters' education. Among the Chinese, boys and girls achieved differentially depending on their parents' concerns about gender and achievement. In terms of actual performance in reading and math-

ematics, Japanese and Chinese children did better than American children in both domains. It is interesting to note that in this study, Japanese girls outperformed American boys on the mathematical tests (Lummis & Stevenson, 1990).

Previous studies of white college students' self-presentation of academic achievement in an interactional context indicated that boys tended to boast and self-aggrandize about their performance, whereas girls tended to be modest. Yet such effects emerged only in public self-presentations. In private presentations, these gender differences disappeared. In general, as social, educational, and occupational opportunities for women of all ethnicities have expanded and equalized in Western societies, findings of gender differences in achievement have declined (Brown, Uebelacker, & Hetherington, 1998).

Aggression

No social behavior is more associated with stereotypical masculinity and the masculine gender role than is aggression. Nor is there any doubt that in the majority of cultures, most violent and antisocial acts tend to be carried out by men. Here I focus on more typical expressions of aggression.

What precisely is aggression? For the layperson, notions of aggression overlap with concepts of assertiveness, dominance, and competitiveness. All these are aspects of the masculine schema. For the psychologist, and especially the social psychologist, aggression involves the intention to do harm to another living being. The key words here are *intention* and *harm*. Psychologists traditionally defined the intention to do harm in terms of direct, physical harm. As we shall see, aggression was thus defined (measured and studied) in a way that biased its frequency, duration, and intensity toward men, yet even then findings were inconsistent.

Across species, females engage in very high levels of aggression to protect offspring and home sites, yet this was overlooked in traditional studies of aggressive behavior (Hood, 1996). If males injured or killed others to protect their territory or access to mates, it was "aggression." If females injured or killed others to protect their offspring or nesting area, it was "maternal instinct." Note how that last point takes us right back to the way language and labeling shapes how we view and interpret behavior.

Feminist psychologists were wise to point out that aggression may in fact be physical or verbal, direct or indirect (White & Kowalski, 1994). With this broader, more realistic definition, our view of the relationship between gender and aggression shifts dramatically. What have we learned about gender and aggression? First, there are serious methodological flaws in the research about human aggression. Most of the early research on aggression was carried out with only male participants, so the stereotypical association between men and aggression was further reinforced (Anselmi & Law, 1998). Moreover, the ethical constraints on overt aggression in the laboratory led to a heavy reliance on self-reports. In keeping with gender role expectations, gendered self-concept, and gender role identification, men from many walks of life were much more likely to report physical aggression (Harris & Knight-Bonoff, 1996a, 1996b). In contrast, observational studies often resulted in contradictory and incompatible results (Cairns & Cairns, 1994). But even observational research has its limitations. You may recall from an earlier chapter that often reports of males "greater aggression" reflect the extreme behavior of only a small number of males in the group (DiPietro, 1981).

Second, regardless of any methodological flaws, it appears to be true that across cultures, men are more physically aggressive compared to women. For example, in both Australia and the United States, boys tended to be more physically aggressive, whereas girls tended to use more indirect aggression (Giancola & Zeichner, 1995; Owens & MacMullin, 1995). Similar findings have emerged in studies conducted in Tonga (Olson, 1994), Argentina (Hines & Fry, 1994), and Scandinavia (Bjorkqvist, 1994). This same pattern of gender differences in aggressive strategies emerged across cultures as varied as Brazil, Finland, Israel, Mexico, and the United States (Burbank, 1994). Within the United States, Harris (1995) found Latino men were more approving of physical aggression, particularly in response to personal insults. However, Latinas also engage in high levels of aggression if such behavior is in keeping with group norms, for example, in gangs (Harris, 1995). Physical and relational aggression were compared among white and African-American children. Regardless of ethnicity, boys were more physically aggressive than girls were, but direct verbal aggression increased with age in both genders. At all ages, girls showed more indirect forms of social aggression, such as withdrawal, rejection and so on (Rys & Bear, 1997).

Third, aggression levels are very vulnerable to situational constraints. For example, Lightdale and Prentice (1994) found equal levels of aggression among video game plays among women and men, but only when the gender of an opponent was uncertain! Men generally show higher levels of aggressive behavior when it is required (rather than chosen) in a laboratory situation, when in public situations, and when the target is also male (Campbell, 1993; Hyde, 1986). When there is no possibility of retaliation, female aggression also approaches male levels. A meta-analysis of over 100 studies revealed that *provocation* in a social situation also equalized the aggression levels expressed by both women and men (Bettencourt & Miller, 1996).

Fourth, aggressive behavior has different social meanings for women and men. In extensive reviews of the literature on gender and the perceptions of aggression, researchers found that women tend to view their aggression as expressive and as a way of dealing with feelings when out of control. Men viewed their aggression as a way of achieving goals and gaining control

(Campbell, 1993; Harris & Knight-Bonoff, 1996a, 1996b). Thus the perception and evaluation of aggression seems strongly related to gender roles and gender stereotypes. In a recent study about children's perception of aggression, boys viewed physical aggression as more hurtful, whereas girls rated social aggression as more hurtful (Galen & Underwood, 1997).

Testosterone and Aggression. Whenever the discussion turns to the subject of gender and aggression, the androgen testosterone is very likely to be mentioned. A common, but erroneous idea regarding testosterone is that it works like dry wood on a campfire: add more wood and the fire burns higher and hotter. It doesn't seem to work that way at all (Bjorkqvist, 1994). The relationship between testosterone and aggressive behavior is much more equivocal and complex. Testosterone levels and aggressive behavior are certainly correlated in lower species, and among humans the peak level years of testosterone are associated with peak levels of antisocial and aggressive behavior (ages 15 to 24). However, the direction of association is not clear (Sapolsky, 1997). For example, male baboons who win fights for higher social status do indeed have higher testosterone levels, but this typically occurs *after* the battle or *after* the new status is achieved (Sapolsky, 2000). In other words, certain behaviors and experiences seem to affect testosterone levels, rather than the other way around (Brody, 1999; Susman, Worrall, Murowchick, Frobose, & Schwab, 1996). This seems to be a difficult reality for many to grasp. Moreover, individual fluctuations in testosterone levels are not related to fluctuations in aggressive behavior. In other words, a person is *not* more likely to behave aggressively when testosterone level is higher. In situations of social stress (such as fights for status), testosterone levels may rise, but so do the levels of several other hormones (cortisol, for instance). To further complicate things, you need to know that testosterone is usually transformed (*aromatized* is the technical term) into other substances, such as estrogen or estradiol, for example. Higher levels of estrogens are also correlated with elevations in aggression (Brody, 1999). Let's take a quick look at some of the other findings regarding aggression and testosterone and see if you don't come away even more confused.

Dabbs and Morris (1990) explored the relationship between testosterone and *antisocial* behavior in over 4,500 male veterans. Higher testosterone levels were associated with a general tendency toward many types of excessive behavior (dominance, competitiveness, substance abuse, more sexual partners, and so on). However, men with higher testosterone levels who were from a higher socioeconomic status engaged in more *prosocial* behavior. Thus, experience and resources seem to modulate any effects of testosterone. Continuing this line of research, Mazur, Booth, and Dabbs (1992) studied the relationship between testosterone levels and the outcomes in a chess competition. In postgame measurements, winners had higher testosterone levels than did losers. However, the eventual *losers* in the finals tournament had significantly higher testosterone levels *before* the matches.

By the way, among women higher testosterone levels are associated with prosocial behavior, positive affect, and a more friendly, expansive personality (Crenshaw & Goldberg, 1996; Harris, Rushton, Hampson, & Jackson, 1996). Overall, testosterone levels seem related to strength, impulsiveness, and adventurousness and these can be shaped into positive or negative behavioral characteristics according to the prevailing gender ideology.

Assertiveness

The ability to stand up for your own rights without denying or trampling the rights of others is a component of the masculine stereotype. Ostensibly, women in our society have been socialized to be more passive. Earlier researchers on gender differences proclaimed that the reason why women were less effective in the occupational and interpersonal realms was their lack of assertiveness (rather than sexism and inequality of opportunity). Do you recognize this same argument from the earlier discussion of achievement? Despite popular beliefs and expectations, the research in this area failed to show consistent gender differences in assertiveness (Deaux & Major, 1998). Multicultural and cross-cultural studies also failed to support the notion of a gender difference in assertiveness. However, cross-cultural studies suggest that men do not respond favorably to assertive women (Rudman, 1998) and that assertiveness is more likely to vary as a function of gender role identification rather than of gender. Thus, regardless of gender, more traditionally feminine individuals will demonstrate lower levels of assertiveness (Wilson & Gallois, 1993).

Conformity

The traditional research literature supported the stereotype of greater conformity and compliance among women, although contradictory findings were widespread. In the laboratory, level of conformity was measured by how frequently a naïve respondent agreed with the erroneous judgments of a group of confederates (Asch, 1951). Women tended to conform more in such scenarios, and this was originally explained in terms of women's "dependency and greater need for harmony." However, conformity levels were strongly influenced by the nature of the stimuli used (estimating line lengths). A classic study found men conformed more when more traditionally feminine objects or tasks were involved (estimating color matches) (Sistrunk & McDavid, 1971). More recent studies have failed to find any conformity at all, suggesting that the conforming behavior may have been a reflection of the behavioral norms in effect during the 1950s (Collin, DiSano, & Malik, 1994).

Empathy

Empathy is usually defined as sensitivity and responsiveness to another's feelings, and such responsiveness is usually associated with the stereotype of the traditional woman in our society (Batson, Turk, Shaw, & Klein, 1995; Glick & Fiske, 1999). It is interesting to note that there has been relatively little research about empathy. Most studies have relied heavily on self-reports, and the relatively strong association of empathy with the feminine stereotype has resulted in findings of large gender differences (Trobst, Collins, & Embree, 1994). It is clear that both men and women judge women to be more empathic than men (Doherty, Orimo, Singelis, Hatfield, & Hebb, 1995). Minority group women are evaluated as being particularly high in empathy, although this too varies according to the method of measurement used, rather than by any essential quality (Watson et al., 1994).

Helping Behavior

The traditional finding was that men were more likely to help others and that women were more likely to seek help (Nadler, 1991). However, the vast majority of social psychological studies involved scenarios of public, short-term encounters between strangers (books dropped on a street, a flat tire, falling while riding a subway train, and so on). These situations increased the likelihood of male helping. Thus *helping behavior* was defined by what men were more likely to do, and so more male helping behavior was observed (Eagly, 1998).

In the real world, the male role does encourage heroic and chivalric helping, especially in risky and dangerous situations. Men clearly help more than women do in such situations. In contrast, the feminine role promotes nurturant and caring helping, such as providing emotional support. Additional feminine elements or expectation involve self-sacrifice and placing greater importance on the needs of others. In our society, women are expected to help others achieve their goals, especially if those others are family members and close friends. Yet this kind of helping remains very difficult for researchers to study. The most recent research on helping behavior rejects the notion of any inherent gender differences in helping behavior. The helping behavior of both women and men is guided by gender role identification. As in the other social behaviors examined here, situational and contextual factors influence helping by women and men (Eagly, 1998). These influential factors include, first, the type of helping required (long versus short term); women are more likely to persist in long-term helping. The second factor is the person who is in need of help (family, close friend, or stranger); men are more likely to help strangers, although this varies by culture. The third factor is the risk level of the helping situation: men are more likely to risk themselves in order to help. The fourth factor is the skills needed to help another: Is physical strength or comforting touch required?

Leadership

The traditional stereotype portrays men as "natural" leaders. Yet the relevant research was characterized by mixed findings. Once again, the question is not whether women and men offer different kinds of leadership, but rather, under what conditions do they behave similarly or differently? Moreover, in examining leadership, one cannot focus on solely on the behavior of the leader. Leadership always occurs in an interactive context. Issues of informal power, formal position, task, group history, and so on must all be considered, along with gender. Laboratory studies of leadership typically involve informal, mixed-sex groups of strangers who meet briefly. Often they work on tasks and problems that are more familiar to men. Moreover, within these mixed-sex groups there is the unavoidable "hidden agenda" of displaying appropriate masculinity and femininity in order to be appealing and attractive to each other. In such situations, display of gender-prescribed behavior and characteristics is self-enhancing and satisfying, and therefore men will more emerge as leaders more frequently (Eagly, Karau, & Makhijani, 1995; Wood et al., 1997).

One study offers some fascinating insights into the impact of culture on dominance and leadership. Researchers compared the decision-making interactions among married couples from three very different cultural backgrounds within the United States. Some couples were Navaho Indians (a relatively matriarchal culture in which women have considerable public power). A second group was comprised of Mormon couples (who tend to have a strongly patriarchal value system). A third group was made up of white Texas farmers (with a relatively egalitarian gender orientation). This researcher evaluated both talking time and whose will tended to prevail in decision making. The results were consistent. The higher the status of women in that culture, the more women expressed dominance and leadership (Strodtbeck, 1998).

Other studies suggest that regardless of gender, those who believe they are capable of performing competently and have high expectations for their own performance are more likely to emerge as leaders. When men and women have equivalent expectations in a situation, no gender differences in the likelihood or style of leadership emerge (Andrews, 1992). With equivalent competence and formal status, dominance rather than gender will predict who will assume leadership.

Conclusions: Culture and the Performance of Gender

Let's return to that confusing encounter between Ramona and Jason at the very beginning of the chapter. Their interchange lies at the nexus of culture, gender, emotion display, communication, and social behavior. Let's use that incident to illuminate some of the concepts discussed in this chapter. Jason approached the party and his meeting with Ramona with the assumption that all the norms and perhaps stereotypes that would guide his behavior in the United States were in effect in the Philippines. They were not! Similarly, Ramona was relying on Filipino cultural and gender norms and perhaps stereotypes to guide her own behavior. The problem with cultural and gender norms is that one never realizes which ones are in effect until violations occur. Jason interpreted Ramona's attentiveness, frequent eye contact, smiling, close interpersonal distance, and touching as indicating romantic or sexual interest. Contrary to the masculine stereotype of emotional insensitivity, Jason was very much aware that Ramona had reciprocated his self-disclosure at an even more personal level. For Jason, this seemingly personal revelation about her family again implied a sexual or romantic interest. Having made this interpretation, he then invoked the masculine gender role norms of assertiveness and sexual initiative by suggesting a significant change in their social relationship (he invited her to a romantic secluded location). For Ramona, a whole other set of norms was in effect. First, one of the most central concepts relevant to Filipino social behavior is the idea of *kapwa* (Enriquez, 1988). There is no word in English that corresponds to it, but it sometimes translated as "others." In English, this implies an exclusionary boundary, the "not me" in an interaction. But in Tagalog (a Filipino language), it implies "the unity of the self with others" (Enriquez, 1988, p. 160). Thus, for Ramona, maintaining connection and inclusion with Jason in the interaction would be paramount. No wonder she was so responsive to him! Also, contrary to the popular stereotype for Asian women, urban Filipino women tend to be assertive, well-educated, achievement oriented, and quite worldly. Also, in Filipino culture, frequent conversations about family and family matters during social encounters are considered very appropriate and desirable, so her family disclosure may not have seemed at all intense or personal to her. Above all, powerful Filipino norms regarding hospitality were in effect for Ramona. These norms include strong prescriptions to be friendly, to be extremely polite, and to go to great lengths to enhance the good feelings of an interaction partner or guest (*kapwa* again). Ramona was observing all these social norms, and they were amplified even more by her role as a relative of the hosts. In the

Philippines, Ramona's attentiveness, smiling, assertive touching, and self-disclosure have no social meaning beyond the politeness required in a spontaneous conversation. Ramona may have been amused, offended, angered, or just confused by Jason's "pass." However, the gender norms of Ramona's society demanded a continued smile and a graceful, nonhostile exit from the situation.

This chapter has centered on a conceptual change within the study of the psychology of gender. This change reflects the massive social changes within our own society. When Western psychologists and sociologists became interested in gender, they observed the rather striking differences in the behavior and statuses of women and men. In contrast to the advice offered in the quotation at the very beginning of the chapter, many tended to believe all of what they saw. They attempted to explain the differences they saw as due to some central essence of masculinity and femininity (Bohan, 1997; DeLameter & Hyde, 1998). They pinpointed the source of these ephemeral differences in emotional expression, communication, personality, and social behavior as residing within the person or within a gender. Yet in all of the areas under examination, findings were inconclusive and contradictory (Deaux, 1999). Thus the notion of essential differences became more and more untenable. Over the years, it has become apparent that powerful social and cultural factors are at work here. These factors may be summarized by concepts of cultural norms and gender-related norms, expectations, situational demands, and stereotypes. Change the social and cultural context or situation, and gender-typed behavior varies predictably. Moreover, many of the ostensible gender differences in emotional expression, communication, and social behavior may be explained as status differences. Any subordinate group, whether a gender group, an ethnic group, a social class, or a group with lower occupational status, seems to display the characteristics traditionally associated with femininity in this society. The coping mechanisms adapted by any subordinate group are adaptive. As a group, women tended to occupy a subordinate status in most areas of social existence, and so subordinate group characteristics and adaptations were misidentified as gender characteristics and adaptations. As the status of women has risen in industrial and postindustrial society, those supposed gender dif-

ferences have declined. However, they still manifest in situations where traditional gender norms are more prominent. Do these concepts hold across other cultures?

Personal values, social roles, and gender were examined among teachers and students across 33 nations. In nations where men had more authority, both men and women tended to endorse the desirability of tradition and conformity to traditional gender roles. These cross-cultural data suggested that modernization was a critical factor in gender-related differences. With greater industrialization, women and men have less differentiated roles, and gender differences in social behavior decline (Matsumoto, 1996; Schwartz, 1994).

In a comparable study, researchers examined modernity, occupational status, and two characteristics that are heavily gender typed (locus of control and emotional expressiveness) across 14 nations. The researchers noted that in the classic work by Williams and Best (1990), men were seen as stronger and more active, but these characteristics were viewed more favorably *only* in nations with lower levels of socioeconomic development. Nations characterized by greater modernity and therefore greater individualism were more liberal and flexible in terms of gender role ideology. Across these societies, women were generally less traditional in gender identification than were men. In more economically developed countries, women viewed themselves more favorably, and this difference appeared related to the fact that they were no longer limited only to domestic roles. These researchers found that regardless of gender, individuals with higher occupational status were more likely to see rewards and gratification as being under their own control (an internal locus of control). They also found individuals with a lower occupational status to be more feeling and relationship oriented (Smith, Dugan, & Trompenaars, 1997).

A study of Canadian college students revealed a comparable relationship among status, communality/expressiveness, and agency/instrumentality. That is, regardless of gender, lower-status individuals were perceived as more communal and less agentic. They also found that in groups, people with less power are more attentive and deferential to those with more power, and they also engage in more approval-seeking behavior. Regardless of gender, individuals with greater status were perceived as assertive and dominant, whereas individuals with lower status were perceived as more deferent and more sensitive (Conway, Pizzamiglio, & Mount, 1996).

Summary

- Over the centuries, scholars have attempted to describe or capture the essential differences between men and women in a variety of ways. Psychologists and sociologists use the terms *masculinity* and *femininity* to refer to the degree to which men and women have incorporated their society's gender ideals into their identity.
- The terms *communal/expressive* and *agentic/instrumental* have been used to summarize the core features of mainstream Western ideals for masculinity and femininity.
- A gender-biased notion of emotional expressiveness is a central feature of the feminine stereotype in mainstream culture. Contextual and situational variables predict variations in emotional expressiveness more reliably than does gender.
- Ostensible gender differences in touch and smiling also vary according to cultural and situational norms.
- Popular writings about strong gender differences in verbal communication reflect white, middle-class norms and expectations. Contextual and

situational factors, especially status, exert strong influences on communication differences.
- The conversations of women and men are quite similar in content. Sexist language has undesirable effects on individuals, especially girls and women.
- The findings related to powerful stereotypes regarding gender differences in several personality traits and their associated social behaviors merit critical evaluation. These include achievement, aggression, assertiveness, conformity, empathy, helping behavior, and leadership.
- Cross-cultural research conducted in societies undergoing rapid sociocultural change in the direction of greater gender equality reveal a pattern of declining gender differences. These findings mirror the changes in our own society.

InfoTrac College Edition

For more information, explore InfoTrac College Edition at

http://www.infotrac-college.com/Wadsworth

Enter search terms: sexist language, agentic and communal, gender and achievement, gender and leadership, gender and language, gender and emotions.

8

Gender and Sexuality
Private Lives and Public Meanings

There is widespread aversion to acknowledging the sexual double standard of a masculinity ideology that values the "sexual stud" . . . and a femininity ideology that constrains women's sexuality and enslaves them to myths of perfectible beauty. ◆ R. F. Levant and G. R. Brooks

Learning Objectives

After studying this chapter, you should be able to:

1. Summarize the gendered aspects of sexual development, mentioning adolescent sexual scripts and the significance of first intercourse.
2. Define *sexual orientation*, and contrast the social meaning of same-sex sexual behavior in the West with its meaning in other societies.
3. Summarize the current findings regarding the origins of sexual orientation.
4. Summarize Masters and Johnson's sexual response model, emphasizing gender similarities and differences, and mentioning how culture influences sexual response.
5. List and explain several gender-related beliefs that influence contemporary sexual attitudes and behavior in Western society.
6. Summarize the gender similarities and differences in autoerotic behavior, and then describe the central features of contemporary Western feminine and masculine eroticism.
7. Explain the significance of fertility and infertility in adult social identity, and then explain how gender and culture influence patterns of contraceptive use and abortion.
8. Describe the gender-related aspects of selected categories of sexual dysfunction.
9. Summarize the gender-related features of two types of commercialized sex.

Encounters with Gender

"Yes, Mrs. Sternwood, yours is a case of hysteria, a fairly common problem. Fortunately, there is now an easy cure. A new electro-mechanical device is reputed to bring rapid relief to women like yourself." Dr. Smith stroked his beard and sighed as he neatly added the usual tedious list of symptoms to his patient's record, "nervousness, insomnia, nymphomaniacal excitement, heaviness in the abdomen, loss of appetite, lascivious thoughts, irritability, weariness." He thought, "This is my second case of 'female complaints' this week. I already prescribed vigorous intercourse several times a week to her husband, but to no avail. So many women seem afflicted." He turned to his patient. "Please lie on the table, with the cloth over your private area. I assure you, the treatment is painless and will take just a few moments." He turned on the various switches and adjusted the new instrument. When it was humming steadily, he approached her and placed the device carefully on her vulva. Ever modest and always the professional, he kept his gaze firmly locked on the view just outside his office window. Horse-drawn carriages and a few of those new automobiles passed by. Within moments, the normally constrained and sedate Mrs. Sternwood was writhing, gasping, and arching her back in a most uncontrollable way. "Oui! Oui! Oui!," she shouted in her native French, and repeatedly called out her husband's name. Dr. Smith nodded his head, "Ah yes, the hysterical paroxysm is complete. The womb has been cleansed." Mrs. Sternwood slowly caught her breath and smiled radiantly. A great feeling of well-being flooded through her. She would be pleased to return for additional treatments. She felt wonderful!

Is this a scene from an old pornographic novel? Is Dr. Smith violating medical ethics and sexually abusing his patient? Did Mrs. Sternwood suffer from a sexual disorder?

Source: Adapted from R. P. Maines (1999), *The technology of orgasm: "Hysteria," the vibrator and women's sexual satisfaction* (Baltimore, MD: Johns Hopkins University Press).

Overview

This chapter examines gender in the context of sexuality, a very private area of life. I also examine the public or social meaning of sexual behavior in terms of gender. For example, sexuality-related concepts such as virginity, prostitution, homosexuality, or sexual dysfunction all have social meanings that vary according to gender, culture, and historical epoch. Sexuality is such a complex and far-reaching aspect of the gendered life that I examine only selected areas of sexual behavior. After a quick look at the development of sexuality, we will study the relationship between gender and sexual orientation. A thorough understanding of the physiological aspects of sexual response will help you evaluate popular ideas and attitudes about the sexuality of women and men. An examination of attempts to control reproduction reveals complex relationships between gender and culture. The chapter ends with a review of selected problems in sexual expression. This covers the very private experience of sexual dysfunction, as well as the public sale and purchase of sexual material and activity (pornography and prostitution).

Developmental Sexuality

The two major themes of childhood sexuality are curiosity and exploration. Questions about where babies come from are common, and curiosity about usually hidden bodily parts also begins in childhood. Comparisons and explorations with same-sex and other-sex playmates are both normal and typical (Schuhrke, 2000). Because their genitals are more obtrusive, genital manipulation and masturbation begin earlier and are more frequent among boys (Schwartz, 1999).

Parents and siblings play a major role in establishing a child's basic attitudes toward the body and sexuality. Across nations, family norms regarding displays of affection, nudity, bodily contact, responses to sexual questions, and reactions and instructions regarding genital touching set the stage for children's basic feelings about their bodies and their later sexuality (Frayser, 1994; Sandfort & Cohen-Kettenis, 2000).

Puberty and Adolescence

Puberty is the process by which the body gradually becomes capable of reproduction. **Menarche, spermarche,** body hair, voice changes, breast development, and other bodily transformations are among the physical signs of sexual maturation. Psychological changes such as an increase in sexual interest and erotic attraction to others also begin in puberty. Autoerotic activities such as romantic or sexual fantasies to accompany masturbation typically begin as well (Leitenberg & Henning, 1995).

In industrialized societies, the socially constructed period of time between childhood and full adulthood is known as *adolescence*. During that life segment, males and females have full reproductive capacity but do not possess the social and economic rights and responsibilities of full adulthood. Since the 1960s, industrial and postindustrial societies have gradually become more permissive regarding nonmarital sexual behavior among both women and men. However, as you will see, many vestiges of the sexual **double standard** remain (Hatfield & Rapson, 1996; Welch, Rostosky, & Kawaguchi, 2000).

Societies vary regarding attitudes toward breast development and menarche. The Mescalero Apache Indians in the southwestern United States hold an annual celebration for all the young women who began to menstruate in the previous year. This ritual is a public affirmation of women's power and fertility (Kelly, 1996). In contrast, menstruation is a private event in European-American society and is surrounded by ambivalent social attitudes (Kowalski & Chapple, 2000; Latteier, 1998; Martin, 1996).

Among girls in Western society, the process of sexual **objectification** begins during adolescence, particularly regarding comparisons to gender ideals for female weight and size (Wiederman & Hurst, 1997, 1998). Physical appearance becomes a central concern for girls (Martin, 1996; Travis, Meginnis, & Bardari, 2000). For boys, puberty and spermarche are not crises or negative experiences. Most boys look forward to adulthood and are not ambivalent about leaving childhood. Male puberty is associated with

---

menarche   **First menstruation.**

spermarche   **First ejaculation.**

double standard   **Equivalent sex-related activity or behavior is differentially approved on the basis of gender. Traditionally, men may engage in considerable casual and nonmarital sex, whereas women are stigmatized and punished for doing so.**

objectification   **Viewing a person as a "thing"; in this context, viewing women's bodies and body parts as the objects of men's fantasies, desires, and control.**

positive masculinity, physical competence, agency, and active sexuality (Sprecher & Regan, 1996).

During adolescence, social messages regarding sexual expression become highly differentiated according to gender. In some societies, young women are veiled and sequestered from men (Stowasser, 1998). People in most industrialized nations consider that young women should inhibit their desires to varying degrees and be wary of sexual overtures until they are in a committed relationship. They must avoid casual sexual encounters and guard against a "loose" reputation. Recognition and acceptance of young women's erotic interests and sexual desires are noticeably missing from the **sexual scripts** for female adolescents in industrialized societies (Anderson & Cyranowski, 1995; Welch et al., 2000). Masculine sexual scripts center on frequent casual sexual encounters (Good & Sherrod, 1997; Levant, 1997). Beliefs in the strength and power of male sexual drive and erotic interests are encouraged (Regan & Dreyer, 1999).

First Intercourse. The meaning of intercourse varies by gender and culture. First intercourse for a man typically signifies a transition to manhood. For women, it signifies a "loss" of her virginity. In some traditional societies, loss of female virginity implies unsuitability for marriage and lowered status as "damaged goods" (Tolman, 1999; Tolman & Brown, 2001). In most industrial societies, heterosexual sexual activity has shifted away from procreation to a more performance and pleasure-oriented ethos. Sexual intercourse is now for love, pleasure, comfort, intimacy, and psychological connection. For example, surveys of middle and high school students in the United States (Cooper & Orcutt, 1997; Kane & Schippers, 1996), Canada (Malo & Tremblay, 1997), and Australia (Rosenthal, Smith, & deVisser, 1999) revealed similar patterns surrounding initiation into heterosexual intercourse. Among those who were sexually active, there were no gender differences in the frequency or recency of sexual activity. In general, young women believed their sexual urges can and should be controlled. They saw teen parenthood as a serious problem and agreed that casual sex was not acceptable for women. Women expressed both positive and negative feelings about their first intercourse. Overall, these studies suggest that young women in industrialized countries now begin intercourse at an earlier age, have more sexual partners, and participate

in a broader range of sexual activities compared to young women of previous decades.

The young men in these studies anticipated and reported substantial peer pressure to have intercourse, and described their first intercourse in very positive terms. Most believed that men are naturally more sexually aggressive and that male sexual desire is relatively indiscriminate and impossible to control. Many subscribed to the belief that men need sex whereas women need love. This belief ostensibly explained male sexual violence. Adherence to this belief was also related to the acceptance of rape myths, the idea that contraception was a woman's responsibility, and the notion that men pursue sex to relieve tensions and have pleasure, whereas women want sex in order to strengthen emotional ties. Similarly, a study of intercourse initiation among Chicano, Latino, black, and white teens within the United States revealed no age differences for timing of first intercourse among women of any ethnicity. However, black teen males had the lowest age of first intercourse. This difference was interpreted in terms of the negative attitudes toward masturbation that prevail in the African-American community (Day, 1992). Masturbation is frowned on and considered a rather deviant activity that is indicative of sexual inadequacy. Thus substantial cultural pressures encourage earlier intercourse among African-American teenage boys (McClean, 1997).

Sexual Orientation

In most societies, establishing and maintaining a sexual relationship with an adult of the other sex is one of the central components of manhood or womanhood. In some societies, one may not be considered a real man or woman until that sexual bond is formalized through a publicly announced marriage. In others, regardless of marriage, true manhood and womanhood are recognized only with the arrival of offspring (Munroe & Munroe, 1994). In most Western societies, the gender ideal is of an exclusive, romantic, heterosexual relationship that culminates in a lifelong monogamous marriage and children. Thus legitimized private sexual activity with a person of the other sex is a core aspect of what defines a woman or a man. Societies vary greatly in the personal and social

---

sexual scripts **The learned guidelines for sexual expression, usually specific to a particular culture.**

The Many Meanings of Same-Sex Sexual Behavior

Latin America: In some Latin societies (such as Mexico and Brazil), not all men who have sex with men are considered homosexual. The behavioral role taken in the sexual encounter is more salient than the gender of the sexual partner. The "receiving" partner is viewed as homosexual, but not the penetrating partner (Almaguer, 1993).

Melanesia: Among the Sambia, young men are required to perform ritualized fellatio on adult men. Appropriate and healthy adult masculinity is believed to depend on their taking in sufficient semen from adult men. Once thus initiated, young men will move on to heterosexual marriage. A similar custom existed in the past among the Azande of Africa (Herdt, 1997).

Lesotho, Africa: The people of Lesotho are called Basotho. Marriage and childbearing are virtually compulsory in Basotho culture. However, "mummy-baby" relationships between female adolescents and young women are recognized as commonplace. They may be celebrated with a public ritual that can include husbands. These relationships are not seen as "lesbian," although extended kissing, body rubbing, emotional exclu-

sivity, and genital contact are all involved. According to Basotho culture, "sex" occurs only with a penis (Gay, 1989; Kendall, 1999).

China: Up through the 1930s, women silk workers constituted a relatively privileged group of Chinese women. Many joined a "marriage resistance" movement and formed extended families. Very close, often sexual, relationships formed in these groups (Sanker, 1986).

North America: In many Native American groups, the "two-spirit person" assumed various cross-gender roles, adopting the clothing and activities of the other gender. A two-spirit person's spouse might be of either sex. Two-spirit people were seen as specially blessed and as intermediaries between the spirit world and the material world. They were also seen as able to assist in healing marital quarrels and enmity.

Greece: In ancient Athenian society, important older men often had younger men as sexual partners. These relationships existed alongside heterosexual marriages and were considered an expression of a man's power and status. Ideals of masculine virility, honor, courage, and

beauty were central in such relationships. In ancient Sparta, a city-state known for its strong militaristic traditions, intimate relationships among warriors were viewed as creating a fiercer and more well-bonded fighting force (Bullough, 1976).

India: The hijras of India are viewed as "female men" who often remove their male genitals. They have sex only with other men, and make a living by singing, dancing, and offering blessings at weddings and at the birth of male children (Herdt, 1997). Recently, several hijras have been elected to public office. Because they have no children for whom to amass wealth or property, they are considered to be less vulnerable to corruption ("Incorruptible eunuchs capture Indian offices, 2001).

Zimbabwe, Africa: At a national book fair, GALZ (Gays and Lesbians of Zimbabwe) were ejected and their display booth destroyed. Robert Mugabe, president of Zimbabwe, declared that homosexuality was a Western (white) vice imported to the African continent by European colonists. Acceptance of same-sex relationships represented moral and social decay (Aarmo, 1999).

---

meanings attached to same-sex sexual behavior (see Box 8.1). In some societies, same-sex sexual activity is viewed as such a heinous violation of religious and social mores that execution is considered the appropriate response (for example, Iran, Kuwait, and Saudi Arabia). In others, imprisonment or a public beating constitute the legal response (as in Pakistan, Romania, and Nigeria) (Amnesty International, 1997). In contrast, the Netherlands has joined Denmark in offering full legal recognition of same-sex marriages (*Advocate*, 2000). In most Western societies, those who prefer erotic activity with same-sex others have, at various times, been considered evil, sinful, con-

fused, disturbed, criminal, or as inhabiting some intermediate category *between* real women and men (Bohan, 1996). This array of attitudes continues today. In contemporary Western society, the socially constructed concept of **sexual orientation** refers to the idea that people can be meaningfully categorized in terms of the gender of their sexual partners (Plummer, 1992).

---

sexual orientation   **The more or less stable pattern of erotic attractions toward and sexual behavior with individuals of the same or the other gender. Those with a bisexual orientation may relate sexually to both women and men.**

Private Acts and Social Identity

Until the 18th century, in European-American culture, same-sex sexual behaviors were seen as sinful acts. In the early 20th century, psychologists helped transform such behaviors into a strongly negative *social identity* (Kitzinger, 2001). That is, same-sex sexual behavior was no longer what a person *did*. It defined what a person *was* (a homosexual or sexual invert) and that person was mentally disordered (Forel, 1908). Scholars seeking to understand same-sex sexual behavior studied groups of incarcerated "criminals" and hospitalized "mental patients." Because same-sex sexual behavior so violated the norms of socially acceptable sexual expression, these inmates and patients were sometimes subjected to medically induced seizures, lobotomies, castration, doses of androgens, doses of estrogens, clitoridectomies, and painful **aversion therapies** (Rosario, 1997). In the earlier versions of the ***Diagnostic and Statistical Manual,*** or **DSM** (American Psychiatric Association, 1952, 1968), homosexuality was listed as a **sociopathic personality disorder.** In the 1950s, psychologist Evelyn Hooker (1957) demonstrated that there were no identifiable differences in the mental functioning of gay men versus heterosexual men. Comparable findings regarding lesbians followed (Armond, 1960). In 1973, a committee of the American Psychiatric Association determined that homosexuality was *not* a mental disorder and removed it from the DSM. In 1975, the American Psychological Association issued a statement of agreement stating that a same-sex orientation implied no mental impairment. In 1993, homosexuality was removed from the World Health Organization's International Classification of Diseases.

All through the 20th century, discrimination and violence against gay men and lesbians continued as both normative and socially acceptable. Appearance or behavior that violated then current gender standards targeted gay men and lesbians for persecution and discrimination. To be lesbian or gay was truly a stigmatized identity (Bohan, 1996). Leaders of the early **homophile** groups such as the Daughters of Bilitis and the Mattachine Society led public demonstrations, making sure their public selves were in strong conformity with current gender norms of dress, speech, and self-presentation. In the United States of the 1960s, the spirit of social activism on behalf of black civil rights and women's rights set the stage for similar activism on behalf of gay rights. In June 1969, police conducted a routine raid on the Stonewall, a gay and **drag** bar in New York's Greenwich Village, beating, threatening, and arresting the patrons. Men in women's clothing and their sympathizers battled police for several days, bringing national and international attention to issues of gay rights and privacy. This was the beginning of the gay rights movement. During the 1980s, a rise in conservative politics and the issue of HIV among gay men were setbacks for gay rights issues. However, in the 1990s cultural change helped unite lesbians and gay men in becoming a highly visible and potent political and social force, particularly in the urban centers of the United States and Canada. Today, most educated and informed people understand that gay men and lesbians are not confused about their gender. In fact, the social norms surrounding masculine sexuality may be exaggerated in the gay male subculture; for example, there may be casual sex, more sexual partners, sexual variety, emphasis on physical appearance, lower priority regarding monogamy, intimacy, and so on (Davies, Hickson, Weatherburn, & Hunt, 1993; Hatala & Prehodka, 1996). Likewise, the social norms surrounding feminine sexuality may be exaggerated in the lesbian subculture, for example, there may be an emphasis on romance and emotional intimacy, idealization of cohabitation and monogamy, couple-oriented social life, a focus on family and children, and so on (Schwartz & Rutter, 1998). In general, lesbians and gay men see themselves as real women and men who differ from the heterosexual majority only in their erotic attractions and in certain aspects of their couple and family roles (Barrett & Logan, 2002; Murphy, 1997). In most other aspects of life, they resemble the heterosexual majority.

---

aversion therapies   **Various conditioning treatments in which an undesirable stimulus (such as, for a homosexual, a nude photo of a young man) is paired with a painful or noxious stimulus.**

Diagnostic and Statistical Manual (DSM)   **The American Psychiatric Association's (APA's) listing and description of the central features of all recognized mental disorders.**

sociopathic personality disorder   **Older term for what is now called *antisocial personality disorder*. Implies a disregard for others, impulsivity, aggressive, and irresponsible behavior.**

homophile   **Having favorable attitudes toward homosexuality or homosexuals.**

drag   **Cross-dressing, usually with a comic or satirical intent.**

Critical Thinking Challenge

Do the following questions seem strange or unusual, and if so, why? Is heterosexuality a reaction to bad experiences with people of one's own sex? Why are heterosexuals so flagrant about their lifestyles, wearing wedding rings, and kissing in public? Why are straight people so adamant about recruiting children to their way of life, insisting on other-sex dating, and flooding the media with representations of heterosexual lovemaking?

Gender-Related Issues Surrounding Sexual Orientation

The Western concept of sexual orientation implies a relatively stable personal characteristic as well as a relatively permanent social identity; namely gay, lesbian, or bisexual (Firestein, 1996). However, these assumptions may be highly questionable, particularly in regard to women, because a majority of self-identified lesbians have had sexual relationships with men (Diamont, Schuster, McGugan, & Lever, 1999).

The Development of Sexual Orientation. Assumptions about the naturalness and universality of heterosexuality have resulted in very little "discourse" about how heterosexual orientation develops (Bem, 1996). However, there are three basic models regarding the origin of a same-sex orientation: biological, environmental, and cognitive.

Research findings purporting a genetic or chromosomal marker for same-sex orientation have been largely discredited for lack of replication, but these notions linger in the popular press and popular imagination (Rice & Anderson, 1999; Wickelgren, 1999). Research reports regarding **concordance** in sexual orientation among twins and siblings appeared promising, but overall findings have been inconsistent (Bailey, Pillar, Neale, & Agyei, 1993; Pattatucci & Hammer, 1995). Studies of differential brain structure such as those of Simon LeVay (1991) also captured the public's imagination, but had serious methodological flaws (Moore & Travis, 2000).

Critical Thinking Challenge

The participants in many concordance studies are recruited via newspaper ads. Does that sound your critical thinking alarm? Why or why not?

Other researchers have claimed the origin of sexual orientation to lie in the influence of prenatal hormones (Long, 1997). When sex hormones were first discovered, people assumed that the bodies of homosexual men were flooded with female hormones and that lesbians had too many masculine hormones. When it became clear that *all* women and men produced both androgens and estrogens, homosexual behavior was hypothesized to be caused by a disturbed proportion of these hormones. It was also believed that highly gender-typed (masculine) men and highly gender-typed (feminine) women were not true homosexuals. There is no evidence to support any differences in hormonal functioning among heterosexual-versus same-sex–oriented individuals, nor is there any hormonal distinctiveness among lesbians or gay men based on their level of gender conformity regarding appearance or comportment (Banks & Gartrell, 1995; Byne, 1995).

Developmentally oriented researchers hypothesized that childhood cross-sex–typed behavior predicted a homosexual orientation for men, but there were no analogous findings for women (Bailey & Zucker, 1995; Baumeister, 2000). Most such studies were retrospective ones. That is, researchers asked already self-identified gay men about their sex-typed childhood behavior. Gay men, growing up in a society that defines a homosexual orientation as related to femininity would be much more likely to remember and admit "cross-sex" childhood behavior. Only two demographic variables correlate reliably with a same-sex orientation: religious devoutness and education. There is less homosexuality among the devout and more among the more highly educated (Pillard & Bailey, 1995).

Critical Thinking Challenge

Why do you think more same-sex sexual activity is reported by more highly educated individuals?

Cognitive-Developmental. Savin-Williams (1995) hypothesized that early maturing children were more likely to function in same-sex groups and therefore more likely to have same-sex encounters early in puberty. Thus early maturers are more likely to develop a homosexual identity, and later maturers were more

---

concordance   **The proportion of twins who share a particular trait, in this case a homosexual orientation.**

likely to become heterosexually oriented. However, the data for lesbians did not fit this model. Most self-identified gay men become aware of their erotic attractions to men during late childhood. Across cultures, women may have a first same-sex relationship at various points during adulthood (Baumeister, 2000; Kitzinger, 1995).

Daryl Bem has attempted to provide a more general approach to the development of sexual orientation (Bem, 1996, 2000). According to the "exotic becomes erotic" (EBE) theory, biological markers do not code directly for sexual orientation, but they do influence basic childhood temperaments. Some children are predisposed toward rough-and-tumble activities (male typical) or quiet activities (female typical). Children prefer to play with those who match them on activity preference level. Gender-conforming children will feel different from other-sex peers, whereas gender nonconforming children feel different from same-sex peers. Feelings of being different from peers of a particular sex result in that group becoming "exotic" because the child experiences heightened physiological arousal around those peers. That is, for the gender-conforming child other-sex interactions result in arousal. For the gender nonconforming child, same-sex peer interactions result in arousal. Later this arousal is transformed into "erotic" arousal. This approach, although innovative, has been criticized as more applicable to masculine development (Peplau, Garnets, Spalding, Conley, & Veniegas, 1998).

Conclusions

The social meaning and interpretation of same-sex sexual behavior depends on the society and historical epoch in which an individual lives (Dykes, 2000). Psychologists do not know how sexual orientation develops. It is a complex phenomenon influenced by interaction among many factors. Hypotheses that same-sex orientation results from some chromosomal, hormonal or neuroanatomical difference have failed the test of replication (Moore & Travis, 2000). There is no evidence to support the idea that an erotic orientation to others of one's own sex is symptomatic of a disturbance in gender identity or any other aspect of mental or emotional functioning (Rothblum & Factor, 2001; Strickland, 1995). An orientation toward erotic behavior with people of one's own sex does not appear to result from problematic childhood socializa-

tion nor from a particular constellation of family dynamics (Bailey, 1996). There is no evidence to support the idea that gay men and lesbians constitute some intermediate step between fully developed men and fully developed women (Rosario, 1997). Moreover, same-sex sexual behavior may not represent equivalent phenomena in both genders in that sexual orientation appears much more flexible and fluid among women (L. M. Diamond, 1998; Baumeister, 2000; Peplau & Garnets, 2000).

Gender, Culture, and Physiological Sexuality: Much Ado About Vasocongestion and Myotonia

The Birds, the Bees, and the Brain

The brain processes and structures that are involved in sexual response are the same for men and women. Sexual arousal begins from awareness of either an internal stimulus (such as an erotic thought or fantasy) or an external one (such as an attractive person). The limbic system and the cerebral cortex are the two main brain structures involved in arousal. The limbic system is involved in the feelings surrounding sexual arousal and behavior (pleasure, affection, connection, and so on). The cortex regulates fantasy, thinking, language, and memory, all of which are central to our experience of sexual activity (see Figure 8.1).

Consideration of what is sexually attractive and arousing brings us immediately to the concept of human diversity, both individual and cultural. A partner's elaborate tattooing or scars may be arousing or repulsive. The feel of silky lingerie or the smell of fresh perspiration may or may not be erotically charged. A pierced ear, a pierced nipple, a pierced penis, or surgically enlarged breasts may revolt or attract, depending on culture or subculture.

Whatever turns you on, the laboratory research of William Masters and Virginia Johnson (1966) has provided considerable insight into how the body responds physiologically when sexually aroused. Although their model has been thoughtfully criticized for its methodological, ethnocentric, and androcentric biases (Tiefer, 1995), it still offers a useful starting point for discussing gender and sexual response.

The Four-Phase Model. There are three important points to remember when considering this model.

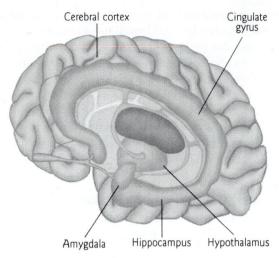

Cerebral cortex   Cingulate gyrus

Amygdala   Hippocampus   Hypothalamus

FIGURE 8.1   These are the parts of the human brain involved in sexual behavior and response.

First, Masters and Johnson described four distinct phases, but these phases blend together smoothly. Second, the same two physical processes are involved in sexual response for *both* women and men; namely, **vasocongestion** and **myotonia.** Third, regardless of gender, and regardless of whether one becomes aroused through an erotic video, masturbation, a vibrator, or other sexual device, a same-sex partner, a partner of the other sex, or anything else, the *physical response* is the same (Masters & Johnson, 1966).

1. *Excitement.* Physical and psychological stimulation lead to diffuse vasocongestion, especially in the pelvic area. In women, beads of *transudate* or plasma fluid appear on the vaginal walls, and these combine to cover the inside of the vagina, the inner labia, and the vaginal opening. The clitoris swells, erects, and elongates, and there are numerous other internal changes. In men, the identical process of vasocongestion in the erectile bodies of the penis produces erection. The scrotal sac pulls upward from the body, and the testes enlarge and become elevated. The erection may occur, subside, and reoccur depending on stimulation. Women's arousal is less subject to disruption or interruption compared to that of men (Masters & Johnson, 1966). The amount and consistency of vaginal lubrication and the speed and rigidity of erection both vary by age, intensity of stimulation, alcohol intake, fatigue, and the situation. Nipple erection occurs in both sexes, but it is more noticeable in women.

Some women develop a rosy sex flush over the upper abdomen and chest. In both sexes, myotonia increases, as do heart rate and blood pressure.

2. *Plateau.* The events just described continue and this provides the pleasure of extended lovemaking. Signs of excitement become more pronounced. In women, the clitoris becomes fully erect and hard, and changes position as it retracts under the clitoral hood. The vaginal opening may become smaller and grips whatever is penetrating. The Bartholin glands secrete a mucuslike fluid. In men, the coronal ridge of the penis enlarges and the head of the penis may turn a purplish color. The testes may double in size, and the Cowper's gland may secrete fluid at the tip of the penis (sometimes referred to as "pre-cum" or, in an earlier time, "love drops"). For both sexes, myotonia increases, especially in the face, neck, arms, and legs. Spasms may cause the hands and feet to become clawlike. Toward the end of the plateau phase, pelvic thrusting becomes involuntary.

3. *Orgasm.* This is subjectively experienced as an intense and highly pleasurable state, often accompanied by a feeling of suspension in time or space. Physical sensations rush all through the body as neuromuscular tensions are suddenly released. This occurs through a series of involuntary and very pleasurable muscular contractions (in 0.8-second intervals) of the vaginal barrel, uterus, and anus in women. In men, these contractions occur in the urethral bulb, urethra, penis, and anus. Orgasms typically last longer in women, because the whole pelvic area is engorged rather than just the genitals, as occurs in men. Women also vary by demonstrating one of three typical sexual response patterns (see Figure 8.2). For both women and men orgasm is accompanied by an extremely high heart rate (100 to 180 beats per minute), high blood pressure, and hyperventilation. Spasms occur in both hands and feet. Facial spasms often produce frowns and grimaces and an involuntary opening of the mouth. Spastic contractions of the arms, legs, back, and lower abdomen may result in aches the next day. Interestingly, verbal descriptions of orgasms by women and men are indistinguishable

---

vasocongestion   **The engorgement/filling of blood vessels, such as those in pelvic and erectile tissue, in response to sexual arousal.**

myotonia   **Increasing levels of muscle tension.**

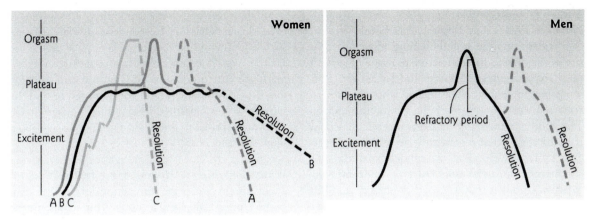

FIGURE 8.2   What are typical orgasm patterns in women and men?

(Vance & Wagner, 1976; Wiest, 1977). Clitoral stimulation is the most direct route to orgasm in women, so manual or oral stimulation is more effective than **missionary position** intercourse. For the majority of men, ejaculation and orgasm occur together, even though they are actually separate processes. Ejaculation consists of the emission and expulsion of semen. During emission, the genital ducts and accessory glands begin to contract, and semen collects in the urethral bulb, which then expands. This expansion leads to a feeling that ejaculation is imminent and unstoppable. Expulsion begins with the contraction of muscles at the base of the penis and around the anus (at those familiar 0.8-second intervals). The earliest contractions expel most of the semen and are experienced as the most pleasurable (Masters & Johnson, 1966).

4. *Resolution.* This involves a slow return to an unaroused state. The muscles return to a relaxed state, and vasocongestion is diffused. Blood pressure, heart rate, and respiration return to normal, and perspiration may appear. Men experience a **refractory period** that varies by age, mood, and type of stimulation available. For example, a 30-minute refractory period is typical for men in their 30s. Women do not experience a refractory period and are thus capable of renewed arousal to orgasm. Preferences during resolution also vary by individual and cultural prescription. Western norms include intimate talk, silence, or sleep (a masculine stereotype). Some want to cuddle, whereas others want to eat, drink, or perhaps smoke.

Gender, Culture, and Sexual Response

Although the physiology of sex may be universal, culture has a powerful influence on many other aspects sexual response. For example, the Dani of New Guinea believe it is inappropriate for a couple to have intercourse until four or five years have passed after the birth of a child (Heider, 1976). Some Australian Aborigine groups prescribe intercourse four or five times a night; for some, every sexual encounter begins with scratching and biting (Munroe & Munroe, 1994). In some Asian groups, the goal of sexual activity is to extend arousal as long as possible so as to balance the physical energy between women and men (Stubbs, 1992). For some sub-Saharan groups, penile insertion in the vagina begins immediately, typically goes on for less than two minutes, and ends with male orgasm. Female orgasm is unknown, and vaginal lubrication is considered unfeminine (Ecker, 1993). Western cultures label all erotic behaviors prior to orgasm as *foreplay*, suggesting a lack of importance. Western languages do not even have a name for the time after orgasm.

About half of women surveyed in the United States report multiple orgasms, especially through

missionary position   **"Man on top of supine woman" position for intercourse. Given this name by indigenous peoples who observed this "unusual" coital position among missionary couples. In many places in the world, side-by-side, and woman-on-top coital positions are more common.**

refractory period   **After male orgasm, the period of time during which erection cannot occur, even with stimulation.**

using a vibrator, oral stimulation, or masturbation (Chalker, 1994; Davis, Black, Lin, & Bonillas, 1996). Subsequent orgasms usually require less effort than the initial one. In some societies, multiple orgasms in men are recognized. Masters and Johnson (1966) identified some men below age 30 who were able to have multiple orgasms without a refractory period. The ability to have "dry" orgasms without an accompanying ejaculation represents a departure from general Western beliefs about masculine sexual response.

Another strongly held belief in contemporary Western culture is that women "take longer" to reach orgasm. This is true when the sexual activity is heterosexual intercourse. However, there is virtually no difference in the time women and men take to reach orgasm during masturbation—that is, less than four minutes (Masters & Johnson, 1966).

Sexual Attitudes and Behavior: The Influence of Gender and Culture

Whereas the physiology of sexual behavior may be universal, the psychological aspects of sexuality are heavily influenced by gender ideology and cultural norms.

Sexual Attitudes and Beliefs

The notion of sexual attitudes implies an evaluative response to some aspect of sexuality. In other words, some behaviors are evaluated as "better," or "more desirable," whereas others may be evaluated as "not at all acceptable." Here I examine how certain culture-based beliefs influence gender-related sexual attitudes.

Sexual Permissiveness. One approach to cultural diversity regarding sexual attitudes is to think of various nations or societies along a continuum from very permissive to very restrictive, but this may be too simplistic. In reality, a society may be permissive regarding some types of sexual behavior but quite restrictive regarding others. For example, researchers surveyed representative samples in 24 industrialized countries regarding their attitudes about four categories of nonmarital sexual expression: premarital sex, teenage sex, extramarital sex, and homosexual sex (Widmer, Treas, & Newcomb, 1998) (see Table 8.1a and 8.1b). As you can see, there is considerable variation across countries regarding the acceptability of each one of these sexual behaviors. Respondents in some nations, such as Germany, may be very accepting of premarital sex, but very rejecting of sex before age 16, or extramarital sex. Attitudes toward same-sex sexual behaviors varies considerably. Are you surprised to find the United States classified as generally conservative? Are you surprised to find Canadians permissive about same-sex behavior?

What Constitutes "Having Sex." In 1997, details about the private erotic interactions of the president of the United States and a young White House intern became public knowledge. One of the interesting debates to emerge from these events had to do with attitudes about what constituted "having sex." This controversy extended into the normally staid worlds of researchers and scientific journal editors. An editor of the prestigious JAMA (*Journal of the American Medical Association*) was fired when he published a study entitled *Would you say you "had sex" if . . . ?* (The journal's editorial board decided that the timing of the study's publication was overly political.) This survey of overwhelmingly white, heterosexual undergraduates ($N = 599$) in the United States revealed many fascinating details of what constitutes "having sex" (see Table 8.2) (Sanders & Reinisch, 1999). Note that about only 60% of the respondents considered oral–genital contact as "having sex." About 20% did not consider penile–anal contact as "having sex." Thus, only penile–vaginal insertion seemed to universally count as "having sex," particularly among men. Similarly, a survey revealed that for the men of some Latino groups, masturbation or oral contact with other men did not constitute "having sex" (Carballo-Dieguez, 1995). The **coital** imperative seems central in ideas about genital sexuality (Daniluk, 1998; Regan & Dreyer, 1999).

Do you recall this chapter's opening vignette? It is clear that Dr. Smith was using a vibrator to induce Mrs. Sternwood's orgasm. However, around the beginning of the 20th century many more physicians, patients, and even husbands would not have defined what happened as a sexual act, because "having sex" was even more rigidly defined solely as penile penetration of the vagina (Maines, 1999).

---

coital   **Having to do with coitus, heterosexual intercourse.**

TABLE 8.1 Variability in Sexual Permissiveness Across Nations

(a) Attitudes toward various forms of nonmarital sexual behaviors in 24 countries

Country	"Is sex before marriage wrong?"		"Is sex before age 16 wrong?"		"Is extramarital sex wrong?"		"Is homosexual sex wrong?"	
	Always Wrong	Not Wrong At All	Always Wrong	Not Wrong At All	Always Wrong	Not Wrong At All	Always Wrong	Not Wrong At All
Australia	13	59	61	9	59	7	55	27
Austria	4	69	36	8	67	2	52	15
Bulgaria	23	57	71	8	51	16	81	10
Canada	12	69	55	9	68	2	39	46
Czech Republic	5	68	59	8	43	9	29	39
East Germany	2	87	27	16	60	4	51	30
West Germany	5	79	34	13	55	4	42	33
Great Britain	12	70	67	3	67	2	58	26
Hungary	19	54	50	7	62	3	83	4
Ireland	35	42	84	1	80	2	71	17
Israel	19	65	67	9	73	4	57	27
Italy	19	59	58	9	67	5	67	19
Japan	19	15	60	3	58	2	65	2
Netherlands	7	77	45	5	63	2	19	65
New Zealand	19	62	71	4	75	1	56	31
North Ireland	31	48	81	2	81	2	80	10
Norway	7	77	55	6	70	1	47	37
Philippines	60	11	77	3	88	1	84	3
Poland	18	60	77	4	74	5	77	14
Russia	13	57	45	11	36	17	57	19
Slovenia	3	82	44	6	57	3	70	8
Spain	20	63	59	14	76	5	45	42
Sweden	4	89	32	17	68	1	56	32
USA	29	41	71	4	80	2	70	19

(b) Countries organized by attitudes toward various types of nonmarital sexual behaviors

Permissive Regarding Teen Sex	Generally Sexually Conservative	Permissive Regarding Same-Sex Relationships	Generally Sexually Moderate	No General Pattern Discerned
Germany	USA	Netherlands	Australia	Japan
Austria	Ireland	Norway	Great Britain	Philippines
Sweden	Northern Ireland	Czech Republic	Hungary	
Slovenia	Poland	Canada	Italy	
		Spain	Bulgaria	
			Russia	
			New Zealand	
			Israel	

Source: Adapted from E. D. Widmer, J. Treas, & R. Newcomb (1998). Attitudes toward nonmarital sex in 24 countries. *Journal of Sex Research.* 35(4). 349–358.

TABLE 8.2   Percentages of Participants Answering Yes to the Question "Would You Say You 'Had Sex' with Someone if the Most Intimate Behavior You Engaged in Was . . . ?"

Specific Behavior	Women	Men	Total
Deep kissing	1.4%	2.9%	2.0%
Oral contact with breasts/nipples	2.3	4.1	3.0
Person touches your breasts/nipples	2.0	4.5	3.0
You touch other's breasts/nipples	1.7	5.7	3.4
Oral contact on other's breasts/nipples	1.4	6.1	3.4
You touch other's genitalia	11.6	17.1	13.9
Person touches your genitalia	12.2	19.2	15.1
Oral contact with your genitals	37.3	43.7	39.9
Oral contact with other's genitals	37.7	43.9	40.2
Penile–anal intercourse	82.3	79.1	81.0
Penile–vaginal intercourse	99.7	99.2	99.5

Source: Adapted from S. A. Sanders and J. M. Reinisch. "Would you say you had sex if . . .?" (1999). *JAMA, 281*(3), 276.

Sexual Norms Change. Up until the 1970s, oral–genital stimulation was considered an unnatural activity that was both sinful and often illegal. Such behavior was associated with gay men, lesbians, and prostitutes, and was considered highly deviant. However, sex researchers and therapists agreed that oral–genital contact heightened intimacy and increased lubrication, thereby facilitating the ease and pleasure of intercourse. Moreover, oral stimulation was usually more effective than coitus for producing orgasm, and it was associated with more intense levels of psychological arousal for both genders. Among middle-class couples, especially white couples, oral–genital contact is now relatively common. About 90% of white married couples in the United States engage in oral–genital sex (Laumann, Gagnon, Michael, & Michaels, 1994). It is the most common sexual technique among same-sex couples, and oral sex is sometimes used as a contraceptive technique among heterosexual adolescents. Outside of romantic relationships, it remains the technique of choice for men with prostitutes (Weinberg, Shaver, & Williams, 1999).

The Double Standard. In many societies premarital, nonmarital, and extramarital sexual expression has been a masculine privilege. Women who engaged in such behavior were typically stigmatized, punished, or even killed. For example, the tradition of "honor killings" allows a man to kill a female blood relative for bringing dishonor to the family. That dishonor is almost invariably sexual. This tradition remains part of the legal code of nations such as Iran, Jordan, Egypt, and parts of Lebanon, Turkey, and Pakistan (Mirhasseini, 1995; Neft & Levine, 1998).

Since the 1960s, one of the most far-reaching changes in sexual attitudes in the industrialized world is in relation to the social acceptance of premarital and nonmarital sexual relationships for both genders. The current norm is often described as "permissiveness with affection," implying that nonmarital sexual expression is acceptable within the context of an ongoing relationship. Extramarital sex is still not generally acceptable, as marital fidelity remains a powerful social and legal ideal for both genders. Although the term *premarital* implies heterosexual relations between two individuals who are "not yet" married, it is clear that many couples engage in sexual intercourse without any intention of marrying. Moreover, many couples increasingly opt for **cohabitation,** rather than a formal marriage (McCormick, 1994). Thus the term *nonmarital* seems more accurate.

Sexual Variety and Experience. There is a consistent gender difference in the number of partners reported by women and men, with women reporting a lower number of sexual partners over a lifetime (Laumann et al., 1994). Women seem more likely to underreport the number of partners, and men to overreport. However, as you have read, women and men may use dif-

cohabitation   Living together, unmarried, in a romantic/sexual relationship.

ferent criteria for judging whether they have "had sex" with a partner (Wiederman, 1997). Changing social norms suggest that younger women, regardless of sexual orientation, are more willing to experiment with more partners (Thompson, 1995).

Gender and Erotic Sexuality

Erotic sexual expression may be either solitary or partnered. Fantasy is an important aspect of eroticism in both types of sexuality.

Autoerotic Behavior: Fantasy and Masturbation

Adolescent males begin to create erotic fantasies somewhat earlier than girls do. Women's erotic fantasies tend to have more sensory imagery and contain more elaborate romantic and sensual content (Leitenberg & Henning, 1995). Men's fantasies tend to center on body parts, overt sexual acts, and themes of power (Michael, Gagnon, Laumann, & Kolata, 1994). Although many believe that fantasies represent the "real desires" of their creators, fantasies actually seem to generate their erotic energy by virtue of their *not* being acted out (Bullough & Bullough, 1994).

Men fantasize more often during masturbation and during nonsexual activity than women do. No gender difference is apparent regarding the frequency of fantasizing during partnered sex. For both women and men, the most popular fantasies involve reliving previous experiences, ideal sex with one's current partner, and sex with another partner (Leitenberg & Henning, 1995).

Over the course of a lifetime, masturbation is probably the most frequent form of human sexual expression. This confirms that for human beings, sexuality has purposes and functions other than reproduction. About 90% of men and 70% of women masturbate at least occasionally (Laumann et al., 1994). There appears to be a recent increase in masturbation rates among women, and many have pointed to the benefits of this change. Yet in mainstream society, sex solely for pleasure and release is more encouraged for men. For women, sex for emotional commitment and reproduction is emphasized (Cyranowski & Anderson, 1998; Sprecher & Regan, 1996).

Let's return to our opening vignette. Up until middle of the 20th century, masturbation was considered sinful, harmful, and dangerous to one's physical and mental health. Mrs. Sternwood apparently accepted the sexual attitudes of her society and was therefore unlikely to relieve her sexual tensions through masturbation. A previous prescription for vigorous intercourse several times weekly was not helpful. Apparently, this couple was unlikely or unwilling to employ any noncoital erotic techniques to facilitate those "uterine paroxysms." Thus it was left to some physicians to "cure" their women patients' "irritability, lascivious thoughts and abdominal heaviness" (Maines, 1999).

Partnered Sexual Expression

In contemporary Western culture, the symbol of erotic sexuality is a young, thin, nude, white woman. One skeptic has described this icon of contemporary eroticism as "tight, light and white" (Wolf, 1991). Thus women's bodies symbolize erotic sexuality in Western culture.

Constructing Feminine Eroticism. Women bodies are viewed as the *object* in erotic activity. Idealized models of women's bodies flood our lives. They fill our television and movie screens, magazine covers, and billboards. Every woman knows what she should look like to be erotically appealing, and of course, *all* real women fail to meet the ideal (Travis et al., 2000). Being a desirable and admired erotic object means spending vast amounts of time, energy, thought, and money in the pursuit of physical perfection (Wiederman & Hurst, 1997, 1998). Hair can and should be repeatedly cut or lengthened, curled or straightened, bound or loosened, darkened or lightened to achieve the "right" look. Whole nail and face "industries" exist to create and maintain the prescribed appearance of those body parts. For African-American women, lighter skin is the hallmark of beauty and sexual attractiveness (Thompson & Keith, 2001; Trepagnier, 1994). The list of flawed female body parts that need continuous correction is long indeed.

Although the face and skin are important for initial attraction, tremendous erotic attention is also focused on the female breast (Haiken, 1999). It is very difficult for most Westerners to realize that there is nothing inherently erotic about the breast. Breasts exist for lactation of infants, yet lactating breasts are considered decidedly nonerotic (Friedman, Weinberg, & Pines, 1998). In societies where women go about their daily tasks bare-breasted, men do not become aroused by viewing breasts.

Critical Thinking Challenge

It might be instructive to have the men and women in your class list all their body parts that they wished looked different from the way they do. What is your prediction about the outcome? Why?

In contrast to an earlier, more sexually repressive time, the current cultural prescription in most Western societies is for women to have orgasms within the sexual encounter itself (Slosarz, 2000). Orgasms are now the mark of the modern woman's eroticism. There appear to be four reasons why more women don't have orgasms during partnered sexual encounters: unfamiliarity with the workings of their own bodies, the overvaluing of modesty and self-control, an overfocus on a partner's pleasure, and an inept or indifferent partner. Also, simple anatomy and the socially approved Western coital position of man-on-top, woman-supine coital position can make orgasm difficult for women. For intercourse, the woman-on-top position allows for greater control of clitoral stimulation, but some couples may have difficulty with the gender-related message thus communicated (Masters & Johnson, 1966). Interestingly, around the world various woman-on-top or side-by-side positions are more common than the missionary position (Langmyhr, 1976; Munroe & Munroe, 1994). Manual or oral stimulation of the clitoris is more effective in producing orgasm, but many women are reluctant to request or pursue such activity, fearing this may be offensive to a male partner. Women who masturbate or who have sex with other women tend to consistently have orgasms because clitoral stimulation is much more likely to be a part of their lovemaking. Requesting oral sex may be difficult or awkward for heterosexual women (Daniluk, 1998).

It's time for another visit to our opening vignette. As you will read in the chapter on gender and physical health (Chapter 11), there is a long Western medical tradition of attributing all manner of bodily problems to a malfunctioning uterus. Many of these problems were considered curable by intercourse and lots of children. Those women whose symptoms persisted after regular marital intercourse and childbirth were considered immature and **hysterical.** Vulvar massage and Freud's "talking cure" were just some of the remedies proposed for this seemingly widespread disorder (Maines, 1999).

Constructing Masculine Eroticism. In many societies, the erect penis, rather than a young woman's body, has been the symbol of erotic sexuality, masculinity, fertility, and power. The gender ideal is that the penis is always erect and ready for sexual activity (Zilbergeld, 1992).

Some **masculinist** scholars see the central problem of Western masculine eroticism as one of *nonrelational sex.* This term refers to the tendency to experience sex as lust, with a minimal requirement for relational intimacy or emotional connection (Good & Sherrod, 1997; Levant, 1997). This allows the targets of sexual desire to be objectified and pursued to meet a set of needs, namely, tension release, physical closeness, nurturance, and an affirmation of adequacy (Brooks, 1995a). This masculine tendency toward nonrelational sex has also been described among ethnic minority men and among gay men (McClean, 1997; Scrivner, 1997). A very positive aspect of this perspective is the more carefree, adventurous, and uninhibited quality that men can bring to the erotic encounter. This can lighten and enliven sexual activity. A more open, casual orientation to erotic experience can also lead to more imaginative exploration and innovation (Good & Sherrod, 2001). However, nonrelational norms can also lead to difficulties with commitment, monogamy, and fidelity. In the public sphere, the negative aspects of this perspective include men's roles as consumers in the sex industry (Stock, 1997). Sexual harassment, sexual abuse, and rape represent the extremes of nonrelational sexuality (Levant & Brooks, 1997; Lisak,

---

hysteria **Vague term traditionally applied to a wide variety of women's symptoms and complaints. Believed to be caused by malfunction or disease of the *hyster* or uterus. By the 19th century it described exaggerated feminine personality traits and mood variations.**

masculinists **Scholars studying various aspects of the masculine gender role; implies advocacy for gender equality.**

1997). However, a majority of men do not harass, abuse, or rape, nor are they unfaithful. Most gender scholars view this tendency toward nonrelational sexual expression as a product of socialization and power arrangements rather than as some inherent quality of men.

Brooks (1997) describes the "centerfold syndrome." First, women are objects of scrutiny, so *looking at* becomes a major feature of masculine sexuality. This sets the stage for turning people into things through pornography and prostitution. Second, masculine sexuality involves comparison with other men so that being the first to "score," having the most conquests, or making it with the sexiest or most attractive woman or man, become goals. The women or men who are the objects of this pursuit can become mere trophies (Scrivner, 1997).

Thus you see that when it comes to erotic sexuality, men can be subject to the unattainable ideal of erotic athlete and women can be subject to the equally unattainable ideal of perfectly endowed erotic object.

Gender and Reproductive Sexuality: A Global Perspective

In Western society, sexuality is often constructed as the immediate experience of the overt genital act. The reality of sexuality extends well beyond copulation to a possible conception, as well as the intense experiences of pregnancy, birthing, and breastfeeding. Beyond that are the many years of intimate care, support, and protection for a child. Obviously, sexual expression can have a very different personal meaning depending on one's gender.

Fertility and Infertility

The issue of fertility may be examined as a set of power differentials based on gender. On the simplest level, only men have the physical power to impregnate (consider how technology has changed this facet of gender relations). In many societies, men's inability to impregnate and father sons may damage both their private self-esteem and their public social standing (Kulczycki, 1999). Research on the impact of infertility on men is sparse but in a qualitative study of infertility among Canadian men, respondents were candid in revealing how sure they were that infertility was

always "a woman's problem." These men spoke movingly about feeling grief, powerlessness, foreboding, and inadequacy when they confronted their loss of this aspect of masculine sexuality (Webb & Daniluk, 1999). In many societies the infertile woman may be merely stigmatized, as in Israel (Remennick, 2000). In others she may be punished or divorced, as among Orthodox Jews or in rural Egypt (Inhorn, 1994) or Camaroon (Feldman- Savelsberg, 1994).

Motherhood is generally seen as a developmentally and psychologically transformative experience, and this is so for women everywhere. In Bangladesh, women are often referred to as the mother of one of their children (usually a male child)—that is, as "Mukti's Ma" (Mita & Simmons, 1995). Japan's postwar nuclear family is often described as L-shaped, with a woman at the crux, her children at the end of the shorter arm, and her husband at the end of the longer arm (Oaks, 1994). Western psychology has held that the desire for and attainment of motherhood is essential to women's sexual maturity and psychological health. In some societies, motherhood may constitute the *only* legitimate role for adult women. This was true in Taliban Afghanistan (Ellis, 2000), in rural Indonesia (Suryakusuma, 1996), and in many nations of sub-Saharan Africa (Coquery-Vidrovitch, 1997).

Voluntary childlessness may not be an option for many women in the world (Riessman, 2000). Even in North American society, there is still considerable pressure to fulfill the *motherhood mandate* (Russo, 1979). An unwillingness or inability to do so may affect a woman's sense of competence, self-esteem, and even her gender identity (Deveraux & Hammerman, 1998). Choosing a life without children has traditionally been viewed as a psychological aberration and a sign of pathology. However, in postindustrial societies, voluntary childlessness is correlated with advanced educational achievements, being firstborn, a history of childhood caretaking, high career aspirations, and strong needs for autonomy, freedom, and independence (Michie & Kahn, 1997).

Critical Thinking Challenge

Consider the term *childless*, and compare it to *armless*, or *sightless*. Some suggest the term *child free*. Does that change the feeling tone surrounding the choice not to have children? Are men also *childless*? Explain.

Culture and Contraception

Try to imagine how your sexual attitudes and behavior would be affected if *every* intercourse could potentially lead to a pregnancy. Would your attitude and behavior be affected if you were of the other gender? Modern effective contraceptive methods have had a powerful impact on women's lives and gender relations on a global scale (Russell & Thompson, 2000). The use of reliable and relatively inexpensive contraception offers women power over their physical, educational, economic, and social destiny (Watkins, 1998).

Societies vary in their attitudes toward, access to, and use of contraceptive methods. In less industrialized and more traditional societies, lower overall rates of contraceptive use prevail, and there is greater reliance on male methods such as withdrawal and condoms. In societies where the norm is for smaller and/or planned families, contraception is almost exclusively a woman's responsibility (Alan Guttmacher Institute, 2001a). Masculine power in initiating and structuring sexual interactions mean that sexually active women must deal with men who may not take responsibility for contraception (Edwards, 1994). In some traditional societies, men are socialized to believe that any restriction on their ability to impregnate derogates their masculinity. For example, a recent study of family planning patterns in Uzbekistan revealed pervasive conflicts between old and new gender and family ideals (Krengel & Greifeld, 2000).

The dissemination of contraceptive information and actual usage depend greatly on the gender arrangements of a society. For example, Guatemalan Indians (about 70% of the population) believe that a woman is predestined to have a certain number of children. Moreover, a woman is subject to great social disapproval from neighbors if she has fewer pregnancies than expected. In public, both women and men may express strong rejection of modern contraceptive methods. But privately, there is increasing acceptance and usage. Guatemalan women prefer to receive contraceptive information from a nonindigenous supervisor who comes to the village only occasionally (Bertrand et al., 1999; Terborgh, 1995).

The increasing use of modern, effective contraceptives is truly a global phenomenon (Neft & Levine, 1998). In western Europe, oral contraceptives are the most popular, whereas the Chinese favor IUDs. In In-

dia, sterilization is preferred (if available). Brazil has no national family planning program, yet increased economic opportunities for women have resulted in a drop in the fertility rate from 6.2 in 1960 to 3.0 in 1990 (Misago & Fonseca, 1999). In Japan, a male-dominated government and medical establishment kept the use of oral contraceptives *illegal* until 1999. In Japan, condoms were sold to housewives door-to-door and were considered a woman's product. Japan has had one of the highest abortion rates in the industrialized world (see Box 8.2). In the United States, about 80% of women of reproductive age use some form of contraception. Sterilization (male or female) is the most popular form of contraception, mostly among married couples. Oral contraceptives follow in popularity, and then the male condom (Alan Guttmacher Institute, 2001a).

Although equivalent proportions of teenagers in the United States and Europe are sexually active, teen pregnancies continue to be a significant social problem in the United States. Fortunately, beginning in the 1990s, rates of teen pregnancy have been gradually declining across all ethnic groups. Increased abstinence, fear of HIV, increased sexual knowledge, an improved economy, and welfare reform have all been cited as major reasons for this welcome development. Researchers have found that neither the age of first intercourse nor the frequency of intercourse have declined, but there has been an identifiable trend toward the use of long-acting and highly effective hormonal contraception such as implants and injectables (Alan Guttmacher Institute, 2001b).

If used properly, modern condoms constitute a relatively reliable and inexpensive contraceptive choice that also provides protection from most sexually transmitted diseases. Yet condom use and nonuse provides another interesting arena for the examination of gender and gender relations in the context of private sexual behavior. In a Canadian study, for example, college students read a diary entry describing a sexual encounter. Participants rated the woman in the scenario much more negatively when she provided the condom for the encounter. Thus, assertive use of condoms by women is still evaluated negatively and constitutes a remnant of the sexual double standard (Hynie & Lydon, 1995). Examination of the demographics of condom use demonstrates that younger

Modern Japan: Contrasts and Controversies in Reproductive and Erotic Sexuality

Modern Japan, an ancient culture and contemporary technological superpower, offers us a compelling picture of how cultural traditions, gender ideology, power politics, and sexuality can combine into a volatile social mixture.

Since the end of World War II, condoms and abortion have been the two major forms of contraception in Japan. About 85% of married couples used condoms, and saleswomen sold them door-to-door to homemakers. Until the beginning of the 21st century, Japanese women had one of the highest abortion rates in the world. About 2/3 of Japanese women had an abortion by age 40. In 1999, after widespread public protests and demonstrations, oral contraceptives were finally approved for general usage.

In the past, high abortion rates were blamed on women's "passivity" regarding sexuality (Coleman, 1983). However, an understanding of Japanese sexual and gender norms reveals how abortion became so acceptable within such a child-oriented society.

Japanese women dislike handling or manipulating their bodies, particularly their genitals. For example, it is traditional to wash underwear separately from other clothing because of its particular "dirti-ness." Predictably, there is a low rate of masturbation among Japanese women. Similarly, IUDs and diaphragms were unacceptable because they also involved the handling of "dirty" parts of the body. Condoms were well accepted because of their low cost, high quality, and minimal medical involvement. Although purchased by wives, condoms were handled by husbands. However, the condom failure rate is considerably higher than that of other contraceptive methods (12% for condoms versus 3% for oral contraceptives). Male sterilization is rare, because vasectomy is believed to promote men's extramarital sex. Medical authorities in Japan have been opposed to oral contraceptives, and some critics contend that physicians enjoyed the lucrative abortion business. Cultural ideals regarding the importance of maintaining bodily harmony led others to argue against introducing additional hormones into the body. Thus abortion became an acceptable, but ambivalent choice. Postabortion religious rituals were common. Traditionally, the spirit of an aborted fetus was believed to have the power to cause misfortune and illness to a woman and her family. Religious rites were performed to appease the fetus and prevent such harm. These rites were con-ducted only once, because it was believed that fetuses and those who died before marriage cannot become true ancestors. Sometimes a special tomb containing a *mizuko jizo* (a small stone statue of the guardian deity of the unborn) was erected and decorated with red bibs, flowers, toys, and so on. Some have complained that the *mizuko* rituals were driven by commercial interests. One physician had a shrine just outside his office for his abortion patients. There is also a Japanese belief in a menopausal syndrome caused by guilt over repeated abortions.

Approval of oral contraceptives was a slow and tedious affair undertaken over many years. Yet Japan's Central Pharmaceutical Affairs Council (CPAC) approved sildenafil (Viagra) within only six months. Reproductive rights advocates pointed out the hypocrisy of the CPAC in citing "health concerns" for their slow action on oral contraceptives. Hundreds of millions of women have used oral contraceptives safely for the last four decades, but almost 200 sildenafil-related deaths have been reported since 1998. The CPAC's deliberations have traditionally been kept secret, and there are only three women on this important 24-member body (Watts, 1999).

---

respondents and men with more education and higher socioeconomic status are more likely to use condoms (Sheeran, Abraham, & Orbell, 1999).

Abortion

There will always be unwanted or unplanned pregnancies (Kulczycki, 1999; Press & Cole, 1999). Difficulty in obtaining contraceptives or male refusal to permit contraceptive use mean that abortion will be used as a method of contraception or family planning in some societies (Kveder, 1999). This is dangerous to a woman's health and can harm families and societies in many ways. Yet around the globe, men control the institutions that provide access to both contraception and pregnancy termination (health care systems, law enforcement, the courts, legislatures, and religious institutions).

It is estimated that about 26 million women have legal abortions each year, and about 20 million have abortions where it is illegal. About 39% of the world's women live under restrictive abortion laws (Alan

Guttmacher Institute, 1999). In developing countries, more married women obtain abortions, especially in Asia, the former Soviet republics in Asia, and some countries in Latin America. However, sub-Saharan African nations do not follow this pattern. In industrialized nations, more unmarried women, especially young women, have abortions. Higher abortion rates in some Asian and eastern European countries reflect the low availability of modern contraceptives. Abortion rates and patterns are complex and vary considerably all over the world. Romania, Cuba, and Vietnam currently have the highest rates of reported abortions in the world (78 to 83 per 1,000 women). The rates in Chile and Peru are also well above international norms (over 50 per 1,000) (Alan Guttmacher Institute, 1999).

In India, now the most populous country in the world, government policies restrict access to reliable contraception. As in many Asian societies, there is a cultural preference for male children, and although abortions for the purpose of sex selection are illegal, there has been a drastic change in the sex ratio of Indian newborns. That is, the global norm for newborns is 952 girls to 1,000 boys. Current figures for India are 927 girls to 1,000 boys. Sex-selective female abortion, neglect of girl infants, and female infanticide are the apparent causes of this sex differential (Reuters Medical News, 2001a).

The decision to abort an unwanted pregnancy is usually a private individual or family decision. However, whether that abortion will be carried out in relatively safe or unsafe conditions is a matter of public policy (Kulczycki, 1999). In Mexico and most of Latin America, abortion is illegal, but clandestine services of varying quality are available. Although physicians and nurses perform abortions on more affluent and urban women, among poor, rural women untrained individuals or the women themselves often use dangerous, primitive, and unsanitary methods, resulting in more than half a million hospitalizations each year (Alan Guttmacher Institute, 1999; Elu, 1999).

Pharmaceutical (rather than surgical) interventions for unwanted pregnancies have been available in Europe for several years. In the United States, the drug mifepristone became available only in the year 2000 and only under close supervision of a physician. Clinical trials demonstrated that a combination of mifepristone and misoprostol was effective in 92% of

cases in terminating unwanted pregnancies at a very early stage (Guttmacher Report on Public Policy, 2000). Presently, low-dose forms of mifepristone and misoprostol are being tested in Vietnam and Tunisia. These new low-dose forms mean women can terminate pregnancies at home without a follow-up visit to a distant and often costly clinic (Reuters Medical News, 2001b).

Relatively little is known about the effects of abortion on men. One study revealed that abortion can be traumatic and stressful for some men. Although many men are supportive through the abortion experience, they may have to deal with their own feelings about the decision. Some men feel they cannot express their feelings of anxiety, helplessness, guilt, regret, and confusion to their partners because they must offer a strong front in support for a partner's decision (Coyle & Enright, 1997).

Gender and Problematic Sexuality

Private Problems: The Sexual Dysfunctions

The term *sexual functioning* implies smooth passage through all the phases of the sexual response cycle (Masters & Johnson, 1966). The term *sexual dysfunction* refers to impaired or incomplete sexual functioning that results in distress (American Psychiatric Association, 1994). The distress part of the definition is very important because what may cause distress in one couple may constitute "good sex" in another. For example, one partner takes 15 minutes of intense stimulation before reaching orgasm. In one couple, this may mean long lovemaking sessions that both find very erotic and satisfying. For another couple, this same behavior results in frustration and bad feelings. Thus the existence of a sexual dysfunction is subjective. Helen Singer Kaplan (1974, 1983) developed an alternate model of sexual response that is more useful in helping individuals with sexual dysfunctions. In this three-phase model each phase corresponds to a particular area of sexual functioning or dysfunction. She included the very important phase of *psychological desire* as a precursor to sexual arousal. She omits the plateau phase from her model because we do not subjectively experience such a phase. She also omits resolution, reasoning that these processes do not involve sexual response, but rather its cessation. See Table 8.3 for a comparison of the Kaplan

TABLE 8.3   Comparison of Two Models of Sexual Functioning and Their Relation to Identified Disorders of Sexual Functioning

W. H. Masters and V. Johnson's Model of Human Sexual Response	Helen Singer Kaplan's Model of Human Sexual Response	Disorders of Sexual Functioning
	Desire	*Disorders of Desire* Hypoactive desire Sexual aversion
Excitement	Arousal	*Disorders of Arousal* Female arousal disorder Male arousal disorder (erectile disorder)
Plateau		
Orgasm	Orgasm	*Orgasm Disorder* Female orgasmic disorder Male orgasmic disorder (premature ejaculation)
Resolution		

model with the Masters and Johnson model. I will discuss only some of the more common sexual dysfunctions.

Certain sexual dysfunctions appear limited to particular societies. In India, normal nocturnal emissions can lead to severe anxiety, hypochondriasis, and erection difficulties in some men. This condition, called Dhat syndrome, typically occurs among men from families with extremely conservative sexual attitudes. Their central anxiety is about uncontrollable semen loss. In Koro syndrome, some Chinese men develop the morbid belief that the penis is retracting into the abdomen and that this is fatal. These men believe their "disease" is caused by masturbation, wet dreams, or excessive intercourse. Until very recently in Western societies, women were more likely to seek treatment for sexual dysfunctions. However, among Asians and Middle Eastern Arabs, men are more likely to seek treatment for a variety of sexual problems and are very reluctant to involve wives. In those societies, women who express concern about their sexual functioning are considered immoral (Bhugra & DeSilva, 1993; Verma, Khaitan, & Singh, 1998).

Disorders of Desire. The term *hypoactive sexual desire disorder (HSDD)* implies a persistent lack of interest in, or desire for sexual activity. Even sexual fantasies are absent. About two times as many women report a lack of interest in sex (Laumann et al., 1994). At present, about 81% of those diagnosed with HSDD

disorder are women. Interestingly, HSDD men may masturbate more than similar women, but both have a low incidence of intercourse (Beck, 1995).

A second disorder of desire is called *sexual aversion.* Those with sexual aversion experience disgust, anxiety, and perhaps panic in response to genital contact. They may be revolted by a partner's touch but have normal desire and enjoy arousal and orgasm in masturbation. They will participate in sexual activity to avoid future encounters (quick masturbation, intercourse, or fellatio). They are uncomfortable with nudity, find a partner's touch repulsive, and dissociate during sexual activity. The number of women diagnosed with sexual aversion disorder greatly outnumbers men. However, it may be that men with aversion disorder simply do not enter relationships nor seek professional intervention. In terms of gender-typed behavior, women with sexual aversion disorder tend to downplay their secondary sexual characteristics by wearing loose, juvenile, or asexual clothing (Ponticas, 1992).

Disorders of Arousal. The term *erectile dysfunction* refers to the man's persistent or recurrent inability to attain or maintain an erection (APA, 1994). In past years, this was a private and shameful problem for a couple (Rowland & Burnett, 2000). Today, the term is practically a household word, especially among middle-aged and older couples. In television and magazine ads, a former presidential candidate urges

FIGURE 8.3 Viagra helped transform what was a private and shameful problem with dark psychological overtones into a publicly discussed medical problem.

couples to seek a simple pharmaceutical intervention for this problem: Viagra! (See Figure 8.3.)

When Viagra (sildenafil citrate) became available in March of 1998, a major aspect of the relationships among gender, sexuality, and aging was transformed (see Figure 8.4). It was said that urologists and family practitioners developed writers' cramp as they struggled to write out millions of prescriptions. The ability to experience and sustain an erection is considered a key to masculine self-esteem. With the introduction of Viagra, male sexual functioning is now virtually assured into old age (as long as general good health continues).

Viagra is an oral medication, taken about 30 to 60 minutes before anticipated intercourse. It inhibits the activity of certain enzymes (phosphodiesterase) that interfere with the maintenance of blood flow into the penis. Sildenafil has no effect in the absence of sexual stimulation. It is effective in about 70% of men with erectile dysfunction, but it will not work for men who have undergone prostatectomy. Cardiac risks are elevated with the use of Viagra, so medical supervision regarding its use and dosage is important (Rose,

1999). Sildenafil will *not* improve erections in normally functioning men.

Given the apparent similarities in the physiological aspects of sexual response, does sildenafil work for women with arousal disorder? Although the neural and vascular events involved in male erection are relatively well understood, the parallel mechanisms in women are not (Berman & Berman, 2000). For example, the fact that vaginal lubrication is result of fluid seepage from blood vessels, rather than a glandular secretion, is very recent knowledge. The "slipperiness" of vaginal fluid is still not clearly understood. The increased blood flow that results in increased clitoral sensation or lubrication does not seem to benefit women with diminished desire. In fact, some women complain of clitoral discomfort and hypersensitivity if they take sildenafil (Kalb, 1999). See Box 8.3 for a discussion of the economics of female sexual dysfunction.

Critical Thinking Challenge

Those appealing ads of middle-aged individuals dancing lovingly together imply that sildenafil citrate improves relationships as well as erections. What do you think about that implication?

Disorders of Orgasm. Disorders of orgasm are defined as persistent or recurrent delays in, or absence of, orgasm following normally sufficient stimulation (APA, 1994). Levels of desire and arousal appear typical, but no orgasm occurs. The problem of **anorgasmia** is more common among women, with 24% of women reporting such difficulties (Laumann et al., 1994). Delayed or absent orgasm is the most common reason why women seek the help of a sex therapist (Rosen & Leiblum, 1995). The origins of this disorder, which is assumed to be psychological, include a history of sexual abuse, sexual trauma, and relationship dissension. However, some organic conditions and medications can interfere with orgasmic ability, most commonly certain antidepressants (Crenshaw & Goldberg, 1996). Masturbation has been found to be effective for anorgasmic women, especially when combined with instructional videos and/or vibrators. However, many women are sexually satisfied without experiencing orgasm (O'Donohue, Dopke, & Swingen, 1997).

---

anorgasmia   **Inability to experience orgasm.**

"We rarely watch television. Most of our free time is devoted to sex."

FIGURE 8.4 Has sildenafil really changed the lifestyles of older couples?

The most common orgasm problem among men is premature ejaculation, and in a recent national survey 28.5% of men reported having such difficulties at least occasionally (Laumann et al., 1994). However some men suffer from ejaculatory delay (8.5%). The origins of such difficulties are usually assumed to be psychological, but well-funded research is underway to find a pharmacological solution for these problems as well (Rowland & Burnett, 2000).

Public Problems: Commercial Sex

The *sex industry* includes pornography (magazines, books, Internet pages, videos, and films), the various types of prostitution (streetwalkers and **hustlers** or **rent-boys,** brothel workers, and escort services), strip and nude clubs, massage and lingerie parlors, 900 lines for telephone sex, Internet-based sexual images, chat rooms, bulletin boards, and interactive sex-related compact discs (Stock, 1997). When commercialized, sexual activity between a buyer and a seller is removed from the context of an intimate relationship and a shared experience. Instead, it exists in the context of a business transaction and profit. Sex is packaged and sold (another form of nonrelational sex). In this context, a partner is merely a means to self-satisfaction. This can lead to a denial of the humanity of the sexual services provider, and the stage may thus be set for exploitation, abuse, and violation (Levant, 1997; Stock, 1997). Overwhelmingly, men are the purchasers of commercial sex, and women's bodies are the main products packaged, marketed, and bought.

---

hustler/rent-boy   Male prostitute who typically serves other men. *Rent-boy* is a British term.

For Love and/or Money: Sildenafil and Female Sexual Dysfunction

In a recent survey, 43% of American women reported sexual function complaints. Thirty-two percent of the women surveyed stated they rarely wanted sex, 26% stated they didn't have orgasms, and 23% said they didn't find sex particularly pleasurable (Laumann, Paik, & Rosen, 1999). If a little blue pill (Viagra) could make Pfizer the second largest pharmaceutical company in the world, with over 14 million prescriptions annually, surely women deserve equality in their potential sex-related purchases. Viagra works by inhibiting the action of an enzyme that interferes with continuing genital vasodilation. If improved vasodilation helps men, shouldn't it help women as well? Put on that critical thinking helmet as you descend into this morass of information.

Comparatively less is known about women's sexual functioning. For example, the nerves and blood vessels critical to women's sexual response are "not yet" well defined (Berman & Berman, 2000). Nevertheless, some physicians prescribe Viagra for their women patients who complain of sexual dysfunction. Controlled clinical trials with sildenafil on 577 European, Australian, and Canadian women demonstrated that Viagra was no more effective than a placebo in improving sexual response (Basson, McInnes, Smith, Hodgson, Spain, & Koppiker,

2000). Nevertheless, there's a huge potential market here.

An Arkansas coffeehouse has become the sole distributor of Niagara, a Swedish beverage that's loaded with caffeine, sugar, ginseng, maté, and other herbs, all guaranteed to give an immediate and super buzz to anyone who ingests them. This soft drink was on the market before Viagra, but no one was buying. Its name similarity to Viagra led clever marketers to tout it as a woman's love potion. A 6.6-ounce bottle sells for $4.50. Customer testimonials are a living and growing monument to the placebo effect (Galarneau, 2001; Killian, 2001).

More sophisticated consumers prefer at least a thin coating of science for their products (Levine, 2000). Two physicians and a pharmacist are marketing Doctor's Lotion on line at $48 a tube. It contains nitroglycerin, a well-known vasodilator long used by cardiac patients. Any testing? They gave it to 50 of their patients, and 95% "reported favorable results." Is there a problem here? Another physician offers two versions of Dr. K's Dream Cream. One contains ground sildenafil and the other contains the amino acid L-arginine, also a vasodilator.

Noting accurately that women's complaints seem more about desire, rather than arousal, one researcher insists that

testosterone supplements should take care of the problem. He presents his ideas at various female sexual dysfunction conferences. These conferences tend to be sponsored by pharmaceutical companies (LaSalandra, 2000). Hmmm.

A whole new array of remedies for female sexual dysfunction is hitting the market (Levine, 2000). They include several vasodilators that are taken orally (VasoFem, Alista, and FemProx). For those unwilling to take one more pill, there are vasodilator creams that can be applied directly to the clitoris (E-1, Alprostadil). Testosterone is available in patches to counteract the synthetic hormones in some oral contraceptives that interfere with normal testosterone production. Some provide estrogen as well. The chemical apomorphine will increase neural impulses from the brain to the genital area. Bupropion is used in anti-smoking treatments, and there are reports that it increases sexual interest. A well-known pharmaceutical company is conducting trials.

The EROS-CTD (Clitoral Therapeutic Device), has recently been approved by the FDA. It is a thimble-sized mini-vibrator that sells for $359 and provides "gentle suction" to the clitoral area. Will we see 21st-century versions of Dr. Smith and Mrs. Sternwood?

Men also purchase sexual materials and services that involve other men or children.

Pornography is usually defined as visual and auditory products created solely for the purpose of sexual arousal. *Erotica* typically implies that there is some artistic or cultural value attached to the arousing material. However, distinctions between pornography and erotica are often difficult (Jones, 1998). Traditional hard-core pornography is designed for men, focuses on body parts, and is devoid of any relational context, except for power and submission. Specialty materials

such as sadomasochistic pornography exaggerate these themes even more. Relatively few women are attracted to traditional pornography for sexual arousal. Most report distaste for the "raw action" of traditional pornography. Materials involving romance, extended foreplay, and intense eroticism are generally more appealing to women, and this too represents a gigantic market. Popular women's magazines and romantic pulp fiction (referred to as "bodice rippers") seem to function as a subtler means to the same goal of sexual arousal. However, the safety and anonymity provided by the Internet may change these norms. A growing array of woman-oriented erotica and pornography is available on the Internet (Kibby & Costello, 1999).

Traditional hard-core pornography is problematic for a number of reasons. On the one hand, these materials present women with unrealistic bodies, often with gigantic breasts or other exaggerated body parts. Women's bodies are presented as sexual playthings, existing only for male sexual pleasure. Pornography is full of images of violence and brutality toward women (gay male pornography contains comparable images of men) and it often implies that women seek out and enjoy such experiences. Repeated scenes of vaginal and anal penetration with dangerous objects distorts men's understanding of women bodies, eroticism, and sexuality. Technological innovations such as interactive CD-ROMs allow the user to act out or practice graphic sexualized violence. There is a long-standing body of laboratory evidence that exposure to images of sexualized violence affects men's attitudes toward and treatment of women (Bauserman, 1998; Donnerstein, Linz, & Penrod, 1987).

The capacities of men's bodies regarding penis size, erection, repeated copulation, and ejaculation are also often misrepresented. These falsehoods distort men's understanding of their own bodies and their sexuality. Finally, the orgasmic ecstasy typically portrayed by such materials contributes to unrealistic expectations regarding real sex with real people.

On the other hand, married couples are the primary consumers of the milder, more romanticized, and more egalitarian pornographic videos available at the neighborhood video store or local cable service. They are often used to "spice up" an ongoing sexual relationship, and seem to promote relational sexual expression, as well as erotic experimentation (Brosius, Weaver, & Staub, 1994). For those without a partner, they can provide accompaniment for an evening devoted to masturbation.

Prostitution involves the offer and purchase of sexual services in a relatively anonymous encounter, with no emotional involvement or obligation. The lowest-status and most visible level of prostitute is the gaudily dressed female or transvestite streetwalker, or the rough-looking hustler or rent-boy. At the other end of the spectrum are the well-educated and refined male and female "escorts" available in every major city.

Prostitution can be problematic for several reasons. It is physically dangerous. Because prostitutes repeatedly place themselves in risky situations with strangers, they are very vulnerable to beatings, rapes, mutilations, and murder by violent or disturbed clients (Weinberg et al., 1999). Prostitutes are also very vulnerable to both contract and spread sexually transmitted diseases, especially HIV. They are more likely to engage in unsafe sexual practices without the protection of a condom (Calhoun & Weaver, 1996). Prostitutes, regardless of their sex, manifest high rates of intravenous drug use, and this also increases HIV risks for the prostitute and his or her **john** (Potterat, Rothenberg, Muth, Darrow, & Phillips-Plummer, 1998). Lastly, prostitution is inevitably intertwined with racism and classism. Poverty, poor education, exploitation, and sexual and physical abuse all contribute to the making of a prostitute (Dalla, 2000). This pattern persists all over the world: From the sex bars of Thailand, to the planeloads of blonde Russian "Natashas" in the Middle East, to the well-regulated storefronts of Amsterdam's sex district, some poor women and men see prostitution as the only way to support themselves and their families (Conradi, 1995; Phoenix, 1999).

Conclusions

Cultural ideas about gender are heavily intertwined with those about sexuality. We typically experience our sexuality as an intensely individual and private aspect of our lives. We experience our sexual attitudes and preferences as emerging "naturally" from within us, yet this chapter reveals sexuality to be heavily shaped by surrounding gender ideology, historical epoch, social norms, power arrangements, culture, and even technology. Acceptable forms of sexual expression, erotic response, fertility, and reproductive control can vary widely from society to society, and these acceptable forms are based on the gender ideology of that particular society. Whatever society one may be born into, gender will guide and influence private sexual behavior as well as evaluations of that behavior. Sex-related social issues such as pornography and prostitution are almost rigidly

---

john **A prostitute's customer, also called a *trick*; in Great Britain, a *punter.***

organized along gender lines, with men as the consumers of commercial sex and women as the main products purchased or used.

Summary

◆ Childhood experiences set the foundation for adult sexuality. For girls, adolescence is marked by ambivalence, objectification, and more restrictive sexuality. For boys, adolescence is marked by positive masculinity, physical competence, and active sexuality. The meaning and experience of first intercourse varies according to gender.

◆ The concept of sexual orientation is a social construction. Attitudes toward same-sex sexual behavior vary by culture and historical epoch. The origins of sexual orientation are unknown. The vast majority of gay men and lesbians are not confused or disturbed about their gender.

◆ Vasocongestion and myotonia are the physical processes involved in sexual response. Masters and Johnson developed a four-phase model of sexual response. Gender and culture influence various aspects of sexual response.

◆ Our beliefs underlie our sexual attitudes and behavior. Recently in Western society, there have been substantial changes in attitudes regarding women's sexuality, oral-genital sex, nonmarital sex, and same-sex relationships. Beliefs about male sexual drive and the coital imperative remain relatively unchanged.

◆ Fantasy and masturbation are the most frequent types of human sexual expression. Contemporary feminine eroticism focuses on the self as a flawed sexual object. Contemporary masculine eroticism focuses on competition and nonrelational sex. Exaggerations of the masculine erotic model contribute to coercive and exploitive sexual expression.

◆ In many societies, fertility may define womanhood and manhood. Voluntary childlessness may not be a choice. Reliable contraception has permanently changed gender relations and women's lives. Cultural forces and gender arrangements determine contraceptive practices and the availability of abortion.

◆ Sexual dysfunctions are private and subjective phenomena. The incidence and distribution of sexual dysfunctions varies by culture and gender.

◆ Pornography and prostitution are public and problematic sex-related behaviors organized along gender lines

InfoTrac College Edition

For more information, explore InfoTrac College Edition at

http://www.infotrac-college.com/Wadsworth

Enter search terms: contraception and gender, adolescent sexuality, sexual orientation, gender and sexuality, gender and abortion.

9

Gender and Education
Choices, Changes, and the Status Quo

Education . . . is often demeaned as a "woman's field." . . . The younger and less privileged the students, the more likely it is that their teacher will be a woman. Within higher education, women are overrepresented in low-status institutions with high teaching loads [and] underrepresented in universities with graduate and research programs. . . . Research is a high-status "male" activity even when women do it; teaching is a low-status "female" activity even when men do it. ◆ F. A. Maher and M. K. Tetrault

Learning Objectives

After studying this chapter, you should be able to:

1. List and describe three important ideas relevant to understanding the relationship between gender and education.
2. Contrast the current educational practices that were described as "shortchanging" girls with the findings regarding practices that seem to harm boys.
3. Summarize how gender influences the educational process in terms of gender arrangements in the elementary grades, gendered textbooks and readers, teacher perceptions and expectations, and career preparation.
4. Summarize the major explanations for the gender imbalance in particular educational domains, and then describe the changes that have been proposed to rectify that imbalance.
5. Summarize the current findings and recommendations regarding gender and study of mathematics.
6. Summarize the current findings regarding gender and computer technology.
7. Summarize the current findings regarding the paucity of women in the physical sciences and engineering.
8. Summarize the important features of the relationship between gender and education in developing countries.

Encounters with Gender

It's the first day of class for the newly revamped physics course. Dr. Jones eagerly begins to apply what was learned in a science curriculum reform workshop. A nonthreatening ice-breaking exercise seems to relax everyone, including Dr. Jones. Everyone who registered is present—30 students, with 6 women among them: a record enrollment and a record number of women. Dr. Jones beams while going over a carefully revised syllabus: labs, tests, and computer work. To implement the new goals of cooperative learning and research, the class is divided into six project teams (this counts for 60% of the course grade). The projects are very challenging, and there's a bonus for the group with the best project. Dr. Jones makes sure to assign one woman to each team, and the groups meet for a first planning session. As the semester proceeds, Dr. Jones is proud to observe that the women students perform as well as the men students on the tests, lab exercises, and computer simulations. However, toward the end of the semester Dr. Jones notes that the women are increasingly absent from class. They soon accumulate poor lab and test grades. By the end of the semester four of the women have dropped the course, one is clearly taking a back seat in her group's research project, and one seems to be the natural leader of her group. Dr. Jones is upset and confused. All that work was invested into changing the physics curriculum and the drop rate is higher than ever. Why is it so difficult for women to perform in advanced science courses? Do their absences indicate a lack of motivation and persistence? Why can't they just stick with it when the going gets tough? What happened here?

Source: Adapted from S. V. Rosser (1997), *Re-engineering Female Friendly Science* (New York: Teachers College Press).

Overview

As a student, you are involved in the process of mastering the knowledge and skills deemed important in your society at this time in history; that is, you are being *educated*. Gender has a persistent influence throughout the whole process of education, and this

ABCs of GENDER (ATTITUDES, BEHAVIORS, AND CONCERNS)   BOX 9.1

The Issue: Some Surprising Facts About Education Around the World

Test your present level of knowledge regarding gender and education. The answers appear after the questions.

1. Which nation has achieved the highest literacy rate among women?
   a. Romania
   b. India
   c. Cuba
   d. South Africa

2. In which ethnic minority do the smallest proportion of women attend college?
   a. Native Americans
   b. Latinas
   c. African Americans
   d. Filipino Americans

3. In the year 2001 in which professional area do women students outnumber men for the first time in history?
   a. Information sciences
   b. Business administration
   c. Medical school
   d. Law school

4. Which U.S. institution of higher learning was the first to admit both women and men?
   a. Harvard University

   b. Oberlin College
   c. Columbia Teachers College
   d. UCLA

5. Which nation has the highest percentage of women physicists?
   a. Canada
   b. Germany
   c. Japan
   d. Hungary

6. Whose pioneering research led to radically changed ideas about the uniqueness of human beings?
   a. Jane Goodall
   b. Dian Fossey
   c. Sue Savage-Rumbaugh
   d. Birute Galdikas

7. Which country has the highest proportion of women attending college?
   a. Sweden
   b. Australia
   c. United States
   d. Israel

Answers:

1. c. Cuba. Whatever the shortcomings of the Castro regime, Cuba now has universal literacy.

2. b. Latinas. Although Latinas have made considerable educational strides, the language difficulties, relative poverty, and gender ideologies of recent groups of immigrants from all areas of Latin America have contributed to low rates of college attendance among Latinas.

3. d. Law school. In 2001 the number of women law students exceeded the number of men for the first time.

4. b. Oberlin College. As you will read later in the chapter, men and women pursued separate programs of study.

5. d. Hungary. Hungary also has a historical tradition of notable women mathematicians.

6. a. Jane Goodall. Human beings were thought to be unique in their ability to fashion tools. Jane Goodall was the first primatologist to observe chimps modifying natural objects for use as tools.

7. c. United States. A higher proportion of women attend college in the United States than anywhere else in the world.

---

process ultimately results in maintaining or changing a society's gender arrangements. Whether a nation's educational system is devoted to providing basic literacy and **numeracy**, or advanced scientific and technological knowledge, gender imbalances persist. This chapter examines various gender-related aspects of education within North American society and around the world. You might begin by tackling the questions in Box 9.1.

Thinking About Gender and Education

Take a moment to reflect on your own ideas about what education is and what the purposes of education are. For most of us, education is a formal process that occurs under the supervision of *experts* who decide

when, how, and what we should learn. In general, we are supposed to learn the skills and knowledge that are relevant to Western industrial and postindustrial society. Large tracts of land, complex physical facilities, and vast amounts of resources are devoted to this process. In developed nations only formally trained and credentialed individuals are allowed to instruct others. However, the Australian Aborigine child who learned from an elder how to find water in a barren desert was also being educated. The Norwegian Laplander child who knows how to get a mother reindeer who has had a stillbirth to accept an orphan calf as her own has been educated. You are in the process

---

numeracy The ability to think and express oneself in quantitative terms.

TABLE 9.1   The Most Important Reasons for Attending College

	Women	Men
My parents wanted me to go	36.4%	32.7%
I could not find a job	5.0	4.8
Wanted to get away from home	17.5	18.0
To be able to get a better job	73.0	72.9
To gain a general education and appreciation of ideas	65.0	53.8
To improve my reading and study skills	41.4	35.4
Nothing better to do	2.2	4.6
To make me a more cultured person	39.2	30.3
To be able to make more money	67.9	74.7
To learn more about things that interest me	75.2	68.7
To prepare myself for graduate or professional school	61.2	49.5
A mentor or role model encouraged me to go	13.6	12.3
To get training for a specific career	75.2	68.3

Source: Adapted from *Fact File* (2000). *Chronicle of Higher Education.* 46(21). A50–51. Originally published in American Council on Education and University of California at Los Angeles, Higher Education Research Institute. *The American Freshman: National Norms for Fall, 1999.*

of learning the "stuff" that is important for you to function effectively in your society. At the moment, that includes learning about gender.

What is the purpose or goal of all this learning? Some students might say something about how a college education prepares the graduate to "get a decent-paying job doing something I like." Others may view education as the means to actualize one's potential. A few others might venture that the purpose of formal education is to pass on valued selections from all accumulated human knowledge to the next generation. Although that may sound rather lofty and perhaps grandiose, it is also true. In Table 9.1, college students offer their top reasons for attending college. Observe the similarities and differences in the reasons offered by college men and women.

Three other ideas can put our discussion of gender and education into perspective. First, we should recognize that whereas the notion of a literate and educated citizenry dates back to the founding of a democratic United States and Canada, the idea of a formal, advanced education for a majority of citizens dates back only to the end of World War II—less than 65 years ago! Prior to that, such education was the privilege of an elite few. Typically, only the *sons* of affluent families merited this privilege. Oberlin College, founded in 1833, was the first institution of higher education in the United States to admit both women and men. Women studied the Ladies' Course and re-

mained segregated from the men. Not until the 1960s did African Americans gain the right to at least potentially equal access to a high-quality education, and not until the 1980s did the number of women attending college in the United States begin to equal the number of college men (Mayberry, 1996). Talk about social change!

Second, although it is commonly believed that individuals choose freely from an array of educational (and occupational) opportunities, powerful norms of appropriate education based on gender, ethnicity, and social class still persist (Cook, 1996).

Third, recognize that from a global perspective even basic *literacy* is out of reach for many people. Literacy can open the door to many other positive changes. However, in most poor nations the *privilege* of literacy and formal education is more available to boys than to girls.

Critical Thinking Challenge

International aid organizations such as UNICEF declare education to be a human right rather than a privilege. How do you see this issue?

Controversies: Past, Present, and Future

The idea that education and challenging intellectual activity could interfere with a woman's reproductive capacities or maternal functioning may seem absurd.

Nevertheless, many educational experts promulgated this belief into the 20th century (Barnes, 1912; Clarke, 1874; Hall, 1903, 1904, 1911). Even today, the gender ideology and gender arrangements of many societies continue to control and restrict the kinds of education available to girls and women. As in the previous chapter, we are witnessing how gender arrangements and hierarchies reach out to influence the entire life course of the individual.

Today, no publicly supported school would announce blatantly different curricula for boy or girl students. Title IX of the Education Amendments of 1972 outlawed gender discrimination in any program that received federal funds. Thus students select or are assigned their courses from the same curriculum, regardless of gender. This implies that from kindergarten through the senior years of high school and college, girls and boys, men and women are exposed to the same educational experience. In the early 1990s, however, a series of reports about education in the United States and western Europe suggested that this was not so. Researchers declared that everyday classroom interactions and arrangements "shortchanged" girls' education (AAUW, 1991, 1992; Sadker & Sadker, 1994). According to these reports, teachers called on boys more often, gave boys more precise and helpful comments, and offered them more praise, criticism, and remediation. In upper-grade schoolrooms, teachers praised boys for their intellectual capabilities, and girls for their neatness and compliance. Girls got better grades, but teachers perceived this as due to girls' greater conscientiousness, rather than talent or ability. The reports also noted that sexual harassment began in late elementary schools and increased all through high school (Murnen & Smolak, 2000). These harassing behaviors ranged from sexual comments and gestures to overt sexual groping and touching. A majority of harassers are male students acting alone or in groups. Although close to equal numbers of girls and boys have experienced sexually harassing behavior, boys tend to view harassment as normative dominance behavior. However, girls experience harassment as hostile and threatening (Hand & Sanchez, 2000). This last concern was viewed as one aspect of the gender-related *hidden curriculum* of the educational system: Masculine intimidation is encouraged and declared normative. Likewise, girls' fearfulness and inhibition are also normalized as appropriate gender-typed behavior. Harassment regarding sexual orientation also becomes widespread, particularly for boys who do not rigidly conform to traditional gender-typed behavior or interests. Findings of a decline in self-esteem among white girls did not hold across ethnic groups (Kling, Hyde, Showers, & Buswell, 1999). The process of women's sexual objectification also begins in middle school. Researchers said that thinness, likeability, conformity, and physical attractiveness constitute a hidden curriculum for young women in many schools. These concerns consume time, energy, and motivation that should go into learning and career preparation.

Extracurricular sports provide boys with a whole additional area of competence and achievement. Sports help retain many boys who are at risk for leaving school, and they offer additional channels for popularity and status (McNeal, 1995). Male athletic contests and the cheerleading that accompanies them communicate important messages about value, power, and gender roles.

Critical Thinking Challenge

Did your high school provide the same status enhancement, public recognition, and college scholarship opportunities for women athletes as it did for men?

Finally, the gender differentials regarding interest in and preparation for careers in mathematics, science, engineering, and information technology remain overwhelming. These issues are so important for personal and occupational success in the 21st century that I will be discussing them at length later in the chapter.

These reports set off a firestorm of debate and conflict. The education gender wars are still quite heated, and much of the current discussion implies that one gender has to lose out. One side insists that girls continue to be shortchanged in schools. Others say that the research cited by the proponents of this view was dated, deeply flawed, and sensationalized. Still other scholars charge that the recent attention paid to girls' education actually harms boys by making the classroom hostile to boys (Sommers, 2000). They suggest that recent discussions of gender and schooling have concentrated on femininity and girls' schooling, as if boys' learning and socialization within the school system were somehow not problematic

(Mac an Ghaill & Haywood, 1998). Proponents of this latter perspective point out that boys' academic underachievement is clearly linked to their more frequent antisocial behavior. Boys with academic difficulties are more likely to commit a serious youth crime and are more likely to end up in the criminal justice system (Caseau et al., 1994). They suggest that the norms of the typical classroom may violate boys' behavioral repertoire. Boys are focused on hierarchy and competition, but the typical classroom requires compliance, cooperation, and affiliation. Nor does having more men in the elementary school classroom necessarily solve this problem. Men who enter teaching usually have a history of successful conformity to the feminized classroom (McIntyre, 1996).

More boys have more trouble learning to read and write. They receive lower grades, are more likely to repeat a grade, and are more likely to be suspended or expelled (Bushweller, 1994; Gurian, 1996). Boys drop out at higher rates and are placed in special education classes more often (Kaufman, Klein, & Frase, 1999). In the United States, schooling seems to fail in educating a substantial proportion of poor white and minority group boys.

Displays of masculine behavior place boys at greater risk of being labeled as "inappropriate" and as emotionally or behaviorally disordered (EBD) (McIntyre & Tong, 1998). The gender disparity in classification as EBD is quite marked, ranging from 3:1 to 8:1 in various samples (Bushweller, 1994), and minority group boys are greatly overrepresented in this group. In Britain and Australia, educators have begun to take action in regard to boys' long-standing underachievement They have called for a return to a more traditional and more highly structured curriculum and pedagogy for all children (Sommers, 2000).

Can a peace treaty end the education gender wars? In reality, when something works for one gender it works for the other as well. For example, involving students in real-life science experiments has been helpful in keeping more girls interested in science, and this clearly works for boys too. Getting rid of harassment and bullying in the classroom and schoolyard benefits both girls and boys. There has been considerable progress in getting more girls to choose a wider range of courses and careers, especially those considered more traditionally masculine. This has resulted in more productive and lucrative careers for women. However, there has been considerably less progress in facilitating boys selecting traditionally feminine courses and careers, both in the United States and Europe (Bailey & Campbell, 2000; Stewart, 1998). For example, in spite of excellent opportunities, good salaries, geographic portability, time flexibility, and benefits, it remains unusual for a young man to announce his interest in elementary school teaching, or a nursing career. As you will see in the next chapter (on gender and work), traditions of gender segregation in education help create a gender-segregated workplace, as does the differential valuation of so-called men's jobs versus women's jobs.

The elementary school classroom is among the most highly gender-segregated workplaces (Cohen, 1992). Stereotypic assumptions about masculine and feminine traits and abilities, low salaries, lack of status, and highly publicized sex abuse cases contribute to the scarcity of men in the primary grades. More men in the classroom might mean greater support for children from single-parent homes, and it could reinforce the belief that men can also be nurturing. The relative invisibility of men in elementary school education also reproduces the notion that young children are the "natural" responsibility of women (Oyler, Jennings, & Lozada, 2001). Interestingly, in most developing nations, teaching is a higher-status occupation, and teachers at all levels are men (Persell, James, Kang, & Snyder, 1999).

Critical Thinking Challenge

About 98% of elementary school teachers are women. Yet about 30% of elementary school principals and 80% of school superintendents are men. What is the gender lesson here?

Gender and the Educational Process

On the surface, girls and boys now appear subject to equivalent educational processes. However, in reality issues of gender impinge on that process in several ways.

Gender Lessons in the Early Grades

As you read in an earlier chapter, self-imposed gender segregation is a well-recognized phenomenon of childhood. Gender antagonism increases when teachers have genders compete against each other in classroom activities. On the playground there is almost complete segregation, with boys invading girls' spaces more often than vice versa. Invaders and harassers are almost always male, and when complained about, they insist their intrusions and verbal insults are all in fun (Thorne, 1993). It is at these junctures that teachers and principals begin to normalize boys' aggressive and intrusive behaviors. Girls' experience of such interactions as unwanted and coercive is often ignored and demeaned. Girls and boys learn that boys' aggression is "natural" and must be tolerated and accommodated.

Gendered Tales and Texts

School readers and textbooks are powerful shapers of children's understanding of who they are in the world and who they might become. For example, despite recent changes in Japan, traditional gender roles persist in children's readers. Stereotypic traits such as beautiful, kind, affectionate, appreciative, caring, gentle, and patient were strongly associated with female characters. Male traits included looking strong and being big/giant, kind, mischievous, fair, knowledgeable, and agile. Men appeared in a wide range of occupational roles, from manual laborer to the professions, but women rarely had any occupations at all (Jassey, 1998). A similar analysis of elementary school readers in the United States revealed that male characters demonstrated only traditionally masculine traits, whereas female characters were much more androgynous. Male characters outnumbered female characters 3:2. Biographies and illustrations featuring boys and men outnumbered those of girls and women 2:1 (Witt, 1996).

In poor countries, schoolbooks are rare and valued objects that facilitate an equally rare and valued ability: literacy. A study of Kenyan schoolbooks revealed significant patterns of stereotyping and misrepresentation. Girls and women were noticeably absent from representations of agricultural work, even though they do most of it in this East African nation (Obura, 1991).

Critical Thinking Challenge

Does the low proportion of female characters and their inaccurate representation really matter? What does this communicate about female visibility and importance to the children using these books?

Classroom Perceptions and Expectations

Gender affects teacher expectations in many ways. One study of the expectations of 6th-grade math teachers revealed that they believed that boys had more talent for mathematics but that girls tried harder. Girls' consistently higher math grades were attributed to extra effort rather than to any mathematical ability (Jussim & Eccles, 1992). The authors also noted that these beliefs represented a continuation of parents' gendered beliefs regarding math abilities (Li, 1999; Muller, 1998). Young pupils seem to absorb these expectations. Compared to girls, elementary school boys expressed greater feelings of competence in mathematics and sports even though their actual test score differences were minimal. Such gender differentials seem to cut across societies. Evidence from Cameroon, Sierra Leone, Malawi, Guinea, and Rwanda suggest that both male and female teachers believe that boys are academically superior (Anderson-Levitt, Bloch, & Soumare, 1994; Brock & Cammish, 1997).

Ethnic and class stereotypes also affect teacher perceptions and expectations. For example, research participants watched videos of "target students." These videos communicated information about ethnicity, gender, and social class, and all three variables affected how target students were evaluated. Ethnicity was found to have the strongest and most consistent effect on differential evaluation. African-American boys received the lowest ratings on work habits, cognitive skills, sociability and emotional maturity, whereas white boys received the highest ratings across all four variables (Murray, 1996).

Concern continues regarding the lower level of academic achievement by African-American boys. Hypothesizing that school success is related to one's level of *identification* with academics, Claude Steele (1992) argued that the relatively poor academic outcomes for African Americans (especially boys) are caused by a system of schooling that leads to *disidentification* with academics. One researcher evaluated levels of disidentification by age, ethnicity, and gender in a nationally representative sample. The findings suggested that only African-American boys demonstrated disidentification across all the content areas considered (Osborne, 1997).

A large-scale study of African-American 10th graders revealed that gender, SES, and achievement in the early grades had the most influence on later student motivation. Girls were significantly more motivated, spent more time on homework, and took more math, science, English, and foreign language courses. SES was highly correlated with motivation level for both genders (Adams & Singh, 1998). When African-American students were asked about whether they believed ethnicity, gender, or social class would have the greatest impact on their ultimate success, about 2/3 of the women respondents reported they believed their gender would subject them to the most restrictions (O'Connor, 1999).

Gender also influences how *teachers* are perceived and evaluated. One study found that college students were more likely to choose a professor of their own gender as a "best professor," but there was no gender effect for their choices of "worst professor" (Basow, 2000). College students in the United States were asked to indicate the desirability of various traits for a teaching applicant whose gender was identifiable by name, or undetermined ("Dr. Lawson"). Although university instruction is seen as a masculine, male-dominated profession, college students valued feminine-identified personality traits in their instructors (warmth, charisma, and personal interest in students). Yet they rated more masculine teaching styles more favorably. These researchers also found the traits and teaching styles of men instructors to constitute the norm. That is, the "male" instructor and Dr. Lawson received equivalent ratings, whereas the "female" instructor was rated differentially on most items (Burns-Glover & Veith, 1995). College students have different expectations for male instructors, believing them to be more competent, more experienced, and tougher. They see young women instructors as less capable than young men teachers, but believe older women to be the best teachers (Bachen, McLoughlin, & Garcia, 1999; Basow & Silberg, 1987).

Critical Thinking Challenge

How would you evaluate these findings regarding perceptions of teachers in light of the quotation that opens this chapter?

Career Preparation

As students begin to think about and prepare for their future occupations, they have to consider some profound questions: "Who am I? How far can I go? What can I, as a woman, or man do?" How do men and women make the choices they do? Invariably the choices made are related to expectations for success and a sense of personal efficacy for the choices they perceive as available, both short term and long term. Students also consider the relation of the perceived options with their self-identity and basic psychological needs. The potential cost of investing time into one choice versus another is also considered. All of these are related to students' gender role schemas (Eccles, 1994). See what Dilbert has to say about these matters (Figure 9.1).

Occupational choices are also always influenced by one's personal experiences, self-perceived abilities, cultural norms, family norms, and peers (Rainey & Borders, 1997; Schoon, 2001). In addition to these more internal factors, external realities also come into play. Popular media presentations influence our overall occupational knowledge and what we consider appropriate work. Economic conditions are also powerful arbiters of occupational choice.

Today, women in industrial and postindustrial societies develop more flexible self-concepts than men do, and they imagine themselves in a broader array of life domains (school, neighborhood, work, home, family, and so on) (Curry et al., 1994). Although women's career aspirations have increased over the past several decades, women still experience greater self-efficacy in women-dominated fields (Phillips & Imhoff, 1997). Boys and men remain more restrictive about appropriate work preparation and selection. Although vocational roles still remain central in men's lives, family and home responsibilities are increasingly demanding attention and consideration as men select and prepare for their occupations.

To examine the interplay of both internal and external factors in one particular segment of the population, researchers examined the development of occupational aspirations and expectations among inner-city boys, from the second through the eighth grades, and found increasing occupational realism with increasing age. Occupational expectations gradually began to mirror actual ethnic and class differences in adult job holdings. These findings suggested that lower occupational expectations were strongly related to increasingly lowered educational expectations. The occupational aspirations of these boys reflected and re-created the world they knew

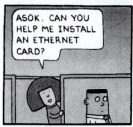

FIGURE 9.1   How do you interpret this many-leveled comment about gender and preparation for the workplace?

(Cook et al., 1996). The myth is that jobs are open to all regardless of color, class, or residence. Talents, interests, and industriousness alone are supposed to decide one's occupation. Schools and popular media support this myth by presenting ethnic models of high achievement, but actually, parental social class remains the most powerful predictor of educational and occupational aspiration. By the way, there was little support for a second popular myth—namely, that most inner-city boys aspire to be athletes and thus downplay their schoolwork. By the eighth grade, fewer than 5% of boys sought to be professional athletes. Also, contrary to the previously mentioned disidentification hypothesis, boys in this study believed that more education *would* pay off for them but were conscious of their seeming inability to achieve academically. Other research explodes another commonly held notion—namely, that collegiate aspirations are associated with greater androgyny among girls. Androgyny was evaluated in two samples of high school women. The women in an upper-level math class were all college bound. A second sample was on a vocational track in a cosmetology class. These researchers found greater androgyny in the cosmetology group, whereas a more traditionally feminine orientation prevailed among the women in the math class (Wulff & Steitz, 1997).

Critical Thinking Challenge

How would you explain the more traditionally feminine gender role orientation for the college-bound women in the math class?

Gender, Math, Science, and Technology: Explorations in the Delta Quadrant

In one manifestation of the popular *Star Trek* television series, the starship *Voyager* is under the command of the competent *and* nurturing Captain Kathryn Janeway. The starship crew is lost in an unexplored area of the universe known as the Delta Quadrant. Each week they encounter previously unknown species, phenomena, and technologies. This makes an interesting metaphor for the relationship among gender and mathematics, science, engineering, and computer technology. In most (but not all) industrialized and postindustrial nations, men have

ZOOM & ENLARGE   **BOX 9.2**

A Very Brief History of Gender and Science

For many centuries, knowledge and truth were portrayed as women, and mathematics is still referred to as *queen of the sciences*. On one side of the Nobel Prize medal is pictured a female Natura (Nature personified). A female Scientia (Science personified) lifts a veil from her face.

Modern science developed in Europe during the 17th and 18th centuries and was conceived of and referred to as a *masculine philosophy*. When the classics constituted the only acceptable form of knowledge and science was considered heretical knowledge, some affluent women were encouraged to pursue science. As research science began to replace the classics as the foremost form of intellectual knowledge, women were actively excluded (Fox, 1999). At least one important philosopher (Immanuel Kant) and one famous scientist (Carl Linnaeus) wrote that a primary qualification for serious intellectual work such as science was *having a beard!* In the 19th century, the

masculinization of science became associated with the notions of private versus public spheres, and science became firmly ensconced in the public sphere. The gender ideology supporting this was that women dealt with the immediate and practical and were thus incapable of considering the abstract and universal. They lacked genius. Francis Galton declared men of science to be "strongly anti-feminine; their mind is directed to facts and abstract theories, and not to persons or human interests" (quoted in Schiebinger, 1999, p. 71).

By the 1940s, womanhood and science had become incompatible. During the 1980s, in keeping with the spirit of the second women's movement, there was a dramatic increase in the proportion of science and engineering degrees awarded to women. For example, the proportion of baccalaureate degrees in engineering awarded to women went from

less than 1% in 1975 to 16% in 1985. However, this trend began to slow in the late 1980s, and continues relatively unchanged today. The mental image of *the scientist* remains male. Women scientists are disparaged if they meet current standards of attractive femininity, and disparaged if they do not. Furthermore, the contemporary culture of science involves unspoken assumptions and values, certain customs, important rituals of conformity, norms of language usage, styles of interaction, modes of dress, and a hierarchy of values and practices that may all be relatively unfamiliar to women. For example, aggressive competitiveness is highly valued in physics, whereas modesty and being soft-spoken are not. Sports culture is often intertwined with academic life to bolster collegiality among men, but this is alienating to many women. How might women scientists adapt to this culture? Should they?

---

traditionally dominated these four areas, and most indications suggest that this gender differential will continue (Box 9.2 offers a historical perspective on gender and the rise of science). These traditionally masculine domains still remain relatively unexplored territory for girls and women in terms of aspiration, education, and achievement. It often appears that many young women feel lost indeed as they consider their place in these areas of study.

Critical Thinking Challenge

Have the women in your gender class felt lost in the domains of mathematics, science, engineering, and computer technology?

Pervasive and Persistent Underrepresentation

Why are girls and women underrepresented in mathematics, science, engineering, and computer class-

rooms? Why do they seem to avoid or leave these domains of study even though these fields will be among the major areas of employment in the decades ahead? They are also the fields that will have great impact on people's lives in the future.

It might be comfortable to believe that stereotypes regarding gender, mathematics, science, and information technology are decreasing and that young boys and that girls now choose their educational pathways freely and without bias, but this seems far from true (Farmer et al., 1999). For example, students in the United States, ages 9 through 13, were asked to choose courses for themselves and for students of the other gender. Boys chose significantly more math and science courses for themselves, and girls chose significantly fewer. When asked to select science courses for the other gender, the stereotype effect was even more powerful. Both genders saw physical science and technology courses as suitable for boys. Life sciences (biology, ecology, and so on) were the only courses judged suitable for girls (Farenga & Joyce, 1999). Table 9.2 offers an overview of some of the majors selected by beginning college students in the United States (American Council on Education, 1999).

Mathematics constitutes the critical filter that facilitates students' entry into scientific and computer studies. Several recent studies continue to document the continued stereotyping of mathematics as a male domain (Barnett & Corazza, 1998; Efklides, Papadaki, Papantoniou, & Kiosseoglou, 1998; Muller, 1998), even among those who are talented in this area (Leung, 1998; Park, Bauer, & Sullivan, 1998). Thus it appears that the current generation of students is likely to carry the same stereotypes into their course and career selections, and the present relationship among gender, mathematics, science, and technology will be reproduced.

Various explanations have been offered to account for women's relatively low level of representation in these areas. *Difference models* claim that men and women behave differently in these domains. *Deficit models* claim that women and men are subject to unequal treatment within these areas (Sonnert & Holton, 1995).

Difference Models. Cognitive and personality factors have been cited as the source for differential course and career selections. Popular ideas about "women's way of knowing" suggest that women are not oriented to the objectivity and rationality required by scientific pursuits (Belenky et al., 1986). Stereotypic beliefs that all women have a more intuitive, synthetic, and holistic cognitive style contribute to the idea that they are not suitable candidates for advanced work in science and mathematics. Also, stereotypic beliefs persist that girls and women have lower career aspirations and that these aspirations are limited to areas defined as feminine. Some claim that girls and women are socialized to be less resilient and to become more easily discouraged. An interaction style that de-emphasizes aggressiveness and competition is also believed to impede success in these areas.

Gender differences in math and science interests have also been cast as a *persistence gap* (Cole & Fiorentine, 1991). According to this perspective, although it is now acceptable for women to pursue high-status careers women fail in these pursuits be-

TABLE 9.2   What Students Expect to Major In

Area of Study	Total	Men	Women
Arts and Humanities	11.1%	10.0%	11.7%
Life Sciences	4.9	4.9	6.8
Business	16.0	18.5	13.9
Education	11.5	6.0	16.0
Engineering	8.1	15.2	2.4
Physical Sciences	2.0	2.8	1.9
Professions	13.3	8.3	17.7
Architecture	1.3	1.9	0.8
Health Technology	0.7	0.3	0.9
Nursing	2.9	0.3	5.1
Predental, Premedical, Preveterinary	4.3	3.1	5.4
Physical Therapy, Occupational Therapy, or other types of therapy	2.5	1.3	3.5
Social Sciences	8.8	5.8	11.3
Political Science	2.2	2.2	2.2
Psychology	4.3	2.1	6.1
Technical	3.9	7.1	1.2
Building Trades	0.5	1.1	0.0
Computer Programming	1.7	3.0	0.6
Electronics	0.3	0.6	0.6
Computer Science	3.8	6.5	1.6
Law Enforcement	1.9	2.7	1.2

Source: Adapted from *Fact File* (2000). *Chronicle of Higher Education*, 46(21), A50–51. Originally published in American Council on Education and University of California at Los Angeles, Higher Education Research Institute, *The American Freshman: National Norms for Fall, 1999.*

cause they do not try hard enough. They are less persistent because they can rely on safety net of marriage. Men continue to achieve social standing almost exclusively via occupational success. Thus they must persist. One study of elite scientists revealed that 80% of the men, but only 34% of the women were primary wage earners (Sonnert & Holton, 1995).

The demands of competing life roles have also been cited as an explanatory variable. As you have read, even professional women remain responsible for most of the domestic labor, child care, and elder care in their families. The culture of the science profession often remains structured on the assumption that there is an unpaid spouse devoted to all these life roles. Researchers have found that compared to men scientists, fewer women are married and substantially fewer have children. Moreover, whereas many of the professional men are married to homemakers, almost all the professional women are married to fellow professionals. For example, in one sample, about 80% of women mathematicians were married to other mathematicians. A substantial proportion of these women believed marriage and family constitute advantages for their careers. They felt that the emotional support and security they experienced contributed to their professional success. Many stated that marriage and children offered both "problems and opportunities" for women scientists (Sonnert & Holton, 1995).

Structural Deficit Models. Women's low participation in these domains has also been explained in terms of discriminatory barriers that blocked women's paths and facilitated men's success. The barriers begin with biased advisement regarding course selection in high schools. Some teachers continue to believe that neither high achievement nor the study of science is consistent with feminine roles (Kahle, Parker, Rennie, & Riley, 1993). Such teacher expectancies have a powerful impact on more vulnerable students. Finally, overt job discrimination constitutes another barrier. These discriminatory policies included restriction to only entry-level jobs, no opportunities for promotion or tenure, and no access to research funding. Less formal barriers involved a lack of access to professional and social networks, few mentors, and **tokenism** (Schiebinger, 1999). A similar pattern of structural impediments has recently been identified in India's educational system (Arora, 2001).

The problem has also been cast as a "leaky pipeline" (Alper, 1993). The idea was that if more girls entered math and science education, more would end up in math/science careers, so the issue was viewed as one of "self-deselection." Too many girls were opting out of math and science at too early an age. The solutions proposed involved childhood socialization to science and math that more resembled that of boys, more training opportunities, and greater financial support (Rosser, 1997).

Another approach was the concept of critical mass for women in science and math. Researchers note that a minority group that has suffered discrimination is easily marginalized when it constitutes only a small presence in a larger, dominant population. The presence and survival of that group is in constant

jeopardy. However, if the minority grows in numbers and influence, the relationship between the majority and minority changes. The minority can ensure its survival. This point of change is called the *critical mass* and seems to be reached at about 15%. Researchers studied 30 academic science departments in five disciplines, comparing those successful in graduating women doctoral students with those that were unsuccessful. They also compared those departments with a critical mass of women faculty with those without. These authors concluded that achievement of a critical mass alone was insufficient. To create real change, there must also be change in the structure of the scientific workplace. Action from above, meaning administrative policies and announcements, was also important in creating a woman-friendly climate. These researchers concluded that the dispersal of women students into male-dominated research groups led to little but a sense of sustained isolation. When women scientists are isolated, their colleagues may impose tougher and higher standards for acceptance and success. Isolated individuals also lack the psychological support, helpful information, and the social knowledge that underlie success. Informal social networks are indispensable to professional development, career advancement, and the scientific process. Isolation also results in stigma, a depletion of self-confidence, and ultimately increasingly poor performance (Etzkowitz et al., 1994).

With this new understanding, let's return to our Dr. Jones's physics class (the vignette at the beginning of the chapter). The study of physics has proven particularly resistant to the entry of women. Physics has been described as a "culture of noisy arrogance . . . that tends to silence women" (Schiebinger, 1999). In 1996 only 3% of full professors of physics in the United States were women, and among physics departments offering only bachelor's degrees, 75% had no women on their faculties (Schiebinger, 1999). No matter how talented or prepared, women registering for a college physics class know they are entering a masculine universe (Stewart, 1998). Most

---

tokenism **The practice of hiring or appointing a single or token number of people from underrepresented groups in order to deflect criticism or comply with affirmative action rules.**

likely Dr. Jones is male and therefore there is no supportive role model for the women students in this alien territory. Although distributing the women students among the research teams may have seemed like a good idea, the highly competitive nature of the groups (remember those bonus points?), coupled with the isolation each woman may have felt as the "token" within her group, may all have combined to produce the poor performance and high dropout rate among the women in the class. Interestingly, when researchers asked college students to imagine themselves as physicists, all the women respondents specifically mentioned isolation as a likely experience (Lips & Asquith, 1995). In Dr. Jones's class, one woman had apparently adapted by taking a "back seat" with the men in her group. The woman who took command of her research group may have been so exceptionally talented and persistent that nothing could keep her from excelling. But surely a student shouldn't have to be brilliant and exceptional to survive in an undergraduate physics class!

What has been done to change the gender balance in science, mathematics, and computer technology? Conferences have been held to develop and share innovative classroom methods to hold the interests of girls, women, and minority group men (Farmer et al., 1999). Undergraduate and graduate programs have attempted to provide mentors. However, keep in mind that mentoring has *not* traditionally been rewarded in faculty tenure and promotion reviews. Some institutions have implemented reforms in student recruitment, as well as in hiring and promotion practices to overcome barriers for women faculty. There have been some attempts to introduce equity in parental leave, including a slowing of the tenure clock to allow for family responsibilities (Wilson, 2000). Other institutions have been careful to avoid tokenism in hiring. Consultants from women's studies and ethnic studies have recommended more collaborative learning through the use of groups, as well as a greater emphasis on practical applications of principles. Internet-based interest groups such as SYSTERS (for women in computer-related work) and university counseling center support programs have also been shown to be helpful in supporting women and ethnic minority men in mathematics, science, and information technology.

The women who succeed in these areas tend to come from wealthier and more highly educated families compared to the men in these fields. They tend to come from families with fathers in scientific or technical occupations. These women are exceptionally talented, with remarkably high SAT and GPA scores (Benbow, Lubinski, Shea, & Eftekhari-Sanjani, 2001). They are often graduates of single-sex schools (also true in Europe). Historically black schools also have a very high proportion of science and math graduates, and these schools are the primary source of African Americans who pursue doctorates in science. However, a disadvantage of women's colleges and historically black institutions is that they are not primarily research institutions, so they lack specialized equipment and laboratory supports (Schiebinger, 1999).

Gender and Mathematics

Math class is tough. ◆ Barbie

There have been persistent findings of lower performance by girls and women on standardized mathematics tests. Brain-based physiological differences were ostensibly the reasons for women's inferior mathematics performance. However, more recent research has revealed a steady narrowing of the gender gap in math scores on standardized tests as girls take more math courses. The gender gap in math performance also disappears if different criteria are used to measure math achievement. For example, girls' course grades and classroom test grades are superior to those of boys up through high school. Furthermore, findings of gender differences in mathematics performance vary widely across cultures. For example, girls tend to demonstrate superior scores on standardized tests in nations as diverse as Finland, Hungary, and Thailand. They tend to demonstrate essentially equal performance in British Columbia (Canada), Hong Kong, Nigeria, Scotland, and Sweden, but tend to score lower than boys in France, Israel, Netherlands, Ontario (Canada), and Swaziland (Baker & Jones, 1993). A recent study of French-speaking Canadian high school students revealed that boys' negative attitudes toward mathematics increased over time, whereas girls' attitudes actually became more favorable (Chouinard et al., 1999).

Generally, there are no gender differences in mathematics performance in elementary school, but girls begin outperforming boys in *computation* in grades 5–6 (10 to 12 years old). However, boys begin outperforming girls on mathematical concepts and applied word problems during this same age period (Hopkins et al., 1997). Across several societies, adolescent boys begin performing better on math achievement tests, and this advantage persists and increases from adolescence onward (Park et al., 1998; Povey, 1998). Girls seem to use rules and algorithms more than boys do. As early as the first grade, girls seem to use different strategies in solving math problems (Carr & Jessup, 1997). Didactic instruction on solving math problems, a less competitive classroom atmosphere, and classroom techniques requiring cooperation all result in better mathematics performance among girls and women compared to similar boys (Seymour, 1995). However, in Europe and North America, boys vastly outnumber girls in classes for the mathematically gifted, often at a ratio of 12:1. We should also note that the ratio of Asian-American students in such classes (22%) far exceeds their proportion in the general population. In contrast, the ratio of African-American students is far below their proportion in the general population (at only 2%). For another insight into the complexities of group differences in mathematics achievement, consider that in one study of gifted math students, 70% of female students and 63% of male students were oldest or only children. Thus birth order is a better predictor of mathematical giftedness than is gender, but little attention is given to this fact (Gallagher, 1993).

The following strategies have been found to produce equivalent math performance in *both* genders: cooperative learning opportunities rather than competitive motivational strategies, frequent individualized and hands-on learning opportunities that require mathematical application, as well as the use of realistic and practical problems in assignments. Another positive strategy includes active career and educational guidance that exposes students to nontraditional careers, and makes explicit the effects of traditional gender socialization regarding mathematics (Juntunen, 1996). Other researchers recommend the occasional use of sex-segregated groups to reduce the public performance of traditional gendered behavior—namely, domination by boys and girls turning to boys for help.

Boys and Girls in Cyberspace

A world of buxom babes and blow 'em up games.

◆ M. J. Ybarra

In North American society, the world of computer technology and information sciences is rather firmly demarcated as masculine turf (Whitley, 1997). A recent study of the effect of gender on children's game software preferences offers a glimpse of how this comes about. Boys and girls (age 10–11) played with four versions of the same computer-based problem game (gender-typed *Pirates* or *Princesses*, a gender-neutral *Honeybears* version, and an abstract *Blocksworld* version). Boys strongly preferred the *Pirates* version over the *Princesses* version. There were no differences among the girls in preference. *Blocksworld* was least preferred by both genders. Previous research revealed that girls performed worse on the *Pirates* version, but there were no gender differences in performance on the identical but gender-neutral *Honeybears* version (Joiner, 1998).

You are already quite familiar with the childhood environmental factors that influence children's orientation to computer technology. Parental beliefs and gender-typed toys, school books and other books, children's movies, teacher expectations, and classroom behavioral norms are all viewed as contributing to a differential involvement with computers. Much of the educational software designed to teach the fundamentals of math is more appealing to boys. Software designers (many are women) assume users will be male (psychologically, the notion of "generic student" still equals "male student"). For example, in one math game students fire guns at correct answers written on passing tanks. Boys like the action, the loud noises, and flashing colors. Girls tend to find all this boring and prefer word-oriented software and practical tasks and puzzles (Schiebinger, 1999).

Critical Thinking Challenge

How would you evaluate the quality of cybergirl Web sites such as girltech.com and chickclick.com?

A recent meta-analysis revealed that boys and men had more rigid gender stereotypes regarding computers, experienced greater self-efficacy, and expressed more positive affect toward computers (Whitley, 1997). The issue of the paucity of women preparing for the cyber industries has even found its way into one of those magazines tucked into the tight pouch behind the seat on a popular airline. In the December 1999 issue of *Sky* Magazine M. J. Ybarra asks the question directly, "Why Won't Women Write Code?" This author claims that even though little girls are as fascinated by computers as their male siblings, by the time they are 16 they will "have lost interest in computers, her youthful promise swallowed by the high-tech gender gap that keeps the fastest growing jobs in the new economy almost as male-dominated as football" (Ybarra, 1999, p. 40). According to the National Science Foundation, the proportion of undergraduate women earning degrees in computer science declined from 36% in 1985 to 28% in 1995 and the postgrad numbers have declined from 3% to 1%. In the United States, more women are studying for the clergy than for computer science!

In the classroom, boys seem to dominate computer use, especially when paired with girls. The arousal level produced by aggressive computer games further serves to alienate girls. Most information technology teachers are men, and teachers (regardless of gender) see computers as more relevant to the careers of boys. Teachers tend to conform to the stereotype of masculine attraction and expertise in technology, and this leads them to encourage boys more in the computer classroom. These tendencies seem to result in less hands-on experience for girls.

Regarding the supposedly "natural" affinity between men and computers, cross-cultural studies offer some interesting insights. Two similar samples in the United Kingdom and Hong Kong were compared on computer attitudes and computer anxiety. In the UK sample, there were no gender differences in computer anxiety, but men had more experience with computers and also more positive attitudes toward computers. In the Hong Kong sample, men also had more computer experience, but there were no gender differences in computer attitudes. However, Hong Kong men reported more computer anxiety. The authors note that in Hong Kong, media depictions with males in dominant positions relative to technology are noticeably absent. They concluded that computers and technology are *not* heavily masculinized in Hong Kong (Brosnan & Lee, 1998). An Israeli study compared the final test scores in microbiology classes using (a) computer simulations or (b) traditional class-

room methods. The typical gender gap in performance disappeared, and this was interpreted as largely because of the lack of competitiveness in the computer-based learning situation (Huppert et al., 1998).

Gender and the Sciences

The findings of longitudinal and cross-sectional studies of gender and science education are relatively consistent. Beginning in middle school, a gender gap appears in science course selection, in standardized science achievement, science literacy tests, and in expressed scientific career interests. This gap widens all through high school and into the college years (Burkam et al., 1997; Eisenhart & Finkel, 1998; O'Sullivan et al., 1997). This culminates in the relative absence of women in the scientific and technical professions. When women do persist in scientific careers, they tend to concentrate and excel in the life sciences (biology, ecology, and so on). The processes thought to contribute to the gender imbalance in science education and career preparations include the mass media stereotype of scientists as "nerdy and male," the oppressive and unwelcoming atmosphere that exists in many science classrooms and programs, the persistent cultural definition of women and minorities as individuals who "leave science," the manipulation of scientific findings for corporate and political gain, and the exclusion of non-Western, nonmale interests and perspectives from science (Rosser, 1997).

The liberal solution is to find ways to give girls, women, and minority group members ways to gain equal access to all that is available to white men and boys. A more radical approach is to confront the bias in the choice and definition of problems scientists address. For example, the influx of women into medical research has changed the way clinical drug trials are conducted (see Chapter 11, on gender and physical well-being). Some researchers have focused on the "culture" of elite scientific workplaces. They note that across disciplines, no matter what quality is perceived as needed at the highest ranks, women seem to fall short. For example, among the sciences physics is ranked as most prestigious, followed by chemistry, engineering, and then biology. The social sciences are at the bottom of the prestige hierarchy. As one descends, the proportion of women becomes greater.

Within physics itself, theoretical physicists have the highest rank. Experimental physicists have lower status, and that is where women physicists aggregate. In engineering, management holds highest rank, then senior and project engineers, then engineering design, then research and development. Lower down are analysis or test engineering, and manufacturing engineering. Again, the proportion of women increases as one descends. However, contradictions abound: Among engineers, electrical engineering is considered more *women's work* because it is "abstract, math-based and clean." But in physics, such abstract work is considered *men's work*. Thus when particular capacities are considered paramount in one field, women with those capacities are rare, but when those same capacities are considered of lower status in another field, women suddenly predominate (Eisenhart & Finkel, 1998).

Engineering represents a particular problem. Researchers examined factors related to persistence among women engineering students and found mathematical ability to be most powerful predictor of persistence in engineering. They found that compared to similar men, women with high mathematical ability simply select fewer math and science courses. They concluded that higher-level math and science courses in the earlier grades are critical in providing the skills needed to persist (Schaefers, Epperson, & Nauta, 1997).

A Global Perspective on Gender and Education

A nation's educational system mirrors the gender arrangements of that society, and therefore education is an arena for both conflict and positive change (see Box 9.3). Education can be a source of empowerment and advancement, or it can serve to reproduce and maintain gender inequities (Persell et al., 1999).

When the military establishment, religious institutions, or an economically privileged class provide education, a small group of people have a great deal of power over the uneducated masses. In the contemporary world, most education is supported by the state and universal access to education is a formal goal for most governments (Schafer, 1999). Thus the entire citizenry of a nation is potentially subject to the values, attitudes, and contents of a particular educational system. Although most of us see state-supported education as benign or benevolent, we should realize that education can be used to preserve and promote oppression. Consider the goals of racially segregated schools in the United States or the special Indian schools in Canada. In these state-supported systems, education served to keep certain groups in a subordinate status. The same was true under apartheid in South Africa or in the colonial schools in the African colonies. Today, many governments in the developing world cannot afford to provide education for their citizens, so INGOs (international nongovernmental organizations) are becoming the major providers of education in those nations (Schafer, 1999). This is significant because these organizations promulgate a *world culture* of human rights and gender equity. Predictably, the activities of these INGOs sometimes provoke conflict within traditional societies and within certain political regimes.

The Developing Nations

Presently there is a worldwide trend toward numerical gender parity at all levels of education. Gender and education have become central themes in virtually all discussion regarding international development. UNICEF sees education as a *human right* that is denied to many women and girls and has declared their education to be a moral imperative (Heward, 1999). The World Bank lends funds for establishing schools for girls. However, such gender parity exists in relatively few parts of the developing world.

For all developing nations, the first step in achieving educational equity is basic literacy (Walter, 1999). In virtually every region of the world, a smaller percentage of women are literate. Nearly 75% of women over age 25 are illiterate in sub-Saharan Africa. About 60% of women in the Middle East, 37% of women in Asia, 21% of women in Latin America, 7% of women in Europe, and 3% of women in the United States are illiterate (see Figure 9.2a and 9.2b). On a global level, male illiteracy is similarly distributed, but female illiteracy is higher in all geographic areas. The literacy gender gap is slowly shrinking over time, and is somewhat smaller among those under 25. In terms of secondary education (the equivalent of high school), the only places where the proportion of women is equal to or greater than that of men are cer-

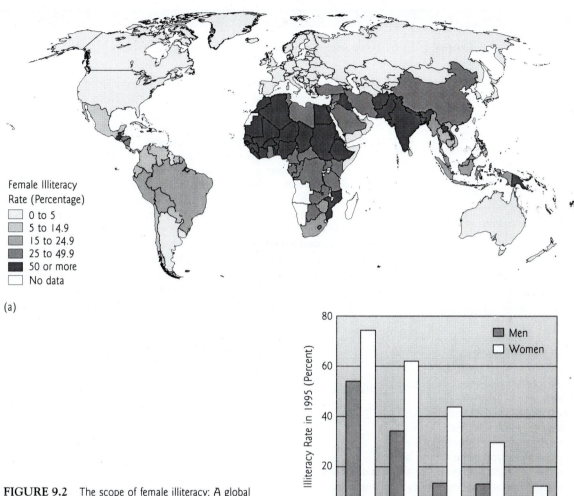

FIGURE 9.2 The scope of female illiteracy: A global perspective. (a) This map shows the distribution and concentration of female illiteracy around the world. (b) All over the globe, the proportion of female illiteracy is always greater.

tain countries in South America, the Caribbean, and in the United States. At the college level, in many South American and European nations, Australia, New Zealand, and Canada, the proportion of women is equal to or higher than that of men. The United States has the highest proportion of women in colleges. In wealthier Middle Eastern countries, higher education is acceptable for women until they marry, but such schooling remains highly segregated (El-Sanabary, 1994). In the Caribbean area, men can

earn relatively high wages without any secondary education (as cab drivers, construction workers, and so on), whereas women need formal education to enter office work and government work. In most developing nations, even when girls and women have access to schooling, several gender-related factors combine to further limit their pursuit of education (Post, 2001). When the Taliban came to power in Afghanistan, one of their first acts was to prohibit girls from receiving any education beyond age 8. You can

SLIDE SHOW   **BOX 9.3**

A Glimpse into Classrooms Around the Industrialized World

We can come to appreciate another type of diversity if we glimpse the status of gender issues in education in several industrial and postindustrial nations.

United Kingdom: UK society is both similar to that of mainstream North America and also quite distinct. Studies conducted in the United Kingdom have not supported the contention that girls and women students receive inadequate attention or feedback in the classroom (Lightbody & Durndell, 1998). All students study the same curriculum up to age 16 and then choose from various areas of study (Colley, 1998). Predictably, students' educational aspirations narrow along gender lines. Sports, mathematics, the physical sciences, and information technology become masculine choices, whereas languages, social sciences, the humanities, and lower-level child-oriented careers become feminine choices. Girls who transgress the traditionally masculine boundaries have congregated in veterinary science and in certain branches of medicine, physiotherapy, dentistry, and law, and they are quite successful. Recent changes require all students to study at least one technical subject up to age 16. Although men in the United Kingdom continue to avoid domains demarcated as traditionally feminine, recent student surveys revealed that men rated flexible job time requirements to accommodate family commitments as more important than women did (Lightbody & Durndell, 1998).

Sweden: Sweden has a strong tradition of full gender equity in terms of education, labor force participation, and gender balance in that nation's legislature and at all levels of government. However, a less intense pattern of gender-typed educational choices eventuates in concentrating more women at the lower ends of the occupational hierarchy. In Sweden today, only nine years of education are compulsory, but 98% of all students apply to the voluntary *gymnasium* (upper secondary school). There, students may choose from among 30 academic or vocational programs. The gender distribution of the areas within these programs remains segregated. Researchers tried to identify the parental role models that influenced student selection of gender-atypical domains. Sons tended more often to select careers that were similar to those of their fathers, thus continuing the gender typing of their occupations. The only variable correlated with the selection of gender-atypical careers was a high parental educational level (Dryler, 1998).

South Korea: South Korea remains overwhelmingly a man's world. With the exception of some Middle Eastern nations, there are fewer women political leaders and business leaders in Korea than anywhere else in the world. Women hold only about 2% of all civil service positions. In terms of education, boys and girls must study in separate classes, and sometimes in separate wings of their

schools. South Korean schools, like Japanese schools, emphasize mathematics, reading, and rote memory, all instilled in an atmosphere of authority and intense pressure. All students must wear uniforms. No makeup or elaborate jewelry is permitted, and no romantic socializing is tolerated. Boys are routinely beaten, but girls seldom receive physical punishment. The images and roles depicted in textbooks promote the relative invisibility and passivity of women, and traditional masculine traits and occupations for men. As in many Asian countries, 14- and 15-year-old students must pass a very stressful high school entrance exam in order to attend college. Inadequate performance on these exams means referral to a vocational school and essentially losing the chance to ever attend college. The passing score for boys in Korea has been about 20 points lower than that required for girls. Recently, the mother of a daughter who was denied college admission based on this overtly discriminatory policy took on an entire nation's cultural ethos. She and her daughter dared to lead national protests that ultimately forced the president of South Korea to end this type of discrimination and initiate a policy of gender equity in college admissions (Kristof, 1996).

Japan: Western educators, psychologists, and industrialists have studied the Japanese educational system extensively. The achievements and abilities of Japa-

read in Box 9.4 more about the Taliban's almost unimaginable oppression of girls and women.

In poor nations, the proportion of resources a nation is willing to devote to educating its citizens usually depends on its openness to Western ideas of citizenship, individualism, and modernity. Even when a developing nation is willing to educate its citizens, the

resources available may be scarce indeed (see Figure 9.3). Interestingly, the two exceptions are Cuba and Sri Lanka. For example, in conservative Pakistan leaders have made defense a priority, rather than education. Most Pakistani women remain illiterate and spend their lives bearing children and in the endless daily domestic labor involved in fetching fuel, water,

BOX 9.3 *(continued)*

nese students in mathematics, engineering, and technology are the stuff of educational legend. However, relatively little is known in the West about Japanese women's junior colleges. There are 592 such colleges in Japan and 91.6% of their students are women. The curriculum is devoted to the cultivation of womanly virtues such as compliance, docility, supportiveness, and strong maternal interests. These schools provide practical, nonprofessional training oriented toward "preparation for family roles." That is, they aim to produce comforting wives for work-weary husbands, nurturing mothers of sons who will excel, and workers skilled at "women's work." This training will qualify graduates to obtain gender-specific, short-term positions as "OLs" (office ladies). OLs provide cheap and temporary labor for periods of high economic growth. Employers prefer junior college graduates for these low-level secretarial *women's positions*. University women are considered *namaiki* (impertinent), whereas junior college graduates are considered more *sunao* (obedient) (McVeigh, 1998).

South Africa: Although located on the African continent, South Africa is unique in its blend of first world and third world features. Its former policy of **apartheid** created a situation in which a small white minority lived a privileged developed-world lifestyle whereas the black and **coloured**

majority were kept in permanent subordination. Separate educational systems provided meager resources for black Africans and segregated schools prepared blacks for a lifetime of service to the white minority. Since apartheid ended in the early 1990s, the nation has attempted to provide social equity and economic opportunity for all its citizens. By 1993 women accounted for 49% of university students, with 63% of women students concentrated in science, education, business, and health care (Budlender, 1997; Unterhalter, 1999). However, women with equivalent education do not earn similar incomes or have jobs of similar status compared to men. The origins of this disparity should be familiar to you by now: gender segregation in career choices, overt job discrimination, and poor child care services. The issue of violence also affects large numbers of women in this country. An articulate women's movement has highlighted these problems, and laws and programs have been initiated to end gender discrimination. The assumption is that access to education is the key to social and economic well-being for all South African citizens, and education is a high priority for the new government.

The traditional South African teacher was educated in a racially exclusive school. Students in segregated classrooms all spoke the same language (English, Afrikaans, or one of several African languages) and came from a similar eco-

nomic background. A very formal classroom manner and physical punishment for troublesome students constituted accepted pedagogy. A central government administrator provided syllabi, textbooks, and exams. Today, a very diverse student body in terms of racial, ethnic, linguistic, and socioeconomic background fills classrooms. The new curriculum demands learner-centered or cooperative teaching methods. Instructors are not allowed to cane unruly students. Professors are preparing the first generation of teachers who will teach in a vastly different and rapidly changing society. At a historically black university (University of the Western Cape), students may take a course on the psychology of gender (Robinson, 1999). Black African students often share gender-related experiences of conflict between their home (rural) background, which is tribe-bound and heavily traditional, versus their Westernized urban lifestyle. In some classes, a traditional dynamic occurs, with men dominating debates and urging women to change themselves and speak out. The women seem to gain solidarity from the opportunity to have men listen to them. Other women protect men from these challenges by raising cases of men being battered, raped, and so on (Shefer, Potgieter, & Strebel, 1999). How does this compare with the discussion dynamics of your gender class?

---

and animal fodder (Heward, 1999). In many nations of Africa and South Asia, young girls must walk many miles each day just to provide basic fuel and water for their families and food for their animals (see Figure 9.4). In Mexico, girls from large, poor families are needed for vital domestic chores and thereby miss schooling opportunities (Post, 2001). Frequent ab-

sences and high dropout rates are the rule for girls in those societies. The status of agricultural production

---

apartheid **Past government policy of white South African government aimed at segregation of its citizens on the basis of color and race. Abandoned under new constitution in 1993.**
coloured **Under apartheid, the term used to classify all South African citizens of mixed racial/ethnic heritage.**

First the Schools, Then the Jobs, Then Their Health: The Girls and Women of Afghanistan

Contributed by Jennifer Holmes, Kennesaw State University

The Afghani people suffered through a hundred years of political and religious unrest, only to be subjected to another decade of oppressive Soviet military occupation during the 1980s (Maley, 1998). With the dissolution of the Soviet Union in 1992, various competing anti-Soviet Islamic rebel groups further contributed to the devastation of Afghanistan. In the midst of this turmoil, a student group, the Taliban (the word means "students of religious studies") quickly grew into a potent military and political force. In 1996, the well-educated Taliban promised to restore order and peace to a devastated Afghanistan. They seized power in Kabul, the capital and came to control about 90% of Afghani territory. The Taliban sect insisted that only the strictest adherence to Islamic law would restore harmony to the nation and guarantee salvation to believers (Maley, 1998). The Taliban taught a puritanical, oppressive, and literal interpretation of the Koran that transformed Afghanistan into an 11th-century theocracy (Shah, 1999).

Prior to the Taliban takeover, Afghanistan was a rapidly developing nation, with remarkable accomplishments in terms of education and employment. Nearly 70% of Kabul's educators were women. About 40% of Kabul's physicians and about 50% of Afghani university students were women (Johnson, 1998; Rasekh, Bauer, Manos, & Iacopino, 1998). Afghani girls and women in the urban centers were free to dress and move about as they wished. They were also free to choose their own educational and occupational pathways and to enjoy the benefits of their achievements and labor. All of that was forcefully transformed to a degree that still remains difficult for many of us to grasp.

Among the very first actions taken by the Taliban was to prohibit girls over age 8 from attending school. Soon after that, women were prohibited from working outside their homes. Because of their many women workers, schools, pharmacies, clinics, and hospitals were forced to close. Women were no longer allowed to leave their homes unless escorted by a male relative and unless they were completely covered from head to toe by the *burqa* (Pan, 1999; Prussel, 1998). This is a large covering that allows the wearer to see out only through a square piece of meshed cloth that is about 5 square inches. With women physicians, nurses, aides, and other health personnel forbidden to work, the girls and women of Af-

ghanistan were unable to receive even basic medical care and health services. The Taliban strictly forbade male doctors to examine and treat women patients.

The "religion police" patrolled the streets of cities carrying whips. They were free to whip, beat, and maim those they determine were violating Islamic law. Men were punished for having beards of insufficient length. Women were punished for exposing an ankle, laughing in public, or wearing shoes that made too much noise. At least one disobedient woman was publicly executed (Shah, 1999). Music, television, and any pictorial depictions of the human body were banned. Windows were painted over to prevent people from looking inside women's homes.

The previous civil war and ongoing religious and political fighting created an entire generation of widows. It was estimated that in 1997 there were about 30,000 widows in Kabul alone (Dupree, 1998). Prohibited from working, these women had no source of income and were forced to become street beggars, always at the mercy of the religion "police." Many starved to death or committed suicide.

---

in a developing nation affects gender and education. In many developing countries, agriculture is the sole means of survival. Women and girls do about 80% of the labor involved in food production, and this labor is almost always unpaid. Typically, any crops or livestock produced are the property of husbands and his family of origin. When not in the fields, girls are needed for housekeeping, child care, and other income-producing activities. On a typical day in sub-

Saharan Africa and South Asia, two thirds of children *not* in school are girls (Stromquist, 1999).

In some societies, attending school conflicts with deeply held beliefs about controlling the sexuality of girls and women (Persell et al., 1999). In such societies, the distance involved in schooling rural girls and women becomes problematic. Distance from family supervision has been identified as a particular impediment to education in Ethiopia, Gambia, Guinea,

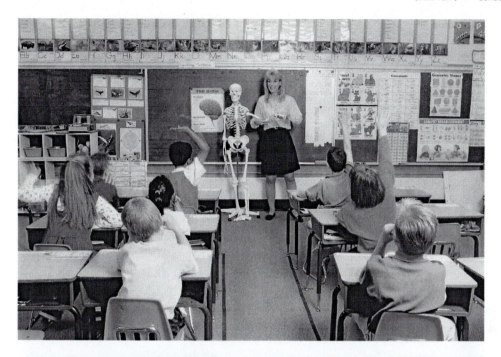

FIGURE 9.3   The education-related problems facing the students in this suburban schoolroom (top) are quite different from those in this classroom in Africa (bottom). As of 1996, for example, only 44% of boys in Mali, Africa, and 34% of Malian girls had *ever* attended school. In both settings, however, gender inequities persist.

In the peak season . . .

Waking at sunrise, a girl in rural Nepal begins her 14-hour day by taking care of the animals and fetching water. After a half-hour for breakfast, she then spends at least two hours gathering fodder. She eats an early lunch before beginning work planting in the paddy, where she will spend at least six hours. In the evening, she again tends the animals, fetches water, takes her dinner and goes to bed at about 7:30 P.M. She has spent 12½ out of 14 waking hours laboring at her chores.

In the slack season . . .

A girl in rural Nepal, rising with the sun, begins her day by taking care of the animals and fetching water. She takes breakfast and then spends at least two hours gathering fodder. The slack season differs from the peak in that, after lunch, she has time for a short rest. Then she goes to collect firewood, a chore that will take five or six hours. In the evening, she again looks after the animals, fetches water, eats dinner and has time for another short rest before going to bed at about 8:00 P.M. Her slack-season chores take 10½ out of 14 waking hours.

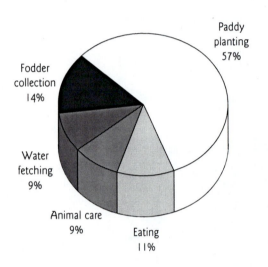

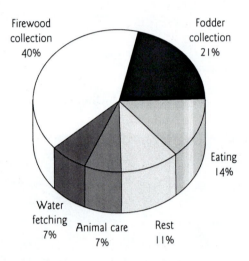

FIGURE 9.4 This view of a working day in the life of a 10-year-old girl in Nepal helps us understand why few girls can attend school in some parts of the world.

Kenya, Mali, Sierra Leone, Tanzania, and Zimbabwe (Brock & Cammish, 1997; Odaga & Ward, 1995).

Investment in the education of girls contributes to social and economic development (UNICEF, 1997). However, this is so only in countries where more economic development and egalitarian gender regimes prevail. In some South Asian nations, education for girls is viewed as a means of inculcating even greater piety and deference. Women's education is correlated with increased demands for isolation, restriction, and greater devotion to the education of sons. For example, in Sri Lanka there is almost universal literacy

and a low birth rate but little economic development. Girls and women there remain subordinated to domestic labor and to domestic violence (Persell et al., 1999). Thus basic education does not *guarantee* empowerment. Consider that in many places in Africa a woman cannot own her own property. She obtains the right to use land from her husband's lineage group (Riphenberg, 1997). Without owning land, she has no access to credit, technical assistance, or membership in farmer's organizations. In Brazil, women obtain almost as many years of education as men and their levels of school enrollment at school are about the same.

However, women occupy inferior positions in professional roles, in political representation, and in access to income and property (Persell et al., 1999). However, in general the education of girls and women is correlated with later marriage, smaller family size preferences, higher rates of contraceptive usage, reduced fertility rates, improved child survival rates, lower crude birth rates, longer life expectancies, lower death rates, and an increased ability to provide basic life needs (Hadden & London, 1996; T. C. Martin, 1995; UNICEF, 1997).

In situations of economic deterioration and social upheaval, parents opt to educate only their sons. In many traditional societies, greater benefits accrue to a family from educating boys, because girls become part of a husband's family. Also, a daughter's household and field labor is much more valuable than a son's. For poor families, drought, economic depression, social turmoil, or a rise in school fees always entail sacrificing a girl's education first (Riphenberg, 1997). At the same time, girls and women often recognize that access to any education is the pathway to increased status and earnings for themselves and their children (Fallon, 1999). Education for girls and women facilitates increased opportunities in the labor market. However, in the factories sprouting all over the developing world, women's wages are typically 60% to 70% of men's wages, and opportunities for advancement are minimal. This is caused mostly by discrimination, not less education. We'll be taking a closer took at the relationship between gendered work patterns and the global economy in the next chapter.

Conclusions

Many of the weaknesses of the North American educational systems may be recast and reanalyzed as gender issues. For boys, higher failure and remediation rates remain problematic. For girls, concentration in lower-status programs of study continues.

Gender equity in mathematics, the physical sciences, engineering, and information technology is not simply a matter of "add women and stir" (Rosser, 1997). Only serious curricular and methodological transformation can rectify the problem of under-representation of women and minority group men (Levinson et al., 1996).

The myth that ethnic, class, and gender factors do not affect educational choices needs to be exposed. Educational policies and practices that continue to marginalize and subordinate individuals on the basis of gender, ethnicity, and social class require change.

In many developing nations, education is promoted as a basic human right that should be available to all. Although literacy and numeracy generally bring overall improvement to the quality of life for all human beings, cultural, economic, and political factors can impede empowerment.

In both industrial and postindustrial nations, full gender equity in education has yet to be realized. As we will see in the next chapter, gender inequities in education result in occupational and economic inequities.

Summary

◆ Education is the process by which the skills and knowledge relevant to a particular culture are learned and applied. An advanced education for all who desire it is a relatively new idea. Norms of gender, ethnicity, and social class influence educational choices and patterns. Basic literacy is still a distant goal for much of the world's population.

◆ A series of reports set off a debate as to whether girls are "shortchanged" by the current educational processes. Recent findings suggest that gender-related factors in the educational process are also detrimental to boys' academic achievement.

◆ The elementary school classroom is characterized by a relative absence of men teachers, by gender-stereotypic texts, and by gender-biased teacher perceptions, expectations, and attributions. There are persistent gender-related and ethnicity-related differentials in career choice and occupational preparation.

◆ Difference models and deficit models have been proposed to explain the relative gender imbalance among students in mathematics, the physical sciences, engineering, and information technology. Several reforms have attempted to rectify this gender imbalance.

◆ Women's mathematical underachievement is not a cultural universal, yet it persists in North American society and in western Europe. A number of psychosocial variables maintain computer technology as a masculine domain. Women scientists have aggregated in the life sciences. Women continue to avoid adequate academic preparation in the fields of physics, engineering, and the information sciences.

◆ Education remains a critical arena in which gender inequities may be maintained or modified. For poor nations, basic literacy and numeracy are major, but often elusive goals. Many factors combine to maintain lower literacy rates among women all over the developing world. Literacy and more years of education are often correlated with other significant social and economic benefits.

◆ In industrial and postindustrial societies, patterns of gender segregation in educational choices continue. These patterns culminate in inequities in occupational and economic achievement.

 InfoTrac College Edition

For more information, explore InfoTrac College Edition at

http://www.infotrac-college.com/Wadsworth

Enter search terms: gender and education, gender and physics, gender and computer science, gender and science.

10

Gender and Work

Segregation Now, Segregation Forever?

Only a tiny minority of us ever are involved in inventing our present, let alone our future. Ordinary men and women—which means almost all of us—struggle along with received truths as well as received ways of being and doing. ◆ Lillian Rubin

Learning Objectives

After studying this chapter, you should be able to:

1. Describe the likely origins of the division of labor by gender, and then provide a brief overview of the history of human labor emphasizing recent social changes.
2. Describe the relationship between masculinity and success in the worker-provider role, mentioning the concept of positionality.
3. Explain three issues relevant to understanding the relationship between gender and work on a global level.
4. Explain how occupational aspirations and expectations are influenced by gender and other sociocultural factors, emphasizing recent findings across nations and within the United States.
5. List and explain seven gender-related factors relevant to the course of career path development.
6. Define and describe the nature of occupational segregation, and then provide an overview of two major approaches that attempt to explain how such segregation is maintained.
7. Explain the relationships among gender stereotyping, gender discrimination, and occupational segregation, and then summarize recent findings regarding gender and compensation.
8. Explain the metaphors of the sticky floor, the glass ceiling, and the high-speed escalator, emphasizing their impact on gender-differential success in managerial positions.
9. Explain how the Tall People parable relates to the struggle for gender equity in the workplace.
10. Describe three factors relevant to understanding the relationship among gender, employment demands, and family needs.
11. Summarize the findings regarding quality of life in the contemporary dual-earner family.
12. Summarize the perspectives and policies regarding parental leave and child care across several nations.

Encounters with Gender

The e-mail from the CEO contained an invitation to lunch. Yes, Max's hard work and expertise in the firm's overseas operations were well recognized. The reward would be a substantial promotion, a three-year appointment in the London Office, a generous salary increase, company-subsidized housing, and relocation expenses. The twins would attend an international school. Of course a long and detailed family discussion was held, but they all knew how long Max had dreamed of such an opportunity. After expressing some ambivalence, all family members agreed to be supportive. Off they went. Within a year, the company's European operations had expanded. After a slow start, the couple had developed a small circle of friends, their new home overlooked the Thames, and they even had a little time for shared leisure activities. The twins were honor students. But after the first year, marital problems were at an impasse. Resign the new position, or there would be a divorce. What went wrong? Why couldn't Max's spouse be more supportive and appreciative?

Overview

An understanding of the relationship between gender and work begins with two basic concepts: the universal division of human labor on the basis of gender, and work success as a core component of adequate masculinity in the industrialized world. A third important principle relates to patterns of occupational segregation. This segregation begins with gender differentiated occupational aspirations, preparations, and expectations. It is maintained via stereotyping and discrimination. Gender segregation persists across virtually all paid work areas as well as within the same field of work, and it is strongly related to status and pay differentials. The manager role merits special discussion because it involves behaviors that heavily imbued with gender-related meanings: leadership, decision making, dominance, and so on. Lastly, we will examine the balance between work roles and family roles. This issue is a continuing concern in developing economies, as well as in industrial and post-industrial nations. This chapter contrasts some varied approaches to this issue.

Human Survival and Human Work: The Gendered Division of Labor

Most sociologists and anthropologists consider the division of labor by gender to be a fundamental aspect of gender role construction and maintenance within traditional societies. That is, physical strength and child-related responsibilities were major determinants of how survival tasks were distributed. Men's greater physical strength was associated with the development and encouragement of social and interpersonal roles that emphasized action, dominance, and leadership. Women's child-related responsibilities were associated with the development and encouragement of roles that emphasized positive emotional expression, interpersonal relating, and the caretaking of others. Distinctive roles and activities for women and men became a fundamental organizational feature of every human society, and thus we have the beginnings of the notion of women's work and men's work. However, remember that the specific content of those roles and activities varies tremendously across societies (Bonvillain, 1998).

A Brief History of Human Work

Recent insights into the earliest human history offer a picture of bands of men and women sharing the work of gathering foodstuffs, hunting small game, fishing, and generally cooperating to ensure the survival of their offspring (Basow, 1992). Most likely, women developed new technology such as slings to carry infants, language to communicate with children, and later,

perhaps, even agriculture. It is likely that groups of men traveled from the home camp to hunt animals, and returned with meat and skins. Most likely, men were the inventors of new technology for hunting and defense, as well as the creators of social hierarchies. In hunting-and-gathering societies, women's work typically provides about 80% of needed food (Mascia-Lees & Black, 2000). In the Old Testament, the Hebrew woman was made virtuous by her work in growing food, making cloth, and running a smoothly functioning household. For most of recorded human history, women and men labored along side each other in the fields and among the herds and flocks. At home, both made their respective contributions to preserving food, making garments and footwear, constructing and maintaining homes, and bringing up children (Carnoy, 1999). And so it continued for thousands of years. When we jump way ahead to the industrial revolution (late 18th century), a momentous social transformation takes place: the separation of workplace and home. Men, boys, and girls left home to work in the factories and mines. Mothers remained at home, growing food, selling any surplus, raising animals, crafting needed household objects, and caring for offspring until the children too, were old enough to work for wages. By the 19th century the notion of *separate spheres* for women and men was declared both God's and nature's plan for (white middle- and upper-class) humanity. Of course, up through the first half of the 20th century, minority and immigrant women were excluded from this master plan.

During World War II, women of all ethnicities moved into the factories to make the goods need for a massive war effort (see Figure 10.1). They worked at every level of the management and manufacturing process. At the end of the war, women were encouraged and sometimes forced to leave those jobs and make way for returning soldiers. By the end of 1946, two million women in the United States had been fired from their factory and management jobs (Barnett & Rivers, 1996). During the 1950s, gender ideology and gender ideals supported these social changes. The emerging gender ideal was the white, middle-class, stay-at-home, suburban mother who was totally devoted to her husband's workplace success, her children's social adjustment, and the voracious consumption of goods and services. The gender ideal for men became the white, middle-class, commuter

FIGURE 10.1   During World War II, women of all ethnicities functioned well in "men's" jobs.

father, heavily devoted to job and monetary success. For middle-class North Americans, the separation of the masculine workplace versus feminine home place, and occupational role versus family role was virtually complete (Coontz, 1997; Parsons & Bales, 1955). By the 1960s, new appliances had reduced household drudgery, and reliable contraception led to smaller families. Agribusiness and supermarkets offered fresh food, prepackaged meals, and other products to all who could afford them. The civil rights movement, the anti-Vietnam War movement, and the second women's movement were all gaining momentum to bring about another wave of socioeconomic change. Beginning in the 1970s, massive numbers of middle-class women joined their working-class peers in the workplace. Women were re-entering the offices, factories, and classrooms on an unprecedented scale. This phenomenon of large numbers of middle-class women working for wages constitutes a major 20th-century social transformation (see Figure 10.2). Today, such employment is the rule rather than the exception, and women comprise well over half the workforce. Although early studies presented women's wages as supplemental and secondary, today such work is viewed as a matter of economic necessity,

both in the two-adult household, and in the large number of single-adult, woman-headed households (Dunn & Skaggs, 1999). Although paid employment has helped to diminish gender inequality, issues of job segregation persist, as do gender-related pay and status differentials. Nor has the issue of women's "double shift" regarding domestic tasks and child care been resolved (Hochschild, 1989). This continuing facet of gender inequity inevitably leads to "work versus family" conflict in many societies.

The feminization of the postindustrial workforce continues for several reasons. First, the decline in manufacturing and the rise in clerical and service occupations contributes to increased opportunities for women. Second, vast numbers of new jobs have been created in the service sector of the economy (retail, catering, clerical, leisure, and other personal services) and these are all traditionally "women's work." A third reason is the decline in male employment brought about early retirement. Some link these changes to a "breakdown" of the family, or to a "crisis of masculinity," or to a "takeover" of men's jobs. Some men are frustrated about their more limited opportunities and prefer to blame women, but women still see men as favored in the workplace. Others suggest this

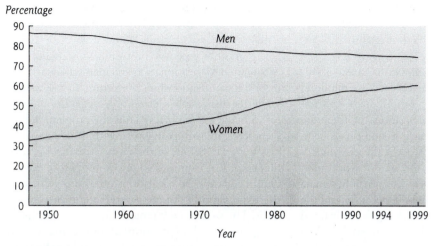

Percentage

FIGURE 10.2   Percentage of population in the workforce of the United States by gender from 1948 to 1999. *Sources:* Adapted from C. Costello & B. K. Kringold (Eds.), (1996), *The American woman 1996–1997* (New York: Norton), p. 47. Updated (from 1994 to 1997) from U.S. Bureau of Labor Statistics (2000, January) *Employment & Earnings, 47*(1), 11, Table A-2.

increase in women workers has had minimal effect on women's occupational subordination and on male dominance in the workplace (R. K. Brown, 1997). After reading and discussing this chapter, you may come to your own conclusions.

Masculinity and the Worker Role

In the industrialized world, the worker role is the principal masculine role and most men continue to define themselves primarily by and through their work (Beeghley, 1996; Ranson, 2001). The major focus of masculine socialization is preparation for the adult role of worker in that both sports and traditional masculine play train boys for future work roles. Industrial and postindustrial societies situate the most meaningful male activities outside the home and family, and adult masculinity, male identity, and male role performance all revolve around work (Cohen, 1993).

Critical Thinking Challenge

What traditional boys' games or activities rehearse the roles of friend, suitor, husband, father, or household maintainer?

Among the most positive aspects of masculinity are the need to succeed, to excel, to be respected at work, and to be a responsible and reliable provider and protector. These features constitute the traditional masculine way of performing nurturance, support, and caretaking within the family and community. Thus the masculine role is largely defined as that of breadwinner and successful worker. The chronically unemployed or underachieving man loses status and identity as an adequate male. Mainstream masculinity is equated with ambition, power, authority, autonomy, and assertiveness (Betcher & Pollak, 1993). Powerful social approval and material rewards attend the performance of these characteristics within the work role. In the industrialized West, across ethnicities and social classes, masculine success is measured by monetary compensation, power, and occupational status. It is not measured by a man's physical attractiveness, the social value of his accomplishments, nor the virtue or success of his offspring. Thus, in the opening vignette we can hardly fault Max for being excited about the opportunity to advance, even if it did uproot the family. After all, such achievement is a valued goal and it was clear that the family actually benefited. Besides, all seemed to be going well for the family. Shouldn't one support a spouse's ambition and enjoy the affluence and leisure provided by success? Why did Max's spouse have such difficulty adjusting to such a privileged life?

Another important and relevant aspect of adequate masculinity is *positionality*. That is, manhood or masculinity is defined by a position superior to that of women. Men in subordinate positions are therefore *less masculine*. We see the conflict around this issue in the notion that higher-status work is the province of men and that even in the same area of work, men should somehow be *over* women. Reciprocally, female subordination and roles involving support for and the facilitation of the goals of others typify traditional women's work (Beneke, 1997). A recent study of Dominican fruit plantation workers offers a dramatic illustration of all these principles. When large-scale plantations (pineapples, melons, and avocados) were first established, men were hired for most types of work. Field work and packinghouse work were declared as men's work. However, women workers gained a reputation for greater compliance and reliability and soon replaced the men at these low-paid jobs. Soon afterward, to reduce costs even further, these agrobusinesses moved to a contract system that involved using local *contratistas* (all men) to hire informal work crews. These contractors hired only men workers who then refused to work at the same jobs as women. Today, work in the fields is considered men's work whereas packinghouse work is considered lower-status *women's work* (Raynolds, 2001).

Traditionally, men proved their manhood by their physical strength and their ability to limit their employers' demands (Meyer, 1999; Quam-Wickham, 1999). Men "did gender" at and through work. However, men's socialization for physicality, autonomy, and competition can be problematic in the postindustrial work world where teamwork and cooperation are required. In today's information-based workplace, physical strength is much less valued in comparison to technical expertise and interpersonal skills. Moreover, most men do not feel very successful, because ironically, the gendered requirement of positionality virtually guarantees that there will always be someone *above* any individual man. Moreover, submerging one's whole sense of self-esteem and value into work can be dangerous. Economic change, large-scale down-sizing, age discrimination, change of work-

place opportunities, and then retirement can all damage self-esteem based solely on occupational role. Finally, *workaholism* or single-minded devotion to success is another potential problem. Work addiction is detrimental to the formation and maintenance of family and social relationships. Returning to the opening vignette, this couple seemed to have additional time for joint social activities. Thus the problem did not seem to be an overinvolvement with work duties.

Work can be one of the most satisfying aspects of life, because it expresses an important part of the self. Our occupation or vocation is often the vehicle for the expression of our creativity, talent, or acquired skills. The workplace is typically the arena for the development and expression of our achievement, strivings, and pursuit of excellence and productivity. Labor that is self-selected or that is aimed at some higher purpose is extremely fulfilling. Nor is there any doubt that money can help make life easier and more enjoyable. Although generous monetary compensation is a heavily endorsed cultural value in the West, the meaning of work can go way beyond that.

Returning for the last time to the opening vignette: What happens to your view of the story if you learn that Max's full name is Maxine and that their three-year London sojourn meant her husband would remain at home, unemployed and relegated to the role of a househusband? For many of us, the idea of a healthy grown man being financially supported by a wife elicits some discomfort, if not disapproval. Also, although it is expected that a wife should fully support her husband's occupational goals and ideals, most of us set limits on the sacrifices a husband should make for his wife's career goals. A man totally devoted to his wife's career advancement and to child care often seems somehow "emasculated." All this should offer some additional insights into how closely the concepts of "manhood" and "successful paid worker" are entwined in Western society's gender construction. It also demonstrates again how gender-related social arrangements influence the life course of individuals.

Critical Thinking Challenge

Survey the nontraditional-age students in your class regarding their accommodations to their spouse's career development. It may prove an eye-opener for both the men and women in your class. Younger students can interview their parents on this issue.

The Work Gap, the Wage Gap, and Women's Microventures

Most students reading this chapter are personally concerned about the relationship between gender and work within industrial and postindustrial economies. However, to broaden our understanding, let's examine three important issues related to gender and work on a global scale.

First, all over the world women's traditional labors have not been constructed as real work at all. Nor have their labors been counted as economic activity. For example, a young married woman in sub-Saharan Africa rises at dawn to feed chickens and milk the family goats. She walks a mile to gather firewood and another mile to fetch water. After preparing, serving, and cleaning up after breakfast for her family, she picks and processes vegetables from the family garden. She makes and mends family clothing. She weaves a large basket for storing grain and brews beer to sell in the local market. In the afternoon, she "helps" her husband in plowing, planting, weeding, picking, and processing corn, which she will also sell the next day. Another wife might "help" her husband in operating a small store. In the economic equation, these husbands are productive farmers and storekeepers, whereas wives are counted as not working and therefore not economically productive (Conway-Turner & Cherrin, 1998). Thus, there is a substantial gender gap in what kinds of activities are counted as *work* in the developing and developed world. Women's labors are often unpaid and part of the *informal labor sector*, which is typically not included in many nations' accounting systems. Men's work is part of the *formal labor sector* and contributes to a nation's gross national product (ILO, 1995; Seager, 1997).

The second issue becomes real if you take a moment to examine where your clothing, electronic devices, and household objects were manufactured. You will find that you are indeed a participating consumer in the global economy! Multinational companies set up manufacturing plants in developing nations because of inexpensive labor costs, and that cheap labor is almost invariably women's labor. For example, women make up about 90% of all lightweight assembly workers in the international garment and electronics industries (ILO, 1995). The Mexican *maquiladora* system provides just one nearby example of this trend. United States–based corporations have established thousands of assembly plants (*maquiladoras*) along the United States–Mexico border and over 80% of the lowest-paid workers are women. Men typically occupy supervisory and managerial positions (Tiano, 1994). These plants are generally exempt from minimum wage requirements, environmental constraints, and worker safety rules (Naumann & Hutchison, 1997).

Now for some good news! All over the world, many women are becoming successful microentrepreneurs and joining the self-employed sector (Neft & Levine, 1997). In 1976, the Grameen Bank program was established in Bangladesh to offer small-scale loans for enterprising individuals to begin and develop small ventures. Most of these microloans went to poor women, often illiterate. This very successful program, and many others like it, have spread all over the world (Fisher, 1996).

Gender and the Contemporary Workplace

Work, workers, and working are all changing (Howard, 1995). Women now constitute at least 40% of the industrialized world's paid workforce (World Bank, 1996), and about 60% of the workforce in the United States (U.S. Bureau of the Census, 1998). Immigration continues to affect the ethnic makeup of the North American workforce. For example, in previous years, Mexican, Puerto Rican, and Native American women traditionally showed lower rates of labor force participation, whereas African-American, Chinese, Japanese, and Filipino women showed rates higher than those of white women. However, all over North America, such ethnic differences are rapidly declining.

Occupational Aspirations and Expectations

Occupational and career development is a lifelong process, and gender is one of the most powerful and persistent influences on this process (Shu & Marini, 1998). Traditional theories of occupational development have been criticized for not adequately taking into account issues of socioeconomic status, gender, ethnicity, or sexual minority status (Cotton, Bynum, & Madhere, 1997). Most theories are described as focusing on white, Western, able-bodied, middle-class, heterosexual men (Patton & McMahon, 1999; Rojewski & Hill, 1998). Such theories assume that an array of career choices is available to all individuals, who are motivated to pursue their personal interests in making certain choices. In reality, political and historical events, religious beliefs, gender roles, ethnicity, sexual orientation, standards of living, and economic opportunities within various nations are likely to produce differences in the ways young people see their futures and direct their lives (Badgett, 1999). For example, a large sample of European and North American adolescents from 11 nations were surveyed about their intended careers, and future interests regarding occupational success, family concerns, social responsibility, and social pleasure. The authors concluded that West European and North American youths showed *more* interest in future education and careers compared to East Europeans. They also found that West Europeans emphasized the importance of social pleasure and vacations compared to East Europeans and Americans, and this pattern was even stronger among boys than among girls. East Europeans and Americans defined success more in terms of fame, money, and professionalism than did West Europeans. Both East Europeans and Americans emphasized the importance of taking responsibility for their families and of being useful to their country, compared to West Europeans. This last finding was explained in terms of the relatively low level of social welfare supports in eastern Europe and the United States, and also the unique role of the United States as a superpower. Overall, boys emphasized the importance of becoming successful in terms of wealth and fame more than girls, and boys were more interested in the material aspects of life. In most countries surveyed, girls valued social pleasure and vacations more than boys. In Germany, girls were more interested in family roles, whereas in Romania boys were more interested in family roles (Nurmi, Liiceanu, & Liberska, 1999).

Critical Thinking Challenge

What recent social, political, and economic events in the United States and Europe might help us understand the differences in the aspirations of these young respondents in the study just described?

Similarly, high school students in the United States who were at academic risk (a majority were mi-

nority group members) were surveyed regarding their occupational aspirations. Compared to the young men in this sample, the women aspired to higher-prestige occupations. The men lacked necessary information about careers, lacked interest in making career choices, were more occupationally discouraged, and perceived more external barriers to their future success (Rojewski & Hill, 1998). In contrast, an examination of vocational identity and career choice among gifted and talented high school students of varied ethnicity revealed that gender-traditional choices were widespread, but women were more likely to "cross over" than were men. Gifted girls tended to lower their occupational aspirations as they entered adolescence, despite doing well academically. Gifted boys tended to have higher expectations and were more likely to aspire to doctoral or professional education. These authors concluded that gifted boys had a clearer and more stable picture of their career interests, talents and goals, whereas girls were more conflicted regarding multiple role expectations (Leung, 1998). When a more typical sample of college students was asked to rate the importance of success in various life domains, and to indicate anticipated obstacles, there was considerable consensus across race, gender, and social class categories. Women attached more importance to attaining family goals, but there were no gender differences in the importance attached to economic success. Students of color rated economic success as more important than did white students. Women and minority students of both genders anticipated discrimination as likely obstacles. The five goals rated most highly *by all* were to have a warm, caring relationship with another adult, to acquire mastery of skills for their occupation, to have a secure financial future, to have a comfortable relationship with their original family, and to be physically fit (Eskilson & Wiley, 1999). In a recent survey of managers, there were interesting and substantial gender differences regarding the types of barriers that corporate professionals expected to affect their careers (see Table 10.1) (Wajcman, 1998).

Critical Thinking Challenge

What do you anticipate as the likely obstacles in your career development?

According to traditional career development theory, men chose careers shortly after adolescence,

TABLE 10.1 Career Barriers Perceived by Men and Women in the Corporate World (reported as percentage of sample)

Perceived Barrier	Men	Women
Inflexible working patterns	6%	14%
Family commitments	44	43
Lack of adequate child care	3	8
Lack of career guidance	45	50
Lack of training provision	9	5
Prejudice of colleagues	11	23
Lack personal motivation/confidence	19	21
Senior management seen as a "club"	32	54
Social pressures	1	10
Sexual discrimination and harassment	1	17
Insufficient education	11	13

Source: J. Wajcman (1998). *Managing like a man: Women and men in corporate management* (University Park: Pennsylvania State University Press), p. 88.

and then advanced in these same careers until retirement. Women's careers were temporary until the full-time career of motherhood and homemaking commenced. These latter roles were unpaid and unstructured. Today, it is clear that meaningful paid work is central to both women's and men's lives. Also, individuals will change career paths several times over the work years, and even again after retirement. Women's career development is more complex than that of men because of the cultural dichotomy of work and family (Patton & McMahon, 1999).

A review of a decade of research on gender and career development led to the conclusion that to fully comprehend the path of career development in both women and men, one must consider the following issues (Phillips & Imhoff, 1997):

◆ Women continue to have somewhat lower career aspirations than do comparably talented men, especially if they hold traditional gender role attitudes. Media images regarding suitable occupations influence both genders.

◆ Young women may be less ready to choose an occupational path. Their occupational choices may be influenced by, subordinated to, or even determined by a spouse's occupational path (Farmer et al., 1997). Choices are also highly influenced by the sex segregation of occupations.

◆ Women with more instrumental and more expressive traits are more likely to choose nontraditional occupations, as will those with more egalitarian attitudes (Kulik, 1998). Parental models, peer attitudes, and school environment are relevant here (Castellino, Lerner, Lerner, & vonEye, 1998).

◆ Unlike men, women are much more likely to "enter" the workforce several times during their lives, and to work part time for extended lengths of time. These patterns can have a detrimental effect in fields characterized by rapid technological change and also in the professions (Davey, 1998; Epstein, Seron, Olglensky, & Saute, 1999).

◆ Variables such as ethnicity, sexual orientation, level of household and child care assistance, and traditionality of occupation all contribute to levels of well-being, burnout, stress, self-esteem, and depression among both women and men. However, the gender inequity in domestic duties, child care responsibilities, and vulnerability to **sexual harassment,** are special burdens for many employed women (Bronstein & Farnsworth, 1998; Chira, 1998).

◆ In general, men still advance faster, further, and with greater compensation. Salary differentials persist, even when education, age, experience, and performance are controlled. Marriage and parenthood are associated with higher salaries for men but with lower salaries for women. Issues such as differential training opportunities, level of occupational mobility, and differential evaluation for promotion are all important factors in the path of career development (Aniseff, Turrittin, & Zeng, 1999).

Gender differentials in seniority levels, lifetime wages, likelihood of part-time employment, total years of employment, and attention to retirement planning all have a powerful impact at retirement. In general, women still lose out on all these economic variables (Dailey, 1998). However, because of their lifelong multiple roles, women typically demonstrate a better adjustment to the postemployment years (Carp, 1997).

---

sexual harassment **Unwelcome and offensive sexual comments, behaviors, advances, requests, demands, or assaults in a workplace (or school setting) by a co-worker or supervisor. (Chapter 14, on gender and power takes an in-depth look at sexual harassment on the job and elsewhere.)**

Occupational Segregation

Women remain employed in a narrower range of occupations and industries compared to men. The areas in which women aggregate are characterized by lower status and lower compensation levels (Dunn & Skaggs, 1999; Heinz, 1999). For example, about 75% of women workers are concentrated in service sector industries: clerical, sales, and service. Some examples of highly gender-segregated occupations are librarian, health technician, elementary school teacher, secretary, clerk, nurse, bank teller, telephone operator, and dental assistant (Dunn, 1996). The most common occupations for men are manager, administrator, truck driver, supervisor construction worker, and carpenter (DeLaat, 1999). Levels of female employment in administrative, managerial, professional, and technical job categories are slowly increasing in most industrialized countries. It is interesting to note that gender integration occurs in different ways in different areas of the world. In eastern Europe, many women have moved into jobs in men's traditional areas, whereas in southern Europe, integration results from men entering women's service and clerical areas (Bakker, 1996).

What exactly do we mean by occupational segregation? Consider the following examples. Women and men in the same occupational category are often differentially employed, and this has significant economic consequences. High-priced restaurants employ men (waiters), whereas low-priced restaurants tend to employ women (waitresses). The faculties of more prestigious research universities still largely consist of men. Less prestigious educational institutions employ more women faculty. See Box 10.1 to get a closer look at the significance of gender segregation within specific occupations.

Men and women in the same occupational category work in different industries, again with economic consequences. Women are often employed in the textile industry, where wages are low, whereas men are in the petroleum industry, where wages are high. Even when men and women appear to have similar jobs, men typically have more **workplace authority** (Albeda & Tilly, 1997). Many college students believe that affirmative action laws and attitude change have brought about gender equality in the workplace, but Table 10.2 demonstrates that both occupational gender segregation and gendered wage differentials are still alive and well in the 21st century.

When women and men have equivalent natural talents, they are segregated into very different occupational pathways. Men with superior fine motor skills become surgeons and diamond cutters. Women with equivalent fine motor skills become seamstresses and assemblers. Men who want to care for children become pediatricians, whereas similar women become child care workers.

The occupational categories in which women are concentrated resemble traditional gender relations within the family: Women assist men, care for children, and clean up after others. Women earn less money and are more economically dependent, thus continuing a major feature of traditional gender relations. In industrialized nations, women's wages range between 63% and 89% of men's, with the greatest wage equality in the Nordic countries (Sweden, Norway, Denmark, Finland).

Explaining Occupational Segregation. There are two basic approaches in explaining the persistence of occupational segregation and its associated wage differentials. The first is more psychological and internal in that it places the source of such concentration within the person and emphasizes such factors as the acceptance of traditional gender socialization, individual preferences and choice, and personality factors (Rasanen, 1997).

A debate began about gender differences in communication styles began in the 1980s (Crawford, 1995; Noble, 1995). Ostensibly, men learned to be assertive, whereas women learned to be conciliatory. Researchers who saw these differences as problematic (mainly in the United States) concluded these tendencies resulted in women being more often ignored, excluded, and/or patronized in workplace interactions.

Because of gender socialization, women may experience the same workplace events as more stressful than do men. A variation of these theme is that women are exposed to more stress, from conflicts between work and family. Later in the chapter, you will see that it is not work itself that is associated with women's greater stress and vulnerability, but rather the second shift of housework and child care responsibilities.

---

workplace authority   Usually defined as the number of subordinates that a manager supervises.

TABLE 10.2   Women's Participation in the Workforce Worldwide

Nations with Highest Level of Participation		Nations with Lowest Level of Participation	
China	80%	Dominican Republic	18%
Niger	80	Syria	17
Rwanda	80	Mali	16
Sweden	80	Pakistan	16
Burundi	79	Yemen	12
Mozambique	78	Jordan	10
Benin	77	Libya	10
Burkina Faso	77	Saudi Arabia	10
Vietnam	77	Afghanistan (pre-Taliban)	9
Laos	76	Algeria	8

Source: N. Neft & A. D. Levine (1997). *Where women stand: An international report on the status of women in 140 countries, 1997–1998* [Women's participation in the workforce, worldwide (percentage of women aged 15–64)] (New York: Random House), pp. 55-56.

Since the 1950s there has been debate regarding which gender is differentially motivated by **intrinsic** or **extrinsic work values**. More recent studies (1980s to the present) have found no gender differences on the intrinsic/extrinsic dimension. Other studies suggested women valued the more social aspects of jobs, whereas men were more concerned with pay and career advancement. Overall, women do tend to attach greater value to working with people, flexible work hours, and opportunities to use special skills in the workplace (Rowe & Snizek, 1995).

Critical Thinking Challenge

Explanations of gender differences in work behavior that focus on internal psychological processes imply that women's work attitudes, for instance, are set *before* they enter the workforce, so occupational segregation may appear justified. Lower earnings and nonadvancement may also be viewed as a "natural" result of these forces.

The second approach to explaining occupational segregation is more external, in that it places the source of such concentration in the structure of the work system and gender differentials in access to rewards. Feminist analysts argue that wage hierarchies are not objectively determined on basis of skill level, experience, and other relevant factors. Instead, the gender of the average worker in that field affects wages. Evidence indicates that a wage penalty exists for workers in female-dominated occupations. (See

Table 10.3.) Occupational prestige and workplace authority are also related to the gender composition of jobs. In the United States, female-dominated professions have less prestige. Wright, Baxter, and Birkelund (1995) compared the level of workplace authority across seven nations and found considerable variability. English-speaking nations had smallest gender gap in workplace authority, and Japan had the largest.

In spite of overall lower pay, prestige and authority, women often report greater levels of job satisfaction than men do. This rather remarkable finding seems to result from women's lower expectations regarding monetary rewards and the fact that they compare themselves to other women rather than to men (Desmarais & Curtis, 1997; Jost, 1997).

Critical Thinking Challenge

Some scholars contend that attempts to decrease occupational segregation by encouraging women to enter areas traditionally dominated by men merely continues the process of devaluing women's traditional work, roles, and interests. What arguments can you make both for and against this point of view?

intrinsic versus extrinsic work values   Work motivated by the pleasure and rewards of the work itself is said to be *intrinsically* motivated. Work motivated by factors such as pay, status, opportunity for advancement, and so on is *extrinsically* motivated.

SLIDE SHOW   BOX 10.1

Engendering Specific Occupations

Waitering and Waitressing: Taking orders and serving food and beverages may be considered women's work because they involve activities that are cultural extensions of feminine family roles: pleasing, supporting, and deferring. But there are often gender-differentiated appearance norms and interaction styles for servers. Male servers are often required to wear a tuxedolike uniform, whereas women are often required to dress as sex objects or wear uniforms that suggest those of domestic workers. A formal service style in high-prestige restaurants requires servers to appear dignified and reserved. This performance is gendered as masculine. The more casual service style of the coffee shop or diner promotes an informal, ever-smiling, friendly form of interaction and is gendered as feminine. Although 80% of table servers are women, it has been difficult for women to gain access to prestigious restaurants. Today's establishments are somewhat more integrated. Terms such as *servers* or *waitrons* are in use, and there may be elaborate systems in place to promote gender equity (E. J. Hall, 1993).

Domestic Work: Traditionally, domestic work was one of the few nonagricultural jobs available to African-American women, especially in the South. Irish immigrant women held these positions in the North. Prior to World War II, large numbers of Chinese and Japanese men were domestic workers, especially in the American West (Le Espiritu, 1998). Today, in middle- and upper-class homes, domestic workers often perform household chores and child care, and over 95% of these workers are women. Such work is

physically strenuous and exposure to chemicals is common. It involves low pay, no advancement or promotion, low status, no prestige, a lack of guaranteed benefits, and often, social stigma (Romero, 1992). Sometimes there is psychological exploitation by the employer of the employee (usually both are women). Such work is often ethnically stratified, with women of color and immigrant women predominating. Often undocumented Latin or Asian women are hired as domestics (Hondagneu-Sotelo, 1997). For the new immigrant, domestic work may mean freedom from pesticides and the other dangers inherent in agricultural work. Both women and men believe that housework and child rearing merits only minimum wage. Some feminists see the hiring of domestic workers as allowing continued male privilege regarding housework and child care. Others see such employment as a steppingstone from agricultural work, and as a venue for acculturation and social mobility. Domestic workers who work for several employers on a contractual basis fare the best, economically and socially. Many Filipinas do domestic work all over the Western world. These workers often employ poorer Filipinas to do their own domestic work back in the Philippines (Parrenas, 2000).

Entrepreneur: Women now own one in three small businesses in the United States and employ about 15.5 million workers (Moore & Buttner, 1997). Woman-owned businesses are newer, smaller, and more likely to be in the service sector. They typically begin as part-time ventures. Women are also more likely to inherit businesses than they were

in the past. Owners of small businesses find it difficult to provide employee benefits and are unlikely to offer child care, but they are more willing to offer flexible work hours to their employees. The fastest-growing states have the largest and fastest-growing woman-owned businesses: California, Texas, New York, and Florida. Here is a more vivid picture of this phenomenon: In Santa Fe, New Mexico, 1 in 10 adult women are business owners. They are artists, gallery owners, café operators, and so on or are otherwise associated with the tourist industry (Mergenhagen, 1996). A recent study of work styles in Martinique (a Caribbean island), revealed high labor market participation by women (48% of women). However, men used their social networks and family members to support their attempts at entrepreneurial expansion. Women used their earnings to simply feed, clothe, and shelter their families, without investing in expansion (Browne, 2000).

Farming: The term *farmer* evokes the mental image of a man. Although we normally think of a farmer as someone who makes a living growing food and/or animals for consumption, it has a deeper meaning. That is, a farmer *owns the land* on which crops and animals are raised, and the farmer enjoys the profits from that activity. However, it has been estimated that girls and women grow half of the food, do about 80% of the world's agricultural work, but own less than 1% of its land. In poor countries in Southeast Asia and Africa, women grow, harvest, process, and prepare all food for their families, and almost all employed women

BOX 10.1 *(continued)*

work in agriculture. Thus many farms in the developing world are woman managed, but not woman owned (Lindsey, 1996).

Medicine: Recently, a large-scale survey of new physicians in the United Kingdom inquired about the personal attributes they had developed. Men felt better equipped with "leadership potential," a "spirit of curiosity," and "tolerance of ambiguity and uncertainty." Women felt more confident in their "ability to inspire confidence in others," "ability to listen," "ability to work in a team," and "caring and compassionate nature." There were no significant differences in self-perceived "ability to recognize own limitations and strengths," or "excitement with the subject of medicine," "open-mindedness," or "perseverance" (Clack & Head, 1999).

A medical anthropologist studied surgeons "doing gender" and describes the masculine ambience that surrounds surgery. The characteristics and ethos of that medical specialty are traditionally masculine: arrogance, aggressiveness, courage, and the ability to make split-second decisions in situations of life and death. However, the number of women surgeons has increased tenfold since the 1970s. This author found that patients, chiefs of surgery, colleagues, and subordinates all had notions of appropriate female conduct, and all had ways for invoking differences. A chief resident reports that virtually all her male colleagues confided their romantic difficulties in her. Another surgeon reported that she had to ask for instruments only one at a time, otherwise nurses branded her as "de-

manding" even though multiple requests were typical of male surgeons. Although it is standard for operating room staff to inquire about surgeons' spouses, partners, children, and so on, male surgeons *never* reciprocate. Women surgeons who fail to reciprocate are labeled "snobbish" and "standoffish." Nurses become quick and extra careful around a volatile, demanding male surgeon but become slow and sullen in the face of comparable female behavior. A common technique for male surgeons who are training residents is "teaching by humiliation." Such behavior is simply not acceptable from female chief residents (Cassell, 1997).

Law: In 1971, only 3% of attorneys were women. This rose to about 25% in 1991, and today about 40% of attorneys are women, most often in the less lucrative areas of law. A survey revealed that women attorneys had the same professional expectations as similar men, but they reported significantly lower job satisfaction, because of their lack of influence and opportunities for promotion (Chiu, 1998). Simpson (1996) sent questionnaires to 700 African-American women attorneys (response rate was 74%). All began paid employment early in their lives, and all were raised with ideals of upward mobility through education and employment. All had role models of working, active, strong mothers. Respondents reported an early awareness of the marginality of black men's employment and stated they were raised to accept that they would be equally responsible for their family's financial solvency. Many named prominent black women who

served as role models. Virtually all engaged in some community service. They credited affirmative action programs for helping them get into and pay for their college and law education.

The Trades: A woman printed the first copies of the Declaration of Independence (M. Martin, 1997). Yet today, despite federal legislation prohibiting discrimination, relatively few women work in the skilled trades. These occupations offer many benefits including wages that are two to three times that typical of "women's work," a paid apprenticeship, potential opportunities for advancement, and considerable mobility (Greene & Stitt-Gohdes, 1997). Skilled workers such as carpenters, computer technicians, electricians, heating and air-conditioning technicians, mechanics, plumbers, and truckers comprise about 65% of the workforce. There is a tremendous and increasing demand for skilled workers. Although federal contracts encourage women contractors, no federal contract has even been withdrawn because of low female employment. The barriers to gender equity in the trades should now be familiar to you: stereotypes, resistance from counselors, employer skepticism, and a lack of awareness of the requirements and rewards of these occupations. For example, women in the construction trades report both great job satisfaction from being responsible for the safety of others and from having supervisor and co-worker support. They also report dissatisfaction with underuse of their skills and with sexual harassment (Goldenhar, Swanson, Hurrell, Ruder, & Deddens, 1998).

TABLE 10.3 Gender Composition of Selected Occupations and Median Weekly Earnings by Gender

Occupation	Number of Men Workers (thousands)	Weekly Median Earnings	Number of Women Workers (thousands)	Weekly Median Earnings
Financial manager	344	1,154	353	703
Engineers, architects, and surveyors	1,865	1,052	219	907
Physicians	335	1,364	125	852
Registered nurses	141	791	1,443	747
Nursing aides	163	367	1,255	318
Teachers (elementary school)	308	785	1,529	697
Administrators, education	282	1,076	420	819
Teachers (college and university)	397	1,038	241	859
Economists	57	977	63	774
Psychologists	55	760	86	623
Social workers	220	661	485	579
Attorneys	386	1,340	191	974
Editors and reporters	113	803	98	709
Real estate salespeople	173	767	191	585
Cashiers	301	296	989	275
General office workers	115	706	233	539
Computer equipment operators	128	610	170	485
Secretaries and stenographers	47	*	2,582	446
Insurance adjusters	112	660	304	501
Security services workers	1,791	613	347	492
Food preparers and servers	1,583	311	1,607	286
Table servers	172	325	480	294
Maids and housemen	87	330	385	289
Janitors and cleaners	1,054	351	442	293
Construction trades workers	4,059	571	85	423
Textile sewing machine operators	94	326	322	273
Truck drivers	2,409	532	85	412
Bus drivers	166	498	119	384
Farm workers	463	311	68	259

Source: Adapted from U.S. Bureau of Labor Statistics (2000, January) *Employment and Earnings, 47*(1), Table 39, pp. 213–218.
Note: This table demonstrates several important concepts related to gender and work. First, a relatively high degree of occupational gender segregation persists. Second, occupations in which women are concentrated tend to have lower compensation levels. Third, even within the same occupation, men are paid more.
*Unable to calculate.

Stereotyping and Discrimination

Through the gender-stereotyping process, similarities among gender group members are exaggerated. Uniqueness, differences, and variability are all downplayed. Such overgeneralization can quickly become the basis of faulty reasoning, biased judgments, and discriminatory actions (Martell, 1996). Individuals gain advantages or disadvantages based on their group membership rather than on their actual characteristics (Biernat & Kobrynowicz, 1999; Heilman,

1995). In terms of work-related characteristics, the basic stereotype is that men are forceful, independent, decisive, ambitious, and strong on achievement-related traits. The basic stereotype is that women are tender, understanding, concerned with others, and are strong on nurturant and affiliative traits. The stereotypic attributes ascribed to women are not those believed to be essential for work success. Consequently, work success is associated with men, not with women.

Gender stereotyping affects employee selection decisions and performance evaluations after hiring. Stereotyping even affects self-perceptions, in that women sometimes limit their job choices or devalue themselves and their contributions in the workplace (Scott & Creighton, 1997). Members of one gender may not apply for a particular job because they are socialized not to desire such jobs, or they may be socialized to believe they would not perform well in the job. They may perceive themselves not to have the qualities stated or assumed to be necessary for the job. For example, researchers in a Dutch study found that personnel ads more often listed traditionally feminine characteristics. However, compared to women participants, men were more confident that they possessed *both* the feminine and masculine characteristics required. Men found all the positions listed about equally attractive, whereas women found jobs described with more "masculine" characteristics (for example, "requires analytical skills") as considerably less attractive (Taris & Bok, 1999).

When openings occur, applicants may apply or be referred on the basis of the stereotypic gender-appropriateness of the job. Men may be referred to more senior roles and women to more menial positions (Benokraitis, 1997; Scott & Creighton, 1997). Some employers may seek to "protect" women by excluding them from better-paying positions that require nighttime hours, for example, or the handling of large amounts of cash at opening and closing times of businesses.

Personnel ads and job descriptions may be written to encourage or discourage applications by members of one gender. The applicant selection criteria may be knowingly or unknowingly biased. Traditional height or strength requirements may no longer be relevant. For example, women were traditionally excluded from telephone/electrical line repairer positions because some extra strength was required to manipulate heavy wooden ladders. Now these ladders are of lighter aluminum.

Gender and gender stereotypes are likely to influence the selection process at every point: in the emphases of biographic data, in the description of educational qualifications, in interview dynamics, in the evaluation of work samples, and in formal presentations (Scott & Creighton, 1998). For example, requirements such as "an assertive interpersonal style," or "an attractive appearance," "attention to detail" all have heavy gender-related meanings and interpretations. In situations of **tokenism**, other qualified applicants may be overlooked or purposely rejected. At interviews, there may be inappropriate (and illegal) questions about marital status, child care arrangements, extensive traveling with colleagues of the other sex, and so on (Wurzburg & Klonoff, 1997).

Critical Thinking Challenge

Has anyone in your class been subjected to such illegal questions? What was the context, and what was her or his response? How did the person feel about that experience? Was any legal action taken?

Compensation Issues

One area of employment-related research that is sure to challenge critical thinking capacity concerns gender differences in self-pay expectations. In one study, college seniors entering a variety of occupations assessed their self-pay expectations. Regardless of field, women reported lower pay expectations both at entry and at their projected career peak than did comparable men. Even in women-dominated fields such as nursing and education, the expected peak self-pay differential was significantly less! Women also believed that their lower pay was fair (Jackson, Gardner, & Sullivan, 1992). A substantial body of research has produced similar results (Desmarais & Curtis, 1997; Jost, 1997). How would you explain these findings?

Does gender socialization result in women becoming less concerned with pay, productivity or maximizing monetary rewards, and seeing themselves as lower in business sophistication? Alternatively, perhaps women are aware that they will *in fact* be paid less than men, and so they compare themselves to other women rather than to men (Bylsma & Major, 1994; Trentham & Larwood, 1998). In support of this perspective, one researcher found that over a 10-year span, after controlling for hours worked, education background, and self-confidence in personal skills, men still received higher salaries than women (Tsui,

---

tokenism Work situation in which members of a particular gender or ethnic group (usually women or ethnic minority group members) comprise less than 15% of the peers group and are hired only to satisfy affirmative action requirements.

1998). In contrast, researchers examined gender and salary attainment among graduates of a historically black business school. They found no gender differences in actual income. However, the response rate in this survey study was only 25% (Dreher & Chargois, 1998).

Critical Thinking Challenge

How would *you* explain results of this last study? Is it sampling error? Is there true gender equity in business? Does ethnicity make the difference?

Gender and Management: All About Sticky Floors, Glass Ceilings. and High-Speed Escalators

The notion of the "sticky floor" refers to the obstacles women (and some minority group members) face in advancing into supervisory and management roles. Despite the great progress made since the 1970s, the concept of manager remains solidly masculine (Wajcman, 1998). Regardless of gender, when college students evaluated "target" managers, the characteristics of the *ideal* manager and *male* manager were the same. However, the qualities of a female manager were quite distinct and varied a great deal (Deal & Stevenson, 1998). In another laboratory study, only women leaders who were appointed as leader, who had expertise, and who were legitimized by a male experimenter could influence the performance of their all-male groups on a masculine task (Yoder, Schleicher, & McDonald, 1998). These authors concluded that when women work in traditionally masculine roles such as management, they are numerically underrepresented, they violate norms regarding the gender-appropriateness of the occupation, and they carry the lower status of women. Each of these factors has been related to negative outcomes in laboratory studies (Eagly, Karau, & Makhijani, 1995). However, lab studies may not generalize to real-world settings, because some studies suggest the evaluation of subordinates is unrelated to gender (Rosenthal, 1996). As you may recall from earlier chapters, many conditions in the laboratory increase the likelihood of gender stereotyping: stranger–stranger interactions, public performance, time constraints, and so on. Nevertheless, in a real-world study, when a matched sample of male

and female executives were compared, women managers had less workplace authority, managed fewer subordinates, and received fewer stock options than similar men did (Lyness & Thompson, 1997).

The *glass ceiling* is defined as the invisible barriers, whether real or perceived, that limit advancement opportunities for women who are already in the managerial elite (Swoboda, 1995). Again, despite tremendous progress, women comprise only 10% of senior managers in the Fortune 500 companies. Fewer than 4% of CEOs (chief executive officers), presidents, executive VPs, and COOs (chief operations officers) are women, as are less than 3% of the top corporate earners. Thus it appears the glass ceiling persists (Martell, Parker, Emich, & Crawford, 1998). Although overt and blatant discrimination may be less common, certain practices and cultural norms seem to create a pattern of *systemic disadvantage* for women (Meyerson & Fletcher, 2000). Furthermore, the glass ceiling is a global issue. For example, Japanese women are among the world's most educated, but are underused. Only a small number of Japanese women have become successful managers and executives in business, government, and education (for example, women comprise only 10% of corporate management) (Renshaw, 1999). What are factors maintain the sticky floor and the glass ceiling? Social norms condition both women and men to view women in terms of personal roles rather than in leadership roles. Yet gender differences in management style are mainly in the eye of the beholder, and similarities outweigh any differences. Are things getting better for women managers? A recent study investigated glass ceiling effects in the United States, Sweden, and Australia. These researchers found a gender gap in level of authority, especially at the middle-management level, but no systematic evidence of a glass ceiling in the United States and rather weak evidence of this phenomenon in the latter nations (Baxter & Wright, 2000).

Many executives still contend that women are less committed to their jobs. They may insist that investing in women corporate managers does not pay off because they leave their jobs because of family responsibilities. A longitudinal study of gender and manager turnover in 20 of the Fortune 500 firms revealed that over the same time period, 26% of women managers had left, compared to 14% of men managers. However, contrary to stereotypes, women did not leave because of family issues. Over half left because they were dissatisfied with their jobs or perceived a lack of career opportunities in their current company. Interestingly, dissatisfaction with pay was *not* a major reason why women left (Stroh, Brett, & Reilly, 1996).

The absence of woman mentors is a persistent issue. Good help from above is frequently mentioned as an important technique for promotion and advancement. For the moment, it appears most mentors will continue to be men (Bierma, 1996). As more and more women rise in the corporate and organizational ranks, it will be interesting to see if more women take on the mentor role to help talented subordinates.

The lack of a visible and politically organized women's movement that challenges barriers is also a factor in maintaining barriers. In a seven-nation comparison, the degree of gender gap in levels of workplace authority varied considerably (United States, Canada, United Kingdom, Australia, Sweden, Norway, and Japan). These researchers concluded that the existence of a politically active women's movement was highly correlated with the frequency with which women occupied authoritative positions in the workplace (Wright et al., 1995).

Occupational segregation often results in women being excluded from lunch, sporting events, or drinks after work. At these informal gatherings friendship bonds and alliances are formed, loyalties are established, and vital work-related information is exchanged.

Women who cross the boundary into traditionally masculine occupations face both greater difficulties and greater rewards. When men cross over into "women's occupations," a rather different phenomenon has been documented. Clearly, there may be some negative social outcomes in terms of status and prestige loss (Henson & Rogers, 2001). However, in the workplace a "high-speed escalator" often propels men to the very top levels of woman-dominated occupations (C. L. Williams, 1995b). Box 10.2 further explores what happens when men cross occupational boundaries. There appears to be a preference for hiring men in women-dominated professions such as nursing, librarianship, and social work. Once hired, men are often catapulted into higher-status positions such as supervision, administration, and policy-making. For example, only about 15% of all elementary school teachers are men, but men make up about 96% of all top-level public school superintendents and assistant superintendents (Maume, 1999).

Conclusions. To achieve gender equity in the workplace, both the sticky floor and the glass ceiling should disappear. High-speed escalators should be shared by the highly competent, regardless of gender. Eradication of the sticky floor, glass ceiling, and the gender-segregated high-speed escalator involves diagnosis, dialogue, and experimentation, all carried out in the culture of a particular organization or agency. For example, one company had a strong tradition of long, unplanned meetings and expectations that managers would be constantly available. These norms were difficult for women managers because of their inequitable home and family responsibilities. Although these problems arise from a male-based culture, the fault is often with existing systems, not with individual recalcitrant men (Meyerson & Fletcher, 2000). Sometimes a parable says it best (adapted from Bailyn, 1997):

> Suppose all the really powerful people were short. Tall people were systematically excluded from all positions of status and privilege. But then tall people called for change and succeeded in gaining some benefits. First, the powerful short people tried having tall people act like short ones. Tall people had to stoop to enter doorways, hunch up in tiny chairs, and so on. Some good-hearted short people attempted to fix the structure in small ways. They added tall doorways in the back of buildings, purchased special desks, and even designed "tall-people tracks" for those unwilling to deal with the norms and demands of the short world. Other short people celebrated the differences and pointed out the positive features of tallness. They placed tall people in jobs where tallness was an asset. All these approaches helped, but no overall change occurred, because the interventions dealt with the symptoms of inequity, not the causes.

Critical Thinking Challenge

Some scholars insist that the sticky floor, glass ceiling, and high-speed escalator will disappear when women stop complaining about the very organizations that hire them. To advance, women must take on and *solve* their organizations' biggest problems (Barr, 1996; Furchtgott-Roth, 1998). How would you evaluate this recommendation?

Men in the World of Women's Work

Contributed by Lisa M. Crowe, Kennesaw State University

Gender ideology perpetuates the notion that each gender is suited to particular kinds of work, and that the work of one gender is more valuable than that of the other. Historically, whatever men do has been considered more important and of greater value than the work of women. What about men who transgress this gender boundary and take on work that is traditionally considered inappropriate or denigrating for men? How do others, especially other men, perceive and evaluate such men? How do occupational transgressors maintain their sense of masculinity and satisfactory self-concept in a workplace dominated by women? How do such men actually fare in gender-atypical occupations?

It may be understandable why many women are drawn to the higher status, power, and compensation of traditional "men's" jobs. Unless that position involves physical strength or overt physical aggression (for example, furniture mover or professional boxer), most contemporary women are applauded for pursuing their achievement goals. However, the reaction is generally not as favorable when men enter "women's" jobs. There is often a loss of status and social acceptability (C. L. Williams, 1995b). Society questions these men's abilities as well as their masculinity. Stereotypes about the gender appropriateness of particular occupations result in ridicule and intolerance for men who dare to "cross over" into generally devalued women's work (Chusmir, 1990). His mental health, rationality, self-esteem, sexuality, sense of adequacy, and ambition may all be seriously challenged by others.

The boy who announces to his parents that he wants to be a hairdresser, dental hygienist, or preschool teacher is unlikely to elicit swells of parental pride. Nursing or librarianship may still elicit ambivalence, concern, or even rejection from family and friends.

Social psychologists have shown us that when members of a socially meaningful minority group make up less than 15 percent of the larger group, prejudice and marginalization are highly likely. These acts of discrimination lead to self-consciousness and underachievement because of the increased sense of surveillance and pressure to perform. Members of numerical minorities may attract extra attention, and this may be seen as favoritism by other members of the group. Resentment ensues and may lead to even more performance pressures. This is the nature of *tokenism*.

Although women tokens often face prejudice and discrimination in schools and the professions, men are often desirable, welcome, and well-protected entrants into women's jobs. In teaching, faculty members and administrators reach out to men and their success may be subtly or overtly facilitated. The positive aura that surrounds the overlapping concepts of "man" and "worker" may all be brought to bear on the evaluation of his work and potential. Most men come to view their hypervisibility as a positive factor rather than as problematic. Women co-workers often seem particularly supportive of men in such situations.

In contrast to the women who lack mentors when they enter male-dominated occupations, men very often find a disproportionate number of male mentors at the very highest levels of their occupations or professions (Bradley, 1989). Thus men take many of their occupational gender privileges into women's career fields. They seldom experience the barriers and marginalization that challenge women in men's career fields.

In virtually every occupation, men earn more money than women do, and men who do women's work typically fare better than their female colleagues (Maume, 1999; C. L. Williams, 1995a). Sometimes organizational forces may propel men up the career ladder, in spite of their personal goals and ambitions. The high-speed *escalator* is an appropriate metaphor for describing the speed at which men may be catapulted up the success and leadership ladder in "women's" occupations.

Thus both women and men experience discrimination when working in gender-atypical settings, but the types and impact of the discrimination are different (Henson & Rogers, 2001). Women tend to be marginalized *within* the workplace, whereas men face negative attitudes and prejudice *outside* the workplace. Within the organization, men in gender-atypical occupations often experience preferential treatment in hiring and promotions. Furthermore, as more men enter gender-atypical jobs, they bring with them their generally higher social status and often there is improvement in the overall reputation, compensation, and benefit packages that surround these jobs.

Gender, Employment, and the Family

Most students are aware that a very lively and profound debate is going on in the industrialized and postindustrial world about how to organize and prioritize responsibilities regarding domestic tasks, child care, family needs, and paid work (Aryee & Luk, 1996; Barnett & Gareis, 2000).

Just Yesterday: Role Overload and Psychological Distress

When large numbers of middle-class women returned to the workplace, psychologists and sociologists first described how paid work led to role overload and psychological distress for women (Hughes & Galinksy, 1994; Ozer, 1995; Pugliesi, 1995). The general finding was that women in dual-earner families demonstrated greater psychological distress and more stress-related symptoms. Women in dual-earner families also reported less job enrichment, less time at work, greater child care difficulties, and more household labor inequity (Beatty, 1996; South & Spitze, 1994). Although many of these studies implied that the new paid work role *itself* was the cause of these difficulties, it soon became clear that conflicts over the level of spouse/partner involvement in household chores, the availability of reliable and affordable child care, differential access to rewarding employment opportunities, and the issue of inflexible workplace policies were the determining agents (Barnett, Raudenbush, Brennan, Pleck, & Marshall, 1995; Barnett & Shen, 1997; Stohs, 1995). It was not paid employment that was causing these difficulties, it was that women came home from a day's work at segregated second-class jobs and then faced a second shift of domestic tasks and responsibilities (Deater-Deckard & Scarr, 1996; Hochschild, 1989; Jena, 1999).

Regardless of gender, working parents (not just women) experience less stress and better work outcomes when they have greater autonomy, more schedule control, fewer demands, greater job security, more supportive supervisors, more supportive workplace cultures, and opportunities for job advancement that are not inhibited by gender or ethnicity (Galinsky, Bond, & Friedman, 1996; Lennon, 1994).

Some believe that men are not just unwilling, but somehow *unable* to fully assume their share of child care and household tasks (Zuo, 1997). However, research findings support the notion that gender is performed and maintained by situations rather than psyches or biology and that men who need to perform both work and family roles can do so very fully and competently. Studies of single fathers and house-husbands demonstrate that men are fully capable of performing job roles, household chores, and child-related roles very adequately—*and* with the same level of stress in the absence of support by others (Fassinger, 1993). Fathers with a "double shift" also reported feeling hampered regarding the hours they could devote to work and limited by the type of assignments they could accept. Their career paths suffered from their inability to accept transfers and the lowered priority given to work. They also described how earnings declined because of these factors (Ranson, 2001). Other men reported problems with supervisors who failed to consider their home and family responsibilities (Greif, DeMaris, & Hood, 1993; Smith, 1998). A recent survey of dual-earner families in the United States revealed that 36% of men were involved in grocery shopping and 27% prepared some meals (Harnack, Story, Martinson, Neumark-Sztainer, & Stang, 1998). Take a look at Box 10.3 to see how families around the world cope with these issues.

It's time for some more critical thinking. As you have read, some theorists contend that women select certain educational pathways, acquire certain skills, and aggregate in certain less demanding and lower-level jobs because they give higher priority to raising a family. This sounds plausible, but traditionally woman-dominated jobs are actually the *least* amenable in this regard. Schoolteachers, clerical workers, sales staff, and service personnel typically have the least flexible work hours. Beginning nurses and health aides must often work nights and weekends. Lower-level service jobs usually offer the least unsupervised time and relatively little sick leave and vacation. Thus jobs considered traditionally men's jobs may actually be *more* compatible with family responsibilities. Furthermore, if structural segregation and job discrimination were not real factors in employment patterns, one would predict that unmarried women would avoid low-paying jobs and seek higher paying male dominated jobs, but they are as likely as married women to be employed in lower-paying, female-dominated occupations (Beeghley, 1996).

The Dual-Earner Family: Jugglers and Balancers Around the Globe

United States: About 60% of those classified as Latinos in the United States are of Mexican descent. The Latino family has been characterized by rigid gender roles. However, recent decades have seen substantial changes in Latino work/family patterns and family structure. These changes are caused by the effects of acculturation, the increasing education level of Latinas, and the rising rates of Latina workforce participation. In one study of working-class, dual-earner Mexican-American families, most women reported their husbands participated somewhat in housework and child care tasks, and more than half endorsed even more participation. Women respondents reported only a moderate level of job–family stress, and job satisfaction level was high (Herrera & DelCampo, 1995). In a recent study, women expressed guilt about not being at home to care for children but felt good about getting help from an extended family structure (Brown et al., 1998).

India: The level of women's employment in India has skyrocketed over the past three decades. The impetus for this change has come from economic need, psychological needs, and state policies aimed at improving the status of women. Today there are two conflicting gender

ideals for Indian women: (a) the dependent homemaker, wife, and mother and (b) the independent, assertive employee. Although urban, educated women have infiltrated more prestigious, male-dominated occupations, the larger picture is much less progressive. Particularly compliant women are more likely to be selected for any existing jobs. Women are still differentially recruited into jobs requiring passivity and dependence. Women's employment patterns are more often determined by issues such as distance from the workplace and work schedules rather than by education, skill, and ambition. Child care and elder care remain women's sole responsibilities. Although men seem to benefit from marital and family support, studies suggest marriage is a barrier to women's employment progress. Women experience more work–family conflict and greater family interference with their work, but have gained more decision-making power (Joshi & Sastry, 1995).

Israel: Israeli society represents a mixture of both traditional and postindustrial values, all permeated with a strong religious orientation. There are pressures in Israeli society for women to develop careers and yet also to fulfill the traditional roles of

full-time wife and mother. Although role conflict is great among Israeli women, less job–family stress is reported. This may be due to the fact that the Israeli Labor Union pays for and provides child care (Rosenbaum & Cohen, 1999).

Japan: In today's Japan, **salarymen** essentially live at their offices and visit at home each night after a very long commute. In 1992, a new law gave all employees the right to time off following the birth of child, and Ota Mutsumi became one of the first men to take parental leave. For three months, he was a housebound homemaker. This event was so momentous and newsworthy that Japanese TV crews followed him around and recorded unusual events such as his changing his daughter's diapers or preparing meals! He reported his greatest stress involved walks in the park because of the lack of acceptance by mothers there. Japanese magazines on child care filled with stories designed to help men handle the "park debut." The author reports his experience changed his attitude toward both work and family. He no longer works overtime. He became active in the parents association for his children's daycare center, and helped organize a neighborhood playhouse for elementary school

Today: Ongoing Negotiations in the Dual-Earner Family

As of the mid-1990s about 60% of couples were dual earners and only about 10% of total households in the United States consisted of the traditional single-earner nuclear family (Parasuraman & Greenhaus, 1997b). Today's collaborative, dual-earner family appears to be a success. Overall, dual-earner families exhibit good emotional and physical health, and thriving children. There is little significant depression

among the women, little work addiction among the men, and generally good relationships with children. Such parents are appropriately worried about their children's future. Two full incomes provide a buffer against the changing economy, and both parents tend

salaryman   **Japanese term adapted from English to describe the very dedicated, loyal office worker or manager in modern Japan (also used in Korea). Implies strong devotion to work organization and worker role, long commutes to home, and minimal involvement with family.**

pupils with working parents. He also produced a Web page for working parents of both genders. In 1996, only 0.16% of Japanese men took parental leave. Very few Japanese men are present at birth of their children, and some critics insist that men's principal role in child care is to hold a video camera (Mutsumi, 1999).

Iran: About 48% of women and 29% of men in Iran are illiterate. Women comprise less than 10% of Iran's workforce. About 80% of employed women are in government jobs, and about 90% work in the capital city, Tehran. The vast majority of employed women are concentrated in teaching, health, and low-skilled clerical or sales work. However, even within these occupations, the number of women declines dramatically as one rises in the hierarchy. There are no day-care centers, nursery schools, or paid sitters for children in Iran, so all child care must come from relatives. Grocery shopping and food preparation are extremely time consuming for Iranian women. Shopping must be done daily. There is essentially no household technology, and no prepackaged products or ready-made foods. Women help each other to hear radio announcements about the distribution of

particular foods. Some social critics insist that paid work just adds to women's burdens, whereas other insist that women with income and provider responsibilities gain power and strength from their income. The unchanged demands regarding familial responsibilities adds to the gender ideology that women are unreliable workers. Employed women are much more likely to exert influence over whom they marry, and to live with their husbands independently of his parents. In upper-class and upper-middle-class families women may use part of their income for themselves (Ghorayshi, 1996).

Germany: Women in both the former East Germany and West Germany voice stronger opposition to traditional gender roles compared to male counterparts. East German communism fostered more progressive employment opportunities for women and had policies that enabled women to fully combine employment with motherhood. This was based on the Marxist philosophy that paid work is a right and duty for all. However, the gender gap in attitudes about gender, work, and family persisted, and the second shift for women was a way of life. West Germany compen-

sated women for leaving the labor market to become full-time homemakers and reinforced traditional values by encouraging them to remain dependent on men for financial support. Again, neither regime ever fundamentally challenged the notion that domestic tasks were women's work (Adler & Brayfield, 1996).

China: Under communism, women moved rapidly from unpaid agricultural work to paid employment. Today about half of the Chinese workforce is female, and many Chinese women are in the professions. For example, about 35% of Chinese scientists are women. Working-class families seem to have a more equal division of household duties compared to professionals, but the husbands of professional women are slowly sharing more domestic tasks. In a study of women university faculty members in China and the United States, Zhang and Farley (1995) found the rates at which husbands cooked, cleaned, and performed other domestic chores was remarkably similar to that found in the United States. However, more American men did food shopping compared to men in China (31% versus 20%).

---

to be more invested in family life (Barnett & Rivers, 1996; Chira, 1998). Other promising findings include the following:

◆ Employed women are generally in better physical and psychological health compared to full-time homemakers. Work has a positive impact on men's health as well (Steil, 1997).
◆ Dual earner and dual-career couples are more cooperative and collaborative. Both men and women

rank balance in work and family roles among the most important issues in accepting new positions (Parasuraman & Greenhaus, 1997a).
◆ Full-time parental employment appears to have no negative impact on children if child care is dependable and of high quality (Caruso, 1996).
◆ Marriage is a central identity to dual-earner men and women. Fatherhood and family life is more central to men in dual-earner couples, and they are more willing to compromise regarding work

"The sun was shining, the bees were humming, the birds were singing.
'We're all going to have a wonderful time!' cried Billy."

FIGURE 10.3   Is this an effective way to achieve a better balance between family and work responsibilities?

demands (Helgesen, 1998). Figure 10.3 offers one version of such compromise. Gender role distinctions in household and child care responsibilities are very gradually shrinking but still not equitable (Brown, Graves, & Williams, 1997; Greenstein, 1996).

However, many gender-related work issues are far from settled. Many corporations still operate as if a man's job were more important to him than his family. They often have travel policies that do not consider family needs. Organizations need to examine the real costs of family relocations in terms of social, emotional, and marital upheaval. Some corporations are changing as they realize that in the postindustrial workplace, "face time" (being physically present at the work site) is not a good measure of productivity. Researchers have demonstrated greater productivity from workers who feel they can control their work hours and places. New work formats such as a compressed workweek and weekly or monthly balancing of work hours are other family-friendly approaches (Barnett & Rivers, 1996).

The notions of a work time and a workplace separate from the home place may gradually become obsolete. In 1996, 20 million Americans earned income from a home-based enterprise, and this is increasing rapidly (Munk, 2000). E-mails at home, faxes on vacation, business meetings by teleconferencing all contribute to this trend. The networked personal computer is central in creating the knowledge-based economy, and for the first time in human history women and men must develop the same set of skills for economic success (Helgesen, 1998).

We're Havin' a Baby

A new baby requires physical, temporal, emotional, and economic space. *Parents* have children, not just *women*. To adjust to a profoundly different family structure and provide everything a new infant requires, some relief from employment responsibilities is needed, and gender is a powerful determinant of how individuals balance infant care with work duties. In general, men are less likely to be associated with the work–family programs offered by their employers. Men are less likely to take paternity leave, less likely to take part-time work, and more likely to disguise why they need flexible schedules (Powell, 1997). In one study, men who were high in family commitment took somewhat longer leaves, but those committed to egalitarian marriages took the longest leaves (Hyde, 1995).

In Canada, all provinces have some maternity leave policy, and some have parental, adoption, and paternity leaves. Ontario has 18 weeks of unpaid parental leave. Quebec has general child care leave of 5 days per year without pay (Truelove, 1996). In Communist China, women have the right to three months' leave with regular pay (Li, 1991). All European countries have paid maternity leave, although length and pay level vary. A majority of European Union members have paid parental leave, but relatively few fathers take it. In Sweden, a couple has the right to 15 months of paid leave to share, at 90% of pay for the first 12 months. About a third of Swedish fathers take parental leave, which is high by international standard, but considered low by Swedish legislators. In the United States, President Bill Clinton signed the first federal Family and Medical Leave Act in 1993. It provides for a minimum standard of 12 weeks of unpaid family leave (which may include elder care). For the law to apply, the mother must work must work for an organization with more than 50 employees for at least one year. At the end of this unpaid leave, she has a right to an equivalent job, but no guarantee of the same job. It is unclear whether this leave policy applies equally to men or whether adoptive parents are fully covered. The true limits of health and other benefits during the leave period are still untested.

Child Care: Patchwork or Piecemeal

Who is minding the baby in the industrialized and postindustrial world? In the United States, a *patchwork* of child care is provided by individuals, churches, public and private groups, corporations, public schools, and so on. Child care is among the most highly sex segregated of service industries (97% women) (Center for the Child Care Workforce, 2002). Wages are quite low, even for college-educated women. Even though research demonstrates that on-site child care increases productivity and reduces worker turnover, relatively few firms provide child care services or benefits directly to employees. Such services are expensive, and the demand varies greatly in an era of small families. Furthermore, other workers may see employer provided child care as discriminatory because relatively few employees benefit.

To examine the origin of this patchwork of services, let's begin with a little recent history. In the United States, the federal government's involvement with child care began during the Depression, mainly to provide unemployed teachers with jobs. During World War II there were 3,000 child care centers serving 600,000 children of mothers working in the defense industries. By 1946, middle-class women were ensconced back in the home and all federal funding for child care was terminated. During the 1970s, several federal laws designated funds for welfare recipients seeking or training for work. They also offered child care–related tax deductions for middle-class families. However, when these taxpayers were required to report the Social Security numbers of child care providers, the number reporting this credit plummeted dramatically. Thus child care workers still remain a major part of the underground economy of the United States (Bloom & Steen, 1996).

Canada too has no national child care legislation or policy. Canadian religious organizations created the first nurseries and crèches, and these were seen as charity for poor families. Up through the 1940s, single parents could place their children in orphanages and visit them on weekends; no alternatives were available. During World War II, the governments of Quebec and Ontario offered child care to defense workers. Ontario has maintained its child care centers, sharing the cost with municipalities. Today, child care is regulated by provincial governments, and is generally described as piecemeal. Although 3- to 5-year-olds are generally well served, there is a great shortage of facilities for infants and older children. Child care locations are often neither near home nor work, and they are extremely rare in rural areas (England, 1996; Truelove, 1996). In both Canada and the United States, the proximity of the child care site is often a major decision point in women's job selection process because women are overwhelmingly the ones who take children to child care (Frone & Yardley, 1996).

An international perspective on child care reveals that underlying the child care policies and practices of every nation are particular attitudes and philosophies regarding women, men, and children (Fincher, 1996). The United States, Canada, and Britain consider child care a *private* parental responsibility. Again, in keeping with the theme of this section of your text, social attitudes and public policies reach out to influence aspects of an individual's life. Child care is defined as an employment issue, not a family issue (Lewis (1997). Publicly supported child care is still viewed as social welfare.

In contrast, the European Union countries have made child care a significant national priority. This commitment is apparent in national child care policies and is complemented by a set of family policies such as parental and family leaves, flexible working hours, and easily available and heavily subsidized child care.

In the Nordic countries and France, child care is viewed as a community issue, and almost all children enter child care. Child care is perceived as an essential and mainstream service. Like education, child care is seen as a public good that results in advantages for the broader society. In Sweden, the provision of easily available, inexpensive, and high-quality child care is considered integral to the retention of women workers (as are parental insurance, flexible working hours, and income tax deductions for child care). All Swedish children from 18 months until school age have access to child care that is based on sound pedagogic principles (Svenska Institute, 2000). How-

ever, social critics have complained that whereas labor and child care policies encourage women into the double role of caretaker and worker, men have made little movement in increasing their domestic and family roles (Kinnunen & Mauno, 1998).

Almost every reader of this text will have to deal directly with the occupational and family issues described in this chapter. Where do you stand on these issues? Take a few minutes to complete the questionnaire in Box 10.4. Consider comparing your responses with those of your classmates.

Summary

◆ The division of the labor needed for survival according to gender is one of the most ancient, fundamental, and enduring aspects of human societies.

◆ Development of a separate masculine workplace versus a feminine home place began with the industrial revolution. Beginning in the 1960s, large numbers of middle-class women re-entered paid employment.

◆ In the industrial world, the masculine gender role centers on success in the worker and provider roles.

◆ Women's labors are often neither perceived as work, nor counted as economic productivity. Economic globalization concentrates women in low-paying jobs. All over the world women are securing low-cost loans that facilitate self-employment.

◆ Occupational segregation and its inequities begin with gender differentiated aspirations, expectations, and career development. The differential career paths of men and women are based on a number of factors.

◆ Occupational segregation by type and level of work is a prominent feature of the contemporary workplace. Gender differentials in prestige, status, advancement opportunities, and compensation all follow from this segregation. Overall, men still receive higher pay for the same work.

◆ The two major explanations for the establishment and maintenance of occupational segregation differ in terms of emphasis. Traditional psychological theories emphasize more internal, socialization-related factors. Structural theories emphasize more external and situational factors.

THE ABCs of GENDER (ATTITUDES, BELIEFS, AND CONCERNS)   BOX 10.4

The Issue: Gender and Work

Your gender _____   Your age _____

For questions 1–7, write down the number that most accurately reflects your response.

1 = Strongly disagree   2 = Disagree   3 = Neither agree nor disagree   4 = Agree   5 = Strongly agree

_____   1. Distinctions between "men's work" and "women's work" are based on biological differences and will always exist, no matter how much societies change.

_____   2. The increasing rate of paid employment for women is a direct cause of many of the negative aspects of postindustrial society such as youth violence, chemical abuse, family dissolution, and so on.

_____   3. My gender has had no influence on my choice of college major or first postcollege occupation.

_____   4. My computer skills are adequate for success in the information-based, postindustrial economy.

_____   5. My foreign language skills are adequate for success in the international postindustrial economy.

_____   6. I am likely to enter a relatively gender-segregated occupation after college.

_____   7. I believe that problems such as the sticky floor, glass ceiling, and high-speed escalator will not influence my occupational success.

8. After one year at my first postcollege job, I expect to be earning $_____ annually.

For questions 9–10, answer a if you are male and b if you are female, using the response ratings 1–5 above.

_____   9a. I would be very comfortable if my wife/partner were unemployed (by choice) and I provided all financial support for her.

_____   9b. I would be very comfortable if my husband/partner were unemployed (by choice) and I provided all financial support for him.

_____   10a. I would expect my wife/partner to give up a desirable job and move to another city so that I could pursue graduate studies (or accept a better job).

_____   10b. I would expect my husband/partner to give up a desirable job and move to another city so that I could pursue graduate studies (or accept a better job).

For questions 11–12, divide the circles below into pie diagrams.

11. Divide pies 1 and 2 to represent your *ideal distribution* of percentage of total time you and your spouse/partner will devote to (a) domestic chores, (b) paid work responsibilities (include commuting time), (c) family activities and responsibilities, and (d) time for self.

12. Divide pies 3 and 4 to represent your *expected distribution* of percentage of total time you and your spouse/partner will devote to (a) domestic chores, (b) paid work responsibilities (include commuting time), (c) family activities and responsibilities, and (d) time for self.

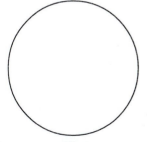 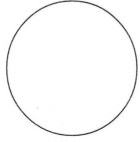 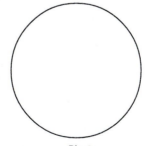 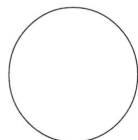

Pie 1	**Pie 2**	**Pie 3**	**Pie 4**
Ideal Distribution for You	**Ideal Distribution for Your Spouse/Partner**	**Expected Distribution for You**	**Expected Distribution for Your Spouse/Partner**

◆ Gender bias, stereotyping, and discrimination are important and complex factors related to gender and paid work. The qualities traditionally associated with management and supervision result in a masculine bias in hiring for these positions. The sticky floor, the glass ceiling, the high-speed escalator, and the parable of the tall and short people are useful metaphors in understanding the relevant gender issues.

◆ The competing demands of job and family are prominent issues in the now normative dual-earner family. Earlier findings of greater distress among employed women were related to second-class and second-shift treatment, rather than to work itself.

Across cultures, families and nations have developed varying ways of viewing and dealing with the issues of parental leave and child care.

InfoTrac College Edition

For more information, explore InfoTrac College Edition at

http://www.infotrac-college.com/Wadsworth

Enter search terms: occupational segregation, glass ceiling, role overload, dual earner, gender and work.

11 Gender and Physical Health

On Labor, Lifestyle, and Longevity

By Linda A. Travis and Grace Galliano

We real cool. We / Left school. We / Lurk late. We /
Strike straight. We / Sing sin. We / Thin gin. We /
Jazz june. We / Die soon. ◆ Gwendolyn Brooks

Learning Objectives

After studying this chapter, you should be able to:

1. Offer a brief history of gender-related factors in health, illness, and treatment, mentioning the accomplishments of the women's health movement.
2. List and explain three important contemporary issues related to gender and health.
3. Explain what is meant by the gender-related context of health, offering examples of how gender influences (a) the health problems individuals are likely to have, (b) interactions with health care providers, (c) the structure and functioning of the health care system, and (d) culture-related health factors.
4. Explain how gender influences occupational and reproductive health difficulties.
5. List and explain the major gender-related lifestyle factors that influence patterns of health and illness, paying special attention to sexual lifestyles in industrial and postindustrial nations and in Africa.
6. Explain the gender-related central paradox regarding morbidity and longevity, and summarize the hypothesized explanations for this phenomenon.
7. Summarize the gender-related factors surrounding coronary disease.
8. Summarize the gender-related factors surrounding cerebral vascular accidents, cancer, and dementia.

Encounters with Gender

Dr. Sarah Smith worked hard in her rural clinic in a developing nation. It took years to earn the villagers' trust, but now every morning, sick mothers and their children walk many miles to line up in the intense heat. One hot day the line was especially long, and her patients had waited for many hours. Suddenly Sarah heard a murmur run through the crowd, and she saw the line of women and children step aside to make way for a young man carrying a little boy. As he walked to the front of the line, Sarah could clearly see that infected wounds on the toddler's leg would require at least two hours of treatment. The father politely explained that his oldest son needed medical attention. He motioned for the little girl on Sarah's examining table to get down, and put his son in her place. Sarah was taken aback by his actions and looked around at the mothers who had been waiting so patiently. Their faces were blank. Sarah's assistant whispered that this father was an important man from a nearby village. Sarah had never felt such conflict. It was unfair to treat this patient ahead of all the others who had waited. Yet she knew that if she asked that he wait his turn, he would be humiliated. She could jeopardize her relationships with the local officials and with the very women who needed her help. The sick little girl she had been treating was quietly crying, and her mother was tearful. How would you want Sarah to respond to this encounter with the traditions of gender? How would you respond?

Overview

This chapter explores the powerful influence of gender and gender roles on how we risk and maintain our health, attend to physical signs and symptoms, and avoid accidents and injuries. Should a health problem arise, our gender influences how and when we interact with the medical system, how we cope with illness and dysfunction, as well as who provides and receives care. You will see that gender influences what health problems we are likely to have, when we are likely to have them, and even how long we live. The chapter ends with a look at four specific health problems; coronary disease, cerebral vascular accidents, cancer, and dementia.

Looking Back and Looking Around Us

Imagine a world in which most parents watch many of their children die. Imagine a world in which a sizable proportion of women die in childbirth, and a sizable proportion of men die because of work-related diseases and injuries. Consider what it would be like to witness whole families, villages, and towns decimated by mysterious poxes, plagues, and fevers. Think of all the injuries, wounds, infections, or even toothaches you or family members have ever had. Not so very long ago, any one of these problems might have resulted in lifelong disability or death. This was the human condition up until relatively recently.

In the more developed world today, we go about our daily lives fully expecting a remarkable array of expertise, medicines, and technology to be readily available should we become ill or have an accident. However, none of this is available for vast numbers of our fellow human beings in the less developed world. A rural clinic such as the one described in the opening vignette is still a rare and invaluable resource in many parts of the world. Funds and personnel for such facilities may come from international organizations, but they depend on the cooperation and acceptance of national and local leaders. Conflicts between the values and customs of a host society and Western medical practices may be common in some parts of the world, and they are not easily resolved. As you project what you would do in Dr. Smith's situation, try to articulate your own guiding values about gender equity. Do they center on abstract principles or the practicalities of ongoing relationships? Do they facilitate short-term or long-term goals?

A Brief History

For centuries, the healing arts were the province of women. Salves, herbal teas, and techniques for treating broken bones were offered by wise women who passed that knowledge on to their daughters. What we now call *reproductive health* was also the province of women, specifically the midwife. However, beginning in the 18th century, science and then medicine gradually became the province of men.

Ideas about the relationship between women's reproductive functions and illness date at least back to ancient Greece, but during the 19th century these notions became codified as "medical knowledge" as well as popular belief (Theriot, 1996). Whereas men's illnesses had varied sources, virtually all of women's ills came to be attributed to disorders of the female reproductive organs. One leading 19th-century physician wrote, "[T]he Almighty, in creating the female sex [has] taken the uterus and built up a woman around it" (cited in Healy, 1995, p. 3). Victorian norms defined "real women," as white and upper class, and such women were quite distinct from men, women of color, and women of the lower social classes. The proper Victorian woman was more fragile and vulnerable than women of the lower classes. She was frequently "indisposed" by menstruation and pregnancy (Kronengold, 1999). Once women's health became defined solely as *maternal health*, nonreproductive problems such as cancers, cardiovascular diseases, osteoporosis, and so on were given relatively little attention, and women's occupational health was virtually ignored (Krieger & Fee, 1996).

Medical scientists also established men's bodies as the human standard, so women's bodies became the exception and "abnormal." Conditions peculiar to women such as pregnancy, childbirth, and menopause came to be seen as inherently pathological (Ehrenreich & English, 1973). Another 19th-century physician wrote, "Woman is a pair of ovaries with a human being attached, whereas man is a human being furnished with a pair of testes" (Virchow, cited in Fausto-Sterling, 1985, p. 90). Medical texts contained anatomical drawings of female structures that were often inaccurate, and medical studies focused on men's bodies and men's diseases (Lawrence & Bendixen, 1992). Medical research continued using only male samples, whereas women were systematically excluded from research studies and drug trials. These exclusions were justified by concerns for women's fertility and developing fetuses (Stanton, 1995). For example, even though a majority of people over 65 are women, the Baltimore Longitudinal Study of Aging included no women (Weisman, 1998). In terms of the health care system itself, the few women admitted to medical school were shunted off to less prestigious areas of medicine. The gender hierarchy of male physicians and female *helpers* became more rigid, and these trends persisted essentially unchanged until the second half of the 20th century.

The women's health movement (WHM) began in the 1960s with the nationwide effort to legalize abortion, but activists soon took up other health issues. The 1973 publication of *Our Bodies, Ourselves* by the Boston Women's Health Collective was an important milestone on the pathway to greater gender equity in medical practice. In 1976, women's groups, health workers, and medical providers united to establish the National Women's Health Network to provide feminist input to national health policy. During the 1980s, the health-related issues of poor and minority women became more prominent via the establishment of the Black Women's Health Project. In 1986, the National Institutes of Health (NIH) began a new policy of greater inclusion of women in **clinical research trials**. But even in the year 2000, new directives were needed make those changes a reality (Democrat & Chronicle, 2000). Federal attention also resulted in the Women's Health Initiative, the largest clinical trial ever conducted. It follows women aged 55 to 79 for up to 12 years and is designed to investigate factors related to cardiovascular disease, breast and colorectal cancers, and osteoporosis.

The WHM raised many important issues regarding gender, health, and illness to the forefront of discussion, consideration, and eventual change. For example, there was a tradition of inappropriate medical interventions such as unnecessary cesarean sections, unnecessary hysterectomies, and overmedication with tranquilizers and antidepressants. Another major achievement of the women's health movement is that detailed, and sometimes intimidating "patient package insert" (PPI) inside every package of medication. It offers a summary of the known problems and contraindications associated with a particular drug. The activities of the WHM also led to the emergence of women-controlled health centers. Today this innovation has been successfully adopted and replaced by hospital-run facilities. Health activists were also successful in changing the procedures surrounding breast cancer biopsy. A finding of cancerous cells used to lead to an immediate mastectomy. Now a two-step procedure allows a woman to discuss treatment options with her physician. New research has confirmed that the benefits of lumpectomies are as beneficial as mastectomies, and the possible overuse of chemotherapy (American Cancer Society, 2002; Kiebert, deHaes, & Van de Velde, 1991; Rowland, 1998). On the international level, female genital mutilation, reproductive rights, and the costs of HIV medications in the developing world remain unresolved issues (Kronengold, 1999). Returning again to the opening vignette, do you believe feminist health activists can be effective in environments where the notion of gender equality clearly violates local cultural values? How can such conflicts be resolved?

Contemporary Issues

You can evaluate your own present level of knowledge about gender and health by completing the questionnaire in Box 11.1. You may find some of the answers rather surprising. Consider researching some of these issues further on the Net or by inviting a knowledgeable professional to your class. For the moment, let's examine some real-life issues related to gender, ethnicity, and the health care system.

There are many things we do, or at least try to do to promote our well-being and prevent problems (for example, adequate sleep, using sun block agents, wearing safety belts, flossing our teeth, and so on). We typically monitor certain aspects of our bodily functioning, and if we perceive some problem we must then interpret our symptoms. Is that lingering cough caused by allergies, a cold, bronchial infection, or lung cancer? Each of us makes a judgment or depends on someone else (usually a woman) to make a judgment. If the symptom is not considered routine, we then consider engaging the medical system to help us deal with it. Thus women are the "health brokers" for the family. They interpret physical signs and symptoms and decide whether and which particular segments of the health care delivery system will be accessed and when. Women are also viewed as the "natural" major caregivers for all others in the family: parents, siblings, spouses, and children. This caregiver role affects well-being, risk for illness, and even mortality (Neal, Ingersoll-Dayton, & Starrels, 1997; Yee & Schulz, 2000). Serious illness in a wife/mother has the most disruptive effect on total family functioning because women have so many family roles. Men who are sud-

---

clinical research trials   Controlled trials in which the effectiveness of new medications or treatments are evaluated. Participants are typically volunteers who meet the criteria for the particular trial.

THE ABCs of GENDER (ATTITUDES, BELIEFS, AND CONCERNS)   BOX 11.1

The Issue: Your Knowledge About Gender and Health

_____ Your gender

_____ Your age

_____

(Other variable of interest)

1. What is the most common surgical procedure performed in the United States?
2. For which gender does the risk for cancer increase with age?
3. Which gender is more vulnerable to dementia? Why?
4. Are African-American or European-American women more likely to develop breast cancer? Are African-American or European-American men more likely to develop prostate cancer?
5. Are men or women more vulnerable to cerebral vascular accidents (strokes)?
6. Are women who die of cancer most likely to die of breast cancer?
7. What is the most common type of cancer among young men?
8. What is the most frequent type of plastic surgery performed in the United States?
9. Can Viagra (sildenafil) improve women's sexual responsiveness?
10. Which ethnic group has the highest rate of diabetes in the world?

Answers

1. Male circumcision.
2. It's a complex pattern. Around menopause, women's cancer rates rise, but beginning at age 60 overall cancer risks equalize for both genders. Risk rises for men up until about 79, and then cancer curves level off for both genders.
3. More women are diagnosed with dementia because the greatest risk factor is age, and women greatly outnumber men among the very old.
4. European-American women are more likely to *develop* breast cancer, but African-American women are more likely to *die* of breast cancer. This outcome appears mostly caused by the differential access to health care associated with poverty. African-American men are more likely to both develop and die of prostate cancer. Biological factors may combine with social factors to produce this outcome.
5. Overall, men and women have about equal numbers of strokes, but the patterns are somewhat different. Young women and old women have slightly more strokes than men do.

But middle-aged men have more strokes than middle-aged women (Wenger, 1998).

6. Because of increases in smoking rates among women, lung cancer has become the leading cause of death from cancer.
7. Testicular cancer.
8. Although many might guess face lifts or breast modifications to be the most common, actually liposuction is.
9. There is no evidence that this drug will increase women's erotic responsiveness; in fact, a placebo is more effective (Reuters Medical News, 2000a). However, sildenafil may help certain women undergoing in vitro fertilization (IVF) successfully conceive a pregnancy. The drug increases blood flow to the endometrium, and when used with estradiol valerate, it promotes endometrial thickness, which may facilitate a successful pregnancy (Sher & Fisch, 2000).
10. About 50% of adult Pima Indians in Arizona have been diagnosed with diabetes.

---

denly placed in caregiver roles may have particular difficulty in handling children's emotions of fear and sadness (Booth & Crouter, 1998). Thus gender influences how and when we interact with the medical system—a medical system that is itself highly organized along gender lines (Zimmerman & Hill, 1999).

A second important issue in contemporary health studies is the continued use of so-called racial descriptors in health data records. Such classification communicates little about a patient's genetic and cultural background. For example, blanket descriptors such as *white* obscure diseases more common among ethnic

groups originating from around the Mediterranean Sea. Classification as *black* can obscure certain conditions more common in the European ancestors of African Americans (Caldwell & Poppenoe, 1995). The risk for hypertension among Latinos varies dramatically by national origin. Mexican women are at low risk, whereas Puerto Rican and Cuban women are at greatest risk perhaps because the Caribbean nations have a sizable population of African origin. Classification as Asian is also problematic. Whereas Japanese- and Chinese-American women have the lowest rates of hypertension, Filipinas have rates almost equal to those of African-American women (Martinez-Maldonado, 1991).

These classifications also distort the truth about health and social class. At all ages, European Americans appear to have the best health, and this approach to organizing data implies some inherent biological characteristic. Such differentials are largely a matter of socioeconomic status, *not* biology (Krieger & Fee, 1996). Many group differences in health status and illness typically disappear when socioeconomic status is controlled (Kim, Bramlett, Wright, & Poon, 1998). Through the 19th century, "scientific" studies supported the notion that social class was a biological distinction and caused by innate, inherited abilities. Thus a high rate of tuberculosis and infectious diseases among immigrant "ethnic Europeans" (referring to those from southern Europe) was viewed as a clear biological inferiority. All through the 20th century, "race," as represented by color, has persisted as a "biological" reality when it is really a social construction.

Critical Thinking Challenge

Despite the misinformation and stereotypes perpetuated by racial descriptors, I use them throughout the chapter because that's how health-related data continue to be arranged. What solutions can you devise to this problem?

A third issue is the problem of making health research data understandable to a lay audience. Confusion and skepticism result when one study "proves" that caffeine causes miscarriages, and then another "proves" the opposite. What do animal studies "prove" about human beings? Furthermore, health studies that contradict accepted norms tend to disappear from public awareness. For example, the findings that maternal drinking harms a fetus are well reported. However, the studies that link a father's drinking with reduced infant birthweight, and the finding that cocaine binds to sperm are not well publicized (Bertin & Beck, 1996).

Gender and the Context of Health, Illness, and Treatment

Physical health, illness, and treatment exist in a complex, interactive framework of biological sex, psychosocial constructions of gender, and cultural practices

(Kronengold, 1999). Once again, in keeping with the theme of this section of the text, these gender-related sociocultural factors combine to shape and influence an *individual's* life course. A complete catalogue of all the gender-related issues regarding the health and illness of men and women is beyond the scope of this chapter, but we will review some selected aspects of this relationship.

Biological Factors

Genetic abnormalities are more likely to be carried by women, but are more likely to be expressed in male offspring. Some examples of this rule include hemophilia, meningitis, muscular dystrophy, and certain types of mental retardation (Travis, 1988). However, autoimmune disorders such as rheumatoid arthritis and systemic lupus erythematosus (SLE) are all more common among women (Chrisler, 2001).

Estrogens seem to provide a protective buffer against heart disease among younger women. In contrast, testosterone and other neuroendocrine factors among men lead to a more intense cardiovascular response to stressors (Wilson, 1999). Read more about this important area of health decision making in Box 11.2.

Social and Cultural Factors

Important components of masculinity include strength and invulnerability. Therefore it is not surprising that men do not perceive themselves as vulnerable to illness. Yet numerous studies reveal that a self-perception of vulnerability is the primary motivator for testicular and breast self-examination, mammography, and prostate cancer screening (McCaul, Branstetter, Schroeder, & Glasgow, 1996; Watson et al., 1998).

In the developing world, complications of pregnancy and childbirth result in high levels of early mortality among women. Chronic female malnutrition is also an issue because men may be fed first, and women deprive themselves to feed their children (Kronengold, 1999). In industrialized societies, women live longer but have more problems with chronic diseases and functional impairments as they age (Dimond, Catanzaro, & Lorensen, 1997).

ZOOM & ENLARGE   **BOX 11.2**

Decisions About Health and Hormones

Ovarian estrogens mediate many reproduction-related processes (such as breast development). Estrogens are produced by the adrenal glands in both women and men, but there is no known function for estrogen in men. The decline in estrogen production at menopause causes a number of short- and long-term changes. Hot flashes and night sweats occur in about 70% of menopausal women and vaginal dryness occurs in about 20%. Vaginal and urethral tissue becomes thinner and drier, predisposing women to more minor infections and more frequent urination. Metabolic changes cause bones to lose calcium, and this makes women more prone to bone fractures. Blood pressure tends to increase, as do levels of circulating blood fat, putting women at greater risk for heart attacks and stroke. The usual medical response for these changes is hormone replacement therapy (HRT). Such hormones must be used appropriately, or abnormal tissue growth can oc-

cur. Some reports suggest HRT is associated with lower risk for colon cancer, and delaying Alzheimer's disease, but this remains unclear (Ziegler et al., 1996). HRT is not appropriate for women with a history of breast or endometrial cancer. For some women HRT may present an increased risk of blood clots. Long-term clinical studies of the impact of HRT continue (Preston, 1998).

Testosterone is key in the development and maintenance of the distinctive bone and muscle distribution of the adult male, as well as his reproductive capacity. Testosterone contributes to men's strength, hair patterns, and balance. It also appears to have antidepressant properties and seems to promote a higher activity level (Roy, 2000). Higher testosterone levels are associated with psychological dominance, physicality, and self-esteem. However, testosterone levels appear to change in response to environmental factors. About a fourth of men

over 65 have low levels of testosterone, but little is known about any beneficial effects of testosterone replacement. Some researchers believe that the impaired muscle strength, loss of balance, and fractures that contribute to frailty in older men are related to testosterone and growth hormone levels. Testosterone has been linked to prostate cancer, although no causal connection has been established. Removing the testes is a treatment for metastatic prostate cancer. Testosterone is also used to treat acne.

DHEA (dehydroepiandrosterone) is an adrenal hormone used by the body to make both estrogen and testosterone. It has been recently touted to prevent cancer, heart disease, improve memory, and reduce fat. It is considered a food additive and is not regulated by the FDA. Some health food stores sell *cytosterol*, a precursor to DHEA that has not been shown to benefit humans. Any health claims for this substance are based on animal studies.

Women are the major users of health and medical services (Wyke, Hunt, & Ford, 1998). They seek care even when healthy (for contraception, pregnancy, and so forth). Overall, women have higher physical illness rates, more disability days, and more physician visits (Lane & Cibula, 2000). Thus gender predicts the level of health self-monitoring as well as the monitoring of the health status of family members. Gender also predicts the timing, frequency, and types of interactions with the health care system (King, 1998; Macintyre & Hunt, 1997)

The gay or lesbian couple facing life-threatening or chronic illness is likely to have social stigma added to their burden. A private relationship may be made public to strangers or to the couple's families of origin. Hospital policies may restrict same-sex partner visitation. Hospital staff may react negatively to expressions of intimacy and concern in same-sex couples (Rolland, 1994).

A Health Care System Organized Along Gender Lines

The existing system of health care in the United States mixes public and private services in a way that leaves almost 20% of the population without any health insurance, and many more just one major illness away from financial ruin. Most of those without adequate health insurance are women and children, especially members of ethnic minority groups (Zimmerman & Hill, 1999).

Only about 20% of practicing physicians are women, and few women have a voice in setting health policy (Zimmerman & Hill, 1999). Yet a majority of health workers are women (85% of hospital workers and 75% overall). Systemically, the relationship between the dominant male physician and his subordinate helpers (nurses, nutritionists, therapists, technicians, and so on) reflects traditional patriarchal norms. However, all this is changing rapidly (Bright

TABLE 11.1 Proportion of Women Entering Medical School in the United States from 1950 to 1998

Years	Number	Percentage
1949–1950	387	5.5%
1959–1960	494	6.0%
1969–1970	929	9.1%
1979–1980	4,575	27.8%
1989–1990	6,404	38.2%
1997–1998	7,325	43.5%
2000–2001	7,659	45.9%
2001–2002	8,039	47.6%

Source: Association of American Medical Colleges (2002).

et al., 1998). Women now comprise about 40% of medical students, less than 10% of full professors, and 3% of medical deans. The number of medical students in the United States who come from ethnic minority groups is also gradually increasing, especially African-American women and Latino and Asian men (Zimmerman & Hill, 1999). Tables 11.1 and 11.2 summarize these trends.

Regarding medical specialty, women comprise about 62% of pediatrics, 60% of ob/gyn (obstetric/gynecology) residents, and about 43% of residents in family practice and psychiatry. However, about 80% of general surgeons are men, as are over 90% of orthopedic surgeons and 95% of thoracic surgeons (Barzansky, Jonas, & Etzel, 1998).

Compared to women physicians, men physicians have been found to be less likely to refer women for screenings or tests. Several studies suggest that they are less likely to refer women patients with equivalent symptoms for kidney transplantation, cardiac catheterization, and bypass surgery (Maynard, Every, & Martin, 1997).

Gender also affects various aspects of patient–physician interaction. Studies of communication patterns revealed that women patients disclose more personal information, ask more questions, and generally talk more. Physicians of both genders interact more with female patients. Women patients and women physicians use more "we" talk, discussing symptoms and treatments in a couple or family context. Male physicians use more technical terms and jargon, interrupt more, and demonstrate less eye contact and less touching (Gabbard-Alley, 2000). The impact of these differences may be significant. A recent British study found that teen pregnancy rates were 25% lower in clinics that had young, women physicians (Hippisley-Cox et al., 2000). In Canada, medical educators have proposed that a gender issues perspective be included in medical training (Lent & Bishop, 1998).

Gender even affects the likelihood of medical malpractice suits. In a large-scale survey of physicians in which a variety of relevant variables were controlled, the researchers found that 49% of male, versus 26% of female physicians, had been sued. These differences are attributed to gendered practice styles and communication patterns (Freeborn, Levinson, & Mullooly, 1999).

Gender enters into every stage of the medical research process. The male-dominated Congress makes budget allocations to the National Institutes of Health (NIH), which funds 90% of all basic biomedical research. Men predominate as heads of NIH study sections, as leaders of medical schools and institutions, as directors of institutes, as chairs of university departments, and as the principal investigators who conduct medical research. There are also gender im-

TABLE 11.2 Gender and Ethnic Backgrounds for Students Entering Medical Schools in the United States

Ethnic Group	Percentage Women			Percentage Men		
	1991–1992	1996–1997	1997–1998	1991–1992	1996–1997	1997–1998
African American	4.2%	5.2%	4.9%	3.3%	3.4%	3.1%
Native American/Alaskan	0.3%	0.4%	0.4%	0.2%	0.4%	0.4%
Native Latino	2.4%	3.2%	2.9%	3.4%	3.9%	3.6%
Asian American/ Pacific Islander	6.4%	7.4%	8.0%	9.5%	10.2%	10.6%

Source: Association of American Medical Colleges (2002).

balances among the journal editors and "peers" who review research findings prior to their publication (Dickersin & Schnaper, 1996).

You have read here about only some of the factors that interact to produce gender differentials in health promotion, **morbidity**, and ultimately mortality. Biological factors account for some of these differences. However, these biological factors interact with very powerful social psychological, cultural, and institutional factors to influence lifelong patterns of health, injury, illness, and eventually, mortality. Let's examine three arenas for such interactions: occupational health, reproductive health, and the health issues related to lifestyle. For additional insights into how culture and gender interact to affect health and illness, look at Box 11.3 on the diversity of gender and health issues in the United States. Box 11.4 offers a view of gender and health issues across national boundaries.

Labor

Early in the 20th century, typical occupations for men were farmer, laborer, miller, stonemason, carpenter, painter, miner, and so on. All these occupations involved hard physical labor as well as long-term exposure to infectious agents and toxic substances. Lung diseases such as asthma, chronic bronchitis, chronic air flow limitation, and tuberculosis frequently resulted from occupational exposure to dust, fumes, or gases.

Serious back injuries, broken bones, and accidental amputations were commonplace among men who performed physical labor, and most men did. Thus musculoskeletal injuries, intractable infections, and chronic diseases and dysfunctions resulted in poor health and frequent early death among working men. The 20th-century shift from manual to white-collar occupations, as well as reduced exposure to infectious diseases are both important determinants of the significant decline in chronic disease among men. The average decline in chronic respiratory problems, heart valve disease, and joint and back problems has been about 66%. About a third of this decline may be attributed to shifts in occupational activities (Costa, 2000). However, men remain concentrated in dangerous and hazardous occupations. These include law en-

forcement, mining, construction, convenience store clerks, and taxicab drivers!

In listing the dangers in men's traditional work roles, the most dangerous one of all was omitted. What do you think it is? (*Hint:* It is discussed in Chapter 14.)

Today, despite lingering traditions of occupational segregation and hierarchical job arrangements, women and men are coming to share the same workplaces, working conditions, and stresses. For example, a study of urban bus drivers in Sweden revealed equivalent physiological stress responses in drivers of both genders (Aronsson & Rissler, 1999). In the United States, two studies of the relationships among gender, job factors, and coronary heart disease found that for both women and men, greater job-decision latitude and fewer work hours were associated with lower levels of risk factors for heart disease. Researchers concluded that psychological strain and physiological illness can result from a work situation in which psychological demands are high, but an individual's sense of control or decision-making latitude are low. People in such jobs may be at higher risk for coronary disease (Bartley et al., 2000; Sorenson, Lewis, & Bishop, 1996). There is also some preliminary evidence from Scotland to suggest that the particular stresses of occupational tokenism may also be associated with increased health risks (Hunt & Emslie, 1998).

Statistics in the United States and Canada reveal that about half of all adolescents are employed full time or part time. There is relatively little research on employment and health outcomes among adolescents, but work injuries represent a particularly important health issue among adolescents. The most significant predictor of work injuries to adolescents has been found to be gender. Adolescent boys are much more likely to sustain work injuries. Carelessness, recklessness, distractibility, rebelliousness, impulsivity, and substance abuse were also relevant predictors and these are all associated with gender norms and ideals for adolescent masculinity (Frone, 1998).

---

morbidity   **Rates of illness and injury.**

SLIDE SHOW

BOX 11.3

Gender, Health, Illness, and Cultural Diversity in the United States

Latino Migrant Farm Workers: Most migrant worker families are of Latino origin, and maintaining adequate health is very difficult for this group because of their substandard living and working conditions. Migrant families receive restricted access to health and human services because of language difficulties, frequent relocation, cultural barriers, and limited economic and political resources. In one health assessment of migrant workers and their families, almost a third tested positive for tuberculosis. Urinary tract infections were the most common problem for women, largely from frequent dehydration as well as limited toilet and bathing facilities in the field. Both women and men suffered from exposure to pesticides and chemicals, extreme heat and dehydration, unsanitary working conditions, and frequent job-related injuries. Although children's immunizations were generally current, dental cavities and head lice were common. The living and working conditions for many migrant workers are comparable to those of developing countries. Latino traditions place men in the dominant role regarding decision making and income disbursement. Nutritious food, dental care, and medica-

tions may be given lower priority than tobacco, alcohol, and fattening foods (Bechtel, Shepherd, & Rogers, 1995).

Laotian Hmong-Americans: To date, there is no adequate explanation for the *sudden unexplained nocturnal deaths* (SUNDS) that occurred (mainly during the 1980s) among Laotian Hmong refugees and immigrants. Ninety-nine percent of SUNDS deaths occurred among men (median age 33), and such unexplained deaths typically occurred within two years of arrival in United States (Landrine & Klonoff, 2001). Autopsies found previously undetectable abnormalities in the cardiac conduction system. Resuscitated survivors almost always report that a "nightmare" with very specific content triggers the syndrome. The nightmare spirit or *dab tsog* (pronounced "da cho") threatens to press the life out of its victim. The sleeper becomes aware of a presence nearby but is completely paralyzed. Hmong who believe in the existence of this evil spirit are most susceptible to later SUNDS. Hmong men in North America experience a great deal of stress. Adaptation to life in the United States has meant the obliteration of virtu-

ally all aspects of the traditional masculine role. Their loss of family and social power has a tremendous impact on most Hmong men. In addition, many Hmong men suffer from "survivor guilt," because relatives who remained in Laos at the end of the Vietnam War were killed. The incidence of SUNDS has dropped considerably with more years of acculturation (Adler, 1994).

Asian Americans: Recent research has revealed a number of significant ethnic group variations in the response to medications. Acetaminophen (Tylenol and so forth) is metabolized more slowly in Asian Indians than in Caucasians. Smoking, alcohol, and oral contraceptives make for additional differences in their responses to this substance. Repeated studies demonstrate that the Chinese need lower doses of morphine to achieve the same pain reduction (Smith & Lin, 1996).

Native Americans: About half of all Native Americans live in poverty. Heart disease has replaced accidents as the leading cause of death over the past few years. Cigarette smoking, diabetes, and obesity are more prevalent among Native Americans than among European-Americans.

Production and Reproduction

Let's examine the other gender-related context for labor: reproduction. In more developed nations, pregnancy itself causes virtually no deaths, but elsewhere about a fourth of the deaths of reproductive-age women are caused by pregnancy complications (L. Doyle, 1995). In more developed countries, the maternal death rate is about 5 per 100,000 live births, but in some African nations it is about 600 per 100,000 live births (Population Reference Bureau, 1999). Although men can maintain their health without controlling their fertility, women cannot. For optimal health, women require contraceptives that

have no debilitating or damaging side effects, and they must be able to pass through pregnancy and childbirth safely. Protracted childbearing with inadequate spacing between pregnancies is simply unhealthy. Uncontrolled childbearing damages women's bodies, their children, and ultimately society (Lane & Cibula, 2000). Table 11.3 presents a statistical picture of the relationship among fertility rate, infant and child mortality, and adult life expectancy in some of the nations mentioned in this chapter.

Who controls fertility? In many societies, organized religion, economics, and government policies have a powerful effect on women's reproductive

BOX 11.3 *(continued)*

and lung cancer rates vary by region and parallel smoking rates. There are significantly higher rates of cervical cancer among Indians living in Arizona and New Mexico. As a group, Native American women have a low rate of cervical screening because of cultural beliefs that these are necessary only during childbearing years. Native American women have a lower incidence of breast cancer than do European-American women. The Pima Indians of Arizona have highest prevalence of diabetes in the world (50% of adults). Alcoholism and the resulting **fetal alcohol syndrome (FAS)** is the leading health problem among the American Indian population. Mortality caused by alcoholism among 45- to 64-year-old women is 54/100,000 women as compared to 8/100,000 of European-American women. Alcoholism is also related to the extremely high rates of domestic violence (abuse of spouses, children, and elders) among Native Americans (Tom-Orme, 1995).

African Americans: Poverty exerts a pervasive influence on the health of African Americans. The lifestyle of poor people contributes mightily to disease and physical dysfunction. Obesity, high-

cholesterol diets, a lack of supermarkets in the central city and the prevalence of fast-food outlets, cultural attitudes toward body size, and high rates of substance abuse, including tobacco, are all major factors causing the poor health of the inner-city poor. Because many African Americans are poor, they are much less likely to have adequate health insurance, and therefore their use of preventive health care services is low. Even when these services are available, a long history of exploitation by the health system community further limits trust and use. These factors contribute to lower rates of mammography, prostate exams, and other routine tests. African-American men have the lowest life expectancy of any ethnic group in the United States. Although European-Americans have a higher incidence of cancer, African Americans have significantly lower survival rates, especially with prostate cancer. Interestingly, hypertension rates are directly related to skin pigmentation, with darker individuals having higher rates. Poor African-American women have double the rate of diabetes that European-Americans do. African Americans are more susceptible to stroke, as well as to syphilis and gonor-

rhea (L. Doyle, 1995). African-American women develop breast cancer at an earlier age, and their mortality from the condition is significantly higher. Diabetes is the fourth major cause of death for African-American women but only seventh for white women. Motor vehicle accidents and homicide rates are particularly high among African-American men, and the rates of HIV/AIDS among black women are about double that of European-Americans. Racism clearly affects physical health (Clark, Anderson, Clark, & Williams, 1999). For example, data taken from a large-scale study of adults revealed that both professional and working-class black adults who reported they had experienced and accepted racial discrimination evidenced higher systolic blood pressure (SBP) compared to those who reported they had experienced and challenged such discrimination (Krieger & Sidney, 1996). An archival study of hospitalized patients records revealed that black patients with congestive heart failure or pneumonia received an overall lower quality of care than other patients with these conditions, with few gender differences (Ayanian, Weissman, Chason-Taber, & Epstein, 1999).

choices. Let's look at three examples. In Latin America, the Catholic Church continues to limit access to both contraceptives and abortion. In contrast, China has attempted to offset the threat of starvation and to regulate economic development by strict enforcement of a one-child policy (Neft & Levine, 1997). A long-standing cultural tradition of son preference has resulted in many infant girls being placed in orphanages. In contrast, the former communist dictatorship of Romania enforced strongly pronatalist policies in order to increase population. Abortions were illegal and, except for spermicides and poor-quality condoms, contraceptives were virtually impos-

sible to obtain. The results were a tremendous increase in illegal abortions, an upsurge in infant and maternal mortality, and institutions filled with abandoned and neglected children (Neft & Levine, 1997). Although social policies regarding reproduction are inevitable, health activists insist that women must be equal participants in policymaking and must have a full array of reproductive choices.

fetal alcohol syndrome **Abnormalities in children whose mothers drank heavily during pregnancy. Syndrome includes facial abnormalities, mental impairment, and stunted growth.**

Gender, Health, and Illness Around the World

Muslims in Israel: Studies have demonstrated differentials in mortality rates around major holidays among Jews, Chinese Buddhists, and Christians in the United States. Anson and Anson (1997) examined gender differences in mortality in the context of three Muslim holidays among Muslims living in Israel. These researchers note the highly gendered nature of Muslim holidays. Men officiate and participate in these religious rites, but women have the heavy burden of preparation. Traditions impose strict social regulation on women regarding what must be prepared and how to serve it. For men, social integration is strengthened. These researchers hypothesized that for women, religious festivals would be associated with a rise in mortality during the festivals and with a decline afterward. For men, there would be a decline in deaths before the festivals and an increase afterward.

Ramadan involves a month-long period of atonement and forgiveness. Food, fluid, and other substances are avoided from sunrise to sunset. Each evening, a festive meal is served to family members, invited kin, and to poor members of the community. This daily fasting during Ramadan is a very important religious duty. Men are expected to spend these days in intensive prayer and reading the Koran. Women spend the days fasting and preparing an elaborate evening meal, which is expected to change daily. As predicted, women's mortality was found to be greater during the month of Ramadan than in the month after. Men's mortality was higher in the two weeks after Ramadan.

Asian Indians: As in other developed nations, heart disease is the single most frequent cause of premature death in adults in the United Kingdom. The incidence of coronary disease (CD) among Indian-Asian men aged 35–54, is one of the highest in the United Kingdom, with Asian-Indian men having four times higher risk of a heart attack compared to European men. Recently, the death rates from CD have increased 8% in men and 14% in women. The stresses of migration, cultural isolation, and economic difficulties are relevant issues, as are other lifestyle factors. Smoking is held responsible for 20% of CD deaths. Indian culture revolves around family and social occasions, and affluence is associated with not having to exert oneself physically. Spirituality is associated with copious amounts of sweet food offerings and social occasions involve sedentary activities. Ghee (clarified butter) and full-fat milk are dietary mainstays. The traditional "conjoint family household" (elderly parents, one or more of their adult sons, their wives, and their children) is often a source of considerable stress (Sookhoo, 1998).

Ashkenazi Jews: About 5% of breast cancers are hereditary, and certain mutations in the BRCA1 and BRCA2 genes have been identified as conferring an 85% lifetime risk of developing breast cancer. These genes increase the risk of male breast cancer as well.

There is a higher frequency of these genetic mutations among Ashkenazi Jews (originating from eastern Europe). Genetic screening can identify those who are at risk.

Negative test results can reassure unaffected members of such families, but positive test results raise a formidable array of ethical and psychological issues (Lalloo et al., 1997).

Egypt: Worldwide, more male infants are conceived and born, but in all countries where boys and girls receive equal care, male infants have between 10 and 30% greater mortality.

In areas where males receive more food and health care than females, the gender ratio may be reversed. Boys get more food, education, health care, and social support.

Girls and women have higher death rates during childhood (because of malnutrition) and during childbearing years. Male wage earners get the greatest share of food, then women and boys, and the least share goes to girls. In Egypt from 1953 to 1985 there was a higher mortality rate among female infants. This has reversed since 1985. Egypt has made tremendous efforts to reduce infant mortality, but problems persist in rural areas and among the urban poor (Lane & Cibula, 2000).

South Korea: Approximately 72% of adult Korean men smoke. Lung cancer rates have skyrocketed from 2.1 per 100,000 men in 1980 to 28.0 per 100,000 men in 1996. Fewer than 2% of Korean women smoke, yet lung cancer rates increased from 1.4 per 100,000 women in 1980, to 6.9 in 1990. This increase is attributed almost totally to the effects of secondhand smoke (Hee, 1999).

TABLE 11.3   Life and Death in the Global Family

Selected Nation	Fertility Rate Per 1,000	Infant Mortality Rate	% of Children Dying by Age 5	Life Expectancy Men	Life Expectancy Women
Egypt	3.1	52.0	6%	64	67
Sierra Leone	6.3	136.0	22%	45	51
Uganda	6.9	81.0	13%	41	42
Zimbabwe	4.0	53.0	11%	40	40
South Africa	3.3	52.0	9%	55	60
Canada	1.5	5.6	1%	76	82
United States	2.0	7.0	1%	74	79
Mexico	3.0	32.0	4%	69	75
Cuba	1.6	7.2	1%	73	78
Brazil	2.3	41.0	5%	59	62
Kuwait	3.2	13	2%	72	73
Israel	2.9	5.8	1%	76	80
Iraq	5.7	127	14%	58	60
Bangladesh	3.3	82	12%	59	58
India	3.4	72	10%	60	61
Afghanistan	6.1	150	26%	46	45
Philippines	3.7	35	5%	66	69
Vietnam	2.7	35	5%	63	69
China	1.8	31	4%	69	73
South Korea	1.6	11	1%	70	77
North Korea	2.3	26	3%	67	73
United Kingdom	1.7	5.9	1%	74	80
Finland	1.7	4.2	1%	73	81
Germany	1.3	4.9	1%	73	80
Russia	1.2	17	2%	61	73
Italy	1.2	5.5	1%	75	81
New Guinea	4.8	77	12%	56	57
Australia	1.7	5.3	1%	76	81
New Zealand	1.9	5.3	1%	74	80

Source: World Population Data Sheet (1999) (Washington, DC: Population Reference Bureau).

Lifestyle: Behavior, Bacteria, and Viruses

In North America, about half of the mortality from the 10 leading causes of death can be traced to aspects of lifestyle. Gender-related lifestyle factors influence patterns of health maintenance and the readiness to take and persist in curative behaviors (Orleans, 2000). Take a look at Table 11.4 to see which leading causes of death have major lifestyle components. In more developed countries, preventable illness and injuries account for 70% of all medical care spending (Copenhaver & Eisler, 1996; Vogt, Hollis, Lichtenstein, et al., 1998). Thus it may be said that behavior, rather than bacteria or viruses, results in a significant amount of disease, disability, and premature death. Exposure to pathogens such as HIV is dependent on behavior and decision making. In the industrial and postindustrial world, success in reducing morbidity and mortality may lie more with the psychologist and sociologist than with the pathologist.

TABLE 11.4   Ten Leading Causes of Death
(by gender, for all ages)

Condition	Rank for Women	Rank for Men
Heart diseases	1	1
Cancers	2	2
CVAs	3	3
Accidents	7	4
Chronic obstructive pulmonary disease	4	5
Pneumonia and influenza	5	6
Diabetes	6	7
Suicide		8
Liver diseases (cirrhosis)		9
Homicide and legal interventions		10
Alzheimer's disease	8	
Kidney diseases	9	
Septicemia	10	

Source: Adapted from Hoyert, Kochanek, & Murphy (1999).

Traditional Masculinity

In general, traditional masculinity appears to be unhealthy. Masculine socialization encourages an aggressive and competitive interpersonal style rather than a cooperative one. In stressful situations, men's socialization results in coping styles that are action oriented and therefore include a much lower threshold for physical aggression and violence. Such actions lead to higher injury and death rates among boys and men (Copenhaver & Eisler, 1996).

Injuries, especially traumatic brain injuries (TBIs), are a leading cause of death from birth to age 45. The ratio of male to female TBIs between puberty and middle age ranges between 2:1 to 3:1 (Farace & Alves, 2000). A significant portion of these injuries is caused by masculine risk-taking behavior, especially regarding speeding, driving while intoxicated and lower rates of safety belt use (Morrongiello & Rennie, 1998; Zimbardo, 1997). Take a look at Table 11.5 to see the traditional masculine behaviors that increase the risks for injury and death. Firearms also account for many deaths and injuries among young men. Gunshot wounds and homicides are a particular issue among African-American boys and men. In the United Kingdom, accidents and violence cause 70%

of men's deaths compared to 35% of women's deaths for those under age 35 (L. Doyle, 1995).

Gender socialization influences what is perceived as stressful, as well as the socially approved responses to such stressors. For example, masculine norms require men to prevail in situations that require physical strength and physical fitness. However, these abilities decline with age and accumulated poor health habits. Second, gender role prescriptions demand that men be decisive and self-assured, but living up to these gender ideals is increasingly difficult in a complex society (Clatterbaugh, 1997). Third, some men may experience significant distress in situations that require the expression of tender feelings. But changing norms regarding romantic relationships and family responsibilities demand exactly such expression (Pleck, 1995).

The poem that appears at the beginning of this chapter is a dramatic comment on the more negative aspects of masculine gender role socialization. Although the language employed suggests contemporary urban African-American vernacular, the sentiments expressed cut across ethnic boundaries.

Performing the Gendered Lifestyle

Compared to women, men are less likely to notice symptoms or report them to a health care provider. Men have a lower frequency of physician office visits, are less likely to have annual physicals, and appear less willing or able to take time from work to go to seek medical assistance. Thus serious illnesses may be diagnosed at a much later stage of development. The "sick role" often involves submissiveness, dependence, and powerlessness, and these characteristics conflict with core aspects of the masculine gender role.

One interpretation of the fact that women visit their health care providers more often is that they are more distressed. An alternative interpretation is that men don't acknowledge their symptoms and are less likely to get assistance at earlier stages of a problem (Copenhaver & Eisler, 1996; Green & Pope, 1999). Compared to women, men tend not to manifest minor illness, but when health problems occur they are often more life threatening. Acute and nonfatal chronic conditions are generally more common among women (for example, varicose veins, gallbladder conditions, chronic colitis, and thyroid condi-

TABLE 11.5   Risky Behaviors Associated with the Masculine Gender Role

Alcohol overuse	Tobacco use
Dangerous sports	Criminal activity
Refusal to seek health care	Use of recreational drugs
Refusal to wear safety belts	Engaging in physical fights
Carrying weapons	Consuming a high-fat diet
Sleep deprivation	Physical overexertion
Refusal to wear sunscreen	Avoiding/ignoring health information
Risky sexual practices	Denying/ignoring symptoms
Risky behavior at workplace	Avoiding/ignoring nutritional information
Avoiding social support	Consuming a high-cholesterol diet
Dangerous driving practices	Neglect of testicular self-examination
Refusal to wear helmets	Driving under the influence of alcohol
Working in dangerous occupations	Using anabolic steroids

Source: Adapted from W. H. Courtenay (2000a), Behavioral factors associated with male disease, injury, and death: Evidence and implications for prevention. *Journal of Men's Studies, 9*(1), 81–142; and W. H. Courtenay (2000b), Constructions of masculinity and their influence on men's well-being: A theory of gender and health, *Social Science and Medicine, 50*(10), 1385–1401.

tions). However, studies done on groups of women and men for whom social and occupational role demands are equal show little difference in rates of illness (Stoudemire, 1998). Thus the differences in morbidity and mortality are related more to gender role requirements, than to any inherent biological factors.

Critical Thinking Challenge

Some researchers have suggested that men's reluctance and resistance in preventive health care is exacerbated by most physicians also being men. How would you test this question?

Until quite recently men had significantly higher levels of tobacco use. The youthful decision to smoke tobacco takes a deadly toll on middle-aged men. The list of tobacco-related diseases and dysfunctions includes cancers of the lung, throat, mouth, lips, and nose. Chronic obstructive respiratory diseases, cardiac disease, cerebral vascular disease, and a host of other problems may be traced back to this traditionally masculine manner of risk taking, pleasure seeking, and stress reduction. However, lung cancer deaths for women increased 150% between 1974 and 1994, but only 20% for men during that same period. Lung cancer surpassed breast cancer as the leading killer of *younger* women in 1987 (about 51,000 die annually).

Recently, at least two genetic factors have been identified that may make women more vulnerable to the **carcinogenic** properties of tobacco smoke (Tobacco smoke and women, 2000; Zang & Winder, 1996).

At all age levels, and within all ethnic groups, men are more likely than women to drink heavily, to report more drinking-related problems, and to use illegal drugs (Miller & Cervantes, 1997; Wilsnack, 1995). The lifetime prevalence of alcoholism for men is about 24%, compared to about 5% for women (Greenfield, 1996). The number of women in alcohol treatment programs has increased, but the ratio of men to women in treatment remains about 10:1. However, alcoholic women are at greater risk of early death. Women tend to advance more rapidly from initial onset of problem drinking to adverse medical problems such as liver disease and cognitive impairment (Greenfield, 1996).

Experiences of childhood abuse have serious health consequences for both women and men. For example, a history of childhood maltreatment is typically associated with poorer overall health, greater physical and emotional functional disability, and a greater number of health risk behaviors (Candib, 1995; Walker et al., 1999).

carcinogenic   Identified as a possible cause of cancer.

FIGURE 11.1 Diet books versus junk foods: Both of these phenomena interact with gender-related factors to influence health and well-being.

Adult experiences of sexual harassment, domestic violence, and sexual assault may also be considered from a physical health perspective. Sexual harassment is associated with nausea, sleeplessness, loss of self-esteem, fear, anger, helplessness, isolation, nervousness, and depression (vanRoosmalen & McDaniel, 1998). Rape and sexual assault may result in STD infection, serious bodily injury, and permanent disability. Battering results in fetal injuries, broken bones, disfigurements, and damage to internal organs (Duncan, Strayton, & Hall, 1999; Koss, Ingram, & Pepper, 2001). In New Guinea, battered women are said to have *ailolo sasi*, a phrase that literally means a "bad stomach." This condition is a mixture of anger, shame, and despair that sometimes leads to suicide (L. Doyle, 1995).

For men, sports-related injuries are often a health issue. Many more men enter emergency rooms with sports-related broken bones, concussions, and chest injuries (Burstyn, 1999). A minority of men use anabolic steroids to increase muscle mass and to ostensibly improve their athleticism. These drugs are associated with hypertension, elevated cholesterol levels, sexual dysfunction, liver damage, thyroid problems, testicle shrinkage, kidney and prostate cancer, baldness, acne, sterility, and lung problems (Pope & Katz, 1992; Klein, 1995).

For many women (and some gay men), weight control is often a central health issue (see Figure 11.1). For some, dieting reduces health risks, whereas for others dieting increases risks. Despite the cultural emphasis on a thin body ideal, the incidence of obesity appears to be increasing in the United States (Brownell & Rodin, 1994; Nestle & Jacobson, 2000). The prevalence of eating disorders, and a subclinical preoccupation with eating and weight represent other gender-related problems that increase with age (Casper, 1998). Although eating disorders are considered a psychiatric illness, they result in damage to the dental, cardiovascular, and gastrointestinal systems, and they can be fatal (Pike & Striegel-Moore, 1997).

Gender and Sexual Lifestyle

Sexually transmitted diseases, including HIV and AIDS, offer prime examples of how gendered behavior and lifestyles can be central in disease transmission. In the Western world, HIV first emerged in the gay male community. Among gay men, traditional masculine sexual norms of risk taking, as well as casual and frequent unprotected sexual activity with numerous partners were all exaggerated, and this facilitated the transmission of HIV throughout that community (Dowsett, 1996). In many developing nations, these same masculine sexual norms as well as feminine norms of passivity and accommodation are spreading HIV and AIDS among heterosexuals (Amaro, 1995; Catania, Binson, Doleini, Moskowitz, & van der Straton, 2001).

Examination of the history of HIV and AIDS in the Western world reveals one more arena in which gender norms and gender bias can influence health policies. Because HIV and AIDS first affected gay men, few resources, and attention were devoted to dealing with the "gay plague." As HIV spread beyond the gay male community, women sex workers were targeted as the primary agents for HIV transmission to male partners and children, even though the odds of man-to-woman transmission are eight times greater than the reverse (Padian, Shiboski, Glass, & Vittinghof, 1997). Today, intravenous drug users, as well as gay and bisexual men, are most affected by HIV (Catania et al., 2001; Mays et al., 2001).

Originally, the listing of HIV-related diseases were based on male experiences of infection (Sherr, 1996). Although the first symptoms of HIV infection are similar in both genders, some important differences then emerge. Over 40% of HIV-infected women experience gynecologic diseases such as **cervical dysplasia**. Cervical diseases seem to progress more rapidly to advanced stages in HIV-infected women. Women infected with both HIV and HPV (human papilloma virus) run a particular risk of cervical cancer (Wallin, Wiklund, Angstrom, et al., 1999). Certain opportunistic infections such as pneumocystis carinii pneumonia (PCP), toxoplasmosis, and lymphoma occur in

both genders, but Kaposi's sarcoma (KS) is common only among gay men. Women are more likely to experience bacterial pneumonia, endocarditis, and septicemia (Catz & Kelly, 2001). It was not until 1992 that the Centers for Disease Control issued revised classifications for HIV infection and expanded the case definition for AIDS. This resulted in the addition of three new clinical conditions to the list of AIDS-related opportunistic infections: pulmonary tuberculosis, recurrent pneumonia, and invasive cervical cancer (Hankins, 1996). This is important because such classification helps determine who may participate in clinical trials for new drugs and other treatments. It also determines who may receive disability payments, and when.

As most students know, properly used condoms offer excellent protection from the HIV virus. Early testing and treatment can also protect against illness progression. Programs designed to increase condom use and HIV testing assumed that the critical factor in changing behavior was information. They ignored issues of power, gender norms, and culture in sexual encounters (Dancy, 1996). Sexual encounters are enacted in a context of highly gendered beliefs and attitudes. Lifelong socialization for sexual assertiveness or sexual passivity, unequal sexual power, fears of disconnection and abandonment and even the threat of violence for demanding that a condom be used are all factors that may contribute to unprotected intercourse (Buzi, Weinman, & Smith, 1998; Jackson et al., 1998–1999). Box 11.5 discusses how cultural norms regarding gender and sexuality can create havoc in societies unprepared to deal with the reality of a sexually transmitted disease.

The decision to use condoms ultimately lies with men. Effecting a change in sexual norms means recognizing the contexts of men's lives, addressing their fears and desires, and encouraging responsibility, communication, and respect for themselves and their partners (Chara & Kuennen, 1994). Fortunately, the message regarding condom use has penetrated some segments of the population. For example, the recent decline in cases of chlamydia and other STDs among college students has been attributed to more awareness of STDs and the greater use of condoms (Yacobi, Tennant, Ferrante, Pal, & Roetzheim, 1999). For

---

cervical dysplasia   **Abnormal growth of cells on the cervix.**

Gender and AIDS in Africa

Uganda and Zimbabwe provide tragically informative case studies of how culture and gender norms can combine to produce devastation in health (see Figure 11.2). In 1999, approximately 2.6 million people died of AIDS, and 85% of these deaths occurred in southern Africa (Hirsch, Vistica, Masland, Dickey, et al., 2000).

The Ugandan population is made up of 60 tribes, and all share a tradition of shame and secrecy regarding sexual matters. Girls may learn from an aunt how to please their husbands, whereas brothers typically learn from an uncle that frequent and casual sex prove manhood. Civil war and urbanization has radically altered lifestyles in Uganda, but traditional sexual attitudes persist. Beginning at about age 14, boys and men are expected to have sex frequently and with many partners. Wives are expected to remain faithful and please their husbands sexually. Men bring HIV to their wives, who in turn pass the infection to their infants. Prostitution is one of the few ways unmarried, widowed, and abandoned women can support themselves and their children. Medicines are essentially unavailable, and certainly unaffordable by the vast majority of Ugandans. Ugandan society has essentially been devastated by HIV and AIDS, and an entire generation of orphans has been created (Hirsch et al., 2000). A new government sex education program is aimed at 5- to 14-year-olds and encourages sexual equality between girls and boys. Its very popular magazine *Straight Talk* is aimed at literate urban youth. Although young people

now have more information regarding sexuality, reproduction, and disease transmission, there has been virtually no change in sexual and gender attitudes (Aliro & Ochieng, 1999).

In Zimbabwe, about 20 to 40% of the population may be infected with HIV. Zimbabwe represents a male-dominated society with a polygamous tradition. Men leave their families in the rural areas and come to the cities to find jobs. Visits to prostitutes are common, and most men have girlfriends in the city. Both prostitutes and girlfriends may have several men contributing to their upkeep and that of their children. Women seldom admit they have had more than one sexual partner. Men also prefer to have "dry sex," considering a lubricated vagina unpleasant. Women employ many unhygienic practices to achieve this. Dry sex causes microtears in the vaginal wall and also increases the likelihood that condoms will break, thus adding to the risk of infection. The resulting infections increase vulnerability to all sexually transmitted pathogens, including HIV. How-

ever, most women are too shy to discuss such practices with health care workers.

Unable to achieve jobs and wealth themselves, young girls seek men with the "three C's" (car, cell phone, and cash). Also, many men believe that sex with a virgin will cure HIV and AIDS. The HIV infection rate among 15- to 20-year-old girls and women is five times that of men the same age, indicating that the girls' and women's partners are older men.

Although government clinics distribute free condoms to attending women, men typically reject their use, because such suggestions or demands from wives, girlfriends, and prostitutes are perceived as inappropriate for women and demeaning for men. Also, many men feel strongly that women in possession of condoms are likely to have sex with other men. Nevertheless, the Zimbabwean government has made a major commitment to distributing condoms to women. The Zimbabwe National Family Planning Council distributes 50 million condoms a year (Ezzell, 2000).

Nations such as Uganda and Zimbabwe simply lack the resources to care for the large numbers of orphans created by the AIDS epidemic.

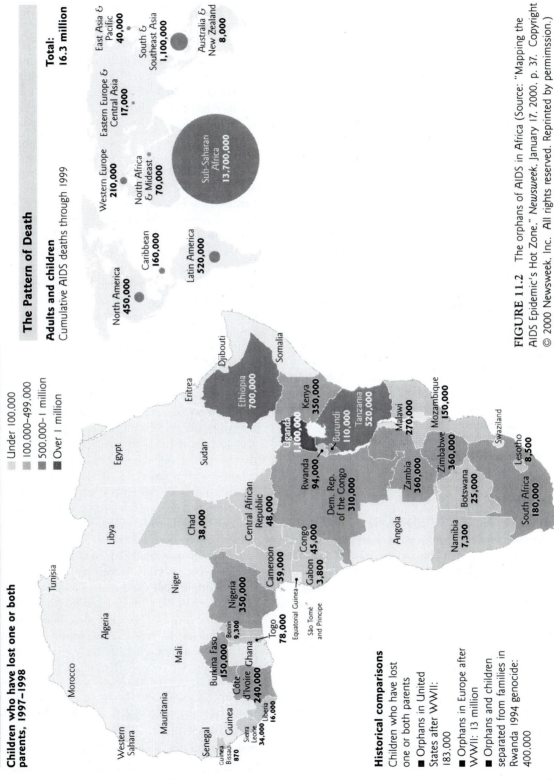

255

The Orphans of AIDS

Children who have lost one or both parents, 1997–1998

Under 100,000
100,000–499,000
500,000–1 million
Over 1 million

Morocco

Western Sahara

Tunisia

Algeria

Libya

Egypt

Mauritania

Mali

Niger

Senegal

Gambia

Guinea Bissau **870**

Guinea

Sierra Leone **34,000**

Liberia **16,000**

Côte d'Ivoire **240,000**

Burkina Faso **150,000**

Ghana

Benin **9,300**

Togo **78,000**

Nigeria **350,000**

Cameroon **59,000**

Equatorial Guinea

São Tomé and Principe

Gabon **3,800**

Congo **45,000**

Chad **38,000**

Central African Republic **48,000**

Sudan

Eritrea

Djibouti

Ethiopia **700,000**

Somalia

Uganda **1,100,000**

Rwanda **94,000**

Burundi **110,000**

Kenya **350,000**

Tanzania **520,000**

Dem. Rep. of the Congo **310,000**

Angola

Zambia **360,000**

Malawi **270,000**

Mozambique **150,000**

Zimbabwe **360,000**

Namibia **7,300**

Botswana **25,000**

South Africa **180,000**

Swaziland

Lesotho **8,500**

Historical comparisons

Children who have lost one or both parents

■ Orphans in United States after WWII: 183,000

■ Orphans in Europe after WWII: 13 million

■ Orphans and children separated from families in Rwanda 1994 genocide: 400,000

The Pattern of Death

Adults and children
Cumulative AIDS deaths through 1999

Total: 16.3 million

North America **450,000**

Caribbean **160,000**

Latin America **520,000**

Western Europe **210,000**

Eastern Europe & Central Asia **17,000**

North Africa & Mideast **70,000**

Sub-Saharan Africa **13,700,000**

East Asia & Pacific **40,000**

South & Southeast Asia **1,100,000**

Australia & New Zealand **8,000**

FIGURE 11.2 The orphans of AIDS in Africa (Source: "Mapping the AIDS Epidemic's Hot Zone," *Newsweek,* January 17, 2000, p. 37. Copyright © 2000 Newsweek, Inc. All rights reserved. Reprinted by permimssion.)

many middle- and upper-class adolescents, condom use implies a more sophisticated masculinity (Cleavenger, Juckett, & Hobbs, 1997).

Critical Thinking Challenge

Do you believe that sexual prowess can cease to be a core element of ideal masculinity? Do you believe that men can (or should) be socialized to value sexual responsibility and restraint more?

Living with and dying of HIV now requires years of caretaking, and this too is a gender-related issue. Gay men are often rejected by their biological families, so close friends of both genders and community organizations become the primary caretakers. However, as HIV has spread beyond the gay male population, the demographics of caregiving have moved to informal care at home (Faithful, 1997). All over the world, the vast majority of caretakers are girls and women. One study described African-American mothers and grandmothers in the rural South caring for their adult children with HIV. These women saw their provision of physical, emotional, and spiritual caregiving as a continuation of what they had always done. Many had grown up in poverty under segregation, and as a survival tactic they had learned to avoid interaction with the white medical and social service hierarchy. Their "church family" remained a very important resource (Boyle, Hodnicki, & Ferrell, 1999).

Longevity

At the beginning of the 20th century, the average life expectancies for both men and women were essentially equal, about 49 years. The leading causes of death were tuberculosis, smallpox, diphtheria, polio, and other infectious diseases. Since then, public health efforts have provided clean water, safe sanitation practices, and wide-scale childhood immunization against disease. In more developed nations, medical science and technology have reduced the complications of pregnancy and childbirth and overcome most infectious diseases. Government regulations, the efforts of organized labor, and employers themselves have reduced the incidence and impact of accidents and illnesses, especially those that were job related. As you have read, gender-related lifestyle issues are now the major challenge to optimal health and longevity in industrial and postindustrial societies.

The Central Paradox

There is a central paradox regarding gender, morbidity, and mortality. Even though women report more illness and more use of health care, their life expectancy is greater. In every developed nation, women outlive men. The lowest life expectancies for women are in Afghanistan, Ethiopia, and Sierra Leone. In Bangladesh, men outlive women. In India and Pakistan, women and men have almost equal life expectancy. Female infanticide, neglect, less breastfeeding, less food, and medical care for female children suggest that what may be a "biological advantage" can be canceled out by social forces (L. Doyle, 1995). In developed nations, the gender gap in life expectancy continues to grow, and the sheer number of women **centenarians** is rapidly increasing. Thus older women far outnumber older men. Above age 85, the ratio is five women for every two men (Gatz, Harris, & Turk-Charles, 1995). Figure 11.3 offers a darkly humorous comment on this extended longevity. Within the United States, however, there are striking differences in life expectancy according to ethnic group (see Table 11.6), with African-American men having the shortest life expectancy.

In more developed nations, vast numbers of women now pass successfully through their reproductive years and thrive well past menopause. Thus they are much more likely to experience health problems that were relatively rare in past generations. Chronic conditions for women over 75 years of age include arthritis, colitis, anemia, migraines, bladder infections, hypertension, hearing, and vision impairment, heart disease, and orthopedic problems, especially those related to osteoporosis (Gatz et al., 1995). However, despite their many age-related medical conditions, for a given level of disability women are less likely to assess their health as poor compared to similar men (Arber & Cooper, 1999). Lifestyle issues also affect life among the very old. For example, a survey revealed that frequent vigorous exercisers and long walkers had significantly higher life satisfaction scores and were cognitively younger than less active short walkers and inactives (Clark, Long, & Schiffman, 1999).

For aging men, the picture is somewhat different. In general, men have higher rates of sensory/structural impairments, life-threatening chronic diseases, and major disabilities caused by chronic conditions. Older

---

centenarian   **Person living to 100 or older.**

"In my day, people died."

FIGURE 11.3 Although this cartoon may seem far-fetched, recent advances in stem-cell research may extend life expectancy to about 150 years. Theoretically it will allow for the replacement of worn-out or malfunctioning organs (Hall, 2000).

men live longer with more serious problems compared to women (Dimond, Catanzaro, & Lorensen, 1997). Widowers who survive into old age typically remarry and live with a new spouse. For those who do not, a social support system is often lacking. Among older single or widowed men, the incidence of depression increases with age, and suicide rates rise (Reynolds, Frank, Mazumdar, Meltzer, et al., 1999).

In accounting for this gender gap in longevity, the conventional wisdom offered is of two types. Some hypothesize a biological, perhaps genetic, source. Others cite hormonal influences such as the protective influence of estrogen among premenopausal women. The wide-scale use of hormone replacement therapy (HRT) may help continue this advantage into the later years. However, the impact of testosterone is an unknown factor in longevity. Testosterone

appears related to increased activity, impulsiveness, irritability, aggressiveness, and an elevated physiological response to stress (Travis, 1988; Wilson, 1999). Even those who adhere to a biological explanation believe that men's longevity can be prolonged by exercise, nutrition, and healthier lifestyle decisions.

A second approach emphasizes gender roles. Accordingly, men work harder, whereas women experience less stress. Furthermore, in the face of difficulties, gender norms prescribe that women may seek help, often from men. Thus women have an easier life and reap the benefits of men's labor.

Critical Thinking Challenge

How would you evaluate either of these two explanations for this gender gap in longevity?

TABLE 11.6 Life Expectancy by Ethnic Group

White women: 80	Black women: 74
White men: 73	Black men: 66

Source: Peters, Kochanek, & Murphy (1998).

Gender and Contemporary Mortality

Ask someone what people die of today, and most are likely to report that men tend to die of heart attacks, whereas women die of breast cancer. Let's examine both of these commonly held beliefs.

Coronary Disease (CD). Because heart disease kills so many middle-aged men in the developed world, it has been called the chief *widow maker*. However, the perception that heart disease is a man's disease is both wrong and dangerous. Coronary disease ultimately claims most women, but at an older age. About half of all women can expect to have serious heart trouble in their lifetimes. About 500,000 women die of CD each year as opposed to the 46,000 women who die of breast cancer. Thus CD is the number one killer and disabler of women in the United States. However, most information regarding prevention, clinical features, therapy, and prognosis are based on studies of middle-aged men. For example, the Physicians Health Study that evaluated the use of daily aspirin to reduce the risk of **myocardial infarctions (MIs)** was conducted on 22,000 healthy *male* physicians (Schumacher & Smith, 1995).

The age patterns of this largely preventable disease are differentiated by gender. The first symptom of heart disease is typically chest pain (angina pectoris), and this is more common among younger men and older women. Women actually have a wider array of first symptoms (LaCharity, 1999). Women tend to have heart attacks much later than do men, about 10 to 20 years after menopause, with death rates peaking after age 65 (Healy, 1995). In contrast to their behavior for most other conditions, women are *slower* to seek care for cardiac symptoms. Women, their friends, their family members, and even their physicians seem to perceive these symptoms differently. Men are more likely to be quickly referred from primary care to a cardiologist. Prompt treatment for myocardial infarctions is critical, but laypeople and health care workers alike are less likely to suspect a heart attack among women. However, once diagnosed as having a heart attack, men and women will receive identical treatment. But it is not clear whether this approach is optimal. Often women don't do as well after a heart attack, because their older age increases the likelihood of **comorbidity.** Other poorly understood factors such as women's smaller artery size may also be significant (Sheifer, Canos, Weinfurt, & Arora, 2000). Women typically take longer to recuperate, are less likely to return to work, experience more mood and sleep disturbances, and have more impaired sexual functioning. Comparable data from England and New Zealand support the finding that women are twice as likely to die after a heart attack; 11 or 12%, versus 5 to 6% for men (Wenger, 1998). After an infarction, women are less likely to participate in cardiac rehabilitation programs. The reasons for this are unknown but may have to do with the content and emphases of such programs. However, when women do participate, they benefit equally (Lieberman, Meana, & Stewart, 1998).

Certain risk factors for heart disease are the same for both genders: family history, high-fat diets leading to high cholesterol levels, tobacco use, lack of exercise, hypertension, diabetes, and obesity. For women, multiple births (more than five children) and estrogen deficiency are additional risk factors. For men, greater cardiac reactivity may make stress more problematic. Interestingly, some studies demonstrate that men who adhere more strongly to traditional masculine gender roles experience more cardiac reactivity when placed in situations that challenge their masculine self-image. Systolic blood pressure (SBP) is especially likely to rise when such men faced with a task classified as appropriate to the "other sex" (Copenhaver & Eisler, 1996; Wright, Murray, Storey, & Williams, 1997). Greater cardiac reactivity has also been found to be related to anger expression, as well as not expressing the more tender emotions such as love, compassion, fear, and hurt. Although a low-fat diet, cholesterol management, lean body weight, stress reduction, and exercise will certainly increase men's longevity, so might substantial changes in the performance of traditional masculine gender roles.

Critical Thinking Challenge

A higher education level is among the best predictors of overall cardiovascular health. Does this mean that attending graduate school will prolong your life and keep you healthier? Why or why not?

Cerebral Vascular Accidents. Cerebral vascular accidents (CVAs or strokes) are the third leading cause of death in the United States. Overall, men and women have about equal numbers of strokes, but again, the pattern is different. Young women and old

---

myocardial infarction   Commonly referred to as a "heart attack."

comorbidity   *Morbidity* refers to illness or injury. *Comorbidity* refers to two or more illnesses that occur together.

women have slightly more strokes than their male counterparts. Middle-aged men have more strokes than do middle-aged women. Regular medical check-ups and other preventive measures have reduced the overall incidence of CVAs, but those that do occur are more likely to be major ones. Although there are several types of CVAs, the symptoms typically include muscle paralysis, numbness, blindness, lost or slurred speech, and balance problems. A family history of CVAs is a powerful risk factor, as is ethnicity. However, other risk factors include many lifestyle issues such as smoking, diet, and stress.

Cancer. Among men aged 15–34, cancer ranks fourth as a cause of death (after accidents, homicide, and suicide). In older, working-age men (35–54) cancer is the second leading cause of death after heart disease. In developed countries, over 60% of cancer deaths occur in people over 65, but an upward trend begins earlier, especially among women. This gender difference in "cancer age" coincides with reductions in sex gland activity, specifically, after age 45 in women and after age 60 in men. During middle age (40–59) cancer risks in women surpass those of men (breast cancer incidence rises around menopause). Breast cancer is the leading cause of death among middle-aged women in the Western world. By age 60, overall cancer risks are equalized in both genders, but thereafter cancer incidence and mortality increase for men. Lifetime incidence probability is about equal for both genders, but the total cancer mortality rate of men is double that of women, largely because of occupational hazards and lifestyle factors such as smoking and alcohol. Compared to women, men have higher rates of cancer with known causes (lung, bladder, stomach, esophagus, mouth, larynx, and so on). For many cancer types that are not sex-specific (colorectal cancers, leukemias, and lymphomas), men have lower survival rates.

Longevity and the Dementias. Contrary to popular belief, dementia (the progressive impairment of memory and other cognitive abilities) is not a normal part of aging. Although some decline in these areas is expected, a steep decline suggests pathology. Recent meta-analyses debunk the idea that women are more susceptible to dementia. However, because there are so many older women, there are many more women

with dementia; that is, age is the greatest risk factor for developing dementia. Dementia is a major reason for the institutionalization of the old (Gatz et al., 1995).

Conclusions

The paradox of gender and physical health is that at all younger ages, women's morbidity rates exceed that of men. However, at all younger ages men's mortality rates exceed those of women for accidents, occupational injuries, heart disease, cancer, CVAs, and pneumonia as well as homicides, suicides, and AIDS. Thus there is a significant gender difference in longevity, based mainly on gender-related lifestyle factors. Later in life, women die of the same diseases as men do. In the industrialized world, the differential patterns in health maintenance, illness, injury, and mortality are strongly associated with gender-related lifestyle factors.

Summary

◆ In past centuries, infectious diseases were the major threats to health. Beginning in the 18th century, women were gradually excluded from the healing arts and from participating in the development of modern medical science. Women's health movement activists have improved gender-relevant health services in many areas.

◆ Contemporary concerns include (a) the importance of understanding gender-related health issues, (b) the distortions and stereotypes perpetuated by "racial" classifications in the organization and presentation of health data, (c) making health data understandable to the lay public, and (d) adequate health care on a global scale.

◆ Health promotion, illness, and the health service system all exist in a complex and highly gendered context or framework. Gender affects virtually every aspects of health, including the biological bases of pathology, medical education, the medical research system, the delivery of health services, and the dissemination of health information.

◆ Job-related factors no longer pose the health threat they once did, but boys and men are still more likely to sustain injuries and illnesses in the workplace. In more industrialized societies, pregnancy and childbirth are safe processes. In the developing world, however, reproductive processes pose a major health threat for women and children. Overall, women still lack the power to influence social policies regarding reproductive health.

◆ In industrialized societies, most illness is caused by behavior and decision-making processes. Key elements of traditional Western masculinity are associated with high rates of injury and illness. Sports injuries, interpersonal aggression, vehicular accidents, tobacco use, substance abuse, unprotected sex with multiple partners, firearms use, high-fat diets, and so forth. All contribute to higher morbidity and mortality rates among men. Lifestyle-related threats to women's health include smoking, substance abuse, unprotected sex with multiple partners, experiences of abuse, and eating disorders. In general, women experience greater morbidity. Moreover, caretaking of those who are ill, disabled, or dying is a traditional feminine role.

◆ In industrial societies, women use the medical system more, are ill more often, and tend to have more chronic conditions. Yet women have a longer life expectancy. Explanations for this gender gap in mortality tend to emphasize either biological factors or gender role issues.

◆ Contrary to popular belief, coronary disease is the major cause of death for both genders, but there is a gender differential in terms of when in the life span these conditions have a maximum impact on mortality.

◆ Cancer affects men and women at different points in the life span, with reproductive cancers peaking after menopause for women. For men, all types of cancer increase after age 60. Gendered lifestyle factors, especially tobacco and alcohol use, influence the types of cancers developed. Because more women live into very old age, more women develop dementias.

InfoTrac College Edition

For more information, explore InfoTrac College Edition at

http://www.infotrac-college.com/Wadsworth

Enter search terms: gender and health, gender and AIDS, gender and coronary disease, masculinity and health, reproductive health.

Gender and Mental Health

On Labels, Culture, and Boundary Violations

There is also no doubt that, within a health care structure dominated by patriarchal values, it was easier to define the problems of women as illness and those of men as deviance, and therefore unrelated to health issues. In this way, the macho image of the "strong" man and the "weak" woman was maintained. ◆ P. M. Prior

Learning Objectives

After studying this chapter, you should be able to:

1. List and explain two traditional concepts that are relevant to understanding the relationship between gender and psychopathology.
2. Summarize the findings related to gender and ethnic biases and the potential for stereotyping in labeling behavior as psychopathological.
3. Explain why women have been viewed as more vulnerable to mental disorder, and then explain why men have recently become more numerous in psychiatric populations.
4. Summarize current thinking about gay and lesbian mental health.
5. Explain the distinction between universally recognized patterns of disordered behavior and culture-bound syndromes, mentioning the influence of gender in six specific culture-bound syndromes.
6. Summarize the relevant data supporting the notion of eating disorders (especially anorexia) as a culture-bound syndrome, mentioning the prevalence of eating disorders in the African-American community and among men.
7. Summarize the factors believed to contribute to the greater incidence of depression among women.
8. Summarize the factors believed to contribute to the greater incidence of substance abuse among men.
9. Summarize the findings regarding the relationship between gender and anxiety disorders.
10. Summarize the findings regarding the relationship between gender and antisocial personality disorder.
11. Summarize the findings regarding gender differences in schizophrenia.

Encounters with Gender

On a sunny Saturday afternoon, Anna, 16 years old, is at home reading a magazine. Her oldest brother, David, age 21, enters the house. Seeing Anna, he directs her to go upstairs to dust and vacuum his room. He tells her that when she's done, she is to wash his car because he is going out that evening. Anna puts her magazine away and quietly cleans up David's room. She washes his car without complaint, and is careful to put hose, bucket, sponge, and towels back in their places. She tells David that she is done and returns to her magazine. How are we to understand Anna's behavior? How are we to understand David's behavior? Is Anna home-bound because she is too fearful to be out in public? Is Anna so depressed she is unable to stand up for herself? Has her self-esteem slipped so low that she obeys blindly? Is compliance her only protection from a tyrannical brother? Is David an abusive man who takes advantage of his sister and perhaps others? Do these siblings live in a dysfunctional family?

Source: Adapted from L. Uba (1994). *Asian-American personality patterns, identity, and mental health.* New York: Guilford, p. II.

Overview

In this chapter, we will explore several gender-related issues surrounding mental health and mental illness (psychopathology). We begin with a quick historical overview, and then explore how dominant groups influence what is considered disordered behavior. A review of some of the controversies surrounding current diagnostic labels follows. Some behavior patterns are considered disordered across virtually all societies, but other disorders are related to the gender constructions of a particular society. Eating disorders may be usefully considered as a culture-bound syndrome. I then discuss two classes of behavior that are viewed as disorders of gender: gender identity disorder (gender dysphoria) and transvestism. Gender-related issues in other selected categories of psychopathology are reviewed. Women predominate in two of these classes of disorders, and men predominate in two others. An overview of sex and gender differences in schizophrenia completes the discussion.

Labels: Past and Present

The notion of *rational man* versus *irrational woman* is a core component in the more traditional construction of gender. Traditional masculinity is associated with strength of mind and rationality, whereas traditional femininity is associated with frailty of mind and irrationality (Brookes, 1998; Malson, 1997).

A second core notion regarding gender and mental illness relates to the reduction of women to their reproductive function. For centuries, in the Western world, the wandering uterus (*hyster*) and diseased ovaries were considered responsible for women's apparent nervousness and vulnerability to psychological disorder (**hysteria**). During the 19th century, an ongoing debate considered whether women's mental illness belonged in the province of the neurologist, *alienist* (early term for psychiatrist), or gynecologist. A 19th-century physician declared that women were especially susceptible to mental disturbances at three different times of life: the onset of menstruation, the childbearing years, and the menopausal years. Given the relatively short life span during the 19th century, that didn't leave many years when women weren't "especially subject" to mental illness. Another 19th-century physician marveled that *any* women at all were healthy mentally, given the sensitivity of their reproductive organs.

If all of women's complaints and symptoms were caused by dysfunctions of the reproductive organs, it followed that **hysterectomy** and **ovariectomy** constituted the proper treatment for women's "mental conditions." Women physicians questioned the relationship between reproductive organs and mental disorder, and some *alienists* and neurologists suspected that hereditary factors and "brain lesions" might be the real causes of mental disorder. Some even pointed to environmental factors such as oppressive roles, the demands of constant child rearing, and restrictive clothing as combining with hereditary factors to produce disorder. Some male gynecologists blamed education as a cause of mental disorder, but women physicians tended to recommend education as a preventive device (Minton, 2000; Theriot, 1996).

Toward the end of the 19th century, the reproductive organ theory of mental disorder was displaced by the nervous system theory. Women's "nerves" were believed to be smaller, more sensitive, and more reactive to the external world. Therefore women were particularly vulnerable to **neurasthenia**. This theory too was replaced, by a psychoanalytic theory emphasizing unconscious mechanisms and the repression of sexual impulses (Freud, 1948).

Contemporary Issues in Labeling

Today the line between physical and mental illness is very blurred. Just as cognitive and behavioral factors are critical to understanding physical diseases and dysfunctions, we see that genetic, neuroanatomical, and physiological factors are critical to understanding mental disorders and dysfunctions (Stam, 1998).

Critical Thinking Challenge

As you read and study this chapter, can you identify those disorders in which the Western tradition of separation between mind and body seems problematic or artificial?

You will see that psychosocial issues of gender are intertwined all through current conceptions of mental health, mental illness, and treatment. For example, interviewer gender is significantly related to respondents' reports of psychiatric symptoms. Respondents of

---

hysteria **A disorder originally said to consist of unexplainable seizures, paralyses, and sensations of choking (*globus hystericus*). Later the label was applied to "feminine" personality or mood, and so forth—that is, highly impressionable, weak-minded, and so on.**

hysterectomy **Surgical procedure in which the uterus is partially or completely removed.**

ovariectomy **Surgical removal of the ovaries.**

neurasthenia **Nineteenth-century "nervous system" disorder characterized by lack of energy, vague aches and pains, and occasional fever.**

both genders report more symptoms when interviewed by women. Women interviewers seem to create conditions more conducive to disclosure and are perceived as more sympathetic than men interviewers (Pollner, 1998).

Although some behavioral patterns are considered disordered across virtually all societies, in other situations social power plays a role. That is, the behavior of a dominant group becomes the norm against which the behavior of subordinate groups is compared. The behavioral and social norms of subordinate groups are often judged to be deficient and therefore disordered. As you have seen, the social norms governing gender are among the most powerful and pervasive (Phelan & Link, 1999). Inge Broverman and her colleagues (1970) carried out a classic study of gender role stereotypes and clinical judgments of mental health. They gave practicing clinicians a list of behavioral traits and asked the respondents to indicate the traits that described a healthy, mature, socially competent man, woman, or adult (sex unspecified). Clinicians described desirable behaviors and characteristics for the healthy adult that closely resembled those for men but that were quite different from those for a woman. This seemed to suggest quite a double bind. To be a healthy adult meant displaying masculine characteristics, but women who were masculine would certainly not be considered healthy. The results also implied that femininity was immature, incompetent, and less healthy. Researchers later questioned the validity of the Broverman study because the questionnaire contained a greater number of desirable masculine traits. When the study was replicated with a more balanced questionnaire, no bias effect emerged (Garb, 1997).

Does this mean there is no gender bias in diagnostic processes? A recent review of studies in this area fails to demonstrate gender bias in the diagnosis of most disorders. However, depressed men are more likely to be diagnosed as having an organic disorder whereas similar women are more likely to be diagnosed as having a functional disorder. There is also reliable evidence to suggest that more pathology is attributed to men described as passive, and to women described as aggressive (Garb, 1997). Although no current evidence suggests that female psychiatric patients are judged as more disturbed than male patients, other types of bias may persist. For example,

physicians prescribe **psychotropic medications** about twice as often for women as for men (Casper, 1998).

The same power differential extends to other subordinate groups. For example, during the 18th century the pursuit of freedom and autonomy was considered patriotic and healthy for white men, but among runaway slaves it was evidence of mental derangement and was labeled *drapetomania* (Thomas & Sullen, 1974).

Until quite recently, in British hospitals, a high rate of psychiatric hospitalizations among Caribbean patients was a well-known phenomenon. However, diagnoses of depression as well as overall hospitalization rates dropped dramatically when a new Caribbean Culture Specific Screen (Abas, Phillips, Carter, Walter, Banerjee, & Levy, 1998) replaced the traditional diagnostic interview instrument (Prior, 1999). In Australia, the general prevalence of psychiatric disorders matches that of other industrialized states, but psychiatric disorders are more prevalent among Aborigines (1% of the population). Up until the 1960s, Aborigine children were forcibly removed from their families and placed with white foster families or in institutions. A survey found 44% of Aborigine psychiatric outpatients and 56% of inpatients had been brought up in foster families or institutions (McKendrick et al., 1990). In a large sample from the United States, African-American and Asian-American patients were more often diagnosed as psychotic compared to Latinos and whites. Black men and Native American men are more likely to be hospitalized than referred to community-based treatment (Flaskerud & Hu, 1992). Take a look at Box 12.1 to see a parallel situation in modern Israel.

Critical Thinking Challenge

Some analysts suggest that the greater prevalence of psychiatric disorder among ethnic minority groups could be caused by the extra stresses associated with minority group status (Cohen, 2000). What do you think?

The Diagnostic and Statistical Manual (DSM) of the American Psychiatric Association is a listing and classification of mental disorders. The DSM-I (1952)

---

psychotropic medication   **Medications that affect cognitive or affective functioning.**

Gender, Psychopathology, and Culture in Modern Israel

The modern state of Israel offers an interesting arena for us to observe the interplay among gender and culture in patterns of psychopathology. There are three cleavages in contemporary Israeli society. Most obvious are the tensions between Jews and Arabs living in Israel. Fewer are aware of the tensions between ultraorthodox Jews (about 10% of the population) and the majority of the population, who live very secular lives. A third social division exists between Ashkenazic Jews (Ashkenazim) who have more recently immigrated from eastern Europe versus Sephardic Jews (Sephardim) from Asia (Iran) and North Africa (Morocco and Ethiopia).

Modern Israel has well-established traditions of psychological and psychiatric research. Recent community-based studies support the typical finding that affective disorders are more often diagnosed among women, whereas personality disorders and substance abuse are more frequently diagnosed among men. The typical inverse relationship between socioeconomic variables and mental disorder is also found. Overall, psychiatric disorders are more frequent among immigrants than among native-born Israelis. Among the immigrant groups, higher rates of psychopathology prevail among the Sephardim, who are generally much poorer than the Ashkenazim. However,

affective disorders (especially depression) are more common among Ashkenazim, and are particularly high among ultraorthodox Ashkenazi men. Sephardim are overrepresented among those diagnosed with schizophrenic disorders, personality disorders, alcoholism, and drug addiction. The homicide rate among Sephardim is twice as high as among Ashkenazim. Studies of attributions for mental illness found that generally Ashkenazim perceive themselves as sick persons suffering from innate and incurable ailments. Sephardim see themselves as basically healthy and attributed their problems to external factors that could be eliminated.

Among Moroccan and Ethiopian Jews, belief in demons and sorcery is widespread, and they see their troubles as caused by these demons. Iranian Jews have extremely high psychiatric morbidity rates characterized by rather peculiar bodily symptomatology. They are often labeled as suffering from *Parsitis*, which may be translated as "the Persian syndrome." Many are referred to psychiatric clinics after no organic basis is found for somatic complaints. Ethiopian Jews often experienced severe trauma on their way to Israel, and many children and adolescents of both genders have developed various forms of PTSD. Among Ethiopians, the abdomen is seen as the con-

tainer for all emotions, and many have developed an eating disorder resembling anorexia nervosa, called "eating arrest." These individuals stop eating, but the usual weight phobia and disturbed body image are not present. Patients often describe an acute sensation of being filled with agony and pain, which they cannot contain any longer. These unbearable troubles seem related to earlier persecutory experiences, survivor guilt, and acculturation problems.

Among the ultraorthodox, boys are more vulnerable to depression at younger ages because of very high demands for emotional and cognitive maturity. Girls become more vulnerable at puberty when their inherent "impurities" around menstruation become apparent and their sexuality is harshly suppressed. For ultraorthodox Jews diagnosed with schizophrenia, delusions usually have a heavy religious content. The child survivors and offspring of Holocaust survivors are also more vulnerable to mental disorder. Recent wars and terrorism have created additional vulnerabilities.

Source: Y. Bilu (1995), Culture and mental illness among Jews in Israel, in I. Al-Issa (Ed.), *Handbook of culture and mental illness: An international perspective* (Madison, CT: International University Press), pp. 129–148.

---

had only 130 pages, the DSM-II (1968) had 134 pages, the DSM-III (1980) had 481 pages, and the current DSM-IV (1994) has 886 pages. Does this increase mean there is really more psychopathology in the world to be labeled? Or does it imply greater refinement and elaboration of details? Perhaps the expanding list of diagnostic categories reflects only the increasing social power of psychologists and psychiatrists (Kupers, 1995). Although more behaviors are being constructed as psychopathological, change also

happens in the other direction as well. For example, in the 19th and early part of the 20th century, same-sex sexual behavior was considered evidence of mental disorder. However, in 1980 the American Psychiatric Association removed homosexuality from the list of disorders in the DSM-III.

In creating the DSM-IV (American Psychiatric Association, 1994), there was great debate regarding several of the proposed diagnostic categories. For example, the diagnostic label "self-defeating personality

Is Pathology in the Eye of the Beholder?

Relying on satire to make their point, some feminist clinicians have proposed additional personality disorders that pathologize traditional masculine behavior in a way comparable to how they saw traditional feminine roles labeled as pathology in the DSM-IV (American Psychiatric Association, 1994). They propose the following "disorders":

※ *Independent personality disorder* includes putting work above relationships (traveling too much on business and working late), having others assume responsibility for one's social life

because of difficulty in expressing affection (for example, requires spouse to do most of child care responsibilities).

※ *Restricted personality disorder* involves limited expression of emotions (for example, failing to cry), repeatedly choosing physical or intellectual activities over emotional activities, engaging others to perform emotional behaviors, and avoiding feeling-related topics by changing the subject, leaving room, acting annoyed, or becoming silent (M. Kaplan, 1983).

※ *Delusional dominating personality disorder* (DDPD) was proposed to counter self-defeating personality disorder (SDPD) (Caplan, 1991). It involves the delusion that one is entitled to the services of any woman with whom one is personally associated, the delusion that physical force is the best way to solve interpersonal problems, the delusion that sexual and aggressive impulses are uncontrollable, and the delusion that women like to suffer and be ordered around.

---

disorder" was considered appropriate for women who were repeatedly victimized by abusive men. Feminists quickly pointed out that there was no equivalent label for men who repeatedly abused women. Should victims be pathologized, but not perpetrators? Ultimately the label was not included. However, "physical abuse of adult" and "sexual abuse of adult" were added to the DSM-IV (APA, 1994). This allowed the diagnosis of pathology in perpetrators of abuse.

Critical Thinking Challenge

Some critics point out that labeling sexual and physical abuse of others as psychopathology is a way of "medicalizing badness" (Prior, 1999). Such labeling suggests that such behavior should be treated rather than punished. What are the interpersonal, social, and legal implications of this approach?

Rancorous debate also ensued over the label "late luteal phase dysphoric disorder." This was finally included in the appendix of the DSM-IV as "premenstrual dysphoric disorder" (known more commonly as PMS, or premenstrual syndrome) and was described as requiring more research. The issue of gender bias in the diagnosis of personality disorders has been a persistent problem (Kupers, 1995). "Histrionic personality disorder," "borderline personality disorder," and

"dependent personality disorder" are all applied disproportionately to women (Widiger, 1998). To understand why this disproportion suggests sexist bias, you should know that the diagnostic criteria for "histrionic personality disorder" include emotional lability (rapid changes in emotional state), overconcern with physical attractiveness, and sexual seductiveness. Presumably, many normal, healthy women could meet the criteria for diagnosis. Feminist clinicians have attempted to draw attention, through satire, to the sexist quality of some of these labels. Take a look at Box 12.2 to see some thought-provoking examples.

Similarly, diagnoses of "attention-deficit hyperactivity disorder (ADHD)," "oppositional defiant disorder," and "conduct disorder" are all disproportionately applied to boys. The criteria for "conduct disorder" may be sexist in that there is an overemphasis on the aggressive behavior that is more normative for boys. The diagnostic criteria for conduct disorders seem to have developed with extremes of masculine behavior in mind (cruelty to animals or people, sexual assault, and so on). These criteria neglect behaviors more typical of conduct disorder in girls, such as early sexual activity and early use of drugs and alcohol. Thus antisocial, abusive, and exploitive behaviors among girls are much more likely to go undetected (Prior, 1999).

TABLE 12.1   Conditions Diagnosed More Frequently in One Gender

Diagnosed More Frequently in Women	*Diagnosed More Frequently in Men*
Most prevalent affective disorders (major depression and dysthymia)	Substance abuse
	Conduct disorders
Anxiety disorders (panic disorder and agoraphobia)	Personality disorders (antisocial, narcissistic, and obsessive-compulsive)
Eating disorders	
Personality disorders (histrionic, borderline, and dependent)	Intermittent explosive disorder
	Pathological gambling

Source: Adapted from C. M. Hartung & T. A. Widiger (1998). Gender differences in the diagnosis of mental disorders: Conclusions and controversies of the DSM-IV, *Psychological Bulletin, 123*(2), 260–278. Adapted from R. C. Kessler, K. A. McGonagle, K. A. Zhao, C. B. Nelson, et al. (1994). Lifetime and 12-month prevalence of DSM-IIIR psychiatric disorders in the United States. Results from the National Co-Morbidity Study, *Archive of General Psychiatry, 51*, 8–19.

Gender Differentials in Psychiatric Diagnoses

When certain conditions are diagnosed more frequently in one gender, issues of stereotypes and bias must be considered (see Table 12.1). Some diagnostic categories seem to serve as an "upper limit" for the very characteristics that are encouraged in each gender. Boys are encouraged to be active, rough, aggressive, sexually adventurous, and rational, but if too aggressive, they may be considered "conduct disordered," and so on. If women are too emotionally expressive, they may be diagnosed with "histrionic personality disorder" or as very depressed (Kupers, 1995; Prior, 1999).

Rosenfield (1999) offers another perspective on the gender differentials in diagnostic labeling. Women appear to demonstrate higher rates of internalizing disorders, such as depression and anxiety. The symptoms of these disorders include a sense of loss, hopelessness, helplessness, and involve attributions of self-blame and self-reproach. Fears take the form of phobias, panic attacks, and free-floating anxiety. Men have higher rates of "externalizing disorders," such as substance abuse and antisocial disorders. Symptoms include the expression of problematic feelings in outward behavior. They involve enduring aggressive and antisocial personality traits as well as problems in forming close, enduring relationships. You may evaluate your own tendencies in dealing with troublesome events or experiences by completing the questionnaire in Box 12.3. In any case, the stereotype of the typical psychiatric patient as a depressed or anxious middle-aged woman persists. Why do you think it is generally believed that women are more vulnerable to psychological disorder?

First, women are more likely to *report* distress. In a Canadian **epidemiological study**, 60% of the women respondents reported very high stress levels, 44% reported anxiety, and 35% rated themselves as depressed (Walters, 1993). However, a recent Scottish study found no gender differences in the reporting of psychological symptoms among respondents of varied ages (MacIntyre, Ford, & Hunt, 1999).

Until very recently, men have been underrepresented in psychiatric statistics because they are discouraged from seeking help and from acknowledging distress (Campbell, 1996). Also, although women and men seem to react to negative life events in similar ways, connecting with others (for example, seeing a therapist) may be more healing for women (Leong & Zachar, 1999; Zlotnick et al., 1996).

Another reason why women have been traditionally overrepresented in psychiatric statistics is because until quite recently substance abuse and antisocial personality disorder were not counted or researched as mental illnesses (Prior, 1999). Men are more than twice as likely as women to have substance dependence. That is, there is a 36% lifetime prevalence of substance abuse problems for men, compared to 18% for women. Similar patterns prevail in the United Kingdom, New Zealand, and Ireland (Prior, 1999).

epidemiology   **Study of the prevalence of mental and physical illness in community samples; a public health approach to illness and health.**

ABCs of GENDER (ATTITUDES, BELIEFS, AND CONCERNS)   BOX 12.3

The Issue: Gender and Personal Coping Styles

_____ Your gender

_____ Your age

_____

(Other variable of interest)

Think about a recent significantly negative personal event that resulted in your feeling depressed or low (perhaps failing a course, the breakup of a love relationship, a serious quarrel, an accident or physical illness, loss of a loved one, or so on). Check any item that describes what you did when you were feeling badly.

_____ 1. I worked alone on a hobby that required concentration.

_____ 2. I wrote about how I was feeling.

_____ 3. I got away from everyone, and tried to sort out my feelings.

_____ 4. I called my friends and arranged to do something fun with them.

_____ 5. I had a lot to drink, or took other drugs.

_____ 6. I told at least one friend about how badly I was feeling.

_____ 7. I provoked an argument with someone, provoked a physical fight, or destroyed something.

_____ 8. I engaged in a strenuous physical activity.

_____ 9. I wrote a letter (e-mail?) to someone describing my feelings.

_____ 10. I did something reckless (drove over the speed limit, swam in a dangerous place, went to a dangerous place, engaged in casual, unprotected sex, or so on).

_____ 11. I listened to loud, exciting music and/or danced.

_____ 12. I made a list of the reasons why I was sad or depressed.

Evaluation

As you have read, many clinical researchers believe there are substantial differences in how women and men express their feelings of depression. Men are more likely engage in distracting, externalizing, high-energy activities. Women are more likely to internalize by ruminating or mulling over their unhappiness. Although the first coping style may sometimes lead to other difficulties (accidents, illness, trouble with police), the second may amplify bad feelings.

Items 1, 4, 5, 7, 8, and 10 are more typical of a _distracting_ style.

Items 2, 3, 6, 9, 11, and 12 are more typical of a _ruminative_ style.

You may want to compile and compare the responses of your class members by gender. Can you think of any variables, other than gender, that might elicit such group differences in coping style? Explain.

Source: Based on S. Nolen-Hoeksema (1990), _Sex differences in depression_ (Stanford, CA: Stanford University Press). Adapted from C. A. Rickabaugh (1998), _Sex and gender: Student projects and exercises_ (Boston: McGraw-Hill), pp. 281–286.

Antisocial personality disorder (ASPD) involves a persistent pattern of violating the rights of others, along with a general lack of conformity to social norms. This pattern is recognized in almost every society (Benjamin, 1993; Robins & Regier, 1991). However, until recently antisocial personality disorder was considered untreatable and therefore often omitted from psychiatric statistics. Changes in categorization practices now suggest slightly higher rates of mental illness among men over the lifetime: 36% for men versus 30% for women (Prior, 1999).

Two additional factors have brought men more into the spotlight of recent psychiatric statistics. First, hospital beds for psychiatric patients are now relatively rare. Therefore greater priority is given to those who demonstrate behavior that is perceived to be dangerous. In other words, only those patients who seem likely to harm others are likely to be hospitalized. The highest risk for violence is associated with substance abuse and antisocial personality disorder—the very categories in which men predominate (Eronen, Angermeyer, & Schulze, 1998; Hiday, Swartz, Swanson, et al., 1998; Steuve & Link, 1998). Second, over the past two decades the suicide rate among young men has been increasing in most Western countries and there are particularly high suicide rates among men with mental disorders (Kelleher, 1998; Lesage et al., 1994).

Other than research on the risk taking surrounding alcohol and substance abuse, there is actually

---

antisocial personality disorder   Personality disorder characterized by pervasive behavioral pattern of disregard for and violation of rights of others.

little research to document the impact of masculine roles on mental health (Lynch & Kilmartin, 1999; Wisch, Mahalick, Hayes, & Nutt, 1995). Over the next decade, assuming current trends continue, men will become the majority of patients in psychiatric institutions, just as they now predominate in prisons (Prior, 1999).

On the international level, it is very difficult to make comparisons because of the diversity in cultural concepts of disorder and also level of health service delivery. However, there is evidence of an increase in the incidence of depression, especially for men in Africa. There are also increasing reports of conditions related to responses to trauma. Diagnosed cases of schizophrenia appear to be on the decline (Sartorius et al., 1989).

Gay and Lesbian Mental Health

During a time when the idea that a same-sex or bisexual orientation was automatically assumed to signify psychopathology, pioneering researcher Evelyn Hooker dared to challenge that psychiatric and psychological truism (Hooker, 1957). Since then research has consistently demonstrated the absence of any relationship between sexual orientation and psychopathology (Gonsiorek, 1996). Although gay men and lesbians do not want their sexual orientation to be pathologized, the social difficulties they suffer because of their sexual orientation *can* cause significant psychological distress (D'Augelli, 1998). The coming-out process, harassment and threats of violence, family rejection, ambivalent support for establishing and maintaining long-term relationships, and alternative family issues are all lifelong concerns for lesbians and gay men (James, 1998). For example, as a group gays and lesbians have somewhat higher rates of depression, substance abuse, and attempted suicide (Oetjen & Rothblum, 2000). These appear related to social isolation and the internalization of negative stereotypes (Shidlo, 1994). The risk of suicide for lesbian and gay adolescents is three to six times greater than among heterosexual youth (Erwin, 1993). These problems are intensified for gay and lesbian ethnic minority youth (Greene, 1994). For gay men, an additional mental health issue concerns the multiple and continuing losses experienced because of AIDS (Marion, 1996).

Cultural Diversity and Mental Disorder

Culture influences which behaviors are identified as "illness" and which as "willfully antisocial" (take another look at the quotation at the beginning of the chapter). Every culture offers guidance regarding the cause of and the healing for nonnormative behavior, as well as an appropriate healer. Belief systems, value orientations, religious practices, medical practices, social organization, and family structure are all involved in constructing concepts of "mental illness."

Let's examine several examples. Cultures differ regarding the value of personal autonomy versus dependence. The fear of dependency (especially for men) has been labeled a core American value. However, in Japan, certain forms of interpersonal dependence are valued for both men and women (Doi, 1973). Depending on one's culture, highly competitive men may be highly revered or deeply despised. Culture determines whether traits of submissiveness or assertiveness are linked with well-being, especially among women. Members of many Asian groups describe emotional states only in terms of bodily organs (remember the "lonely liver" in Chapter 2?). Members of these societies will express mental or emotional distress by high levels of physical complaints and symptoms (Wing-Foo & Lee-Peng, 1995; Ying, Lee, Tsui, Yeh, & Huang, 2000). A house-bound woman may be labeled as **agoraphobic** in the West but as *virtuous* in some Muslim nations (Guarnaccia, 1997). Do you recall Anna and David's behavior in the opening vignette? In North America, a healthy teenager alone at home with a magazine on a sunny weekend afternoon might seem a little unusual. David's authoritative commands to Anna would strike most of us as nonnormative and perhaps abusive. Anna's response to her brother certainly seems unusual. Yet if Anna were a first-generation Egyptian-American daughter of devout Muslims, or the daughter of recent Korean immigrants, her behavior would be both appropriate and commendable. Her obedience to her eldest brother would be in keeping with the family norms of both of these ethnic groups. Her behavior would not indicate poor self-esteem or depression-induced passivity. David, too, was behaving within acceptable family norms for both these ethnic groups.

---

agoraphobia **Intense and irrational fear of not being able to escape a public situation.**

However, if Anna were African American or third-generation Japanese-American, her behavior would seem pathological within her cultural context. How would David's behavior be evaluated within your ethnic group or an ethnic group with which you are familiar?

However, in virtually all societies certain acute or chronic breakdowns in functioning have been identified. These more or less universally identified illnesses include what Western psychiatry labels *schizophrenia, bipolar disorder, major depression*, and *obsessive-compulsive disorder*, but these are not universal labels or classifications (Lefley, 1999). For example, among the Inuit of northern Quebec Province, four classes of disorders are recognized: epilepsy, dissociative symptoms, depression, and a state of agitation and incoherent behavior that seems equivalent to schizophrenia (Kirmayer, Fletcher, & Boothroyd, 1997).

Culture-Bound Syndromes

Although some syndromes of mental disorder may be universal, there are also some seemingly unique syndromes found only in specific cultural settings (Hughes & Wintrob, 1996). As you read about these "culture-bound" syndromes (Yap, 1967, 1974), consider their gender-related components.

Nervios (ataquée de nervios). Nervios is a condition experienced mainly by women in Latino societies. Symptoms include uncontrollable screaming, frequent crying, dizziness, headache, fatigue, weakness, and stomach problems, as well as feelings of worry, anger, and sadness. Chronic domestic problems seem to be the precipitating factor. The symptoms resemble those of panic attacks, but some features are different. *Ataqués* are usually provoked by an upsetting event, but panic attacks occur in situations that are not inherently upsetting. *Ataqués* also lack the acute fear of future attacks that is a hallmark of panic attacks. Researchers note that *ataqués* allow a loss of impulse control and the expression of rage. These are normally prohibited for Latinas (Guarnaccia, Rivera, Franco, & Neighbors, 1996).

Dhat Syndrome. In some Asian cultures, there is a preoccupation with semen loss (*dhat* syndrome). Semen preservation is considered a guarantee of health,

longevity, and power. In some communities, nocturnal emissions may lead to severe anxiety, hypochondriasis, and erectile difficulty. A specific fear is that semen is mixing with urine. It is associated with mood disorder and primarily affects young unmarried men in cultures that discourage premarital sexual activity (D'Ardenne, 1996).

Koro (genital retraction syndrome, or Suoyang). This mental disorder is characterized by a man's belief that his penis is retracting into his abdomen and death will ensue because of this. It occurs mainly in mainland China, but it is also found among South African Zulu and Greek Cypriot men. Western clinicians consider it to be an acute anxiety state associated with sexual dysfunction. In China, outbreaks of this condition seem to accompany massive economic or social upheavals (Gang-Ming, Guo-Qian, Li, & Tseng, 1995).

Windigo Psychosis. This condition, affecting mainly men of the Cree Inuit, Algonquin, and Ojibwa Indians of Canada, is characterized by cannibalistic delusions. The sufferer believes he has been transformed into a giant monster that eats humans. This delusion appears derived from tribal mythology about survival in the Arctic (Carson, Butcher, & Coleman, 1988).

Taijin Kyofusho. This condition, *taijin kyofusho*, is unique to the Japanese, especially among adolescents and young adults. It refers to an intense fear of facing or interacting with other people. The fear, sometimes psychotic in intensity, centers on offending or hurting the feelings of others owing to imagined shortcomings within themselves. These shortcomings or flaws may include blushing, making eye contact, or emitting a body odor (Guarnaccia, 1997).

Latah. This occurs mainly among women in Southeast Asia. Those affected break into obscenities and **echolalia** following an event that startles them. They may also follow commands automatically or repetitively imitate another person (Lefley, 1999).

Many of us may find the notion of culture-bound syndromes as exotic and related to the unique preoc-

---

echolalia   **Repetition or echoing of what others say.**

cupations of other societies. It is often more difficult to see certain disorders that are prevalent in Western industrial and postindustrial society as equally culture bound. The conditions commonly known as *premenstrual syndrome (PMS)* may be considered a culture-bound phenomenon, as may eating disorders (Lee, 1996).

Eating Disorders as a Culture-Bound Syndrome

In the West, writings about "fasting girls" date back to the 5th century, and this behavior was viewed as just one pathway in the quest for spiritual piety (Lee, 1996). Over the centuries, several saints, including Joan the Meatless, Christina the Astonishing, and Catherine of Siena, attracted ecclesiastical attention because of their seemingly miraculous ability to live without food. Up through the 12th and 13th century, fasting remained a means for expelling demons, expunging evil thoughts, giving hope, and achieving salvation (Malson, 1997). Thus the social meaning of food, dietary restraint and fasting was quite different in medieval society than in contemporary society. By the 16th century, admiration for "holy anorexia" shifted to vilification when people discovered that those women who survived such fasting actually did consume small amounts of food and liquid (Hepworth, 1999). As you have read, during the 18th century the rise of logical positivism and medical science led to increasing distinctions between "rational man" versus "irrational woman" and "normative man" versus "pathological woman." During the 19th century "inappetency" became a relatively common nervous symptom of women suffering from "hysteria." Cases of emaciation and food refusal seemed to occur in girls and very young adolescents from ages 7 to 16, and this too differs from the typical profile of the contemporary patient diagnosed as eating disordered. The formerly spiritual act of self-starvation became a medicalized phenomenon in 1874 when Dr. William Gull renamed it *anorexia nervosa*. In the absence of an observable, physical cause, self-starvation became a concern of psychiatry. Freud's view of anorexia was that the "nutritional instinct" was impaired because the person could not accept her sexual impulses (Freud, 1933). For Freud and his followers, extreme thinness symbolized the rejection of womanhood and femininity. Loss of feminine body shape and the ces-

sation of menstrual periods seemed to confirm this for the psychoanalyst.

During the 1930s, self-starvation was labeled Simmonds disease and misattributed to a pituitary dysfunction. In the 1940s, psychological explanations for anorexia were again in favor. During the 1950s, anorexics were exposed to some of the excesses of psychiatry such as electroconvulsive shock treatments and forced feedings. Hilde Bruch (1978) and Salvador Minuchin (Minuchin, Rosman, & Baker, 1978) hypothesized a relationship between family dysfunction and anorexia. Pathological mothers were targeted as the causal agent for the disorder. Fathers were invisible in this literature, as was any analysis of the family as a patriarchal structure (Hepworth, 1999). For the feminist therapist, anorexia is related to women's subordinate social position, the expression of anger, and the need for control (Katzman, Weiss, & Wolchik, 1986).

Current research literature on anorexia emphasizes intestinal, hypothalamic, endocrinal, neurological, and even genetic predispositions (see Figure 12.1). Yet it is still uncertain whether physiological signs and symptoms precede or follow anorexic behavior (Walsh & Devlin, 1998). Anorexia has also been described as an affective disorder, a cognitive dysfunction, and as a distortion in body image (Martz, Handley, & Eisler, 1995; Striegel-Moore & Cachelin, 1999). Both anorexia and bulimia are viewed as related to familial pathology, especially to sexual abuse during childhood, but the findings regarding this association are inconclusive (DeGroot & Rodin, 1999; Figueroa, Silk, Hutch & Lohr, 1997).

What is clear is that cultural ideals and stereotypes for women's bodies in the West are getting thinner and thinner. North American society seems obsessed with weight and supports an entire weight loss industry, aimed mainly at women. The steep rise in the number of diet-focused books and articles in women-oriented publications and programs as well as the increasingly unrealistic body ideals presented in the media all contribute to the problem.

Medical experts agree that anorexia is a serious disorder, estimated to affect between 0.5% to 1% of adolescent women. The associated fatality rate is about 5% (Walsh & Devlin, 1998). Serious physical changes occur in anorexics, including amenorrhea (cessation of menstruation), hypothermia, cardiac

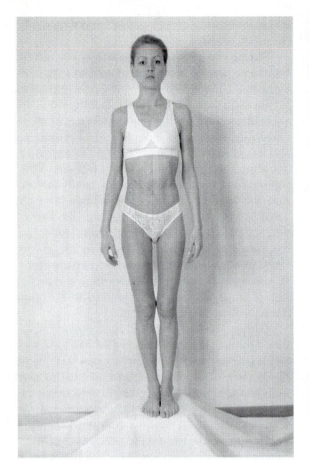 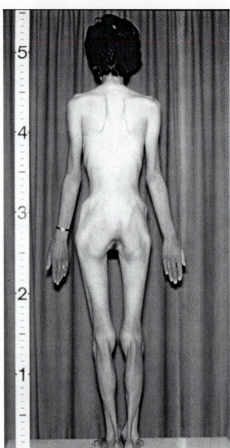

FIGURE 12.1   Anorexia damages multiple organ systems in the body yet is characterized by persistent distortions of body image.

abnormalities, hypotension, edema, lanugo (a fine covering of body hair), and various metabolic changes. About 95% of those diagnosed with anorexia are girls and women, and rates of anorexia and bulimia have increased since the 1960s. The prevalence of eating disorders is believed to be higher in some groups, such as ballet dancers, models, actresses, and so on. Anorexia and bulimia are reported to be more common among private school students, the professional and upper classes, and among white women. Eating disorders are a complex phenomenon and seem to be related to cultural definitions of femininity, perfectionism, body image, and individual control issues.

An established body of research suggests that African Americans have a greater tolerance for diversity of body type and shape, and that African-American women value physical traits other than thinness (Parker, 1995). Anorexic and bulimic symptoms were traditionally rare among African Americans, but when they did occur they were correlated with conflicted ethnic identity (Harris & Kuba, 1997). However, more recent studies found significant correlations among body mass, body dissatisfaction, low self-esteem, and bulimic symptoms among African-American women (Lester & Petrie, 1998).

Up until recently, eating disorders were assumed to be rare outside of North America, western Europe, and Australasia, and among *white* South Africans. A large sample of South African students were recently surveyed regarding their eating attitudes and behaviors. A comparable percentage of both black and white female students had scores within the clinical range on several eating disorder scales (Le Grange, Telch, & Tibbs, 1998). These researchers concluded that the risk of eating disorders increases in developing nations as Western gender ideals proliferate. Moreover, there are growing reports of eating disorders in Hong Kong, China, Taiwan, Malaysia, India, Singapore, and Japan (Lee,1996; Reuters Medical News, 2001e). Eating disorders found in nonindustrialized nations usually occur among the daughters of urban entrepreneurs and the professional elite (Littlewood, 1995).

A paradoxical feature of eating disorders is that many of the factors that usually protect against psychopathology actually become risk factors. For example, social class is usually inversely related to the risk for mental illness, but eating disorders are more common among middle- and upper-class women. Higher intelligence is usually more protective, but eating disorders are especially prevalent among college students. Emotional intelligence generally facilitates the rejection of stereotypes, but the eating disordered blindly pursue ideal body stereotypes. The factors that *do* seem to protect from eating disorders include positive self-regard, high self-esteem, good coping skills, a sense of self-efficacy, social support, identification with feminist values, and a strong racial identity (Murnen & Smolak, 1997; Rogers, Fesnick, Mitchell, & Blum, 1997; Snyder & Hasbrouck, 1996).

Men and Eating Disorders

The cultural pressures for female thinness extend to white men as well. In one study, white college men believed they would be ridiculed if they dated women who were heavier than the ideal body size. The black men surveyed did not express such concerns (Powell & Kahn, 1995).

When women and men with binge eating disorders were compared, they did not differ on measures of eating disturbance, shape and weight concerns, interpersonal problems, or self-esteem. However, more men met the criteria for at least one other psychiatric diagnosis, and more men had a lifetime diagnosis of substance dependence. Women reported binge eating

in response to negative emotions, especially anxiety, anger and frustration, and depression. Men reported no specific triggers for bingeing (Tanofsky, Wilfley, Spunnell, Welch, & Brownell, 1997).

Studies of boys and men with eating disorders are rare. In one archival study of eating-disordered men in the United States, 46% (62) of the sample were bulimic, 22% (30) were anorexic, and 32% (43) met the criteria for eating disorder "not otherwise specified." Co-morbid psychiatric disorders such as depression (54%), substance abuse (37%), and personality disorder (26%) were common. A substantial proportion of these men were in "high-risk" occupations such as modeling or acting. Sexual orientation was also a salient issue. Of the bulimic patients, 42% were identified as either homosexual or bisexual, and 58% were identified as asexual. Homosexuality or bisexuality seems to be a risk factor for eating disordered men, especially bulimics (Anderson, 1999; Carlat, Camargo, & Herzog, 1997).

Disorders of Gender

In Western culture, individuals who experience a profound incongruity between their anatomical sex and their *core gender identity* (inner sense of oneself as a man or woman) are labeled as suffering from a mental disorder—namely, *gender identity disorder* (or gender dysphoria) (American Psychiatric Association, 1994). Gender-dysphoric individuals do not experience themselves as disturbed, but rather as in need of a "correction" in their assigned gender and gender roles (Griggs, 1998). In other cultures, the violation of gender boundaries by dressing and adopting the social roles and public identity of the other gender may have quite different social meanings. For example, among many Native American tribes, the "two-spirit person" served as a mediator in disputes between men and women and also as an intermediary between the physical and spiritual worlds (L. E. Brown, 1997). In American Samoa, the *fa'afafine* view themselves as women and have a tradition of elaborate and public beauty contests. They typically pursue traditional women's jobs and customarily provide off-color entertainment at bridal showers and weddings (Mageo, 1992). Samoan society regards the *fa'afafine* as a third gender (Poosa, 1992).

Transgenderism

Gender-dysphoric individuals typically report a life-long and deeply held feeling that some bodily error has been made—that they should have been born as a member of the other sex. They may experience revulsion at their own genitals or secondary sex characteristics, and have recurrent fantasies about engaging in behaviors associated with the other gender (Morris, 1974). Estimates of the prevalence of gender identity disorder vary greatly, but typical estimates are that 1 in 30,000 men and 1 in 100,000 women are gender dysphoric to varying degrees (American Psychiatric Association, 1994). It is unclear why this condition is more prevalent among males, but at least one study found more extreme cross-gender behavior among the girls who were referred to treatment (Zucker, Bradley, & Sanikhani, 1997).

Some gender-dysphoric individuals manage to live out the conventional roles congruent with their original gender assignment. However, if and when discomfort about their anatomic sex and social identity becomes unbearable, gender-dysphoric individuals may go to great lengths to attempt to live as a member of their self-perceived true gender. Some may don the clothing and ornamentation of the other gender, at first in private and then in public. Wearing the clothing associated with the other gender typically elicits feelings of comfort, calmness, and a sense of inherent "rightness." Other gender-dysphoric individuals may seek hormonal supplements to give their bodies the contours and secondary sexual characteristics of the other sex (breasts or facial hair). They may practice the socially prescribed postures, gestures, and vocal qualities of the other gender, and thus become masters of the acceptable public performance of their preferred gender. If sufficiently affluent and well motivated, many seek sex reassignment surgery. (See Figure 12.2.) But not all who seek gender reassignment pursue genital surgery for sex reassignment (Griggs, 1998). They are satisfied to have the social identity and bodily contours of the "right gender" but without the genital anatomy that usually goes with that social identity.

The most comprehensive studies of transsexuals come from the Netherlands (Cohen, deRuiter, Ringelberg, & Cohen-Kettenis, 1997). The Dutch health services reimburse the cost of sex reassignment surgery, and individuals can assume a new legal identity after completing the surgery and treatment. Researchers there claim a higher prevalence of **transsexualism** (1 in 12,000 men and 1 in 30,000 women). Only Singapore has higher recorded rates. Interestingly, in central and eastern Europe the sex ratio for those identified as gender dysphoric is actually reversed, but no reasons for this difference has been identified (Prior, 1999).

The origins or causes of gender dysphoria are unknown. For the vast majority of such individuals, chromosomal, hormonal, and anatomical features are all typical. Nor is the condition associated with other psychiatric conditions. Tests of various biological and psychological hypotheses regarding the cause of this phenomenon have produced inconclusive results (Green, 2000).

The complex process of gender reassignment begins with gradually adopting the dress, mannerisms, and general lifestyle of the desired gender. A specially trained counselor may aid in this part of the transition. The next step is hormone therapy. The candidate for reassignment must live successfully for about a year as a member of the other gender. Many gender-dysphoric individuals are satisfied with finally having their inner sense of self confirmed by their outward appearance and interactions with others. Others actively seek the final step in the reassignment process, surgical intervention to reconstruct the genitals (Brown & Rounsley, 1996).

Transvestism

Transvestism is the wearing of clothing and ornamentation associated with the other gender. Historically, female cross-dressing was apparently more common, but male cross-dressing currently receives more attention (Bullough & Bullough, 1993). Depending on the culture, this boundary violation can have spiritual, entertainment, or artistic significance. Even within Western societies, individuals engage in cross-dressing for a variety of reasons. The male female impersonator or *drag queen* has long been a staple of entertainment within the gay male subculture. Within

---

transsexualism **Extremely high level of gender dysphoria; moves the individual to seek surgical intervention for the purpose of sex reassignment.**

(a)

(b)

FIGURE 12.2 (a) Computer scientist Lynn Conway, a postoperative transsexual woman who underwent sex reassignment in 1968 (http://www.lynnconway.com). (b) Leslie Feinberg, activist, writer, and public speaker in the transgender movement (http://www.transgenderwarrior.org). Rather than disturbed or disordered, transgendered individuals view themselves as having a potentially correctible condition. Life as a member of their self-perceived gender is experienced as a desirable solution to an error of gender assignment.

mainstream society, the cross-dressed comedian is always sure to get laughs.

It is difficult to get a sense of the prevalence of this behavior. Cross-dressing heterosexual men come to the attention of mental health professionals when their partners discover their interests. It is difficult to ascertain whether there is any overt disturbance in functioning or personality among male cross-dressers.

Psychologists and psychiatrists have been concerned with those men for whom seeing, touching, and wearing articles of women's clothing results in sexual arousal. In contrast to the gender-dysphoric individual for whom cross-dressing is calming and self-confirming, the *fetishistic transvestite* uses articles of women's clothing to produce orgasm through masturbation. The person prefers clothing over contact or interaction with an actual sexual partner (Brown, 1995).

Gender Issues in Other Disorders

There are several classes of mental disorder in which there is a significant gender differential. An examination of these disorders allows a glimpse at the interaction among biological, psychological, and social factors.

Affective Disorders

The term *affect* refers to one's mood or emotion as observed or inferred by another person. Affective disorders involve an apparent disturbance of mood, either in the direction of euphoria and high activity (mania) or toward sadness and low activity (depression). Depression, which is among the most common of all psychiatric disorders, has been called "the common cold of psychiatry." Between 8% and 18% of the general population experience at least one major depressive episode over a lifetime. **Bipolar illness** is equally prevalent in both genders, but the most common types of depression (major depression and dysthymia), are at least twice as common among women (Nolen-Hoeksema, 2001; Schraedley, Gotlib, & Hayward, 1999). Cross-national studies suggest a gender differential in depressive illness from 2:1 to 4:1, depending on the sample and assessment technique (Culbertson, 1997; Gater, Tansella, Korten, Tiemans, et al., 1997). Explanations for this differential must include both psychological and physiological factors.

The biological underpinnings of depression are relatively well understood today. They include a genetic proclivity, hormonal influences (especially cortisol, thyroid, and estrogen), and neurotransmitter disturbances (especially norepinephrine, serotonin, dopamine acetylcholine, and the neuropeptides) (Young & Korszun, 1999). However, these neuroendocrine responses are invariably precipitated by life events. Depression is most often associated with prolonged and intense feelings of sadness and dejection. These emotions are accompanied by feelings of loss, helplessness, powerlessness, and self-reproach. For many severely depressed individuals, something seems to "click" in the brain and general despondency becomes true depression (a physical state) that requires medical intervention. Depression also affects bodily systems and the immune system, making one more vulnerable to dysfunction and disease (Healy, 1995).

Gender differentials in depression begin at adolescence (Compas, Oppedisano, Connor, Gerhardt, et al., 1997; Hankin, Abramson, Moffitt, & Silva, 1998; Nolen-Hoeksema & Girgus, 1994). In a survey of a large, ethnically diverse sample of adolescents, girls reported higher levels of depressive symptoms. Physical and sexual abuse are strongly linked with depression for both boys and girls, with an even stronger association among boys (Schraedley et al., 1999). A comparable multiethnic study found higher depression scores among girls with early pubertal development and among boys with later development. Latinos reported more depressive symptoms than any other group, regardless of socioeconomic status. The largest gender differential in depressed mood was among whites, with white males having the lowest scores of any group (Siegel et al., 1998).

Critical Thinking Challenge

Do you tend to attribute the increase in rates of depressive symptoms among adolescent women to the physiological changes of puberty, or to the psychosocial pressures that young women experience? To something else? To what do you attribute the strong depression differential between white women and men? Explain your reasoning.

An APA task force on depression attributed women's greater risk for depression to socioeconomic, biological, and emotional variables. Personality factors, certain cognitive styles, and a lack of problem-solving strategies were all associated with depressive states. Major contributing factors included sexual and physical abuse. Poverty too was identified as a "pathway to depression." Compared to men, women are more likely to experience sexual harassment, stalking, sexual assault, domestic violence, and other sexist events. These experiences also contribute to higher rates of depression and related disorders (Gold, Lucenko, Elhai, Swingle, & Sellers, 1999; Klonoff, Landrine, & Campbell, 2000; Lenhart, 1996). The general risk factors for depression are being female, low socioeconomic status, family history, loss, physical illness, and old age (Gladstone, Kaslow, Seeley, & Lewisohn, 1997; Thoits, 1994/1995).

The task force also suggested that men's depression was masked by their use of alcohol and illegal drugs. When distressed, men are more likely to engage in reckless and risky behavior, substance abuse, casual sex, or criminal behavior. This eliminates them from clinical statistics and concentrates them in social deviance or crime statistics. Masculine distress is also highly associated with the patterns of physical illness and early mortality described in the previous chapter (Vaillant, 1998). Whereas women internalize

---

bipolar disorder   Affective disorder characterized by recurrent cycles of mania alternating with depression.

their feelings more and blame themselves for incompetence or failure, men tend to blame others for their difficulties, which leads to anger and acting out (A. J. Clark, 1998; Real, 1997).

In spite of the difficulty involved in developing assessment instruments that work across cultures, the gender differential regarding adult depression has been confirmed cross-nationally (United States, Sweden, Germany, Canada, New Zealand, Puerto Rico, and Korea). However, such studies have also found depression levels to be rising among young men (Klermon & Weissman, 1989; Weissman, Bland, Joyce, Newman, Wells, & Wittchen, 1993).

Masculinity and Affect. Many psychological theories emphasize the importance of emotional self-awareness and emotional expression in healthy functioning. However, traditional masculine socialization encourages men to devalue and restrict their emotional experience (Wisch et al., 1995). The end result of this socialization can resemble descriptions of *alexithymia*. This is a condition characterized by unawareness of feelings, difficulty describing feelings, a concrete and reality-based cognitive style, and an impoverished emotional and fantasy life. The *alexithymia* construct originally referred to the emotion-related deficits encountered among stroke patients. However, the construct has recently been applied to "normals." Mild levels of these characteristics have been found in Canadian college men (Levant, 1996). A study of American college men found that men reporting greater gender role conflict also acknowledged greater levels of alexithymia and a more intense fear of intimacy (Fischer & Good, 1997). These authors and others have noted that the verbal expression of feelings that is required in "talk" therapy may represent a sociocultural bias that favors women (Campbell, 1996).

Critical Thinking Challenge

Traditional feminine socialization encourages high levels of emotional self-awareness and the expression of particular feelings. When this is exaggerated, a "diagnosis" is declared, requiring intervention (Kaplan, 1983, referring to the DSM-III). Traditional masculine socialization encourages emotional unawareness and the lack of expression of particular feelings. When this is exaggerated, "normality" is declared. Does this evaluation have merit?

Substance Use Disorders

Substance use disorders include both abuse of and dependence on alcohol, legal drugs, and illegal drugs. Take a look at Table 12.2 to examine the gender differential in substance abuse patterns. Traditional gender role construction both normalizes and encourages alcohol abuse among men, while condemning all substance abuse among women (Gomberg, 1993). Alcohol abuse begins earlier, and remains three to six times more common in men. Across all ethnic groups and at all ages, men exceed women in rates of drinking, heavy drinking, and alcohol-related disorders (Miller & Cervantes, 1997; Nelson, Heath, & Kessler, 1998). Both alcohol abuse and binge drinking are more common among European-Americans than among members of ethnic minorities (Office of Applied Alcohol Studies, 1997). At any one time, alcoholics occupy about half the psychiatric hospital beds in the United States (Brooks & Silverstein, 1995).

Studies of alcohol's impact on behavior go all the way back to 1880 but there was little research on women and alcohol until the 1970s. Much of this differential in attention was prompted by the higher prevalence of alcoholism among men and also the social problems associated with men's drinking (crime, interpersonal violence, accidents, and work problems). Also, more men alcoholics were accessible for study in prisons and veterans' hospitals. Women's

TABLE 12.2   *Gender Ratios for Substance Abuse–Related Disorders*

Disorder	Gender Ratio
Alcoholism	M > W
Amphetamine	M > W
Caffeine	M > W
Marijuana	M > W
Cocaine	M = W
Hallucinogens	M > W
Inhalant	M > W
Nicotine	M > W
Opioids	M > W
Phencyclidine (PCP, angel dust)	M > W
Sedatives, hypnotics, antianxiety, etc.	W > M
Polysubstance	?

Source: Adapted from C. M. Hartung & T. A. Widiger. (1998). Gender differences in the diagnosis of mental disorders: Conclusions and controversies of the DSM-IV, *Psychological Bulletin. 123*(2), 260–278.

drinking was generally more invisible and of concern only when it affected their wife and mother roles. During the 1970s, public interest in women's alcohol abuse arose in response to concern over fetal alcohol syndrome as a distinctive problem in women's alcohol abuse (Wilsnack, 1995).

There is a complex pattern of gender differences among substance abusers. Regarding psychiatric comorbidity, antisocial personality is more common among men alcoholics whereas depression is more common among women alcoholics (Clark, Pollack, Bukstein, Mezzich, Bromberger, & Donovan, 1997; Schutte, Hearst, & Moos, 1997). Alcoholic men are more likely to be regularly employed. Multiple substance abuse and the abuse of prescription drugs may be more common among women (Wechsberg, Craddock, & Hubbard, 1998). Substance-abusing men are much less likely to live with a substance-abusing partner than are similar women (Mendelson & Mello, 1998).

Physiological factors contribute to the higher incidence of alcohol dependence among men. Androgens enhance the activity of a particular liver enzyme that helps eliminate alcohol. Thus men are less susceptible to the immediate subjective negative consequences of alcohol, and this favors earlier development of dependence. This enzyme is less active in women, discouraging heavy drinking. However, this same enzyme allows greater absorption, and therefore women run a greater risk of alcohol toxicity. Alcoholic women shorten their lives by 15 years, and their death rate is five times that of general population of women. Alcoholic men's death rate is three times that of the general population of men (Graham, Wilsnack, Dawson, & Vogeltanz, 1998).

Stress reduction has long been a popular explanation for alcohol abuse. The traditionally masculine coping styles that center on denial of psychological pain, avoidance of certain feelings, and acting-out behavior is also highly associated with heavier drinking (Lash, Copenhaver, & Eisler, 1998; McCreary et al., 1999). Alcohol abuse among men may be usefully considered a form of self-medication (Cooper, Russell, Skinner, Frone, & Mudar, 1992). Heavy drinking in one's social group ("drinking buddies") is also an important factor in the development of alcohol problems (Brooks & Silverstein, 1995). On col-

lege campuses, binge drinking, and other alcohol-related rituals are a particular issue for young men (Smith & Mathews, 1997). For both women and men physical and sexual victimization during childhood is highly predictive of adult substance abuse (Gold et al., 1999). Across ethnic minority groups, there is a reliable relationship among alcohol, the likelihood of violence and various types of victimization in adulthood (Friedman, Kramer, Kreisher, & Granick, 1996; Novins, Beals, Shone, & Manson, 1996).

Most cocaine-dependent individuals have a family history of alcohol dependence, as do most **opioid** abusers. Opioid users of both genders are seven times more likely to have psychiatric comorbidity, especially mood disorders. Because substance abuse, especially of illegal substances, is such a violation of the feminine gender role, it has been hypothesized that women substance abusers are more psychiatrically disturbed, but the relevant evidence is inconclusive (Luthar, Cushing, & Rounsaville, 1996). Women more often report initiating heroin use to decrease pain or because a partner used. Men report initiating heroin use because of curiosity or to gain peer acceptance. Other reasons given for drug use by both men and women include depression, feeling unsociable, family and job pressures, and health problems. Men more frequently used alcohol or marijuana before narcotic use. The prognosis for opioid dependence is poor, but women more often pursue psychological help for these problems (Chatham, Hiller, Rowan-Szal, Joe, & Simpson, 1999).

Treatment. Information on gender and treatment outcomes for substance abuse is scarce, and it is uncertain whether treatment programs designed specifically for women have a better success rate than do traditional mixed programs (Greenfield, 1996). Although the proportion of women in alcohol treatment programs has increased in recent years, the general ratio remains about 10 men to 1 woman. Compared to men, women have lower retention and success rates in federal drug treatment programs, but this may stem from the male-oriented nature of such programs (Greenfield, 1996).

---

opioids   Narcotic substances, including opium, heroin, methadone, and so on.

Anxiety Disorders

Women, especially younger women, appear more prone to essentially all anxiety disorders, and this gender differential emerges early in life (Horwath & Weissman, 1997; Lewisohn, Gotlib, Lewisohn, Seeley, et al., 1998). Although phobic objects tend to be the same for both genders, about 70% of those affected by phobias are women. **Simple phobia** is twice as common among women, and agoraphobia occurs in 8% of women and 3% of men. Within the United States, panic disorder occurs in 20 in 1,000 women and about 8 in 1,000 men. There are somewhat higher rates among African Americans. Generalized anxiety disorder is also more common in women, as is posttraumatic stress disorder. Obsessive compulsive disorder is generally higher in women, but when gender comparisons were controlled for marital status, employment status, job status, ethnicity, and age, prevalence rates were equalized (Horwath & Weissman, 1997). Although social phobia has a greater lifetime prevalence among women, more men seek treatment for this condition (Weinstock, 1999).

The rate for anxiety disorders varies widely across nations, from 0.7 in Australia to 4.5 in London and 4.8 in Santander, Spain (Horwath & Weissman, 1997). Icelandic researchers found that phobia (not depression) was the most commonly reported psychopathological disorder among the women of that nation. For men, alcohol abuse was most common, then phobias, followed by drug abuse. Divorced or separated individuals were at greater risk, as were women homemakers, and disabled or unemployed persons (Arnarson, Gudmundsdottir, & Boyle, 1998).

Antisocial Personality Disorder

Personality disorders are defined as inflexible, long-standing maladaptive traits that significantly impair functioning in an individual's personal or social life (American Psychiatric Association, 1994). The person diagnosed with antisocial personality disorder (ASPD) demonstrates a persistent pattern of "reckless disregard for the rights and feelings of others" (Benjamin, 1993, p. 193). Most individuals who engage in "antisocial" behaviors are not diagnosable as ASPD. The construct of antisocial personality disorder refers to a chronic pattern of behavior that is amoral, im-

pulsive, and socially deviant (Sutker, Bugg, & West, 1993). There is no apparent cognitive or affective loss or disruption in ASPD. Terms such as *irresponsibility, emotional detachment, irritability, aggressiveness, impulsivity, sexual promiscuity,* and *lack of remorse* are the characteristic descriptors for this diagnostic category. *Impulsive anger, hostility, cunning, interpersonal antagonism, belligerence,* as well as the willingness and ability to "con" others in relationships are also typical descriptors. These individuals exhibit a shallow emotional style and have no lasting ties or commitments. They tend to avoid softer emotions such as warmth or intimacy, viewing them as signs of weakness (Sperry & Mosak, 1993).

A diagnosis of antisocial personality disorder (ASPD) appears to be applicable to about 3% of men in the general population and 1% of women (Kaylor, 1999). Individuals who manifest ASPD are believed to be responsible for an inordinate amount of crime, violence, and social distress. In the industrial and postindustrial West, the strong value placed on individualism and patriarchy is believed to contribute to the relatively high prevalence of this condition (Kaylor, 1999).

Critical Thinking Challenge

Impaired social, cognitive, and affective functioning, as well as distress are the hallmark characteristics of mental disorders. ASPD has *none* of those characteristics. So how could ASPD be considered a mental disorder (Benjamin, 1993)?

The notion of ASPD has been criticized as "moral judgment masquerading as a clinical diagnosis" (Blackburn, 1988) and also as a "wastebasket" and "myth." Yet it is highly researched and repeatedly described with great consistency (Sutker et al., 1993). For example, two hundred years ago Pinel (1801/1997) described a disorder characterized by aberrant affect and impulsive rage, but with no deficit in reasoning. Later in the 19th century, the term "moral insanity" was used to summarize the central features of ASPD (Meyer, 1993). Cleckley (1941) outlined the basic characteristics of ASPD, using descriptors such

---

simple phobia **Intense and irrational fear of a specific object or event (spiders, public speaking, and so forth).**

as "superficial charm," "absence of nervousness," "lack of remorse," "lack of insight," "unreliability," "untruthfulness," "impersonal sex life," and "aimlessness in life." Although many people with ASPD are in prisons, the condition is more often associated with recurrent job troubles, violence, multiple moving traffic offenses, and severe marital problems. In one epidemiological sample, of those evaluated as demonstrating ASPD 47% had two or more arrests (Robins & Regier, 1991). The core features of ASPD may also be characteristic of hard-driving and ambitious businesspeople, politicians, and other professionals. Although past thinking has made ASPD synonymous with criminality, there may be greater overlap with substance abuse. Across ethnic groups, a diagnosis of ASPD is most associated with masculine gender, younger age, less education, and lower socioeconomic status.

Diagnoses of antisocial personality are made much more often among men, perhaps at a ratio of 6:1 (Sperry & Mosak, 1993). ASPD is reliably associated with low levels of anxiety, high need for stimulation, and frequent sensation seeking. Individuals diagnosed with ASPD appear devoted to the pursuit of exciting, dangerous, and reckless activities that produce high levels of **autonomic arousal** (Quay, 1993; Raine, Lenez, Bihrle, LaCasse, & Coletti, 2000)

ASPD may be underdiagnosed among women. Some clinical researchers speculate that histrionic and antisocial personalities constitute sex-typed versions of the same condition, and that ASPD is more readily seen among men because it is congruent with the masculine role (Sutker et al., 1993). Given any proclivity for this condition, traditional masculine gender role socialization seems to facilitate its development. Women may act out their antisocial proclivities with sexual promiscuity, child neglect, substance abuse, and petty crimes (Pajer, 1998; Widiger, 1998).

In the past, ASPD was hypothesized to be associated with excess serum testosterone, but research studies have been inconclusive (Aromaki, Lindman, & Erikson, 1999). The classic hypothesis regarding the physiological foundations of ASPD is its association with very low levels of autonomic arousal. This low reactivity has been thought to explain some of the prominent features of ASPD: resistance to punishment, high sensation seeking, risk taking, sexual promiscuity, and the lack of remorse or guilt. Recent physiological studies have confirmed the reduced autonomic activity and revealed prefrontal and frontal lobe dysfunctions but this evidence is not strong (Raine et al., 2000).

Schizophrenia

Early in the 20th century, Emil Kraepelin (1919) first labeled and categorized the severe mental illnesses now collectively termed *schizophrenia*, and he quickly observed gender differences in the manifestation and course of the disorder. Nevertheless, until the 1990s most studies of schizophrenia were conducted on male patients (Hartung & Widiger, 1998). Even today, no gender distinctions are made in the treatment guidelines for schizophrenia (Seeman, 2000). One of the early theories regarding the causes of schizophrenia focused on pathological interactions between mother and child (Bateson, Jackson, Haley, & Weakland, 1956; Jackson & Weakland, 1959). This theory minimized the impact of fathers and other environmental influences. Feminists cited the widespread acceptance of this approach as a prime example of the tradition of the mother blaming that was all too common in the history of psychiatry and clinical psychology. Although the precise origins of schizophrenia remain a mystery, there is strong and reliable evidence that schizophrenia has an organic basis. Schizophrenia is now viewed as a neurodevelopmental disorder that probably begins at conception and results from a combination of genetic impairment, prenatal infection, trauma, and stress. These factors affect many aspects of fetal neural development, and the impact is seen 15 to 30 years later in psychotic behavior (Walkup & Gallagher, 1999). An overview of current findings regarding the relationship between gender and schizophrenia provides a number of insights.

There is reliable evidence that the neuroanatomical changes accompanying schizophrenia vary according to sex. For example, schizophrenic men were found to exhibit significantly less cerebral asymmetry (differences between the left and right hemispheres), compared to control participants, whereas schizo-

---

autonomic arousal   Part of nervous system that controls involuntary functions such as heart rate, glands, and so on. Fear-inducing stimuli normally elicit strong autonomic arousal.

phrenic women exhibited significantly more asymmetry. Other studies of schizophrenic men reveal various temporal lobe differences in comparison to both normals and schizophrenic women (Reite, Sheeder, Teale, et al., 1997; Rojas, Teale, Sheeder, et al., 1997). Although most studies find decreased cortical gray matter and enlarged ventricles among schizophrenics of both genders, the effect is greater among affected men. However, a relatively recent study found no sex differences in this relatively well-known neuroanatomical phenomenon (Lauriello et al., 1997).

Although studies of schizophrenia in the West reliably demonstrate an earlier onset among men, Chinese researchers consistently find an earlier age of onset among affected women. This may be attributable to the pattern of early marriage in China, which generally protects men from diagnoses of mental illness (Lieberman et al., 1996; Lieberman & Fisher, 1999).

Although schizophrenia is milder in women during the first decade, symptoms increase in severity later on. Younger schizophrenic women respond more quickly and more thoroughly to antipsychotic medications. Women more often demonstrate adverse effects to antipsychotic drugs (Lindamer & Jeste, 1999). In men, symptoms tend to lessen in severity during the later years. This difference has been attributed to sex differences in age-related changes in the action of certain neurotransmitters (Castle, Sham, & Murray, 1998, in a British sample; Lindamer, Lohr, Harris, & Jeste, 1997, in an American sample).

In general, women diagnosed as schizophrenic demonstrate better functioning both before and after diagnosis and treatment. Schizophrenic women are more likely to marry, to have children, and to maintain social relationships both before and after onset than are comparable men (Rasanen et al., 1999, in a Finnish sample; Torgalsboen, 1999, in a Norwegian sample).

Schizophrenic women generally have a more benign course, with fewer hospitalizations and lower risk of suicide. It is uncertain whether these effects are due to greater treatment compliance by women patients or to certain neuroendocrine effects (Klinkenberg & Calsyn, 1998). Schizophrenic men have more negative symptoms (behavioral deficits, such as social withdrawal), whereas women tend to have more positive symptoms (behavioral excesses such as hallucinations) (Haas & Garrett, 1998; Harrison, Croudace, Mason, Glazebrook, & Medley, 1996).

Conclusions

The traditional Western notion of separation between the physical and the mental has become less and less useful as the physiological underpinnings of mental disorders are uncovered. The traditional Western notion of masculine strength of mind and feminine weakness of mind is unsupported by the facts of psychiatric impairment. Psychopathology emerges as a result of interaction among biological, environmental, cultural, and individual factors. Some types of psychopathology are recognized by all human societies. However, the form and prevalence of many types of psychopathology are heavily influenced by gender and culture. In the industrialized West, each gender predominates in some diagnostic categories of psychopathology and these categories appear related to socially constructed gender norms.

Summary

◆ Two notions have influenced traditional thinking about gender, mental health, and mental illness. The first was the supposed contrast between the rational man versus the irrational woman. The second was the notion that women's minds and mental functioning were totally subordinated to their reproductive functions.

◆ Traditional gender biases in the detection and diagnosis of psychopathology have declined, but the biases and stresses surrounding ethnicity, minority status, and poverty appear to persist in a variety of cultures.

◆ The behaviors designated as psychopathological have varied over time. The stereotype of women's greater vulnerability to psychopathology continues for a number of reasons, but this is changing as the number of men classified as having significant psychiatric impairment increases.

◆ Some patterns of behavior are universally recognized as disordered, whereas certain other patterns of behavior may be designated as culture-bound syndromes. Eating disorders, especially anorexia, may be usefully viewed as a culture-bound syndrome.

◆ Most forms of depression are at least twice as prevalent among women, and this has been attributed to physiological, social, and individual factors. Traditional feminine gender norms facilitate high affect, high self-awareness, and a more ruminative cognitive style.

◆ Substance abuse is about five to six times more prevalent among men, and has been attributed physiological, social, and individual factors. Traditional masculine gender norms facilitate denial, avoidance, and a more active, distracting cognitive style.

◆ Women predominate in almost all anxiety disorders, but the rates of anxiety disorders vary across nations.

◆ Men predominate in antisocial personality disorder, although gender bias may be at work here.

◆ There are significant gender variations in the findings surrounding schizophrenia. These include neuroanatomical differences, as well as differential developmental and behavioral patterns.

InfoTrac College Edition

For more information, explore InfoTrac College Edition at

http://www.infotrac-college.com/Wadsworth

Enter search terms: gender and mental health, gender and depression, eating disorders, transgender, gender and alcohol.

13 Gender and the Media

Tribal Tales for the 21st Century

A democratic civilization will save itself only if it makes the language of the image into a stimulus for critical reflection—not an invitation for hypnosis. ◆ Umberto Eco

Learning Objectives

After studying this chapter, you should be able to:

1. Define media and briefly explain the factors involved in reading media messages.
2. Explain how media may be said to represent tribal stories, emphasizing how these mediated representations help construct reality and prescribe ideals for members of a society.
3. List and briefly explain nine current issues surrounding gender and the media.
4. Summarize the research findings regarding media and gender socialization, and then explain why the conclusions surrounding this research remain so tentative.
5. List seven points demonstrating that advertisements extend far beyond the mere promotion of products and services, and then connect these points to gender construction and performance.
6. Summarize the contributions of Jean Kilbourne and Erving Goffman to our understanding of gender representations in advertising.
7. Summarize the research findings regarding television as an "educator" in our personal lives.
8. Explain how and why representations of lesbians and gay men in the media have changed.
9. Explain why pornographic media merit special attention in understanding gender representations.
10. List and summarize the findings regarding five other relatively gender-segregated media formats, emphasizing the Internet's potential as a gender-free medium.

Encounters with Gender

A wife and husband are both successful creative artists. For decades, he has been a world-renowned filmmaker. He has faced criminal charges because of his films, but nevertheless he continues his creative work. She has been the most popular singer in the history of her nation, but for the past 20 years she has been banned completely from performing in public. Like all women performers, she has been condemned to total silence in her homeland. Yet accolades from admiring critics and fans all over the globe continue. In her native country, a new generation idolizes her, even though they have never seen or heard her in live performance. Because the sale of pop music cassettes and CDs is a criminal offense in her homeland, they have only recordings from two decades ago. Government reforms now permit her to sing again, but only *outside* of her native country and only if accompanied on tour by her husband. Tearful, cheering thousands recently filled Toronto and Vancouver stadiums to hear her sing. When she returns home, she too may face criminal charges. At each concert, she ends with a song that asks, "Why is it these days that singing is a crime?" (Ditmars, 2000).

We live in an age of truly global media. Free-flowing, instantaneous communication is rapidly becoming a universal norm. Can you imagine a society in which public communication and expression via the media is restricted to only one gender?

Overview

In this chapter we examine how an environment saturated with media interacts with and influences gender construction and performance. First, we try to understand what media representations mean in human experience, and then we take a look some of the issues that surround gender and contemporary media. An exploration of how media influences gender socialization follows, after which we examine gender representations in selected media formats, specifically advertising and television programming. Finally, we review media formats that are more or less gender segregated: pornography, televised sports, soap operas, magazines, films, and the Internet. The gender issues surrounding mass media on a global scale are considered all through the chapter.

Tuning In

The Latin word *medium* means "middle," and its plural, *media*, refers to the technological processes that lie in the middle of the communication pathway between senders and receivers (that's you and me) of a message (Croteau & Hoynes, 2000). Gender influences all aspects of this pathway. Gender influences the process by which messages are created or selected for sending, who is sending messages, how the message is constructed, and the medium chosen for transmission. Within the receiver, the process of creating meaning in response to media messages is called "reading the message," and this too is influenced by gender. In other words, the same message may be individually or socially constructed to mean different things for members of each gender (Grossberg, Wastella, & Whitney, 1998). Gender also influences level of attention, awareness, as well as affective response to media messages. The term *mass media* refers to the gigantic, anonymous audience that receives messages in today's media saturated world. The same videos and CDs sell around the world (Davis & Davis, 1995). Nearly every country in the world now has at least one television channel. Even in remote areas, people may gather around the village radio or television set on a daily basis (Furnham & Mak, 1999).

To put all this in perspective, let's go back about 30,000 years to consider some of the earliest media representations. Imagine a small group or clan of early human beings gathered around the communal fire. The shellfish, plants, nuts, and berries have been consumed, and a few remaining bones gnawed (Nemecek, 2000). Talented members of the group head into the recesses of a cave and begin to draw animal figures on the wall and ceiling. The animals are disproportionately large and fat, as well as unrealistically accessible and vulnerable. Human figures wielding spears and arrows are added to the drawing, and this particular representation of an important human experience is complete. At about the same moment in human history, other talented members of the group mold clay and carve stone into clearly female figures with exaggerated bellies, hips, breasts, and buttocks. These figures

too are about another important human experience: sex, fertility, birth, and nourishment of the young (see Figure 13.1).

Although we have no absolute way of knowing the original purpose or meanings of any of these artifacts, it seems clear that both creations communicated important "messages" to those who were familiar with them. It's safe to say these media products simultaneously accomplished two goals. First, they told important "stories" of the human group: the need for reproductive success, and success in the hunt. Such media also represented important ideals: the ideal hunt and hunter, and the ideal fertility of the human group. At some basic level, that's exactly what the arts and contemporary media still do. They tell the "important stories of our tribe" (how we grow, suffer, love, prevail, and so on), and they also describe and prescribe social ideals (how we should behave, feel, succeed, and so on). In addition, they "discourse" about the relationships among members of the human group.

Critical Thinking Challenge

In your mind's eye, is the cave artist a man or a woman? Is the sculptor or stone-carver a man or a woman? What do you believe influenced your imagery?

In the 21st century, most human beings live in an ocean of media: radio, television, newspapers, cassette tapes, magazines, books, movies, toys, recorded music, video games, computer software, advertisements on billboards, and in magazines, flyers, and direct mail. Even this textbook may be considered a form of media. Human civilization is awash in communicated messages, both auditory and visual. Yet most of the time we wade through it all, relatively unaware (Croteau & Hoynes, 2000). Think about your typical week—how many hours a day do you have the television going? Do you actively watch, or is it merely background for your daily life? Consider the number of hours you spend with your car and home radio, or looking at billboards, street ads, newspaper ads, and similar types of advertising. What about all that forest of paper that comes to you in the mail each day? How many magazines, catalogues, and other printed materials do you look at each week? The Internet is all about the transmission of messages of many types.

The mass media are critical agents in many types of socialization, including gender socialization

FIGURE 13.1   "Venus" figures such as the one pictured at left have been found in many places in the world. Similarly, cave paintings such as the one above have also been found on virtually every continent.

(Croteau & Hoynes, 2000). By high school graduation day, students may have spent more time in front of a television set than in the classroom. The media also tell us what our society is like and suggest how we should *be* in it. For example, although crime rates have decreased dramatically over the last several years, the number of crimes reported on local television news has actually increased (Joliffe, 1996). This creates the illusion that crime is rampant, and many people in the United States live in fear of violent crime. The visual images of the perpetrators are typically of young men, often minority group members. The visual images of the victims and survivors are often girls and women. Even though men are more often the victims of violence, television news programs are much more likely to describe or show female victims. Thus a whole reality and social world are constructed for the receiver or viewer, and certain stereotypes and role expectations are reinforced (Brown, 1996).

Critical Thinking Challenge

How many popular movies begin with the plot line "A young woman is brutally murdered, and . . ."? How does this repetitive media representation affect women (and men)?

We should also realize that media influence how we interact with the world. In the recent past, people had to be physically present at events to experience them. Today, we are accustomed to having significant events electronically mediated. Media act as the bridge between people's private lives and the public world. However, processing via the media changes events, because only those aspects that "work" in a media presentation are available for receivers. Unless you had an older sibling, friend, or relative, you first absorbed the image of "college student" through the media. Is your personal experience of being a real college student at odds with its media representation? How?

The various media present powerful models and ideals. The media prescribe and enforce a particular ideology, "belief system," or "worldview." The media tell us about appropriate, ideal, and stigmatized roles for women and men, boys and girls, spouses and workers, criminals, and lovers, and so forth (Croteau & Hoynes, 2000).

Social, spiritual, and political leaders often point to media as agents in particular social problems but seldom point to media as agents in positive social change. The relationships between violence and song lyrics, between pornography and sex crimes, between domestic violence and the cinematic glorification of aggression, all continue to be debated and researched. The relationships between media representations and human rights, reproductive rights, worker dignity, better health practices, and improved human relationships are often ignored. Media images "teach" many things.

Current Issues Surrounding Gender and the Mass Media

Media are now an inseparable part of people's lives. Media representations and mediated events structure our personal sense of history. The media provide the imagery and soundtrack of people's memories: a song associated with falling in love, a video or photographic image related to some international tragedy, and so on.

Critical Thinking Challenge

How have the media images surrounding the terrorist attack on September 11, 2001, influenced your understanding of and response to that event? Has that event changed your view of the world or your life plans? Was gender involved in that event?

Media and Gender Socialization. Although parents and peers appear to be the critical agents in the gender socialization of children, media are an equally potent influence (Calvert, 1999). In the industrialized world, toys, books, videotapes, comic books, CDs, electronic games, and so on all constitute major aspects of the contemporary child's formative environment. What do children learn about their potential and place in the world from these mediated representations?

Gender, Media, and Private Life. Until relatively recently, the only guidelines and models available for how to conduct relationships with others, especially intimate relationships, came from parents, relatives, and immediate community. Mass media, especially books, film, and video, offer the privilege of observing many diverse models for personal relationships. This change has influenced our ideas and ideals regarding important relationships. A recent study revealed that teens applied media ideals to their personal relationships. Even teenagers who were already outside mainstream ideals (such as teen mothers) aspired to the interpersonal ideology presented in popular media (Steele, 1999).

Media Presentations Offer a Hegemonic Ideology. The term "hegemonic ideology" refers to the belief that there is an inevitable order of power and domination among the groups that make up society. This ordering is so strong that it often seems natural. Here are several examples. Men dominate virtually all political talk shows . In a study of gender and source selection and use in journalistic stories, 68% of news sources were men, compared to only 20% who were women. References involving male sources were significantly longer and more often described as "informed" or "reliable" (Zoch & Turk, 1998).

Media Can Normalize the Unusual. A day's worth of television talk shows suggests that men who sleep with their wife's sisters, stripper grandmothers, mother–daughter prostitute teams, cross-dressers, and violent racists are all relatively commonplace. They aren't.

The Globalization of Gender Construction. All over the world, control and creation of media products are in men's hands. Men's game-playing (sports) receives as much media attention as do international events. Youth, cleavage, and stereotyping continue to mark the place of women in much of the global media. By representing powerful women as sexual objects, their contributions are trivialized. By representing powerful men solely in terms of their public achievements, their full humanity is demeaned.

Media as Cultural Colonialism. Media products from the United States are exported everywhere and have great potency in the global community. Let's consider several examples. The majority of the human race does not speak English, yet 80% of all Internet sites and traffic are in English (Nunberg, 2000). Presently, over 800 million people in 210 nations view world events as constructed by CNN in Atlanta, Georgia (Croteau & Hoynes, 2000). The gender images and ideals of today's U.S. movie listings will flood Europe, Latin America, Asia, and Africa within the next few years. In Germany, almost 90% of films shown in theatres are American films. In

China, an arrested dissident insisted that his government should have to "read him his rights," as he had seen in American police shows. In India, millions mourned the death of Lucille Ball because her show was a national favorite (Grossberg et al., 1998). The gender representations in these media products have the potential to improve or worsen the human condition (Rhode, 1997).

Media Violence as a Cause or Major Contributor to Societal Violence. The causes of violence are multiple, but the question remains as to whether media violence contributes to social mayhem, to desensitization regarding violence, and to increased fear of victimization. Questions of violence and victimization are often structured along gender lines.

Influence of Pornography. Although the impact of pornography was originally debated on moral, religious, and ethical grounds, feminists argue that pornographic images lead to the physical and sexual abuse of women. Is Robin Morgan's (1980) conclusion that "pornography is the theory, and rape is the practice" a valid one?

Later on in the chapter, we'll explore some of these issues in greater detail.

Critical Thinking Challenge

Take a look at today's print or electronic news. What messages about gender may be read there?

Children's Media

The media environment for children growing up in relatively affluent societies consists of toys, books, television programs, television commercials, interactive electronic games, Internet interaction, big-screen movies, small-screen videotapes, comic strips, and comic books. All of these are agents in the gender socialization of children (Beal, 1994; Witt, 2000). For example, the Mighty Morphin' Power Rangers have excellent manners and preach cooperation and mutual respect. However, they spend much of their time kicking, punching, karate-chopping, and shooting enemies (Cantor, 1998). What messages do children absorb from these media icons?

Early researchers in this area concluded that children who watch more television tend to hold more

rigidly to gender stereotypes (McGhee & Frueh, 1980; Zemach & Cohen, 1986). Traditional television commercials aimed at children represented women as passive, deferent, of lower intelligence, of low credibility, and as being punished for strong effort. Men were represented as constructive, powerful, autonomous, and achieving (Witt, 2000). Has anything changed?

Critical Thinking Challenge

Are there any female characters among the puppet cast of *Sesame Street*? Are you aware that Miss Piggy is the only female character among the Muppets? Do you believe any of this really matters? Why or why not?

Browne (1998) compared gender stereotypes in advertising on children's television in the 1990s in both Australia and the United States. The relative invisibility of girls and women persists, in that the ratio of boys to girls in ads was 2:1. In both nations, boys were presented as more knowledgeable, active, aggressive, and instrumental than were girls. Men were more often shown working outside home, and women were still shown in domestic roles. This researcher concluded there was essentially an equal degree of stereotyping in both nations.

A content analysis of children's educational programming, revealed stereotyping across age ranges, and a more traditional presentation of gender roles for young children than for teens. Although male characters in programs for older children were less stereotyped, female characters remained equally stereotyped across programs for all age ranges. Despite improvements in children's programming, women are still underrepresented, appear in a narrower set of roles, and are represented in more unimportant and limited ways (Barner, 1999).

Critical Thinking Challenge

Barner (1999) concluded that most child-oriented fare centers on the adventures of a school-age boy or boylike creatures. Can you think of any exceptions?

Violence in Children's Media

Research and public debate about the impact of the high levels of aggression and violence in children's media has continued for many decades (Furnham &

Mak, 1999). Some scholars argue that aggressive play fosters imitative violence, perpetuates war, and encourages interpersonal aggression, and so on. Others contend that aggression-filled games teach role taking and allow children (especially boys) to come to terms with war, violence, and death (Kinder, 1999). Violent entertainment also allows boys to express strong emotions, although boys normally curtail their affect (Goldstein, 1998). Still others argue that aggressive play is natural, inevitable, and essentially universal among males of all primate species (Sagan & Druyan, 1992). Media producers say children want to be aroused, and violence is arousing. Some psychologists contend that only already aggressive children prefer to watch media violence.

Research support is strongest regarding children's desire for arousal (Cantor, 1998). There is also some limited support for the notion that those who already have a more aggressive disposition are more attracted to violent entertainment. It is very difficult to test the notion that some inherently male quality makes violent entertainment attractive, because most violent media products have males as central characters. In any case, violent entertainment is certainly not new. Think about those classic fairy tales. In the past, cruel and sadistic stories of children abused by stepmothers (why never stepfathers?), lost in forests, eaten by animals, drowned, and burnt by fires, were probably meant to be instructional and ensure survival (Tator, 1998).

Whatever the origin of violence in children's media, the gender difference in this area is striking (Goldstein, 1998). The differential in the activity levels of boys and girls may help explain the initial attraction of violent games for boys. Developmental researchers have shown that with increasing age, preschool girls show a growing preference for romantic and adventure tales, whereas boys increasingly prefer violent tales (Collins-Standley, Gan, Hsin-Ju, & Zillman, 1996).

Animated cartoons are particularly popular among children, and researchers continue to document their high levels of aggression and gender stereotyping. In general, male characters are more prominent, more aggressive, appear more often, talk more, and perform more varied activities. The few female characters are usually less knowledgeable and are secondary to male characters. Female characters tend to be more emotional, affectionate, frail, and more domestic. There is a significant relationship between children noticing gender-stereotypic behaviors in cartoon characters and reporting more traditional job expectations for self and others, particularly among boys (Thompson & Zerbinos, 1995, 1997).

Interactive Electronic Games

> They are an invitation to illiteracy.
> They create an atmosphere of cruelty and deceit.
> They stimulate unwholesome fantasies.
> They suggest criminal or sexually abnormal ideas and furnish a rationalization for them.
> They supply all the forms and details for antisocial activity.
> They tip the scales toward maladjustment.

Is the preceding quotation taken from a research study of the effects of current video games? Actually, not. It was adapted from the words of psychiatrist Frederic Wertham in his 1954 book, *The Seduction of the Innocent.* These warnings are about the harmful effects of the violence portrayed in the comic books of that era. Over the decades, public outcry shifted from concern about the violence depicted in regular comic books, to the blood and gore of horror comics, and then to the negative impact of television violence. Today interactive electronic games are under the same scrutiny. Aside from their intense visual and sound quality, the attribute most associated with contemporary video games is their high level of graphic violence. Something about that violence seems particularly attractive to boys and men. In 1993, two versions of *Mortal Kombat* appeared: a blood-dripping, decapitation-filled one by Sega and a sanitized version by Nintendo. The Sega version outsold its competitor by 7:1 (Goldstein, 1998). One examination of Nintendo and Sega Genesis games revealed that about 80% of the games centered on aggression or violence. Moreover, 21% of the games sampled depicted violence specifically against women. There were no women in 41% of games with characters, and in 28% of the games, women were solely sex objects (Dietz, 1998). The central themes of the current generation of video games involve someone getting killed, finding out why someone has been killed or evil beings taking over the world.

In addition to the graphic violence, the video game characteristics that are appealing to boys include the uncertainty, speeded responses, multiple levels of difficulty, intense sound effects, and immediate sensory feedback. In general, girls seem to find the high intensity and violence boring, rather than stimulating or challenging (Cassell & Jenkins, 1998).

Video games are overwhelmingly a masculine pastime from childhood through the college years (Subrahmanyam & Greenfield, 1998). However, creators and marketers of game software are very interested in attracting girls into this potentially huge consumer market. In addition to their entertainment function, video games provide strong motivation for computer mastery and interaction. Because most commercially available video games do not reflect the tastes and interests of half the potential game-playing population, girls may begin school with less familiarity and motivation regarding computer use. Early attempts to make video games more interesting to girls consisted of having female protagonists and creating nonviolent content. Packaging was also changed (more pink and purple), but such efforts were not effective. The first entertainment software to actually garner a mass market for girls was *Barbie Fashion Designer* (1996), which sold 500,000 copies in its first two months and continues to be a best-seller.

As interactive video games move to the center of children's media, interesting questions regarding the gendering of computer software arise. Is there something inherently masculine about this medium? Must software be so highly gendered? Will software focusing only on beauty, fashion, hairstyles, and social protocol appeal to girls? What features of *Where in the World Is Carmen San Diego?* explain its strong appeal to both girls and boys? Popular thinking about gender and video games promulgate stereotypes of girls as being essentially different from boys and as being highly appearance oriented (deCastell & Bryson, 1998). In this schema, boys retain their stereotypic qualities of being competitive, aggressive, and technologically inclined (Gilmour, 1999).

The work of MIT researcher Yasmin Kafai (1999) has provided some insights into the relationship between gender and video game culture. She notes that most research in this area has focused on and exaggerated gender differences and has failed to pursue more interesting questions about the range and versatility of children's play behavior. She notes that young children already bring gender-stereotypic notions and values to their video game experience. These are garnered from their previous experience of family roles, community norms, as well as hours of stereotypic movies, television programming and commercials, books, toys, and so on.

Kafai (1999) reports what happens when urban girls and boys (aged 9–10) are allowed to create their own video games. Adventure games comprised the most popular game genre among both girls and boys. Teaching games were popular only among girls. Interestingly, sports games were the least popular category for both genders.

Kafai (1999) also notes some recurrent themes in the process of game creation. First, most of the boy-created games contained some conflict between good and evil. Only one girl-created game had this feature. Even though there were equal levels of obstacles to be avoided or overcome, girls' games had fewer evil characters. Second, action was the major component in almost all the adventure games created. This researcher concludes that the commercial video game industry (dominated by men) mistakenly equated action with violence. Once committed to the pathway of violent imagery, later games merely built on and escalated this feature. Because girls continue to be seen as somehow "opposite" from boys, commercially produced "girl games" come to lack any action at all (violent or not). Third, girls seem to prefer computer use for more reality-oriented goals rather than fantasy goals, so that mystery-based themes are much more appealing to girls (Kafai, 1999).

Conclusions

Children clearly accept and internalize stereotypical presentations. They come to "understand" that Superwoman simply cannot do the same things as Superman. However, demonstrating that gender-stereotypical children's media has a causal influence on later gender-role stereotyping and behavioral rigidity remains problematic. In evaluating the effects of stereotypical television commercials and programming, there simply is no natural "no television" control group for comparison. Second, the correlational approaches that characterize this research make determination of the direction of causality very difficult. Third, relevant studies focus on stereotypical attitudes rather than overt behavior, and this too weakens any conclusions (Beal, 1994).

Youth-Oriented Media

Other than television, the two mass media most associated with teenagers and young adults are magazines and music videos. The best-known magazine for teenage girls is *Seventeen*. This magazine has worldwide distribution, with separate versions for specific nations. An analysis of the contents of the North American version of *Seventeen* Magazine from 1945 to 1995 revealed some changes, but there was still an idealization of traditional social roles and interests for teenage girls (Schlenker, Caron, & Halteman, 1998). However, an analysis of *Seventeen*'s feature articles and advice columns revealed substantial changes in the representation of female sexuality. There was recognition of female desire, with men no longer portrayed solely as sexual agents and women not solely the objects or victims of masculine sexuality. There was recognition of girls' ambivalence about sexuality, and a more open attitude toward homosexuality, masturbation, and oral sex. There was an emphasis on female agency and control of sexual expression. Issues of choice and values were presented. Discussions of sexual behavior had a strong interpersonal and relational orientation, but recreational sex remained unacceptable (Carpenter, 1998).

Research on music videos such as those shown on MTV reveals an overemphasis on seminudity, and primary gender identities for women as sex objects or sexual predators (Signorelli, McLeod, & Healy, 1994). Earlier analyses of music videos demonstrated a high level of occupational stereotyping in representations of women. Rock and rap videos are high in sexual and violent imagery regarding women, and they have received the most research attention as well as public condemnation (Alexander, 1997).

Country music is the top radio format in the United States (CMA Marketing, 1998). A content analysis of country music videos revealed rather progressive portrayals of women artists but more stereotypic portrayals of men artists. Women megastars in country music are a relatively new phenomenon, and the ratio of male to female artists (even megastars) remains at about 3:1. There were more gender-egalitarian portrayals in the videos of women, but scanty dress and suggestive poses were central. In country music videos there is essentially no violence against women, nor do women appear as sexual predators or prostitutes. However, men artists sometimes incorporate condescending or traditional portrayals of women (Andsager & Roe, 1999).

Do you recall the popular singer mentioned at the beginning of the chapter? This vignette recounts the true story of Iranian pop icon Faegheh Atashin (known as Googoosh). In the 1970s, her star status in Iran was compared to that of Elvis in the United States. After Iran was taken over by religious fundamentalists, all public singing by women was outlawed. Women's singing was declared to have a corrupting influence on men. Googoosh could sing only for small groups of women in private. However, her fans and Iranian expatriates have kept her voice and image alive via several Web sites (in both English and Farsi). Her world tour was a political and cultural focus point for Iranians who now live all over the globe (Ditmars, 2000).

Historically, men have dominated the music profession. Whether a rock band or a symphony orchestra, most simply refused to employ women. Women's music was only for friends and family at home. Ostensibly women were too weak to play professionally, or they might spoil their appearance by doing so. Today there are many more women performers across all musical genres (O'Neill, 1997). However, popular music, especially rock and rap music, remains largely a male culture that emphasizes masculine activities and styles. Women still have a marginal, decorative or less creative role, for example, as backup singers, adoring fans, and so on. Men continue to dominate the music business and the organizations surrounding music—management, performance, recording, disc jockeys, journalists, production, and so forth (O'Neill, 1997).

Gender Constructions in Ad-Land

The traditional definition of advertising involves the use of verbal, visual, and auditory materials to sell or promote some product or idea. We are inundated with advertising in our daily lives: radio and television commercials, newspaper and magazine ads, billboards, flyers, posters, direct mail, e-mails, telephone solicitations, the sides of buses and tops of taxicabs, and even the borders of Internet home pages. More of the gross national product of the United States is spent on advertising than on education (Cortese, 1999). However, advertising is much more than the promotion of products and services.

◆ Advertising is about people's dreams, longings, and desires, and the imagery surrounding these wishes is often highly gender typed (Cortese, 1999). Advertising attempts to link our heart-felt emotions to products, and it has the capacity to trivialize our most profound feelings and experiences (Kilbourne, 1999).

◆ Advertising is a form of persuasion, and persuasive techniques vary in effectiveness according to gender (Eagly, 1987). For example, in response to concerns about rising rates of smoking among women, the Association of European Cancer Leagues has changed its advertising approach. It now uses ads emphasizing how smoking contributes to the formation of facial wrinkles and other signs of aging (Reuters Medical News, 2001).

◆ Advertising is a display of cultural heritage and group power. It tracks the sociological history of a group or nation. In television ads, women have only recently come to be heard as authoritative voiceovers, and Asians are still most often shown as children (Coltrane & Messineo, 2000). Even animated product spokespeople (such as that battery bunny) tend to be overwhelmingly male (Peirce & McBride, 1999).

◆ Advertising uses cultural symbols, signs, and frames to quickly invoke "commercial realities." These may include "the good old days," "the happy family," "carefree youth," "powerful person," and so on. These cultural symbols too are often highly gendered (Coltrane & Messineo, 2000).

◆ Advertising captures the symbolic significance of idealized rituals and allows consumers to place themselves in desired social roles. For example, beer-drinking men attract voluptuous women. Happy, healthy children consume fast foods (Kates & Shaw-Gorlock, 1999).

◆ Advertising makes the ideology and values of the target audience more salient. In advertising, women are always youthful with unblemished skin. They are often disoriented or defenseless, with undignified facial expressions and with postures communicating subordination (Schutzman, 1999).

◆ Everyone believes that only "other people" are influenced by advertising (Kilbourne, 1999; Schutzman, 1999).

The relatively consistent findings are that in advertising, men are represented as authoritative, expert, occupation oriented, and are located outside the home and family. Women are represented as passive, dependent, incompetent, and domestic, or as sexual objects. Such gender representations have been documented in medical ads (Craig, 1992), television toy ads (Rajecki, Dame, Creek, Barrickman, & Reid, 1993), and general magazine ads (Walsh-Childers, 1996). Furthermore, these representations persist on a global scale. Similar patterns of gender stereotyping have been identified in Australian radio ads (Hurtz & Durkin, 1997), and in television ads in societies as diverse as Denmark, France, Hong Kong, Indonesia, Mexico, and Portugal (Furnham & Mak, 1999), as well as in Kenya (Mwangi, 1996). Television programming and news accounts in Communist China offer similar gender representations (Ming, 2000).

There has been relatively little examination of male roles in advertising. The image of the solitary man "functioning in isolation" is a profound cultural symbol and represents the Western gender ideals of strong individualism, self-reliance, and the pursuit of self-interest. In a study of ads taken from six magazines with male audiences, an emphasis on clear occupational roles was prominent. The most frequent occupations and roles represented were athlete, cowboy, outdoorsman, fisherman, biker, pirate, beach bum, swimmer, and yachtsman. The most frequent locations represented were business office, bar, sporting event, family or living room, and hotel room. It was also apparent that muscularity has now come to represent masculinity. The ideal man is young, handsome, and displays a perfect athletic physique. This trend toward muscularity is apparent even in children's action figures (Kolbe & Albanese, 1997); see Figure 13.2.

Studying Gender Representations in Advertising

Research and discussion about gender and advertising may be traced back to the work of Jean Kilbourne. Beginning with a collection of slides representing ads then current (1968, *Killing Us Softly*), Kilbourne (1999) has continued to chronicle the advertising imagery surrounding the representation of gender. She records how cigarettes came to symbolize indepen-

FIGURE 13.2 These popular children's "action heroes" represent the new masculine ideal of heavy muscularity.

dence for women and how beer and cars came to represent adequate masculinity. Additional understanding about gender representation in advertising came through the work of sociologist Erving Goffman (1979). He identified five patterns of gender-related "behavior displays" in ads (see Figure 13.3):

- *Relative size* (especially height). Men are almost always larger or taller than women, or placed above women in ads.
- *Feminine touch*. Women trace, cradle, or caress objects or products, whereas men grasp or hold them.
- *Function ranking*. If there is action or activity in the image, men have the active or executive role.
- *Ritualization of subordination*. Women are frequently kneeling, lying down, bent over, or off balance relative to men in ads.
- *Licensed withdrawal*. Women are psychologically withdrawn from involvement. They stare off to

vacant space, whereas men are much more likely to look directly at the observer.

Later research (Archer, Iritani, Kimes, & Barrios, 1983) recognized the phenomenon of *faceism* in the repertoire of gender conventions in advertising. This term refers to the representation of men via their faces, whereas women are more likely to have their whole body or only isolated body parts shown (see Figure 13.4).

Critical Thinking Challenge

Some critics have stated this last phenomenon should more properly be called *bodyism*. Why do you think they suggest this descriptor?

Fashion magazine ads seem to provide exaggerated versions of these trends (Crane, 1999). Fashion magazines have incorporated images from rock music culture, drug culture, homoerotic culture, and pornography. A second trend in fashion photography is for women to appear as empowered and androgynous. This is communicated via business suits and other vaguely feminized male attire. A third trend is to present contradictory identities of achievement orientation and seductive sensuality. Although fashion magazines now present a wider range of social identities and "agendas" than in previous decades, the emphasis on physical attributes and sexuality has remained relatively unchanged. Women continue to be presented in sexualized and demeaning poses. Interestingly, younger women tend to "read" these ritualized stances as signifying the woman being "in control" of sexuality (Crane, 1999).

Although "cheesecake" imagery (young, scantily clad women) has been a long tradition in advertising, the use of "beefcake" imagery (young, muscular, scantily clad men) is a relatively recent innovation. The persistent finding has been that cheesecake ads are effective in attracting attention, but do not improve either recall or attitude toward the product brand. Researchers studied the responses of undergraduate women and men to beefcake and cheesecake ads. Women reported negative responses to cheesecake ads, but men did not show a parallel negativity to beefcake ads (Jones, Stanland, & Gelb, 1998).

(a) Relative size

(b) Masculine grasp

(c) Ritualization of
subordination

(d) Licensed withdrawal

FIGURE 13.3 These ads capture some of the gender advertisements described
in Erving Goffman's work.

FIGURE 13.4   Compare these photographs/magazine covers on the issue of faceism/bodyism.

Television as Love, Sex, and Family Life Educator

All television is educational; the only question is: What is it teaching?

◆ FCC Commissioner Nicholas Johnson

Television repeatedly portrays a certain version of reality, and over time viewers come to adopt that version as reality (Gerbner, Gross, Morgan, & Signorielli, 1994). Although television programming provides "instruction" about many aspects of reality, here we discuss the influence of television programming on ideas about human relationships, especially relationships in which sex and gender are the most salient features. (See Box 13.1 for a glimpse of gender representations on the global television screen.) Television is a sexuality educator. Its frankness, accessibility, and popularity allow sexual learning without embarrassment or risk,

SLIDE SHOW BOX 13.1

Gender Representations on the Global Television Screen

India: As the status and purchasing power of urban Indian women has risen, television has become very popular. In India, as elsewhere, advertising makes the prevailing social ideology appear natural, desirable, and permanent. Ads legitimize and idealize women's confinement to the home by presenting them only in the context of domestic duties and products. The use of particular products is presented as a crowning achievement. One ad showed a woman pushing an undesired washing machine out the window of a high-rise apartment, so she could use a product to wash by hand. Single women are typically shown in Western garb and outside the home, whereas married women are usually shown at home in the traditional sari. Motherhood is presented as the most desired vocation for women, and use of a particular product is equated with "good mothering." Women in these ads are always fair complexioned, but such coloring is actually rare in India. Women in televi-sion ads are almost always Hindu (with *bindi*, the traditional forehead marking for married women). Minority Moslem and Christian women are virtually invisible in Indian advertising (Roy, 1998).

Israel: Although Israeli society is often perceived as offering women more oppor-tunities, women actually predominate only in the private sphere. An examina-tion of Israeli advertising images between 1979 and 1994 revealed an increased use of disembodied body parts for both gen-ders. Overall, the numeric representation of women had increased, and women were now shown in higher-status occu-pations, but still in lower-status occupa-tions compared to men. Women were sexualized more often by being shown in bed or on the floor (First, 1998).

South Africa: Not all ads sell products. Some are labeled *public service announce-ments* (PSAs) and seek to inform or change attitudes or behaviors. An antirape PSA in South Africa was banned by that nation's Advertising Standards Authority. In the ad, South Africa–born Hollywood star Charlize Theron speaks directly into the camera about men and rape in South Africa. She begins by stating that she is often asked what the men are like in South Africa. She then recounts some shocking facts. More women are raped in South Africa than any other country in the world, that one in three South African women will be raped in their lifetimes, every 26 seconds a South African woman is raped, and lastly, South African men don't think it is their problem. She con-cludes that it's not easy to say what South African men are like because there are so few of them. The payoff line in the ad is "Real men don't rape." A great pub-lic outcry arose against the banning of this PSA. On October 10, 1999, the *South African Times* labeled the Chair of the Advertising Standards Authority a *mampara* (a blundering idiot).

---

yet its messages are often limited, stereotypical, and potentially harmful (Botta, 1999). The most com-monly televised messages are that sex is for the young, single, and very attractive. According to television, men are always thinking about sex and are always ready and willing. Sexual encounters are spontaneous, romantic, and risk free. Hours spent in television view-ing appears correlated with stronger endorsement of recreational sex, higher expectations regarding the sexual activity of peers, and more extensive sexual ex-perience, especially for women (Ward & Rivadeneyra, 1999).

Adolescents devote more time to television than to any other mass media (Nielsen Media Research, 1998). One recent study identified several trends in prime-time network television programming. Sex-related messages (sex talk) was commonplace in tele-vision entertainment. Fully 67% of the shows sampled contained sex talk. Actual sexual behavior was less common, and occurred most often between unmarried individuals who had some established relationship. Talk regarding risks and responsibilities of sexual be-havior occurred in only about 10% of the programs sampled (Kunkel et al., 1999).

Television sitcoms represent commonly held be-liefs about how women and men should act as parents and spouses. In contrast to the sitcom ideology of the past, a central message of current sitcoms is that within the family, greater gender similarity, greater gender equality, and lower male dominance results in a happier, more stable, and more satisfying family life (Olson & Douglas, 1997).

The new images of men in the current media de-serve particular attention. Television, magazines, and popular films all seem to be exploring the "new fa-therhood," and they often present idealized images of the new involved father. However, there is also the media image of the "deadbeat dad." He is presented as

BOX 13.1 *(continued)*

Japan: The first television program was broadcast in 1953, and television sets were soon revered as one of the "three sacred treasures" (washing machines and refrigerators were the other two). Television has gradually become the center of Japanese family life, taking the place of the Japanese father, who typically works late every night, far away from home. Gender stereotyping and other forms of gender bias persist on Japanese television. Even though women comprise the vast majority of viewers, men appear at ratio of 2:1 over women. The women portrayed range from teens to their early 20s. Women over 40 are rarities. The age range for men is wider. In ads, women are most often shown in traditional roles as wives and mothers. However, semiclad women and illicit sex are common themes in programming. Although women have made some progress in the Japanese television industry, they constitute only about 6% of national and 18% of commercial newscasters and em-

cees. Feminist groups are in the forefront of formal attempts to improve presentations of women on Japanese television (Suzuki, 1995).

Morocco: Television advertising and television programming has had a tremendous impact on adolescent gender roles and gender expectations. There have been substantial changes in the norms regulating mate selection, courtship, and the place of sexual expression within marriage. These changes have moved urban Moroccan society rapidly toward Western norms (Davis & Davis, 1995).

Bangladesh: Since 1989, Communications for Change (formerly Martha Stuart Communications) has offered funds, equipment, training, and a supportive platform for "participatory video." In these programs, poor people, most often women, can quickly produce videos to effect social change. For example, at mar-

riage Bangladeshi women typically leave their home villages to live with their husband's family. In cases of domestic violence, village courts seldom offer justice because the husband's friends and family control them. One local women's group videotapes battered women and others who witnessed the violence. Showing the tapes in court discourages false testimony by the batterer's family and friends. Another woman videotaped the campaign speeches of local politicians. After election, these videotapes were shown publicly and used to pressure elected officials to keep their promises to villagers. During a cholera outbreak, a video team quickly produced a health tape about how insects spread bacteria. It showed how local food vendors and restaurant owners failed to protect food from flies and other pests. Public playing of the tapes brought a quick change in behavior (Stuart & Berry, 1996).

---

mean, selfish, and indifferent (Dienhart, 1998). One television critic reviewed the current images of men on prime-time television and summarized their representation as "dumb as posts and proud of it." He found that men were depicted as "rude, crude, sex-crazed, sexist, childish, and blindingly egotistical." This critic concluded that most well-written adult shows seemed aimed at women audiences, and that as long as men are in power, men can be safely ridiculed (Gates, 2000).

Gays and Lesbians in the Mass Media

Since the 1970s, the representation of gay men and lesbians in the mass media has both increased and changed in a more positive direction. Several factors have contributed to this media trend. The discovery that past and present artists were gay has become a source for pride. Second, AIDS activists and human

rights activists have made excellent use of the media as a means of advocacy. Third, the gay and lesbian community is emerging as a consumer market of great potential, partially because they have fewer children and therefore more spending power. New research on the consumer habits of this community is burgeoning. It is estimated that there are about 19 million gay people in the United States alone, with tremendous spending power. Businesses catering to the lesbian and gay community have expanded beyond clubs and bookstores to media, merchandise catalogues, and vacation companies as well as legal, medical, financial, and communication services. One survey compared gay and lesbian consumers to a heterosexual sample regarding media usage, and found that as a group, gays and lesbians read a somewhat different array of newspapers and magazines, watch different television shows, listen to different radio programs, and are more likely to use catalogues and online resources. Differences between gay men and lesbians as consumers were also noted. As a marketing group, lesbians do not exhibit the same upscale characteristics of gay men. They have less education and are older (Burnett, 2000). Although the stereotype depicts gays and lesbians as having more disposable income, good taste, and a desire to purchase high-quality products, there are contradictions. This community includes gay men living with AIDS, gay men of color, disabled gays, and those with little education. Lesbians experience the same economic disadvantages as other women (Kates, 1999).

Some believe that media of particular interest to the lesbian and gay communities should be clearly demarcated as "alternative." Others hold that such material should be fully available on a par with more mainstream media productions. For example, Blockbuster's video rental stores used to have an "Alternative Life Style" section. Now all videos and DVDs with any "gender transgressive" content are fully integrated into mainstream categories. There is at least one television show dedicated to lesbian and gay issues, *In the Life*. It airs on public television stations. A cable offering of the controversial British show *Queer as Folk* also broke new ground in this area. A few large urban areas have gay- and lesbian-oriented cable stations. There are now a considerable number of gay and lesbian magazines available at chain bookstores, and they have large national audiences (*The Advocate*, *Out*, *Girlfriend*, and so on). There are gay newspapers available in most major cities in North America. Openly lesbian and gay music performers perform for both alternative and mainstream audiences (Doty & Gove, 1997). National ad campaigns present openly gay representations (Ikea, Lee Jeans, American Express, and so on); see Figure 13.5. Yet although "lesbian chic" may be fashionable among the sophisticated, discrimination and hate crimes against gay men and lesbians continue (Horne & Lewis, 1997).

Relatively Gender-Segregated Media

Some media formats absorb the interest of mainly one gender. Pornography is probably the most highly gender-segregated media format because most porno-

FIGURE 13.5   Ads such as this openly seek to attract gay and lesbian consumers.

graphic materials are produced by men, for men. Although there have been changes in the pornography industry, it remains an overwhelmingly masculine medium involving the use of women's bodies to fuel masculine fantasies and promote their sexual satisfaction.

On a global scale, women watch more television than men do, but the important exception to this rule is sports programming (Kennedy, 2000). Sports have always served to separate men from women through athletic contests that emphasize men's physical size and strength (Dufur, 1999). Today, televised sports continue that separation. Another example of gender-segregated television programming involves soap operas or *telenovelas*. Also, although women comprise the vast majority of the audience for daily talk shows, men are the main viewers of weekend political talk shows. In terms of printed media, most magazines are highly gender specific in their appeal. Box 13.2 considers various explorations of gender on the global silver screen. Although the Internet appears to have the

Gender on the Global Silver Screen

Several years ago, in an episode of the popular, but quirky television program *Northern Exposure*, a Native American anthropologist was interviewing non-Indians about the "myths that guided their lives." None of his European-American respondents could answer his inquiries. They seemed confused and kept insisting they didn't believe in "myths." Toward the end of the program it became very clear that popular movies provided the mythic characters and situations that guide the consciousness of most Westerners. There is something special about sitting quietly in the dark with strangers, the smell of popcorn, with latecomers reduced to dark, shadowy figures who pass between you and the screen. The sound is loud and intense, and the screen images are over 10 feet high. Music and action are always perfect and precise. That's where our societal mythology is made and absorbed.

Mention the words *gender* and *movies* in the same sentence, and most people will immediately think of the contrast between "chick flicks" and "guy flicks" (also known as "shoot 'em ups") (Oliver, Weaver, & Sargent, 2000). But there's much more to this issue.

Recently the National Film Institute ranked the best comedy films ever made. The two top winners were *Some Like it Hot* and *Tootsie*. Is it a coincidence that both films involve cross-dressing men and a host of other "gender transgressions"? Below is a listing of other recent films that deal with issues of gender. By the time you read this, there are likely to be many more. Consider having classmates select some of these films for viewing and then reporting about the gender issues involved in each of them.

Orlando

Thelma and Louise

M. Butterfly

The Crying Game

Being John Malkovich

Boys Don't Cry

The Fight Club

American Beauty

Alien (Did you know that the part of Ripley was written for a male actor? Nothing was changed when Sigourney Weaver was selected for the role.)

Farewell My Concubine (Chinese)

The King of Masks (Chinese)

Raise the Red Lantern (Chinese)

Shall We Dance? (Japanese)

Antonia's Line (Dutch)

My Life in Pink (Belgian)

---

potential to be a gender-free medium, masculine norms continue to shape its content and communications patterns. Let's take a closer look at each of these relatively gender-segregated media formats.

Pornography

Although media can be used to transmit many types of messages, the gendered messages of pornography have been of particular concern. Pornography is usually defined as sexual material created for the sole purpose of sexual arousal and commercial gain. However, feminist scholars insist that debasing and degrading imagery, especially of women and children, is also a defining component of pornography (Cowan & Dunn, 1994; Griffin, 1981). Sexual material created for some artistic or spiritual purpose is termed *erotica*. The distinction between erotica and pornography seemingly rests on the intentions of the person who

created the material. However, the inherent difficulty of distinguishing between the two has resulted in mass protests, controversial U.S. Supreme Court decisions, arrests of museum directors, and numerous lawsuits (Hardy, 1998).

Sexually explicit materials have been around since antiquity and have been used for sociopolitical criticism as well as titillation. Modern pornography dates back to 17th- and 18th-century Britain and France. Classic 18th-century pornographic texts such as *Fanny Hill* often described the exploits of resourceful and independent women who supported themselves as prostitutes and madams. Women speak up for themselves in these texts and seek their own pleasure. Female pleasure, with and without men, was a common theme (Mourao, 1999). Up through the 19th century, pornographic materials were available only to the wealthy classes. During the 1960s drawings, photographs, magazines, and films were expensive and available only through specialized outlets. Today, commercial pornography constitutes a global multibillion industry, dominated by men. Women's "images" are used to propel sales and rentals, but the profits end up in the hands of a few men who control the production and distribution of this product.

The development of video technology and the Internet has changed the pornography industry. Now such materials are relatively inexpensive and easily available to anyone with a VCR or Internet access (Gardos & Mosher, 1999). The audience for pornography has changed as well. There is some evidence that couples are the major renters of pornographic videos and that they watch the videos as part of their sexual repertoire. In addition to videotapes, the Internet is now a major source of pornographic imagery, and here the traditional boundary between pornography producers and consumers dissolves. For example, in chat rooms participants create pornographic narratives as they engage in "net sex" (Blair, 1998).

Pornography is often described as a highly masculine genre because of its preoccupation with genitalia and overt sexual activity, to the virtual exclusion of any socioemotional context (Barron & Kimmel, 2000). In one study, participants viewed standard pornographic videos versus more woman-oriented videos (they tend to contain more elaborate plots and an interpersonal context for the sexual activity). Overall, women responded more positively to the woman-oriented videos, whereas men responded favorably to both types of videos (Mosher & McIan, 1994).

There is a large body of classic research that sought to evaluate whether exposure to pornography, especially violent pornography, affected men's attitudes and behavior toward women and children (for example, see Donnerstein et al., 1987; Kelley, Dawson, & Musialowsky, 1989; Zillman & Bryant, 1989). However, there is still little consensus on this matter (Barak, Fisher, Belfry, & Lashambe, 1999; Cowan & Dunn, 1994; Mourao, 1999).

Although about 90% of contemporary pornography is nonviolent, the messages in material that does contain coercive or violent themes communicates that women enjoy being raped and otherwise brutalized. Researchers have found that after repeated exposure to pornography, men trivialized rape, overestimated the prevalence of unusual sexual acts,

displayed callousness toward women and their sexuality and concerns, were more dissatisfied with their sexual relationships, and had reduced trust in their intimate partners (Gardos & Mosher, 1999). However, the question remains whether all this influences actual behavior. Although an early Danish study revealed a negative correlation between availability of pornography and sex crimes (Kutchinsky, 1973), more recent studies revealed a positive correlation between the availability of pornography and sex crimes (Weaver, 1994). Other researchers found that child molesters and rapists frequently used pornography prior to and during sexual assaults (Marshall, 1988). The general conclusion is that pornography, especially violent pornography, can activate sexually callous perceptions and aggressive behaviors (Gardos & Mosher, 1999). Actually, these effects can occur even with nonsexual content, thus implying that it is the *violent* rather than the sexual content that is problematic (Grossberg et al., 1998; Zillman & Weaver, 1999). Yet many contemporary movies and videos abound with "tasteful" or even eroticized rape scenes. Movie imagery of graphic violence against women is also a Hollywood mainstay (Hardy, 1998).

Critical Thinking Challenge

If many rapists and child molesters use pornography as part of their deviant activities, does it follow that pornography leads or causes some men to rape or molest?

Pornography may also be viewed as the highly fictionalized and highly gendered "story" of male and female sexuality. We have already mentioned the pornography-related message that in spite of their protestations, women enjoy sexual violation. Consider two other examples. "Cum shots" are a centerpiece of pornography. Special effects are now used to create the illusion of longer, more copious, and more forceful ejaculations. The reading of this message varies by gender. For men, such imagery may imply acceptance and idealization of male sexuality. Women found such images degrading and a turnoff (Gardos & Mosher, 1999). Another mainstay of traditional pornography involves women engaging in masturbatory acts that involve the insertion of objects (often dangerous objects) into the vagina. In pornography, sexual activity between women also focuses on pen-

Top Sites

Remarkably, 70 percent of e-porn traffic occurs during the 9-to-5 workday. The most popular stops:

	Millions of hits, April 2000	Average Minutes
PornCity	3.38	10.5
Kara's Playground	3.06	3.2
Erotism	1.67	7.1
Schoolgirls4U	1.63	.57
ErosVillage	1.56	6.9
Amateur Pages	1.28	4.8
Ygal	1.27	.4
TeenSteam	1.25	2.7
CunTV	1.24	1.2
High Society	1.13	.54

Surfers by Age

2–11	2.2%	35–49	31.7
12–17	15.3	50–54	6.8
18–20	6.9	55–64	6.0
21–24	6.8	65–99	2.9
25–34	21.6		

By Education

Grammar school	0.4%
Some high school	4.4
High-school graduate	26.1
Some college	24.0
Associate degree	9.2
Bachelor's degree	22.3
Graduate degree	13.7

By Income

0–$24,999	7.3%
25,000–49,999	27.6
50,000–74,999	27.5
75,000–99,999	14.9
100,000–149,999	9.0
150,000	3.5

By Gender

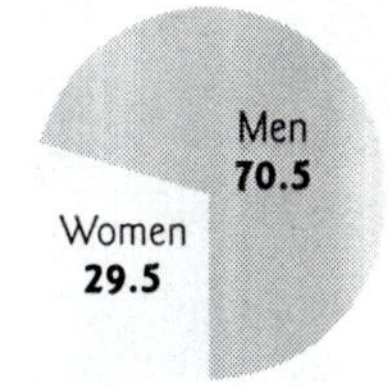

Men 70.5
Women 29.5

FIGURE 13.6 Internet pornography represents a significant area of usage. (*Source:* "Internet pornography," 2000, June 12, *Newsweek*, p. 76.)

etrative acts. All these sexual "stories" are misrepresentations of reality.

Pornography is often dealt with as an undifferentiated mass, but this tendency may cloud important distinctions. For example, a recent study compared the level of sexual violence and victim gender in pornographic magazines, videos, and Usenet (Internet newsgroup) pornography. There was little difference in the levels of sexual violence between magazines and videos, although both tended to portray sexual violence as consensual. However, Usenet pornography differed markedly and portrayed men as victimizers much more often (Barron & Kimmel, 2000). These researchers concluded that Internet pornography continues to eroticize male dominance and to increase misogyny (see Figure 13.6). They described Usenet groups as equivalent to "all-male locker rooms" in which the sexual derogation of women is used to maintain *hegemonic masculinity* (Bird, 1996). That is, this media format represents and idealizes emotional detachment, competitiveness among men, and the sexual objectification of women. On one Usenet site, exhibitionists used video/phone technology to create "shows" in which erections and ejaculations were the central features. The vast majority of participants were white men, although some couples and individual women also participated (Kibby & Costello, 1999). Clearly Usenet groups provide the

greatest access to pornography at the lowest cost, and participants are both producers and consumers.

Critical Thinking Challenge

Pulp romance novels, often referred to as *bodice-rippers* have been labeled as "women's pornography" (Snitow, 1995). Examine some samples from this world of the "creamy thigh," and "throbbing manhood" to draw your own conclusions.

On Sports, Soaps, and Talk

Media sports are still an overwhelmingly masculine pursuit. Broadcasts of skating and gymnastics may attract women, and tennis may attract about equal numbers of viewers of both genders, but all over the world, the biggest and most lucrative athletic contests have male audiences. Soccer, wrestling, boxing, football, and baseball broadcasts are for men (Figure 13.7). In one study of gender issues and televised sports, researchers compared the verbal commentary accompanying two men's and two women's athletic events. They found little overtly sexist commentary but did find more "gender marking" (references to "women athletes" and "women tennis players," and so on) and a hierarchy of naming by gender and by race (white men were referred to by last names, whereas women and minority men were referred to by first names).

FIGURE 13.7   In spite of recent inroads by women athletes, broadcast sports such as soccer and football remain a masculine domain.

These researchers concluded that sports commentary both marks women's sports and infantilizes women athletes (Messner, Duncan, & Jensen, 1993). Over the last 10 years, women athletes have received more coverage, but they still remain relatively invisible. Women sports reporters, sportswriters, and commentators are still relatively rare and continue to face sexist discrimination in their professions (Dufur, 1999).

Soap opera viewers are overwhelmingly female. Overall, viewers tend to be less educated, have lower incomes, and are often members of ethnic minorities (Gerbner et al., 1994). The overtly sexual content of soaps increased 35% between 1985 and 1994, but concerns about safer sex continue to be notably absent (Greenberg & Woods, 1999). Other soap opera sexual norms are more troublesome: Date rapes are frequently transformed into romantic episodes, and HIV infections are most often acquired from drug use (Rogers, 1995). The pursuit of pregnancy is a frequent theme, and unusual inseminations abound (Greenberg & Woods, 1999). There has been a recent increase in representations of strong ethnic women on the soaps, but they typically return to their "proper place" of subservient devotion to white men (Jenrette, McIntosh, & Winterberger, 1999).

On contemporary television talk shows, discussion of important social issues such as racism, social violence, domestic conflict, alternative sexuality, welfare rights, and religious freedom may be distorted by the requirements of a mediated presentation designed primarily as entertainment. These shows blur the boundaries among news, information, and entertainment (Shattuc, 1997). Televised versions of events and concepts must be short, simple, and entertaining. They present individual personal experience as a source of knowledge (Shattuc, 1997). Unique and unusual personal experiences are simply *not* a reliable source for grasping complex gender-related issues.

Tabloid talk shows ("trash talk") constitute a popular subgenre of this media format. These shows are significant agents in the normalization of the unusual. At least three homicides have been related to guest appearances on such shows (Gamson, 1998).

Magazines

Two recent studies provide a useful glimpse into the gender-related nature of popular magazines. Vigorito and Curry (1998) examined the role presentations in almost 8,000 popular magazine illustrations. These researchers noted that most scientific studies of gender depictions have focused on women. Treating men as if they had no gender can make their privileged status invisible (Katz, 1995). In man-oriented magazines, men of all races are shown overwhelmingly in occupational roles. Such magazines contain many figures with exaggerated physical gender traits (muscles, hair, beards, and so forth). Depictions of men in majority male reader magazines emphasized dominance, control, and unemotional relationships. Men were rarely portrayed as spouses or parents in men's magazines. However, woman-oriented magazines typically contain many portrayals of nurturing men. Women's magazines showed significantly more images of men with babies, as lovers, and as family members, and so on (Vigorito & Curry, 1998).

Berns (1999) examined the representation of domestic violence in 10 popular women's magazines from 1970 to 1997 and found 111 relevant articles. Analysis revealed that articles about domestic violence in women's magazines continued to ignore the role of the abuser and of society. The emphasis on immediate intervention was seldom balanced with a discussion of long-term needs for prevention or social change. Articles written by survivors of domestic violence emphasized how they escaped these situations. Articles written by others emphasized why women stayed in abusive relationships. Only four of the articles reviewed focused any attention on the batterer. Three of these focused on "warning signs" and advised women to simply avoid these men. Only one of the articles placed responsibility on the batterer or implied that men needed to change their behaviors.

The Internet as a Gender-Free Medium

At the beginning of the 20th century, the telephone radically changed the way people interacted. Today, the Internet is precipitating an equally radical change. However, in addition to communication and information, the Internet can also provide social escapism, diversion, entertainment, and relaxation (Korgaonkar & Wolin, 1999). Ostensibly, the invisibility of the Internet disrupts the visual or auditory cues that elicit gender and ethnic biases (Ebo, 1998). However, critics insist that the Internet will not change gender-induced biases, because the philosophy, covert tendencies, and culture of the medium are already highly masculinized (Ebo, 1998). For example, computer-mediated communication (CMC) clearly offers no visual or auditory cues regarding gender, and this diminishing of social cues should lessen gender-influenced inequalities. Yet research findings suggest that men dominate Usenet and e-mail discussion groups (Crowston & Kammeres, 1998). Men even dominate Usenet groups devoted to women and feminism. Researchers have found that women and men were interested in different discussion topics and that the communicative style of a message has an effect on interest in participation. Both men and women were less interested in participating after reading messages composed in a stereotypically masculine style (adversarial with strong assertions, self-promotion, presuppositions, rhetorical questions, authoritative tone, challenges, and humor/irony) rather than a stereotypic feminine style (attenuated assertions, apologies, explicit justifications, true questions, personal tone, and support of others. However, the more masculine style is becoming more normative for Internet communication (Crowston & Kammeres, 1998).

Summary

- Regardless of its form, all media transmit messages about human experience and ideals. The media are critical agents in gender socialization. Media has an impact on how we experience reality, and the media have great potential for positive or negative influence.

- Nine issues surround the relationship between gender and the media on the personal, interpersonal, and cultural levels.

- Classic research on the representation of gender across children's media demonstrated a persistent pattern of subordination of girls' abilities and activities compared to those of boys. In general, this pattern still continues.

- Relatively high levels of aggression and violence are common in children's media, especially in interactive electronic games. Kafai (1999) offers some useful insights into video game culture. Research conclusions are tentative and problematic regarding the impact of violent models on children's development and actual behavior.

- Magazines and music videos comprise important media formats for teenagers in the West. Gender stereotyping and the derogation of women and women's roles still permeate these media formats.

- Advertising is more than the promotion of goods and services. The work of Jean Kilbourne (1968) and Erving Goffman (1979) began the scientific studies of gender representation in advertising. The patterns identified by these two researchers persist in this medium.

- Television programming often functions as an educator in matters of gender, love, sexuality, and family life. Television offers powerful models and ideals of adolescence, love, courtship, marriage, and family.

- The representation of lesbians and gay men in the media has both increased and changed and become more positive over the last two decades. This community represents an affluent market for media advertisers.

- Some forms of media are relatively segregated by gender. Pornography is an overwhelmingly male medium, and researchers have attempted to determine if the sex and gender messages contained within pornography affect how men treat women and children. Broadcast sports are also a male domain across the globe.

- Soap operas and talk shows constitute an overwhelmingly female media domains. Illicit sexuality is a soap opera mainstay, and talk shows blur the boundaries between information and entertainment. Tabloid talk shows normalize very unusual behavior. Popular magazines are typically oriented toward one gender or the other. Although the Internet has potential as a gender-free medium, current trends make this unlikely.

InfoTrac College Edition

For more information, explore InfoTrac College Edition at

http://www.infotrac-college.com/Wadsworth

Enter search terms: gender and media, gender and advertising, pornography, violence and media.

14 Gender and Power

The Personal and the Political

Men are members of a social group and a social category that is invested with power. This has the consequence that membership in that group or category brings power, if only by association. ◆ J. Hearn

Learning Objectives

After studying this chapter, you should be able to:

1. Define *power*, and explain the relationship between power and masculinity.
2. Describe the various facets of the relationship between gender and power.
3. Define *sexual harassment*, and summarize the problems in determining the prevalence of this form of coercive power.
4. Describe the important characteristics of harassers and the harassed, and then summarize the various explanations for the occurrence of sexual harassment.
5. Distinguish between rape and sexual assault, and summarize the methodological problems in determining the prevalence of sexual assault.
6. List and explain the types of sexual assault, and summarize the findings regarding the impact of sexual assault.
7. Explain how traditional attitudes toward domestic violence were reflected in two relevant legal principles, and then summarize the accomplishments of feminists in regard to domestic violence.
8. Summarize the controversy surrounding domestic violence as a gendered phenomenon.
9. Summarize current findings regarding the characteristics of batterers and their targets.
10. Briefly summarize at the issues related to gender and the legal system.
11. Briefly summarize recent progress in women's access to political power.
12. Briefly summarize the current status of gender equity in the U.S. military.
13. List and explain the current issues related to gender and organized religion.

Encounters with Gender

Ann, her husband Bob, Ann's sister Carol, and her husband David were off on a weekend in the woods. By the second day, the rising tension between Carol and David was evident to all. David's initial teasing had escalated to ridicule, and Carol alternately ignored or placated him, or confronted his taunts. Ann took David aside and told him that his comments were hurtful, and asked him to please stop. Bob tried to distract David by engaging him in activities.

Finally Bob got away from the tension by driving to town to pick up some groceries for their dinner. Ann went out for a short hike, and as she returned to the cabin, she could hear David's menacing voice. As Ann entered, she saw David slap her sister as he screamed and cursed her. As David drew his arm back to hit Carol again, Ann yelled and jumped between them. She tried to pull David away, but he shoved her across the room onto a sofa. Carol arose, trying to keep David from attacking Ann. Screaming obscenities at both of them, David slammed out of the cabin. Ann ran to the phone to call the police, but Carol begged her not to do so. It would just make things worse, and David would calm down quickly. Ann was furious at David's behavior, and vowed to take her sister home with them immediately. Carol warned that if Ann told Bob what had happened, he and David would surely get into a fight. She implored Ann not to say anything. Carol explained this had been going on for a while, and she was planning to leave David soon. Ann reluctantly agreed to say nothing, and they somehow got through the evening.

As they packed the car early the next morning, Carol displayed that fake, nervous smile that Ann always hated. Bob was irritated and confused at Ann's silence and withdrawal. Ann was feeling worse and worse about herself, and terrified for her sister's safety. She also felt angry with Carol for bringing this problem into their family. Ann tried hard not to cry, but she felt herself sinking deeply into her sister's world of fear and acquiescence. Ann felt she had betrayed her sister, herself, and even her husband by hiding what had happened. She saw clearly that David's violence was now not only controlling Carol, but her as well. It was even having an impact on Bob, even if he didn't know exactly what happened. David was solicitous and affectionate toward Carol as they loaded the last of the baggage into the car.

How do you feel about Carol? How do you feel about David? What would you have done if you were Ann? How would you want Bob to respond to David's abusive behavior?

Overview

This chapter analyzes a central aspect of human gender relations—namely, the gender differential in power. Sexual harassment and sexual assault may both be viewed as exaggerated expressions of masculine power via the sexual channel. Battering also represents the use of men's physical power to dominate relationships with intimate partners. This material can be distressing for some students because of their own personal encounters with coercion and violence. Masculine power may also be observed in most of society's important structures and institutions: the legal system, the political system, the military, and organized religion. A global perspective lets us evaluate the progress made toward sharing power more equitably.

Power: A Gendered Analysis

The first part of this chapter covers some of the darkest and most painful aspects of gender relations. For some students, delving into topics such as harassment, sexual assault, and interpersonal violence will be merely disturbing and perhaps infuriating. For others, both men and women, such reading and discussion may be very painful, stirring up reminders of their own personal experiences or those of loved ones. For many of the men in the class, there may be feelings of defensiveness, shame, or even guilt. An honest discussion of these topics is likely to elicit many deeply felt emotions. Your classroom can provide a safe environment in which students can express their feelings in an honest, respectful, and compassionate way. Your instructor is likely to know of campus and community resources for students who feel particularly troubled by these topics. Your instructor may also be able to guide students who want to channel their anger and frustration into positive action on your campus and in your community.

Power and Masculinity

Power may be defined as the ability to influence what happens in interactions, the ability to limit access to resources, and the ability to define experiences for others (for example, was it "friendly flirting" or "sexual harassment"?). Those with power can negotiate directly for what they want. The powerless must use indirect means, such as lying low, being passive, hinting, being nice, withdrawing, pleasing, and so on (Kurth, Spiller, & Travis, 2000).

In everyday interactions, dominance behavior (direct demands or threats) elicits negative evaluations of women, but not of men (Copeland, Driskell, & Salas, 1995). On another level of analysis, even in the most egalitarian of societies, and for as long as archeologists can tell, it is mainly men who enact and enforce laws, lead governments, instigate and wage wars, reveal and interpret God, amass fortunes, and threaten others. Around the world, men control the courtroom, the corporate boardroom, the computer lab, the medical center, and the university classroom (Beeghley, 1996). At every level, powerful men shape and determine the course of others' lives. Living arrangements, economic arrangements, and social institutions have all been constructed to maintain the power and control that one gender has over the other.

Critical Thinking Challenge

It is unlikely that the men around you see themselves as having much "power." How would you explain this seeming contradiction?

Masculine power and privilege are maintained and reproduced by gender ideology, social structures, persuasion, and economic influence. When those strategies and structures fail, those in power may employ threats, force, and violence (Hearn, 1998). It is not that all men are violent all the time, or that only men are violent; rather, traditional gender construction leads men to dominate the phenomenon of violence and to specialize in violence. In many societies, violence is a way of demonstrating masculinity. Violence is a highly gendered activity and may be viewed as the performance of *hypermasculinity* (Hearn, 1998).

We should also remember that prior to the 1970s, many of the phenomena discussed in the first part of this chapter simply did not "exist." That is, although the interactions and events described here certainly took place, they had no name. Consider the supervisor who fondled a woman worker, or a husband who beat his wife. It was a private matter that involved the "natural" relationship between men and women, husbands and wives. The targets of these displays of gender-related power typically had little recourse. Some women were resourceful enough to defend themselves and deal effectively with perpetrators. A few were connected to other men who had even more power than the perpetrators, and who could therefore intervene and protect them. Some women had their own resources and managed to simply escape coercive situations. Many suffered in silence, fear, and subordination. Beginning in the 1970s, activists confronted, challenged, and deconstructed a great deal of masculine privilege and interpersonal power. The sexual exploitation of a subordinate worker or a student came to be labeled *sexual harassment*. Forced sexual contact between people who knew each other became labeled *date rape* or *acquaintance rape*. The beating, choking, and torturing of intimate partners was labeled *battering* or *wife abuse*. Social, legal, economic, and political structures were modified so that women could make policy on their own behalf, seek legal protection, work with dignity, and claim their human right to live without violence. All over the world, this task is far from complete, but it certainly has begun. Feminist men and women may have changed the relevant laws and institutions in many nations, but basic changes in gender ideology have yet to occur in many places.

An Analysis of Gender and Power

Certain aspects of masculine power seem so "normal" as to be as invisible as the air we breathe. For example, Messerschmidt (1993, p. 1) declares the obvious: "It is no secret who commits the vast majority of crime. Arrest, self-report, and victimization data all reflect that men and boys both perpetuate more . . . crimes . . . than do women and girls." Thus gender is an explanatory variable for crime, but it is seldom mentioned. Feminists emphasize the fact that the fear of masculine crime controls many aspects of women's lives, but there has been little attention to the fact that the masculine sex role demands repetitive demonstrations of masculinity. Delinquency and criminality may be viewed as such demonstrations.

Manifestations of masculine power are often dealt with as separate, unconnected entities. A gender analysis makes it clear that sexual harassment, sexual abuse, sexual assault, and battering are all related to the construction of the masculine gender role (Bowker, 1998). Moreover, power relations in the family are directly linked to the levels and severity of intimate violence: the more patriarchal the society, and the greater women's economic dependence, the more likely are all forms of domestic violence (Websdale & Chesney-Lind, 1998).

Critical Thinking Challenge

Who determines if a particular act is labeled as *violence*? Female genital mutilation (FGM) continues to be of concern to African women, yet white Western feminists "named" and defined it as violence. Is FGM an institutionalized form of violence, a health and human rights issue, or just a cultural practice?

Women's vulnerability to male violence has an insidious quality. Normally, human beings fear violence at the hand of *strangers*. For women, however, violence is more likely to come from those with whom they are most intimate. We think of homes as a secure refuge from violence and exploitation. Yet for women all over the world, the home is the most likely site for violence (Hearn, 1998).

The norms of masculine power assertion through violence are so deeply entrenched in most human societies that victims of male violence tend to blame themselves for it. Perpetrators tend to blame others for their own behavior, and "others" tend to blame the victim (Cowan, 2000). Thus, the rape survivor blames herself for agreeing to "go for a drive," the batterer blames his wife for the remark that preceded his assault, and citizens blame the crime victim who went for a walk in the park alone (Lamb, 1996).

Around the world, certain women are defined as deserving victims of masculine violence. In some societies, she may be the widow without grown sons. In others, she is the young bride whose husband declares her dowry as inadequate. In many Western societies, people see prostitutes and other sex workers as deserving of such treatment (Farley & Barkon, 1998).

Women are not passive recipients of violence. They tolerate violence for a number of economic, structural, and ideological reasons. They use various strategies to minimize men's violence. Some women can defend themselves physically. Others enlist the help of authorities or other family members. Many women do manage to leave abusive relationships and to support their children. However, in many societies women simply lack adequate power to control or even influence men's behavior (Hearn, 1998).

Coercive Power

Coercive power is the ability to impose one's will by force, threats, or deceit. Three manifestations of coercive power discussed here are (a) sexual harassment in the workplace and in academic settings, (b) rape and sexual assault, and (c) domestic violence.

Sexual Harassment

Sexual attractions in the workplace and at school are common as well as understandable (see Figure 14.1). Such interests can be positive, motivating, and a source of energy for both individuals and organizations. Mild flirting and humor can alleviate boredom and help humanize bureaucracies (Wajcman, 1998). Sexuality cannot be banished from everyday interactions, and sexual harassment laws and policies do *not* mean that men and women can't joke or have fun in employment or academic situations (Levy & Paludi, 1997). Sexual harassment, in contrast, involves repetitive unwanted and unwelcome sex- or gender-related attention or actions that interfere with a person's functioning and sense of well-being. The inability of a particular group, usually women, to control exposure to these unwanted behaviors shows that power is involved in sexual harassment. The concept of sexual harassment may be confusing because the term is often used in different ways. The legal definition of sexual harassment construes certain behaviors

FIGURE 14.1 The most common scenario for sexual harassment in both the workplace and in academia involves male superiors and female subordinates.

as a form of sex discrimination (Levy & Paludi, 1997). However, there is also the personal experience of sexual harassment, which may or may not overlap with its legal definition (Fitzgerald & Omerod, 1993; Levy & Paludi, 1997). This discussion will not cover everyday harassing behaviors in the schools and schoolyards, or on public streets.

In the classic sexual harassment scenario, someone with social or economic power (an employer, supervisor, instructor, or so forth) suggests or insists to a subordinate that sexual activity is required as a condition for continued employment, advancement, or the avoidance of negative consequences. This is called *quid pro quo* ("this for that") harassment. A second type involves the maintenance of a hostile environment. This could include degrading employment policies (for example, requiring only women servers to wear revealing clothing) or exposure to sexually offensive remarks, behaviors, materials, and so on (for example, the pornographic slides included in a class lecture). Social scientists have mainly been concerned with the prevalence, severity, and impact of the experience of sexual harassment. That is, they have examined experiences or situations in which sex-related or gender-related remarks, jokes, touching, requests, threats, and so on have been used to subordinate, demean, or control another person (Fitzgerald, Swan, & Magley, 1997). In this discussion, *sexual harassment* refers to the experience of unwanted sex-related behavior at work or at school that the target perceives as offensive, excessive, and threatening to a sense of well-being (Pryor & Whalen, 1997). Most often the perpetrator is a man, and the target a woman, but situations involving same-sex sexual harassment (SSSH) make it clear that the real issues here are those of power and gender, rather than sexual or romantic interest (Tangri & Hayes, 1997). Although the discussion here centers on experiences of sexual harassment, I mention some court cases that have clarified or solidified the issues involved.

Was Too, Was Not, Was Too, Was Not. The question of whether particular events or interactions constitute sexual harassment moves people to reconsider many important aspects of gender and gender relations. The issues here are those of relationship status, power, and gender-related perceptions (Leeser & O'Donohue, 1997). For example, when 4,000 university students, faculty, and staff were surveyed, there was almost universal agreement that sexual bribery, explicit propositions, and physical sexual advances constituted sexual harassment. However, strong gender differences arose regarding the perception of sexist comments, coarse language, and sexual jokes as harassment. Women respondents were sensitive to the status differences (for example, professor versus classmate) between the harasser and the harassed (Frazier, Cochran, & Olson, 1995). Women tended to view sexual harassment as an abuse of power, whereas men tended to view it as flirtation and flattery (Levy & Paludi, 1997). In general, men are more likely to believe that sexual harassment is not a problem and that women exaggerate its prevalence (Gutek & O'Connor, 1995). Men are also more likely to attribute responsibility for harassment to the target. Men tend to base their perception of whether sexual

harassment has occurred on the target's reactions, whereas women based their perception on the perpetrator's behavior, regardless of the target's response (Henry & Meltzoff, 1998). According to the American Psychological Association (1993) men and women have different perceptions regarding what is sexually harassing. It was argued that a *reasonable woman* standard should replace the traditional *reasonable person* standard to determine if sexual harassment has occurred because certain remarks and behaviors are particularly threatening to women given their realistic concerns regarding men's economic power and sexual violence (Blumenthal, 1998; Rutter, 2000). Thus, in evaluating whether sexual harassment has occurred, the *impact on the target* matters more than the *actor's intentions*. Interestingly, in a multination study the strongest gender differences in the perception of various scenarios as sexual harassment emerged in samples from the United States and Brazil. There were no gender differences in such perceptions among Australian and German respondents (Pryor et al., 1997).

Prevalence of Sexual Harassment. Experiences of sexual harassment may be underreported and underestimated. A typical estimate is that one out of two women will have an experience of harassment, depending on the definition used, the population surveyed, measures used, and the time frame evaluated (Henry & Meltzoff, 1998). The estimated prevalence for men is about 15% (DuBois, Knapp, Faley, & Kustis, 1998; Levy & Paludi, 1997). There are significant differences according to occupational group. University faculty, staff, and administrators are more likely to experience harassment than are students. Women working in blue-collar trades are more at risk than are white-collar or pink-collar workers (Levy & Paludi, 1997). Until recently, the medical profession was defined as masculine turf and sexual harassment was apparently widespread (Dickerstein, 1996). For example, Dr. Frances Conley, one of the nation's first female neurosurgeons, resigned her professorship at Stanford Medical School, citing an extensive history of experiences of sexual harassment. She was subjected to touching and groping by her male colleagues, as well as to degrading sexual comments. Dr. Conley was successful in regaining her position after several "administrative changes" were made.

The Harassed and the Harasser. Financial need and a previous history of personal victimization increase a person's vulnerability to sexual harassment. Targets are more likely to be single or divorced, better educated (they are more likely to complain), and very dependent on their job (Tang & McCollum, 1996).

There is no single "personality type" who can be predicted to sexually harass. However, men who harass are likely to be older, married, and of the same ethnicity as their targets. Harassers typically harass more than one woman, and hold calloused and adversarial attitudes toward women. They also tend to value and emphasize male social and sexual dominance. They are often surprised that their attention was not welcomed. Harassers typically believe that complaints of harassment are not authentic. They tend to have low self-esteem and are insensitive to the perspectives of others. Thus harassers are not deviant or pathological. Instead, they overconform to the masculine gender role (Bondurant & White, 1996; Tang & McCollum, 1996).

Women harassers are rare (Levy & Paludi, 1997). Most of men's experiences with sexual harassment involve other men (DuBois et al., 1998; Stockdale, Visio, & Batra, 1999). Same-sex sexual harassment (SSSH) usually occurs because the targeted men do not fit the offenders' gender role stereotype of heterosexual hypermasculinity. The most common type of SSSH involves sexual jokes and teasing. More serious and disturbing are threats and attempted assaults. For example, Joseph Oncale was a small, quiet, slightly built young man who began a job on an offshore drilling rig. Over many months, the other men on the work crew repeatedly tormented him with insults, crude sexual jokes, numerous pranks, teasing, physical and sexual threats, and finally, overtly assaultive behavior. These behaviors centered around Oncale's deviation from the hypermasculine gender norms and stereotypes that were normative in his workplace. Oncale sued his employer, alleging responsibility for a hostile environment of sexual harassment. The U.S. Supreme Court ruled that the plaintiff did in fact experience SSSH (*Oncale v. Sundowner Offshore Servs. Inc.*, 1998), and he was able to recoup substantial monetary damages.

The Impact of Sexual Harassment. A significant body of research has documented the impact of sexual harassment experiences. In academia, sexually harassed students cope by avoiding or dropping classes, avoiding the perpetrator, bringing friends to meetings, mentioning boyfriends, changing majors, or dropping out (Biaggio & Brownell, 1996). In the workplace, targets of harassment change jobs, demonstrate decreased morale, higher absenteeism, lower job satisfaction, performance decrements, and damage to their other interpersonal relationships. They typically report poorer emotional health, depression, helplessness, strong fear reactions, a sense of loss of control, disrupted private lives, and decreased motivation. Physical health outcomes typically include headaches, sleep disturbances, disordered eating, gastrointestinal disorders, nausea, weight loss or gain, and crying spells. For both women and men, experiences of harassment injure the sense of self and create self-doubt (Rosen & Martin, 1998; Shrier, 1996).

Explanations and Remedies for Sexual Harassment. Sexual scripts may spill over into work and academic situations (Gutek, 1985). Central to the masculine sexual script are frequent demonstrations of sexual competence and a sense of entitlement. Thus, some men are likely to initiate such behavior in nonsexual/nonromantic contexts. Three traditional masculine sexual scripts and their complementary feminine scripts (see Table 14.1) add to the likelihood of harassment occurring (Kurth et al., 2000).

Another approach emphasizes the situations or environmental factors that facilitate or impede sexual harassment (Humlin, Fitzgerald, & Drasgow, 1996). In most organizational contexts, women occupy subordinate positions. In such contexts, behaviors begin to reflect and amplify status differences and gender roles. When the job positions within an organization are gender integrated, the traditional societal gender hierarchy is not replicated within the organization. Second, because work is central to masculine gender identity, introducing women into male-dominated jobs and professions is likely to elicit a particularly hostile type of sexual harassment. Male-dominated jobs are seen as requiring special traits and abilities, and these traits and abilities make men superior. The influx and success of women into these realms removes the mystique surrounding such jobs, and male superiority is threatened. Third, highly gender-segregated jobs facilitate the development of a "masculine

TABLE 14.1   Sexual Scripts Contributing to Sexual Harassment

Masculine Scripts	Feminine Scripts
Seducer: Pursuer and appreciator of women. All female subordinates are sexual objects.	*Sexual object:* Women must always be sexually alluring through their appearance and demeanor.
Initiator: Stronger sex drives make men the natural initiators of sexual encounters. Men have the burden to initiate and risk rejection. Women are burdened with fending off unwanted approaches without hurting the man's self-esteem.	*Passivity:* Women should quietly endure offensive or disturbing behavior from men because female submissiveness is normal and natural.
Dominator: Women who enter male domains do not deserve protective treatment. Men may mark territory with pornography or physical aggression (pinches, etc.) to establish dominance and control over that domain.	*Dependence:* Women's vulnerable economic position limits their freedom to complain or take other action.

Source: Adapted from S. B. Kurth, B. B. Spiller, & C. B. Travis (2000). Consent, power, and sexual scripts: Deconstructing sexual harassment, in C. B. Travis & J. W. White (Eds.), *Sexuality, society, and feminism* (Washington, DC: American Psychological Association), pp. 323–354.

culture." If only a few women hold certain jobs, they achieve *token status*, and this promotes even more stereotyping. If dramatic power asymmetries exist in the distribution of jobs, those in positions of greater power stereotype subordinates even more. Fourth, if some men have a greater propensity for sexual harassment, they are more likely to act on their propensities when the norms of a particular workplace prime these harassing tendencies, as when, for example, a supervisor models, condones, or ignores such behavior (Pryor, Giedd, & Williams, 1995).

Rape and Sexual Assault

> [Rape] is nothing more or less than a process of intimidation by which all men keep all women in a state of fear. ◆ Susan Brownmiller

Concerns about sexual abuse, rape, and sexual assault have been at the forefront of the women's and children's rights movements (Haaken & Lamb, 2000). Child sexual abuse is a profound betrayal of the trust and protective bond that normally exists between a child and caring adults. Adults have infinite power over children, and a small number of adults exploit that power for their own sexual pleasure (Haugaard, 2000). Between 95% and 97% of perpetrators are men (Fergusson & Mullen, 1999). Some women offenders have been identified, but their offenses are typically highly correlated with overt mental disorder. This is not true of men who sexually abuse children. Other women offenders claim to carry out their activities under a man's domination (Laumann et al., 1994). The targets of child sexual abuse may be of either gender (Johnston & Johnston, 1997). This discussion will focus more on adult sexual assault.

In many jurisdictions, the term *rape* has a narrow legal meaning. It refers solely to forceful vaginal penetration by a penis. The term *sexual assault* covers a wider array of coercive sexual acts, including acts perpetrated against men, and so it may be more useful to this discussion.

Prevalence of Sexual Assault. Estimating the prevalence of sexual assault is problematic. Varying definitions of "forced sexual contact" for women can yield prevalence estimates ranging from 10% to 50% (DeKeseredy, 1997; Lohr, Adams, & Davis, 1997). Sampling biases constitute another difficult issue. American college students are the typical populations studied, and their experiences may not be at all representative. Studies of "rapists" are very problematic. They tend to rely on highly unrepresentative samples of convicted offenders. Another approach involves surveying college men about whether they engaged in certain coercive behaviors. Here the range varies from 15% to 25% depending on the methodology employed (Calhoun, Bernat, Clum, & Frame, 1997; Lohr et al., 1997). Epidemiological studies with well-accepted definitions appear to be the most useful regarding prevalence estimates, and they generally reveal that 20% of women in North America have experienced some form of sexual assault (Tjaden & Thoennes, 2000).

Perspectives on Sexual Assault. Traditionally, rape was viewed as a property crime, and offenders compensated a father or husband for damage to their property.(Brownmiller, 1975). Up through the twentieth century, some states required eyewitness testimony before authorities would take a woman's rape complaint seriously. Early rape research placed responsibility for sexual assault on the target, who "generate[d] the potentiality for criminal behavior" (Amir, 1971, as cited in Currie, 1998). These beliefs were based on the idea that men's sex drive was so powerful that they could not control themselves. If a woman's clothing, appearance, or behavior aroused a man to this point, she must accept the consequences (Donat & White, 2000). Types of rape include the following:

Acquaintance or date rape. This is the most common assault scenario, but the least likely to be reported. A woman may fear being blamed for trusting her assailant. Drug or alcohol use may cloud her memory, or she may fear retaliation from the assailant.

Statutory rape. This refers to sexual activity with a person below the age of consent. States, provinces, and nations vary on what is considered the age of consent for sexual activity. It may range from 12 to 16.

Stranger rape. Most rape prevention programs are focused on this relatively rare crime. It is the most likely type of assault to be reported and to receive publicity.

Marital rape. The marital rape exemption was codified in British law in the 17th century. According to this legal doctrine, upon marriage a woman had contracted to engage in sexual relations with her husband and she could not retract this. Today, all states and provinces have eliminated the exemption for marital rape. However, debate on this issue continues in the United Nations. Most marital rapes take place in the context of battering (Monson & Langhinrichsen-Rohling, 1998).

Male rape. Two or more heterosexual adult males perpetrate the typical male sexual assault. The typical target is an adolescent or young adult male, and the goal is to degrade and humiliate him (Washington, 1999). Serious physical injury is very common. Jails, prisons, and war situations are common sites for male rapes (Hickson et al., 1994).

Gang rapes. Usually perpetrated by two or more members of a bonded group, such as an athletic team, gang, or fraternity.

Researchers have attempted to explore the cognitive distortions typical of sex offenders such as convicted rapists. Offenders interpret many social cues as indicating sexual interest, and claim that targets actually wanted and enjoyed the sexual encounter (Ward, Hudson, Johnston, & Marshall, 1997). The sexual attitudes of assaultive men emphasize their sexual entitlement and how their powerful sexual impulses must be fulfilled. Convicted offenders usually blame their targets for their incarceration (Hanson & Scott, 1995).

The image of the rapist as an impulsive and deranged stranger persists. The reality is that about 80% of rapists know their targets, are not psychiatrically disturbed, and typically plan their attacks (Ellis, 1994). Furthermore, the documented mass rapes in Nazi Germany, Bangladesh, Bosnia, Croatia, and Rwanda remind us that rape is a military tactic and a central component of "ethnic cleansing" and other genocidal policies (Websdale & Chesney-Lind, 1998). Because *men* define war as warriors fighting each other for the protection of women back home, the "gender war" at the front lines becomes invisible. Activists have been successful in getting the United Nations to recognize rape as a violation of human rights. In very poor nations, or where the government is authoritarian, fundamentalist, or militaristic, interventions regarding sexual violence are unlikely to exist. In Pakistan, a woman must have four male witnesses before her rape complaint will be heard (Beyer, 2001). In Bolivia, rape charges cannot be made unless the victim was a minor and a virgin (Kelly & Radford, 1998).

The vast majority of convicted rapists are not mentally disordered. However, they typically report a history of family violence, and an early and varied sexual history with many partners. Juvenile sex offenders appear to have absorbed distorted ideas about sex, relationships, and the glamour of violent sex (Coleman, 1997). Adult offenders tend to be domineering with women, highly self-centered, and low in empathy (Dean & Malamuth, 1997; White & Koss, 1993).

The Impact of Sexual Assault. The physical impact of sexual assault can run from minimal injury to overt mutilation, lethal infection, and permanent disability. The psychological impact of sexual assault depends on the meaning of the experience to the woman or girl, her level of emotional support, and her individual coping mechanisms. There is a significant shift in the survivor's cognitive and affective worldview. The world is no longer safe, and previously neutral social situations take on a malevolent air. Survivors may internalize blame or minimize the event. Other residuals include intrusive memories, anxiety, depression, distrust of one's own reality, self-harm, chronic pain, sleep disorders, and eating disorders (Brillon, Marchand, & Stephenson, 1999; Janoff-Bulman, 1992; Schwartz & Leggett, 1999). One study of an unusual cluster of suicides in a small Inuit community in Manitoba revealed that four of the five women suicides had been previously sexually assaulted (Wilkie, Macdonald, & Hildahl, 1998).

There are now rape crisis centers in almost all major cities of North America. Thirty years of Take Back the Night marches have attempted to shift the responsibility for assault to the perpetrators and to assert women's rights to move freely about their lives and communities, but there is still an emphasis on safety advice for women. Few efforts are aimed at stopping men and boys from committing sexualized aggression and assault (Foubert, 2000). Preventive campaigns aimed at boys and men have been somewhat successful in Scotland, Australia, and Scandinavia (Kelly & Radford, 1998). However, certain forms of sexual violence remain normalized. Most countries do not recognize marital rape, and during war sexual violence toward "enemy women" is tolerated if not encouraged. Refugee and displaced women are among the most vulnerable groups on the planet. In refugee camps, the staff may be indifferent, insisting that rape is seldom fatal and that it is a "normal" part of refugee life. Typically, no protection is offered to girls and women as they go out to gather firewood, fetch water, and so on. Adverse publicity and the small but growing number of women leaders within the United Nations are gradually changing these policies. Recognition of rape as a global human rights issue is slow (Cohen, 2000).

Current explanations for sexual assault emphasize one of several elements. Some accounts emphasize individual pathology. Others emphasize sociocultural factors that normalize sexual coercion and encourage the development of a masculine sexuality that is predatory rather than psychologically connective (Hall, Sue, Narang, & Lilly, 2000). For example, a large sample of Australian high school boys had more restrictive attitudes toward women's roles, endorsed more sexist ideas for relationships, and agreed that forced sex was acceptable in some situations. Both boys and girls believed men rape because of unmet sexual needs (Davis & Lee, 1996). A national survey conducted in the Central African Republic revealed that nearly 22% of women respondents reported their first intercourse met the legal definition of sexual assault (Chapko, Somse, Kimball, Hawkins, & Massanga, 1999).

Domestic Violence

Some scholars argue that the use of gender-neutral labels such as *domestic violence, family violence, couple violence,* or *marital violence* obscures the reality of the problem. Box 14.1 discusses a recent controversy centered on whether domestic violence is a gender-related phenomenon or a situation of mutual combat. Based on the weight of the research evidence, battering is not gender neutral because the flow of violence is overwhelmingly unidirectional (Kurz, 1998). It is men who batter girlfriends (courtship violence), wives, and partners. Some women do batter their male partners, and members of same-sex couples are not immune from battering (Frieze & Davis, 2000). But overall, battering involves the assertion of men's physical power over an intimate female partner (see Figure 14.2). This assertion occurs in the context of a legal and political tradition that upholds men's power in families.

BOX 14.1

A Recent Controversy in Domestic Violence Research

Some researchers believe that battering is not gendered unidirectional violence. They describe domestic violence as a situation of mutual combat (DeMaris, 1992). Using a survey instrument called the Conflict Tactics Scale (CTS), these researchers reported that women were violent almost as often as men were (12.8% of men and 11.7% of women) (Strauss, 1993; Strauss, Gelles, & Steinmetz, 1980). Many textbooks and popular writings still refer to these findings.

However, the methodology of these studies appears fundamentally flawed. The CTS simply counts aggressive acts without any context, so that a shove, slap, punch, or kick from a 5-foot, 1-inch, 110-pound woman becomes equivalent to one from a 6-foot, 1-inch, 210-pound man who may have been "practicing" aggression since boyhood. Furthermore, the CTS failed to inquire if women initiated the physical aggression or whether their acts were self-defensive or retaliatory (Frieze & Davis, 2000). The fear of imminent death and rape compounds the impact of violence on women and must also be considered. Other research makes it clear that men consistently underreport their violence and that women's violent acts are more often in self-defense. Men are also more likely to use dangerous, repetitive, and injurious forms of violence (Johnson, 1998).

The National Violence Against Women Survey was conducted in 1995 and revealed that married and cohabiting women reported significantly more intimate physical assault and stalking than did comparable men, both over a lifetime and in the previous 12 months. Table 14.2 summarizes some of the findings. Women reported more physical assault, more frequent and longer-lasting victimization, greater fear of bodily injury, more time lost from work, more injuries, and more frequent use of medical, mental health, and justice system services than did male respondents (Duncan et al., 2000; Rudman, 2000). These findings contradict studies of gender similarity in domestic violence rates (Kernie, Wolf, & Holt, 2000; Tjaden & Thoennes, 2000).

TABLE 14.2   Percentage of Men and Women Victimized by a Current or Former Marital/Opposite-Sex Cohabiting Partner in Lifetime by Type of Violence

Type of Violence	Men (n = 6,934)	Women (n = 7,278)
Forcible rape	0.2	4.5
Physical assault total	7.0	20.4
Threw something	4.4	7.8
Pushed, grabbed, shoved	5.1	16.9
Pulled hair	2.3	8.5
Slapped, hit	5.3	14.9
Kicked, bit	2.6	5.3
Choked, tried to drown	0.5	6.0
Hit with object	3.2	4.9
Beat up	0.5	8.4
Threatened with gun or knife	1.8	5.2
Used gun or knife	0.9	1.4
Stalking	0.5	4.1
Any of the above	7.3	21.7

Source: Adapted from P. Tjaden & N. Thoennes (2000). Prevalence and consequences of male-to-female and female-to-male intimate partner violence as measured by the National Violence Against Women Survey. *Violence Against Women, 6*(2), 142–161.

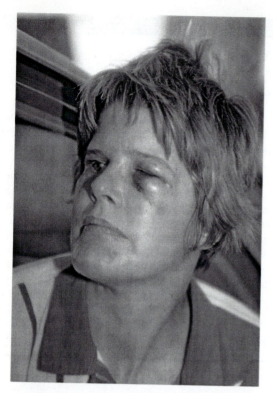

FIGURE 14.2 All over the world, domestic violence threatens the safety and security of far too many women and children.

The legal doctrine of *coverture* completely merged a married woman with her husband. She had no legal rights regarding property, inheritance, earnings, credit, contracts, child custody, protection, and so on. Legally, she and any children were her husband's property, just as buildings, slaves, livestock, and land were. A husband was free to use or abuse his private property as he wished. Up until end of the 19th century, British police were prohibited from intervening in marital disputes. Wife beating was a man's prerogative, a private matter, and even the poorest man could *own* a wife. In the United States, *coverture* was finally abolished late in the 19th century, but wife beating was not made illegal in all states until 1920 (Marcus, 1994).

The English common-law concept of the "rule of thumb" allowed a husband to "correct" his wife as he saw fit provided he did not use a stick thicker than his thumb (Websdale, 1998). The spirit of these legal concepts lingers with us today. There is still reluc-

tance to prosecute violent acts against wives. Rape, robbery, and aggravated assault are fully prosecutable if perpetrated against a stranger, but when the victim is a wife there is still doubt (Marcus, 1994).

Traditional psychological and sociological literature attempted to "locate" battering in the individual psychopathology of both batterer and victim (Currie, 1998). Ostensibly, battered women had low self-esteem, were psychiatrically unstable, were inadequate wives, and had innumerable psychophysiological complaints. A woman's masochism was what kept her in an abusive relationship. These factors were seen as the *causes* of battering, rather than as the *results* of repetitive battering traumas.

Later theory and research emphasized the batterer's psychopathology. Perpetrators were emotionally dependent, suffered from depression and excessive jealousy, and had low self-esteem as well as poor social skills. Batterers grew up in families in which physical punishment and abuse were normative. Perpetrators were impulsive, improperly socialized, and could not help their outbursts of rage. They were responding to unbearable economic and social stresses or lacked nonviolent alternatives for expressing themselves. A large-scale British study found that the public viewed battering as the behavior of abnormal people. Marriage counseling was seen as the appropriate intervention, rather than legal or sociopolitical change. An alternative view was that battering is "simply a crime" and should be treated as such (Dell & Korotana, 2000).

In the 1970s, a grassroots movement arose among feminist activists to educate the public about battering. They established shelters and provided other services for battered women and their children. Shelter locations were secret, and elaborate steps were taken to ensure that enraged husbands and boyfriends could not find their partners. When a proportion of battered women chose to return to their battering partners, the classic question quickly became "Why do they stay?" Even today, it is rare for discussions of domestic violence to begin "Why do they repeatedly batter the women they love?" In other words, the issue of battering remained immune from analysis as a gendered assertion of physical, economic, and social power. The opening vignette for this chapter is relevant here. From a safe and rational distance, the problem of domestic violence seems simple: He hits her, she should leave. Perhaps the vignette provided just a glimpse of the interpersonal dangers and complexities of domestic violence. One man's violence immediately ripples to touch many other people. All the apparent solutions have short-term and long-term consequences. Carol was trying to prevent a possible escalation of violence by not telling her sister's husband Bob about David's violence. Ann was suddenly pulled into continuing the secrecy. Bob was affected by the tension that surrounded the battering. In battering situations, there is overt danger to the battered woman *and* to many others. There is power in physical violence, and many are controlled by it. Some who work in the field of domestic violence believe the question should really be "How does anyone ever successfully get away?"

During the 1980s and 1990s, several significant reforms were enacted. In many cities, discretion regarding arrest was removed from the investigating police officer. An officer *must* arrest a batterer if there is reasonable evidence of domestic violence, and judges are now more likely to respond with jail time and other supervision for batterers. These mandatory arrest policies have reduced domestic violence incidents in some urban areas in the United States, but not in others. In Canada, prompt arrest, prosecution, and relevant "treatment" for batterers appear to have reduced recidivism (Johnson, 1998). Researchers have concluded that mandatory arrest is not a perfect response but is better than just separating the partners or referring them to counseling. However, a battered woman remains realistically fearful of retribution from an enraged partner. After all, of battered women who are murdered, 75% are killed while attempting to leave an abusive relationship (Tjaden & Thoennes, 2000).

The United Nations issued the Declaration on the Elimination of All Forms of Violence Against Women (1993) and has reframed violence against women as a human rights issue that demands attention on a global scale. However, as you can see from Box 14.2, progress regarding domestic violence is very slow and uneven around the world.

The Batterer. According to Israeli researchers, violent men are both impulse ridden and overcontrolled. Their descriptions of violent incidents are characterized by minimization, denial, and a projection of blame onto their victims. They experience themselves as being at war, and see the partner as an enemy who repeatedly probes their weak spots (Eiskovitz & Buchbinder, 1997). Another study chronicled batterers' cognitive distortions and gendered assumptions. One batterer saw his verbal abuse, ripping his wife's clothing, and throwing objects at her as examples of how he "just didn't hit women." Batterers minimize the impact of their behavior when they explain that they "just" slapped, kicked, punched, or pinned a spouse or partner (Dell & Korotana, 2000). Some batterers view their attacks as a way of letting out violent feelings, getting a partner's attention, getting revenge, teasing, and trying to upset the other. A frequent theme is "showing who was boss." For these men, battering was goal-oriented aggression designed to maintain an gendered power imbalance (Copenhaver, Lash, & Eisler, 2000). Batterers have been found to demonstrate a higher need-for-power compared to other men (Barnett, Lee, & Thelen, 1997; Eckhardt, Barbour, & Davison, 1998).

Why Do Women Endure Domestic Violence? A woman may remain in abusive relationships for a number of reasons. She may be unable to economically provide for a family. Gender differentials in education, job skills, and earnings become very salient here. She may still love her partner and still believe that she can stop his violence. Each violent episode is followed by a honeymoon period of remorse and solicitous affection, and she may believe that is how "he really feels" (Walker, 1984). In the opening vignette, David's postabuse behavior was very typical of battering situations. Promises of reform and rededication to the marriage abound. Soon afterward, a period of gradual tension building recurs, culminating in another violent episode. Over time, the level of violence generally escalates (Walker, 1984). A battered woman may be too terrified to leave because of his threats to kill her, their children, or other family members. She may have little support to leave. Often *her complaints*, rather than the battering, are viewed as disruptive to orderly community life. A renewed idealization of "old-fashioned families" that stayed together ignores the fact that abused women had few options in the past (Herzberger, 1996). This is still true in many places in the world (Beyer,

SLIDE SHOW   **BOX 14.2**

A Global Perspective on Domestic Violence

Russia: Rates of battering and spousal homicides are skyrocketing in the new Russia. A woman is nearly three times more likely to be murdered by an intimate partner in Russia than in the United States. Although the majority of Russian women are employed, they are concentrated in low-paying factory jobs, and are thus unable to support children on their own. There is limited child care, a rising drug culture, and the highest rate of alcoholism in the industrialized world. The sheer number of available weapons has increased dramatically. Scarce housing means that battered women must continue to live with their batterers. Community resources for battered women are few and weak. The police force is poorly paid, demoralized, and ineffective in battering situations (Gondolf & Shestakov, 1997).

Brazil: In the major cities, special women's police stations have been established to deal with domestic violence. Traditionally, police rarely investigated domestic violence cases and women were seen as responsible for the violence.

Moreover, the murder of adulterous wives or female partners was rarely punished because such homicides were viewed as crimes of honor. Feminists have changed public attitudes about the acceptability of wife beating, but prosecution is rare. Women police officers receive some special training, but there is little budgetary support for these programs. When officers investigate domestic incidents, they can do little about the leniency shown for batterers or the continued disrespect for battered women (Thomas, 1994).

Lebanon: Lebanon represents a society in transition, in that Western influences are both powerful and derided. Beirut, Lebanon is a very cosmopolitan city, with Muslims as the dominant and socially progressive majority. The Christian-Armenian minority is much more isolated from Western influences. In general, Middle Eastern family structure is very patriarchal and men are expected to dominate women. Although both ethnic groups subscribe to traditional Arab values, battering appears to be much more common among Christian-Armenians in Lebanon. Hus-

bands may impose their will on family members through physical violence. The typical reasons for such abuse are unmet gender role expectations, conflicts with a husband's relatives, and alcohol abuse (Keenan, El-Hadad, & Balian, 1998).

Romania: Since overthrowing its totalitarian regime in 1989, this nation has undergone rapid change, but battering is pervasive and deeply ingrained. Although Marxism ostensibly made no distinction between what is private and what is public, the former communist nations have very poor records of protection for women and children in what was considered the private matter of domestic violence. There is nothing in the Romanian criminal code regarding domestic violence, and media coverage of the problem is virtually nonexistent. Only most the severe cases are ever reported, and police are trained only to calm disputants. There are no shelters or other services, and any court cases seem to disappear. There is little attention to women's rights, and women have few positions of power. It is estimated that repetitive domestic vio-

---

2001). Over time, exposure to violence has a powerful impact on a survivor's cognitions. Repetitive traumas lead to a cognitive shift that reduces logical thinking and problem-solving abilities. Targets of repeated violence come to believe that they caused the violence and that their experience is not unusual.

Conclusions. About 20% of North American women will experience a physical assault of some type over a lifetime, most likely from someone they know intimately. Around the world, battering is most prevalent in societies where norms and beliefs are supportive of masculine power and privilege in relation to women as intimate partners (Johnson, 1998; Lacayo, 2001).

Institutionalized Power

The Legal System

A nation's laws describe the rights, responsibilities, and restrictions of its citizens. Laws facilitate a safe and orderly daily life for citizens. Let's examine several issues that show the interaction between gender and legal systems on a global level.

The laws of many nations codify ongoing discrimination against women (Choo, 2000). For example, only 44 nations have laws against domestic violence, yet 20 to 50% of all women are likely to experience such violence. In Kuwait, women still cannot vote (Meyer, Rizzo, & Ali, 1998). In Saudi Arabia, women are not allowed to drive and are pro-

BOX 14.2 *(continued)*

lence affects from 20% to 50% of Romanian women (Knickrehm & Teske, 2000).

Serbia: The democratization of eastern Europe meant very different things for men and women in the former Yugoslavia. For men, this meant multiparty elections and a free market economy. For women, it meant predatory capitalism, organized crime, and loss of social rights. A resurrected patriarchal religious ideology demanded a return to "old values." Women were blamed for both declining public morality and men's criminal behavior. The new Serbian nationalism and militarism was constructed around violent masculinity. Television programs showed dead Serbians in Bosnia and Croatia, and enraged Serbian men apparently took this out on their wives and children. Young Serbian men joined the paramilitary units responsible for atrocities such as rape and "ethnic cleansing" (genocide). Returnees from these wars kept guns and grenades in their homes, and alcohol abuse was rampant. Men's participation in these wars increased violence against women at home, especially

violence by sons against mothers. Moreover, almost 500,000 Serbian refugees were housed in private homes. The extra work of accommodating them fell on women. The pressures of supporting distraught Bosnian relatives resulted in increased violence against women refugees and their women hosts (Mrsevic & Hughes, 1997).

Chile: Under dictatorship (1973–1990), the core values of total obedience and respect for those in power legitimized both child abuse and wife battering. Blows to the head were considered an especially effective means to ensure children's compliance to the rules of both father and the state. Yet mothers were held responsible for both child abuse and its prevention. During the late 1980s, Chilean violence scholars were influenced by research emanating from the United States that blamed and pathologized battered women. When the Chilean dictatorship was overthrown in 1990, interventions into domestic violence evolved quickly under feminist influence. The Women's Secretariat was established in

1990, and domestic violence legislation was finally approved in 1994. However, no changes have been made in the Chilean judiciary to implement that legislation (Bacigalupe, 2000).

Quebec: Estimates of battering in Quebec are similar to those elsewhere in North America (about 30% report some incident). Montreal had one of the first programs for convicted batterers. Program founders were critical of the "pathology and stress" formulations about battering and adopted a feminist perspective that emphasized men's power and control over women. They produced bilingual documents identifying battering as a criminal act, the need for batterers to take responsibility for their acts, and the need for preventive measures that go beyond personal therapies. The number of men who call the 24-hour crisis hotline has increased substantially over the years. The program has been criticized for emphasizing men's suffering and the trauma of masculine socialization, rather than the impact of battering on women (Dankwort & Rausch, 2000).

---

hibited from entering careers in government, law, and engineering (Beyer, 2001). When the Ukrainian economy was privatized, 80% of downsized workers were women. Today, in France, Bolivia, and Madagascar women are still barred from working night shifts (night shifts often pay more). In Bangladesh and Kenya, citizenship is passed to children only through fathers. In Jordan, Morocco, and Syria, laws permit "honor killings," the murder of women by their male relatives for alleged sexual offenses (Choo, 2000). These offenses include marrying against a family's wishes. Most African legal systems are based on very patriarchal tribal traditions. Nevertheless, Lesotho, Malawi, Namibia, and South Africa have passed bills

enshrining human rights and the notion of gender equality (Maluwa, 1999).

When U.S. Supreme Court Justice Sandra Day O'Connor graduated near the top of her law school class, she could find work only as a legal secretary. Today two women sit on the nation's highest court. About half of all current law students in the United States are women, as are about 29% of practicing attorneys. Their presence seems to have improved the public's perception of lawyers. (Carter, 2000). Surveys suggest that opportunities for women in the legal profession are substantial, but the work ethic in law firms is designed for working men with stay-at-home spouses. Women who have children and who work part time simply cannot compete in a profession that measures advancement through billable hours (Samborn, 2000).

Critical Thinking Challenge

What is your attitude toward the legal profession? Although many remain skeptical of lawyers, we should remember that it was through the efforts of attorneys that equal pay and equal education became rights, domestic violence became a crime, and women could choose what to do about an unwanted pregnancy.

The Criminal Justice System. Law enforcement is a stereotypically masculine profession. The first women officers in Los Angeles wore no uniform, carried no weapon, and kept their badges in a pocketbook. During both world wars, women successfully performed many police duties, but their employment was terminated when peace ensued. During the 1950s and 1960s women officers performed clerical, communications, and "meter maid" duties. A few worked as decoys and plainclothes officers, but their status was still marginal. During the 1970s, a series of lawsuits against the New York City Police Department, as well as new federal equal employment legislation, put law enforcement agencies on notice regarding their discriminatory policies. The FBI and Secret Service hired their first women agents in 1972 (Gold, 1999). Table 14.3 offers a quick glance at two indices of the level of gender equity in law enforcement in the United States. The vast majority of those who make and enforce the law are men, and men also comprise the vast majority of those arrested and incarcerated for breaking the law. Currently, women constitute about 7.5% of the incarcerated population (Kurshan, 1996).

Historically, most of the crimes for which women were incarcerated were sex related: prostitution, promiscuity, serial premarital pregnancies, adultery, venereal disease, vagrancy, and abortion (Kushan, 1996). After the Civil War, all men and black women convicted of crimes were sent to prison. White women convicted of crimes were remanded to reformatories, which were generally more humane than penitentiaries. These early reformatories offered more freedom of movement and more work opportunities. Children up to 2 years old could stay with their mothers within the institution. Some reformatories were

TABLE 14.3   Women and Policing

(a) Police Agencies with Largest Percentages of Women in Top Command

Dayton, OH	37.5%
Travis County, TX	36.4%
Pittsburgh, PA	30.0%
King County, WA	28.0%
Atlanta, GA	26.1%

(b) Agencies with Largest and Smallest Percentages of Women Police Officers

Madison, WI	29.7%
Cook County, IL	26.2%
Washington, DC	24.6%
Philadelphia, PA	23.8%
Detroit, MI	23.4%
.	.
.	.
.	.
South Carolina Highway Patrol	2.5%
Augusta, ME Police	2.5%
West Virginia State Police	2.1%
Oklahoma Highway Patrol	1.6%
North Carolina State Highway Patrol	1.4%

Source: Adapted from *Equality Denied, The Status of Women in Policing,* 1998. Copyright 1999, National Center for Women and Policing, a division of Feminist Majority Foundation, as cited in M. E. Gold (1999), *Top cops* (Chicago: Brittany Publications).

staffed and administered by women. Petty theft was the most common crime, and inmates were mainly Irish-American working-class women who abused alcohol. During 1930s, reformatories and penitentiaries were merged. Today, most of the prison population of both genders consists of poor people of color who have been convicted of crimes related to substance abuse (Kurshan, 1996).

Another large segment of incarcerated women are those who have seriously injured or killed a battering spouse. For example, of the women on Death Row, about half are there for killing an abusive spouse or partner (Rosenblatt, 1996). These facts present an interesting dilemma of gender: Men who commit capital crimes such as murder and manslaughter are considered to pose the greatest risks to public safety. However, most criminologists agree that women who have killed their abusive spouses represent a very low risk to public safety (Faith, 1996).

Many scholars point to poverty as a major causal factor in criminal activity, arrest, conviction, and incarceration. Women are every nation's most impoverished group, yet they commit the fewest crimes (Faith, 1996). How would you account for this?

Political Power

In the majority of human societies, political power has been a masculine domain. In democratic societies, once women achieved the vote the next debate quickly centered on their "proper role" relative to political power. All over the world, the debate about gender and political power continues (Norris, 1997). Table 14.4 chronicles the slow ascent to positions of political power of women in the United States.

The first public political role for women identified in the Western democracies, was that of First Lady. In the United States, the earliest press coverage limited the First Lady to the role of spousal escort. By the middle of the 19th century, a protocol role emerged. That is, the president's wife became the leader of fashionable American society and she presided over ceremonial and social functions. In early 20th century, gender role expectations had shifted, and the First Lady was required to lead women in their volunteer and charitable works in the community. With Eleanor Roosevelt, the First Lady took on a new, unofficial, and still controversial policymaking role. A recent study of media coverage of First Ladies suggested that the more politically active a First Lady, the more negative is the journalistic coverage. With every new presidential election, most of the relevant media coverage focuses on what the First Lady's role *should be* rather than on the actual substance of her work. The public appears to want a president's wife to be active but relegated to "soft" issues such as children, education, and health (Scharrer & Bissell, 2000). However, in 2000 Hillary Rodham Clinton made political history by being elected senator from New York State. In 2001, Laura Bush also made history. She became the first presidential spouse to use the president's weekly radio address to the nation to speak out against the Taliban's oppression of women in Afghanistan. She also called for a role for women in the power structure of postwar Afghanistan. Thus

TABLE 14.4   Gender and Political Power: Pioneers

Pioneer	Event or Accomplishment
Elizabeth Cady Stanton	Ran unsuccessfully for Congress in 1866 (New York).
Jeanette Rankin	First to win a congressional seat. Served 1917–1919 and 1941–1942 (Montana).
Nancy Landon Kassebaum	First woman elected to Senate in 1978 (Kansas).
Nellie T. Ross	First woman governor, 1925 (Wyoming).
Shirley Chisholm	First African-American woman elected to House, 1968 (New York).
Geraldine Ferraro	First woman to run for vice president, 1984 (New York).
Ileana Ros-Lehtinen	First Latina woman elected to House, 1991 (Florida).
Carol Moseley-Braun	First African-American woman elected to Senate, 1992 (Illinois).
Hillary Rodham Clinton	First former First Lady to be elected senator (New York).
Nancy Pelosi	First woman to serve as House minority whip. She is in line to take over as Speaker of the House.

Source: Adapted from S. Thomas (1998). Introduction: Women and elective office: Past, present and future, in S. Thomas & C. Wilcox (Eds.), *Women and elective office: Past, present and future* (New York: Oxford University Press), pp. 1–14.

for the first time, a First Lady has spoken out about U.S. foreign policy (Allen, 2001).

Can you speculate about the role expectations for a future First Gentleman or First Husband?

When it comes to the public's perception of political leaders, gender stereotypes seem to run rampant. Men leaders are seen as more competent regarding foreign policy, defense spending, foreign trade, crime, and economics. Women leaders are viewed as more liberal, practical, emotional, honest, hardworking, compassionate, and less likely to use military force. The fact that Margaret Thatcher, Golda Meir, and Indira Gandhi did not hesitate to use military force has not altered this stereotype.

FIGURE 14.3   Note the gender representation in the Swedish legislature.

Women political leaders are more often viewed as agents of change. Citizens of both genders tend to become uneasy when women leaders focus on the "hard" areas of foreign policy, labor, banking, and trade (Scharrer & Bissell, 2000). In general, elected officials who are women are viewed as less knowledgeable on defense and crime and more credible on "compassion" issues. However, women legislators see themselves as more hardworking, more patient, and attending more to details, better prepared in daily tasks, more able to deal with women constituents, and more concerned with the long-term ramifications of legislation (Thomas, 1997).

Gender stereotyping is likely to persist in the political arena because the typical voter is not well motivated to acquire much information about campaign issues. The voter depends more on the visual cues provided by television, and gender is the most obvious cue. One experimental study revealed that women candidates did best when their advertising exposed voters to their stereotypical strengths. The

woman candidate who called for more enforcement of gender discrimination laws was taken more seriously than one who called for more aggressive monitoring of terrorist groups (Iyengar, Valentino, Ansolabehere, & Simon, 1997).

The gender imbalance in government offices is evident at every level and is most dramatic at the highest levels (Norris, 1997). Women's representation in the U.S. Congress is still lower than in similar assemblies in Canada, Austria, Germany, Netherlands, Denmark, Sweden, Norway, and Finland (Apfelbaum, 1993). (See Figures 14.3 and 14.4.)

A gender balance in elected office is important for many reasons. A democratic government cannot be legitimate if all its citizens do not have a proportional interest and stake in serving their community and nation. Second, if all citizens have equal opportunity to affect decisions, they will have greater trust and support for that leadership. Third, women comprise a great pool of untapped talent. Fourth, women need to have full access to public office so that their somewhat

FIGURE 14.4 Nancy Pelosi is House Minority Whip. If she becomes Speaker of the House she will become the highest-ranking elected woman.

different life experiences and concerns are represented there. But traditional gender socialization regarding power and leadership means women do not see themselves as viable political candidates (Thomas, 1998). The challenge regarding political power is to convince more women to run for office. Today, in the United States, when women do run for office, they win as often as men do (Duerst-Lahti, 1998).

The Military

Military power often elicits contradictory and ambivalent attitudes. For many, the glorious warrior is a central icon in human imagination and history. Traditionally, the defense of the homeland and the protection of women and children against the enemy were noble and honorable pursuits for the best of a society's young men (Klein, 1999). However, in reality the vast majority of war tasks have no warrior ethos, and modern warfare kills more civilians than soldiers. Thus, for many the military is about training some people to kill others, the killing and maiming of youth, the squandering of a nation's resources, and a guarantor of grief for women and children (Bourke, 1999).

The U.S. military is also the nation's largest vocational and managerial training institution. It is an institution within which poor and disadvantaged youth can learn, advance, prosper, gain status, and earn respect. Since the end of World War II, the U.S. military has also served as a human relations laboratory in which egalitarian ideals are announced as official policy and enforced from the top down. As a result the military is probably the most ethnically integrated institution in American society. The path to gender equity in the military has been slower and has had many bumps and diversions, but the momentum is unstoppable. Women now contribute their skills and service at virtually every level of the military (Sadler, 1997).

In today's complex world, in addition to waging war the U.S. military is often involved in keeping the peace and relieving human suffering. However, deeply held gender ideology continues to link men with war and women with peace. Traditionally, war was a major arena where men could prove their masculinity, and masculinity was the sole required qualification for participation and success. Women give and sustain life; they do not take life. Combat is about killing people, and it remains difficult for many people to imagine wives, mothers, and daughters doing that. Also, femininity is heavily disparaged in the military. For example, male recruits are usually called "girls" until they prove their capabilities (Peach, 1996).

The U.S. military is presently unmatched in its level of racial integration and ethnic minority achievement. Even though ethnic minority accomplishment is now a part of the military's institutional culture, the resolution of gender issues is still incomplete (Dansbury, 1998). However, the war in Afghanistan has brought about significant movement in this regard.

Let's begin with a little recent history. In 1948, President Truman signed an executive order calling for an end to segregation in the military and a goal of full racial equality. That executive order also gave women a permanent place in the U.S. military, but with many limitations. Only 2% of a branch's total personnel could be women, and only 10% of its officers. Laws and policies allowed overt discrimination in enlistment procedures, discharge policies, dependency benefits, promotion opportunities, and job restrictions. In 1967, Congress repealed many of these restrictions, but participation in direct combat was still prohibited. Nonetheless, the number of women, especially ethnic minority women, seeking military experience) grew rapidly and by the mid 1990s, women constituted over 13% of active duty personnel (13.4% of officers and 13.2% of enlisted members). In 1993, a new policy allowed women to compete for virtually all assignments, and this gave women a greater potential for participating in combat assignments.

The Gulf War made clear that it was impossible to distinguish between combat and support roles. For example, although Air Force women could not fly fighter planes, they could fly the tankers that refueled fighter planes in enemy airspace. Also, "noncombat" ships were highly likely to become targets of attack, but their crews could not shoot back. In Desert Storm, women made up slightly over 7%, or 41,000 of the deployed U.S. forces (Pierce, 1998). Thirteen military women were killed, with five killed in action. Two

were captured. The successful performance of these women in combat situations challenged deeply held ideas about war, women, men, and the military. Strength differences were overcome by teamwork, and there were few significant cohesion problems. According to one military professional, in all-man units, the important process of male bonding occurs, but in integrated units *unit bonding* occurs. Unit bonding depends more on shared risks, hardships, and other intense experiences, rather than on gender. Members of integrated units seem to develop brother–sister bonds rather than sexual ones, and there is accumulating evidence that women and men can interact effectively in nonsexual ways (Cornum, 1996). By 1994 women were flying combat aircraft and were assigned to combat ships. Ultimately, advocates moved to end all restrictions and to make all assignments on the basis of ability, not gender. However, the Navy continues to exclude women from nuclear submarines, mine sweepers, and SEAL Commando units (Peach, 1996).

In the war in Afghanistan, progress shifted from a listing of newsworthy service "firsts" to quiet and regular progress in all areas of the military. Women now comprise 16% of armed services personnel. The greatest concentration is in the high technology-oriented Air Force, where they make up 19% of all personnel. A full 99% of all Air Force positions and 91% of all Army positions are now open to women. However, women are still restricted from infantry, artillery, armored units, and submarine duty. Nor do women serve in the Special Forces. By the end of 2001, only 10 women flew Navy fighter planes (*Newsweek*, October 29, 2001). (See Figure 14.5.)

For many, the benefits and personal rewards that accompany military service (travel, personal development, sense of community and purpose, gender equity in pay, health, retirement, and so on) are unequaled in the private sector. Although sexual harassment scandals still receive a great deal of press and research attention, today's military is actively dealing with many diversity issues. These include the integration of gays and lesbians, as well as issues of racial identity issues as the number of multiracial individuals increases. Other gender issues include the economic impact of so many more women in the military, their impact on military effectiveness, the expansion of job specialties, the impact of pregnancy and single parenthood, gender differences in work absences, gender

FIGURE 14.5 Women are steadily being integrated into all levels and all types of military positions including those involving direct combat.

equity in promotions, and the gender issues surrounding daily life in foreign cultures. For example, in Indonesia and Saudi Arabia, military women must cover their bodies completely when they go off-base (*Newsweek*, October 29, 2001).

There are many cogent arguments both for and against a fully gender-integrated military, as summarized in Table 14.5. A study of a fully gender-integrated unit of peacekeepers in Bosnia revealed no differences in performance and war-fighting spirit. Sexual attractions and relationships were not a problem when troops were deployed with a specific mission. The pregnancy rate among those in the Bosnian operation was substantially below that elsewhere in the U.S. military in Europe (Priest, 1998). However, military women may not use their health services to obtain abortions.

Organized Religion

Religious traditions exert tremendous power over the individuals who comprise any society. These beliefs and traditions both influence and reflect the gender ideology of that human group. Here we describe several overarching themes that are relevant to gender, religion, and spirituality on a global level.

Gender Construction. A society's gender system is reflected in the core symbols and beliefs of that society's religious traditions. The gender of the central deity or deities, the gender hierarchy that may be suggested by creation and founding myths, the ideal relationship between women and men prescribed by narratives about important religious personages, sacred writings related to gender roles, and so on all influence the maintenance of gender within the society adhering to a particular spiritual tradition. For example, Shakerism, Spiritualism, Christian Science, and Theosophy all de-emphasized a masculine deity, denied the need for an ordained clergy, and denied that motherhood was the only acceptable role for women. These religious traditions tended to have more gender balance among their leaders (Thurman, 1997). The mainline sects of the Jewish, Christian, and Islamic traditions are heavily patriarchal, with a clearly masculine deity, creation myths that subordinate women

TABLE 14.5   Arguments for and Against a Gender-Integrated Military

In Favor	Against
Since the all-volunteer force began in 1970s, it has become clear that women recruits have more education, higher test scores, and fewer performance problems than comparable men.	The extra screening involved in selecting women with adequate physical capacity for combat is both costly and time consuming.
Regarding physical and psychological fitness for combat, only *some* women and *some* men meet the standards for strength and stamina. Regardless of gender, many recruits do not meet these standards. Some women are qualified for combat roles, but by excluding all women, they are treated as an undifferentiated class.	Concerns about pregnancy make for inefficiency.
	Although many individual women soldiers have been effective, in general, there is a substantial problem with sexual misconduct and harassment. This leads to dangerous loss of morale.
The modern military requires more than physical strength; bravery, intelligence, and technical skills are also critical.	The military is a coercive institution full of intense pressures and undesirable tasks. To be fair, there must be complete equality in all tasks. When training and performance standards are modified for women, this sense of fairness is violated.
Physical size and strength have little to do with firing weapons at a distance. For hand-to-hand combat, the redesign of weapons can offset the need for physical strength.	The American public is simply not ready to accept the idea of women in combat.
Regarding vulnerability to rape; in war, *both* men and women are vulnerable to rape. Women have survived as prisoners of war. Women always have to deal with the threat of rape in their everyday lives.	No matter the rules and restrictions, sexual and romantic relationships will develop. The jealousies, courtship rituals, and favoritism typical of romantic relationships are disruptive and destructive of a sense of fairness.
The belief that women lose more time from duty because of pregnancies is unfounded. Men lose more time because of desertion, chemical abuse, incarceration, and going AWOL.	The normal course of sexual attraction and romantic involvement is not compatible with military functioning and goals.
Single parenthood and the impact of maternal deployment on young children are real issues, but it is irrational to exclude women who are not parents and then include men who are parents.	In close situations, there will be resentment and competition among men for the fewer women available.
The American public seems accepting of women in combat roles. Surveys of military women real that they favor women choosing combat roles, but not requiring combat roles for women. The death of 11 women soldiers in the Gulf War and two in the bombing of the U.S.S. *Cole* was accepted by the American public.	Women's involvement in the military strengthens a basically immoral institution. Women should devote themselves to nonviolent alternatives to war.
If women are to truly have equal rights, they must have equal responsibilities.	Combat roles are antithetical to women's roles as peace makers rather than warriors.
Exclusion from combat roles denies women opportunities for advancement, specialized training, and leadership roles.	

Sources: Adapted from B. L. Moore & S. C. Webb, (2000), Perceptions of equal opportunity among women and minority Army personnel, *Sociological Inquiry*, 70(2), 215–239; D. Priest (1998). Sexual integration has not harmed the military, in B. Leone (Ed.), *Working women: Opposing viewpoints* (San Diego: Greenhaven Press). pp. 129–139; J. Webb (1998). Sexual integration has harmed the military, in B. Leone (Ed.), *Working women: Opposing viewpoints* (San Diego, CA: Greenhaven Press), pp. 137–146.

to men, narratives that prescribe power and control for men, and narrow models for women of either the long-suffering wife/mother or of sexual sinner.

Recent world events have sparked a new interest in Islamic traditions of gender. Many Muslim nations blend and overlap secular and religious laws. With the rise of Islamic fundamentalism all over the world, religious doctrines have sometimes overpowered secular laws. Some of the more repressive rules of Islamic law (the *Shari'a*) are based on the Koran, but many others actually have their origins in tribal customs that *predate* the development of Islam. For example, if a woman is murdered, compensation is only half that prescribed for men victims. Daughters may inherit only half of what their brothers are due. Women may have only one spouse, whereas men are allowed up to four. In Iran, girls as young as 9 may be given in marriage (Beyer, 2001).

Agents versus Symbols. In patriarchal religious traditions, men function as active and powerful agents of the divine, whereas women often serve as only symbols (Sered, 1999). Great tension arises when women seek to claim any agent roles within patriarchal traditions. For example, if sexual restraint is important within a religious tradition then men define what constitutes sexual transgression and prescribe appropriate punishments. Women become the *symbol* of that restraint, and female virginity becomes an obsessive focus. Mary may birth a son, but she is still a virgin. Women's genitals are mutilated to ensure "purity" and lack of erotic pleasure. Women must completely cover their bodies so that men will not sin (Sered, 1999; Beyer, 2001).

Critical Thinking Challenge

Why do you think biblical characters such as Delilah, Jezebel, and Mary Magdalene are more well known than Sarah, Hagar, Rachel, Ruth, Naomi, Esther, or Miriam?

Religious activists have attempted to claim agentic roles for women within established religions. In 1970, only about 3% of clergy in the United States were women. By 1990, the percentage was about 10%, and by 2000 almost one third of enrolled divinity students were women (see Figure 14.6). Full gender equity exists within a denomination when there are no positions from which women are barred and when women are proportionally represented at all levels, but ordination alone does not imply full clergy rights. For example, way back in 1853 Congregationalists ordained a woman, but since then the rare women clergy have served only in the smallest

FIGURE 14.6 Scenes such as this one with a woman minister are still quite rare in most organized religions.

congregations and at the lowest pay. The Roman Catholic Church will ordain no women as priests, but women pastors lead at least 300 parishes in the United States. Catholic women serve as chaplains in hospitals, colleges, and prisons. In general, laypeople still resist women clergy, and there has been conflict over women's ordination in almost every denomination (Chaves, 1997). On a global level, women's voices are now influential in Judaism, Christianity, Islam, and Hinduism, but at the same time fundamentalism has resurfaced, perhaps in order to reassert patriarchy (Sered, 1999).

Formality. Across cultures and epochs, the less formal and developed a religious tradition, the more equitable is the gender balance in the significant roles of that tradition (King, 1993). In many preindustrial societies, women are ritual experts and specialists in health care, and childbirth, but these roles have disappeared as societies westernize and modernize. For example, in Okinawa women dominated the official mainstream religion for 500 years. Okinawan priestesses owned their land and passed it to their daughters, but Japanese law demanded registration by "male heads of households," and priestesses quickly lost their land and power to male relatives (Sered, 1999). In general, the more institutionalized a religion becomes, the more are women excluded from positions of authority and power. Women typically hold higher status in archaic, ancient, tribal, and noninstitutionalized forms of religion (shamanism, Quakers, and so on). Consider the female visionaries in Germanic pagan religion, and the oracles, sibyls, prophetesses, and fortune-tellers of ancient Greece and Rome. There were women priests in ancient Egypt, Sumeria, Babylonia, Greece, and Japan. Today, women are seeking higher status in many of the world's established religions (Murphy, 1998; Young, 1994).

Beginnings. Abraham, Moses, Mahavira, Buddha, Zoroaster, Jesus, and Muhammed were all men, but women had prominent roles in the founding and development of all these religions. The general pattern is that once a religion becomes established and organized, men assume leadership and control, whereas women are relegated to the periphery and are often subjugated by the very religious tradition they helped create. For example, Muhammed's wife and daughter had critical roles in the founding and spread of Islam. Women converts spread the New Testament gospel all over the Roman world. More recently, a man named Dada Lkhraj founded the Brahma Kumari religion in India. His teachings cast women as superior to men and gave special encouragement to women. Lkhraj entrusted the movement to a group of nine women, and these women spread his teachings beyond India. In India, all Brahma Kumari centers are run by "sisters," and women converts have far outnumbered men. Brahma "brothers" do all domestic work except for cooking. This leaves the sisters free to teach, lead meditation groups, and function as spiritual directors. However, as this religion spreads overseas men are gradually taking over the movement (Howell, 1998).

Religiosity of Women. Across cultures, established religions depend mightily on the religiosity of women to continue (Dorahy et al., 1998). For example, the ratio of women to men who attend Christian churches ranges from 2:1 to 7:1. Even in churches where there is an all-male ordained leadership, the inner circle of laity who run things is likely to be mostly women. In many African-American churches, women are 75% to 90% of the participants. Interestingly, Christian congregations outside western Europe and North America have a better gender balance—for example, in Poland (Mathewes-Green, 1999). Feminists have researched pre-Christian women's spirituality, documented the antiwoman stance of many religious traditions, and attempted to create more gender-inclusive rituals, but they have tended to ignore the greater religiosity of women (Walter & Davie, 1998).

Critical Thinking Challenge

How would *you* account for women's greater religiosity and heavy involvement in patriarchal religions?

Conclusions

The term *power elite,* coined by sociologist C. Wright Mills (1956), referred to the men at the top of corporate, political, and military worlds. In his work, Mills ignored women because there were so few among the power elite. In the last presidential administration, more women than ever before served at the highest posts, and their appointments garnered a great deal of publicity. In the current administration, the Cabinet and the White House staff are well integrated by gender, and this receives little media attention. Box 14.3 offers a glimpse of two remarkable women who are potent symbols of increasing gender equity in the power elite.

The corporate board room is now at least sprinkled with women. There are slow increments in the number of women in Congress and state legislatures. It seems safe to conclude that in North America, the power elite is no longer an all-male bastion. However,

ZOOM & ENLARGE   **BOX 14.3**

A Tale of Two Women: The Strongest Link

This is the story of two women who work among the most powerful people on the planet. Their story is even more remarkable because of the person to whom they are mutually linked.

In 1996, Madeleine Albright became the first woman to become secretary of state for the United States, and she always approached her unique status with both humor and serious determination. After being sworn in, Albright was asked how it felt to be both a woman and a secretary of state. She replied that she had been a woman for 60 years and a secretary of state for six hours. She suggested it was best to wait to see how the two went together. In her capacity as secretary of state, she always made it a point to speak out about the social, political, and economic rights of women. She led the fight to have long-standing practices such as domestic violence,

honor crimes, genital mutilation, dowry murders, female infanticide, wartime rapes, and the sale of women labeled as crimes that must be stopped rather than as cultural differences (Albright, 2000).

Condoleezza Rice serves the current administration and the nation as national security adviser. Her achievements constitute a living tribute to the progress women and minorities have made in sharing power in the United States.

Rice was born to two schoolteachers in then-segregated Birmingham, Alabama. Her family moved to Denver, Colorado, and she entered the University of Denver at age 15 with a career in music in mind. There she met Dr. Josef Korbel, a Czech refugee who was then head of that institution's School of International Relations. Under his mentorship, her interests shifted to international affairs. She became an expert on all things Russian and

Soviet. Their close relationship extended for many years, and she was a guest in his home many times. She came to know all the members of the Korbel family quite well. At age 19, she began a master's degree at Notre Dame. A doctorate at the University of Denver soon followed. At age 26, she joined the faculty of Stanford University and quickly rose to the position of provost. "Condi" was tapped to join the National Security Council under George Bush Sr. In the current administration, she serves as national security adviser, and she works among the American domestic and foreign policy elite (Nordlinger, 1999).

How are these two women linked? Dr. Josef Korbel was Madeline Albright's father. Thus we see that some men in powerful positions are willing to mentor exceptional women whether in the private or public sphere.

highly masculine behavioral norms still predominate in that rarefied zone at the top (Zweigenhaft & Domhoff, 1998).

Summary

◆ The concepts of power and masculinity are closely intertwined. Feminists have provided an analysis of power as a gender-related phenomenon.

◆ Sexual harassment is an unwelcome and repetitive pattern of sex-related behavior that interferes with functioning or well-being. Such illegal behavior appears fairly prevalent in the workplace and academia. Explanations for sexual harassment, including same-sex sexual harassment emphasize overconformity to the masculine role and power relations.

◆ The term *sexual assault* has a broader meaning than rape. Six types of sexual assault have been identified: acquaintance rape, statutory rape,

stranger rape, marital rape, male rape, and gang rape. Sexual assault is physically and psychologically traumatic. Current explanations for sexual assault emphasize socialization for a predatory masculine sexuality.

◆ Domestic violence is the physical abuse of an intimate partner. It is ensconced in traditional ideas about marriage and masculine privilege. Legal reforms and grassroots social programs have provided greater protection for battered women. Batterers overadhere to notions of masculine power in relationships. Battered women tolerate abuse for a number of socioeconomic reasons.

◆ Around the world, legal systems continue to represent entrenched masculine power. Women have made considerable progress in gaining power in the various aspects of the legal system in North America.

◆ Political power remains a resolutely masculine domain all over the world. Gender stereotypes influence the perception of political leaders. The gradual entry of women into international leadership is slowly changing the perception of certain gendered cultural practices as crimes and issues of human rights.

◆ In most societies, the warrior role is a masculine pursuit. The U.S. military is the most ethnically integrated institution and continues to undergo a process of gender integration. There are many cogent and convincing arguments both for and against a fully gender-integrated military.

◆ Organized religion is a powerful force in the social construction of gender. Four themes describe the relationship between gender and power in organized religion around the world.

InfoTrac College Edition

For more information, explore InfoTrac College Edition at

http://www.infotrac-college.com/Wadsworth

Enter search terms: power and masculinity, sexual harassment, sexual assault, domestic violence, gender and politics.

15

Gender and the Future

A Global View

Where there is no vision, the people perish. ◆ *Proverbs 29:18*

Encounters with Gender

The monitor screen and coffee bean grinder/brewer came on at their preset times. The morning global Web report offered the usual mix of issues. Robin still loved to listen to the young newscaster's lilting South African accent. Mars base director Lydia Katrinova was interviewed, and she described how a large-scale environmental controls tragedy had been successfully averted. To reach the largest number of viewers, she chose to speak in Mandarin Chinese, so the Russian, English, and Spanish translations sped across the bottom of the screen. In central and southern Africa, AIDS, drought, and environmental degradation had severely reduced the population of many countries. Ambitious military leaders continued to take over vast new territories for their respective factions. Groups of brutal young men, well stocked with weapons and stolen food, medical, and other aid supplies, waged endless and self-destructive wars. In New York City, the prime minister of Afghanistan was addressing the United Nations about her nation's achievement of universal literacy. She contrasted this with neighboring nations where illiteracy remained at an appalling 80%. In Canada, the newly elected prime minister took the oath of office. His life partner, Jacques Breton, stood beaming beside him, along with their six adopted children. The president of Argentina, Maria Moreno, had just concluded the South Atlantic Free Trade Agreement (SAFTA) with the nations of western Africa, and a wonderful shot of the men and women who led those 15 nations appeared, with all wearing the traditional garb of their respective nations. What a rainbow of human diversity! In Washington, DC, Secretary of Technology Amanda Cho-Ming was retiring on her 85th birthday, and the new secretary, Bradley Smith, was on hand. Smith, an African American, was credited with transforming South Central Los Angeles into the new Edu/Tech Innovation Center for the Americas (ETICA).

This vignette represents one possible gender-related vision of the future. What is your vision of gender and gender relations in the future?

Overview

This chapter projects into the future the various trends and patterns discernible in current understandings of gender and gender relations. Most likely, issues of gender and gender relations will be very different for various human groups. Many of the topics discussed earlier in the text are reconsidered in terms of your likely future life. Larger social issues are reconsidered in terms of developments on a global scale.

Gender and the Future: Whose Future?

All through this text, you have read a great deal about the many facets of gender in the past and present. This chapter allows some speculation about the *possible futures* for gender, gender roles, and gender relations. We speak of *futures* in the plural, because future gender roles and gender relations are likely to be very different for various human groups.

A baby born today in Botswana or Afghanistan will face gender-related issues quite different from those faced by a baby born in New Zealand or Sweden. Sociopolitical forces and individual internal decisions will affect the course of gender and gender relations all over the world. Let's begin close to home. Let's begin with you.

There are several ways to look at the future of gender. Most immediately, we might consider the impact of gender, gender roles, and gender relations in *your personal future*. Here you might think about the options available to you, given your gender. As you have read, the illusion persists in North American society that we choose freely from among a whole array of life options. In reality, family and ethnic traditions, current social norms, and certain economic, political, and technological realities will influence your individual choices and pathways. If you are an older student, you may be aware that these factors have already constricted the choices available to you in the future. If you are a college student of traditional age, your previous socialization will influence your choice of college major as well as your postgraduation jobs. Do you believe gender-related factors will influence your ability to advance in your occupation or profession? The issues should be familiar to you by now. How will your own self-concept and need for achievement influence your occupational accomplishments? How much will gender bias or privilege influence your success?

Moreover, given your gender how long are you likely to live? How long are you likely to work? What are likely to be your health concerns when you are 50 years old, 75 years old, or 95 years old? What are likely to be your living arrangements after age 75? What is most likely to be the eventual cause of your death? What choices are you likely to have regarding contraception, conception, birthing, and the rearing of your children? Many have hopes that new medical technology and pharmaceutical innovation will make the controversy regarding the choice of pregnancy termination a historical artifact. Thirty years after *Roe v. Wade*, the battle over reproductive rights may simply become more complex (Wingert & Tesoriero, 2000). You will be dealing with issues of human cloning and medical research involving fetal tissue (Cibelli, Lanza, West, & Ezell, 2001; Green, 2001).

Critical Thinking Challenge

Now that you have considered these questions for yourself, try to imagine yourself a man or woman of your age in Peru or Zimbabwe. How are you likely to answer them? Based on what you understand about life in those nations, do some of the questions seem irrelevant?

The interpersonal level of gender provides a whole new arena for consideration of the future. Let's begin with the influence of gender in our intimate relationships. Depending on your gender, how many intimate partners or spouses are you likely to have over your lifetime? At present, men tend to have more sexual and romantic partners over the course of a lifetime (Laumann, Gagnon, Michael, & Michaels, 1994). Do you believe these norms are likely to equalize within your lifetime? Do you believe the norm for men to marry women who are younger, smaller, less

affluent, and less educated than themselves will change substantially?

Your relationship with your spouse or intimate partner(s) may occupy considerable emotional and social space in your future life. If relationship prescriptions truly become more egalitarian, prepare for even more careful and time-consuming negotiations regarding relationship power, decision-making power, priorities for needs, conflicting lifestyle choices, and a myriad of other subtle issues. For a committed, egalitarian couple, life together may be more exciting, but it will require much more conscious effort and consideration. If an egalitarian relationship is a life goal for you, I wish you and your partner good luck, exceptional communication skills (especially listening skills in both partners), and a true willingness to negotiate.

Critical Thinking Challenge

Most of us take for granted the social norm that our "close friends" are individuals of *our own gender*. Exceptions to this social norm are so rare that they usually merit considerable comment. Do you believe this norm is likely to change in *your* future? Why or why not?

Will more diverse family forms eventually become the normative "family model"? That is, will the term *family* no longer evoke the "larger male adult, smaller female adult, and two biologically related children" icon? Take a moment to consider the future possibilities. How does it feel to consider the possible alternatives? Is it confusing and overwhelming, or exciting?

For those with a same-sex sexual orientation, many issues will remain unresolved into the future. The social and legal controversies surrounding legal recognition of same-sex relationships are ultimately issues of sex and gender. A "marriage" is legally and socially defined as occurring between people of different sexes. Interestingly, many of the court cases surrounding same-sex relationships involve redefinitions of critical human gender-related roles. These include the roles of "spouse," "parent," "relative," "family," and so on. An important question is whether equivalent legal, social, and personal recognition and rights will be granted to same-sex relationships. The goal for gay rights activists is for gay and lesbian relationships to finally become *ordinary* (Quindlen, 2000). Or do you predict a turn back to more traditional attitudes

	Permits marriage	Permits civil unions	Lacks anti-gay-marriage law	Domestic partner benefits for state employees	Has granted adoptions to individuals	Has granted adoptions to same-sex couples	Has granted second-parent adoptions	Has school non-discrimination law	School law includes gender identity	Has non-discrimination law	Non-discrimination law includes gender identity	Includes sexual orientation in hate crimes law	Hate crimes law includes gender identity	Repealed sodomy laws
D.C.			✔		✔	✔	✔	✔	✔	✔	✔	✔	✔	✔
Vermont	✔	✔	✔	✔	✔	✔	✔	✔		✔		✔	✔	✔
California			✔	✔	✔	✔	✓	✔	✔	✔		✔	✔	✔
Connecticut		✔		✔	✔		✔	✔		✔	✔	✔		✔
New Jersey		✔			✔	✔	✔	✔		✔	✔	✔		✔
Minnesota					✔		✓	✔	✔	✔	✔	✔	✔	✔
Rhode Island		✔		✔	✔	✔	✓			✔	✔	✔		✔
Massachusetts		✔			✔	✔	✔	✔		✔	✔	✔		
New York		✔	✔		✔	✔	✔					✔		✔
New Hampshire		✔		✔			✓			✔		✔		✔
Oregon		✔	✔	✔			✓					✔		✔
Washington				✔	✔	✔	✓					✔		✔

✔ indicates statewide law   ✓ indicates law in some areas

FIGURE 15.1   Here is a glance at the current status regarding recognition and rights of gay and lesbian families. What changes do you envision in the near future? *Source:* Lisa Bennett (2001, Winter). Living on a fault line, *Human Rights Campaign Quarterly,* p. 11.

toward same-sex relationships? The chart in Figure 15.1 summarizes the current status of legal protections for gay and lesbian families in 11 states and Washington, DC.

On the more public aspects of interpersonal relations, the whole issue of "gender as performance" comes quickly into the spotlight. As women and men come to occupy more and more of the same social roles and spaces in Western society, the normally gendered performances of everyday life and interaction are likely to become indistinguishable. Will men and women come to be equally expressive of the same range of emotions? Would you predict the norms for performance in such areas as empathy, helping behavior and leadership will move toward the more traditionally feminine or more traditionally masculine? Will there be balance at some ideal midpoint? Perhaps new forms of public behavior and interaction style will emerge and become normative. Do you be-

lieve the language use and conversational patterns of both genders will become indistinguishable?

Gender-related research findings continue to be translated and often "mistranslated" for the public. The usurping of research findings for their ostensible "entertainment value" also continues. For two recent examples, take a look at Box 15.1.

Critical Thinking Challenge

Despite 30 years of advocacy for the elimination of sexist language, in the aftermath of the World Trade Center attack, newscasters consistently referred to "firemen" and "policemen." Why does sexist language persist?

On the social level, we can re-examine many of the topics covered in previous chapters and ask a whole set of new questions for the future. For example, the issue of gender and sexuality in the future raises

On Current Representations of Gender Research: Some Things Just Don't Seem to Change

Just when you believe that things have changed and that people take a more sensible and critical approach to gender research findings, another wave of pseudo-information rolls in. Here are two recent examples.

A major segment of a popular morning news show was ostensibly devoted to the question "Are women better listeners than men?" A neuroradiologist appeared on the program to explain that his research team used a functional brain-imaging technique that revealed gender differences in the processing of meaningful auditory stimulation (readings from a thriller novel) in a sample of 20 women and 20 men. Researchers found that women tended to demonstrate more neural responses in both cortical hemispheres, whereas responses in men were more concentrated in the left hemisphere. Television programmers translated this finding as showing that women are better listeners because they use more of their brain. Once again, we observe the power of stereotyping, confirmation bias, and pseudoscience as entertainment. Before the program segment even began, local newscasters began joking with network program hosts about gender stereotypes regarding attending and listening. Women announcers began smiling and

nodding knowingly, whereas men announcers began joking defensively and asking speakers to repeat themselves because "naturally, they weren't listening."

First, note the biases implicit in the "scientific question" as presented to the public. A finding of some gender difference was immediately transformed into one gender being *better* or *worse* at something than the other gender. This is quite a leap. Moreover, the "gender performance" alluded to is a popular stereotype: Women complain men don't listen to them. Men complain women that women talk too much about topics that do not merit attention. Clearly, some men and women have communication difficulties. This difficulty is attributed to their *gender* rather than to anything else (such as roles or status). A complex laboratory finding of differences in a particular form of neural processing in a small sample is seized on to "explain" this anecdotal observation or experience. Attributing this anecdotal observation to neural "differences" implies that it is somehow *natural or immutable* (like the fact that humans are not physically equipped to fly). However, the laboratory finding has little to do with social interactions for which we all have been social-

ized over a lifetime. A giant and misleading leap is made when the finding is "translated" into an amusing confirmation of stereotypic expectations for gender-related behavior. Now women can continue to attribute communication failures to "the way men are," rather than to communication performances that can be modified. Men can continue to ignore and devalue what women say. The gender game continues.

As a second example, a recent magazine contained an article entitled "Women Smell Better" (Women smell better, 2002). Can you guess what this article is about? The provocatively entitled article is actually about the inroads women are making into the traditionally male-dominated wine industry. Among the factors required for success in this endeavor is a superior sense of smell (and therefore of taste). The title refers to the well-known finding that there is a relationship between estrogen levels and sensitivity to olfactory stimulation. Again, this differential sensitivity does not mean that all women are "better" at detecting odors than all or even most men. By the way, why do you think women were traditionally so rare as leaders in the grape-growing and wine-making industries?

---

some dire specters. The poor nations of sub-Saharan Africa continue to be decimated by HIV and AIDS. In Botswana, Swaziland, and Zimbabwe about one third of the adult population is infected with HIV. The AIDS pandemic has created 13.2 million orphans, of which 95% live in sub-Saharan Africa. South Africa has the largest number of people living with HIV in the world: 4.2 million people (CARE, 2000). This spread is caused by largely highly gendered sexual norms, as well as by the developmental

status of these nations. The World Health Organization (WHO) and UNAIDS have finally begun to publicly recognize the role that traditional notions of masculinity play in the spread of HIV, both in terms of sexual behavior and drug-injecting behavior (Reuters, 2000b). In most of the world, HIV infection rates are much higher among men. However, in sub-Saharan Africa rates are higher among women. According to a recent report issued by UNAIDS, "Male behavior also contributes to HIV infections in women, who often have less power to determine where, when and how sex takes place" (AIDS Epidemic Update, 2000). Although drugs exist that can slow down the progression of HIV infection into full-blown AIDS, their costs are still out of reach for poor nations. Even when low-cost versions of these drugs are available, there is no simple solution. Drug cocktail therapies are highly individual and require very knowledgeable health professionals to supervise them. Patients too must be able to understand and self-monitor a very complex drug regimen. The right drugs must get to the right patients, and civil unrest makes this unlikely. Even if peace were to prevail, knowledgeable health workers would have to be able to monitor thousands of people dispersed all through a rural landscape with few roads. In the meantime, warring factions steal medical supplies to sell them to support their ongoing military campaigns. The future is bleak indeed for the children, women, and men of the African continent. Nothing short of an inexpensive and easily distributed vaccine is likely to help.

Critical Thinking Challenge

As you have read, profoundly gendered cultural beliefs, attitudes and behaviors are very difficult to change. Efforts to change the sexual behaviors that spread HIV have been aimed mainly at women of childbearing age. A focus on men's behavior has just barely begun. Why are governments and health agencies so reluctant to address the sexual and drug use behavior of men?

All over the world, the threat of sexual violence continues to poison the lives of women and men and the relationships between them. The possibility of sexual violence continues to constrain and control women's lives and freedoms. This highly negative aspect of gender relations is also based on highly gendered sexual norms regarding power assertion. It also rests on the deeply entrenched norm of discouraging physical competence among women. Can you envision physical self-defense training (judo, karate, and so on) being adopted as a normal aspect of physical education for all children? As a parent, would you be willing to devote as much expense and effort to self-defense training for your children as you might for sports activities or dance lessons? Do you believe that if every young girl knew how to physically protect her-

self from attack, this aspect of the power dynamic between the genders would shift? What changes would you envision in boys' socialization toward the goal of eradicating the threat of sexual violence?

In the modern industrialized and postindustrial world, the issues of education and occupation are inextricably bound. The contemporary bonds that tie them together are *technology* and *meaningfulness*. As long as women continue to conceptualize femininity as antithetical to technology and its mathematical and scientific supports, they will be relegated to a more narrow range of educational pathways. This will inevitably result in a narrower range of occupational possibilities. This, in turn, predicts lower earnings and lower-status work for many women compared to what will be available for the technologically astute (Geewax, 2000). As long as men continue to equate adequate masculinity solely with monetary achievement, rather than with personally and socially meaningful work, they too will be relegated to a narrower range of educational pathways. Men will also be more subject to potential occupational and personal stagnation. In postindustrial societies, economic development, political freedom, scientific innovation, and technological development all facilitate the expression of one's occupational potential. It seems socially desirable not to have gender norms constrain and limit an individual's potential in both these domains.

On the global level, inhabitants of developing nations will continue to struggle to achieve basic literacy. Young girls will continue to be systematically excluded from even basic schooling (Nussbaum, 2000). The developing global economy will continue to provide low-paid factory work for millions of poor men and women. Young men who enter factory work are likely to have more formal education and to be perceived as possessing the characteristics required for leadership and managerial roles. Women in developing nations tend to have less control over their reproductive lives and to be perceived as compliant and less ambitious. Thus the traditional gender occupational hierarchy is being reproduced in the developing world. Men will become supervisors and managers, and women will continue to occupy the lowest levels of the labor market.

The issues of gender and health are also very likely to be salient in the future. In developing na-

FIGURE 15.2   How likely is this change in what is considered newsworthy?

tions, adequate food, clean water, minimal health care, and a nontoxic environment are issues for children of both genders. Will both boys and girls have equal access to the resources available? In postindustrial societies, it remains to be seen if the masculine gender role will change to reduce the need to engage in dangerous and life-threatening activities to demonstrate adequate masculinity. Medicine and biotechnology will certainly provide improved means to repair the gender-related illnesses and disabilities that occur over a lifetime. But surely it would be more desirable to *prevent* the injuries and illnesses that reflect gender norms and prescriptions (Mollica, 2000).

Traditionally, women have lived their whole lives with a sense of personal vulnerability to violence. The events of September 11, 2001, demonstrated that men and women are equally vulnerable to the violence of global terrorism. Issues of war and domestic terrorism will continue to have a bearing on the health and lives of all men, women, and children, no matter where they live.

For women in postindustrial societies, changes in gender role conceptualizations have "improved" their mental health. However, in places such as Afghanistan, almost 10 years of severe Taliban oppression of girls and women resulted in high levels of clinical depression and suicide (Lacayo, 2001). The new Af-

ghanistan is still taking shape as you read this, and full rights for women are a central concern (Simons, 2001). A worldwide trend toward religious fundamentalism is growing. Will the sexism and oppression that seem to accompany such movements grow or recede over the next several decades?

How will the worlds of women and men be represented equally in the media of the 21st century? See Figure 15.2 for one humorous vision of the newspaper of the future. The Internet and its associated technology is changing many aspects of media production and distribution. As long as men dominate this personal technology, its potential power will reflect the needs and interests of men, rather than of both genders.

As stated in an earlier chapter, a core component of masculinity is power, whether private and interpersonal or public and political. If there is to be true gender equity in the future, changes will ripple into the most insulated areas of private and public life. Imagine a world without domestic violence. What changes in gender socialization and social legislation would have to occur to achieve this? Imagine an everyday world in which, *all over the world*, more than half of police, judges, attorneys, mayors, state legislators, agency executives, cabinet secretaries, and chief executives were women. How would it feel to be a man

THE ABCs of GENDER (ATTITUDES, BEHAVIORS, AND CONCERNS)   **BOX 15.2**

The Issue: The Gender Environment of Your Everyday Life

What is the gender distribution of those who make up your everyday life? Does the gender distribution of these individuals reflect anything about your attitudes, beliefs, values, and concerns regarding gender?

What is the gender of . . .	Woman	Man	Not Applicable
My main physician or other health care provider?			
A second often used health care provider?			
My dentist?			
My attorney?			
My tax adviser or tax preparer?			
My optometrist or ophthalmologist?			
My family financial adviser?			
My minister?			
My therapist or counselor?			
My hairdresser?			
My college or university president?			
My favorite professor?			
Another professor whom I most respect?			
The majority of professors in my major department?			
The chair of my major department?			
My president, prime minister, or national equivalent?			
My senator or equivalent?			
My congressional representative, member of Parliament, or equivalent?			
My state senator or equivalent?			
My state representative, provincial representative, or equivalent?			
My mayor or equivalent?			
My mentor(s)?			
My hero or ideal? (Most admired person)			

in such a world? How would it feel to be a woman in such a world? How would such a world look and feel to a growing boy or girl?

Additional Explorations

Through Box 15.2, you can evaluate your own current gendered environment. If your social environment made up of a preponderance of people of one gender or the other, how would you explain this? Consider if there is any benefit for you and your family in creating a more gender-balanced environment. Does the present gender balance in your life reflect your values or attitudes? Do you want to change any aspects of your gender environment?

This text has not covered every area where gender has an impact. Space, time, and academic calendar considerations have required omission or curtailed discussion of certain topics. You and your classmates might want to consider the following future-oriented topics and issues for further investigation.

Gender and Environmentalism. How is gender intertwined with the forces of environmental destruction and revitalization? A guiding principle of the environmental movement is to *think globally, and act locally*. How is gender involved in efforts to improve the environment in your local community?

Gender and Space Exploration. One large step for *humankind*? Will human exploration of space remain

BOX 15.2 *(continued)*

What is the gender of . . .	Woman	Man	Not Applicable
Last real estate agent used?			
The person in whom I am most likely to confide a troubling personal problem?			
The person from whom I am most likely to request computer-related help?			
The person from whom I am most likely to request advice regarding a physical health concern?			
My immediate work supervisor?			
My work supervisor at an intermediary level?			
My work supervisor at the highest level?			
An adult relative whom I respect?			
An author whose work I enjoy or admire?			
A music maker whose work I enjoy or admire?			
My plumber, electrician, or housepainter?			
My wallpaper installer?			
My domestic helper(s)?			
My auto mechanic?			
The authors of my current college textbooks?			
The historical personage with whom I would most like to have a leisurely lunch?			
The current celebrity or famous person with whom I would most like to have a leisurely lunch?			
My closest friend?			
The person with whom I laugh the most?			
My favorite relative?			
The person I fear the most?			
The person I most respect?			

a predominantly masculine domain? Would this area of knowledge and research look different if there were true gender equity at all levels of space exploration (from budgetary appropriations, to the technicians at the launch pad, to the astronauts)? The opening vignette suggested that a woman might lead the first human settlement on Mars. Do you think this is likely?

Gender and the Sports Industry. Why is masculine *play* a multibillion-dollar global business? Why is the human pursuit of physical and athletic competition an overwhelmingly masculine endeavor? Why are the physical limits of masculine strength and ability of such interest to other men? Why don't women's play

or other gender-typed interests merit the same attention worldwide? On televised news broadcasts, sports are given as much air time as international affairs, and more time than weather conditions. Why? Can you design an original sport or game in which women's particular physical abilities were featured and emphasized?

Gender and the Arts. A thorough discussion of gender and the visual arts (painting, sculpture, and so on) was omitted from this text. Also, check this month's best-seller lists, both fiction and nonfiction. What is the gender representation of the authors reflected there? What is the gender distribution of the conductors and musicians of your local symphony orchestra?

Gender and Architecture. Hypothesized gender differences in spatial abilities have been cited as an explanation for the relative rarity of women in architecture. How would you evaluate this claim?

Gender and the Behavioral Sciences. Check a representative sample of the psychology, sociology, and anthropology journals in your institution's library. What is the gender distribution of authors in the various subfields of inquiry? What is the gender representation of authors in the areas of psychology, sociology, or anthropology that is of greatest interest to you (other than the psychology of gender, of course)?

Gender and International Development. The priorities of such organizations as the United Nations, the International Monetary Fund, and so on have been said to reflect highly gender-related interests. Consider researching the gender issues regarding international loan projects, and the policies that surround them.

Closing Thoughts

The implicit theme of this book-long discussion of gender is that of *change* in the boundaries that have separated the genders. There have been *changes* in gender roles and gender relations over the past centuries, and there is an ongoing pressure toward *change* in contemporary societies everywhere. The ideological bias that permeates this book is that the change toward greater egalitarianism between the genders is more desirable than change in the other direction. Your author can only hope that you will employ your critical thinking skills in contemplating these ideas about gender in the future.

Your study of gender began with a quotation about the impact of truth, lies, and commonly accepted false beliefs. Here is one last thought as you complete your course of study.

> If you don't like the way the world is, you change it. You have an obligation to change it. You just do it one step at a time. ◆ Marian Wright Edelman

InfoTrac College Edition

For more information, explore InfoTrac College Edition at

http://www.infotrac-college.com/Wadsworth

Enter search terms: gender and music, gender and art, gender and sports, gender and international development.

References

Aarmo, M. (1999). How homosexuality became "Un-African": The case of Zimbabwe. In E. Blackwood & S. E. Wieringa (Eds.), *Female desires: Same-sex relation and transgender practices across cultures* (pp. 255–280). New York: Columbia University Press.

Abas, M., Phillips, C., Carter, J., Walter, J., Banerjee, S., & Levy, R. (1998). Culturally sensitive validation for depression in older African Caribbean people living in south London. *British Journal of Psychiatry, 173,* 249–254.

Abell, S. C., & Richards, M. W. (1996). The relationship between body shape and satisfaction and self-esteem. *Journal of Youth and Adolescence, 25,* 691–703.

Abernathy, T. J., & others. (1995). The relationship between smoking and self-esteem. *Adolescence, 30*(120), 899–907.

Adams, C. R., & Singh, K. (1998). Direct and indirect effects of school learning variables on the academic achievement of African-American 10th graders. *Journal of Negro Education, 67*(1), 48–65.

Adams, K. L., & Ware, N. C. (1995). Sexism and the English language: The linguistic implications of being a woman. In J. Freeman (Ed.), *Women: A feminist perspective* (pp. 331–346). Mountain View, CA: Mayfield.

Adler, A. (1927). *Understanding human nature.* New York: Doubleday Anchor.

Adler, L. L., & Gielen, U. D. (1994). *Cross-cultural topics in psychology.* Westport, CT: Praeger.

Adler, M. A., & Brayfield, A. (1996). East–West differences in attitudes about employment and family in Germany. *Sociological Quarterly, 37*(2), 245–260.

Adler, N. E., & Coriell, M. (1997). Socioeconomic status and women's health. In S. J. Gallant & G. P. Keita (Eds.), *Health care for women: Psychological, social and behavioral influences* (pp. 11–23). Washington, DC: American Psychiatric Press.

Adler, S. R. (1994). Ethnomedical pathogenesis and Hmong immigrants' sudden nocturnal deaths. *Culture, Medicine and Psychiatry, 18*(1), 23–59.

Adler, S. R. (1995). Refugee stress and folk belief: Hmong sudden deaths. *Social Science & Medicine, 40*(12), 1623–1629.

Advocate. (2000, October 24). The Dutch say "I do." *Advocate,* p. 13.

Agbayani-Siewart, P., & Revilla, L. (1995). Filipino-Americans. In P. G. Min (Ed.), *Asian-Americans* (pp. 134–168). Thousand Oaks, CA: Sage.

Agonito, R. (1977). *History of ideas on women.* New York: Paragon Press.

Ahrons, C. R., & Miller, R. B. (1993). A longitudinal analysis of the effect of the ex-spouse relationship on paternal involvement. *The Journal of Orthopsychiatry, 63,* 441–450.

Aiping, M. (1999). To have a son: The one-child family policy and economic change in rural China. In J. West, Z. Minghua, C. Xianggun, & C. Yuan (Eds.), *Women of China* (pp. 137–155). New York: St. Martin's Press.

Alan Guttmacher Institute. (1999). Facts in brief: Induced abortion worldwide. Available online at www.agi-usa.org/pubs/. Retrieved on April 15, 2002.

Alan Guttmacher Institute. (2001a). Facts in brief: Contraceptive use. Available online at www.agi-usa.org/pubs/. Retrieved on May 7, 2001.

Alan Guttmacher Institute. (2001b). Why is teenage pregnancy declining? The roles of sexual activity and contraceptive use. Available online at www.agi-usa.org/pubs/. Retrieved on April 30, 2001.

Al-Attia, H. (1996). Gender identity and role in a pedigree of Arabs with intersex due to 5 alpha reductase-deficiency. *Psychoneuroendocrinology, 21*(8), 651–657.

Albeda, R., & Tilly, C. (1997). *Glass ceilings and bottomless pits: Women's work and women's poverty.* Boston: South End Press.

Albright, M. K. (2000). Women in American foreign policy. *SAIS Review, 20*(2), 65–70.

Alexander, G. M., & Hines, M. (1994). Gender labels and play styles: Their relative contributions to children's selection of playmates. *Child Development, 65,* 869–879.

Alexander, S. (1997, March 28). *Paradox and self-identity: Images in music videos.* Paper presented at the annual conference of the Popular Culture Association, San Antonio, Texas.

Ali, A., Richardson, D. C., & Toner, B. B. (1998). Feminine gender role and illness behavior in irritable bowel syndrome. *Journal of Gender, Culture and Health, 3*(1), 59–65.

Aliro, O. K., & Ochieng, H. M. K. (1999). Male adolescence and sex education in Uganda. In Panos [Institute] (Ed.), *AIDS and men* (pp. 99–109). London: Second Edition Books.

Alivisatos, B., & Petrides, M. (1997). Functional activation of the human brain during mental rotation. *Neuropsychologica, 35,* 111–118.

Alksnis, C., Desmarais, S., & Wood, E. (1996). Gender differences in scripts for different types of dates. *Sex Roles, 34*(5/6), 321–339.

Allen, R. E. (Ed.). (1991). *Greek philosophy: Thales to Aristotle* (3rd rev. ed.). New York: Free Press.

Allen, L. S., & Gorski, R. A. (1992). Sexual orientation and the size of the anterior commissure in the human brain. *Proceeding of the National Academy of Sciences, 89,* 7199–7202.

Allen, M. (2001, November 18). Laura Bush gives radio address; First Lady says fight is for dignity of Afghan women. *Washington Post,* Section A, 1–2.

Allen, P. (1996). *The concept of women.* Montreal, Quebec: Eden Press.

Almaguer, T. (1993). Chicano men: A cartography of homosexual identity and behavior. In H. Abelove, M. Barale, & D. Halperin (Eds.), *The Lesbian and Gay Studies Reader* (pp. 255–273). London: Routledge.

Alper, J. (1993). The pipeline is leaking women all the way along. *Science, 260,* 409–411.

Altman, J., & Ginat, J. (1996). *Polygamous families in contemporary society.* New York: Cambridge University Press.

Alvesson, M., & Billing, Y. D. (1998). *Understanding gender and organization.* Thousand Oaks, CA: Sage.

Amaro, H. (1995). Love sex and power: Considering women's realities in HIV prevention. *American Psychologist, 50,* 437–447.

Amato, P. R. (1998). More than money? Men's contribution to their children's lives. In A. Booth & A. C. Crouther (Eds.), *Men in families* (pp. 244–278). Mahwah, NJ: Erlbaum.

American Anthropological Association (AAA). (1998). AAA statement on "race." *Anthropology Newsletter, 39,* 3.

American Association of University Women (AAUW). (1991). *Shortchanging girls, shortchanging America.* Washington, DC: Author.

American Association of University Women (AAUW). (1992). *The AAUW report: How schools shortchange girls.* Washington, DC: American Association of University Women Foundation and National Education Association.

American Cancer Society. (2002). Types of breast cancer treatment. Available online at http://www.nccn.org/. Retrieved on April 15, 2002.

American Council on Education. (2000). Fact File (2000). *Chronicle of Higher Education, 46*(21), A50–A51. Original work published 1999.

American Psychiatric Association (APA). (1952). *Diagnostic and statistical manual of mental disorders* (1st ed.). Washington, DC: Author.

American Psychiatric Association (APA). (1968). *Diagnostic and statistical manual of mental disorders* (2nd ed.). Washington, DC: Author.

American Psychiatric Association (APA). (1973). *Diagnostic and statistical manual of mental disorders* (2nd ed., revised). Washington, DC: Author.

American Psychiatric Association (APA). (1980). *Diagnostic and statistical manual of mental disorders* (3rd ed.). Washington, DC: Author.

American Psychiatric Association (APA). (1994). *Diagnostic and statistical manual of mental disorders* (4th ed.). Washington, DC: Author.

Amir, M. (1971). *Patterns of forcible rape.* Chicago: University of Chicago Press.

Amnesty International. (1997). *Breaking the silence: Human rights violations based on sexual orientation.* London: Author.

Amponsah, B., & Krekling, S. (1997). Sex differences in visual-spatial performance among Ghanaian and Norwegian adults. *Journal of Cross Cultural Psychology, 28*(1), 81–92.

Anderson, A. E. (1999). Eating disorders in gay men. *Psychiatric Annals, 29*(4), 206–212.

Anderson, B., & Cyranowski, J. (1995). Women's sexuality: Behaviors, responses and individual differences. *Journal of Consulting and Clinical Psychology, 63,* 891–906.

Anderson, K. J., & Leaper, C. (1998). Meta-analyses of gender effects on conversational interruption: Who, what, when, where, and how. *Sex Roles, 39*(3–4), 225–251.

Anderson-Levitt, K., Bloch, K. M., & Soumare, A. (1994). *Inside classrooms in Guinea: Girls' experiences.* Washington, DC: World Bank.

Andrews, P. H. (1992). Sex and gender differences in group communication: Impact. *Small Group Research, 23*(1), 74–95.

Andsager, J. L., & Roe, K. (1999). Country music video in country's year of the woman. *Journal of Communication, 49*(1), 69–82.

Angier, N. (1999). *Woman: An intimate geography.* Boston: Houghton Mifflin.

Aniseff, P., Turrittin, A. H., & Zeng, L. (1999). Social and geographical mobility 20 years after high school. In W. R. Heinz (Ed.), *From Education to Work: Cross-National Perspectives* (pp. 25–41). London: Cambridge University Press.

Anonymous. (1997). Afghanistan: Women kept out of hospitals. *Off Our Backs, 27*(11), 5.

Ansbacher, H. L., & Ansbacher, R. R. (Eds.). (1965). *The individual psychology of Alfred Adler.* New York: Basic Books.

Anselmi, D. L., & Law, A. L. (1998). *Questions of gender: Perspectives and paradoxes.* New York: McGraw-Hill.

Anson, O., & Anson, J. (1997). Surviving the holidays: Gender differences in mortality in the context of three Moslem holidays. *Sex Roles, 37*(5–6), 381–399.

Apfelbaum, E. (1993). Norwegian and French women in high leadership positions. The importance of cultural contexts upon gendered relations. *Psychology of Women Quarterly, 17*(4), 409–429.

Arber, S., & Cooper, H. (1999). Gender differences in health in later life: The new paradox. *Social Science and Medicine, 48*(1), 61–76.

Archer, D., Iritani, B., Kimes, D. D., & Barrios, M. (1983). Faceism: Five studies of sex differences in facial prominence. *Journal of Personality and Social Psychology, 45,* 725-735.

Archer, J. (1988). *The behavioral biology of aggression.* Cambridge, England: Cambridge University Press.

Aries, E. (1996a). *Men and women in interaction: Reconsidering the differences.* New York: Oxford University Press.

Aries, E. (1996b). *Women, men and gender: Ongoing debates.* New Haven, CT: Yale University Press.

Aristotle. (Trans. 1912). *De generatione animalium* (Trans. A. Platt). *The Oxford Translation of Aristotle.* Oxford, England: Clarendon Press.

Armond, V. (1960). Some personality variables in overt female homosexuality. *Journal of Projective Techniques, 24,* 293–309.

Armstrong, K. A. (1995). The problems of using race to understand sexual behavior. *SIECUS Report, 23*(3), 8–10.

Arnason, E. O., Gudmundsdottir, A., & Boyle, G. J. (1998). Six-month prevalence of phobic symptoms in Iceland: An epidemiological postal survey. *Journal of Clinical Psychology, 54*(2), 257–265.

Arney, G. (2000, November 25)g. Bangladesh's third sex. *BBC News.* Available online at http://news.bbc.co.uk/ hi/english/world/from_our_own_ correspondent/newsid_1038000/ 1038875.stm. Retrieved on April 24, 2001.

Aromaki, A. S., Lindman, R. E., & Eriksson, C. J. P. (1999). Testosterone, aggressiveness, and antisocial personality. *Aggressive Behavior, 25*(2), 113–123.

Aronsson, G., & Rissler, A. (1998). Psychophysiological stress reactions in female and male urban bus drivers. *Journal of Occupational Health Psychology, 3*(2), 122–125.

Arora, S. (2001). Women participation in science and technology with reference to higher education. *Social-Science International, 17*(1), 107–113.

Arora, D. (1999). Structural adjustment programs and gender concerns in India. *Journal of Contemporary Asia, 29*(3), 328–352.

Aryee, S., & Luk, U. (1996). Balancing two parts of adult life experience: Work and family identity among dual-earner couples. *Human Relations, 49*(4), 465–487.

Asch, S. E. (1951). Effects of group pressure upon the modification and distortion of judgement. In H. Guetzkow (Ed.), *Groups, leadership and men.* Pittsburgh: Carnegie Press.

Asch, S. E. (1956). Studies of independence and conformity: A minority of one against a unanimous majority. *Psychological Monographs, 70*(9), Whole No. 416.

Association of American Medical Colleges. (2002). Table B8, Women Enrollment and Graduates in U.S. Medical Schools. From DW: Student Section, 1992–93 to present. Information obtained from Collins Mikesell, Sr. Research Associate, Section for Student Services, Association of American Medical Colleges, 2501 M Street, NW, Washington, DC 20037, cmikesell@aamc.org.

Atkinson, J. W. (1964). *An introduction to motivation.* Princeton, NJ: Van Nostrand.

Aukett, R., Ritchie, J., & Mill, K. (1988). Gender differences in friendship patterns. *Sex Roles, 19*(1–2), 57–66.

Axtel, R. E. (1993). *Do's and taboos around the world.* New York: Wiley.

Ayanian, J. Z., Weissman, J. S., Chason-Taber, S., & Epstein, A. M. (1999). Quality of care by race and gender for congestive heart failure and pneumonia. *Medical Care, 37*(12), 1260–1269.

Babbie, E. (2001). *The practice of social research* (9th ed.). Belmont, CA: Wadsworth.

Baca-Zinn, M., Hondagnew-Sotelo, P., & Messner, M. A. (1997). *Through the prism of difference: Readings on sex and gender* (pp. 13–22). Boston: Allyn and Bacon.

Bachen, C. M., McLoughlin, M. M., & Garcia, S. S. (1999). Assessing the role of gender in college student's evaluation of faculty. *Communication Education, 48,* 193–210.

Bacigalupe, G. (2000). Family violence in Chile: Political and legal dimensions in a period of democratic transition. *Violence Against Women, 6*(4), 427–448.

Badgett, M. V. L. (1999). Employment and sexual orientation: Disclosure and discrimination in the workplace. In A. L. Ellis & E. D. B. Riggle (Eds.), *Sexual identity on the job: Issues and services* (pp. 29–52). New York: Haworth Press.

Badinter, E. (1997). *XY: On masculine identity.* New York: Columbia University Press.

Bailey, S. M., & Campbell, P. B. (1999). *The gender wars in education.* Groton, MA: Campbeil-Kibler Associates.

Bailey, J. M. (1995). Biological perspectives on sexual orientation. In A. R. D'Augelli & C. J. Patterson (Eds.), *Lesbian, gay, and bisexual identities over the lifespan* (pp. 104–135). New York: Oxford University Press.

Bailey, J. M. (1996). Gender identity. In R. C. Savin-Williams & K. M. Cohen (Eds.), *The lives of lesbians, gays and bisexuals* (pp. 71–93). Fort Worth, TX: Harcourt Brace.

Bailey, J. M., & Bell, A. P. (1993). Familiality of female and male homosexuality. *Behavior Genetics, 23,* 313–720.

Bailey, J. M., & Zucker, K. J. (1995). Childhood sex-typed behaviors and sexual orientation: A conceptual analysis and quantitative review. *Developmental Psychology, 31,* 43–55.

Bailey, J. M., Gaulin, S., Agyei, Y., & Gladue, B. A. (1994). Effects of gender and sexual orientation on evolutionarily relevant aspects of human mating. *Journal of Personality and Social Psychology, 66,* 1081–1093.

Bailey, J. M., Pillar, R. C., Neale, M. C., & Agyei, Y. (1993). Heritable factors influence sexual orientation in women. *Archives of General Psychiatry, 50,* 217–223.

Bailey, L. (2000). Gender shows: First time mothers and embodied selves. *Gender and Society, 15*(1), 110–129.

Bailey, S. M., & Campbell, P. B. (1999). The gender wars in education. Groton, MA: Campbeil-Kibler Associates.

Bailyn, L. (1997). The impact of corporate culture on work–family integration. In S. Parasuraman & J. H. Greenhaus (Eds.), *Integrating work and family* (pp. 207–219). Westport, CT: Quorum Books.

Bakan, D. (1966). *The duality of human existence.* Chicago: Rand McNally.

Baker, D. P., & Jones, D. P. (1993). Creating gender equality: Cross-national gender stratification and mathematical performance. *Sociology of Education, 66,* 91–103.

Bakker, I. (1994). Introduction: Engendering macro-economic policy reform in the era of global restructuring and adjustment. In I. Bakker (Ed.), *Strategic silence: Gender and economic policy.* London: Zed Books.

Bakker, I. (1994). Introduction: Engendering macro-economic policy reform in the era of global restructuring and adjustment. In Isabella Bakker (Ed.), *Strategic silence: gender and economic policy* (pp. 1–29). London: Zed Books.

Bakker, A., van Kesteren, P. J. M., Gooren, L. J. G., & Bezemer, P. D. (1993). The prevalence of transexualism in the Netherlands. *Acta Psychiatrica Scandinavia, 87,* 237–238.

Banaji, M. R. (2001). Ordinary prejudice. *Psychological Science Agenda, 14*(1), 8–10.

Bandura, A. (1977). *Social learning theory.* Englewood Cliffs, NJ: Prentice Hall.

Bandura, A. (1986). *Social foundations of thought and action: A social cognitive theory.* Englewood Cliffs, NJ: Prentice Hall.

Bank, S. P., & Kahn, M. D. (1997). *The sibling bond.* New York: Basic Books.

Bankole, A., Singh, S., & Haas, T. (1999). Characteristics of women obtain induced abortion: A worldwide view. *International Family Planning Perspectives, 25*(2), 68–77.

Banks, A., & Gartrell, N. (1995). Hormones and sexual orientation: A questionable link. *Journal of Homosexuality, 28,* 247–268.

Barak, A., Fisher, W. A., Belfry, S., & Lashambe, D. R. (1999). Sex, guys and cyberspace: Effects of Internet pornography and individual differences on men's attitudes toward women. *Journal of Psychology and Human Sexuality, 11*(1), 63–92.

Barbach, L. (1982). *For each other: Sharing intimacy.* New York: Anchor Press/Doubleday.

Barbach, L. (2000). *The pause: Positive approaches to premenopause and menopause* (2nd ed.). New York: Plume.

Barbee, A. P., Cunningham, M. R., Winstead, B. A., Derlega, V. J., Gulley, M. R., Yankedon, P. A., & Druen, P. B. (1993). Effects of gender role expectations on the social support process. *Journal of Social Issues, 49,* 175–190.

Barer, B. M. (1994). Men and women aging differently. *International Development*, 38(1), 29–40.

Barinaga, M. (1994). Women in science '94: Surprises across the cultural divide. *Science, 263*, 1468–1472.

Barner, M. R. (1999). Gender stereotyping and intended audience age: An analysis of children's educational TV programming. *Communication Research Reports, 16*(2), 193–202.

Barnes, E. (1912). *Woman in modern society.* New York: B. W. Huebsch.

Barnett, L. B., & Corazza, L. (1998). Identification of mathematical talent and programmatic efforts to facilitate development of talent. *European Journal for High Ability, 9*(1), 48–61.

Barnett, O. W., Lee, C. Y., & Thelen, R. E. (1997). Gender differences in attributions of self-defense and control in interpartner aggression. *Violence Against Women, 3*(5), 462–481.

Barnett, R. C., & Gareis, K. C. (2000). Reduced hours, job role quality and life satisfaction among married women physicians with children. *Psychology of Women Quarterly, 24*(4), 358–364.

Barnett, R. C., & Rivers, C. (1996). *She works, he works: How two-income families are happier, healthier, and better off.* San Francisco: HarperCollins.

Barnett, R. C., & Shen, Y. C. (1997). Gender, high and low schedule control housework tasks, and psychological distress: A study of dual-earner couples. *Journal of Family Issues, 18*(4), 403–428.

Barnett, R. C., Raudenbush, S. W., Brennan, R. T., Pleck, J. H., & Marshall, N. C. (1995). Change in job and marital experiences and change in psychological distress: A longitudinal study of dual-career couples. *Journal of Personality and Social Psychology, 69*, 839–850.

Barr, S. (1996, September). Up against the glass. *American Management Association*, pp. 12–17.

Barret, B., & Logan, C. (2001). *Counseling gay men and lesbians: A practice primer.* Pacific Grove, CA: Brooks/Cole.

Barron, M., & Kimmel, M. (2000). Sexual violence in three pornography media: Toward a sociological explanation. *Journal of Sex Research, 37*(2), 161–168.

Bartholet, J. (2000, January 17). The plague years. *Newsweek*, pp. 32–38.

Barzandty, B., Jonas, H. S., & Etzel, S. I. (1998). Educational programs in U.S.

medical schools, 1997–1998. *JAMA, 280*, 803–808.

Basinger, J. (2000). Girls catch up with boys in math, report finds, but overall student gains have slowed. *Chronicle of Higher Education*, August 25, pp. 1–2.

Basow, S. (1992). *Gender: Stereotypes and roles* (3rd ed.). Pacific Grove, CA: Brooks/Cole.

Basow, S. A. (2000). Best and worst professors: Gender patterns in student choices. *Sex Roles, 43*(5/6), 407–418.

Basow, S. A., & Silberg, N. T. (1987). Student evaluations of college professors: Are female and male professors rated differently? *Journal of Educational Psychology, 79*, 308–314.

Bassett, M. T., & Krieger, N. (1986). Social class and black–white differences in breast cancer survival. *American Journal of Public Health, 76*(12), 1400–1403.

Basson, R., McInnes, R., Smith, M. D., Hodgson, G., Spain, T., & Knoppiker, N. (2000). Efficacy and safety on sildenafil in estrogenized women with sexual dysfunction associated with female sexual arousal disorder. *Obstetrics and Gynecology, 95* (4, Suppl. 1), 54.

Bateson, G., Jackson, D. D., Haley, J., & Weakland, J. (1956). Toward a theory of schizophrenia. *Behavioral Science, 1,* 251–264.

Batson, C. D., Turk, L. L., Shaw, L. I., & Klein, T. R. (1995). Information function of empathic emotion: Learning that we value the other's welfare. *Journal of Personality and Social Psychology, 68,* 619–631.

Baumeister, R. F. (1988). Should we stop studying sex differences altogether? *American Psychologist, 43*, 1092–1095.

Baumeister, R. F. (2000). Gender differences in erotic plasticity. The female sex drive as socially flexible and responsive. *Psychological Bulletin, 126*, 347–374.

Baumeister, R. F., & Sommer, K. L. (1997). What do men want? Gender differences and two spheres of belongingness: Comment on Cross and Madson. *Psychological Bulletin, 122*(1), 38–44.

Bauserman, R. (1998). Egalitarian, sexist and aggressive sexual materials: Attitude effects and viewer responses. *Journal of Sex Research, 35*(3), 244–253.

Bauserman, R., & Rind, B. (1997). Psychological correlates of male child and adolescent sexual experiences with adults: A

review of the non-clinical literature. *Archives of Sexual Behavior, 26*(2), 105–141.

Baxter, J., & Wright, E. O. (2000). The glass ceiling hypothesis: A comparative study of the United States, Sweden and Australia. *Gender & Society, 14*(3), 275–294.

Beal, C. R. (1994). *Boys and girls: The development of gender roles.* New York: McGraw-Hill.

Beals, A. R., & Eason, M. A. (1993). Siblings in North America and South Asia. In C. W. Nuckolls (Ed.), *Siblings in South Asia* (pp. 71–101). New York: Guilford.

Beatty, C. A. (1996). The stress of managerial and professional women: Is the price too high? *Journal of Organizational Behavior, 17*(3), 233–251.

Bechtel, G. A., Shepherd, M. A., & Rogers, P. W. (1995). Family, culture, and health practices among migrant farm workers. *Journal of Community Health Nursing, 12,* 15–22.

Beck, J. G. (1995). Hypoactive sexual desire disorder: An overview. *Journal of Consulting and Clinical Psychology, 63*, 919–927.

Beeghley, L. (1996). *What does your wife do? Gender and the transformation of family life.* Boulder, CO: Westview Press.

Belenky, M. F., Clinchy, B. M., Goldberger, N. R., & Tarule, J. M. (1986). *Women's ways of knowing: The development of self, voice, and mind.* New York: Basic Books.

Bem, D. J. (1996). Exotic becomes erotic: A developmental theory of sexual orientation. *Psychological Review, 103*, 320–335.

Bem, D. J. (2000). Exotic becomes erotic: Interpreting the biological correlates of sexual orientation. *Archives of Sexual Behavior, 29*(6), 531–548.

Bem, S. L. (1974). The measurement of psychological androgyny. *Journal of Consulting and Clinical Psychology, 42*, 155–162.

Bem, S. L. (1981). Gender schema theory: A cognitive account of sex typing. *Psychological Review, 88*, 354–364.

Bem, S. L. (1983). Gender schema theory and its implications for child-development: Raising gender-aschematic children in a gender-schematic society. *Signs, 8*, 598–616.

Bem, S. L. (1985). Androgyny and gender schema theory: A conceptual and empirical integration. In T. B. Sonderegger

(Ed.), *Nebraska Symposium on Motivation 1984: Psychology and Gender* (pp. 179–226). Lincoln: University of Nebraska Press.

Bem, S. L. (1989). Genital knowledge and gender constancy. *Child Development, 60,* 649–662.

Bem, S. L. (1993). *The lenses of gender.* New Haven, CT: Yale University Press.

Benbow, C. P., & Stanley, J. C. (1980). Sex differences in mathematical ability: Fact or artifact? *Science, 210,* 1262–1264.

Benbow, C. P., & Stanley, J. C. (1983). Sex differences in mathematical reasoning ability: More facts. *Science, 222,* 1029–1031.

Benbow, C. P., Lubinski, D., Shea, D. L., & Eftekhari-Sanjani, H. (2000). Sex differences in mathematical ability at age 13: Their status 20 years later. *Psychological Science, 11*(6), 474–480.

Beneke, T. (1997). *Proving manhood.* Berkeley: University of California Press.

Benenson, J. F., Apostoleris, N. H., & Parnass, J. (1997). Age and sex differences in dyadic and group interaction. *Developmental Psychology, 33*(3), 538–543.

Benenson, J. F., Del Bianco, R., Philippoussis, M., & Apostoleris, N. H. (1997). Girls' expression of their own perspectives in the presence of varying numbers of boys. *International Journal of Behavioral Development, 21*(2), 389–405.

Benenson, J. F., Liroff, E. R., Pascal, S. J., & Cioppa, G. D. (1997). Propulsion: A behavioral expression of masculinity. *British Journal of Developmental Psychology, 15* (Pt. 1), 37–50.

Benjamin, L. S. (1993). *Interpersonal diagnosis and treatment of personality disorders.* New York: Guilford Press.

Bennett, L. (2001, Winter). Living on a fault line. *Human Rights Campaign Quarterly, 11.*

Benokraitis, N. V. (Ed.). (1997). *Subtle sexism: Current practice and prospects for change.* Thousand Oaks, CA: Sage.

Beren, S. E., Grilo, C. M., Hayden, H. A., & Wilfley, D. E. (1996). The influence of sexual orientation on body dissatisfaction in adult men and women. *International Journal of Eating Disorders, 20,* 135–141.

Bergum, V. (1997). *A child on her mind: The experience of becoming a mother.* Westport, CT: Bergin & Garvey.

Berman, L. A., & Berman, J. R. (2000). Viagra and beyond: Where sex educators and therapists fit in from a multidisciplinary perspective. *Journal of Sex Education and Therapy, 25*(1), 17–25.

Berman, M. E., Tracy, J. I., & Coccaro, E. F. (1997). The serotonin hypothesis of aggression revisited. *Clinical Psychological Review, 17*(6), 651–665.

Bernadett-Shapiro, S., Ehrenshaft, D., & Shapiro, J. L. (1996). Father participation in childcare and the development of empathy in sons. *Family Therapy, 23*(2), 77–93.

Berndt, T. J., & Keefe, K. (1995). Friends influences on adolescents' adjustment to school. *Child Development, 66*(5), 1312–1329.

Berns, N. (1999). My problem and how I solved it: Domestic violence in women's marriages. *Sociological Quarterly, 40*(1), 85–108.

Berry, J. W., Dasen, P. R., & Saraswathi, T. S. (Eds.). (1997). *Handbook of cross-cultural psychology. Vol. 2: Basic processes and human development* (2nd ed.). Boston, MA: Allyn and Bacon.

Berry, J. W., Poortinga, Y. H., Segall, M. H., & Dasen, P. R. (1992). *Cross-cultural psychology: Research and applications.* New York: Cambridge University Press.

Berry, J. W., Segall, M. H., & Kagitcibasi (Eds.). (1997). *Handbook of cross-cultural psychology. Vol. 3: Social behavior and applications* (2nd ed.). Boston: Allyn and Bacon.

Bertin, J. E., & Beck, L. R. (1996). Of headlines and hypotheses: The role of gender in popular press coverage of women's health and biology. In K. L. Moss (Ed.), *Man-made medicine: Women's health, public policy, and reform* (pp. 37–56). Durham, NC: Duke University Press.

Bertrand, J., de Salazar, S. G., Mazariegos, L., Salanic, V., Rice, J., & Sow, C. K. (1999). Promoting birthspacing among the Maya-Quiché of Guatemala. *International Family Planning Perspectives (IFFP), 25*(4), 160–167.

Best, D. L., & Williams, J. E. (1997). Sex, gender and culture. In J. W. Berry, M. H. Segall, & C. Kagitcibasi (Eds.), *Handbook of cross-cultural psychology* (pp. 163–212). Boston: Allyn and Bacon.

Betcher, R. W., & Pollack, W. S. (1993). *In a time of fallen heroes.* New York: Guilford.

Bettencourt, B. A., & Miller, N. (1996). Gender differences in aggression as a function of provocation: A meta-analysis. *Psychological Bulletin, 119,* 422–447.

Beumont, P., & Vandereycken, W. (1998). Challenges and risks for health care professionals. In W. Vandereycken & P. J. V. Beumont (Eds.), *Treating eating disorders* (pp. 1–29). New York: New York University Press.

Beutel, A. M., & Marini, M. M. (1995). Gender and values. *American Sociological Review, 60,* 436–448.

Beyer, S. (2001, November 25). The women of Islam. *Time.com.* Available online at http://www.time.com/. Retrieved on March 29, 2002.

Bhugra, D., & DaSilva, P. (1993). Sexual dysfunction across cultures. *International Review of Psychiatry, 5,* 243–252.

Biaggio, M., & Brownell, A. (1996). Addressing sexual harassment: Strategies for prevention and change. In M. A. Paludi (Ed.), *Sexual harassment on college campuses* (pp. 215–234). New York: State University of New York (SUNY) Press.

Bierhoff, H. W. (1996). Heterosexual partnerships: Initiation, maintenance and disengagement. In A. E. Auhagen & M. vonSalisch (Eds.), *The diversity of human relationships* (pp. 173–196). New York: Cambridge University Press.

Bierma, L. L. (1996). How executive women learn corporate culture. *Human Resource Development Quarterly, 7*(2), 145–164.

Biernat, M., & Kobrynowicz, D. (1999). A shifting standards perspective on the complexity of gender stereotypes and gender stereotyping. In W. B. Swann, Jr., J. H. Langloss, & L. A. Gilbert (Eds.), *Sexism and stereotypes: The gender science of Janet Taylor Spence* (pp. 75–106). Washington, DC: American Psychological Association.

Bigg, D. S. (1993). Brief for Amicus Curiae. *American Psychological Association in support of neither party in the case of Teresa Harris v. Forklift Systems, Inc.* Washington, DC: American Psychological Association.

Biller, H. B., & Kimpton, J. L. (1997). The father and the school-aged child. In M. E. Lamb (Ed.), *The role of the father in child development* (3rd ed., pp. 143–161). New York: Wiley.

Bilu, Y. (1995). Culture and mental illness among Jews in Israel. In I. Al-Issa (Ed.),

Handbook of culture and mental illness: An international perspective (pp. 129–148). Madison, CT: International University Press.

Bily, S., & Manoochehri, G. (1995). Breaking the glass ceiling. *American Business Review, 13*(2), 33–39.

Bird, S. R. (1996). Welcome to the men's club: Homosociability and the maintenance of hegemonic masculinity. *Gender and Society, 10,* 120–132.

Bischoping, K. (1993). Gender differences in conversation topics, 1922–1990. *Sex Roles, 28*(1–2), 1–18.

Bjorklund, D. F., & Shackelford, T. K. (1999). Differences in parental investment contribute to important differences between men and women. *Current Directions in Psychological Science, 8*(3), 86–89.

Bjorkquist, K. (1994). Sex differences in physical, verbal, and indirect aggression: A review of recent research. *Sex Roles, 30,* 177–188.

Blackburn, R. (1988). On moral judgments and personality disorders: The myth of psychopathic personality revisited. *British Journal of Psychiatry, 153,* 505–512.

Blackwood, E. (2000). Culture and women's sexualities. *Journal of Social Issues, 56*(2), 223–238.

Blackwood, E., & Wieringa, S. E. (Eds.). (1999). *Female desires: Same-sex relations and transgender practices across cultures.* New York: Columbia University Press.

Blair, C. (1998). Netsex: Empowerment through discourse. In B. Ebo (Ed.), *Cyberghetto or cybertopia? Race, class and gender on the Internet* (pp. 205–217). Westport, CT: Praeger.

Blair, H. A., & Sanford, K. (1999). T.V. & zines: Media and the construction of gender for early adolescents. *Alberta Journal of Educational Research, 45*(1), 103–105.

Blair, S. L., & Lichter, D. T. (1991). Measuring the division of household labor: Gender segregation of housework among American couples. *Journal of Family Issues, 12,* 91–113.

Blakemore, J. E. O. (1998). The influence of gender and parental attitudes on preschool children's interest in babies: Observations in natural settings. *Sex Roles, 38* (1–2), 73–93.

Blanchard, R., & Klassen, P. (1997). H-Y antigen and homosexuality in men. *Journal of Theoretical Biology, 18*(5), 313–318.

Blankenhorn, D. (1995). *Fatherless America: Confronting our most urgent social problem.* New York: Basic Books.

Bleier, R. (1984). *Science and gender.* New York: Pergamon Press.

Block, C. E. (2000). Dyadic and gender differences in perceptions of the grandparent–grandchild relationship. *International Journal of Aging and Human Development, 51*(2), 85–104.

Block, M. H., & Adler, S. M. (1994). African children's play and the emergence of the sexual division of labor. In J. L. Roopnarine, J. E. Johnson, & F. H. Hooper (Eds.), *Children's play in diverse cultures* (pp. 149–178). New York: State University of New York (SUNY) Press.

Block, M. H., & Robins, R. W. (1993). A longitudinal study of consistency and change in self-esteem from early adolescence to early adulthood. *Child Development, 64,* 909–923.

Blonder, L. X. (1991). Human neuropsychology and the concept of culture. In J. B. Lancaster (Ed.), *Human nature: An interdisciplinary biosocial perspective* (pp. 83–116). Hawthorne, NY: Aldine deGruyter.

Bloom, D. E., & Steen, T. P. (1996). Minding the baby in the United States. In K. England (Ed.), *Who will mind the baby?* (pp. 23–35). London: Routledge.

Bluestone, N. H. (1987). *Women and the ideal society: Plato's republic and modern myths of gender.* Amherst: University of Massachusetts Press.

Blumenthal, J. A. (1998). The reasonable woman standard: A meta-analytic review of gender differences in perceptions of sexual harassment. *Law and Human Behavior, 22*(1), 33–57.

Bly, R. (1990). *Iron John.* Reading, MA: Addison Wesley.

Bohan, J. S. (1996). *Psychology and sexual orientation: Coming to terms.* New York: Routledge.

Bohan, J. S. (1997). *The psychology of sexual orientation.* New York: Routledge.

Bolansky, E. S., & Boggiano, A. K. (1994). Predicting helpful behaviors: The role of gender and instrumental/expressive self-schemata. *Sex Roles, 30,* 647–661.

Bondurant, B., & White, J. W. (1996). Men who sexually harass: An embedded perspective. In D. K. Shrier (Ed.), *Sexual harassment in the workplace: Psychiatric issue* (pp. 59–78). Washington, DC: American Psychiatric Press.

Bonvillain, N. (1998). *Women and men: Cultural constructs of gender* (2nd ed.). Upper Saddle River, NJ: Prentice Hall.

Bookwala, J., Yee, J. L., & Schulz, R. (2000). Caregiving and detrimental mental and physical health outcomes. In G. M. Williamson, D. R. Shaffer, & P. A. Parmelee (Eds.), *Physical illness and depression in older adults* (pp. 93–131). New York: Kluwer.

Booth, A., & Crouter, A. C. (1998). *Men in families: When do they get involved? What difference does it make?* Mahwah, NJ: Lawrence Erlbaum.

Bornstein, M. H., Tamis-de Monda, C. S., Pascual, L., Hayes, O., & Maurice. (1996). Ideas about parenting in Argentina, France and the U.S. *International Journal of Behavioral Development, 19*(2), 347–367.

Borysenko, J. (1996). *A woman's book of life.* New York: Riverhead Books.

Bosacki, S., Innerd, W., & Towson, S. (1997). Field independence–dependence and self-esteem in preadolescents: Does gender make a difference? *Journal of Youth and Adolescence, 26*(6), 691–703.

Boston, M. B., & Levy, G. D. (1991). Changes and differences in preschoolers understanding of gender scripts. *Cognitive Development, 6,* 417–432.

Botta, R. A. (1999). Television images and adolescent girls' body image disturbance. *Journal of Communication, 49*(2), 22–41.

Bourke, J. (1999). *An intimate history of killing.* New York: Basic Books.

Bowker, L. H. (Ed.). (1998). *Masculinities and violence.* Thousand Oaks, CA: Sage.

Boyle, J. S., Hodnicki, D. R., & Ferrell, J. A. (1999). Patterns of resistance: African-American mothers and adult children with HIV illness. *Scholarly Inquiry for Nursing Practice: An International Journal, 13*(2), 111–133.

Brabeck, M. M. (1996). The moral self, values and circles of belonging. In K. F. Wyche & F. J. Crosby (Eds.), *Women's ethnicities: Journey through psychology* (pp. 145–166). New York: Westview Press.

Bradbury, T. N., Campbell, S. M., & Fincham, F. D. (1995). Longitudinal and behavioral analysis of masculinity and femininity in marriages. *Journal of Personality and Social Psychology, 68*(2), 328–341.

Bradley, H. (1989). *Men's work, women's work: A sociological history of the sexual di-*

vision of labour in employment. Minneapolis: University of Minnesota Press.

Brain, R. (1976). *Friends and Lovers*. New York: Basic Books.

Brannon, L. (1996). *Gender: Psychological perspectives*. Boston: Allyn and Bacon.

Brannon, L. (1999). *Gender: Psychological perspectives* (2nd ed.). Boston: Allyn and Bacon.

Brehm, S. S. (1992). *Intimate relationships* (2nd ed.). New York: McGraw-Hill.

Brian, R. (1976). *Friends and lovers*. New York: Basic Books.

Bridges, J. S. (1993). Pink or blue: Gender-stereotypic perceptions of infants as conveyed by birth congratulations cards. *Psychology of Women Quarterly, 17*(2), 193–205.

Bright, C. M., Duefield, C. A., & Stone, V. E. (1998). Perceived barriers and biases in the medical education experience by gender and race. *Journal of the National Medical Association, 90*(11), 681–688.

Brillon, P., Marchand, A., & Stephesson, R. (1999). Influence of cognitive factors on sexual assault recovery. Descriptive review and methodological concerns. *Scandinavian Journal of Behavior Therapy, 28*(3), 119–137.

Brislin, R., Cushner, K., Cherrie, C., & Yong, M. (1986). *Intercultural interactions: A practical guide*. Newbury Park, CA: Sage.

Brock, C., & Cammish, N. (1997). Factors affecting female participation in education in seven developing countries (2nd ed.). *Education Research*, Serial No. 9.

Brody, L. R. (1999). *Gender, emotion and the family*. Cambridge, MA: Harvard University Press.

Brody, L. R., Lovas, G. S., & Hay, D. H. (1995). Gender differences in anger and fear as a function of situational context. *Sex Roles, 32*, 47–78.

Bromberger, J. T., & Matthews, K. A. (1996). A "feminine" model of vulnerability to depressive symptoms. A longitudinal investigation of middle-aged women. *Journal of Personality and Social Psychology, 70*, 591–598.

Bronstein, P. A., & Farnsworth, L. (1998). Gender differences in faculty experiences in interpersonal climate and processes for advancement. *Research in Higher Education, 39*, 557–572.

Brooke, J. (1998, August 23). Utah struggles with a revival of polygamy. *New York Times*, p. 12.

Brookes, B. (1998). Women and mental health: A historical introduction. In S. E. Romans, *Folding back the shadows: A perspective on women's mental health* (pp. 1–22). Otago, NZ: University of Otago Press.

Brooks, G. R. (1995a). *The centerfold syndrome*. San Francisco: Jossey-Bass.

Brooks, G. R. (1995b). *Nine parts of desire: The hidden world of Islamic women*. New York: Doubleday Anchor Books.

Brooks, G. R. (1997). The centerfold syndrome. In R. F. Levant & G. R. Brooks (Eds.), *Men and sex: New psychological perspectives* (pp. 28–59). New York: Wiley.

Brooks, G. R. (2001). *A new psychotherapy for traditional men*. San Francisco: Jossey-Bass.

Brooks, G. R., & Silverstein, L. B. (1995). Understanding the dark side of masculinity: An interactive systems model. In R. F. Levant & W. S. Pollack (Eds.), *A new psychology of men* (pp. 280–333). New York: Basic Books.

Brosius, H. B., Weaver, J. B., & Staub, J. F. (1994). Exploring the social and sexual "reality" of contemporary pornography. *Journal of Sex Research, 30*(2), 161–170.

Brosnan, M., & Lee, W. (1998). A cross-cultural comparison of gender differences in computer attitudes and anxieties: The United Kingdom and Hong Kong. *Computers in Human Behavior, 14*(4), 559–577.

Broude, G. (1980). Extramarital sex norms in cross-cultural perspective. *Behavioral Science Research, 15*, 181–218.

Broude, G. (1983). Male–female relationships in cross-cultural perspective: A study of sex and intimacy. *Behavioral Science Research, 18*, 154–181.

Broverman, I. K., Broverman, D. M., Clarkson, F. E., Rosenkrantz, P. L., & Vogel, S. R. (1970). Sex role stereotypes and clinical judgements of mental health. *Journal of Counseling and Clinical Psychology, 34*, 1–7.

Broverman, I. K., Vogel, S. R., Broverman, D. M., Clarkson, F. E., & Rosenkrantz, P. S. (1972). Sex-role stereotypes: A current appraisal. *Journal of Social Issues, 28*(2), 59–78.

Brown, C. (1997, April 14). Hollywood lesbians: It's a girl world. *Newsweek*, 68–69.

Brown, G. R. (1995, April). Cross-dressing men often lead double lives. *Meninger Letter*, pp. 4–5.

Brown, J. W. (1996). Media victims. In P. M. Lester (Ed.), *Images that injure* (pp. 205–213). Westport, CT: Praeger.

Brown, L. B., Uebelacker, L., & Heatherington, L. (1998). Men, women and the self-presentation of achievement. *Sex Roles, 38*(3–4), 253–268.

Brown, L. E. (1997). *Two-spirit people*. Binghamton, NY: Haworth Press.

Brown, M. L., & Rounsley, C. A. (1996). *True selves: Understanding transsexualism: For families, friends, coworkers and helping professionals*. San Francisco: Jossey-Bass.

Brown, R. K. (1997). *The changing shape of work*. New York: St. Martin's Press.

Brown, R. P., & Josephs, R. A. (1999). A burden of proof: Stereotype relevance and gender differences in math performance. *Journal of Professional and Social Psychology, 76*(2), 246–257.

Brown, T. L., Graves, T. A., & Williams, S. A. (1997). Dual-earner families: The impact of gender and culture on this normative family structure and implications for therapy. *Family Therapy, 24*(3), 177–189.

Browne, A., Salomon, A., & Bassuk, S. S. (1999). The impact of recent partner violence on poor women's capacity to maintain work. *Violence Against Women, 5*(4), 393–426.

Browne, B. A. (1997a). Gender and beliefs about workforce discrimination in the US and Australia. *Journal of Social Psychology, 137*, 107–116.

Browne, B. A. (1997b). Gender and preference for job attributes: A cross-cultural comparison. *Sex Roles, 37*, 61–71.

Browne, B. A. (1998). Gender stereotypes in advertising on children's television in the 1990's: A cross analysis. *Journal of Advertising, 27*(1), 83–96.

Browne, K. E. (2000). Workstyle and network management: Gendered patterns and economic consequences in Martinique. *Gender and Society, 14*(3), 435–456.

Brownell, K. D., & Rodin, J. (1994). The dieting maelstrom: Is it possible and advisable to lose weight? *American Psychologist, 49*, 781–791.

Browning, J. R., Hatfield, E., Kessler, D., & Levine, T. (2000). Sexual motives, gender and sexual behavior. *Archives of Sexual Behavior, 29*(2), 135–153.

Brownmiller, S. (1975). *Against our will: Men, women and rape*. New York: Simon & Schuster.

Bruch, H. (1978). *The golden cage*. Cambridge, MA: Harvard University Press.

Brumberg, J. J. (1997). *The body project*. New York: Random House.

Brush, L. D. (1999). Gender, work, who cares? In M. M. Ferree, J. Lorber, & B. B. Hess (Eds.), *Revisioning gender* (pp. 161–189). Thousand Oaks, CA: Sage.

Budlender, D. (Ed.). (1997). *The Second Women's Budget*. Cape Town: Institute for Democracy in South Africa.

Bullough, V. L. (1976). *Sexual variance in society and history*. Chicago: University of Chicago Press.

Bullough, V. L., & Brundage, J. (Eds.). (1982). *Sexual practices and the medieval Church*. Buffalo, NY: Prometheus.

Bullough, V. L., & Bullough, B. (1993). *Cross-dressing, sex and gender*. Philadelphia: University of Pennsylvania Press.

Bullough, V. L., & Bullough, B. L. (1994). *Human sexuality: An encyclopedia*. New York: Garland.

Buntaine, R. L., & Costenbader, V. K. (1997). Self-reported differences in the experience and expression of anger between girls and boys. *Sex Roles, 36*(9), 625–637.

Burbank, V. K. (1994). Cross-cultural perspectives on aggression in women and girls: An introduction. *Sex Roles, 30,* 169–176.

Burkam, D. T., Lee, V. E., & Smerdon, B. A. (1997). Gender and science learning early in high school: Subject matter and laboratory experiences. *American Educational Research Journal, 34*(2), 297–331.

Burke, P. (1996). *Gender shock*. New York: Basic Books.

Burke, R. J. (1997). Alternate family structures: A career advantage? *Psychological Reports, 81*(3, Pt. 1), 812–814.

Burn, S. M. (1996). *The social psychology of gender*. New York: McGraw-Hill.

Burnett, J. J. (2000). Gays: Feelings about advertising and media used. *Journal of Advertising Research, 40*(1–2), 75–84.

Burns, A. (2000). Position statement on gender relations and gender differences. *Psychology, Evolution, and Gender, 2*(1), 87–90.

Burns, A., & Homel, R. (1989). Gender division of tasks by parents and their children. *Psychology of Women Quarterly, 13,* 113–125.

Burns-Glover, A. L., & Veith, D. J. (1995). Revisiting gender and teaching evaluations: Sex still makes a difference. *Journal of Social Behavior and Personality, 10*(6), 69–80.

Burr, V. (1998). *Gender and social psychology*. London: Routledge.

Burstyn, V. (1999). *The rites of men: Manhood, politics, and the culture of sport*. Toronto: University of Toronto Press.

Bushweller, K. (1994). Turning our backs on boys. *American School Board Journal, 181*(5), 20–25.

Buss, D. M. (1994). *The evolution of desire: Strategies of human mating*. New York: Basic Books.

Buss, D. M. (1995). Psychological sex differences: Origins through sexual selection. *American Psychologist, 50,* 164–168.

Buss, D. M., & Kenricks, D. (1998). Evolutionary social psychology. In D. Gilbert, S. Fiske, & G. Lindzey (Eds.), *The handbook of social psychology* (Vol. 2, 4th ed., pp. 554–594). New York: McGraw-Hill.

Bussey, A., & Bandura, A. (1992). Self-regulatory mechanisms governing gender development. *Child Development, 63,* 1236–1250.

Butler, A. C. (2000). Trends in same-gender sexual partnering, 1988–1998. *Journal of Sex Research, 37*(4), 333–343.

Buunk, B. P., & Mutsaers, W. (1999). The nature of the relationship between remarried individuals and former spouses and its impact on marital satisfaction. *Journal of Family Psychology, 13*(2), 165–174.

Buzi, R. S., Weinman, M. L., & Smith, P. B. (1998). Ethnic differences in STD rates among female adolescents. *Adolescence, 33*(130), 313–318.

Byer, C. O., Shainberg, L. W., & Galliano, G. (1999). *Dimensions of human sexuality* (5th ed.). New York: McGraw-Hill.

Bylsma, W. H., & Major, B. (1994). Social comparisons and contentment: Exploring the psychological costs of the gender wage gap. *Psychology of Women Quarterly, 18*(2), 241–249.

Byne, W. (1995). Science and belief: Psychological research on sexual orientation. *Journal of Homosexuality, 28,* 303–344.

Byrnes, J. P., & Takahira, S. (1991). Explaining gender differences on SAT-math items. *Developmental Psychology, 29,* 805–810.

Cairns, E., & Darby, J. (1998). The conflict in Northern Ireland: Causes, consequences, and controls. *American Psychologist, 53*(7), 754–760.

Cairns, R. B., & Cairns, B. D. (1994). *Lifelines and risks: Pathways of youth in our time*. Cambridge, England: Cambridge University Press.

Caldwell, S. H., & Popperoe, R. (1995). Perceptions and misperceptions of skin color. *Annals of Internal Medicine, 122,* 614–617.

Calhoun, K. S., Bernat, J. A., Clum, G. A., & Frame, C. L. (1997). Sexual coercion and attraction to sexual aggression in a community sample of young men. *Journal of Interpersonal Violence, 12*(1), 396–406.

Calhoun, T., & Weaver, G. (1996). Rational decision-making among male street prostitutes. *Deviant Behavior: An Interdisciplinary Journal, 17,* 209–222.

Calvert, S. L. (1999). *Children's journeys through the information age*. New York: McGraw-Hill.

Camilleri, C., & Malewska-Peyre, H. (1997). Socialization and identity strategies. In J. W. Berry, P. R. Dasen, & T. S. Saraswathi (Eds.), *Handbook of cross-cultural psychology* (Vol. 2, pp. 41–67). Boston: Allyn and Bacon.

Campbell, A. (1993). *Men, women, and aggression*. New York: Basic Books.

Campbell, J. L. (1996). Traditional men in therapy: Obstacles and recommendations. *Journal of Psychological Practice, 2*(3), 40–45.

Campbell, L. D., Connidis, I. A., & Davies, L. (1999). Sibling ties in later life. *Journal of Family Issues, 20*(1), 114–148.

Campenni, C. E. (1999). Gender stereotyping of children's toys: A comparison of parents and non-parents. *Sex Roles, 40,* 121–138.

Cancian, F. M., & Oliker, S. J. (2000). *Caring and gender*. Thousand Oaks, CA: Pine Forge Press.

Candib, L. M. (1995). Incest and sexual abuse. In L. M. Candib, *Medicine and the family* (pp. 81–115). New York: Basic Books.

Cantor, D. W., & Bernay, T. (1992). *Women in power: The secrets of leadership*. New York: Houghton Mifflin.

Cantor, J. (1998). Children's attraction to violent television programming. In J. Goldstein (Ed.), *Why we watch* (pp. 88–115). New York: Oxford University Press.

Caplan, P. J. (1989). *Don't blame mother*. New York: Harper & Row.

Caplan, P. J. (1991). Delusional dominating personality disorder (DDPD). *Feminism and Psychology, 1*, 171–174.

Caplan, P. J., & Caplan, J. B. (1994). *Thinking critically about research on sex and gender*. New York: HarperCollins.

Caplan, P. J., & Caplan, J. B. (1997). Do sex-related cognitive differences exist, and why do people seek them out? In P. J. Caplan, M. Crawford, J. S. Hyde, & J. T. E. Richardson (Eds.), *Gender differences in human cognition* (pp. 52–77). New York: Oxford University Press.

Carballo-Dieguez, A. (1995). The sexual identity and behavior of Puerto Rican men who have sex with men. In G. M. Herek & B. Greene (Eds.), *AIDS, identity and community: The HIV epidemic and lesbians and gay men* (pp. 105–114). Thousand Oaks, CA: Sage.

CARE Information Center. (2000). AIDS Epidemic Update. Available online at www.care.org/. Retrieved on April 15, 2002.

Carlat, D. J., Camargo, C. A., Jr., & Herzog, D. B. (1997). Eating disorders in males: A report on 135 patients. *American Journal of Psychiatry, 154*(8), 1127–1132.

Carli, L. L., LaFleur, S. J., & Loeber, C. C. (1995). Nonverbal behavior, gender, and influence. *Journal of Personality and Social Psychology, 68*(6), 1030–1041.

Carlson, B. E., & Videka-Sherman, L. (1990). An empirical test of androgyny in the middle years: Evidence from a national survey. *Sex Roles, 23*(5–6), 305–324.

Carnoy, M. (1999). The family, flexible work and social cohesion at risk. *International Labor Review, 138*(4), 411–429.

Carp, F. M. (1997). Retirement and women. In J. M. Coyle (Ed.), *Handbook on women and aging* (pp. 112–128). Westport, CT: Greenwood Press.

Carpenter, L. M. (1998). From girls into women: Scripts for sexuality and romance in *Seventeen* magazine 1974–1994. *Journal of Sex Research, 35*(2), 158–168.

Carr, M., & Jessup, D. L. (1997). Gender difference in first-grade mathematics strategy use: Social and metacognitive influences. *Journal of Educational Psychology, 89*(2), 318–328.

Carr, M., Jessup, D. L., & Fuller, D. (1999). Gender differences in first grade mathematics strategy use: Parent and teacher

contributions. *Journal for Research in Mathematics Education, 30*(1), 20–46.

Carroll, J. M., & Russell, H. A. (1996). Do facial expressions signal specific emotions? Judging emotion from the face in context. *Journal of Personality and Social Psychology, 70*, 205–218.

Carroll, M. D. (1998). But fingerprints don't lie, eh? *Psychology of Women Quarterly, 22*, 739–749.

Carson, R. C., Butcher, J. N., & Coleman, J. C. (1988). *Abnormal psychology and modern life* (8th ed.). Glenview, IL: Scott Foresman.

Carstensen, L. L., & Charles, S. T. (1998). Emotion in the second half of life. *New Directions in Psychological Science, 7*(5), 144–149.

Carter, S. (1987). *Men who can't love*. New York: M. Evans.

Carter, T. (2000). Paths need paving. *ABA Journal, 86*, 34–39.

Caruso, D. (1996). Maternal employment status, mother–infant interaction and infant development in day-care and non-day care groups. *Child and Youth Care Forum, 25*(2), 125–134.

Caseau, D. L., Luckasson, R., & Kroth, R. I. (1994). Special education sevices for girls with serious emotional disturbance: A case of gender bias? *Behavioral Disorders, 20*(1), 51–60.

Casey, M. B. (1996). Understanding individual differences in spatial ability within females: A nature–nurture interactionist framework. *Developmental Review, 16*(3), 241–260.

Casey, M. B., Nuttall, R., & Pezaris, E. (1997). Mediators of gender differences in mathematics college entrance scores: A comparison of spatial skills with internalized beliefs and anxiety. *Developmental Psychology, 33*(4), 669–680.

Cash, T. F., & Henry, P. E. (1995). Women's body images: The results of a national survey in the U.S.A. *Sex Roles, 33*(1–2), 19–28.

Casper, R. C. (1998). The psychopharmacology of women. In R. C. Casper (Ed.), *Women's health: Hormones, emotions, and behavior* (pp. 192–218). London: Cambridge University Press.

Cassell, J. (1997). Doing gender, doing surgery: Women surgeons in a man's profession. *Human Organization, 56*(1), 47–52.

Cassell, J., & Jenkins, H. (1998). *From Barbie to Mortal Kombat: Gender and

computer games*. Cambridge, MA: MIT Press.

Castellino, D. R., Lerner, J. W., Lerner, R. M., & von Eye, A. (1998). Maternal employment and education: Predictors of young adolescent career trajectories. *Applied Developmental Science, 2*(3), 114–126.

Castle, D., Sham, P., & Murray, R. (1998). Differences in distribution of ages of onset in males and females with schizophrenia. *Schizophrenia Research, 33*(3), 179–183.

Catania, J. A., Binson, D., Doleini, M. M., Moskowitz, J. T., & van der Straton, A. (2001). Frontiers in the behavioral epidemiology of HIV/STDs. In A. Baum, T. A. Revenson, & J. E. Singer (Eds.), *Handbook of health psychology* (pp. 777–800). Mahwah, NJ: Erlbaum.

Catsambis, S. (1999). The path to math: Gender and social ethnic differences in mathematics participation from middle school to high school. In L. A. Peplau, S. C. DeBro, R. C. Veniegas, & P. L. Taylor, (Eds.), *Gender, culture and ethnicity* (pp. 102–120). Mountain View, CA: Mayfield.

Catz, S. L., & Kelly, J. A. (2001). Living with HIV disease. In A. Baum, T. A. Revenson, & J. E. Singer (Eds.), *Handbook of health psychology* (pp. 841–850). Mahwah, NJ: Erlbaum.

Center for American Women and Politics. (2000). Election 2000: Results for women. Available online at www.cawp.rutgers.edu. Retrieved on April 15, 2002.

Cener for the Child Care Workforce and Human Services Policy Center. (2002). Estimating the size and components of the U.S. child care workforce and caregiving population. Washington, DC. Available online at http://www.ccw.org/pubs/workforceestimatereport.pdf. Retrieved on May 18, 2002.

Chalker, R. (1994). Updating the model of female sexuality. *SIECUS Report, 22*, 1–6.

Chant, S., & McIlwaine, C. (1998). *Three generations, two genders, one world: Women and men in a changing century*. London: Zed Press.

Chapko, M. K., Somse, P., Kimball, A. M., Hawkins, R. V., & Massanga, M. (1999). Predictors of rape in the Central African Republic. *Health Care for Women International, 20*(1), 71–79.

Chapman, A. B. (1997). The black search for love and devotion. In H. P. McAdoo

(Ed.), *Black families* (3rd ed. (pp. 273–283). Thousand Oaks, CA: Sage.

Chara, P. J., & Kuennen, L. M. (1994). Diverging gender attitudes regarding casual sex: A cross-sectional study. *Psychological Reports, 74,* 57–58.

Charlin, A. J. (1998). On the flexibility of fatherhood. In A. Booth & A. C. Crouter (Eds.), *Men in familes* (pp. 41–46). Mahwah, NJ: Erlbaum.

Chase, C. (1998a). Hermaphrodites with attitudes: Mapping the emergence of intersex political activism. *Gay and Lesbian Quarterly, 4,* 189–211.

Chase, C. (1998b). Surgical progress is not the answer to intersexuality. *Journal of Clinical Ethics, 9*(4), 385–392.

Chatham, L. R., Hiller, M. L., Rowan-Szal, G. A., Joe, G. W., & Simpson, D. D. (1999). Gender differences at admission and follow-up in a sample of methadone maintenance clients. *Substance Use and Misuse, 34*(8), 1137–1165.

Chaves, M. (1997). *Ordaining women.* Cambridge, MA: Harvard University Press.

Chen, X., Liu, M., & Li, D. (2000). Parental warmth, control and indulgence and their relations to adjustment in Chinese children: A longitudinal study. *Journal of Family Psychology, 14*(3), 401–419.

Cheung, C., & Liu, E. S. (1997). Impacts of social pressure and social support on distress among single parents in China. *Journal of Divorce and Remarriage, 26*(3–4), 65–82.

Chia, R. C., Moore, J. L., Lam, K. N., Chuang, C. J., & Cheng, B. S. (1994). Cultural differences in gender role attitudes between Chinese and American students. *Sex Roles, 31,* 23–30.

Chira, S. (1998). *A mother's place: Taking the debate about working mothers beyond guilt and shame.* New York: HarperCollins.

Chiu, C. (1998). Do professional women have lower job satisfaction than professional men? Lawyers as a case study. *Sex Roles, 38*(7–8), 521–537.

Chivers, M. L., & Bailey, J. M. (2000). Sexual orientation of female-to-male transsexuals: A comparison of homosexual and non-homosexual types. *Archives of Sexual Behavior, 29*(3), 259–278.

Chodorow, N. (1978). *The reproduction of mothering: Psychoanalysis and the sociology of gender.* Berkeley: University of California Press.

Choo, K. (2000). Unequal under the law. *ABA Journal, 86,* 48–50.

Chouinard, R., Vezeau, C., Bouffard, T., & Jenkins, B. (1999). Gender differences in the development of mathematics attitudes. *Journal of Research and Development in Education, 32*(3), 184–192.

Chrisler, J. C. (2001). Gendered bodies and physical health. In R. K. Unger (Ed.), *Handbook of the psychology of women* (pp. 289–302). New York: Wiley.

Chrisler, J. C., Johnston, I. K., Champagne, N. M., & Preston, K. E. (1994). Menstrual joy: The construct and its consequences. *Psychology of Women Quarterly, 18*(3), 375–388.

Christopherson, E. R. (1989). Injury control. *American Psychologist, 44,* 237–241.

Chu, H., & Lu, T. Hsi, C.(Eds.). (1967) *Reflections on things at hand: The Neo-Confucian anthology.* Translated, with notes, by W. Chan. New York: Columbia University Press.

Chubb, N. H., Fertman, C. I., & Ross, J. L. (1997). Adolescent self-esteem and locus of control: A longitudinal study of gender and age differences. *Adolescence, 32*(125), 113–129.

Chusmir, L. H. (1990). Men who make nontraditional career choices. *Journal of Counseling and Development, 69,* 11–16.

Cibelli, J. B., Lanza, R. P., West, M. D., & Ezzell, C. (2001). The first human cloned embryo. *Scientific American, 286*(1), 44–51.

Cicchetti, D., & Toth, S. L. (1998). The development of depression in children and adolescents. *American Psychologist, 53*(2), 221–241.

Cicerelli, V. G. (1995). *Sibling relationships across the lifespan.* New York: Plenum.

Clack, G. B., & Head, J. O. (1999). Gender differences in medical graduates' assessment of their attributes. *Medical Education, 33*(2), 101–105.

Claes, M. E. (1992). Friendship and personal adjustment during adolescence. *Journal of Adolescence, 15*(1), 39–55.

Clark, A. (1998). Resistant boys and modern languages: A case of underachievement. In A. Clark & E. Millard (Eds.), *Gender in the secondary curriculum* (pp. 27–42). New York: Routledge.

Clark, A. J. (1998). *Defense mechanisms and the counseling process.* Thousand Oaks, CA: Sage.

Clark, D. B., Pollack, N., & Bukstein, O. M., Mezzich, A. C., Bromberger, J. T., & Donovan, J. E. (1997). Gender and comorbid psychopathology in adolescents with alcohol dependence. *Journal of the American Academy of Child and Adolescent Psychiatry, 36*(9), 1195–1203.

Clark, R. A. (1998). A comparison of topics and objectives in a cross section of young men's and women's everyday conversations. In D. J. Canary & K. Dindia (Eds.), *Sex differences and similarities in communication* (pp. 303–319). Mahwah, NJ: Erlbaum.

Clark, R., Anderson, N. B., Clark, V. R., & Williams, D. R. (1999). Racism as a stressor for African Americans. *American Psychologist, 54*(10), 805–816.

Clark, S. D., Long, M. M., & Schiffman, L. G. (1999). The mind body connection. *Journal of Social Behavior & Personality, 14*(2) 221–240.

Clarke, E. (1874). *Sex in education, or, a fair chance for the girls.* Boston: Osgood.

Clatterbaugh, K. (1997). *Contemporary perspectives on masculinity.* Boulder, CO: Westview Press.

Cleavenger, R. L., Juckett, G., & Hobbs, G. (1996). Trends in chlamydia and other sexually transmitted diseases in a university health service. *Journal of American College Health, 44*(6), 263–265.

Cleckley, H. M. (1941). *The mask of sanity.* St. Louis: Mosby.

Clopton, N. A., & Sorrell, G. T. (1993). Gender differences in moral reasoning. Stable or situational? *Psychology of Women Quarterly, 17,* 85–101.

CMA Marketing. (1998). Country Music Association. Available online at http://www.countrymusic.org/marketing/industry_statistics_listener_analysis2000.asp. Retrieved on April 21, 2002.

Cohan, S. (1997). *Masked men: Masculinity and the movies in the fifties.* Bloomington: Indiana University Press.

Cohen, D. (1992). Why there are so few male teachers in the early grades. *Teacher Magazine, 2,* 14–15.

Cohen, R. (2000). "What's so terrible about rape?" and other attitudes at the United Nations. *SAIS Review, 20, 2,* 73–77.

Cohen, T. F. (1993). What do fathers provide? In J. C. Hood (Ed.), *Men, work, and family* (pp. 1–22). Newbury Park, CA: Sage.

Cohen, T. F. (1998). What do fathers provide? Reconsidering the economic and nurturant dimensions of men as parents. In D. L. Anselmi & A. L. Law (Eds.), *Questions of gender: Perspectives and paradoxes* (pp. 569–581). New York: McGraw-Hill.

Cohler, B. J. (1998). Psychoanalysis and the life course: Development and intervention. In I. H. Nordhus, G. R. VandenBos, S. Berg, & P. Fromholt (Eds.), *Clinical geropsychology* (pp. 61–78). Washington, DC: American Psychological Association.

Cohn, L. D. (1991). Sex differences in the course of personality development. *Psychological Bulletin, 109,* 252–266.

Colapinto, J. (2000). *As nature made him: The boy who was raised as a girl.* New York: HarperCollins.

Cole, C. M., O'Boyle, M., Emory, L. E., & Meyer, W. J. 3rd. Comorbidity of gender dysphoria and other major psychiatric diagnoses. *Archives of Sexual Behavior, 26*(1), 13–26.

Cole, J. R., & Zuckerman, H. (1991). Marriage, motherhood and research performance in science. In H. Zuckerman & J. R. Cole (Eds.), *The outer circle: Women in the scientific community* (pp. 205–226). New York: Norton.

Cole, M. (1996). *Cultural psychology.* Cambridge, MA: Belknap Press of Harvard.

Cole, S., & Fiorentine, R. (1991). Discrimination against women in science: The confusion of outcome with process. In H. Zuckerman & J. R. Cole (Eds.), *The outer circle: Women in the scientific community* (pp. 205–226). New York: Norton.

Coleman, H. (1997). Gaps and silences: The culture of adolescent sex offenders. *Journal of Child and Youth Care, 11*(1), 1–13.

Coleman, J. (1999). *Love, sex and marriage: A historical thesaurus.* Amsterdam: Rodopi.

Coleman, S. (1983). *Family planning in Japanese society: Traditional birth control in a modern urban culture.* Princeton, NJ: Princeton University Press.

Collaer, M. L., & Hines, M. (1995). Human behavioral sex differences: A role for gonadal hormones during early development. *Psychological Bulletin, 118*(1), 55–107.

Colley, A. (1998). Gender and subject choice in secondary education. In J. Radford (Eds.), *Gender and choice in education and occupation* (pp. 18–30). New York: Routledge.

Collin, C. A., DiSano, F., & Malik, R. (1994). Effects of confederate and subject gender on conformity in a color classification task. *Social Behavior and Personality, 22*(4), 355–364.

Collins, D. H. (1991). The meaning of motherhood in Black culture and Black mother–daughter relationships. In P. Bell-Scott et al. (Eds.), *Double stitch: Black women write about mothers and daughters* (pp. 42–60). Boston: Beacon Press.

Collins, D. W., & Kimura, D. (1997). A large sex difference on a two-dimensional mental rotation task. *Behavioral Neuroscience, 111*(4), 845–849.

Collins, P. H. (1994). Shifting the center: Race, class and feminist theorizing about motherhood. In E. N. Glenn, G. Chang, & L. R. Forcey (Eds.), *Mothering: ideology, experience, and agency.* New York: Routledge.

Collins, P. H.. (1998). Toward a new vision: Race, class, and gender as categories of analysis and connection. In D. L. Anselmi, & A. L. Law (Eds.), *Questions of gender: Perspectives and paradoxes* (pp. 35–45). New York: McGraw-Hill.

Collins-Standley, T., Gan, S. Y., Hsin-Ju, J., & Zillman, D. (1996). Choice of romantic, violent and scary fairy-tale books by preschool girls and boys. *Child Study Journal, 26*(4), 279–302.

Coltrane, S. (1996). *Family man: Fatherhood, housework, and gender equity.* New York: Oxford University Press.

Coltrane, S. (1998a). *Gender and families.* Thousand Oaks, CA: Pine Forge.

Coltrane, S. (1998b). Theorizing masculinities in contemporary social science. In D. L. Anselmi & A. L. Law, *Questions of gender: Perspectives and paradoxes* (pp. 76–88). New York: McGraw-Hill.

Coltrane, S., & Messineo, M. (2000). The perpetuation of subtle prejudice: Race and gender imagery in the 1990s television advertising. *Sex Roles, 42*(5/6), 363–389.

Comas-Diaz, L. (1987). Feminist therapy with mainland Puerto Rican women. *Psychology of Women Quarterly, 11*(3/4), 461–474.

Compas, B. E., Oppedisano, G., Connor, J. K., Gerhardt, C. A., Hinden, B. R., Achenbach, T. M., & Hammen, C. (1997). Gender differences in depressive symptoms in adolescence: Comparison of national samples in clinically referred and non-referred youths. *Journal of Counseling and Clinical Psychology, 65*(4), 617–626.

Condry, J. C., & Condry, S. (1976). Sex differences: A study of the eye of the beholder. *Child Development, 47,* 812–819.

Condry, J., & Ross, D. (1985). Sex and aggression: The influence of gender label on the perception of aggression in children. *Child Development, 56,* 225–233.

Cone, J. H. (1991). *Martin & Malcolm & America: A dream or a nightmare.* Maryknoll, NY: Orbis Books.

Conley, F. K. (1998). *Walking out on the boys.* New York: Farrar, Straus, & Giroux.

Connell, R. W. (1998). Masculinities and globalization. *Men and Masculinities, 1*(1), 3–23.

Conradi, P. (1995, August 6). Dutch sex industry prepares to become a red-tape district. *New York Sunday Times,* p. 16.

Conway, M., & Vartanian, L. R. (2000). A status account of gender stereotypes: Beyond commonality and agency. *Sex Roles, 43*(3–4), 181–199.

Conway, M., Giannopolous, C., & Stiefenhofer, K. (1990). Response styles to sadness are related to sex and sex role orientation. *Sex Roles, 22,* 579–588.

Conway, M., Pizzamiglio, M. T., & Mount, L. (1996). Status communality and agency: Implications for stereotypes of gender and other groups. *Journal of Personality and Social Psychology, 71*(1), 25–38.

Conway-Long, D. (1994). Ethnographies and Masculinities. In Harry Brod & Michael Kaufman (Eds.), Theorizing Masculinities (pp. 61–81). Thousand Oaks, CA: Sage.

Conway-Turner, K., & Cherrin, S. (1998). *Women, families and feminist politics: A global exploration.* New York: Haworth Press.

Cook, R. J. (1995). International human rights and women's reproductive health. In J. Peters & A. Wolper (Eds.), *Women's rights, human rights: International feminist perspectives* (pp. 256–278). New York: Routledge.

Cook, T. D., Church, M. B., Ajanaku, S., Shadish, W. R., Kim, J., & Cohen, R. (1996). The development of occupational aspirations and expectations among inner-city boys. *Child Development, 67,* 3368–3385.

Coontz, S. (1997). *The way we really are.* New York: Basic Books.

Cooper, C. R., & Denner, J. (1998). Theories linking culture and psychology: Universal and community-specific processes. *Annual Review of Psychology, 49,* 559–584.

Cooper, M. L., & Orcutt, H. K. (1997). Drinking and sexual experience on first dates among adolescents. *Journal of Abnormal Psychology, 106*(2), 191–202.

Cooper, M. L., Russell, M., Skinner, J. B., Frone, M. R., & Mudar, P. (1992). Stress and alcohol use: Moderating effects of gender, coping, and alcohol expectancies. *Journal of Abnormal Psychology, 101*, 139–152.

Copeland, C. L., Driskell, J. E., & Salas, E. (1995). Gender and reactions to dominance. *Journal of Social Behavior and Personality, 10*, 53–68.

Copenhaver, M. M., & Eisler, R. M. (1996). Masculine gender role stress: A perspective on men's health. In P. Kato & T. Mann (Eds.), *Handbook of diversity issues in health psychology* (pp. 219–133). New York: Plenum.

Copenhaver, M. M., Lash, S. J., & Eisler, R. M. (2000). Masculine gender-role stress, anger and male intimate abusiveness: Implications for men's relationships. *Sex Roles, 42*(5–6), 405–414.

Coquery-Vidrovitch, C. (1997). *African women.* New York: Westview Press.

Corbett, K. (1998). Cross-gendered, identifications and homosexual boyhood: Toward a more complex theory of gender. *American Journal of Orthopsychiatry, 68*(3), 352–360.

Cornell, D. (2000). *Feminism and pornography.* New York: Oxford University Press.

Cornum, R. (1996). Soldiering: The enemy doesn't care if you're female. In J. H. Stiehm (Ed.), *It's our military too!* (pp. 3–23). Philadelphia: Temple University Press.

Cortese, A. J. (1999). *Provocateur: Images of women and minorities in advertising.* Lanham, MD: Rowman and Littlefield.

Cose, E. (1999, June 7). The good news about black America. *Newsweek*, 29–40.

Costa, D. L. (2000). Understanding the 20th century decline in chronic conditions among older men. *Demography, 37*(1), 53–72.

Costello, C. B., & Krimgold, B. K. (1998). *The American woman 1996–1997. Where we stand: Women and work.* New York: Norton.

Cotton, L., Bynum, D. R., & Madhere, S. (1997). Socialization forces and the stability of work values from late adolescence to early adulthood. *Psychological Reports, 80*(1), 115–124.

Courtenay, W. H. (2000a). Behavioral factors associated with male disease, injury, and death: Evidence and implications for prevention. *Journal of Men's Studies, 9*(1), 81–142.

Courtenay, W. H. (2000b). Constructions of masculinity and their influence on men's well-being: A theory of gender and health. *Social Science and Medicine, 50*(10), 1385–1401.

Cover. (1997). *Chrysalis: The Journal of Transgressive Gender Identities, 2*, 5.

Cowan, G. (2000). Beliefs about the causes of four types of rape. *Sex Roles, 42*(9–10), 807–823.

Cowan, G., & Dunn, K. F. (1994). What themes in pornography lead to perceptions of the degradation of women? *Journal of Sex Research, 31*(1), 11–21.

Cowan, P., & Cowan, C. P. (1998). New families: Modern couples as new pioneers. In M. A. Mason, S. Skolnick, & S. D. Sugarman (Eds.), *All our families: New policies for a new century.* New York: Oxford University Press.

Coyle, C. T., & Enright, R. D. (1997). Forgiveness intervention with post-abortion men. *Journal of Counseling and Clinical Psychology, 65*(6), 1042–1046.

Craig, R. S. (1992). Women as home caregivers: Gender portrayal in OTC drug commercials. *Journal of Drug Education, 22*(4), 303–312.

Cramer, P., & Skidd, J. E. (1992). Correlates of self-worth in preschoolers: The role of gender-stereotyped behavior. *Sex Roles 26*, 369–390.

Crandall, C. S., & Martinez, R. (1996). Culture, ideology, and artifact attitudes. *Personality and Social Psychology Bulletin, 22*(11), 1165–1176.

Crandall, R. (1997). *Handbook of gender research.* Corte Madera, CA: Select Press.

Crane, D. (1999). Gender and hegemony in fashion magazines. *Sociological Quarterly, 40*(4), 541–563.

Crawford, J., Kippax, S., Onxy, J., Gault, U., & Benton, P. (1992). *Emotion and gender: Constructing meaning from memory.* London: Sage.

Crawford, M. (1994). Rethinking the romance: Teaching the context and function of gender stereotypes in the psychology of women course. *Teaching of Psychology, 21*(3), 151–153.

Crawford, M. (1995). *Talking differences: On gender and language.* London: Sage.

Crawford, M. (1997). Agreeing to differ: Feminist and epistemologies and women's ways of knowing. In M. M. Gergen & S. N. Davis (Eds.), *Toward a new psychology of gender* (pp. 267–284). New York: Routledge.

Crawford, M., & Chafin, R. (1997). The meaning of difference: Cognition in social and cultural contexts. In P. J. Caplan, M. Crawford, J. S. Hyde, & J. T. E. Richardson (Eds.), *Gender differences in human cognition* (pp. 81–130). New York: Oxford University Press.

Creel, H. G. (1953). *Chinese thought from Confucius to Mao-Tse-Tung.* Chicago: University of Chicago Press.

Crenshaw, T. L., & Goldberg, J. P. (1996). *Sexual pharmacology: Drugs that affect sexual functioning.* New York: Norton.

Crick, N. R., Bigbee, M. A., & Howes, C. (1996). Gender differences in children's normative beliefs about aggression: How do I hurt thee? Let me count the ways. *Child Development, 67*(3), 1003–1014.

Cronk, L. (1993). Parental favoritism toward daughters. *American Scientist, 81*, 272–279.

Crooks, R., & Baur, K. (2002). *Our sexuality* (8th ed.). Pacific Grove, CA: Wadsworth.

Crose, R. (1997). *Why women live longer than men.* San Francisco: Jossey-Bass.

Crose, R., Leventhal, E. A., Haug, M. R., & Burns, E. A. (1997). The challenges of aging. In G. P. Keita, R. Royak-Schaler, & S. J. Gallant (Eds.), *Healthcare for women* (pp. 221–234). Washington, DC: American Psychological Association.

Cross, S. E., & Madson, L. (1997a). Elaboration of models of the self: Reply to Baumeister and Sommer (1997) and Martin and Ruble (1997). *Psychological Bulletin, 122*(1), 51–55.

Cross, S. E., & Madson, L. (1997b). Models of the self: Self-construals and gender. *Psychological Bulletin, 122*(1), 5–37.

Croteau, D., & Hoynes, W. (1998). *Media/society: Industries, images and audiences.* Thousand Oaks, CA: Pine Forge Press.

Croteau, D., & Hoynes, W. (1999). *Media/society* (2nd ed.). Thousand Oaks, CA: Sage.

Crouch, R. A. (1998). Betwixt and between: The past and the future of intersexuality. *Journal of Clinical Ethics, 9*(4), 372–384.

Crouter, A. C., MacDermid, S. M., McHale, S. M., & Perry-Jenkins, M.

(1990). Parental monitoring and perceptions of children's school performance and conduct in dual and single earner families. *Developmental Psychology, 26,* 649–657.

Crouter, A. C., Manke, B. A., & McHale, S. M. (1995). The family context of gender intensification in early adolescence. *Child Development, 66,* 317–329.

Crowston, K., & Kammeres, E. (1998). Communicative style and gender differences in computer-mediated communications. In B. Ebo (Ed.), *Cyberghetto or cybertopia* (pp. 185–203). Westport, CT: Praeger.

Culbertson, F. M. (1997). Depression and gender. *American Psychologist, 52,* 25–31.

Curran, L., & Abrams, L. S. (2000). Making men into dads: Fatherhood, the state, and welfare reform. *Gender and Society, 14*(5), 662–678.

Currie, D. H. (1998). Violent men or violent women? Whose definition counts? In R. K. Bergen (Ed.), *Issues in intimate violence* (pp. 97–111). Thousand Oaks, CA: Sage.

Curry, C., Trew, K., Turner, I., & Hunter, J. (1994). The effect of life domains on girls' possible selves. *Adolescence, 29*(113), 133–150.

Cyranowski, J. M., & Anderson, B. L. (1998). Schemata, sexuality and romantic attachment. *Journal of Personality and Social Psychology, 74,* 1364–1379.

D'Amico, M., Barron, L. J., & Sissons, M. E. (1995). Gender differences in attributions about microcomputer learning in elementary school. *Sex Roles, 33*(5/6), 353–385.

d'Ardenne, P. (1996). Sexual health for men in culturally diverse communities–some psychological considerations. *Journal of Sex and Marital Therapy, 11*(3), 289–296.

D'Augelli, A. R. (1994). Lesbian and gay male development: Steps toward an analysis of lesbians' and gay men's lives. In B. Greene & G. M. Herek (Eds.), *Lesbian and gay psychology* (pp. 118–132). Thousand Oaks, CA: Sage.

D'Augelli, A. R. (1998). Developmental implications of victimization of lesbian, gay, and bisexual youths. In G. M. Herek (Ed.), *Stigma and sexual orientation* (pp. 187–210). Thousand Oaks, CA: Sage.

D'Emilio, D., & Freedman, E. (1988). *Intimate matters: A history of sexuality in America.* New York: Harper & Row.

Dabbs, J. M., & Hargrove, M. F. (1997). Age, testosterone, and behavior among female prison inmates. *Psychosomatic Medicine, 59,* 477–480.

Dabbs, J. M., & Morris, R. (1990). Testosterone, social class and antisocial behavior in a sample of 4,462 men. *Psychological Science, 1*(3), 209–211.

Dabbs, J. M., Jr. (1992). Testosterone measurements in social and clinical psychology. *Journal of Social and Clinical Psychology, 11*(3), 302–321.

Dailey, N. (1998). *When baby-boom women retire.* Westport, CT: Praeger.

Dalla, R. L. (2000). Exposing the "pretty woman" myth: A qualitative examination of the lives of female street walking prostitutes. *Journal of Sex Research, 37*(4), 344–353.

Dancy, B. (1996). What African-American women know, do, and feel about AIDS: A function of age and education. *AIDS Education and Prevention, 8,* 26–36.

Daniel, A. (1981). *Bali: Behind the mask.* New York: Knopf.

Daniluk, J. C. (1998). *Women's sexuality across the lifespan.* New York: Guilford Press.

Dankwort, J., & Rausch, R. (2000). Men at work to end wife abuse in Quebec. *Violence Against Women, 6*(9), 936–959.

Dansbury, M. (1998). Cultural diversity and gender issues. In C. Cronin (Ed.), *Military psychology: An introduction* (pp. 175–193). New York: Simon & Schuster.

Darwin, C. (1859). *On the origin of the species by means of natural selection, or the preservation of favored races in the struggle for life.* London: Murray.

Darwin, C. (1872). *The expression of the emotions in man and animals.* Chicago: University of Chicago Press.

Darwin, C. (1879). *The descent of man and selection in relation to sex.* London: Murray.

Davey, F. H. (1998). Young women's expected and preferred patterns of employment and childcare. *Sex Roles, 38*(1–2), 95–102.

Davies, P. M., Hickson, F. C. I., Weatherburn, P., & Hunt, A. J. (1993). *Sex, gay men and AIDS.* London: Falmer Press.

Davies, S., Katz, J., & Jackson, J. L. (1999). Sexual desire discrepancies: Effects on sexual and relationship satisfaction in heterosexual dating couples. *Archives of Sexual Behavior, 28*(6), 553–567.

Davis, C. M., Black, J., Lin, H., & Bonillas, C. (1996). Characteristics of vibrator use among women. *Journal of Sex Research, 33*(4), 313–320.

Davis, K. (1994). What's in a voice? Methods and metaphors. *Feminism and Psychology, 4,* 353–361.

Davis, P. J. (1999). Gender differences in autobiographical memory for childhood emotional expression. *Journal of Personality and Social Psychology, 76*(3), 498–510.

Davis, S. N., & Gergen, M. M. (1997). Toward a new psychology of gender: Opening conversations. In M. M. Gergen & S. N. Davis (Eds.), *Toward a new psychology of gender* (pp. 1–27). New York: Routledge Press.

Davis, S. N., Crawford, M., & Sebrecht, J. (2001). *Coming into her own.* New York: Wiley/Jossey-Bass.

Davis, S. S., & Davis, D. A. (1995). The mosque and the satellite. *Journal of Youth and Adolescence, 24*(5), 577–593.

Davis, T. L. (1995). Gender differences in masking negative emotions: Ability or motivation? *Developmental Psychology, 31,* 660–667.

Davis, T., & Lee, C. (1996). Sexual assault: Myths and stereotypes among Australian adolescents. *Sex Roles, 34,* 787–803.

Dawood, K., Pillard, R. C., Horvath, C., Revelle, W., & Bailey, J. M. (2000). Familial aspects of male homosexuality. *Archives of Sexual Behavior, 29*(2), 155–164.

Day, R. (1992). The transition to first intercourse among racially and culturally diverse youth. *Journal of Marriage and the Family, 54,* 749–762.

Deal, J. J., & Stevenson, M. A. (1998). Perceptions of female and male managers in the 1990's: Plus ça change. . . . *Sex Roles, 38*(3–4), 287–300.

Dean, K. E., & Malamuth, N. (1997). Characteristics of men who aggress sexually and of men who imagine aggressing: Risk and moderating variables. *Journal of Personality and Social Psychology, 72,* 449–455.

Deater-Deckard, K., & Scarr, S. (1996). Parenting stress among dual-earner mothers and fathers: Are there gender differences? *Journal of Family Psychology, 10*(1), 45–59.

Deaux, K. (1999). An overview of research on gender: Four themes from three decades. In W. B. Swann, Jr., J. H. Langlois, & L. A. Gilbert (Eds.), *Sexism and stereotypes in modern society* (pp. 11–34).

Washington, DC: American Psychological Association.

Deaux, K., & LaFrance, M. (1998). Gender. In D. Gilbert, S. Fiske, & G. Lindzey (Eds.), *Handbook of social psychology* (pp. 788–827). New York: McGraw-Hill.

Deaux, K., & Major, B. (1998). A social-psychological model of gender. In D. Anselmi & A. L. Law (Eds.), *Questions of gender* (pp. 367–375). New York.

deBowman, O. C. (2000). Peruvian female industrialists and the globalization project: Deindustrialization and women's independence. *Gender and Society, 14*(4), 540–559.

deCastell, S., & Bryson, M. (1998). Retooling play: Dystopia, dysphoria and difference. In J. Cassell & H. Jenkins (Eds.), *From Barbie to Mortal Kombat* (pp. 232–261). Cambridge, MA: MIT Press.

Deffenbacher, J. L., & Swaim, R. C. (1999). Anger expression in Mexican-American and white non-Hispanic adolescents. *Journal of Counseling Psychology, 46*(1), 61–69.

DeGroot, J., & Rodin, G. M. (1999). The relationship between eating disorders and childhood trauma. *Psychiatric Annals, 29*(4), 225–229.

DeJong, F. H., Muntjewerff, M. W., Louwerse, A. L., & Van de Poll, N. E. (1988). Sexual behavior and sexual orientation of the female rat after hormonal treatment during various stages of development. *Hormones and Behavior, 22,* 100–115.

DeKeseredy, W. S. (1997). Measuring sexual abuse in Canadian university/college dating relationships: The contribution of a national representative sample survey. In M. D. Schwartz (Ed.), *Researching sexual violence against women. A methodological and personal perspective* (pp. 43–53). Thousand Oaks, CA: Sage.

Dekker, I., & Barling, J. (1998). Personal and organizational predictors of workplace sexual harassment of women by men. *Journal of Occupational Health Psychology, 3*(1), 7–18.

Del Castillo, A. (1993). Covert cultural norms and sex/gender meaning: A Mexico City case. *Urban Anthropology and Studies of Cultural Systems and World Economic Development, 22,* 237–258.

DeLaat, J. (1999). *Gender in the workplace: A case study approach.* Thousand Oaks, CA: Sage.

DeLamater, J. D., & Hyde, J. S. (1998). Essentialism vs. social constructionism in the study of human sexuality. *The Journal of Sex Research, 35*(1), 10–18.

Dell, P., & Korotana, O. (2000). Accounting for domestic violence. *Violence Against Women, 6*(3), 286–310.

DeMaris, A. (1992). Male versus female initiation of aggression: The case of courtship violence. In E. C. Viano (Ed.), *Intimate violence: Interdisciplinary perspectives* (pp. 111–120). Washington, DC: Hemisphere Publishing.

deMarrais, K. B., Nelson, P. A., & Baker, J. H. (1994). Meaning in mud: Yup'ik Eskimo girls at play. In J. L. Roopnarine, J. E. Johnson, & F. H. Hooper (Eds.), *Children's play in diverse cultures* (pp. 179–209). Albany: State University of New York (SUNY) Press.

DeMeis, D. K., & Perkins, H. W. (1996). "Supermoms" of the nineties: Homemaker and employed mothers' performance and perceptions of the motherhood role. *Journal of Family Issues, 17*(6), 776–792.

Democrat & Chronicle. (2000, April 30). Reports: Drug trials slight women. *Democrat & Chronicle* (Rochester, NY), p. 10A.

Denmark, F. (1994). Engendering psychology. *American Psychologist, 49,* 329–334.

Denmark, F. L., Russo, N. F., Frieze, I. H., & Sechzer, J. A. (1988). Guidelines for avoiding sexism in psychological research. *American Psychologist, 43,* 582–585.

Desmarais, S., & Curtis, J. (1997). Gender differences in pay histories and views on pay entitlement among university students. *Sex Roles, 37*(9–10), 623–642.

Deutsch, A. (2001, March 31). Dutch laws let gay couples tie knot. *Democrat and Chronicle* (Rochester, NY), p. A12.

Deutsch, F. M. (1999). *Halving it all: How equally shared parenting works.* Cambridge, MA: Harvard University Press.

Deutsch, F. M. (2001). Equally shared parenting. *Current Directions in Psychological Science, 10*(1), 25–28.

Deutsch, F. M., & Saxon, S. E. (1998). Traditional ideologies, nontraditional lives. *Sex Roles, 38*(5–6), 331–361.

Deutsch, F. M., Lussier, J. B., & Servis, L. J. (1993). Husbands at home: Predictors of paternal participation in childcare and housework. *Journal of Personality and Social Psychology, 65,* 1154–1166.

Devereaux, L. L., & Hammerman, A. J. (1998). *Infertility and identity.* San Francisco: Jossey-Bass.

Devor, H. (1997). *FTM: Female-to-male transsexuals in society.* Bloomington: Indiana University Press.

deWaal, F. (1998). *Bonobo: The forgotten ape.* Berkeley: University of California Press.

DeWeerth, C., & Kalma, A. (1995). Gender differences in awareness of courtship initiation tactics. *Sex Roles 32*(11/12), 717–734.

Diamond, J. (1998). *Why is sex fun?* Boulder, CO: Basic Books.

Diamond, L. M. (1998). Development of sexual orientation among adolescent and young adult women. *Developmental Psychology, 34*(5), 1085–1094.

Diamond, M. (1997). Sexual identity and sexual orientation in children with traumatized or ambiguous genitalia. *Journal of Sex Research, 34*(2), 199–211.

Diamond, M., & Sigmundson, H. K. (1997a). Management of intersexuality: Guidelines for dealing with persons with ambiguous genitalia. *Archives of Pediatrics and Adolescent Medicine, 151,* 1046–1050.

Diamond, M., & Sigmundson, K. H. (1997b). Sex reassignment at birth: Long-term review and clinical implications. *Archives of Pediatrics and Adolescent Medicine, 151,* 298–305.

Diamont, A. L., Schuster, M. A., McGugan, K., & Lever, J. (1999). Lesbians' sexual history with men. *Archives of Sexual Behavior, 159,* 2730–2736.

Dickersin, K., & Schnaper, L. (1996). Reinventing medical research. In K. L. Moss (Ed.), *Man-made medicine: Women's health, public policy, and reform* (pp. 57–78). Durham, NC: Duke University Press.

Dickerstein, L. J. (1996). Sexual harassment in medicine. In D. K. Shrier (Ed.), *Sexual harassment in the workplace: Psychiatric issues* (pp. 223–243). Washington, DC: American Psychiatric Press.

Diehl, L. A. (1997). The paradox of G. Stanley Hall: Foe of coeducation and educator of women. In L. T. Be (Ed.), *A history of psychology* (2nd ed., pp. 266–280). New York: McGraw-Hill.

Dienhart, A. (1998). *Reshaping fatherhood: The social construction of shared parenting.* Thousand Oaks, CA: Sage.

Dietz, T. L. (1998). An examination of violence and gender role portrayal in video games: Implications for gender socialization and aggressive behavior. *Sex Roles*, 38(5–6), 425–442.

Dimond, M., Catanzaro, M., & Lorensen, M. (1997). Chronic illness issues and the older adult. In E. Swanson & T. Tripp-Reimer (Eds.), *Chronic illness and the older adult* (pp. 1–30). New York: Springer.

Dindia, K., & Allen, M. (1992). Sex differences in self-disclosure: A meta-analysis. *Psychological Bulletin*, 112(1), 106–124.

Dinh, K. T., Sarason, B. R., & Sarason, I. G. (1994). Parent–child relationships in Vietnamese immigrant families. *Journal of Family Psychology*, 8, 471–488.

Dion, K. K., & Dion, K. L. (1993a). Individualistic and collectivistic perspectives on gender and the cultural context of love and intimacy. *Journal of Social Issues*, 49, 53–69.

Dion, K. L., & Dion, K. K. (1993b). Gender and ethnocultural comparisons in styles of love. *Psychology of Women Quarterly*, 17, 463–473.

DiPietro, J. A. (1981). Rough and tumble play: A function of gender. *Developmental Psychology*, 17, 50–58.

Ditmars, H. (2000). World tour for a diva long banned from singing. *New York Times*, 149, 51, 475, E1–E2. Available online at http://www.nytimes.com/library/arts/080900abroad-googoosh.html. Retrieved April 21, 2002.

Dittman, R. W. (1997). Sexual behavior and sexual orientation in females with CAH. In L. Ellis & L. Ebertz (Eds.), *Sexual orientation: Toward biological understanding* (pp. 53–69). Westport, CT: Praeger.

Dittman, R. W. (1998). Ambiguous genitalia, gender identity problems, and sex reassignment. *Journal of Sex and Marital Therapy*, 24, 255–271.

Dittman, R. W., Kappes, M. E., & Kappes, H. M. (1992). Sexual behavior in adolescent and adult females with CAH. *Psychoneuroendocrinology*, 17, 1–18.

Dodge, H. H. (1995). Movements out of poverty among elderly widows. *Journal of Gerontology*, 50B(4), S240–S249.

Doherty, R. W., Orimoto, L., Singelis, T. M., Hatfield, E., & Hebb, J. (1995). Emotional contagion: Gender and occupational differences. *Psychology of Women Quarterly*, 19, 355–371.

Doherty, W. Kouneski, E. F., & Erickson, M. F. (1998). Responsible fathering: An overview and conceptual framework. *Journal of Marriage and the Family*, 60, 277–292.

Doi, T. (1973). *The anatomy of dependence*. Tokyo: Kodansha.

Doi, T. (1986). *The anatomy of self: The individual versus society*. Tokyo: Kodansha.

Dollison, R. A. (1998). A comparison of the effect of single-sex and co-educational schooling arrangements on the self-esteem and mathematics achievement of adolescent females. Unpublished manuscript: University of South Alabama.

Donat, P. L., & White, J. W. (2000). Re-examining the issue of non-consent in acquaintance rape. In C. B. Travis & J. W. White (Eds.), *Sexuality, society, and feminism* (pp. 355–375). Washington, DC: American Psychiatric Press.

Donnerstein, E., Linz, D., & Penrod, S. (1987). *The question of pornography*. New York: Free Press.

Dorahy, M. J., Lewis, C. A., Schumaker, J. F., Akuamoah-Boateng, R., Duze, M. C., & Sibiya, T. E. (1998). Across-cultural analysis of religion and life satisfaction. *Mental Health, Religion, and Culture*, 1(1), 37–43.

Doty, A., & Gove, B. (1997). Queer representation in the mass media. In A. Medhurst & S. R. Munt (Eds.), *Lesbian and gay studies: A critical introduction* (pp. 84–88). London: Cassell.

Dowsett, G. W. (1996). *Practicing desire: Homosexual sex in the era of AIDS*. Stanford, CA: Stanford University Press.

Doyle, J. A. (1995). *The male experience*. Wisconsin: Brown and Benchmark.

Doyle, L. (1995). *What makes women sick? Gender and the political economy of health*. New Brunswick, NJ: Rutgers University Press.

Dreger, A. D. (1998a). Ambiguous sex or ambivalent medicine? *Hastings Center Report*, 28(3), 24–35.

Dreger, A. D. (1998b). *Hermaphrodites and the medical invention of sex*. Cambridge, MA: Harvard University Press.

Dreger, A. D. (1998c). The history of intersexuality from the age of gonads to the age of consent. *Journal of Clinical Ethics*, 9(4), 345–356.

Dreger, A. D. (1999). *Intersex in the age of ethics*. Hagerstown, PA: University Publishing Group.

Dreher, G. F., & Chargois, J. A. (1998). Gender, mentoring experiences and salary attainment among graduates of an historically black university. *Journal of Vocational Behavior*, 53, 401–416.

Dreher, G. F., & Cox, T. H., Jr. (1996). Race, gender and opportunity: A study of compensation attainment and the establishment of mentoring relationships. *Journal of Applied Psychology*, 81(3), 297–308.

Dresser, N. (1996). *Multicultural manners*. New York: Wiley.

Dryler, H. (1998). Parental role models, gender and educational choice. *British Journal of Sociology*, 49(3), 375–399.

Dube, L. (1997). Women and kinship: Comparative perspective on gender in South and South-East Asia. New York: United Nations Publications.

Dubeck, P. J., & Borman, K. (Eds.). (1996). *Women and work: A handbook*. New York: Garland.

DuBois, C. L. Z., Knapp, D. E., Faley, R. H., & Kustis, G. A. (1998). An empirical examination of same and other-gender sexual harassment in the workplace. *Sex Roles*, 39(9–10), 731–749.

Duden, B. (1991). *The woman beneath the skin*. Cambridge, MA: Harvard University Press.

Duerst-Lahti, G. (1998). The bottleneck: Women becoming candidates. In S. Thomas & C. Wilcox (Eds.), *Women and elective office* (pp. 15–25). New York: Oxford University Press.

Duffy, J., Gunther, G., & Walters, L. (1997). Gender and mathematical problem solving. *Sex Roles*, 37(7–8), 477–494.

Dufur, M. J. (1999). Gender and sport. In J. S. Chavetz (Ed.), *Handbook of the sociology of gender* (pp. 583–599). New York: Kluwer Academic.

Dukes, R. L., & Martinez, R. (1994). The impact of ethgender on self-esteem among adolescents. *Adolescence*, 29(113), 105–115.

Duncan, M. M., Strayton, C. D., & Hall, C. B. (1999). Police reports on domestic incidents involving intimate partners: Injuries and medical help-seeking. *Women and Health*, 30(1), 1–14.

Dunn, D. (1996). Gender-segregated occupations. In P. J. Dubeck & K. Borman (Eds.), *Women and work: A handbook* (pp. 91–93). New York: Garland.

Dunn, D., & Skaggs, S. (1999). Gender and paid work in industrial nations. In J. S. Chavetz (Ed.), *Handbook of the sociology of gender* (pp. 321–342). New York: Kluwer Academic.

Dunnegin, T., McNall, M., & Mortimer, J. T. (1993). The problem of metaphorical non-equivalence in cross-cultural survey research. Comparing the mental health statuses of Hmong refugees and general population adolescents. *Journal of Cross-Cultural Psychology, 24,* 344–365.

Dupree, N. H. (1998). Afghan women under the Taliban. In W. Maley (Ed.), *Fundamentalism reborn?* (pp. 145–166). New York: NYU Press.

Dykes, B. (2000). Problems in defining cross-cultural "kinds of homosexuality" and a solution. *Journal of Homosexuality, 38*(3), 1–18.

Eagly, A. (1987). *Sex differences in social behavior: A social role interpretation.* Mahwah, NJ: Erlbaum.

Eagly, A. (1998). Gender and altruism. In D. L. Anselmi & A. L. Law (Eds.), *Questions of gender* (pp. 405–417). New York: McGraw-Hill.

Eagly, A. H. (1983). Gender and social influence: A social psychological analysis. *American Psychologist, 38,* 971–981.

Eagly, A. H. (1995). The science and politics of comparing women and men. *American Psychologist, 50*(3), 145–158.

Eagly, A. H. (1996). Differences between women and men. *American Psychologist, 51,* 158–159.

Eagly, A. H., Karau, S. J., & Makhijani, M. G. (1995). Gender and the effectiveness of leaders. *Psychological Bulletin, 117,* 125–145.

Ebo, B. L. (1998). *Cyberghetto or cybertopia: Race, class and gender on the Internet.* Westport, CT: Praeger.

Eccles, J. S. (1994). Understanding women's educational and occupational choices. Applying the Eccles et al., model of achievement-related choices. *Psychology of Women Quarterly, 18*(4), 585–609.

Eccles, J. S., & Bryan, J. (1994). Adolescence: Critical crossroads in the path of gender-role development. In M. R. Stevenson (Ed.), *Gender roles through the lifespan: A multidisciplinary perspective* (pp. 111–147). Muncie, IN: Ball State University Press.

Eccles, J. S., Barber, B., & Jozefowicz, D. (1999). Linking gender to educational,

occupational and recreational choices: Applying the Eccles et al. model of achievement-related choices. In W. B. Swann, Jr., J. H. Langlois, & L. A. Gilbert (Eds.), *Sexism and stereotypes in modern society* (pp. 153–192). Washington, DC: American Psychological Association.

Ecker, N. (1993). Culture and sexual scripts out of Africa. *SIECUS Reports, 22*(2), 16.

Eckhardt, C. I., Barbour, K. A., & Davison, G. C. (1998). Articulated thoughts of maritally violent and nonviolent men during anger arousal. *Journal of Consulting and Clinical Psychology, 66*(2), 259–269.

Edidin, P. (2000, March 19). Cabbies' curious cognition. *New York Times, Week in Review,* p. 2.

Edwards, S. R. (1994). The role of men in contraceptive decision-making: current knowledge and future implications. *Family Planning Perspectives, 26*(2), 77–82.

Edwards, S. R. (1994). The role of men in contraceptive decision making: Current knowledge and future implications. *Family Planning Perspectives, 26*(2), 77–82.

Efklides, A., Papadaki, M., Papantoniou, G., & Kiosseoglu, G. (1998). Individual differences in school mathematics performance and feelings of difficulty: The effects of cognitive ability, affect, age and gender. European *Journal of Psychology of Education, 14*(1), 57–69.

Ehrenreich, B., & English, D. (1973). *Complaints and disorders: The sexual politics of sickness.* Old Westbury, NY: Feminist Press.

Eisenhart, M. A., & Finkel, E. (1998). *Women's science: Learning and succeeding from the margins.* Chicago: University of Chicago Press.

Eisikovitz, Z. C., & Buchbinder, E. (1997). *Toward a phenomenological intervention with violence in intimate relationships.* Thousand Oaks, CA: Sage.

Eisler, R. M. (1995). The relationship between masculine gender role stress and men's health risk: The validation of a construct. In R. F. Levant & W. S. Pollack (Eds.), *A new psychology of men* (pp. 207–227). New York: HarperCollins.

Ekman, P., & Friesen, W. V. (1975). *Unmasking the face.* Englewood Cliffs, NJ: Prentice Hall.

El Abd, S., Turk, J., & Hill, P. (1995). Annotation: Psychological characteristics of

Turner syndrome. *Journal of Child Psychology and Psychiatry, 36*(7), 1109–1125.

Elbedour, S., Shulman, S., & Kedem, P. (1997). Adolescent intimacy: A cross cultural study. *Journal of Cross-Cultural Psychology, 28*(1), 5–22.

Elliot, F. R. (1996). *Gender, family, and society.* New York: St. Martin's Press.

Ellis, A. L., & Riggle, E. D. B. (Eds.). (1996). *Sexual identity on the job: Issues and services.* New York: Harrington Park Press.

Ellis, D. (2000). *Women of the Afghan war.* New York: Praeger.

Ellis, G. M. (1994). Acquaintance rape. *Perspectives in Psychiatric Care, 30,* 1, 11–16.

Ellis, H. (1934). *Psychology of sex.* London: Heineman.

Ellis, L., & Ebertz, L. (Eds.). (1997). *Sexual orientation: Toward biological understanding.* Westport, CT: Praeger.

El-Sanabary, N. (1994). Female education in Saudi Arabia and the reproduction of gender division. *Gender and Education, 6*(2), 141–150.

Elu, M. D. (1999). Between political debate and women's suffering: Abortion in Mexico. In A. I. Mundigo & C. Indriso (Eds.), *Abortion in the developing world* (pp. 245–258). London: Zed Books.

Emery, R. E., Kitzmann, K. M., & Waldron, M. (1999). Psychological interventions for separated and divorced families. In E. M. Hetherington (Ed.), *Coping with divorce, single parenting, and remarriage* (pp. 323–344). Mahwah, NJ: Erlbaum.

Endicott, K. (1992). Fathering in an egalitarian society. In B. S. Hewlett (Ed.), *Father–child relations* (pp. 281–295). New York: Aldine deGruyter.

England, K. (1996). Who will mind the baby? In K. England (Ed.), *Who will mind the baby?* (pp. 3–19). London: Routledge.

Enriquez, V. G. (1986). Kapwa: A core concept in Filipino social psychology. In Virgilio Enriquez (Ed.), *Philippine world view.* Singapore: Institute of Southeast Asian Studies.

Ephron, D. (1986). *Funny Sauce.* New York: Viking.

Epstein, C. F., Seron, C., Oglensky, B., & Saute, R. (1999). *The part-time paradox: Time, norms, professional life, family and gender.* New York: Routledge.

Erikson, E. H. (1975). *Life history and the historical moment.* New York: Norton.

Erikson, E. H. (1985). *The life cycle completed.* New York: Norton.

Erkut, S., Marx, F., Fields, J., & Sing, R. (1998). *Raising confident and competent girls: Implications of diversity.* Wellesley, MA: Center for Research on Women.

Eronen, M., Angermeyer, M. C., & Schulze, B. (1998). The psychiatric epidemiology of violent behavior. *Social Psychiatry and Psychiatric Epidemiology, 33*(Suppl. 1), s13–s23.

Erwin, K. (1993). Interpreting the evidence: Competing paradigms and the emergence of lesbian and gay suicide as a social fact. *International Journal of Health Services, 23*(3), 437–453.

Eskilson, A., & Wiley, M. G. (1999). Solving for X: Aspirations and expectations of college students. *Journal of Youth and Adolescence, 28*(1), 51–70.

Essawi, M., Gad, Y. Z., El-Rouby, O., Temtany, S. A., Sabour, Y. A., & El-Awady, M. (1997). Molecular analysis of androgen-resistance syndromes in Egyptian patients. *Disease Markers, 13,* 99–105.

Estioko-Griffin, A., & Griffin, P. B. (1997). Woman the hunter: The Agta. In C. B. Brettell & C. F. Sargent (Eds.), *Gender in cross-cultural perspectives.* Englewood Cliffs, NJ: Prentice Hall.

Etaugh, C. (1993). Women in the middle and later years. In F. L. Denmark & M. A. Paludi (Eds.), *Psychology of women: Handbook of issues and theories.* Westport, CT: Greenwood.

Etzkowitz, H., Kemelgor, J., Neuschatz, M., Uzzi, B., & Alonzo, J. (1994). The paradox of critical mass for women in science. *Science, 266,* 51–54.

Ezzell, C. (2000). Care for a dying continent. *Scientific America, 282*(5), 96–105.

Fabes, R. A., & Martin, C. L. (1991). Gender and age stereotypes of emotionality. *Personality and Social Psychology Bulletin, 17,* 532–540.

Fabes, R. A., Shepard, S., Guthrie, I. K., & Martin, C. L. (1997). Roles of temperamental arousal and gender segregated play in young children's social adjustment. *Developmental Psychology, 33*(4), 693–702.

Fact File. (2000). *Chronicle of Higher Education, 46*(21), A50–51. Original work published in American Council on Education and University of California at Los Angeles, Higher Education Research Institute, *The American Freshman: National Norms for Fall, 1999.*

Fagot, B. I. (1994). Peer relations and the development of competence in boys and girls. In C. Leaper (Ed.), *Childhood gender segregation: Causes and consequences* (pp. 53–66). San Francisco: Jossey-Bass.

Fagot, B. I., & Hagan, R. (1991). Observations of parent reactions to sex-stereotyped behaviors: Age and sex effects. *Child Development, 62,* 617–628.

Fagot, B. I., & Leinbach, M. D. (1993). Gender-role development in young children: From discrimination to labeling. *Developmental Review, 13,* 205–224.

Fagot, B. I., & Leinbach, M. D. (1995). Gender knowledge in egalitarian and traditional families. *Sex Roles, 32,* 513–526.

Fagot, B. I., Leinbach, M. D., & O'Boyle, C. (1992). Gender labeling, gender stereotyping and parenting behaviors. *Developmental Psychology, 28,* 225–230.

Faith, K. (1996). The politics of confinement and resistance: The imprisonment of women. In E. Rosenblatt (Ed.), *Criminal injustice: Confronting the prison crisis* (pp. 165–184). Boston: South End Press.

Faithful, J. (1997). HIV-positive and AIDS infected women: Challenges to mothering. *American Journal of Orthopsychiatry, 67,* 144–151.

Fallon, K. M. (1999). Education and perceptions of social status and power among women in Larteh, Ghana. *Africa Today, 6,* 67–91.

Fancher, R. E. (1997). Gall, Flourens, and phrenology. In L. T. Benjamin (Ed.), *A history of psychology* (pp. 81–87). New York: McGraw-Hill.

Farace, E., & Alves, W. (2000). Do women fare worse? A metaanalysis of gender differences in outcome after traumatic brain injury. *Journal of Neurosurgery, 93*(4), 539–545.

Farenga, S. J., & Joyce, B. A. (1999). Intentions of young students to enroll in science courses in the future: An examination of gender differences. *Science Education, 83,* 55–75.

Farley, M. (1998, December 26). In Lugo Lake marriage is a ticklish affair. *Los Angeles Times,* pp. A1, A5, A6.

Farley, M., & Barkon, H. (1998). Prostitution, violence, and post traumatic stress disorder. *Women and Health, 27, 3,* 37–49.

Farmer, H. S., & Associates. (1997). *Diversity and women's career advancement: From adolescence to adulthood.* Thousand Oaks, CA: Sage.

Farmer, H. S., Wardrop, J. L., & Rotella, S. C. (1999). Antecedent factors differentiating women and men in science/nonscience careers. *Psychology of Women, 23*(2), 763–780.

Farrell, B. G. (1999). *Family: The making of an idea, an institution and a controversy in American culture.* Boulder, CO: Westview.

Fassinger, P. A. (1993). Meanings of housework for single fathers and mothers. In J. C. Hood (Ed.), *Men, work, and family* (pp. 195–216). Newbury Park, CA: Sage.

Fausto-Sterling, A. (1985). *Myths of gender: Biological theories about women and men.* New York: Basic Books, HarperCollins.

Fausto-Sterling, A. (1992). *Myths of gender: Biological theories about women and men* (Rev. ed.). New York: Basic Books.

Fausto-Sterling, A. (2000). *Sexing the body.* New York: Basic Books.

Favreau, O. E. (1993). Do the Ns justify the means? Null hypothesis testing applied to sex and other differences. *Canadian Psychology, 34*(1), 64–78.

Favreau, O. E. (1997). Sex and gender comparisons: Does null hypothesis testing create a false dichotomy? *Feminism and Psychology, 7*(1), 63–81.

Fehr, B. A. (1996). *Friendship processes.* Thousand Oaks, CA: Sage.

Fehr, B., Baldwin, M., Collins, L., Patterson, S., & Benditt, R. (1999). Anger in close relationships: An interpersonal script analysis. *Journal of Social Psychology Behavior, 25*(3), 299–312.

Feingold, A. (1992). Gender differences in mate selection preferences: A text of the parental investment model. *Psychological Bulletin, 112*(1), 125–139.

Feingold, A. (1994a). Gender differences in personality: A meta analysis. *Psychological Bulletin, 116,* 429–456.

Feingold, A. (1994b). Gender differences in variability in intellectual abilities: A cross-cultural perspective. *Sex Roles, 30,* 81–82.

Feldman-Savelsberg, P. (1994). Plundered kitchens and empty wombs: Fear of infertility in the Cameroonian grassfields. *Social Science and Medicine, 29*(4), 463–474.

Felmlee, D. (1994). Who's on top? Power in romantic relationships. *Sex Roles, 31,* 275–295.

Ferguson, D. M., & Mullen, P. E. (1999). *Childhood sexual abuse: An evidence based perspective*. Thousand Oaks, CA: Sage.

Ferguson, S. J. (2000). Challenging traditional marriage: New married Chinese-American and Japanese-American women. *Gender and Society, 14*(1), 136–159.

Ferron, C. (1997). Boy image in adolescence. Cross-cultural research. Results of the preliminary phase of a quantitative survey. *Adolescence, 32*(127), 735–745.

Field, D., Hockey, J., & Small, N. (Eds.). (1997). *Death, gender and ethnicity*. London: Routledge.

Field, D., Hockey, J., & Small, N. (Eds.). (1997). *Death, gender and ethnicity*. New York: Routledge.

Field, T. M. (1994). The effects of a mother's physical and emotional unavailability on emotion regulation. In N. A. Fox (Eds.), The development of emotion regulation: Biological and behavioral considerations. *Monographs of the Society for Research in Child Development, 59*(2), Serial No. 240.

Field, T. M. (1995). Psychologically depressed parents. In M. H. Bornstein (Eds.), *Handbook of parenting* (Vol. 4, pp. 85–101). Mahwah, NJ: Erlbaum.

Figueroa, E. F., Silk, K. R., Huth, A., & Lohr, N. E. (1987). History of childhood sexual abuse and general psychopathology. *Comparative Psychiatry, 38*(1), 23–30.

Filardo, E. K. (1996). Gender patterns in African-American and white adolescents social interactions in same-race, mixed-gender groups. *Journal of Personality and Social Psychology, 71*, 71–82.

Fincher, R. (1996). The state and childcare: An international review from a geographical perspective. In K. England (Ed.), *Who will mind the baby?* (pp. 143–167). London: Routledge.

Fine, M. A., Coleman, M., & Ganong, L. H. (1999). A social constructionist multi-method approach to understanding the stepparent role. In E. Mavis Hetherington (Ed.), *Coping with divorce, single parenting and remarriage* (pp. 273–294). Mahwah, NJ: Erlbaum.

Firestein, B. A. (Ed.). (1996). *Bisexuality*. Thousand Oaks, CA: Sage.

First, A. (1998). Nothing new under the sun? A comparison of images of women in Israeli advertisements in 1979 and 1994. *Sex Roles, 38*(11–12), 1065–1077.

Fischer, A. (1993). Sex differences in emotionality: Fact or stereotype? *Feminism and Psychology, 3*, 303–318.

Fischer, A. R., & Good, G. E. (1997). Men and psychotherapy: An investigation of alexithymia, intimacy, and masculine gender roles. *Psychotherapy, 34*(2), 160–170.

Fisher, J. (1996). Sustainable development and women: The role of NGOs. In J. Turpin & L. A. Lorentzen (Eds.), *The gendered new world order: Militarism, development and the environment* (pp. 95–112). New York: Routledge.

Fisher, C. B., Jackson, J. F., & Villarrunel, F. A. (1998). The study of African-American and Latin-American children and youth. In R. M. Lerner (Vol. Ed.), *Handbook of child psychology* (Vol. 1, 5th ed. (pp. 1145–1208). New York: Wiley.

Fiske, S. T. (1993a). Controlling other people: The impact of power on stereotyping. *American Psychologist, 48*, 621–628.

Fiske, S. T. (1993b). Social cognition and social perception. *Annual Review of Psychology, 44*, 155–194.

Fiske, S. T., & Neuberg, S. L. (1990). A continuum model of impression formation, from category-based to individuality processes: Influence of information and motivation on attention and interpretation. In M. P. Zanna (Ed.), *Advances in experimental social psychology* (Vol. 23). New York: Academic Press.

Fitzgerald, L. F., & Ormerod, A. J. (1993). Breaking silence: The sexual harassment of women in academia and the workplace. In F. Denmark & M. Paludi (Eds.), *Psychology of women: A handbook of issues and theories* (pp. 553–581). Westport, CT: Greenwood Press.

Fitzgerald, L. F., Drasgow, F., & Magley, V. J. (1999). Sexual harassment in the armed forces: A test of an integrated model. *Military Psychology, 11*(3), 329–343.

Fitzgerald, L. F., Swan, S., & Magley, V. J. (1997). But was it really sexual harassment? Legal, behavioral and psychological definitions of the workplace victimization of women. In W. O'Donohue (Ed.), *Sexual harassment theory, research and treatment* (pp. 5–28). Boston: Allyn and Bacon.

Fivush, R., Brotman, M. A., Buckner, J. P., & Goodman, S. H. (2000). Gender differences in parent–child emotion narratives. *Sex Roles, 42*(3–4), 223–253.

Fivush, R., & Reese, E. (1992). The social construction of autobiographical memory. In M. A. Conway, D. C. Rubin, H. Spinner, & W. A. Wagenaar (Eds.). *Theoretical perspectives on autobiographical memory* (pp. 115–132). Dordrecht, the Netherlands: Kluwer Academic.

Flaks, D. K., Ficher, I., Masterpasqua, F., & Joseph, G. (1995). Lesbians choosing motherhood: A comparative study of lesbian and heterosexual parents and their children. *Developmental Psychology, 32*(1), 105–114.

Flanagon, D., Baker-Ward, L., & Graham, L. (1995). Talk about preschool: Patterns of topic discussion and elaboration related to gender and ethnicity. *Sex roles, 32*, 1–15.

Flaskerud, J. D., & Hu, Li-tze. (1992). Relationship of ethnicity to psychiatric diagnosis. *Journal of Nervous and Mental Disease, 180*, 296–303.

Flowers, J. (1998). Improving female enrollment in teacher education. *The Technology Teacher: A Journal of the American Industrial Arts, 58*(2), 21–25.

Fong, C., & Yung, J. (1995–1996). In search of the right spouse: Interracial marriage among Chinese and Japanese Americans. *Amerasia Journal, 21*, 77–98.

Forel, A. (1908). *The sexual question: A scientific psychological, hygienic and sociological study* (C. F. Marshall, Trans.). New York: Physicians and Surgeons Books.

Foreman, M. (Ed.). (1999). *AIDS and men: Taking risks or taking responsibility?* London: Panos/Zed.

Foster, B. T. (1976). Friendship in rural Thailand. *Ethnography, 15*, 251–267.

Foubert, J. D. (2000). The longitudinal effects of a rape prevention program on fraternity men's attitudes, behavioral intent and behavior. *Journal of American College Health, 48*(4), 158–163.

Fowers, B. J. (1991). His and her marriage: A multivariate study of gender and marital satisfaction. *Sex Roles, 24*(3–4), 209–221.

Fowers, B. J., & Richardson, F. C. (1996). Why is multiculturalism good? *American Psychologist, 51*, 609–621.

Fox, D. J. (1999). Masculinity and fatherhood ?: An ethnographic account of the contradictions of fatherhood in a rural Jamaican town. *Men and Masculinities, 2*(1), 66–86.

Frable, D. E. S. (1997). Gender, racial, ethnic, sexual and class identity. *Annual Review of Psychology, 48*, 139–162.

Franchetti, M., & Conradi, P. (1996, June 9). Europe's roaring trade in sex slaves. *London Times*.

Franklin, J. H. (1997). African-American families: A historical note. In H. P. McAdoo (Ed.), *Black families* (3rd ed. (pp. 5–40). Thousand Oaks, CA: Sage.

Franzoi, S. L., & Koehler, V. (1998). Age and gender differences in body attitudes: A comparison of young and elderly adults. *International Journal of Aging and Human Development, 47*(1), 1–10.

Frayser, S. G. (1994). Defining normal childhood sexuality: An anthropological approach. *Annual Review of Sex Research, 5*, 173–217.

Frazier, P. A., Cochran, C. C., & Olson, A. M. (1995). Social science research on lay definitions of sexual harassment. *Journal of Social Issues, 51*(1), 21–38.

Freeborn, D. K., Levinson, W., & Mullooly, J. P. (1999). Medical malpractice and its consequences. Does physician gender play a role? *Journal of Gender, Culture and Health, 4*(3), 201–214.

Freiberg, P. (1991). Self-esteem gender gap widens in adolescence. *APA Monitor, 22*(4), 29.

Freud, S. (1924a). The dissolution of the Oedipus complex. In J. Strachey (Ed.), *The standard edition of the complete psychological works of Sigmund Freud* (Vol. 19). London: Hogarth Press.

Freud, S. (1924b). Some consequences of the anatomical distinction between the sexes. In J. Strachey (Ed.), *The standard edition of the complete psychological works of Sigmund Freud* (Vol. 19). London: Hogarth Press.

Freud, S. (1933). Femininity. In J. Strachey (Ed.), The standard edition of the complete psychological works of Sigmund Freud (Vol. 19). London: Hogarth Press.

Freud, S. (1948). Some psychological consequences of the anatomical distinction between the sexes. In *Collected Papers* (Vol. 5). London: Hogarth Press.

Freud, S. (1965). *New introductory lectures on psychoanalysis (1915–1917)* (Trans. J. Strachey). New York: Norton.

Friedman, A. S., Kramer, S., Kreisher, C., & Granick, S. (1996). The relationships of substance abuse to illegal and violent behavior in a community sample of young adult African-American men and women. *Journal of Substance Abuse, 8*(4), 379–402.

Friedman, A., & Pines, A. M. (1992). Increase in Arab women's perceived power in the second half of life. *Sex Roles, 26*, 1–9.

Friedman, A., & Todd, J. (1998). *The effect of modernization on women's power: Kenyan women tell a story*. Tel Aviv: Tel Aviv University Press.

Friedman, A., Weinberg, H., & Pines, A. M. (1998). Sexuality and motherhood: Mutually exclusive perception women. *Sex Roles, 38*(9–10), 781–800.

Friedman, H. S., Tucker, J. S., Schwartz, J. E., Tomlinson-Keasey, C., Martin, L. R., Wingard, D. L., & Criqui, M. H. (1995). Psychosocial and behavioral predictors of longevity: The aging and death of the "Termites." *American Psychologist, 50*(2), 69–78.

Frieze, I. H., & Davis, K. (2000). Introduction to stalking and obsessive behavior in everyday life. *Violence and Victims, 15*(1), 3–5.

Frone, M. R. (1998). Predictors of work injuries among employed adolescents. *Journal of Applied Psychology, 83*(4), 565–576.

Frone, M. R., & Yardley, J. K. (1996). Workplace family-supportive programmes: Predictions of employed parents' importance ratings. *Journal of Occupational and Organizational Psychology, 69*, 351–366.

Fuller-Thompson, E., Minkler, M., & Driver, D. (1997). A profile of grandparents raising grandchildren in the United States. *The Gerontologist, 37*(3), 406–411.

Furchtgott-Roth, D. (1998). Working women do not face barriers to advancement. In M. E. Williams, B. Stalcup, & K. L. Swisher (Eds.), *Working women: Opposing viewpoint* (pp. 73–78). San Diego: Greenhaven Press.

Furnham, A., & Mak, T. (1999). Sex role stereotyping in television commercials: A review and comparison of fourteen studies done on five continents over 25 years. *Sex Roles, 41*(5–6), 413–438.

Gabbard-Alley, A. S. (2000). Explaining illness: An examination of message strategies and gender. In B. B. Whaley (Ed.), *Explaining illness: Research, theory, and strategies* (pp. 147–170). Mahwah, NJ: Erlbaum.

Gailey, C. W. (1987). Evolutionary perspectives on gender hierarchy. In B. B. Hess & M. M. Ferree (Eds.), *Analyzing gender:*

A handbook of social science research (pp. 32–67). Newbury Park, CA: Sage.

Gaincola, P. R., & Zeichner, A. (1995). An investigation of gender differences in alcohol related aggression. *Journal of Studies on Alcohol, 68*, 675–684.

Galambos, N. L., Almeeda, D. M., & Peterson, A. C. (1990). Masculinity, femininity and sex role attitudes in early adolescence: Exploiting gender intensification. *Child Development, 61*(6), 1905–1914.

Galarneau, A. Z. (2001, May 1). Niagara, the drink touted for romance. *The Buffalo News*, p. B5.

Galen, B. R., & Underwood, M. K. (1997). A developmental investigation of social aggression among children. *Developmental Psychology, 33*, 589–600.

Galinsky, E., Bond, J. T., & Friedman, D. E. (1996). The role of employers in addressing the needs of employed parents. *Journal of Social Issues, 52*(3), 111–136.

Gallagher, J. J. (1993). An intersection of public policy and social science: Gifted students and education in mathematics and science. In L. A. Penner, G. M. Batsche, H. M. Knoff, & D. L. Nelson (Eds.), *The challenges in mathematics and science education* (pp. 15–47). Washington, DC: American Psychological Association.

Galotti, K. M. (1989). Gender differences in self reported moral reasoning: A review and new evidence. *Journal of Youth and Adolescence, 18*, 475–487.

Gamson, J. (1998). *Freaks talk back: Tabloid talkshows and sexual nonconformity*. Chicago: University of Chicago Press.

Gans, H. (1998). Deconstructing the underclass. In P. S. Rothenberg (Ed.), *Race, class & gender in the United States: A integrated study* (pp. 67–72). New York: St. Martin's Press.

Gany-Ming, M., Guo-Qian, C., Li, L., & Tseng, W. (1995). Koro epidemic in southern China. In T. Lin, W. Tseng, & E. Yeh (Eds.), *Chinese societies and mental health*. Hong Kong: Oxford University Press.

Gao, G., & Ting-Toomey, S. (1998). *Communicating effectively with the Chinese*. Thousand Oaks, CA: Sage.

Garb, H. N. (1997). Race bias, social class bias, and gender bias in clinical judgement. *Clinical Psychology: Science and Practice, 4*(2), 99–120.

Garbarino, J., & Kostelny, K. (1996). What do we need to know to understand children in war and community violence? In R. J. Apfel & B. Simon (Eds.), *Minefields in their hearts: The mental health of children in war and communal violence* (pp. 33–51). New Haven, CT: Yale University Press.

Garbarino, J. (1996). The effects of political violence on Palestinian children's behavior problems: A risk accumulation model. *Child Development, 67,* 33–45.

Gardiner, H. W., & Gardiner, O. S. (1991). Women in Thailand. In L. L. Adler (Ed.), *Women in cross-cultural perspective* (pp. 175–188). New York: Praeger.

Gardos, P. S., & Mosher, D. L. (1999). Gender differences in reactions to viewing pornographic vignettes: Essential or interpretive? *Journal of Psychology and Human Sexuality, 11*(2), 65–84.

Garnets, L. D., & Kimmel, D. C. (Eds.). (1993). *Psychological perspectives on lesbian and gay male experiences.* New York: Columbia University Press.

Gater, R., Tansella, M., Korten, A., Tiemans, B. J., Mavreas, V. G., & Olatawura, M. O. (1998). Sex differences in the prevalence and detection of depressive and anxiety disorders in general health care settings: Report from the World Health Organization collaborative study on psychological problems in general health care. *Archives of General Psychiatry, 55*(5), 405–413.

Gates, A. (2000, April 9). Men on T.V.: Dumb as posts and proud of it. *New York Times,* Section 2, p. 1.

Gatz, M., Harris, J. R., & Turk-Charles, S. (1995). *The meaning of health for older women.* Washington, DC: American Psychological Association.

Gavey, N., McPhillips, K., & Braun, V. (1999). Interruptus coitus: Heterosexuals accounting for intercourse. *Sexualities, 2*(1), 35–68.

Gay, J. (1989). "Mummies and babies" and friends and lovers in Lesotho. *Journal of Homosexuality, 11,* 97–116.

Geary, D. C. (1996). Sexual selection and sex differences in mathematical abilities. *Behavior and Brain Sciences, 19*(2), 229–284.

Geary, D. C. (1999). Evolution and developmental sex differences. *Current Directions in Psychological Science, 8*(44), 115–120.

Geary, D. C. (Ed.). (1998). *Male, female: The evolution of human sex differences.* Washington, DC: American Psychological Association.

Geewax, M. (2000, September 4). "Good old days" are now for workers. *Austin-American Statesman,* pp. A1, A16.

Gerbner, G., Gross, L., Morgan, M., & Signorelli, N. (1994). Growing up with television: The cultivation perspective. In J. Bryant & D. Zillman (Eds.), *Media effects: Advances in theory and research* (pp. 17–41). Mahwah, NJ: Erlbaum.

Gergen, M. (1994). Epistemology, gender and history: Positioning the lenses of gender. *Psychological Inquiry, 5,* 86–92.

Gergen, M. (1997). Life stories: Pieces of a dream. In M. M. Gergen & S. N. Davis (Eds.), *Toward a new psychology of gender: A reader* (pp. 203–221). New York: Routledge.

Gergen, M. M., & Davis, S. N. (Eds.). (1997). *Toward a new psychology of gender.* New York: Routledge.

Gerson, K. (1997). Dilemmas of involved fatherhood. In E. Disch (Ed.), *Reconstructing gender: A multicultural anthology* (pp. 272–281). Mountain View, CA: Mayfield.

Gerson, M., Alpert, J. L., & Richardson, M. (1997). Mothering: The view from psychological research. In T. Roberts (Ed.), *The Lanahan readings on the psychology of women* (pp. 136–148). Baltimore: Lanahan.

Geschwind, N., & Galaburda, A. S. (1987). *Cerebral lateralization.* Cambridge, MA: MIT Press.

Ghorayshi, P. (1996). Women, paid work, and the family in the Islamic Republic of Iran. *Journal of Comparative Family Studies, 27*(3), 453–466.

Giancola, P. R., & Zeichner, A. (1995). Alcohol-related aggression in males and females: effects of blood alcohol concentration, subjective intoxication, personality, and provocation. *Alcoholism: Clinical and Experimental Research 19*(1), 130–134.

Gibber, J. R. (1981). *Infant-directed behaviors in male and female rhesus monkeys.* Unpublished doctoral dissertation, University of Wisconsin-Madison.

Gibbons, J. L., Hamby, B. A., & Dennis, W. D. (1997). Researching gender-role ideologies internationally and cross-culturally. *Psychology of Women Quarterly, 21*(1), 151–170.

Gibbons, J. L., Stiles, D. A., & Shkodriani, G. M. (1991). Adolescent's attitudes toward family and gender roles: An international comparison. *Sex Roles, 25,* 625–643.

Gibson, R. C. (1993). The black American retirement experience. In J. S. Jackson, L. M. Chatters, & R. J. Taylor (Eds.), *Aging in black America* (pp. 277–297). Newbury Park, CA: Sage.

Gilbert, N. (1998). Working families: Hearth to market. In M. A. Mason, A. Skolnick, & S. D. Sugarman (Eds.), *All our families: New policies for a new century* (pp. 193–216). New York: Oxford University Press.

Gilligan, C. (1982). *In a different voice.* Cambridge, MA: Harvard University Press.

Gilligan, C., & Attanucci, J. (1988). Two moral orientations. In C. Gilligan, J. V. Ward, J. M. Taylor, & B. Bardige (Eds.), *Mapping the moral domain: A contribution of women's thinking to psychological theory and education* (pp. 73–86). Cambridge, MA: Harvard University Press.

Gilmore, D. (1990). *Manhood in the making: Cultural concepts of masculinity.* New Haven, CT: Yale University Press.

Gilmour, H. (1999). What girls want: The intersections of leisure and power in female computer game play. In M. Kinder (Ed.), *Kids' media culture* (pp. 239–262). Durham, NC: Duke University Press.

Ginorio, A. B., Guiterrez, L., Cauce, A. M., & Acosta, M. (1995). Psychological issues for Latinos. In H. Landrine (Ed.), *Bringing cultural diversity to feminist psychology: Theory research, practice* (pp. 241–263). Washington, DC: American Psychological Association.

Gladstone, T. R. G., Kaslow, N. J., Seeley, J. R., & Lewisohn, P. M. (1997). Sex differences, attributional style, and depressive symptoms among adolescents. *Journal of Abnormal Child Psychology, 25*(4), 297–305.

Glanze, W. D., Anderson, K. N., & Anderson, L. E. (1994). *Mosky Medical Encyclopedia.* New York: Penguin.

Glenn, E. N., & Feldberg, R. L. (1995). Clinical work: The female occupation. In J. Freeman (Ed.), *Women: A feminist perspective* (5th ed., pp. 262–286). Mountain View, CA: Mayfield.

Glick, P. (1991). Trait-based and sex-based discrimination in occupational prestige, occupational salary and hiring. *Sex Roles*, 25(5–6), 351–378.

Glick, P., & Fiske, S. T. (1999). Sexism & other "isms": Independence, status and the ambivalent content of stereotypes. In W. B. Swann, Jr., J. H. Langlois, & L. A. Gilbert (Eds.), *Sexism and stereotypes in modern society* (pp. 193–222). Washington, DC: American Psychological Association.

Glick, P., Wilk, K., & Perrault, M. (1995). Images of occupations: Components of gender and status in occupational stereotypes. *Sex Roles*, 32(9–10), 565–582.

Goffman, E. (1979). *Gender advertisements.* Cambridge, MA: Harvard University Press.

Gold, M. E. (1999). *Top cops.* Chicago: Brittany.

Gold, S. N., Lucenko, B. A., Elhai, J. D., Swingle, J. M., & Sellers, A. H. (1999). A comparison of psychological/psychiatric symptomatology of women and men sexually abused as children. *Child Abuse and Neglect*, 23(7), 683–692.

Goldenhar, L. M., Swanson, N. G., Hurrell, J. J., Ruder, A., & Deddens, J. (1998). Stressors and adverse outcomes for female construction workers. *Journal of Occupational Health Psychology*, 3(1), 19–32.

Goldstein, J. (1998). Immortal combat: War toys and violent video games. In J. Goldstein (Ed.), *Why we watch* (pp. 53–68). New York: Oxford.

Golombok, S., & Tasker, F. (1996). Do parents influence the sexual orientation of their children? Findings from a longitudinal study of lesbian families. *Developmental Psychology*, 33, 3–11.

Gomberg, E. (1993). Women and alcohol: Use and abuse. *Journal of Nervous and Mental Diseases*, 181, 211–219.

Gomez, C. A., & Marin, B. V. (1996). Gender, culture, and power: Barriers to HIV-prevention strategies for women. *Journal of Sex Research*, 33(4), 355–362.

Gondolf, E. W., & Shestakov, D. (1997). Spousal homicide in Russia. *Violence Against Women*, 3(5), 533–546.

Gonsiorek, J. C. (1996). Mental health & sexual orientation. In R. C. Savin-Williams & K. M. Cohen (Eds.), *The lives of lesbians, gays, and bisexuals* (pp. 462–478). Fort Worth, TX: Harcourt Brace.

Gonyea, J. G. (1994). Making gender visible in public policy. In E. H. Thompson (Ed.), *Older men's lives* (pp. 237–255). Thousand Oaks, CA: Sage.

Good, G. E., & Sherrod, N. B. (1997). Men's resolution of nonrelational sex across the lifespan. In R. F. Levant & G. R. Brooks (Eds.), *Men and sex: New psychological perspectives* (pp. 181–204). New York: Wiley.

Good, G. E., & Sherrod, N. B. (2001). The psychology of men and masculinity: Research status and future directions. In R. K. Unger (Ed.), *The handbook of the psychology of women and gender* (pp. 201–214). New York: Wiley.

Goodall, J. (1990). *Through a window: My thirty years with the chimpanzees of Gombe.* Boston: Houghton Mifflin.

Goodnow, J. J. (1996). From household practices to parents' ideas about work and interpersonal relationships. In S. Harkness & C. Super (Eds.), *Parents' cultural belief systems* (pp. 313–344). New York: Guilford Press.

Goodstein, R., & Gielen, U. P. (1998). Some conceptual similarities and differences between cross-cultural and multicultural psychology. *International Psychologist*, 38(2), 42–43.

Goodwin, M. H. (1994). Social differentiation and alliance formation in an African-American children's peer group. In M. R. Stevenson (Ed.), *Gender roles through the lifespan: A multidisciplinary perspective.* Muncie, IN: Ball State University Press.

Gooren, L. (1995) Biomedical concepts of homosexuality: Folk belief in a white coat. *Journal of Homosexuality*, 28, 237–246.

Gordon H. W., & Lee, P. L. (1993). A relationship between gonadotropins and visuospatial function. *Neuropsychologia*, 24, 563–576.

Gottfried, A. E., Gottfried, A. W., & Bathhurst, K. (1995). Maternal and dual-earner employment status and parenting. In M. H. Bornstein (Ed.), *Handbook of parenting* (Vol. 2, pp. 139–160). Mahwah, NJ: Erlbaum.

Gottman, J. M. (1994). *What predicts divorce? The relationship between processes and marital outcomes.* Mahwah, NJ: Erlbaum.

Gottman, J. M., & Carriere, S. (1994). Why can't men and women get along? In D. J. Canary & L. Stafford (Eds.), *Communication and relational maintenance* (pp. 203–227). San Diego: Academic Press.

Graber, J. A., Brooks-Gunn, J., & Galen, B. R. (1998). *Betwixt and between: Sexuality in the context of adolescent transitions.* New York: Cambridge University Press.

Gradman, T. J. (1994). Masculine identity from work to retirement. In E. H. Thompson, Jr. (Ed.), *Older men's lives* (pp. 104–121). Thousand Oaks, CA: Sage.

Graham, K., Wilsnack, K. R., Dawson, D., & Vogeltanz, N. (1998). Should alcohol consumption measure be adjusted for gender differences. *Addiction*, 93(8), 1137–1147.

Gray, J. (1992). *Men are from Mars, women are from Venus.* New York: HarperCollins.

Gray, P., & Feldman, J. (1997). Patterns of age mixing and gender mixing among children and adolescents at an ungraded democratic school. *Merrill-Palmer Quarterly*, 43(1), 67–86.

Green, C. A., & Pope, C. R. (1999). Gender, psychosocial factors and the use of medical services: A longitudinal analysis. *Social Science and Medicine*, 48(10), 1363–1372.

Green, R. (2000). Family cooccurence of "gender dysphoria": Ten sibling or parent–child pairs. *Archives of Social Behavior*, 29(5), 499–508.

Green, R. M. (2001). The ethical considerations. *Scientific American*, 268(1), 48–50.

Greenberg, B. S., & Woods, M. G. (1999). The soaps: Their sex, gratifications and outcomes. *Journal of Sex Research*, 36(3), 250–257.

Greenberg, S. H. (2001, October 29). Get out of my way: Women soldiers, making quiet progress, now hold dangerous combat positions. *Newsweek*, pp. 34–35.

Greene, B. (1994). Ethnic minority lesbians and gay men: Mental health and treatment issues. *Journal of Counseling and Clinical Psychology*, 62(2), 243–251.

Greene, C. K., & Stitt-Gohdes, W. L. (1997). Factors that influence women's choices to work in the trades. *Journal of Career Development*, 23(4), 265–278.

Greenfield, S. F. (1996). Women and substance use disorders. In M. F. Jensvold, U. Halbreich, & J. A. Hamilton (Eds.), *Psychopharmacology and women* (pp. 299–322). Washington, DC: American Psychiatric Press.

Greenberg, S. H. (2001, October 29). Get out of my way: Women soldiers, making quiet progress, now hold dangerous combat positions. *Newsweek*, pp. 34–35.

Greenstein, T. N. (1996). Husband's participation in domestic labor: Interactive effects of wives' and husbands' gender ideologies. *Journal of Marriage and the Family, 58*(3), 585–595.

Greif, G. L., DeMaris, A., & Hood, J. C. (1993). Balancing work and single fatherhood. In J. C. Hood (Ed.), *Men, work, and family* (pp. 176–194). Newbury Park, CA: Sage.

Greimel, E. R., Padilla, G. V., & Grant, M. M. (1998). Gender differences in outcomes among patients with cancer. *Psycho-Oncology, 7*(3), 197–206.

Griffin, S. (1981). *Pornography and silence: Culture's revenge against nature.* New York: Harper & Row.

Griffiths, P. E. (1997). *What emotions really are.* Chicago: University of Chicago Press.

Griggs, C. (1998). *Changing sex and changing clothes.* New York: Oxford University Press.

Grimshaw, G. M., Sitarenios, G., & Finegan, J. K. (1995). Mental rotation at 7 years: Relations with prenatal testosterone levels and spatial play experience. *Brain and Cognition, 29,* 85–100.

Grisaru, N., Lezer, S., & Belmaker, R. H. (1997). Ritual female genital surgery among Ethiopian Jews. *Archives of Sexual Behavior, 26*(2), 211–215.

Gross, J., Carstensen, L. L., Pasupathi, M., Tsai, J., Skorpen, C., & Hsu, H. (1997). Emotion and aging: Experience, expression & control. *Psychology and Aging, 12,* 590–599.

Grossberg, L., Wastella, E., & Whitney, D. C. (1998). *Mediamaking: Mass media in a popular culture.* Thousand Oaks, CA: Sage.

Grotpeter, J. K., & Crick, N. R. (1996). Relational aggression, overt aggression and friendship. *Child Development, 67*(5), 2328–2338.

Guarnaccia, P. J. (1997). A cross-cultural perspective on anxiety disorders. In S. Friedman (Ed.), *Cultural issues in the treatment of anxiety* (pp. 3–20). New York: Guilford Press.

Guarnaccia, P. J., Rivera, M., Franco, F., & Nei, Cghbors. (1996). The experiences of ataqué de nervios: Toward an anthropology of emotions in Puerto Rico. *Culture, Medicine, & Psychiatry, 20*(3), 343–367.

Gubrium, J. F., & Holstein, J. A. (1997). *The new language of qualitative method.* New York: Oxford University Press.

Guerrero, L. K., & Reiter, R. L. (1998). Expressing emotion: Sex differences in social skills and communicative responses to anger, sadness and jealousy. In J. Canary & K. Dindia (Eds.), *Sex differences and similarities in communication* (pp. 321–349). Mahwah, NJ: Erlbaum.

Guinier, L., Fine, M., & Balin, J. (1997). *Becoming gentlemen: Women, law school, and institutional change.* Boston: Beacon Press.

Gur, R. C., Mozley, L. H., Mozley, P. D., Risnick, S. M., Karp, J. S. Alavi, A., Arnold, S. E., & Gur, R. E. (1995). Sex differences in regional glucose metabolism during a resting state. *Science, 267,* 528–531.

Gurian, M. (1996). *The wonder of boys.* New York: Tarcher/Putnam.

Gutek, B. A. (1985). *Sex and the workplace: Impact of sexual behavior and harassment on women, men and organizations.* San Francisco: Jossey-Bass.

Gutek, B. A., & O'Connor, M. (1995). The empirical basis for the reasonable woman standard. *Journal of Social Issues, 51*(1), 151–166.

Gutherie, R. V. (1998). *Even the rat was white* (2nd ed.). Boston: Allyn and Bacon.

Gutman, H. G. (1976). *The black family in slavery and freedom, 1750–1925.* New York: Pantheon.

Guttmacher Report on Public Policy. (2001). Mifepristone rollout begins: FDA okays new contraceptive shot. Available online at www.agi-usa.org/pubs. Retrieved on April 30, 2001.

Guttman, D. (1987). *Reclaimed powers: Toward a new psychology of men and women in later life.* New York: Basic Books.

Haaken, J. (1988). Field dependence research: A historical analysis of a psychological construct. *Signs, 13*(2), 311–330.

Haaken, J., & Lamb, S. (2000). The politics of child sexual abuse research. *Society, 37,* 4, 7–14.

Haas, G. L., & Garratt, L. S. (1998). Gender differences in social functioning in schizophrenia. In K. T. Mueser & N. Tarrier (Eds.), *Handbook of social functioning in schizophrenia* (pp. 149–180). Boston: Allyn and Bacon.

Hadden, K. P., & London, B. (1996). Educating girls in the third world: The demographic, basic needs and economic benefits. *International Journal of Comparative Sociology, 37*(1–2), 31–46.

Haiken, E. (1997). *Venus envy: A history of cosmetic surgery.* Baltimore: Johns Hopkins University Press, 1997.

Hall, E. J. (1993). Waitering/waitressing: Engendering the work of table servers. *Gender and Society, 7,* 329–346.

Hall, G. C. N., Sue, S., Narang, D. S., & Lilly, R. S. (2000). Culture-specific models of men's sexual aggression: Intra- and interpersonal determinants. *Cultural Diversity and Ethnic Minority Psychology, 6*(3), 252–267.

Hall, G. S. (1903). Coeducation in the high school. *National Education Association Journal of Proceedings and Addresses, 42,* 442–455.

Hall, G. S. (1904a). *Adolescence.* New York: Appleton.

Hall, G. S. (1904b). Coeducation. *National Education Association Journal of Proceedings and Addresses, 42,* 442–455.

Hall, G. S. (1911). *Educational problems* (Vol. 2). New York: Appleton.

Hall, G. S. (1922). Flapper americana novissima. *Atlantic Monthly, 129,* 771–780.

Hall, J. A. (1978). Gender effects in decoding nonverbal cues. *Psychological Bulletin, 85*(4), 845–857.

Hall, J. A. (1984). *Non-verbal sex differences. Communication accuracy and expressive style.* Baltimore, MD: Johns Hopkins University Press.

Hall, J. A. (1987). On explaining gender differences: The case of nonverbal communication. In P. Shaver & C. Hendrick (Eds.), *Sex and gender. Vol. 7: Review of personality and social psychology* (pp. 177–200). Beverly Hills, CA: Sage.

Hall, J. A. (1998). How big are non-verbal sex differences? The case of smiling and sensitivity to nonverbal cues. In D. J. Canary & K. Dindia (Eds.), *Sex differences and similarities in communication* (pp. 155–177). Mahwah, NJ: Erlbaum.

Hall, J. A., & Kimura, D. (1994). Dermatoglyphic asymmetry and sexual orientation in men. *Behavioral Neuroscience, 108,* 1203–1206.

Hall, J. A., Halberstadt, A. G., & O'Brien, C. E. (1997). "Subordination" and nonverbal sensitivity: A study and synthesis of findings based on trait measures. *Sex Roles, 37,* 295–317.

Hall, S. S. (2000, January 30). The recycled generation. *New York Times Magazine, 149,* 30–39.

Halpern, C. J. T., Udry, J. R., Suchindran, C., & Campbell, B. (2000). Adolescent males willingness to report masturbation. *Journal of Sex Research, 37*(4), 327–332.

Halpern, D. F. (1992). *Sex differences in cognitive abilities* (2nd ed.). Mahwah, NJ: Erlbaum.

Halpern, D. F. (1994). Stereotypes, science, censorship, and the study of sex differences. *Feminism & Psychology, 4*(4), 523–530.

Halpern, D. F. (1996). Sex, brains, hands and spatial cognition. *Developmental Review, 16*(3), 261–270.

Halpern, D. F. (1996a). Changing data, changing minds: What the data on cognitive sex differences tell us and what we hear. *Learning and Individual Differences, 8,* 73–82.

Halpern, D. F. (1996b). Public policy implications of sex differences in cognitive abilities. *Psychology, Public Policy, and Law, 2*(3–4), 561–574.

Halpern, D. F. (1997a). *Critical thinking across the curriculum: A brief edition of thought and knowledge.* Mahwah, NJ: Erlbaum.

Halpern, D. F. (1997b). Sex differences in intelligence. *American Psychologist, 52*(10), 1091–1102.

Halpern, D. F. (1998a). Recipe for a sexually dimorphic brain: Ingredients include ovarian and testicular hormones. *Behavioral and Brain Sciences, 21*(3), 330–331.

Halpern, D. F. (1998b). Stereotypes, science, censorship, and the study of sex differences. In D. L. Anselmi & A. L. Law (Eds.), *Questions of gender* (pp. 99–103). New York: McGraw-Hill.

Halpern, D. F., & Crothers, M. (1997). Sex, sexual orientation, and cognition. In L. Ellis & L. Ebertz (Eds.), *Sexual orientation: Toward biological understanding* (pp. 181–199). Westport, CT: Praeger.

Hamelin, K., & Ramachandran, C. (1993). Kangaroo care. *Canadian Nurse, 89*(3), 15–17.

Hamer, D. H., Hu, S., Magnuson, V. L., Hu, N., & Pattalucci, A. M. L. (1993). A linkage between DNA markers on the X chromosome and male sexual orientation. *Science, 261,* 321–327.

Hamilton, B. (1996). Ethnicity and the family life cycle: The Chinese-American family. *Family Therapy, 23*(3), 199–212.

Hamilton, M. C. (1991). Masculine bias in the attribution of personhood: People = male, male = people. *Psychology of Women Quarterly, 15,* 393–402.

Hand, J. Z., & Sanchez, L. (2000). Badgering or bantering? Gender differences in experience of and reactions to, sexual harassment among U.S. high school students. *Gender and Society, 14*(6), 718–746.

Hankin, B. L., Abramson, L. Y., Moffitt, T. E., & Silva, P. A., et al. (1998). Development of depression from preadolescence to young adulthood: Emerging gender differences in a 10-year longitudinal study. *Journal of Abnormal Psychology, 107*(1), 128–140.

Hankins, C. (1996). Sexual transmission of HIV to women in industrialized countries. *World Health Statistics Quarterly, 49,* 106–114.

Hansen, K. V. (1992). Our eyes behold each other. In P. M. Nardi (Ed.), *Men's friendships* (pp. 35–49). Newbury Park, CA: Sage.

Hanson, R. K., & Scott, H. (1995). Assessing perspective taking among sexual offenders, non-sexual criminals and non-offenders. *Sexual Abuse: A Journal of Research and Treatment, 7,* 259–278.

Hara, H., & Minagawa, M. (1996). From productive dependents to precious guests: Historical changes in Japanese children. In D. W. Shwalb & B. J. Shwalb (Eds.), *Japanese childrearing: Two generations of scholarship* (pp. 9–30). New York: Guilford Press.

Hardy, S. (1998). *The reader, the author, his woman and her lover: Soft-core pornography and heterosexual men.* Herndon, VA: Cassell.

Hare-Mustin, R. T., & Marecek, J. (1998). Asking the right questions: Feminist psychology and sex differences. In D. L. Anselmi & A. L. Law (Eds.), *Questions of gender* (pp. 104–108). New York: McGraw-Hill.

Hare-Mustin, R. T., & Marecek, J. (Eds.). (1990). *Making a difference: Psychology and the construction of gender.* New Haven, CT: Yale University Press.

Harkness, S., & Super, C. M. (1992). The cultural foundations of fathers roles: Evidence from Kenya and the United States. In B. S. Hewlett (Ed.). *Father-child relations: Cultural and biosocial contexts* (pp. 191–211). New York: Aldine deGruyter.

Harmon, R. J., Bender, B. G., Linden, M. G., & Robinson, A. (1998). Transition from adolescence to early adulthood: Adaptation and psychiatric status of women with 47 XXX. *Journal of the Academy of Child and Adolescent Psychiatry, 37*(3), 286–291.

Harnack, L., Story, M., Martinson, B., Neumark-Sztainer, D., & Stang, J. (1998). Guess who's cooking? The role of men in meal planning, shopping, and preparation in US families. *Journal of the American Dietetic Association, 98*(9), 995–1000.

Harre, R. (1997a). Are emotions significant in psychology only as motives? *Journal for the Theory of Social Behavior, 27*(4), 503–505.

Harre, R. (1997b). Emotions across cultures. *World Psychology, 3*(1/2), 89–106.

Harris, A. C. (1994). Ethnicity as a determinant of sex role identity: A replication study of item selection for the Bem Sex Role Inventory. *Sex Roles, 31,* 241–273.

Harris, D. J., & Kuba, S. A. (1997). Ethnocultural identity and eating disorders in women of color. *Professional Psychology, 1,* 6–17.

Harris, D. J., & Kuba, S. A. (1997). Ethnocultural identity and eating disorders in women of color. *Professional Psychology: Research and Practice, 28*(4), 341–347.

Harris, J. A., Rushton, J. P., Hampson, E., & Jackson, D. N. (1996). Salivary testosterone and self-report aggressive and prosocial personality characteristics in men and women. *Aggressive Behavior, 22*(5), 321–331.

Harris, J. R. (1998). *The nurture assumption: Why children turn out the way they do.* New York: Free Press.

Harris, M. B., & Knight-Bonoff, K. (1996a). Gender and aggression I: Perceptions of aggression. *Sex Roles, 35,* 1–25.

Harris, M. B., & Knight-Bonoff, K. (1996b). Gender and aggression II: Personal aggressiveness. *Sex Roles, 35,* 27–42.

Harris, R. J., & Firestone, J. M. (1998). Changes in predictions of gender role ideologies among women: A multivariate analysis. *Sex Roles, 38*(3–4), 239–252.

Harrison, A. O., Stewart, R. B., Myambo, K., & Teueraishe, C. (1995). Perceptions of social networks among adolescents from Zimbabwe and the United States. *Journal of Black Psychology, 21*(4), 382–407.

Harrison, G., Croudace, T., Mason, P., Glazebrook, C., & Medley, I. (1996). Predicting the long-term outcomes of schizophrenia. *Psychological Medicine, 26*(4), 697–705.

Harrison, J. (1995). Roles, identities, and sexual orientation: Homosexuality, heterosexuality, and bisexuality. In R. F. Levant & W. S. Pollack (Eds.), *A new psychology of men* (pp. 359–381). New York: HarperCollins.

Hartung, C. M., & Widiger, T. A. (1998). Gender differences in the diagnosis of mental disorders: Conclusions and controversies of the DSM-IV. *Psychological Bulletin, 123*(3), 260–278.

Hartup, W. W., & Stevens, N. (1997). Friendships and adaptation in the life course. *Psychological Bulletin, 121,* 355–370.

Hartup, W. W., & Stevens, N. (1999). Friendships and adaptation across the lifespan. *Current Directions in Psychological Science, 8*(3), 76–79.

Hatala, M. N., & Prehodka, J. (1996). Context analysis of gay male and lesbians personal advertisements. *Psychological Reports, 78,* 371–374.

Hatfield, E., & Rapson, R. L. (1996). *Love and sex: Cross-cultural perspectives.* Boston: Allyn and Bacon.

Hatfield, E., & Sprecher, S. (1995). Men's and women's preferences in marital partners in the US, Russia, and Japan. *Journal of Cross-Cultural Psychology, 26,* 728–750.

Haugaard, J. J. (2000). The challenge of defining child sexual abuse. *American Psychologist, 55*(9), 1036–1039.

Haviland, W. A. (1991). *Anthropology* (6th ed.). Fort Worth, TX: Holt, Rinehart, & Winston.

Havranek, C. (1998, November). The new sex surgeries. *Cosmopolitan,* 146–150.

Hawkes, G. R., & Taylor, M. (1999). Power structure in Mexican & Mexican-American farm labor families. In L. A. Peplau, S. C. DeBro, R. C. Veniegas, & P. L. Taylor (Eds.), *Gender, culture and ethnicity: Current research about women and men* (pp. 200–207). Mountain View, CA: Mayfield.

Hay, D. F., Castle, J., Stimpson, C. A., & Davie, L. (1995). The social construction of character in toddlerhood. In M. Killen & D. Hart (Eds.), *Morality in everyday life: Developmental aspects* (pp. 23–51). Cambridge, England: Cambridge University Press.

Hays, S. (1996). *The cultural contradictions of motherhood.* New Haven, CT: Yale University Press.

Headles, S., & Elfin, M. (1996). *The cost of being female.* New York: Praeger.

Healy, B. (1995). *A new prescription for women's health: Getting the best medical care in a man's world.* New York: Penguin.

Hearn, J. (1998). *The violence of men.* Thousand Oaks, CA: Sage.

Hecht, H., & Proffitt, D. R. (1995). The price of expertise: Effects of experience on the water level task. *Psychological Society, 6*(2), 90–95.

Hee, S. J. (1999). Lung cancer in Korea. *Journal of Epidemiology, 28,* 824–828.

Heider, K. G. (1976). *Dani sexuality: A low energy system.* Man 11(2), 188–201.

Heilman, M. E. (1995). Sex stereotypes and their effects in the workplace: What we know and what we don't know. *Journal of Social Behavior and Personality, 10*(6), 3–26.

Heinz, W. R. (1999). Job-entry patterns in a life-course perspective. In W. R. Heinz (Ed.), *From education to work: Cross-national perspectives* (pp. 214–233). London: Cambridge University Press.

Heiss, J. (1992). Social roles. In M. Rosenberg & R. Turner (Eds.), *Social psychology: Sociological perspectives* (pp. 94–129). New Brunswick, NJ: Transaction.

Helgesen, S. (1998). *Everyday revolutionaries.* New York: Bantam Doubleday Dell.

Hendrick, C., & Hendrick, S. (1996). Gender and the experience of heterosexual love. In J. T. Wood (Ed.), *Gendered relationships* (pp. 131–148). Mountain View, CA: Mayfield.

Henley, N. M. (1989). Molehill or mountain? What we know and don't know about sex bias in language. In M. Crawford & M. Gentry (Eds.), *Gender and thought: Psychological perspectives.* New York: Springer.

Henley, N. M., & Freeman, J. (1995). The sexual politics of interpersonal behavior. In J. Freeman (Ed.), *Women: A feminist perspective* (5th ed., pp. 79–91). Mountain View, CA: Mayfield.

Henley, N. M., & LaFrance, M. (1996). On oppressing hypotheses: Or differences in nonverbal sensitivity revisited. In L. H. Radtke & H. J. Stam (Eds.), *Power/gender: Social relations in theory and practice. Inquiries in social construction* (pp. 287–311). Thousand Oaks, CA: Sage.

Henley, N. M., & LaFrance, M. (1997). Gender as culture: Difference and dominance. In T. Roberts (Ed.), *The Lanahan readings on the psychology of women* (pp. 553–567). Baltimore, MD: Lanahan.

Henriques, G., Calhoun, L., & Cann, A. (1996). Ethnic differences in women's body satisfaction: An experimental investigation. *Journal of Social Psychology, 136,* 689–697.

Henry, J., & Metzoff, J. (1998). Perceptions of sexual harassment as a function of target's response type and observers sex. *Sex Roles, 39*(3–4), 253–310.

Henson, K. D., & Rogers, J. K. (2001). "Why Marcia, you've changed!" Male clerical temporary workers doing masculinity in a feminized occupation. *Gender and Society, 15*(2) 218–238.

Hepworth, J. (Ed.) (1999). *The social construction of anorexia nervosa.* Thousand Oaks, CA: Sage.

Herdt, G. (1981). *Guardians of the flute.* New York: McGraw-Hill.

Herdt, G. (1997). *Same sex, different cultures.* Boulder, CO: Westview Press.

Herold, E. S., & Marshall, S. K. (1996). Adolescent sexual development. In G. R. Adams, R. Montemayor, & T. P. Gullotta (Eds.), *Psychosocial development during adolescence: Advances in adolescent development* (Vol. 8, pp. 62–94). Thousand Oaks, CA: Sage.

Herrera, R. S., & DelCampo, R. L. (1995). Beyond the superwoman syndrome: Work satisfaction and family functioning among working-class, Mexican American women. *Hispanic Journal of Behavioral Sciences, 17*(1), 49–60.

Herrmann, D. J., Crawford, M., & Holdsworth, M. (1992). Gender-linked differences in everyday memory performance. *British Journal of Psychology, 83,* 221–231.

Herzberger, S. (1996). *Violence within the family: Social psychological perspectives.* Boulder, CO: Westview Press.

Hetherington, E. M. (1999a). Should we stay together for the sake of the children? In E. M. Hetherington (Ed.), *Coping with divorce, single parenting: A risk and resiliency perspective* (pp. 93–116). Mahwah, NJ: Erlbaum.

Hetherington, E. M. (1999b). Social capital and the development of youth from nondivorced, divorced and remarried families. In W. A. Collins & B. Laursen (Eds.), *Relationships as developmental contexts.* The Minnesota symposia on child psychology (vol. 30., pp. 177–209). Mahwah, NJ: Erlbaum.

Hetherington, E. M., & Stanley-Hagen, M. M. (1997). The effects of divorce on fathers and their children. In M. E. Lamb (Ed.), *The role of the father in child development* (pp. 191–211). New York: Wiley.

Heward, C. (1999). Closing the gender gap? The informal sector in Pakistan. In C. Heward & S. Bunwaree (Eds.), *Gender, education and development: Beyond access to empowerment* (pp. 203–217). London: Zed Books.

Hibbard, D. R., & Buhrmester, D. (1997). The role of peers in the socialization of gender related social interaction styles. *Sex Roles, 39*(3–4), 185–202.

Hickson, F., Davis, P., Hunt, A., Weatherbum, P., McManus, T., & Coxon, A. (1994). Gay men as victims of non-consensual sex. *Archives of Sexual Behavior, 23*(3), 281–294.

Hiday, V. A., Swartz, M. S., Swanson, J. W., Borum, R., & Wagner, H. R. (1998). Male–female differences in the setting and construction of violence among people with severe mental illness. *Social Psychiatry and Psychiatric Epidemiology 33*, S68–S74.

Hill, A. J., & Franklin, J. A. (1998). Mothers, daughters, and dieting: Investigating the transmission of weight control. *British Journal of Clinical Psychology, 37*(1), 3–13.

Hines, M. (1993). Hormonal and neural correlates of sex-typed behavioral development in human beings. In M. Haug, R. E. Whalen, C. Aron, & K. L. Olsen (Eds.), *The development of sex differences and similarities in behavior* (pp. 131–149). Netherlands: Kluwer Academic Publishers.

Hines, N. J., & Fry, D. P. (1994). Indirect modes of aggression among women of Buenos Aires, Argentina. *Sex Roles, 30*, 213–236.

Hippisley-Cox, J., Allen, J., Pringle, M., Churchill, D., McPhearson, M., Bradley, S., & Ebdon, D. (2000). Association between teenage pregnancy rates and the age and sex of general practitioners: Cross sectional survey in Trent 1994–7. *British Medical Journal, 320*, 842–845.

Hira, F. J., & Falkender, P. J. (1997). Perceiving wisdom: Do age and gender play a part? *International Journal of Aging and Human Development, 44*(2), 85–101.

Hirdman, Y. (1998). State policy and gender contracts: The Swedish experience. In E. Drew, R. Emerek, & E. Mahon, *Women, work, and the family in Europe* (pp. 36–46). London: Routledge.

Hochschild, A. (1989). *The second shift: Working parents and the revolution at home.* New York: Viking.

Hockey, J. (1997). Women in grief: Cultural representation and social practice. In D. Field, J. Hockey, & N. Small (Eds.), *Death, gender and ethnicity* (pp. 89–107). New York: Routledge.

Hogan, J. D. (1999). Further reflection on autonomy. In M. B. Nadien & F. L. Denmark (Eds.), *Females and autonomy* (pp. 155–168). Boston: Allyn and Bacon.

Hojgaard, L. (1998). Workplace culture, family supportive policies and gender differences. In E. Drew, R. Emerek, & E. Mahom (Eds.), *Women, work, and the family in Europe* (pp. 140–149). London: Routledge.

Holt, S. B. (1968). *The genetics of dermal ridges.* Springfield, IL: Thomas.

Hondagneu-Sotelo, P. (1997). Overcoming patriarchal constraints: The reconstruction of gender relations among Mexican immigrant women and men. In M. B. Zinn, P. Hondagnew-Sotelo, & M. A. Messner (Eds.), *Through the prism of difference* (pp. 477–485). Boston: Allyn and Bacon.

Hood, K. E. (1996). Intractable tangles of sex and gender in women's aggressive development: An optimistic view. In D. M. Stoff & R. B. Cairns (Eds.), *Aggression and violence: Genetic, neurobiological and biosocial perspectives* (pp. 309–335). Mahwah, NJ: Erlbaum.

Hooker, E. (1957). The adjustment of the male overt homosexual. *Journal of Projective Techniques, 21*, 18–31.

Hooker, E. (1958). Male homosexuality in the Rorschach. *Journal of Projective Techniques, 22*, 33–54. Hoerek, E. (1993). Reflections of a 40-year exploration: A scientific view on homosexuality. *American Psychologist, 48*(4), 450–453.

hooks, b. (1981). *Ain't I a woman? Black women and feminism.* Boston: South End Press.

hooks, b. (1989). *Talking back: Thinking feminist, thinking black.* Boston: South End Press.

hooks, b. (1990). *Yearning: Race, gender, and cultural politics.* Boston: South End Press.

Hopkins, K. B., McGillicuddy, A. V., & DeLisi, R. (1997). Student gender and teaching methods as sources of variability in children's computational arithmetic performance. *Journal of Genetic Psychology, 158*(3), 333–345.

Horne, P., & Lewis, R. (1997). Visual culture. In A. Medhurst & S. R. Munt (Eds.), *Lesbian and gay studies* (pp. 99–112). London: Cassell.

Horner, M. (1972). Toward an understanding of achievement-related conflicts in women. *Journal of Social Issues, 28*(2), 157–175.

Horner, M. (1970). Femininity and successful achievement: A basic inconsistency. In J. Bardwick, E. Douvan, M. Horner, & D. Guttman (Eds.), *Feminine personality and conflict* (pp. 45–76). Pacific Grove, CA: Brooks/Cole.

Horney, K. (1939). *New ways in psychoanalysis.* New York: Norton.

Horney, K. (1967). *Feminine psychology.* New York: Norton.

Hort, B. E., Leinbach, M. D., & Fagot, B. I. (1991). Is there coherence among the cognitive components of gender aquisition? *Sex Roles, 24*(3–4), 195–207.

Hortacsu, N. (1997). Family and couple-initiated marriages in Turkey. *Genetic, Social, and General Psychology Monographs, 123*(3), 325–342.

Horwath, E., & Weissman, M. M. (1997). Epidemiology of anxiety disorders across cultural groups. In S. Friedman (Ed.), *Cultural issues in the treatment of anxiety* (pp. 21–39). New York: Guilford Press.

Hossain, Z., & Roopnarine, J. L. (1993). Division of household labor and childcare in dual-earner African-American families with infants. *Sex Roles, 29*(9–10), 571–583.

Houston, M. (1994). When black women talk with white women: Why dialogues are difficult. In A. Gonzalez, M. Houston, & V. Chen (Eds.), *Our voices: Essays in culture, ethnicity, and communication* (pp. 133–139). Los Angeles: Roxbury.

Howard, A. (1995). A framework for work change. In A. Howard (Ed.), *The changing nature of work* (pp. 3–41). San Francisco: Jossey-Bass.

Howard, J. A., & Hollander, J. A. (1996). *Gendered situation: Gendered selves.* Thousand Oaks, CA: Sage.

Howell, J. D. (1998). Gender role experimentation in new religious movements:

Clarification of the Brahma Kumari case. *Journal for the Scientific Study of Religion, 37*(3), 453–461.

Hoyenga, K. B., Hoyenga, K. T. (1993). *Gender-related differences: Origins and outcomes.* Boston: Allyn and Bacon.

Hoyert, D. L., Kochanek, K. D., & Murphy, S. L. (1999). Deaths: Final data for 1997. *National Vital Statistics Reports, 47*(19), 5.

Hsi, C., & Tsu-ch'ien, L. (Eds.). (1967). *Reflections on things at hand: The Neo-Confucian anthology.* Translated, with notes, by W. Chan. New York: Columbia University Press.

Huang, J. (1993). An investigation of gender differences in cognitive abilities among Chinese high school students. *Personality and Individual Differences, 15*(6), 717–719.

Hubbard, R. (1998). The political nature of human nature. In D. L. Anselmi & A. L. Law (Eds.), *Questions of gender* (pp. 146–153). New York: McGraw-Hill.

Hudak, M. A. (1993). Gender schema theory revisited: Men's stereotypes of American women. *Sex Roles, 28,* 279–293.

Hudley, C. (1998). Urban minority adolescents' perceptions of classroom climate. Unpublished manuscript, University of California at Santa Barbara.

Hughes, C. C., & Wintrob, R. M. (1996). Culture bound syndromes and the cultural context of clinical psychiatry. *American Psychiatric Press Review of Psychiatry, 14,* 565–597.

Hughes, D. L., & Galinsky, E. (1994). Gender, job and family conditions, and psychological symptoms. *Psychology of Women Quarterly, 18,* 251–270.

Huguet, P., & Monteil, J. (1995). The influence of social comparison with less fortunate others on task performance: The role of gender motivations or appropriate norms. *Sex Roles, 33,* 753–765.

Humlin, C. L., Fitzgerald, L. F., & Drasgow, F. (1996). Organizational influences on sexual harassment. In M. S. Stockdale (Ed.), *Sexual harassment in the workplace: Perspectives, frontiers, and response strategies* (pp. 127–150). Thousand Oaks, CA: Sage.

Hunt, K., & Emslie, C. (1998). Men's work, women's work? Occupational sex ratios and health. In K. Orth-Gomer, M. Chesney, & N. K. Wenger (Eds.), *Women, stress, and heart disease* (pp. 87–107). Mahwah, NJ: Erlbaum.

Hunter, A. G. (1997). Counting on grandmothers: Black mothers and fathers reliance on grandmothers for parenting support. *Journal of Family Issues, 18,* 251–269.

Hunter, J., & Mallon, G. P. (2000). Lesbian, gay and bisexual adolescent development: Dancing with your feet tied together. In B. Greene & G. L. Croom (Eds.), *Education, research and practice in lesbian, gay, bisexual, and transgendered psychology* (pp. 226–243). Thousand Oaks, CA: Sage.

Huntsinger, C. S., Jose, P. E., Liaw, F., & Ching, W. (1997). Cultural differences in early mathematics learning: A comparison of Euro-American, Chinese-American, and Taiwanese-Chinese families. *International Journal of Behavioral Development, 21*(2), 371–388.

Huon, G., Lim, J., & Gunewardene, A. (2000). Social influences and female adolescents dieting. *Journal of Adolescence, 23,* 229–232.

Huppert, J., Yaacoby, J., & Lazarowitz, R. (1998). Learning microbiology with computer simulations: students' academic achievement by method and gender. *Research in Science and Technological Education, 16*(2), 231–245.

Hurtz, W., & Durkin, K. (1997). Gender role stereotyping in Australian radio commercials. *Sex Roles, 36,* 103–114.

Hurwich, J., & Tori, C. D. (2000). Consequences of impending national change: Symptoms of psychological distress among homosexual men living in Hong Kong. *Journal of Homosexuality, 38*(3), 85–96.

Huston, A. C., & Alvarez, M. M. (1990). The socialization context of gender role development in early adolescence. In R. Montemayor, G. R. Adams, et al. (Eds.), *From childhood to adolescence: A transitional period? Advances in adolescent development: An annual book series* (vol. 2, pp. 156–179). Thousand Oaks, CA: Sage.

Hutchinson, R., & McNall, M. (1994). Early marriage in a Hmong cohort. *Journal of Marriage and the Family, 56,* 579–590.

Hyde, J. S. (1984). Children's understanding of sexist language. *Developmental Psychology, 20,* 697–706.

Hyde, J. S. (1986). Gender differences in aggression. In J. S. Hyde & M. C. Linn (Eds.), *The psychology of gender: Advances through meta-analysis* (pp. 51–56). Baltimore: Johns Hopkins University Press.

Hyde, J. S. (1993). Meta-analysis in the psychology of women. In F. L. Denmark & M. A. Paludi (Eds.), *Psychology of women: A handbook of issues and theories.* Westport, CT: Greenwood.

Hyde, J. S. (1994). Can meta-analysis make feminist transformation in psychology? *Psychology of Women Quarterly, 18,* 451–462.

Hyde, J. S. (1995). Women and maternity leave: Empirical data and public policy. *Psychology of Women Quarterly, 19*(3), 299–314.

Hyde, J. S. (1998). Measuring feminist attitudes: A possible rapproachement between feminist theory and empirical data? *Psychology of Women Quarterly, 22*(3), 361–362.

Hyde, J. S., & Jaffee, S. R. (2000). Becoming a heterosexual adult: The experiences of young women. *Journal of Social Issues, 56*(2), 283–296.

Hyde, J. S., & Linn, M. C. (Eds.). (1986). *The psychology of gender: Advances through meta-analysis.* Baltimore: Johns Hopkins University Press.

Hyde, J. S., & McKinley, N. M. (1997). Gender differences in cognition: Results from meta-analyses. In P. J. Caplan, M. Crawford, J. S. Hyde, & J. T. E. Richardson (Eds.), *Gender differences in human cognition* (pp. 30–51). New York: Oxford University Press.

Hyde, J. S., & Plant, A. E. (1995). Magnitude of psychological gender differences: Another side to the story. *American Psychologist, 50*(3), 159–161.

Hyde, J. S., Fennema, E., & Lamon, S. J. (1990). Gender differences in mathematics performance: A meta-analysis. *Psychological Bulletin, 107*(2), 139–155.

Hynie, M., & Lyndon, J. E. (1995). Women's perceptions of female contraceptive behavior. *Psychology of Women Quarterly, 19*(4), 563–581.

Ickes, W. (1993). Traditional gender roles: Do they make and then break our relationships? *Journal of Social Work, 49*(3), 71–85.

Imamglu, E. O., & Yasak, Y. (1997). Dimensions of marital relationships as perceived by Turkish husbands and wives. *Genetic, Social, and General Psychology Monographs, 123*(2), 211–232.

Immerman, R. S., & Mackey, W. C. (1998). A proposed relationship between circumcision and neural reorganization. *Journal of Genetic Psychology, 159*(3), 367–378.

Imperato-McGinley, J., Guerrero, L., Gautier, T., & Peterson, R. E. (1974). Steroid 5 alpha-reductase deficiency in men: An inherited form of male pseudohermaphroditism. *Science, 186,* 1213–1215.

Imperato-McGinley, J., Miller, M., Wilson, J. D., Peterson, R. E., Shackleton, C., & Gajdusek, D. C. (1991). A cluster of male pseudohermaphrodites with alpha-5 reductase deficiency in Papua New Guinea. *Clinical Endocrinology, 34,* 293–298.

Imperato-McGinley, J., Peterson, R., Gautier, T., & Sturla, E. (1979). Androgens and the evolution of male-gender identity among male pseudohermaphrodites with 5-alpha reductase deficiency. *New England Journal of Medicine, 300,* 1233–1237.

"Incorruptible" eunuchs capture Indian offices. (2001). *Contemporary Sexuality, 35*(2), 8.

Inhorn, M. C. (1994). Kabsa (aka mushahara) and threatened infertility in Egypt. *Social Science and Medicine, 39*(4), 487–505.

Inman, C. (1986). Closeness in the doing: Male friendship. In J. T. Wood (Ed.), *Gendered relationships: A reader* (pp. 95–110). Mountain View, CA: Mayfield.

Institute for Women's Policy Research. (1999, February,). Employment earnings and economic change. Available online at iwpr.org/RESEARCH.HTM.

Iyengar, S., Valentino, N. A., Ansolabehere, S., & Simon, A. F. (1997). Running as a woman: Gender stereotyping in political campaigns. In P. Norris (Ed.), *Women, media and politics* (pp. 77–98). New York: Oxford University Press.

Jackson, D. D., & Weakland, J. H. (1959). Schizophrenic symptoms and family interaction. *Archives of General Psychiatry, 1,* 618–621.

Jackson, L. A., & McGill, O. D. (1996). Body type preferences and body characteristics associated with bodies by African-Americans and Anglo-Americans. *Sex Roles, 35,* 295–307.

Jackson, L. A., Gardner, P., & Sullivan, L. (1992). Explaining gender differences in self-pay expectations: Social comparisons, standards, and perceptions of fair play. *Journal of Applied Psychology, 77,* 651–663.

Jackson, L. A., Millson, M., Calazavara, L., Strathdee, S., Walmsley, S., & Rachlis, A. (1998–1999). Community HIV prevention: What can we learn from the personal experiences of HIV-positive women living in metropolitan Toronto, Canada. *International Quarterly of Community Health Education, 18*(3), 307–330.

Jacobs, J. E., & Eccles, J. S. (1992). The impact of mothers gender-role stereotypic beliefs on mothers' and children's ability perceptions. *Journal of Personality and Social Psychology, 63,* 932–944.

Jacobson, J. L. (1992). Women's reproductive health: The silent emergency. *New Frontiers in Education, 22,* 1–54.

Jakobs, E., Manstead, A. S. R., & Fischer, A. H. (1999). Social motives and emotional feelings as determinants of facial displays: The case of smiling. *Personality and Social Behavior, 25*(4), 424–435.

James, J. B., Lewkowicz, C., Libhaber, J., & Lachman, M. (1995). Rethinking the gender crossover hypothesis: A test of a new model. *Sex Roles, 32,* 185–207.

James, S. E. (1998). Fulfilling the promise: Community response to the needs of sexual minority youth and families. *American Journal of Orthopsychiatry, 63*(3), 447–454.

James, T. W., & Kimura, D. (1997). Sex differences in remembering the locations of objects in an array: Location shifts versus location exchanges. *Evolution and Human Behavior, 18,* 155–163.

Jandt, F. E. (1998). *Intercultural communication* (2nd ed.). Thousand Oaks, CA: Sage.

Jankowiak, W. R., & Fischer, E. F. (1998). A cross-cultural perspective on romantic love. In J. Jenkins & K. Oatley (Ed.), *Human emotions: A reader* (pp. 55–62). Malden, MA: Blackwell.

Janoff-Bulman, R. (1992). Shattered assumptions: Toward a new psychology of trauma. New York: Free Press.

Jansen, J. J. (1997). *The dual nature of Islamic fundamentalism.* Ithaca, NY: Cornell University Press.

Jassey, I. A. (1998). Gender in elementary school texts. *Japan Quarterly, 16,* 87–93.

Jeffrey, P., & Jeffery, R. (1996). *Don't marry me to a plowman! Women's everyday lives in rural North India.* Boulder, CO: Westview Press.

Jegalian, K., & Lahn, B. T. (2001). Why the Y is so weird. *Scientific American, 284*(2), 56.

Jena, S. P. K. (1999). Job, life satisfaction and occupational stress of women. *Social Science International, 15*(1), 75–80.

Jenrette, J., McIntosh, S., & Winterberger, S. (1999). "Carlotta": Changing images of Hispanic-American women in daytime soap operas. *Journal of Popular Culture, 33*(2), 37–48.

Jensen, J. T., Harvey, S. M., & Beckman, L. J. (2000). Acceptability of suction curettage and mifepristone abortion in the United States: A prospective comparison study. *American Journal of Obstetrics and Gynecology, 182*(6), 1292–1299.

Jhalley, S. (1995). Image based culture: Advertising and popular culture. In G. Dines & J. M. Humez (Eds.), *Gender, race and class in media* (pp. 77–87). Thousand Oaks, CA: Sage.

John, D., & Shelton, B. A. (1997). The production of gender among black and white women and men: The case of household labor. *Sex Roles, 36,* 171–193.

Johnson, A. G. (1997). *The gender knot: Unraveling our patriarchal legacy.* Philadelphia: Temple University Press.

Johnson, C. *Afghanistan: A land in shadow.* London: Oxfam.

Johnson, F. L. (1996). Friendships among women: Closeness in dialogue. In J. T. Wood (Ed.), *Gendered relationships* (pp. 79–94). Mountain View, CA: Mayfield.

Johnson, H. (1998). Rethinking survey research on violence against women. In R. E. Dobash & R. P. Dobash (Eds.), *Rethinking violence against women* (pp. 23–51). Thousand Oaks, CA: Sage.

Johnson, R., Jr., Rohrbaugh, J. W., & Ross, J. L. (1993). Altered brain development in Turner's syndrome: An event-related potential study. *Neurology, 43,* 801–808.

Johnston, F. A., & Johnston, S. A. (1997). A cognitive approach to validation of the fixated-regressed typology of child molesters. *Journal of Clinical Psychology, 53*(4), 361–368.

Joiner, R. W. (1998). The effect of gender on children's software preferences. *Journal of Computer Assisted Learning, 14,* 195–198.

Joliffe, L. (1996). The disposable sex: Men in the news. In P. M. Lester (Ed.), *Images that injure: Pictorial stereotypes in the media* (pp. 97–103). Westport, CT: Praeger.

Jones, M. (1998, March 9). Can art photography be kiddie porn? *Newsweek*, p. 58.

Jones, M. Y., Staland, A. J. S., & Gelb, B. D. (1998). Beefcake and cheesecake: Insights for advertisers. *Journal of Advertising, 27*(2), 33–50.

Jonker, G. (1997). Death, gender and memory. In D. Field, J. Hockey, & N. Small (Eds.), *Death, gender, and ethnicity* (pp. 187–201). New York: Routledge.

Joseph, R. (2000). The evolution of sex differences in language, sexuality and visual-spatial skills. *Archives of Sexual Behavior, 29*(1), 35–66.

Joshi, A., & Sastry, N. (1995). Work and family: Conflict and its resolution. *Indian Journal of Gender Studies, 2*(2), 227–241.

Joshi, M. S., & MacLean, M. (1997). Maternal expectations of child development in India, Japan, and England. *Journal of Cross-Cultural Psychology, 28*(2), 219–234.

Jost, J. T. (1997). An experimental replication of the depressed entitlement effect among women. *Psychology of Women Quarterly, 21*, 387–393.

Judd, C. M., & Park, B. (1993). Definition and assessment of accuracy in social stereotypes. *Psychological Review, 100*, 109–128.

Jung, C. G. (1959a). The archetypes of the collective unconscious. In *The collected works of C. G. Jung* (Vol. 9, Pt. 1). Princeton: Princeton University Press.

Jung, C. G. (1959b). *The basic writings of C. G. Jung.* New York: Modern Library.

Jung, C. G. (1959c). Concerning the archetype with special reference to the anima concept. In *The collected works of C. G. Jung* (Vol. 9, Pt. 1). Princeton: Princeton University Press.

Jung, C. G. (1960). The stages of life. In *The collected works of C. G. Jung* (Vol. 6). Princeton: Princeton University Press.

Juntunen, C. (1996). Relationship between a feminine approach to career counseling and career self-efficacy beliefs. *Journal of Employment Counseling, 33*, 130–143.

Juraska, J. M. (1998). Neural plasticity and the development of sex differences. *Annual Review of Sex Research, 9*, 20–38.

Juraska, J. M., Nunez, J. L., Koss, W. A., & Christopher, A. M. (1998). Effect of neonatal cryoanesthesia in male and female rats on hypocampal anatomy and water maze performance. *Society for Neuroscience Abstracts, 24*, 177.

Jussim, L., & Eccles, J. S. (1992). Teacher expectations: II. Construction and reflection of student achievement. *Journal of Personality & Social Psychology, 63*(6), 947–961.

Kafai, Y. B. (1999). Video game designs by girls and boys: Variability and consistency of gender differences. In M. Kinder (Ed.), *Kids' media culture* (pp. 293–314). Durham, NC: Duke University Press.

Kagan, J. (1994). *Galen's prophecy: Temperament in human nature.* New York: Basic Books.

Kagan, J., & Snidman, N. (1996). Temperamental factors in human development. *American Psychologist, 46*, 856–862.

Kagan, J., Arcus, D., Snidman, N., Feng, W. Y., Hendler, J., & Greene, S. (1994). Reactivity in infants: A cross-national comparison. *Developmental Psychology, 30*, 342–345.

Kagan-Krieger, S. (1998). Brief report: Women with Turner syndrome: A maturational and developmental perspective. *Journal of Adult Development, 5*(2), 125–135.

Kagitcibasi, C. (1996). *Family and human development across cultures: A view from the other side.* Mahwah, NJ: Erlbaum.

Kagitcibasi, C. (1997). Individualism and collectivism. In J. W. Berry, M. H. Segall, & C. Kagitcibasi (Eds.), *Handbook of cross-cultural psychology. Vol. 3: Social behavior and applications* (pp. 1–49). Boston: Allyn and Bacon.

Kahle, J. B., Parker, L. H., Rennie, L. J., & Riley, D. (1993). Gender differences in science education: Building a model. *Educational Psychologist, 28*(4), 379–404.

Kalb, C. (1999, November 15). Viagra may still be mostly a guy thing. *Newsweek*, p. 66.

Kane, E., & Schippers, M. (1996). Men's and women's beliefs about gender and sexuality. *Gender & Society, 10*, 650–665.

Kanter, D. (1993). *Men and women of the corporation.* New York: Basic Books.

Kaplan, H. S. (1983). *The evolution of sexual disorders.* New York: Brunner/Mazel.

Kaplan, H. S. (1974). *The new sex therapy: Active treatment of sexual dysfunctions.* New York: Simon & Schuster.

Kaplan, M. (1983). A woman's view on the DSM-III. *American Psychologist, 38*, 786–792.

Kaschak, E. (1992). *Engendered lives.* New York: Basic Books.

Kashima, Y., Yamaguchi, S., Kim, U., Choi, S., Gelfand, M. J., & Yuki, M. (1995). Culture, gender and self: A perspective from individualism–collectivism research. *Journal of Personality & Social Psychology, 69*, 925–937.

Kasinsky, R. G. (1998). Tailhook and the construction of sexual harassment in the media: "Rowdy Navy boys" and the women who made a difference. *Violence Against Women, 41*(1), 81–99.

Kasser, T., & Sharma, Y. S. (1999). Reproductive freedom, educational equality and females' preference for resource-acquisition characteristics in mates. *Psychological Science, 10*(4), 374–377.

Kassindja, F., & Bashir, L. M. (1998). *Do they hear you when you cry?* New York: Random House.

Kates, S. M. (1999). Making the ad perfectly queer: Marketing "normality" to the gay men's community? *Journal of Advertising, 28*(1), 25–38.

Kates, S. M., & Shaw-Garlock, G. (1999). The ever-entangling web: A study of ideologies and discourses in advertising to women. *Journal of Advertising, 28*(2), 33–49.

Katz, P. (1995). Advertising and the construction of violent white masculinity. In G. Dines & M. Humez (Eds.), *Gender, race and class in media: A text reader.* Thousand Oaks, CA: Sage.

Katz, P., & Kasanak, K. R. (1994). Developmental aspects of gender-role flexibility and traditionality in middle childhood and adolescence. *Developmental Psychology, 30*, 272–282.

Katzman, M. A., Weiss, L., & Wolchik, S. A. (1986). Speak, don't eat! Teaching women to express their feelings. In D. Howard (Ed.), *A guide to dynamics of family therapy* (pp. 143–158). New York: Harrington Press.

Kaufman, M. (1993a). *Cracking the armor: Power, pain and the lives of men.* Toronto: Penguin/Viking.

Kaufman, M. (1993b). Men, feminism, and men's contradictory experiences of power. In H. Brod & M. Kaufman (Eds.), *Theorizing masculinities* (pp. 142–163). Thousand Oaks, CA: Sage.

Kaufman, P., Klein, S., & Frase, M. (1999). *Dropout rates in the United States.* National Center for Education Statistics (NCES) Number 1999082. Washington, DC: U.S. Department of Education.

Kaylor, L. (1999). Antisocial personality disorder: Diagnostic, ethical, and treatment issues. *Issues in Mental Health Nursing, 20*(3), 247–258.

Keenan, C. K., El-Hadad, A., & Balian, S. A. (1998). Factors associated with domestic violence in low-income Lebanese families. *Journal of Nursing Scholarship, 30*(4) 357–362.

Kelleher, M. (1998). Youth suicide in the Republic of Ireland. *British Journal of Psychiatry, 173*, 194–197.

Kelly, G. F. (1996). *Sexuality today: The human perspective* (5th ed.). Madison, WI: Brown & Benchmark.

Kelley, K., Dawson, L., & Musialowski, D. M. (1989). The three faces of sexual explicitness: The good, the bad and the useful. In D. Zillman & J. Bryant (Eds.), *Pornography: Research advances and policy considerations* (pp. 57–85). Mahwah, NJ: Erlbaum.

Kelly, L., & Radford, J. (1998). Sexual violence against women and girls. In R. E. Dobash & R. P. Dobash (Eds.), *Rethinking violence against women* (pp. 53–76). Thousand Oaks, CA: Sage.

Kelly, R. (1976). Witchcraft and sexual relations: An exploration in the social and semantic implications of the structure of belief. In P. Brown & G. Buchbinder (Eds.), *Man and woman in the New Guinea highlands* (pp. 36–53). Washington, DC: American Anthropological Association.

Kendall, C. N., Leishman, B., Rogerson, S., & Walker, S. (2000). Same-sex relationships in Western Australia. *E-law: Murdoch University Electronic Journal of Law, 7*, 4. Available online at www.murdoch.edu.au/elaw/issues.

Kendall, K. (1999). Women in Lesotho and the Western construction of homophobia. In E. Blackwood & S. E. Wieringa (Eds.), *Female desires: Same-sex relations and transgender practices across cultures* (pp. 157–180). New York: Columbia University Press.

Kennedy, D. (1993). Nonsexist language: A progress report. *Canadian Journal of Education, 18*(3), 223–238.

Kennedy, E. (2000). "You talk a good game." *Men and Masculinities, 3*(1), 57–84.

Kennedy, E. J., Carsky, M., & Zuckerman, M. E. W. (1996). The "mommy track:" Impact of family life on women in the professorate. In D. J. Dubeck & K. Borman (Eds.), *Women and work: A*

handbook (pp. 424–427). New York: Garland.

Kernie, M. A., Wolf, M. E., & Holt, V. L. (2000). Rates and relative risk of hospital admission among women in violent intimate partner relationships. *American Journal of Public Health, 90*(9), 1416–1420.

Kessler, R. C., McGonagle, K. A., Zhao, K. A., Nelson, C. B., Hughes, M., Eshleman, S., Wittchen, H. U., & Kendler, K. S. (1994). Lifetime and 12-month prevalence of DSM-IIIR psychiatric disorders in the United States. Results from the National Co-morbidity study. *Archives of General Psychiatry, 51*, 8–19.

Kessler, R. C., McGonagle, K. A., Zhao, K. O., & Nelson, C. B., et al. (1994). Lifetime and 12-month prevalence of DSM-III-R psychiatric disorders in the United States: Results from the National Comorbidity Study. *Archives of General Psychiatry, 51*, 8–19.

Kessler, S. J. (1998). *Lessons from the intersexed.* New Brunswick, NJ: Rutgers University Press.

Kibby, M., & Costello, B. (1999). Displaying the phallus: Masculinity and performance of sexuality on the Internet. *Men and Masculinities, 1*(4), 352–364.

Kibria, N. (1993). *Family tightrope: The changing lives of Vietnamese Americans.* Princeton, NJ: Princeton University Press.

Kidder, L. H., & Fine, M. (1997). Qualitative inquiry in psychology: A radical tradition. In D. Fox & I. Prilleltensby (Eds.), *Critical psychology: An introduction* (pp. 34–50). London: Sage.

Kiebert, G. M, De Haes, J. C. J. M., & van de Velde, C. J. H. (1991). The impact of breast conserving treatment and mastectomy on the quality of life of early stage breast cancer patients: A review. *Journal of Clinical Oncology, 9*, 1059–1070.

Kilbourne, J. (1979). *Killing us softly: Advertising's image of women.* [Film]. Northampton, MA: Media Education Foundation.

Kilbourne, J. (1999). *Deadly persuasion: Why women and girls must fight the addictive power of advertising.* New York: Free Press.

Kilian, C. (2001, April 17). After the fall: Torrent of demand for ladies' love potion Niagara. *The New York Post*, p. 45.

Kilmartin, C. T. (1994). *The masculine self.* New York: Macmillan.

Kim, J. S., Bramlett, M. H., Wright, L. K., & Poon, L. W. (1998). Racial differences in health status and health behaviors of older adults. *Nursing Research, 47*(4), 243–250.

Kim, K. C., & Kim, S. (1995). Family and work roles of Korean immigrants in the U.S. In H. I. McCubbin, E. A. Thompson, A. I. Thompson, & J. E. Fromer (Eds.), *Resiliency of ethnic minority families: Nature and immigrant American families* (pp. 225–242). Madison: University of Wisconsin, Board of Regents.

Kim, M., & Alvarez, R. (1995). Women-only colleges: Some unanticipated consequences. *Journal of Higher Learning, 66*(6), 641–668.

Kimball, M. M. (1995). *Feminist visions of gender similarities and differences.* New York: Haworth Press.

Kimmel, D. C. (2000). Including sexual orientation in life-span developmental psychology. In B. Greene & G. L. Croom (Eds.), *Education, research, and practice in lesbian, gay, bisexual and transgendered psychology* (pp. 59–73). Thousand Oaks, CA: Sage.

Kimmel, M. S. (1996a). *Manhood in America: A cultural history.* New York: Free Press.

Kimmel, M. S. (1996b). The struggle for men's souls. *Tikkun, 11*(2), 15–16.

Kimmel, M. S. (1997). Masculinity as homophobia: Fear, shame, and silence in the construction of gender identity. In M. M. Gergen & S. N. Davis (Eds.), *Toward a new psychology of gender* (pp. 223–242). New York: Routledge.

Kimmel, M. S. (2000a). *The gendered society.* New York: Oxford University Press.

Kimmel, M. S. (2000b, Spring/Summer). What about the boys? *Wellesley Center for Women Research Report*, pp. 1–3.

Kimmel, M. S., & Messner, M. A. (Eds.). (2001). *Men's lives* (4th ed.). Boston: Allyn and Bacon.

Kimura, D. (1999). *Sex and cognition.* Cambridge, MA: MIT Press.

Kimura, D., & Carson, M. W. (1995). Dermatoglyphic asymmetry: Relation to sex, handedness and cognitive pattern. *Personality & Individual Differences, 19*, 471–478.

Kimura, D., & Hampson, E. (1994). Cognitive pattern in men and women is influenced by fluctuations in sex hormones. *Current Directions in Psychological Science, 3*, 57–61.

Kimweli, D. M. S., & Richards, A. G. (1999). Choice of a major and students' appreciation of their major. *College Student Journal, 26*, 16–26.

Kinder, M. (1999). Kids' media culture: An introduction. In M. Kinder (Ed.), *Kids' media culture* (pp. 1–28). Durham, NC: Duke University Press.

King, V. (1994). Nonresident father involvement and child well-being: Can dads make a difference? *Journal of Family Issues, 15*(1), 78–96.

King, A. C. (1998). Section editor's overview. In E. A. Blechman & K. D. Brownell (Eds.), *Behavioral medicine and women: A comprehensive handbook* (pp. 191–197). New York: Guilford Press.

King, U. (1993). *Women and spirituality.* University Park: Pennsylvania State University.

Kinnear, A. (1995). Introduction of microcomputers: A case study of use and children's perceptions. *Journal of Education Computing Research, 13*, 27–40.

Kinnunen, U., & Mauno, S. (1998). Antecedents and outcomes of work–family conflict among employed women and men in Finland. *Human Relations, 51*(2), 157–177.

Kinsey, A., Pomeroy, W., & Martin, C. (1948). *Sexual behavior in the human male.* Philadelphia: Saunders.

Kinsey, A., Pomeroy, W., Martin, C., & Gebhard, P. (1953). *Sexual behavior in the human female.* Philadelphia: Saunders.

Kipnis, K., & Diamond, M. (1998). Pediatric ethics and the surgical assignment of sex. *Journal of Clinical Ethics, 9*(4), 398–410.

Kirmayer, L. J., Fletcher, C. M., & Boothroyd, L. J. (1997). Inuit attitudes toward deviant behaviors: A vignette study. *Journal of Nervous and Mental Disease, 185*(2), 78–86.

Kitzinger, C. (2000). Sexualities. In R. K. Unger (Ed.), *Handbook of the psychology of women and gender* (pp. 272–285). New York: Wiley.

Kitzinger, S. (1995). *Ourselves as mothers: The universal experience of motherhood.* Reading, MA: Addison-Wesley.

Klein, A. M. (1995). Life's too short to die small. In D. Sabo & F. D. Gordon (Eds.), *Men's health and illness* (pp. 105–120). London: Sage.

Klein, M. (1948). *Contributions to psychoanalysis, 1912–1945.* London: Hogarth Press.

Klein, U. (1999). "Our best boys." *Men and Masculinities, 2*(1), 47–65.

Klermon, G. K., & Weissman, M. M. (1989). Increasing rates of depression. *JAMA, 261*, 2229–2235.

Kling, K. C., Hyde, J. S., Showers, C. J., & Buswell, B. N. (1999). Gender differences in self-esteem: A meta-analysis. *Psychological Bulletin, 125*(4), 470–500.

Klinkenberg, W. D., & Calsyn, R. J. (1998). Gender differences in the receipt of aftercare and psychiatric hospitalization among adults with severe mental illness. *Comprehensive Psychiatry, 39*(3), 137–142.

Klonoff, E. A., Landrine, H., & Campbell, R. (2000). Sexist discrimination may account for well-known gender differences in psychiatric symptoms. *Psychology of Women Quarterly, 24*, 93–99.

Knickrem, K. M., & Teske, R. L. (2000). Attitudes toward domestic violence among Romanian and U. S. university students: A cross-cultural comparison. *Women and Politics, 21*(3), 27–46.

Koepke, L., Hare, J., & Moran, P. B. (1992). Relationship quality in a sample of lesbian couples with children and childfree lesbian couples. *Family Relations, 41*, 224–229.

Koff, E., & Benavage, A. (1998). Breast size perception and satisfaction, body image and psychological functioning in Caucasian and Asian-American college women. *Sex Roles, 38*(7–8), 655–673.

Kohlberg, L. (1966). A cognitive-developmental analysis of children's sex-role concepts and attitudes. In E. E. Maccoby (Ed.), *The development of sex differences* (pp. 52–173). Stanford, CA: Stanford University Press.

Kohlberg, L. (1984). *The psychology of moral development.* San Francisco: Harper & Row.

Kolbe, R. H., & Albanese, P. J. (1997). The functional integration of sole-male images into magazine advertments. *Sex Roles, 36*(11–12), 813–835.

Kopper, B. A., & Emerson, D. L. (1991). Women and anger. Sex and sex-role comparisons in the expression of anger. *Psychology of Women Quarterly, 15*, 7–14.

Kopper, B. A., & Emerson, D. L. (1996). The experience and expression of anger: Relationships with gender, gender role socialization, depression and mental health functioning. *Journal of Counseling Psychology, 43*, 158–165.

Korgaonkar, P. K., & Wolin, L. D. (1999). A multivariate analysis of web usage. *Journal of Advertising Research, 39*(2), 53–68.

Koss, M. P., Ingram, M., & Pepper, S. L. (2001). Male partner violence: Relevance to health care providers. In A. Baum, T. A. Revenson, & J. E. Singer (Eds.), *Handbook of health psychology* (pp. 541–558). Mahwah, NJ: Erlbaum.

Kowalsik, R. M., & Chapple, T. (2000). The social stigma of menstruation: Fact or fiction. *Psychology of Women Quarterly, 24*, 74–80.

Kraepelin, E. (1919). *Dementia praecox* (Trans. R. M. Barclay). Edinburgh: Livingstone.

Kramer, B. J., & Kipnis, S. (1995). Eldercare and work-role conflict: Toward an understanding of gender differences in caregiver burden. *The Gerontologist, 35*(30), 340–348.

Kramer, C. (1997). Perceptions of female and male speech. *Language & Speech, 20*, 151–161.

Kramer, J. H., Delis, D. C., Kaplan, E., O'Donnell, L., & Prifitera, A. (1997). Developmental sex differences in verbal learning. *Neuropsychology, 11*(4), 577–584.

Krengel, M., & Greifeld, K. (2000). Uzbekistan in transition: Changing concepts in family planning and reproductive health. In A. Russell, E. J. Sobo, & M. S. Thompson (Eds.), *Contraception across cultures* (pp. 199–220).

Krieger, N., & Fee, E. (1996). Man-made medicine and women's health: The biopolitics of sex/gender and race/ethnicity. In K. L. Moss (Ed.), *Man-made medicine: Women's health, public policy, and reform* (pp. 15–36). Durham, NC: Duke University Press.

Krieger, N., & Sidney, S. (1996). Racial discrimination and blood pressure: The CARDIA study of young black and white adults. *American Journal of Public Health, 86*(10), 1370–1378.

Kring, A. M., & Gordon, A. H. (1998). Sex differences in emotion: Expression, experience and physiology. *Journal of Personality & Social Psychology, 74*(3), 686–703.

Kristof, N. D. (1996, July 13). In sexist South Korea, the girls even the score. *New York Times,* Section 1, p. 4.

Kronengold, J. J. (1999). Gender and health status. In J. S. Chafetz (Ed.), *Handbook of the sociology of gender* (pp.

459–481). New York: Kluwer Academic/ Plenum.

Krugman, S. (1995). Male development and the transformation of shame. In R. F. Levant & W. S. Pollack (Eds.), *A new psychology of men* (pp. 91–126). New York: Basic Books.

Krull, D. S., & Dill, J. C. (1998). Do smiles elicit more inferences than do frowns? The effects of emotional valence on the production of spontaneous inferences. *Personality & Social Psychology Bulletin, 24,* 289–300.

Kuhn, J. A., Arellano, C., & Chavez, E. L. (1999). Correlates of sexual assault in Mexican-American and White non-Hispanic adolescent males. *Violence and Victims, 13*(1), 11–20.

Kulczycki, A. (1999). *The abortion debate in the world arena.* New York: Routledge.

Kulik, L. (1998). Occupational sex typing and occupational prestige: A comparative study of adolescents and adults in Israel. *Youth and Society, 30*(2), 164–181.

Kulik, L. (2000). The impact of gender and age on attitudes and reactions to unemployment: The Israeli case. *Sex Roles, 43*(1–1), 85–104.

Kunkel, D., Cope, K. M., Farinola, W. J. M., Biely, E., Rollin, E., & Donnerstein, E. (1999). *Sex on TV: Content context.* Menlo Park, CA: Kaiser Family Foundation.

Kupers, T. A. (1995). The politics of psychiatry. Gender and sexual preference in DSM-IV. *Masculinities, 3,* 597–605.

Kupersmidt, J. B., DeRosier, M. E., & Patterson, C. P. (1995). Similarities as the basis for children's friendships: The role of sociometric status and withdrawn behavior, academic achievement and demographic characteristics. *Journal of Social & Personal Relationships, 12,* 439–452.

Kurdek, L. A. (1993). The allocation of household labor in gay, lesbian, and heterosexual married couples. *Journal of Social Issues, 49*(3), 127–139.

Kurdek, L. A. (1994). The nature and correlates of relationship quality in gay, lesbian, and heterosexual cohabiting couples: A test of individual difference, interdependence and discrepancy models. In B. Greene & G. M. Herek (Eds.), *Lesbian and gay psychology* (pp. 133–155). Thousand Oaks, CA: Sage.

Kurth, S. B., Spiller, B. B., & Travis, C. B. (2000). Consent, power and sexual scripts: Deconstructing sexual harassment. In C. B. Travis & J. W. White (Eds.), *Sexuality society and feminism* (pp. 323–354). Washington, DC: American Psychological Association.

Kurz, D. (1998). Old problems and new directions in the study of violence against women. In R. K. Bergen (Ed.), *Issues in intimate violence* (pp. 197–208). Thousand Oaks, CA: Sage.

Kushan, N. (1996). Behind the walls: The history and current reality of women's imprisonment. In E. Rosenblatt (Ed.), *Criminal injustice: The history and current reality of women's imprisonment* (pp. 136–163). Boston: South End Press.

Kutchinsky, B. (1973). Eroticism without censorship. *International Journal of Criminology and Penology, 1,* 217–225.

Kveder, D. O. (1998). Abortion in Ljubljana, Slovenia: A method of contraception or an emergency procedure? In A. I. Mundigo & C. Intriso (Eds.), *Abortion in the developing world* (pp. 447–464). London: Zed Books.

La Fromboise, T. D., Heyle, A. M., & Ozer, E. J. (1999). Changing and diverse roles of women in American Indian cultures. In L. A. Peplau, S. C. De Bro, & R. C. Veniegas, & P. L. Taylor (Eds.), *Gender, culture, and ethnicity* (pp. 48–61). Mountain View, CA: Mayfield.

La Mar, L., & Kite, M. (1998). Sex differences in attitudes toward gay men and lesbians: A multidimensional perspective. *Journal of Sex Research, 35*(2), 189–196.

Lacayo, R. (2001, December 3). About face: Lifting the veil. *Time, 158,* pp. 36–41, 46–47.

LaCharity, L. A. (1999). The experiences of younger women with coronary artery disease. *Journal of Women's Health and Gender-Based Medicine, 8*(6), 773–785.

Ladd-Taylor, M. & Umansky, L. (1998). *"Bad" mothers: The politics of blame in twentieth century America.* New York: New York University Press.

Laird, J. (1993). Lesbian and gay families. In F. Walsh (Ed.), *Normal family processes* (2nd ed., pp. 282–328). New York: Guilford.

Lakoff, R. (1973). Language and women's place. *Language in Society, 2,* 45–79.

Lakoff, R. (1975). *Language and women's place.* New York: Harper & Row.

Lakoff, R. (1978). Women's language. In D. Butturff & E. L. Epstein (Eds.), *Women's language and style* (pp. 139–158). Akron, OH: University of Akron.

Lalloo, F., Cochrane, S., Bulman, B., Varley, J., Elles, R., Howell, A., & Evans, D. G. R. (1998). An evaluation of common breast cancer gene mutations in a population of Ashkenazie Jews. *Journal of Medical Genetics, 35,* 10–12.

Lamb, M. E. (1997a). Fathers and child development: An introductory overview and guide. In M. E. Lamb (Ed.), *The role of the father in child development* (pp. 1–18). New York: Wiley.

Lamb, M. E. (Ed.). (1997b). *The role of the father in child development* (3rd ed.). New York: Wiley.

Lamb, M. E. (Ed.). (1999). *Parenting and child development in "nontraditional" families.* Mahwah, NJ: Erlbaum.

Lamb, S. (1996). The trouble with blame: Victims, perpetrators and responsibility. Cambridge, MA: Harvard University Press.

Lambda Legal Defense and Education Fund. (2001). *Overview of state adoptive laws.* Available online at www.lambdalegal.org.

Landrine, H. (Ed.). (1995). *Bringing cultural diversity to feminist psychology.* Washington, DC: American Psychological Association.

Landrine, H., & Klonoff, E. A. (2001). Cultural diversity and health psychology. In A. Baum, T. A. Revenson, & J. E. Singer (Eds.), *Handbook of Health Psychology* (pp. 851–892). Mahwah, NJ: Erlbaum.

Landrine, H., & Klonoff, E. A. (Eds.). (1997). *Discrimination against women: Prevalence, consequences, remedies.* Thousand Oaks, CA: Sage.

Landrine, H., Klonoff, E. A., & Brown-Collins, A. (1992). Cultural diversity and methodology in feminist psychology: Critique, proposal, and empirical example. *Psychology of Women Quarterly, 16,* 145–163.

Landrine, H., Klonoff, E. A., Gibbs, J., Manning, V., & Lund, M. (1995). Physical and psychiatric correlates of gender discrimination: An application of the schedule of sexist events. *Psychology Women Quarterly, 19,* 473–492.

Lane, S. D., & Cibula, D. A. (2000). Gender and health. In G. L. Albrecht, R. Fitzpatrick, & S. C. Scrimshaw (Eds.), *The handbook of social studies in health and medicine* (chap. 1.9). London: Sage.

Langmyhr, G. (1976). Varieties of coital positions: Advantages and disadvantages.

Medical Aspects of Human Sexuality, June, 128–139.

LaRossa, R. (1997). Fatherhood and social change. *Family Relations, 37,* 451–457.

LaSalandra, M. (2000, October 24). Docs, feminist differs on cause of FSD. *Boston Herald,* p. 2.

Lash, S. J., Copenhaver, M. M., & Eisler, R. M. (1998). Masculine gender role stress and substance abuse among substance dependent males. *Journal of Gender, Culture, and Health, 3*(3), 183–190.

Latterier, C. (1998). *Breasts: The women's perspective on an American obsession.* Binghampton, NY: Haworth Press.

Laughlin, C. D. (1991). Pre- and perinatal brain development and enculturation. *Human Nature, 2*(3), 171–213.

Laumann, E., Gagnon, J., Michael, R., & Michaels, S. (1994). *The social organization of sexuality: Sex practices in the United States.* Chicago: University of Chicago Press.

Laumann, E., Paik, A., & Rosen, R. (1999). Sexual dysfunction in the United States, prevalence and predictors. *JAMA, 281,* 537–544.

Lauriello, J. Hoff, A., Wieneke, M. H., Blankfeld, H., Faustman, W. O., Rosenbloom, M., DeMent, S., Sullivan, E., Lim, K. O., & Pfefferbaum, A. (1997). Similar extent of brain dysmorphology in severely ill women and men with schizophrenia. *American Journal of Psychiatry, 154*(6), 819–825.

Laursen, B., & Bukowski, W. M. (1997). A developmental guide to the organization of close relationships. *International Journal of Behavioral Development, 21*(4), 747–770.

Lavale, M., & Pelletier, R. (1992). Ecological value of Bem's gender schema theory explored through females' traditional and nontraditional occupational contexts. *Psychological Reports, 70,* 79–82.

Lawrence, S. C., & Bendixen, K. (1992). His and hers: Male and female anatomy in anatomy texts for U.S. medical students. *Social Science and Medicine, 35*(7), 925–934.

Lazur, R. F., & Majors, R. (1995). Men of color: Ethnocultural variations of male gender role strain. In R. F. Levant & W. Pollack (Eds.), *A new psychology of men* (pp. 337–358). New York: Basic Books.

Leaper, C., & Gleason, J. B. (1996). The relationship of play activity and gender to parent and child sex-typed communica-

tion. *International Journal of Behavioral Development, 19*(4), 689–703.

Leaper, C., Carson, M., Baker, C., Holliday, H., & Meyers, S. (1995). Self-disclosure and listener verbal support in same-gender and cross-gender friends conversations. *Sex Roles, 33*(5–6), 387–404.

Lee, C. (1999). Health, stress and coping among women caregivers: A review. *Journal of Health Psychology, 4*(1), 27–40.

Lee, C. (1997). Social context, depression and the transition to motherhood. *British Journal of Health Psychology, 2,* 93–108.

Lee, J. (1991). *Gay midlife and maturity.* Binghamton, NY: Haworth Press.

Lee, L. C. (1998). An overview. In L. C. Lee & N. W. S. Zane (Eds.), *Handbook of Asian-American psychology* (pp. 1–19). Thousand Oaks, CA: Sage.

Lee, S. (1996). Reconsidering the status of anorexia nervosa as a Western culture bound syndrome. *Social Science and Medicine, 42*(1), 21–34.

Lee, S. (1997). A Chinese perspective of somatoform disorders. *Journal of Psychosomatic Research, 43,* 115–119.

Lee, S., & Hsu, L. K. (1995). Eating disorders in Hong Kong. In T. Lin, W. Tseng, & E. Yeh (Eds.), *Chinese societies and mental health* (pp. 197–208). Hong Kong: Oxford University Press.

Lee, T. R., Mancini, J. A., & Maxwell, J. W. (1990). Sibling relationships in adulthood: Contact persons and motivation. *Journal of Marriage & the Family, 52,* 431–440.

Lee, V. E., & Bryk, A. S. (1989). Effects of single sex schools: Response to Marsh. *Journal of Educational Psychology, 81,* 647–650.

Lee, Y., & Sung, K. (1998). Cultural influences on caregiving burden: Cases of Koreans and Americans. *International Journal of Aging & Human Development, 46*(2), 125–141.

Leeser, J., & O'Donohue, W. (1997). Normative issues in defining sexual harassment. In W. O'Donohue (Ed.), *Sexual harassment: Theory, research and treatment* (pp. 29–49). Boston: Allyn and Bacon.

Le Espiritu, Y. (1996). *Asian-American women and men.* Thousand Oaks, CA: Sage.

Le Espiritu, Y. (1998). All men are not created equal: Asian men in US history. In M. S. Kimmel & M. A. Messner (Eds.), *Men's lives* (pp. 35–44). Boston: Allyn and Bacon.

Lefley, H. P. (1999). Mental health systems in cross-cultural context. In A. V. Horvath & T. L. Scheid (Eds.), *A handbook for the study of mental health* (pp. 566–589). London: Cambridge University Press.

Lefley, H. P. (1999). Mental health systems in cross-cultural context. In A. W. Horwitz & T. L. Scheid (Eds.), *A handbook for the study of mental health* (pp. 566–584). London: Cambridge University Press.

Le Grange, D., Telch, C. F., & Tibbs, J. (1998). Eating attitudes and behaviors in 1,435 South African Caucasian and non-Caucasian college students. *American Journal of Psychiatry, 155*(2), 250–254.

Leibenluft, E. (Ed.). (1999). *Gender differences in mood and anxiety disorders: From bench to bedside.* Washington, DC: American Psychiatric Press.

Leinbach, M. D., & Fagot, B. I. (1993). Categorical habituation to male and female faces: Gender schematic processing in infancy. *Infant Behavior & Development, 16,* 317–332.

Leitenberg, H., & Henning, K. (1995). Sexual fantasy. *Psychological Bulletin, 117*(3), 469–496.

Leland, J., & Chambers, V. (1999, July 12). Generation Ñ. *Newsweek,* pp. 52–58.

Lemish, D. (2000). The whore and the other: Israeli images of female immigrants from the former USSR. *Gender and Society, 14*(2), 333–349.

Lenhart, S. (1996). Physical and mental health aspects of sexual harassment. In D. K. Shrier (Ed.), *Sexual harassment in the workplace and academia* (pp. 21–38). Washington, DC: American Psychological Association.

Lennon, M. C. (1994). Women, work and well being: The importance of work conditions. *Journal of Health and Social Behavior, 35,* 235–247.

Lennon, M. C. (1994). Women, work, and well-being: The importance of work conditions. *Journal of Health and Social Behavior, 35,* 235–247.

Lenny, E. (1991). Sex roles: The measurement of masculinity, femininity, and androgyny. In J. P. Robinson, P. R. Shauer, & L. S. Wrightsman (Eds.), *Measures of personality and social psychological attitudes* (pp. 573–660). New York: Academic Press.

Lent, B., & Bishop, J. E. H. (1998). Sense and sensitivity: Developing a gender issues perspective in medical education. *Journal of Women's Health, 7*(3), 339–342.

Leong, F. T. L., & Zachar, P. (1999). Gender and opinions about mental illness as predictions of attitudes toward seeking professional psychological help. *British Journal of Guidance and Counseling, 27*(1), 123–132.

LePore, P. C., & Warren, J. R. (1997). A comparison of single-sex and coed vocational Catholic schooling: Evidence from the national educational longitudinal study of 1988. *American Educational Research Journal, 34*(3), 485–511.

Lepowsky, M. (1998). The influence of culture on behavior and the case of aggression: Women, men and aggression in an egalitarian society. In D. L. Anselmi & A. L. Law (Eds.), *Questions of gender: Perspectives and paradoxes.* New York: McGraw-Hill.

Lesage, A., Boyer, R., Grunberg, F., Vanier, C., et al. (1994). Suicide and mental disorders: A case-control study of young men. *American Journal of Psychiatry, 151*(7), 1063–1068.

Lester, R., & Petrie, T. A. (1998). Physical, psychological and societal correlates of bulimic symptomatology among African-American college women. *Journal of Counseling Psychology, 45*(3), 315–321.

Leung, S. A. (1998). Vocational identity and career choice congruence of gifted and talented high school students. *Counseling Psychology Quarterly, 11*(3), 325–335.

Levant, R. F. (1995). Toward the reconstruction of masculinity. In R. F. Levant & W. S. Pollack (Eds.), *A new psychology of men* (pp. 229–251). New York: Basic Books.

Levant, R. F. (1996). The new psychology of men. *Professional Psychology, 27,* 259–265.

Levant, R. F. (1997). Non-relational sexuality in men. In R. F. Levant & G. R. Brooks (Eds.), *Men and sex: New psychological perspectives* (pp. 9–27). New York: Wiley.

Levant, R. F., & Brooks, G. R. (Eds.) (1997). *Men and sex: New psychological perspectives.* New York: Wiley.

LeVay, S. (1991). A difference in hypothalamic structure between heterosexual and homosexual men. *Science, 253,* 1034–1037.

Levin, B. L., Blanch, A. K., & Jennings, A. (Eds.). (1998). *Women's mental health services: A public health pespective.* Thousand Oaks, CA: Sage.

Levin, R. J. (1993). The mechanism of human female arousal. *Annual Review of Sex Research, 3,* 1–48.

Levine, H. (2000, December 3). Search for the perfect "O," women get thrill in a pill: Newest sexual revolution takes place in the lab. *New York Post,* p. O25.

Levinger, G. (1994). Feeling good and feeling close. *Personal Relationships, 1*(2), 165–184.

Levinson, B. A. (1996). Social differences and schooled identity at a Mexican *secundaria.* In B. A. Levinson, D. E. Foley, & D. C Holland (Eds.), *The cultural production of the educated person* (pp. 211–238). Albany: State University of New York (SUNY) Press.

Levinson, B. A., Foley, D. E., & Holland, D. C. (Eds.). (1996). *The cultural production of the educated person.* Albany: State University of New York (SUNY) Press.

Levinson, D. J. (1978). *The seasons of a man's life.* New York: Ballantine.

Levy, A., & Paludi, M. A. (1997). *Workplace sexual harassment.* Englewood Cliffs, NJ: Prentice Hall.

Levy, G. D. (1994). High and low gender schematic children's release from proactive interference. *Sex Roles, 30,* 93–108.

Levy, G. D., & Fivush, R. (1993). Scripts and gender: A new approach for examining gender-role development. *Developmental Review, 13,* 126–146.

Levy, J., & Heller, W. (1998). Gender differences in human neuropsychological function. In B. M. Clinchy & J. K. Norem (Eds.), *The gender and psychology reader* (pp. 188–219). New York: New York University Press.

Lewinsohn, P. M., Gotlib, I. H., Lewinsohn, M., Seeley, J. R., & Allen, N. B. (1998). Gender differences in anxiety disorders and anxiety symptoms in adolescents. *Journal of Abnormal Psychology, 107*(1), 109–117.

Lewis, C., Maka, Z., & Papacosta, A. (1997). Why do fathers become disengaged from their children's lives? Maternal and paternal accounts of divorce in Greece. *Journal of Divorce and Remarriage, 28*(1–2), 89–117.

Lewis, S. (1997). An international perspective on work–family issues. In S. Parsuraman & J. H. Greenhaus (Eds.), *Integrating work and family* (pp. 91–103). Westport, CT: Quorum Books.

Li, Q. (1999). Teachers' beliefs and gender differences in mathematics: A review. *Educational Research, 41*(4), 63–76.

Li, S. (1991). The growth of household industry in rural Wenzhou. In P. Nolan & D. Fureng (Eds.), *Market forces in China: Competition and small business—the Wenzhou debate* (pp. 108–125). Atlantic Highlands, NJ: Zed Press.

Lieberman, J. A., Alvir, J. M., Koreen, A., Geisler, S. Chakos, M., Scheitman, B., & Woerner, M. (1996). Psychobiologic correlates of treatment response in schizophrenia. *Neuropsychopharmacology 14,* 13S–21S.

Lieberman, L., Meana, M., & Stewart, D. (1998). Cardiac rehabilitation: Gender differences in factors influencing participation. *Journal of Women's Health, 7*(6), 717–723.

Lieberman, M. A., & Fisher, L. (1999). The impact of a parent's dementia on adult offspring and their spouses: The contribution of family characteristics. *Journal of Mental Health and Aging, 5*(3), 207–222.

Liebert, R. M., & Spiegler, M. D. (1994). *Personality: Strategies and issues.* Pacific Grove, CA: Brooks/Cole.

Lightbody, P., & Durndell, A. (1998). Using stereotypes to dispel negative perceptions of careers in science and technology. In J. Radford (Ed.), *Gender and choice in education and occupation* (pp. 37–58). London: Routledge.

Lightdale, J. R., & Prentice, D. A. (1994). Rethinking sex differences in aggression: Aggressive behavior in the absence of social roles. *Personality & Social Psychology Bulletin, 20,* 34–44.

Lindamer, L. A., & Jeste, D. V. (1999). Gender and response to antipsychotic medication. In J. M. Herrera, W. B. Lawson, & J. J. Sramek (Eds.), *Cross-cultural psychiatry* (pp. 343–353). New York: Wiley.

Lindamer, L. A., Lohr, J. B., Harris, M. J., & Jeste, D. V. (1997). Gender, estrogen and schizophrenia. *Psychopharmacology Bulletin, 33*(2), 221–228.

Lindeman, M., Harakka, T., & Kangas-Jarvinen, L. (1997). Age and gender differences in adolescents' reactions to conflict situations: Aggression, prosociality and withdrawal. *Journal of Youth & Adolescence, 26*(3), 339–351.

Linden, M. S., Lecrubier, Y., Bellantuono, C., Benkert, O., Kisely, S., & Simon, G. (1999). The prescribing of psychotropic drugs by primary care physicians: An international collaborative study. *Journal of Clinical Psychopharmacology, 19*(2), 132–140.

Linden, M. S., Bender, B. G., & Robinson, A. (1995). Sex chromosomal tetrasomy and pentasomy. *Pediatrics, 96*(4), 672–682.

Lindsey, L. L. (1996). Full time homemaker as unpaid laborer. In P. J. Dubeck & K. Borman (Eds.), *Women and work* (pp. 98–102). New York: Garland.

Lips, H. M., & Asquith, K. (1995). Students' possible selves as scientists. *GATES: An International Journal Promoting Great Access to Technology, Engineering and Science, 21*(1), 1–7.

Lisak, D. (1997). Male gender socialization and the perpetration of sexual abuse. In R. F. Levant & G. R. Brooks (Eds.), *Men and sex: New psychological perspectives* (pp. 156–180). New York: Wiley.

Littlewood, R. (1995). Psychopathology and personal agency: Modernity, culture change and eating disorders in South Asia society. *British Journal of Modern Psychology, 68*, 45–63.

Lobel, T. E., & Bar, E. (1997). Perceptions of masculinity and femininity of kibbutz and urban adolescents. *Sex Roles, 37*(3–4), 283–289.

Lobel, T. E., Bar-David, E., Gruber, R., Lau, S., & Bar-Tal, Y. (2000). Gender schema and social judgements: A developmental study of children from Hong Kong. *Sex Roles, 43*(1–2), 19–42.

Loeber, R., & Hay, D. (1997). Key issues in the development of aggression and violence from childhood to early adulthood. *Annual Review of Psychology, 48*, 371–410.

Lohr, B., Adams, H. E., & Davis, J. M. (1997). Sexual arousal to erotic and aggressive stimuli in sexually coercive and non-coercive men. *Journal of Abnormal Psychology, 106*(2), 230–242.

Longmire, L., & Merrill, L. (Eds.). (2001). *Untying the tongue: Gender, power and the word.* Westport, CT: Praeger.

Lonner, W. J., & Malpass, R. (1994). *Psychology and culture.* Boston: Allyn and Bacon.

Lopata, H. Z. (1996). *Current widowhood: Myths and realities.* Thousand Oaks, CA: Sage.

Lorber, J. (1994). *Paradoxes of gender.* New Haven, CT: Yale University Press.

Lorber, J. (1997). Believing is seeing: Biology as ideology. In M. Baca-Zinn, P. Hondagnew-Sotelo, & M. A. Messner (Eds.), *Through the prism of difference* (pp. 13–22). Boston: Allyn and Bacon.

Lott, J. T. 1998. *Asian Americans: From racial categories to multiple identities.* Walnut Creek, CA: Altamira Press.

Lowenthal, M. F., & Haven, C. (1998). Interaction and adaptation: Intimacy as a critical variable. In M. P. Lawton & T. A. Saltho (Eds.), *Essential Papers on the psychology of aging* (pp. 445–462). New York: New York University Press.

Lummis, M., & Stevenson, H. W. (1990). Gender differences in beliefs and achievement: A cross-cultural study. *Developmental Psychology, 26*, 254–263.

Lupton, D., & Barclay, L. (1997). *Constructing fatherhood.* Thousand Oaks, CA: Sage.

Luthar, S. S., Cushing, G., & Rounsaville, B. J. (1996). Gender differences among opiate abusers: Pathways to disorder and profiles of psychopathology. *Drug and Alcohol Dependence, 43*(3), 179–189.

Lynch, J., & Kilmartin, C. T. (1999). *The pain behind the mask: Overcoming masculine depression.* Binghamton, NY: Haworth Press.

Lyness, K. S., & Thompson, D. E. (1997). Above the glass ceiling? A comparison of matched samples of female and male executives. *Journal of Applied Psychology, 82*(3), 359–375.

Lytle, L. J., Bakken, L., & Romig, C. (1997). Adolescent female identity development. *Sex Roles, 37*(3–4), 175–192.

Mac an Ghaill, M., & Haywood, C. (1998). Gendered relations beyond the curriculum: Peer group, family and work. In A. Clark & E. Millard (Eds.), *Gender in the secondary curriculum* (pp. 213–225). New York: Routledge.

Maccoby, E. (1998). *The two sexes: Growing up apart: Coming together.* Cambridge, MA: Belknap Press.

Maccoby, E., & Jacklin, C. (1974). *The psychology of sex differences.* Palo Alto, CA: Stanford University Press.

Macintyre, S., Ford, G., & Hunt, K. (1999). Do women "over-report" morbidity? Men's and women's responses to structured prompting on a standard question

on long-standing illness. *Social Science and Medicine, 48*(1), 89–98.

Macintyre, S., & Hunt, K. (1997). Socioeconomic position, gender, and health. *Journal of Health Psychology, 2*, 315–334.

MacIntyre, T. (1997). Gender differences in cognition: A minefield of research issues. *Irish Journal of Psychology, 18*(4), 386–396.

Mackey, R. A., Diemer, M. A., & O'Brien, B. A. (2000). Psychological intimacy in the lasting relationships of heterosexual and same-gender couples. *Sex Roles, 43*(3–4), 201–227.

Madden, M. E., & Russo, N. F. (1997). *Women in the curriculum: Psychology.* Towson, MD: National Center for Curriculum Transformation Resources on Women.

Mageo, J. M. (1992). Male transvestism and cultural change in Samoa. *American Ethnologist, 2*(3), 443–459.

Maher, F. A., & Tetrault, M. K. (1994). *The feminist classroom.* New York: Basic Books.

Mahler, M. S., Pine, F., & Bergman, A. (1975). *The psychological birth of the human infant.* New York: Basic Books.

Maines, R. P. (1999). *The technology of orgasm: "Hysteria," the vibrator and women's sexual satisfaction.* Baltimore, MD: Johns Hopkins University Press.

Major, B. (1993). Gender, entitlement and the distribution of family labor. *Journal of Social Issues, 49*(3), 141–159.

Major, B., & Cozzarelli, C. (1992). Psychological predictors of adjustment to abortion. *Journal of Social Issues, 48*(3), 121–142.

Major, B., Schmidlin, A. M., & Williams, L. (1990). Gender patterns in social touch: The impact of setting and age. *Journal of Personality & Social Psychology, 58*, 634–643.

Majors, R., & Billson, J. M. (1992). *Cool pose: The dilemma of black manhood in America.* New York: Lexington.

Maley, W. (1998). Interpreting the Taliban. In W. Maley (Ed.), *Fundamentalism reborn?* (pp. 1–28). New York: New York University Press.

Malloy, B. L., & Herzberger, S. D. (1998). Body image and self-esteem: A comparison of African-American and Caucasian women. *Sex Roles, 38*(7–8), 631–638.

Malo, J., & Tremblay, R. E. (1997). The impact of parental alcoholism and maternal social position on boys' school adjustment, pubertal maturation, and sexual behavior: A test of two competing hypotheses. *Journal of Child Psychology & Psychiatry & Allied Disciplines, 38*(2), 187–197.

Malson, H. (1997). *The thin woman: Feminism, post-structuralism, and the social psychology of anorexia nervosa.* New York: Routledge.

Maluwa, T. (1999). Implementing the principle of gender equality through the law: Some lessons from southern Africa. *International Journal of Discrimination, 3*(4), 249–268.

Manalansan, M. (1997). At the frontiers of narrative: The mapping of Filipino gay men's lives in the United States. In M. P. P. Root (Ed.), *Filipino Americans: Transformation and identity* (pp. 247–256). Thousand Oaks, CA: Sage.

Mann, T. (1996). Why do we need a health psychology of gender or sexual orientation? In P. M. Kato & T. Mann (Eds.), *Handbook of diversity issues in health psychology* (pp. 187–197). New York: Plenum Press.

Mann, V. A., Sasanuma, S., Sakuma, N., & Masaki, S. (1990). Sex differences in cognitive abilities: A cross-cultural perspective. *Neuropsychologia, 28*(10), 1063–1077.

Marcus, I. (1994). Reframing "Domestic violence": Terrors in the home. In M. A. Fineman & R. Mykitiuk (Eds.), *The public nature of public violence* (pp. 11–35). New York: Routledge.

Marecek, J. (1995). Gender politics and psychology's ways of knowing. *American Psychologist, 50,* 162–163.

Marini, M., Fan, P. L., Finley, E., & Beutel, A. (1996). Gender and job values. *Sociology of Education, 69*(1), 49–65.

Marino, R., Browne, J., & Minichiello, V. (2000). An instrument to measure safer sex strategies used by male sex workers. *Archives of Sexual Behavior, 29*(3), 217–228.

Marion, M. (1996). Living in an era of multiple loss and trauma: Understanding global loss in the gay community. In C. J. Alexander (Ed.), *Gay and lesbian mental health* (pp. 61–93). New York: Harrington Park Press.

Marks, N. F. (1996). Caregiving across the lifespan: National prevalence and predictors. *Family Relations, 45,* 27–36.

Marsh, H. W. (1989). Effects of attending single-sex and coeducational high schools on achievement, attitudes, behaviors and sex differences. *Journal of Educational Psychology, 81,* 70–85.

Marshall, W. (1988). Use of sexually explicit stimuli by rapists, child molesters and non-offenders. *Journal of Sex Research, 25*(2). 267–288.

Martell, R. F. (1996). What mediates gender bias in work behavior ratings? *Sex Roles, 35,* 153–169.

Martell, R. F., Parker, C., Emich, C. G., & Crawford, M. S. (1998). Sex stereotyping in the executive suite: "Much ado about something." *Journal of Social Behavior & Personality, 13,* 127–138.

Martianen, P., & Valkonen, T. (1996). Mortality after the death of a spouse: Rates and causes of death in a large Finnish cohort. *American Journal of Public Health, 86,* 1087–1093.

Martin, C. L. (1990). Attitudes and expectations about children with nontraditional and traditional gender roles. *Sex Roles, 22*(3–4), 151–165.

Martin, C. L. (1995). Stereotypes about children with traditional and nontraditional gender roles. *Sex Roles, 33,* 727–751.

Martin, C. L., & Ruble, D. N. (1997). A developmental perspective of self-construals and sex differences: Comment on Cross and Madson. *Psychological Bulletin, 122*(1), 45–50.

Martin, E. (1987). *The woman in the body.* Boston: Beacon Press.

Martin, J. R. (1998). Methodological essentialism, false difference, and other dangerous traps. In B. M. Clinchy & J. K. Norem (Eds.), *The gender and psychology reader* (pp. 10–33). New York: New York University Press.

Martin, K. A. (1996). *Puberty, sexuality and the self.* New York: Routledge.

Martin, M. (Ed.). (1997). *Hard-hatted women: Life on the job.* Seattle: Seal Press.

Martin, T. C. (1995). Women's education and fertility: Results from 26 demographic and health surveys. *Studies in Family Planning, 26,* 187–202.

Martz, D. M., Handley, K. B., & Eisler, R. M. (1995). The relationship between feminine gender role stress, body image, and eating disorders. *Psychology of Women Quarterly, 19*(4), 493–508.

Marusic, I., & Bratko, D. (1998). Relations of masculinity and femininity with personality dimensions of the 5-factor model. *Sex Roles, 37*(1–2), 29–44.

Mascia-Lees, F. E., & Black, N. J. (2000). *Gender and anthropology.* Prospect Heights, IL: Waveland Press.

Mascia-Lees, F. E., Sharpe, P., & Cohen, C. B. (1996). The post-modernist turn in anthropology: Cautions from a feminist perspective. In B. Laslett, S., G. Kohlstedt, H. Longino, & E. Hammonds (Eds.), *Gender and scientific authority* (pp. 48–74). Chicago: University of Chicago Press.

Masters, M. S., & Sanders, B. (1993). Is the gender differences in mental rotation disappearing? *Behavior Genetics, 23,* 337–341.

Masters, W., & Johnson, V. (1966). *Human sexual response.* Boston: Little, Brown.

Mathewes-Green, F. (1999). *At the corner of east and now: A modern life in ancient Christian orthodoxy.* Los Angeles: Tarcher.

Matsumato, D. (1994). *People: Psychology from a cultural perspective.* Pacific Grove, CA: Brooks/Cole.

Matsumato, D. (1996). *Culture and psychology.* Pacific Grove, CA: Brooks/Cole.

Matsumato, D., Pun, K. K., Nakatani, M., Kadowaki, D., Weissman, M., McCarter, L., Fletcher, D., & Takeuchi, S. (1995). Cultural differences in attitudes, values, and beliefs about osteoporosis first and second generation Japanese-American women. *Women & Health, 23,* 39–56.

Matsumato, D., Weissman, M. D., Preston, K., Brown, B., & Kupperbusch, C. (1997). Context-specific measurement of individualism–collectivism on the individual level. *Journal of Cross-Cultural Psychology, 28*(6), 743–767.

Matteson, P. S. (1995). *Advocating for the self: Women's decisions concerning contraception.* Binghamton, NY: Haworth Press.

Maume, D. J., Jr. (1999). Glass ceilings and glass escalators. *Work & Occupations, 26*(4), 483–509.

Mayberry, K. J. (Ed.). (1996). *Teaching what you're not: Identity politics in higher education.* New York: New York University.

Maynard, C. (1997). *Jobs people do.* New York: DK Publishing.

Maynard, C., Every, N. R., & Martin, J. S. (1997). Association of gender and survival inpatients with acute myocardial infarction. *Archives of Internal Medicine, 157,* 1379–1384.

Mays, V. M., So, B. T., Cochran, S. D., Detels, R., Benjamin, R., Allen, E., &

Kwon, S. (2001). HIV disease in ethnic minorities: Implications of racial/ethnic differences in disease susceptibility and drug dosage response for HIV infection and treatment. In A. Baum, T. A. Revenson, & J. E. Singer (Eds.), *Handbook of health psychology* (pp. 801–816). Mahwah, NJ: Erlbaum.

Mazur, A., Booth, A., & Dabbs, J. M. (1992). Testosterone and chess competition. *Social Psychology Quarterly, 55, 1,* 70–77.

McAdams, D. P. (1993). *The stories we live by: Personal myths and the making of the self.* New York: Guilford.

McAdoo, H. P. (Ed.). (1997a). *Black families.* Thousand Oaks, CA: Sage.

McAdoo, H. P. (1997b). Upward mobility across generations on African-American families. In H. P. McAdoo (Ed.), *Black families* (3rd ed., pp. 139–162). Thousand Oaks, CA: Sage.

McAdoo, J. (1997). The roles of African-American fathers in the socialization of their children. In H. P. McAdoo (Ed.), *Black families* (3rd ed., pp. 183–197). Thousand Oaks, CA: Sage.

McAninch, C. B., Milch, R., Crumbo, G. B., & Funtowicz, M. N. (1996). Children's perceptions of gender-role congruent and incongruent behavior in peers: Fisher Price meets Price-Waterhouse. *Sex Roles, 35(9/10),* 619–638.

McCall, L., & Yacovone, D. (Eds.). (1998). *A shared experience: Women, men and the history of gender.* New York: New York University Press.

McCaul, K., Branstetter, A., Schroeder, D., & Glasgow, R. (1996). What is the relationship between breast cancer risk and mammography? *Health Psychology, 15,* 423–429.

McClean, V. (1997). African-American men and nonrelational sex. In R. F. Levant & G. R. Brooks (Eds.), *Men and sex: New psychological perspectives* (pp. 205–228). New York: Wiley.

McCormick, N. B. (1994). *Sexual salvation: Affirming women's sexual rights and pleasure.* Westport, CT: Praeger.

McCormick, W. C., Uomoto, J., Young, H., Graves, A. B., Vitaliano, P., Mortimer, J. A., Edland, S. D., & Larson, E. B. (1996). Attitudes toward use of nursing homes and home care in older Japanese-Americans. *Journal of the American Gerontological Society, 44,* 769–777.

McCreary, D. R., Newcomb, M. D., & Sadava, S. W. (1998). Dimensions of the male gender role: A confirmatory analysis in men and women. *Sex Roles, 39(1–2),* 81–95.

McGhee, P. E., & Frueh, T. (1980). Television viewing and the learning of sex role stereotypes. *Sex Roles, 6,* 179–188.

McGrath, E., & Keita, G. P., & Strickland. (1990). *Women and depression: Risk factors and treatment issues.* Washington, DC: American Psychological Association.

McGuinness, D. (1993). Gender differences in cognitive style: Implications for mathematics performance and achievement. In L. A. Penner, G. M. Batsche, H. M. Knoff, & D. L. Nelson (Eds.), *The challenge in mathematics and science education* (pp. 251–274). Washington, DC: American Psychological Association.

McHale, S. M., & Crouter, A. C. (1992). You can't always get what you want: Incongruence between sex-role attitudes and family work-roles and its implications for marriage. *Journal of Marriage & the Family, 54,* 537–547.

McHugh, M. C., Koeske, R. D., & Frieze, I. H. (1986). Issues to consider in conducting nonsexist psychological research: A guide for researchers. *American Psychologist, 41,* 879–890.

McHugh, M. C., Koeske, R. D., & Frieze, I. H. (1997). Issues to consider in conducting non-sexist and psychological research: A guide for researchers. In T. Roberts (Ed.), *The Lanahan readings on the psychology of women* (pp. 483–502). Baltimore, MD: Lanahan.

McIntyre, T. (1996). Guidelines for providing appropriate services to culturally diverse students with emotional and/or behavioral disorders. *Behavioral Disorders, 21(2),* 137–144.

McIntyre, T. (1997). Gender differences in cognition: A minefield of research issues. *Irish Journal of Psychology, 18(4),* 386–396.

McIntyre, T., & Tong, V. (1998). Where the boys are: Do cross-gender misunderstandings of language use and behavior patterns contribute to the overrepresentation of males in programs for students with emotional and behavioral disorders? *Education & Treatment of Children, 21(3),* 321–322.

McKendrick, J. H., Thorpe, M., Cutter, T. N., Austin, G., Roberts, W., Duke, M., & Chiu, E. (1990). A unique mental health network for Victorian Aboriginal people. *Medical Journal of Australia, 153,* 349–351.

McKenzie, K. J., & Crowcroft, N. S. (1994). Race, ethnicity, culture, and science. *British Medical Journal, 309,* 286–287.

McKenzie-Mohr, D., & Zanna, M. (1995). Treating women as sexual objects: Look to the (gender-schematic) male who has viewed pornography. *Personality & Social Psychology Bulletin, 9,* 885–892.

McKnight, J. (1997). *Straight science: Homosexuality, evolution, and adaptation.* New York: Routledge.

McLanahan, S. S., & Sandefur, G. (1995). *Growing up with a single parent.* Cambridge, MA: Harvard University Press.

McLean, C., Carey, M., & White, C. (1996). *Men's ways of being.* Boulder, CO: Westview Press.

McLeod, A. C., Crawford, I., & Zechmeister, J. (1999). Heterosexual undergraduates' attitudes toward gay fathers and their children. *Journal of Psychology & Human Sexuality, 11(1),* 43–62.

McMahon, M. (1995). *Engendering motherhood: Identity and self-transformation in women's lives.* New York: Guilford.

McNeal, R. B. (1995). Extracurricular activities and high school dropouts. *Sociology of Education, 68,* 62–80.

McNeil, D. W., Kee, M., & Zvolensky, M. J. (1999). Culturally related anxiety and ethnic identity in Navajo college students. *Cultural Diversity and Ethnic Minority Psychology, 5,* 56–64.

McVeigh, B. (1996). Cultivating "femininity" and "internationalism": Rituals and routine at a Japanese women's junior college. *Ethos, 24(2),* 314–349.

McWilliams, S., & Howard, J. A. (1993). Solidarity and hierarchy in cross-sex friendships. *Journal of Social Issues, 49(3),* 191–202.

Mealey, L. (2000). *Sex differences: Development and evolutionary strategies.* San Diego: Academic Press.

Meeus, W., & Dekovic, M. (1995). Identity development, parental and peer support in adolescence. Results of a national Dutch study. *Adolescence, 30,* 931–944.

Meleis, A. I., Lipson, J. G., & Paul, S. M. (1992). Ethnicity and health among 5 Middle Eastern immigrant groups. *Nursing Research, 41,* 98–103.

Mendelson, J. H., & Mello, N. K. (1998). Diagnostic evaluation of alcohol and drug abuse problems in women. *Psychopharmacology Bulletin, 34*(3), 279–281.

Mergenhagen, P. (1996). Her own boss. *American Demographics, 18,* 36–41.

Messerschmidt, J. (2000). *Nine lives: Adolescent masculinities.* Boulder, CO: Westview.

Messerschmidt, J. W. (1993). *Masculinities and crime: Critique and reconceptualization of theory.* Lanham, MD: Rowman & Littlefield.

Messner, M. A. (1997). Boyhood, organized sports and the construction of masculinities. In E. Disch (Ed.), *Reconstructing gender* (pp. 57–73). Mountain View, CA: Mayfield.

Messner, M. A. (2000). Barbie girls versus sea monsters: Children constructing gender. *Gender and Society, 14*(6), 765–784.

Messner, M. A., Duncan, M. C., & Jensen, K. (1993). Separating the men from the girls: The gendered language of television sports. *Gender and Society, 7*(1), 121–137.

Messner, M. M., & Sabo, D. F. (Eds.). (1990). *Sport, men and the gender order: Critical feminist perspectives.* Champaign, IL: Human Kinetics.

Meyer, K., Rizzo, H., & Ali, Y. (1998). Islam and the extension of citizenship rights to women in Kuwait. *Journal for the Scientific Study of Religion, 37*(1), 131–144.

Meyer, R. G. (1993). *The clinician's handbook.* Boston: Allyn and Bacon.

Meyer, S. (1999). Work, play and power: Masculine culture on the automotive shop floor (1930–1960). *Men and Masculinities, 2*(2), 115–134.

Meyer-Bahlberg, H. (1998). Gender assignment in intersexuality. *Journal of Psychology & Human Sexuality, 10*(2), 1–21.

Meyer-Bahlberg, H., Ehrhardt, A., Rosen, L., Gruen, R., Veridiano, N., Vann, F., & Neuwalder, H. (1995). Prenatal estrogens and the development of homosexual orientation. *Developmental Psychology, 31,* 12–21.

Meyer-Bahlburg, H., Gruen, R. S., New, M. I., & Bell, J. J. (1996). Gender change from female to male in classical congenital adrenal hyperplasia. *Hormones and Behavior, 30,* 319–332.

Meyerson, D. F., & Fletcher, J. K. (2000). A modest manifesto for shattering the glass ceiling. *Harvard Business Review, 78*(1), 127–136.

Michael, J. (1996). Prosthetic gender and universal intellect: Stephen Hawking's law. In P. Smith (Ed.), *Boys: Masculinities in contemporary culture* (pp. 199–215). New York: Westview Press.

Michael, R. T., Gagnon, J. H., Laumann, E. D., & Kolata, G. (1994). *Sex in America: A definitive survey.* Boston: Little, Brown.

Michie, H., & Cahn, N. R. (1997). *Confinements: Fertility and infertility in contemporary culture.* New Brunswick, NJ: Rutgers University Press.

Mill, J. S. (1869). *The subjection of women.* London: Longmans, Green, Reader and Dyer. Available online at http://www.knuten.liu.se/~bjoch509/works/mill/women.txt. Retrieved on April 21, 2002.

Miller, B. D. (Ed.). (1993). *Sex and gender hierarchies.* New York: Cambridge University Press.

Miller, C., & Swift, K. (1991). *Updated words and women: New language in new times.* New York: HarperCollins.

Miller, E. M. (2000). Homosexuality, birth order, and evolution: Toward an equilibrium reproductive economics of homosexuality. *Archives of Sexual Behavior, 29*(1), 1–34.

Miller, J. G. (1999). Cultural psychology: Implications for basic psychological theory. *Psychological Science, 10*(2), 85–91.

Miller, W. R., & Cervantes, E. A. (1997). Gender and patterns of alcohol problems: Pretreatment responses of women and men to the Comprehensive Drinker Profile. *Journal of Clinical Psychology, 53*(3), 263–277.

Mills, C. W. (1956). *The power elite.* New York: Oxford University Press.

Min, P. G. (1995a). *Asian-Americans: Contemporary trends and issues.* Thousand Oaks, CA: Sage.

Min, P. G. (1995b). Major issues relating to Asian-American experiences. In P. G. Min (Ed.), *Asian-Americans* (pp. 38–57). Thousand Oaks, CA: Sage.

Ming, X. (2000). Sexual prejudices in the media. *Women of China,* 18–19.

Minter, S. (1999). Diagnosis and treatment of gender identity disorder in children. In M. Rottnek (Ed.), *Sissies and tomboys: Gender non-conformity and homosexual childhood* (pp. 9–33). New York: New York University Press.

Minton, H. L. (2000). Psychology and gender at the turn of the century. *American Psychologist, 55*(6), 613–615.

Mintz, S. (1998). From patriarchy to androgyny and other myths: Placing men's family roles in historical perspective. In A. Booth & A. C. Crouter (Eds.), *Men in families* (pp. 3–30). Mahwah, NJ: Erlbaum.

Minuchin, S. (1974). *Families and family therapy.* Cambridge, MA: Harvard University Press.

Minuchin, S., Rosman, B., & Baker, L. (1978). *Psychosomatic families: Anorexia in context.* Cambridge, MA: Harvard University Press.

Mirhasseini, A. (1995). After the revolution: Violations of women's human rights in Iran. In J. Peters & A. Wolper (Eds.), *Women's rights, human rights: International feminist perspectives* (pp. 72–77). New York: Routledge.

Misago, C., & Fonseca, W. (1999). Determinants and medical characteristics of induced abortion among poor urban women in North-East Brazil. In A. I. Mundigo & C. Indriso (Eds.), *Abortion in the developing world* (pp. 217–227). London: Zed Books (World Health Organization).

Mischel, W. (1966). A social-learning view of sex differences in behavior. In E. E. Maccoby (Ed.), *The development of sex differences* (pp. 56–81). Stanford, CA: Stanford University Press.

Mischel, W. (1993). *Introduction to personality* (5th ed.). Fort Worth, TX: Harcourt Brace Jovanovich.

Miskind, M. E., Rodin, J., Silberstein, L. R., & Striegel-Moore, R. H. (1987). The embodiment of masculinity. In M. S. Kimmel (Ed.), *Changing men: New directions in research on men and masculinity.* Newbury Park, CA: Sage.

Mita, R., & Simmons, R. (1995). Diffusion of the culture of contraception: Program effects on young women in rural Bangladesh. *Studies in Family Planning, 26*(1), 1–13.

Mitchell, V., & Helson, R. (1990). Women's prime of life: Is it the fifties? *Psychology of Women Quarterly, 14,* 451–470.

Mitter, S. (1997). Innovations in work organization and technology. In E. Date-Bar (Ed.), *Promoting gender equality at work: Turning vision into reality for the twenty-first century* (pp. 105–129). London: Zed Books.

Moen, I. (1993). Functional lateralization of the perception of Norwegian word tones—evidence from a dichotic listening experiment. *Brain & Language, 44*(4), 400–413.

Moffat, S. D., & Hampson, E. (1996). A curvilinear relationship between testosterone and spatial cognition in humans: Possible influence of hand preference. *Psychoneuroendocrinology, 21,* 323–337.

Moghaddam, F. M., & Harré, R. (1995). But is it science? Traditional and alternative approaches to the study of social behavior. *World Psychology, 1,* 47–78.

Moghaddam, F. M., & Studer, C. (1997). Cross-cultural psychology: The frustrated gadfly's promises, potentialities, and failures. In D. Fox & I. Prilleltensky (Eds.), *Critical psychology: An introduction* (pp. 185–201). London: Sage.

Mohiuddin, Y. N. (1997). Gender inequality in the Pakistan labor market: Myth and reality. In J. M. Rives & M. Yousefi (Eds.), *Economic dimensions of gender inequality* (pp. 167–184). Westport, CT: Praeger.

Mok, T. A. (1999). Asian-American dating: Important factors in partner choice. *Cultural Diversity and Ethnic Minority Psychology, 5*(2), 103–117.

Molinari, V. (Ed.). (2000). *Professional psychology in long-term care: A comprehensive guide.* New York: Heatherleigh Press.

Moller, L. C., & Serbin, L. A. (1996). Antecedents of toddler gender segregation: Cognitive consonance, gender-typed toy preferences and behavioral compatibility. *Sex Roles, 35,* 445–460.

Mollica, R. F. (2000). Invisible wounds. *Scientific American, 282*(6), 54–57.

Money, J. (1994). *Sex errors of the body and related syndromes: A guide to counseling children, adolescents, and their families* (2nd ed.). Baltimore, MD: Brookes.

Money, J. (1997). *Principles of developmental sexology.* New York: Continuum.

Money, J., & Ehrhardt, A. (1972). *Men and women, boy and girl.* Baltimore: Johns Hopkins University Press.

Money, J., Hampson, J. G., & Hampson, J. L. (1955). Hermaphroditism: Recommendations concerning assignment of sex, change of sex, and psychologic management. *Bulletin of Johns Hopkins Hospital, 97,* 284–300.

Money, J., Hampson, J. G., & Hampson, J. L. (1956). Sexual incongruities and psychopathology: The evidence of human hermaphroditism. *Bulletin of the Johns Hopkins Hospital, 98,* 43–57.

Money, J., Hampson, J. G., & Hampson, J. L. (1957). Imprinting and the establishment of gender role. *Archives of Neurology and Psychiatry, 77,* 333–336.

Monson, C. M., & Langhinrichsen-Rohling, J. (1998). Sexual and nonsexual marital aggression: Legal considerations, epidemiology and an integrated typology of perpetrators. *Aggression and Violent Behavior, 3*(4), 369–389.

Monsour, M. (1992). Meanings of intimacy in cross- and same sex friendships. *Journal of Social & Personal Relationships, 9,* 277–295.

Moore, B. L., & Webb, S. C. (2000). Perceptions of equal opportunity among women and minority Army personnel. *Sociological Inquiry, 70*(2), 215–239.

Moore, D. P., & Buttner, E. H. (1997). *Women entrepreneurs: Moving beyond the glass ceiling.* Thousand Oaks, CA: Sage.

Moore, D. S., & Travis, C. B. (2000). Biological models and sexual politics. In C. B. Travis & J. W. White (Eds.), *Sexuality, society and feminism* (pp. 35–56). Washington, DC: American Psychological Association.

Morawski, J. G. (1990). Toward the unimagined: Feminism and epistemology in psychology. In R. T. Hare-Mustin & J. Marecek (Eds.), *Making a difference: Psychology and the construction of gender* (pp. 150–183). New Haven, CT: Yale University Press.

Morawski, J. G. (1994). *Practicing feminisms, reconstructing psychology: Notes on a liminal science.* Ann Arbor: University of Michigan Press.

Morgan, R. (1980). Theory and practice: Pornography and rape. In L. Lederer (Ed.), *Take back the night.* New York: Morrow.

Morman, M. T., & Floyd, K. (1998). "I love you, man": Overt expressions of affection in male–male interaction. *Sex Roles, 38*(9–10), 871–881.

Morrell, C. M. (2000). *Unwomanly conduct: The challenges of intentional childlessness.* New York: Routledge.

Morris, J. (1974). *Conundrum.* New York: Harcourt Brace Jovanovich.

Morrongiello, B. A., & Rennie, H. (1998). Why do boys engage in more risk taking than girls? The role of attributions, beliefs, and risk appraisals. *Journal of Pediatric Psychology, 23*(1), 33–43.

Morse, J. (1998, November 9). Gender bender: A cross-dressing teenager must leave, says a school. *Time Magazine, 152*(19). Available online at http://www.time.com/time/magazine/1998/dom/981109/nation.gender_bender44a.html. Retrieved April 21, 2002.

Mosher, D. L., & Maclan, P. (1994). College men and women respond to X-rated videos intended for male or female audiences. *Journal of Sex Research, 31*(2), 99–114.

Mosse, J. C. (1993). *Half the world, half a chance: An introduction to gender and development.* Oxford, England: Oxfam.

Mourao, M. (1999). The representation of female desire in early modern pornographic texts, 1660–1745. *Signs, 24*(3), 573–602.

Moya, M., Exposito, F., & Ruiz, J. (2000). Close relationships, gender, and career salience. *Sex Roles, 42*(9–10), 825–846.

Mrsevic, Z., & Hughes, D. M. (1997). Violence against women in Belgrade, Serbia: SOS hotline 1990–1993. *Violence Against Women, 3*(2), 101–128.

Muesar, K. T., & Tarrier, N. (Eds.). (1998). *Handbook of social functioning in schizophrenia.* Boston: Allyn and Bacon.

Muller, C. (1998). Gender differences in parental involvement and adolescents mathematics achievement. *Sociology of Education, 71*(4), 336–356.

Munk, N. (2000, March 5). The price of freedom. *New York Times Magazine,* pp. 50–54.

Munroe, R. L., & Munroe, R. H. (1994). *Cross-cultural human development.* Prospect Heights, IL: Waveland Press.

Munroe, R. L., & Munroe, R. H. (1997). A comparative anthropological perspective. In J. W. Berry, Y. H. Poortinga, & J. Handey (Eds.), *Handbook of cross-cultural psychology. Vol. 1: Theory and method* (pp. 171–213). Boston: Allyn and Bacon.

Murnen, S. K., & Smolak, L. (1997). Femininity, masculinity and disordered eating: A meta analytic review. *International Journal of Eating Disorders, 22*(3), 231–242.

Murphy, B. C. (1997). Difference and diversity: Gay and lesbian couples. In M. Duberman (Ed.), *A queer world* (pp. 345–357). New York: New York University Press.

Murphy, B. O., & Zorri, T. E. (1996). Gendered interaction in professional relationships. In J. T. Wood (Ed.),

Gendered relationships: A reader (pp. 213–232).

Murphy, C. (1998). Is the Bible bad news for women? Wilson Quarterly, 22(3), 14–33.

Murr, A. (1998, August 10). Secrets in the desert. Newsweek, p. 37.

Murray, C. B. (1996). Estimating achievement performance: A confirmation bias. Journal of Black Psychology, 22(1), 67–85.

Mutsumi, O. (1999). Dad takes child-care leave. Japan Quarterly, 46(1), 83–89.

Mwangi, M. W. (1996). Gender roles portrayed in Kenyan television commercials. Sex Roles, 34, 205–214. Nadeau, R. L. (1996). S/He brain. Westport, CT: Praeger.

Nader, E., Dubrow, N., & Stamm, B. H. (Eds.). (1999). Honoring differences: Cultural issues in the treatment of trauma and loss. Philadelphia: Brunner/Mazel.

Nadler, A. (1991). Help seeking behavior: Psychological costs and instrumental benefits. In M. S. Clark (Ed.), Prosocial behavior (pp. 290–311). Newbury Park, CA: Sage.

Nandon, S. M., Koverola, C., & Schluderman, E. H. (1998). Antecedents to prostitution: Childhood victimization. Journal of Interpersonal Violence, 13, 206–221.

Nardi, P. M. (Ed.). (1992a). Men's friendships. Newbury Park, CA: Sage.

Nardi, P. M. (1992b). Sex, friendships, and gender roles among gay men. In P. M. Nardi (Ed.), Men's friendships (pp. 173–185). Newbury Park, CA: Sage.

Natarajan, A. (1996). Medical ethics and truth telling in the case of androgen insensitivity syndrome. Canadian Medical Association Journal, 154, 568–570.

National Vital Statistics Report. (1999). Births: Final data for 1997 (Vol. 47, pp. 1–13).

Naumann, A. K., & Hutchinson, M. (1997). The integration of women into the Mexican labor force since NAFTA. American Behavioral Scientist, 40, 950–956.

Neal, M. B., Ingersoll-Dayton, B., & Starrels, M. E. (1997). Gender and relationship differences in care-giving patterns and consequences among employed caregivers. The Gerontologist, 3, 804–816.

Neft, N., & Levine, A. D. (1997). Where women stand: An international report on the status of women in 140 countries 1197–1998. New York: Random House.

Nelson, C. B., Heath, A. C., & Kessler, R. C. (1998). Temporal progression of alcohol dependence symptoms in the United States household population: Results from the National Co-morbidity Survey. Journal of Consulting and Clinical Psychology, 66, 474–483.

Nemecek, S. (2000). Who were the first Americans? Scientific American, 283(3), 80–87.

Nestle, M., & Jacobson, M. (2000). Halting the obesity epidemic: A public health policy approach. Public Health Reports, 115(1), 12–24.

NICHD Early Child Care Research Network. (2000). Factors associated with father caregiving activities and sensitivity with young children. Journal of Family Psychology, 14(2), 200–219.

Nielsen Media Research. (1998). 1998 Report on television. New York: Author.

Nock, S. L. (1998). Marriage in men's lives. New York: Oxford University Press.

Nohara, M. (1996). Preschool boys and girls use "no" differently. Journal of Child Language, 23(2), 417–429.

Nolen-Hoeksema, S. (1990). Sex differences in depression. Stanford, CA: Stanford University Press.

Nolen-Hoeksema, S. (1995). Gender differences in coping with depression across the lifespan. Depression, 3, 81–90.

Nolen-Hoeksema, S. (2001). Gender differences in depression. Current Directions, 10(5), 173–176.

Nolen-Hoeksema, S., & Girgus, J. S. (1994). The emergence of gender differences on depression during adolescence. Psychological Bulletin, 115(3), 424–443.

Noll, S. M., & Fredrickson, B. L. (1998). A mediational model linking self-objectification, body shame, and disordered eating. Psychology of Women Quarterly, 22(4), 623–636.

Nordlinger, J. (1999). Star in waiting: Meet George W's foreign policy czarina. National Review, 51(16), 35–37.

Nordvik, H., & Amponsah, B. (1998). Gender differences in spatial abilities and spatial activity among university students in an egalitarian educational system. Sex Roles, 38(11–12), 1009–1023.

Norris, P. (1997). Women leaders worldwide: A splash of color in the photo op. In P. Norris (Ed.), Women, media and politics (pp. 149–165). New York: Oxford University Press.

Novins, D. K., Beals, J., Shone, J. H., & Manson, S. M. (1996). Substance abuse treatment of American Indian adolescents: Comorbid symptomatology gender differences and treatment patterns. American Academy of Child Adolescent Psychiatry, 35(12), 1593–1601

Nsamenang, B. A. (1992). Perceptions of parenting among the Nso of Cameroon. In B. S. Hewlett (Ed.), Father–child relations: Cultural and biosocial contexts (pp. 321–344). New York: Aldine deGruyter.

Nummenmaa, A. R., & Nummenmaa, T. (1997). Intergenerational roots of Finnish women's sex-atypical careers. International Journal of Behavioral Development, 21(1), 1–14.

Nunberg, G. (2000, March 27). Will the Internet always speak English? The American Prospect, 11, 10. Available online at http://www.prospect.org/print/V11/10/nunberg-g.html. Retrieved on April 22, 2002.

Nurmi, J., Liiceneau, A., & Liberska, H. (1999). Future oriented interests. In F. D. Alsaker & A. Flammer (Eds.), The adolescent experience: European and American adolescents in the 1990s (pp. 85–98). Mahwah, NJ: Erlbaum.

Nussbaum, M. (2000). Globalization debates ignores the education of women. Chronicle of Higher Education, 47(2), 16–17.

Nyborg, H. (1994). Hormones, sex, and society: The science of physiology. Westport, CT: Praeger.

Oaks, L. (1994). Fetal spirithood and fetal personhood. Women's Studies International Forum, 17(5), 511–523.

Obura, A. (1991). Changing images—portrayals of girls and women in Kenyan textbooks. Nairobi: ACTS Press.

O'Connell, A. N. (1976). The relationship between life style and identity synthesis and resynthesis in traditional, neo-traditional and non-traditional women. Journal of Personality, 44, 675–688.

O'Connell, A. N., & Russo, N. F. (1983). Models of achievement: Reflections of eminent women in psychology (Vol. 1). New York: Columbia University Press.

O'Connell-Davidson, J. (1998). Prostitution, power and freedom. Ann Arbor: University of Michigan Press.

O'Connor, C. (1999). Race, class and gender in America: Narratives of opportunity among low-income African-American youths. Sociology of Education, 72(3), 137–157.

O'Connor, P. (1992). *Friendships between women: A critical review*. New York: Guilford Press.

Odaga, A., & Ward, H. (1995). *Girls and schools in sub-Saharan Africa*. Washington, DC: World Bank.

O'Donohue, W., Dopke, C. A., & Swingen, D. N. (1997). Psychotherapy for female sexual dysfunction. *Clinical Psychology Review, 17*(5), 537–566.

Oetjen, H., & Rothblum, E. D. (2000). When lesbians aren't gay: Factors affecting depression among lesbians. *Journal of Homosexuality, 39*(1), 49–74.

Office of Applied Studies. (1997). *The 1996 national household survey on drug abuse*. Rockville MD: Substance Abuse and Mental Health Services Administration.

Ogasawara, Y. (1996). Meanings of chocolate: Power and gender in Valentine's gift giving. *International Journal of Japanese Sociology, 5*, 41–61.

Okagaki, L., & Frensch, P. A. (1994). Effects of videogame playing on measures of spatial performance: Gender effects in late adolescence. *Journal of Applied Developmental Psychology, 15*, 33–58.

Oliver, M. B., Weaver, J. B., & Sargent, S. L. (2000). An examination of factors related to sex differences in enjoyment of sad films. *Journal of Broadcasting and Electronic Media, 44*, 282.

Oliver, W. (1994). *The violent social world of black men*. San Francisco: Jossey-Bass.

Olson, B., & Douglas, W. (1997). The family on television: Evaluation of gender roles in situation comedy. *Sex Roles, 36*, 409–427.

Olson, E. (1994). Female voices of aggression in Tonga. *Sex Roles, 30*, 237–248.

Oncale v. Sundowner Offshore Services, Inc., 523 U.S. 75 (1998).

O'Neil, J. (2000, May 30). Viagra and women: A frosty reception. *New York Times*, Section F, p. 8, col. 5.

O'Neill, S. A. (1997). Gender and music. In D. J. Hargreaves & A. C. North (Eds.), *The social psychology of music* (pp. 46–63). Oxford, England: Oxford University Press.

Opie, C. (1998). Whose turn next? Gender issues in information technology. In A. Clark & E. Millard (Eds.), *Gender in the secondary curriculum*. New York: Routledge.

Orbuch, T. L., Venoff, J., & Hunter, A. G. (1999). Black couples, white couples: The early days of marriage. In E. M.

Hetherington (Ed.), *Coping with divorce, single parenting, and remarriage* (pp. 23–44). Mahwah, NJ: Erlbaum.

Orleans, C. T. (2000). Promoting the maintenance of health behavior change: Recommendations for the next generation of research and practice. *Health Psychology, 19*(1), 76–83.

Orth-Gomer, K., Chesney, M., & Wenger, K. (1998). *Women, stress, and heart disease*. Mahwah, NJ: Erlbaum.

Osborne, J. W. (1997). Race and academic disidentification. *Journal of Educational Psychology, 89*(4), 728–735.

O'Sullivan, C. Y., Reese, C. M., & Mazzeo, J. (1997). *NAEP 1996 science report card for the nation and the states*. (NCES 97-497). Washington, DC: U.S. Department of Education, National Center for Education Statistics.

Ottati, V., Terkidsen, N., & Hubbard, C. (1997). Happy faces elicit heuristic processing in a televised impression formation task: A cognitive timing account. *Personality & Social Psychology Bulletin, 23*, 1144–1156.

Owen, M. (1996). *The world of widows*. New York: Zed Books.

Owens, L. D., & MacMullin, C. E. (1995). Gender differences in aggression in children and adolescents in South Australia school. *International Journal of Adolescence, 6*, 21–35.

Oyler, C., Jennings, G. T., & Lozada, P. (2001). Silenced gender: The construction of a male primary educator. *Teaching and Teacher Education, 17*(3), 367–379.

Ozer, E. M. (1995). The impact of childcare responsibility and self-efficacy on the psychological health of professional working mothers. *Psychology of Women Quarterly, 19*(3), 315–336.

Padian, N. S., Shiboski, S., Glass, S., & Vittinghof, E. (1997). Heterosexual transmission of HIV in northern California: Results from a 10 year study. *American Journal of Epidemiology, 146*, 350–357.

Padma-Nathan, H. (1998). The pharmacological management of erectile dysfunction: Sildenafil citrate (Viagra). *Journal of Sex Education and Theory, 23*(3), 207–216.

Pajer, K. A. (1998). What happens to "bad" girls? A review of the adult outcomes of antisocial adolescent girls. *American Journal of Psychiatry, 155*(7), 862–870.

Paludi, M. (Ed.). (1998). *The psychology of sexual victimization: A handbook*. Westport, CT: Greenwood Press.

Pan, P. P. (1999, November 29). Shelter from a bloodstained land: Almost unnoticed, newest refugees from Afghanistan fight for a life. *The Washington Post*, pp. B1, B7.

Parasuraman, S., & Greenhaus, J. H. (1997a). The changing world of work and family. In S. Parasuraman & J. H. Greenhaus (Eds.), *Integrating work and family* (pp. 3–15). Westport, CT: Quorum Books.

Parasuraman, S., & Greenhaus, J. H. (1997b). *Integrating work & family*. Westport, CT: Quorum Books.

Park, H., Bauer, S. C., & Sullivan, L. M. (1998). Gender differences among top performing elementary school students in math ability. *Journal of Research & Development in Education, 31*(3), 133–141.

Park, J., & Liao, T. F. (2000). The effect of multiple roles of South Korean married women professors: Role changes and the factors which influence potential role gratification and strain. *Sex-Roles, 43*(7–8), 571–591.

Parke, R. D. (1996). *Fatherhood*. Cambridge, MA: Harvard University Press.

Parker, R. (1995). *Torn in two: The experience of maternal ambivalence*. London: Virago Press.

Parker, S., & de Vries, B. (1993). Patterns of friendship for women and men in same- and cross-sex relationships. *Journal of Social and Personal Relationships, 10*(4), 617–626.

Parker, S., Nichter, M., Vuckovic, N., Sims, C. & Riterbaugh, C. (1995). Body image and weight concerns among African American and white adolescent females: Differences that make a difference. *Human Organization, 54*(2), 103–114.

Parks, C. A. (1998). Lesbian parenthood: A review of the literature. *American Journal of Orthopsychiatry, 68*(3), 376–389.

Parlee, M. B. (1997). Feminism and psychology. In M. M. Gergen, & S. N. Davis (Ed.), *Toward a new psychology of gender* (pp. 65–95). Florence, KY: Taylor & Francis/Routledge.

Parrenas, R. S. (2000). Migrant Filipina domestic worker and the international division of reproductive labor. *Gender & Society, 14*(4), 560–580.

Parsons, T., & Bales, R. F. (1955). *Family, socialization, and interaction process*. Glencoe, IL: Free Press.

Pattatucci, A. M. L., & Hammer, D. H. (1995). Developmental and familiarity of sexual orientation in females. *Behavior-Genetics, 25*(5), 407–420.

Patterson, C. J. (1992). Children of lesbian and gay parents. *Child Development, 63*, 1025–1042.

Patterson, C. J. (1995a). Families of the baby boom: Parents' division of labor and children's adjustment. *Developmental Psychology, 31*(1), 115–123.

Patterson, C. J. (1995b). Sexual orientation and human development: An overview. *Developmental Psychology, 31*, 3–11.

Patterson, C. J. (1996). Lesbian and gay parents and their chldren. In R. C. Savin-Williams, & K. M. Cohen (Eds.), *The lives of lesbians, gays and bisexuals: Children to adults* (pp. 274–304). Fort Worth, TX: Harcourt Brace.

Patterson, C. J. (2000). Family relationships of lesbians and gay men. *Journal of Marriage and the Family, 62*(4), 1052–1069.

Patterson, C. J., & Chan, R. W. (1997). Gay fathers. In M. E. Lamb (Ed.), *The role of the father in child development* (3rd ed., pp. 245–260). New York: Wiley.

Patterson, C. J., Hurt, S., & Mason, C. D. (1998). Families of the lesbian baby-boom: Children's contact with grandparents and other adults. *American Journal of Orthopsychiatry, 68*(3), 390–399.

Patton, W., & McMahon, M. (1999). *Career development and systems theory*. Pacific Grove, CA: Brooks/Cole.

Pavlidis, K., McCauley, E., & Sybert, V. (1995). Psychosocial and sexual functioning of adult women with Turner syndrome, *Clinical Genetics, 47*, 85-89.

Peach, L. J. (1996). Gender ideology in the ethics of women in combat. In J. H. Stiehm (Ed.), *It's our military too!* (pp. 156–194). Philadelphia: Temple University Press.

Pederson, P. (Ed.). (1999). *Multiculturalism as a fourth force*. Philadelphia: Brunner/Mazel.

Peirce, K., & McBride, M. (1999). Aunt Jemima isn't keeping up with the Energizer bunny: Stereotyping of animated spokes-characters in advertising. *Sex Roles, 40*(11–12), 959–968.

Pennebaker, J., & Roberts, T. (1992). Toward a his and hers theory of emotion:

Gender differences in visceral perception. *Journal of Social & Clinical Psychology, 11*, 199–212.

Peplau, L. A., & Campbell, S. M. (1989). The balance of power in dating and marriage. In J. Freeman (Ed.), *Women: A feminist perspective* (4th ed., pp. 121–137). Mountain View, CA: Mayfield.

Peplau, L. A. (1991). Lesbian and gay relationships. In J. C. Gonsiorek & J. D. Weinrich (Eds.), *Homosexuality* (pp. 177–196). Newbury Park, CA: Sage.

Peplau, L. A., & Garnets, L. D. (2000). A new paradigm for understanding women's sexuality and sexual orientation. *Journal of Social Issues, 56*(2), 329–350.

Peplau, L. A., Garnets, L. D., Spalding, L. R., Conley, T. D., & Veniegas, R. C. (1998). A critique of Bem's exotic becomes erotic theory of sexual orientation. *Psychology Review, 105*, 387–394.

Perkins, K. (1992). Psychosocial implications of women and retirement. *Social Work, 37*(6), 526–532.

Perry, C. M., & Johnson, C. L. (1994). Families and support networks among African American oldest-old. *International Journal of Aging and Human Development, 38*(1), 41–50.

Persell, C. H., James, C., Kang, T., & Snyder, K. (1999). Gender and education: A global perspective. In J. S. Chavetz (Ed.), *Handbook of the sociology of gender* (pp. 407–440). New York: Kluwer.

Peters, K. D., Kochanek, M. A., & Murphy, S. L. (1998). Report of final mortality statistics, 1996. *National Vital Statistics Reports, 47*(9), 6.

Peterson, C. C. (1999). Grandfathers and grandmothers satisfaction with the grandparenting role: Seeking new answers to old questions. *International Journal of Aging and Human Development, 49*(1), 61–78.

Peterson, G. (1996). Childbirth: The ordinary miracle: Effects of devaluation of child birth on women's self-esteem and family relationships. *Pre- & Peri-natal Psychology Journal, 11*, 101–109.

Peterson, R. R. (1996). Re-evaluation of the economic consequences of divorce. *American Sociological Review, 61*(3), 528–533.

Peterson, V. S., & Runyon, A. S. (1993). *Global gender issues*. Boulder, CO: Westview.

Phelan, J. C., & Link, B. G. (1999). The labeling theory of mental disorder (I) in the application of psychiatric labels. In A. V. Horwitz & T. L. Scheid (Eds.), *A handbook for the study of mental health*. London: Cambridge University Press.

Phillips, R. D., & Gilroy, F. D. (1985). Sex-role stereotypes and clinical judgments of mental health: The Brovermans' findings revisited. *Sex Roles, 12*, 179–193.

Phillips, S. D., & Imhoff, A. R. (1997). Women and career development: A decade of research. *Annual Review of Psychology, 48*, 31–59.

Phoenix, J. (1999). *Making sense of prostitution*. London: Routledge.

Piaget, J., & Inhelder, B. (1956). *The child's conception of space*. London: Routledge & Kegan Paul.

Pierce, P. F. (1998). Retention of Air Force women serving during Desert Shield and Desert Storm. *Military Psychology, 10*, 3, 195–213.

Pike, K. M., & Striegel-Moore, R. H. (1997). Disordered eating and eating disorders. In S. J. Gallant, G. P. Keita, & R. Royak-Schaler (Eds.), *Healthcare for women* (pp. 97–114). Washington, DC: American Psychological Association.

Pillard, R. C. (1998). The search for a genetic influence on sexual orientation. In V. A. Rosario (Ed.), *Science and homosexuality* (pp. 226–240). New York: Routledge.

Pillard, R. C., & Bailey, J. M. (1995). A biologic perspective on sexual orientation. *Psychiatry Clinic North America, 18*, 71–84.

Pina, D., & Bengston, V. L. (1993). The division of household labor and wives' happiness: Ideology, employment and perception of support. *Journal of Marriage and the Family, 55*(4), 901–912.

Pinel, P. (1801/1997). Treating the insane. In L. T. Benjamin, Jr. (Ed.), *A history of psychology: Original sources and contemporary research* (2nd ed., pp. 93–97). New York: McGraw-Hill.

Plant, E. A., Hyde, J. S., Ketner, D., & Devine, P. G. (2000). The gender stereotyping of emotions. *Psychology of Women Quarterly, 24*, 81–92.

Plantenga, J., & Hansen, J. (1999). Assessing equal opportunities in the European Union. *International Labour Review, 138*(4), 351–379.

Pleck, J. H. (1981a). Men's power with women, other men and society. In R. A.

Lewis (Ed.), *Men in different times* (pp. 234–244). Englewood Cliffs, NJ: Prentice Hall.

Pleck, J. H. (1981b). *The myth of masculinity*. Cambridge, MA: MIT Press.

Pleck, J. H. (1995). The gender role strain paradigm: An update. In R. F. Levant & W. S. Pollack (Eds.), *A new psychology of men* (pp. 11–32). New York: Basic Books.

Pleck, J. H., Sonenstein, F. L., & Ku, L. C. (1993). Masculinity ideology: Its impact on adolescent males heterosexual relationships. *Journal of Social Issues, 49*(3), 11–29.

Plummer, K. (Ed.). (1992). *Modern homosexuality*. London: Routledge.

Plutchik, R. (1993). Emotions and their vicissitudes: Emotions & psychopathology. In M. Lewis & J. M. Haviland (Eds.), *Handbook of emotions* (pp. 53–66). New York: Guilford Press.

Poasa, K. (1992). The Samoan *fa'afafine*: One case study and discussion of transsexualism. *Journal of Psychology and Human Sexuality, 5*(3), 39–51.

Pollack, W. (1998). *Real boys: Rescuing our sons from the myths of boyhood*. New York: Random House.

Pollack, W. S., & Levant, R. F. (Eds.). (2001). *New psychotherapy for men*. San Francisco: Jossey-Bass.

Pollitt, K. (1999, May 3). The end of an era at Radcliffe. *Newsweek*, p. 66.

Pollner, M. (1998). The effects of interviewer gender in mental health interviews. *Journal of Nervous and Mental Disease, 186*(6), 369–373.

Pomerleau, A., Bolduc, D., Malcuit, G., & Cossette, L. (1990). Pink or blue: Environmental stereotypes in the first two years of life. *Sex Roles, 22*, 359–367.

Ponticas, Y. (1992). Sexual aversion versus hypoactive sexual desire: A diagnostic challenge. *Psychiatric Medicine, 10*(2), 273–282.

Ponton, L. E. (1997). *The Romance of risk: Why teenagers do the things they do*. New York: Basic Books.

Pope, H. G., & Katz, K. L. (1992). Psychiatric effects of anabolic steriods. *Psychiatric Annals, 22*, 24–29.

Pope, H. G., Gruber, A. J., Mangweth, B., Bureau, B., deCol, C., Jouvent, R., & Hudson, J. I. (2000). Body image perception among men in three countries. *American Journal of Psychiatry, 157*(8), 1297–1302.

Popenoe, D. (1996). *Life without father*. New York: Free Press.

Population Reference Bureau. (1999). *World Population Data Sheet*. Washington, DC: Author.

Post, D. (2001). Region, poverty, subship and gender inequality in Mexican education: Will targeted welfare policy make a difference for girls? *Gender and Education, 15*(3), 468–489.

Potterat, J. J., Rothenberg, R. B., Muth, S. Q., Darrow, W. M., & Phillips-Plummer, L. (1998). Network structural dynamics and infectious disease propagation. *Journal of Sex Research, 35*(4), 333–340.

Povey, H. (1998). "That spark from heaven" or "of the earth": Girls and boys and knowing mathematics. In A. Clark & E. Millard (Eds.), *Gender in the secondary curriculum* (pp. 131–144). New York: Routledge.

Powell, A. D., & Kahn, A. S. (1995). Racial differences in women's desire to be thin. *Journal of Eating Disorders, 17*, 191–195.

Powell, E. (2001). Where do lefties go? *Discover, 22*(1), 28.

Powell, G. N. (1997). The sex difference in employees inclinations regarding work-family programs: Why does it exist, should we care, and what should be done about it (if anything?). In S. Parasuraman & J. H. Greenhaus (Eds.), *Integrating work and family* (pp. 167–175). Westport, CT: Quorum Books.

Powlishta, K. K. (1995). Intergroup processes in childhood. Social categorization and sex role development. *Developmental Psychology, 31*, 781–788.

Powlishta, K. K. (2000). The effect of target age on the activation of gender stereotypes. *Sex Roles, 42*(3–4), 271–282.

Pratto, F., & Hegarty, P. (2000). The political psychology of reproductive strategies. *Psychological Science, 11*(1), 57–62.

Pratto, F., Stallworthe, L. M., Sidanius, J., & Siers, B. (1997). The gender gap in occupational role attainment: A social dominance approach. *Journal of Personality and Social Psychology, 72*, 37–53.

Press, A. L., & Cole, E. R. (1999). *Speaking of abortion*. Chicago: University of Chicago Press.

Preston, L. (1998). Female physicians more likely to use hormone therapy. *Emory Report, 50*, 25. Available online at http://www.emory.edu/EMORY_REPORT/erarchive/1998/March/ermarch.23/

3_2398Doctors.html. Retrieved on May 20, 2002.

Preves, S. E. (1998). For the sake of the children: De-stigmatizing intersexuality. *Journal of Clinical Ethics, 9*(4), 411–420.

Priest, D. (1998). Sexual integration has not harmed the military. In B. Leone (Ed.), *Working women: Opposing viewpoints* (pp. 129–136). San Diego: Greenhaven Press.

Prior, P. M. (1999). *Gender and mental health*. New York: New York University Press.

Prussel, D. (1998). Feminists take on UNOCAL. *The Progressive, 62*, 1–15.

Pryor, J. B., & Whalen, N. J. (1997). A typology of sexual harassment: Characteristics of harassers and the social circumstances under which sexual harassment occurs. In W. O'Donohue (Ed.), *Sexual harassment: Therapy, research and treatment* (pp. 129–151). Boston: Allyn and Bacon.

Pryor, J. B., DeSouza, E. R., Fitness, J., Hutz, C., Kumpf, M., Lubbert, K., Pesonen, O., & Erber, M. W. (1997). Gender differences in the interpretation of socio-sexual behavior: A cross-cultural perspective on sexual harassment. *Journal of Cross-Cultural Psychology, 28*(5), 509–534.

Pryor, J. B., Giedd, J. L., & Williams, K. B. (1995). A social psychological model for predicting sexual harassment. *Journal of Social Issues, 51*, 69–84.

Pugliesi, K. (1995). Work and well-being: Gender differences in the psychological consequences of employment. *Journal of Health and Social Behavior, 36*, 57–71.

Quam-Wickham, N. (1999). Rereading man's conquest of nature: Skill, myths and the historical construction of masculinity in Western extractive industries. *Men and Masculinities, 2*(2), 135–151.

Quay, H. C. (1993). The psychobiology of undersocialized aggressive conduct disorder: A theoretical perspective. *Developmental Psychopathology, 5*, 165–180.

Queen, S. A., & Habenstein, R. W. (1967). *The family in various cultures*. Philadelphia: Lippincott.

Query, J. L., Jr., & Flint, L. J. (1996). The caregiving relationship. In N. Vanzetti & S. Duck (Eds.), *A lifetime of relationships* (pp. 455–483). Pacific Grove, CA: Brooks/Cole.

Quindlen, A. (2000, September 11). The right to be ordinary. *Newsweek*, p. 82.

Raabe, P. H. (1998). Women, work and family in Czech Republic and comparisons with West. *Community, Work & Family, 1*(1), 51–63.

Raag, T., & Rackliff, C. L. (1998). Preschoolers' awareness of social expectations of gender: Relationship to toy choices. *Sex Roles, 38*(9–10), 685–700.

Radke-Yarrow, M. (1998). *Children of depressed mothers: From early childhood to maturity.* New York: Cambridge University Press.

Raesaenen, S., Hakko, H., Herva, A., Isohanni, M., Nieminen, P., & Moring, J. (1999). Gender differences in long-stay psychiatric inpatients. *International Journal of Mental Health, 28*(1), 69–85.

Raffaeli, M., & Larsen, R. W. (Eds.). (1999). *Homeless and working youth around the world: Exploring developmental issues.* San Francisco: Jossey-Bass.

Rahman, Q., & Silber, K. (2000). Sexual orientation and the sleep–wake cycle: A preliminary investigation. *Archives of Sexual Behavior, 29*(2), 127–134.

Raine, A., Lenez, T., Bihrle, S., LaCasse, L., & Coletti, P. (2000). Reduced prefrontal gray matter volume and reduced autonomic activity in antisocial personality disorder. *Archives of General Psychiatry, 57*(2), 119–127.

Rainey, L. M., & Borders, L. D. (1997). Influential factors in career orientation and career aspirations of early adolescent girls. *Journal of Counseling Psychology, 44*(2), 160–172.

Rajecki, D. W., Dame, J. A., Creek, K. J., Barrickman, P. J., et al. (1993). Gender casting in television toy advertisements: Distributions, message content analysis and evaluations. *Journal of Consumer Psychology, 2*(3), 307–327.

Ranson, G. (2001). Men at work: Change or no-change in the era of the "new father." *Men and Masculinities, 4*(1), 3–26.

Rantalaiho, L. (1997). Contextualising gender. In L. Rantalaiho & T. Heiskanen (Eds.), *Gendered practices in working life* (pp. 15–30). New York: St. Martin's Press.

Rantalaiho, L., & Heiskanen, T. (1997). *Gendered practices in working life.* New York: St. Martin's Press.

Rasanen, L. (1997). Desegregation: How to climb invisible walls. In L. Rantalaiho & T. Heiskanen (Eds.), *Gendered practices in working life* (pp. 159–173). New York: St. Martin's Press.

Rasanen, S., Hakko, H., Herva, A., Isohanni, M., Nieminen, P., & Moring, J. (1999). Gender differences in long-stay psychiatric inpatients. *International Journal of Mental Health 28*(1), 69–85.

Rasekh, Z., Bauer, H. M., Manos, M. M., & Iacopino, V. (1998). Women's health and human rights in Afghanistan. *Journal of the American Medical Association, 280,* 449–455.

Raudenbush, B., & Zellner, D. A. (1997). Nobody's satisfied: Effects of abnormal eating behaviors and actual and perceived weight status on body image satisfaction in males and females. *Journal of Social and Clinical Psychology, 16,* 95–110.

Rawlins, W. K. (1992). *Friendship matters.* Hawthorne, NY: Aldine deGruyter.

Ray, G. E., & Cohen, R. (1996). Children's friendships: Expectations for prototypical versus actual best friends. *Child Study Journal 26*(3), 209–227.

Ray, R. (1999). *Fields of protest: Women's movements in India.* Minneapolis: University of Minnesota Press.

Raynolds, L. T. (2001). New plantations, new workers: Gender and production politics in the Dominican Republic. *Gender and Society, 15*(1), 7–28.

Real, T. (1997). *I don't want to talk about it: Overcoming the secret legacy of male depression.* New York: Scribner.

Regan, P. C., & Dreyer, C. S. (1999). Lust? Love? Status? Young adults motives for engaging in casual sex. *Journal of Psychology & Human Sexuality, 11*(1), 1–24.

Reid, M., & Hammersley, R. (2000). Sociopsychobiological issues in understanding gender relations and gender differences. *Psychology, Evolution, and Gender, 2*(2), 167–173.

Reilly, J. M., & Woodhouse, C. R. J. (1989). Small penis and the male sexual role. *Journal of Urology, 142,* 569–571.

Reina, R. (1959). Two patterns of friendship in a Guatemalan community. *American Anthropologist, 61,* 44–50.

Reine, A., Venables, P., & Williams, M. (1990). Relationships between central and autonomic measures of arousal at age 15 years and criminality at age 24 years. *Archives of General Psychiatry, 47,* 1003–1007.

Reiner, W. G. (1996). Case study: Sex reassignment in a teenage girl. *Journal of the Academy of Child & Adolescent Psychiatry, 35*(6), 799–603.

Reiss, I. (1986). *Journey into sexuality: An explanatory voyage.* Englewood Cliffs, NJ: Prentice Hall.

Reite, M., Sheeder, J., Teale, P., Adams, M., Richardson, D., Simon, J., Jones, R. H., & Rojas, D. C. (1997). Magnetic resonance imaging evidence of sex differences in cerebral lateralization in schizophrenia. *Archives of General Psychiatry, 54*(5), 433–440.

Remennick, L. (2000). Childless in the land of imperative motherhood. Stigma and coping among infertile Israeli women. *Sex Roles, 43*(11/12), 821–842.

Renshaw, J. R. (1999). Women in management roles. *Japan Quarterly, 23,* 15–24.

Renzetti, C. M., & Curran, D. J. (1995). *Women, men and society* (2nd ed.). Boston: Allyn and Bacon.

Reuters, H. (2000). Placebo best, Viagra for treatment of sexual dysfunction in women. Available online at http://www.womenshealth.medscape. Retrieved on May 24, 2000.

Reuters Medical News. (2000a). Anorexia bulimia rates have soared in Asia. Available online at http://www.womenshealth.medscape. Retrieved on September 29, 2001.

Reuters Medical News. (2000b). Global HIV infection exceeds predictors by 50%. Available online at http://www.womenshealth.medscape.com. Retrieved on November 11, 2000.

Reuters Medical News. (2000c). Male mortality rate higher than female rate in almost all species. Available online at http://www.womenshealth.medscape.com. Retrieved on February 2, 2001.

Reuters Medical News. (2000d). You weren't listening dear . . . Available online at http://www.womenshealth.medscape.com. Retrieved on November 28, 2000.

Reuters Medical News. (2001a). Ratio of female to male children in India has dropped drastically. Available online at http://www.womenshealth.medscape.com. Retrieved on April 5, 2001.

Reuters Medical News. (2001b). Simplified medical abortion feasible in developing countries. Available online at http://www.womenshealth.medscape.com. Retrieved on May 5, 2001.

Reynolds, C. F., Frank, E., Mazumdar, S., Meltzer, C. D., Mulsant, B. H., Pollock, B. G., Schulgerg, H. C., Schulz, R.,

Shear, M. K., & Smith, G.(1999). In R. Schulz, G. Maddox, & M. P. Lawton (Eds.), *Annual review of gerontology and geriatrics.* Vol. 18: *Intervention research with older adults* (pp. 48–74). New York: Springer.

Rhode, D. L. (1997). *Speaking of sex: The denial of gender inequality.* Cambridge, MA: Harvard University Press.

Rice, G. C., & Anderson, C., Risch, N., & Ebers, G. (1999). Male homosexuality: Absence of linkage to microsatellite markers at Xq28. *Science, 284,* 665–667.

Richards, M. H, Crowe, P. A., Larson, R., & Swarr, A. (1998). Developmental patterns and gender differences in the experience of peer companionship during adolescence. *Child Development, 69*(1), 154–163.

Richardson, F. C., & Fowers, B. J. (1997). Critical theory, post-modernism and hermeneutics. Insights for critical psychology. In D. Fox & I. Prilleltensky (Eds.), *Critical psychology: An introduction* (pp. 265–283). Thousand Oaks, CA: Sage.

Richardson, J. T. E. (1997). Introduction to the study of gender differences in cognition. In P. J. Caplan, M. Crawford, J. S. Hyde, & J. T. E. Richardson (Eds.), *Gender differences in human cognition* (pp. 3–29). New York: Oxford University Press.

Richman-Loo, N., & Weber, R. (1996). Gender and weapons design. In J. H. Stiehms (Ed.), *It's our military too!* (pp. 136–155). Philadelphia: Temple University Press.

Rickabaugh, C. A. (1998). *Sex and gender: Student projects and exercises.* New York: McGraw-Hill.

Ridgeway, C. L., & Diekema, D. (1992). Are gender differences status differences? In C. L. Ridgeway (Ed.), *Gender, interaction and inequality* (pp. 157–179). New York: Springer.

Riessman, C. K. (2000). Stigma and everyday resistance practices: Childless women in South India. *Gender and Society, 14*(1), 111–135.

Riger, S. (1992). Epistemological debates, feminist voices: Science, social values and the study of women. *American Psychologist, 47,* 730–746.

Rind, B., & Tromovitch, P. (1997). A meta-analytic review of findings from national samples on psychological correlates of child sexual abuse. *Journal of Sex Research, 34*(3), 237–255.

Rind, B., Tromovitch, P., & Bauserman, R. (1998). A meta-analytic examination of assumed properties of child sexual abuse using college samples. *Psychological Bulletin, 124*(1), 22–53.

Riphenberg, C. (1997). Women's status and cultural expression: Changing gender relations and structural adjustment in Zimbabwe. *Africa Today, 44*(1), 33–50.

Risman, B. J. (1989). Can men "mother"? Life as a single father. In J. Risman & P. Schwartz (Eds.), *Gender in intimate relationships: A microstructural approach* (pp. 155–164). Belmont, CA: Wadsworth.

Robins, L., & Regier, D. (Eds.). (1991). *Psychiatric disorders in America: The epidemiological catchment area study.* New York: Free Press.

Robinson, M. (1999). Initial teacher education in a changing South Africa: Experiences, reflections, and challenges. *Journal of Education for Teaching, 25*(3), 191–201.

Robinson, N. M., Abbott, R. D., Berninger, V. W., & Busse, J. (1996). The structure of abilities in math-precocious young children: Gender similarities and differences. *Journal of Educational Psychology, 88*(2), 341–352.

Rogers, D. D. (1995). Daze of our lives: The soap operas as feminine text. In G. Dines & J. M. Humez (Eds.), *Gender, race, and class in media: A text reader* (pp. 325–331). Thousand Oaks, CA: Sage.

Rogers, L., Resnick, M. D., Mitchell, J. E., & Blum, R. W. (1997). The relationship between socioeconomic status and eating-disordered behaviors in a community sample of adolescent girls. *International Journal of Eating Disorders, 22,* 15–23.

Rogers, M. F. (1999). *Barbie culture.* Thousand Oaks, CA: Sage.

Rohner, R. P. (1998). Father love and child development: History and current evidence. *Current Directions in Psychological Science, 7*(5), 157–161.

Rojas, D. C., Teale, P., Sheeder, J., Simon, J., & Reite, M. (1997). Sex-specific expressions of Heschl's gyrus function and structural abnormalities in paranoid schizophrenia. *American Journal of Psychiatry, 154*(12), 1655–1662.

Rojewski, J. W., & Hill, R. B. (1998). Influence of gender and academic risk behavior on career decision making and occupational choice in early adolescence. *Journal of Education for Students at Risk, 3*(3), 265–287.

Rolland, J. R. (1994). *Families, illness and disability.* New York: Basic Books.

Romaine, S. (1999). *Communicating gender.* Mahwah, NJ: Erlbaum.

Romans, S. E. (1998). *Folding back the shadows: A perspective on women's mental health.* Dunedin, New Zealand: University of Otago Press.

Romero, M. (1992). *Maid in the USA.* New York: Routledge.

Root, M. P. (1998). Women. In L. C. Lee & N. W. S. Zane (Eds.), *Handbook of Asian American psychology* (pp. 211–231). Thousand Oaks, CA: Sage.

Rosaldo, M. Z. (1974). Women, culture and society: A theoretical overview. In M. Z. Rosaldo & L. Lamphere (Eds.), *Women, culture and society* (pp. 17–42). Stanford, CA: Stanford University Press.

Rosario, V. A. (1997). *Science and the homosexualities.* New York: Routledge.

Rosario, V. A. (1998). Homosexual bio-histories: Genetic nostalgias and the quest for paternity. In V. A. Rosario (Ed.), *Science and homosexualities* (pp. 1–23). New York: Routledge.

Rose, S. (1995). Women's friendships. In J. C. Chisler & A. H. Hemstreet (Eds.), *Variations on a theme: Diversity and the psychology of women* (pp. 79–105). New York: State University of New York (SUNY) Press.

Rose, S., & Frieze, I. H. (1993). Young singles' contemporary dating scripts. *Sex Roles, 28,* 499–509.

Rose, S., Zand, D., & Cini, M. (1994). Lesbian courtship rituals. In E. D. Rothblum & K. A. Brehony (Eds.), *The Boston marriage today* (pp. 70–85). Amherst: University of Massachusetts Press.

Rose, V. L. (1999). Guidelines for the use of sildenafil. *American Family Physician, 59*(4), 1054.

Rosen, L. N. (1998). Psychological effects of sexual harassment: Appraisal of harassment, and organizational climate among US army soldiers. *Military Medicine, 163*(2), 63–67.

Rosen, L. N., & Martin, L. (1998). Incidence and perceptions of sexual harassment among male and female U.S. Army soldiers. *Military Psychology, 10*(4), 239–257.

Rosen, R. C., & Leiblum, S. R. (1995a). *Case studies in sex therapy.* New York: Guilford.

Rosen, R. C., & Leiblum, S. R. (1995b). Treatment of sexual disorders in the

1990's: An integrated approach. *Journal of Counseling and Clinical Psychology,* 63(6), 877–890.

Rosenbaum, M., & Cohen, E. (1999). Egalitarian marriages, spousal support, resourcefulness, and psychological distress among Israeli working women. *Journal of Vocational Behavior,* 54(1), 102–113.

Rosenblatt, E. (Ed.). (1996). *Criminal injustices: Confronting the prison crisis.* Boston: South End Press.

Rosenfield, S. (1999). Splitting the difference: Gender, the self and mental health. In C. S. Aneshensel & J. C. Phelan (Eds.), *Handbook of the sociology of mental health* (pp. 209–225). New York: Kluwer Academic.

Rosenthal, D. A., Smith, A. M. A., & de Visser, R. (1999). Personal and social factors influencing age at first intercourse. *Archives of Sexual Behavior,* 28(4), 319–333.

Rosenthal, P. (1996). Gender and managers' casual attributions for subordinate performance: A field story. *Sex Roles,* 34(1–2), 1–15.

Rosenthal, R. (1991). *Meta-analytic procedures for social research* (Rev. ed.). Newbury Park, CA: Sage.

Rosser, S. V. (1997). *Re-engineering female friendly science.* New York: Teachers College Press.

Rothblum, E. D., & Factor, R. (2001). Lesbians and their sister as a control group: Demographic and mental health factors. *Psychological Science,* 12(1), 63–69.

Rottnick, M. (Ed.) (1999). *Sissies and tomboys: Gender nonconformity and homosexual childhood.* New York: New York University Press.

Rotundo, A. (1993). *American manhood.* New York: Basic Books.

Rovet, J., Netley, C., Bailey, J., Keenan, M., & Stewart, D. (1995). Intelligence and achievement in children with extra X aneuploidy. A longitudinal perspective. *American Journal of Medical Genetics,* 60, 356–363.

Rowe, R., & Snizek, W. E. (1995). Gender differences in work values: Perpetuating the myth. *Work and Occupations,* 22(2), 215–229.

Rowland, D. L., & Burnett, A. L. (2000). Pharmacotherapy in the treatment of male sexual dysfunction. *Journal of Sex Research,* 37(3), 226–243.

Rowland, J. H. (1998). Breast cancer: Psychosocial aspects. In E. A. Blechman & K. D. Brownell (Eds.), *Behavioral medicine and women* (pp. 577–587). New York: Guilford Press.

Roy, A. (1998). Images of domesticity and motherhood in Indian television commercials: A critical study. *Journal of Popular Culture,* 32(3), 117–134.

Roy, N. J. (2000, April). The he hormones. *New York Times Magazine,* 2, 46–51, 58–59, 69, 79.

Rudman, L. A. (1998). Self-promotion as a risk factor for women: The costs and benefits of counter stereotypical impression management. *Journal of Personality & Social Psychology,* 74, 629–645.

Rugg, M. (1995). La difference vive. *Nature,* 373, 561–562.

Ruhm, C. J. (1996). Gender differences in employment behavior during late middle age. *Journal of Gerontology,* 51B, 511–517.

Russell, A., & Thompson, M. S. (2000). Introduction: Contraception across cultures. In A. Russell, E. J. Sobo, & M. S. Thompson (Eds.), *Contraception across cultures: Technologies, choices and constraints* (pp. 3–22). New York: Berg.

Russell, J. A. (1994). Is there universal recognition of emotion from facial expression? A review of the cross-cultural studies. *Psychological Bulletin,* 115, 102–141.

Russo, N. F. (1979). Overview: Sex roles, fertility and the motherhood mandate. *Psychology of Women Quarterly,* 4, 7–15.

Rutter, P. (2000). Reasonable woman/Reasonable man: The emergence of a modern archetype of gender equality in political life. In T. Singer (Ed.), *The vision thing: Myth, politics and psyche in the world* (pp. 241–250). Florence, KY: Taylor & Francis/Routledge.

Rutter, V., & Schwartz, P. (1996). Same sex couples: Courtship, commitment and context. In A. E. Auhagen & M. von Salisch (Eds.), *The diversity of human relationships* (pp. 197–226). New York: Cambridge University Press.

Rys, G. S., & Bear, G. G. (1997). Relational aggression and peer relations: Gender and developmental issues. *Merrill-Palmer Quarterly,* 43(1), 87–106.

Sacker, D., Firth, R., Fitzpatrick, K., Lynch, K., & Bartley, M. (2000). Comparing health inequality in men and women: Prospective study of mortality 1986–96. *British Medical Journal,* 320, 1303–1307.

Sacks, K. B. (1998). How Jews became white. In P. S. Rotherberg (Ed.), *Race, class, and gender in the United States* (pp. 100–114). New York: St. Martin's Press.

Sadker, M., & Sadker, D. (1994). *Failing at fairness: How America's schools cheat girls.* New York: Scribner.

Sadler, G. C. (1997). Women in combat: The U. S. military and the impact of the Persian Gulf War. In L. Weinsteim & C. C. White (Eds.), *Wives and warriors: Women in the military in the U.S. and Canada* (pp. 79–97). Westport, CT: Bergin & Garvey.

Sagan, C., & Druyan, A. (1992). *Shadows of forgotten ancestors.* New York: Random House.

Salmela-Aro, K., & Nurmi, J. E. (1996). Uncertainty and confidence in interpersonal projects: Consequences for social relationships and well-being. *Journal of Social and Personal Relationships,* 13(1), 109–122.

Salmela-Aro, K., Nurmi, J., Saisto, T., & Halmesmaki, E. (2000). Women's and men's personal goals during the transition to parenthood. *Journal of Family Psychology,* 14(2), 171–186.

Samborn, H. V. (2000). Higher hurdles for women. *ABA Journal,* 86, 30–33.

Samorar, L. A., Porter, R. C., & Stefani, L. A. (1998). *Communication between cultures* (3rd ed.). Belmont, CA: Wadsworth.

Sanders, G., & Wright, M. (1997). Sexual orientation differences in cerebral asymmetry and in the performance of sexually dimorphic cognitive and motor tasks. *Archives of Sexual Behavior,* 26(5), 463–480.

Sanders, S. A., & Reinisch, J. M. (1999). Would you say you "had sex" if . . . . *JAMA,* 281(3), 275–277.

Sandfort, T. G. M., & Cohen-Kettenis, P. T. (2000). Sexual behavior in Dutch and Belgian children as observed by their mothers. *Journal of Psychology and Human Sexuality,* 12(1–2), 105–115.

Sandnabba, N. K., & Ahlberg, C. (1999). Parents' attitudes and expectations about children's cross-gender behavior. *Sex Roles,* 40(3–4), 249–263.

Sangree, W. H. (1992). Grandparenthood and modernization: The changing status of male and female elders in Tiriki, Kenya and Irigwe, Nigeria. *Journal of Cross-cultural Gerontology,* 7(4), 331–361.

Sanker, A. (1986). Sisters and brothers, lovers and enemies: Marriage resistance in southern Kwangtung. In E. Blackwood (Ed.), *The many faces of homosexuality: Anthropological approaches to homosexual behavior* (pp. 69–83). New York: Harrington Park Press.

Santrock, J. (1994). *The authoritative guide to self-help books*. New York: Guilford Press.

Santrock, J. W. (1998). *Child development* (8th ed.). New York: McGraw-Hill.

Sapolsky, R. (1997). Testosterone rules. *Discover, 18*(3), 44–50.

Sapolsky, R. M. (2000). The trouble with testosterone: Will boys just be boys? In M. S. Kimmel (Ed.), *The gendered society reader* (pp. 14–19). New York: Oxford University Press.

Saris, R. N., & Johnston-Robledo, I. (2000). Poor women are still shut out of mainstream psychology. *Psychology of Women Quarterly, 24*(3), 233–235.

Sartorius, N. (1989). Recent research activities in WHO's mental health programme. *Psychological Medicine, 19,* 233–244.

Sattel, J. W. (1998). Men, inexpressiveness, and power. In B. M. Clinchy & J. K. Norem (Eds.), *The gender and psychology reader* (pp. 498–504). New York: New York University Press.

Sattler, D., Shabatay, V., & Kramer, G. P. (1998). *Abnormal psychology in context: Voices and perspectives*. Boston: Houghton Mifflin.

Saucier, D. M., & Kimura, D. (1998). Intrapersonal motor but not extra-personal targeting skill is enhanced during the midluteal phase of the menstrual cycle. *Developmental Neuropsychology, 14,* 385–398.

Savage, R. M., & Gouvier, W. D. (1992). Rey Auditory-Verbal Learning Test: The effects of age and gender norms for delayed recall and story recognition trials. *Archives of Clinical Neuropsychology, 7,* 407–414.

Savin-Williams, R. C. (1995). Lesbian, gay male, and bisexual adolescence. In A. R. D'Augelli & C. J. Patterson (Eds.), *Lesbian, gay, and bisexual identities over the lifespan* (pp. 165–189). New York: Oxford University Press.

Schaefers, K. G., Epperson, D. L., & Nauta, M. M. (1997). Women's career development: Can theoretically derived variables predict persistence in engineering majors? *Journal of Counseling Psychology, 44*(2), 173–183.

Schafer, M. J. (1999). International non-governmental organizations and third world education in 1990: A cross-national study. *Sociology of Education, 72*(2), 69–88.

Schairer, C., Lubin, J., Troisi, R., Sturgeon, S., Brinton, L., & Hoover, R. (2000). Menopausal estrogen and estrogen-progestin replacement therapy and breast cancer risk. *Journal of the American Medical Association, 283*(4), 485–491.

Scharrer, E., & Bissell, K. (2000). Overcoming traditional boundaries. The role of political activity in media coverage of first ladies. *Women and Politics, 21*(1), 55–83.

Schiebinger, L. (1999). *Has feminism changed science?* Cambridge, MA: Harvard University Press.

Schiebinger, L. (2000). *Feminism and the body*. New York: Oxford University Press.

Schlenker, J. A., Caron, S. L., & Halteman, W. A. (1998). A feminist analysis of *Seventeen* magazine: A content analysis from 1945–1995. *Sex Roles, 38*(1–2), 135–145.

Schmidt, S. L., Oliveira, R. M., Rocha, F. R., & Abreu-Villaca, Y. (2000). Influences of handedness and gender on the grooved peg board test. *Brains and Cognition, 44,* 445–454.

Schnarch, B. (1992). Neither man nor woman: *Berdache*—A case for non-dichotomous gender construction. *Anthropologica, 34*(1), 105–121.

Schoeber, J. M. (1998). Feminizing genitoplasty for intersex infants. In M. D. Stringer, K. T. Oldham, P. D. E. Mouriquand, & E. R. Howard (Eds.), *Pediatric surgery and urology: Long term outcomes* (pp. 549–558). London: Saunders.

Schoon, I. (2001). Teenage job aspirations and career attainment in adulthood: A 17-year follow-up study of teenagers who aspired to become scientists, health professionals or engineers. *International Journal of Behavioral Development, 25*(2), 124–132.

Schraedley, P. K., Gotlib, I. H., & Hayward, C. (1999). Gender differences in correlates of depressive symptoms in adolescents. *Journal of Adolescent Health, 25*(2), 98–108.

Schuhrke, B. (2000). Young children's curiosity about other people's genitals. *Journal of Psychology and Human Sexuality, 12*(1–2), 27–48.

Schultz, D. P., & Schultz, S. E. (1996). *A history of modern psychology*. Fort Worth, TX: Harcourt Brace.

Schutte, K. K., Hearst, J., & Moos, R. H. (1997). Gender differences in the relations between depressive symptoms and drinking behavior among problem drinkers: A three-way study. *Journal of Consulting and Clinical Psychology, 65*(3), 392–404.

Schutzman, M. (1999). *The real thing: Performance, hysteria, and advertising*. Hanover, NH: Wesleyan University Press.

Schwartz, I. M. (1999). Sexual activity prior to coital interaction: A comparison between males and females. *Archives of Sexual Behavior, 28,* 63–69.

Schwartz, M. D., & Leggett, M. S. (1999). Bad dates or emotional trauma? The aftermath of campus sexual assault. *Violence Against Women, 5*(3), 251–271.

Schwartz, P. (1994). *Peer marriage*. New York: Free Press.

Schwartz, P., & Rutter, V. (1998). *The gender of sexuality*. Thousand Oaks, CA: Sage.

Scott, N., & Creighton, P. (1997). Gender issues in employment selection. In J. Radford (Ed.), *Gender and choice in education and occupation* (pp. 104–140). New York: Routledge.

Scrivner, R. (1997). Gay men and non-relational sex. In R. F. Levant & G. R. Brooks (Eds.), *Men and sex* (pp. 229–256). New York: Wiley.

Seager, J. (1997). *The state of women in the world atlas*. New York: Penguin USA.

Sears, S. R., & Hennessey, A. C. (1996). Students' perceived closeness to professors: The effect of school, professor gender and student gender. *Sex Roles, 35*(9–10), 651–655.

Seattle-Post-Intelligencer. (1999, May 4). Hussein's wife says she broke tradition, p. A3.

Sedikides, C., Oliver, M. B., & Campbell, W. C. (1994). Perceived benefits and costs of romantic relationships for women and men: Implications for exchange theory. *Personal Relationships, 1,* 5–21.

Seeman, M. V. (2000). *Women and psychosis*. Conference Report *Medscape.Women's Health, 5*(2). Available online at *http://*

www.medscape.com/. Retrieved on April 21, 2002.

Segall, M. H., Lonner, W. J., & Berry, J. W. (1998). Cross-cultural psychology as a scholarly discipline. *American Psychologist, 53*(10), 1101–1110.

Seidler, V. J. (1992). Rejection, vulnerability and friendship. In P. M. Nardi (Ed.), *Men's friendships* (pp. 15–33). Newbury Park, CA: Sage.

Seidlitz, L., & Diener, E. (1998). Sex differences in the recall of affective experiences. *Journal of Personality & Social Psychology, 74*, 262–271.

Sellers, S. L. (2001). Social mobility and psychological distress: Differences among black American men and women. *African-American Research Perspectives, 7*(1), 117–147.

Seltzer, J. A., & Brandreth, Y. (1994). What fathers say about involvement with children after separation. *Journal of Family Issues 15*(1), 49–77.

Serbin, L. A., Powlishta, K. K., & Gulko, J. (1993). The development of sex typing in middle childhood. *Monographs of the Society for Research in Child Development, 58*(2, Serial No. 232), 1–73.

Sered, S. S. (1999). "Woman" as a symbol and women as agents. In M. M. Ferree, J. Lorber, & B. B. Hess (Eds.), *Revisioning gender* (pp. 193–218). Thousand Oaks, CA: Sage.

Seward, R., Yeats, D., Seward, J., & Stanley-Stevens, L. (1993). Fathers' time spent with their children: A longitudinal assessment. *Family Planning Perspectives, 27*, 275–283.

Seymour, E. (1995). The loss of women from science, mathematics, and engineering undergraduate majors: An explanatory account. *Science Education, 74*(4), 437–473.

Shaffer, D. R., Pegalis, L. J., & Bazzini, D. G. (1996). When boy meets girl (revisited): Gender, gender role orientation and prospect of future interaction as determinants of self-disclosure among same- and opposite-sex acquaintances. *Personality and Social Psychology Bulletin, 22*(5), 495–506.

Shah, A. (1999). Taliban holds first public execution of a woman. *The Independent*, p. 19.

Sharps, M. J., Welton, A. L., & Price, J. L. (1993). Gender and task in the determination of spatial cognitive performance.

Psychology of Women Quarterly, 17, 71–83.

Shashaani, L. (1994). Gender differences in computer experience and its influence on computer attitudes. *Journal of Educational Computing Research, 11*(4), 347–367.

Shattuc, J. C. (1997). *The talking cure: TV talk shows and women*. New York: Routledge.

Shaywitz, B. A., Shaywitz, S. E., Pugh, K. R., Constable, R. T., Skudlarski, P., Fulbright, R. K., Bronen, R. A., Fletcher, J. M., Shankweiler, D. P., Katz, L., & Gore, J. C. (1995). Sex differences in the functional organization of the brain for language. *Nature, 373*, 607–609.

Sheeran, P., Abraham, C., & Orbell, S. (1999). Psychosocial correlates of heterosexual condom use. *Psychological Bulletin, 125*(1), 90–132.

Shefer, T., Potgieter, C., & Strebel, A. (1999). Teaching gender at a South African university. *Feminism & Psychology, 9*(2), 127–133.

Sheifer, S. E., Canos, M. R., Weinfurt, K. P., Arora, U. K., Mendelsohn, F. O., Gersh, B. J., & Weissman, N. J. (2000). Sex differences in coronary artery size assessed by intravascular ultrasound. *American Heart Journal, 139*(4), 649–653.

Sher, G., & Fisch, J. D. (2000). Vaginal sildenafil (Viagra): a preliminary report of a novel method to improve uterine artery blood flow and endometrial development in patients undergoing IVF. *Human Reproduction, 15*(4), 806–809.

Sherr, L. (1996). Tomorrow's era: Gender, psychology and HIV infection. In L. Sherr, C. Harkins, & L. Bennet (Eds.), *AIDS as a gender issue: Psychological perspectives* (pp. 16–14). New York: Taylor & Francis.

Shidlo, A. (1994). Internalized homophobia: Conceptual and empirical issues in measurement. In B. Greene & G. M. Herek (Eds.), *Lesbian and gay psychology* (pp. 176–205). Thousand Oaks, CA: Sage.

Shields, S. A. (1975a). Functionalism, Darwinism and the psychology of women: A study in social myth. *American Psychologist, 30*, 739–754.

Shields, S. A. (1975b). Ms. Pilgrim's progress: The contributions of Leta Stetter Hollingworth to the psychology of women. *American Psychologist, 30*, 852–857.

Shields, S. A. (1982). The variability hypothesis: The history of a biological model of sex difference in intelligence. *Signs, 7*, 769–797.

Shields, S. A. (1990). Conceptualizing the biology–culture relationship in emotion: An analogy with gender. *Cognition and Emotion, 4*, 359–374.

Shields, S. A. (1991). Gender in the psychology of emotion: A selective research review. In K. T. Strongman (Ed.), *International review of studies on emotion* (Vol. 1, pp. 227–245). Chichester, England: Wiley.

Shields, S. A. (1995). The role of emotion belief and values in gender development. In N. Eisenberg (Ed.), *Social development* (pp. 212–232). Thousand Oaks, CA: Sage.

Shields, S. A. (1998). Gender in the psychology of emotions: A selective research review. In D. L. Anselmi & A. L. Law (Eds.), *Questions of gender: Perspectives and paradoxes* (pp. 376–389). New York: McGraw-Hill.

Shields, S. A. (1999). Thinking about gender, thinking about theory: gender and emotional experience. In A. Fischer (Ed.), *Gender and emotion*. Cambridge, England: Cambridge University Press.

Shinagawa, L. H. (1996). The impact of immigration on the demography of Asian Pacific Americans. In B. O. Hiong & R. Lee (Eds.), *Reframing the immigration debate* (pp. 59–126). Los Angeles: Leadership Education for Asian Pacifics & UCLA Asian American Studies Center.

Shotlund, R. L., & Hunter, B. A. (1995). Women's "token resistant" and compliant sexual behaviors are related to uncertain sexual intentions and rape. *Personality & Social Psychological Bulletin, 21*, 226–236.

Shrier, D. K. (Ed.). (1996). Sexual harassment in the workplace and academia: Psychiatric issues. *Clinical Practice Series*, No. 38. Washington, DC: American Psychiatric Press.

Shu, X., & Marini, M. M. (1998). Gender related changes in occupational aspirations. *Sociology of Education, 71*(1), 43–67.

Shulman, S., & Seiffge-Krenke, I. (1997). *Fathers and adolescents*. New York: Routledge.

Siegel, J. M., Aneshensel, C. S., Taub, B., Cartwell, D. P., & Driscoll, A. K. (1998).

Adolescent depressed mood in a multiethnic sample. *Journal of Youth and Adolescence, 27*(4), 423–427.

Signorella, M., Bigler, R. S., & Liben, L. (1993). Developmental differences in children's gender schemata about others: A meta-analytic review. *Developmental Review, 13*(2), 147–183.

Signorielli, N., McLeod, D., & Healy, E. (1994). Gender stereotypes in MTV commercials: The beat goes on. *Journal of Broadcasting and Electronic Media, 38*(1), 91–101.

Silverstein, L. B. (1996a). Evolutionary psychology and the search for sex differences. *American Psychologist, 51*, 160–161.

Silverstein, L. B. (1996b). Fathering is a feminist issue. *Psychology of Women Quarterly, 20*(1), 3–38.

Silverstein, L. B., & Auerbach, C. F. (1999). Deconstructing the essential father. *American Psychologist, 54*(6), 397–407.

Silverstein, L. B., & Phares, V. (1996). Expanding the mother–child paradigm: An examination of dissertation research 1986–1994. *Psychology of Women Quarterly, 20*(1), 39–54.

Silverthorne, Z. A., & Quinsey, V. (2000). Sexual partner age preferences of homosexual and heterosexual men and women. *Archives of Sexual Behavior, 29*(1), 67–76.

Simic, A. (1978). Aging and the aged in cultural perspective. In B. G. Myerhoff & A. Simic (Eds.), *Life's career-aging: Cultural variations in growing old* (pp. 9–22). Beverly Hills, CA: Sage.

Simon, A. (1998). The relationship between stereotypes and attitudes toward lesbians and gays. In G. M. Herek (Ed.), *Stigmas and sexual orientation* (pp. 62–81). *Psychological perspectives on lesbian and gay issues* (Vol. 4). Thousand Oaks, CA: Sage.

Simons, M. (2001, December 8). Professional women from Afghanistan meet to press for full rights. *New York Times*, Section B, p. 3.

Simpson, G. (1996). Factors influencing the choice of law as a career by black women. *Journal of Career Development, 22*(3), 197–209.

Singh, D., Vidaurri, M., Zambarano, R. J., & Dabbs, J. M., Jr. (1999). Lesbian erotic role identification: Behavioral, morphological and hormonal correlates. *Journal*

of *Professional and Social Psychology, 76*, 1035–1049.

Sistrunk, F., & McDavid, J. W. (1971). Sex variables in conforming behavior. *Journal of Personality & Social Psychology, 17*, 200–207.

Skaalvik, E. M., & Rankin, R. J. (1994). Gender differences in mathematics and verbal achievement, self-perception and motivation. *British Journal of Educational Psychology, 64*(3), 419–428.

Skuse, D. H., James, R. S., Bishop, D. V. M., Coppin, B., et al. (1997, June). Evidence from Turner's syndrome of an imprinted X-linked locus affecting cognitive function. *Nature, 387*(6634), 705–708.

Slijper, F. M. E., Drop, S. L. S., Molenaar, J. C., deMuinck, K. S., & Sabine, M. P. F. (1998). Long term psychological evaluation of intersex children. *Archives of Sexual Behavior, 27*(2), 125–144.

Slosarz, W. J. (2000). Analysis of sexual behavior acceptance in Poland. *Journal of Psychology and Human Sexuality, 12*(3), 79–87.

Smith, C. D. (1998). "Men don't do this sort of thing:" A case study of the social isolation of househusbands. *Men & Masculinities, 1*(2), 138–172.

Smith, G. (1996). Dichotomies in the making of men. In C. McLean, M. Carey, & C. White (Eds.), *Men's ways of being* (pp. 29–50). New York: Westview Press.

Smith, L. (Ed.). (1999). *Nike is a goddess.* New York: Publisher Group West.

Smith, L. M. (1996). *Sex and revolution: Women in socialist Cuba.* New York: Oxford University Press.

Smith, L., & Mathews, J. (1997, December 7). In Virginia, a sobering lesson doesn't sink in: Binge drinking remains common on campuses despite recent tragedies. *The Washington Post*, B1, B7.

Smith, M., & Lin, K. (1996). Gender and ethnic differences in the pharmacogenetics of psychotropics. In M. F. Jensvold, U. Halbreich, & J. A. Hamilton (Eds.), *Psychopharmacology and women.* Washington, DC: American Psychiatric Association.

Smith, P. (Ed.). (1996). *Boys.* Boulder, CO: Westview Press.

Smith, P. B., Dugan, S., & Trompenaars, F. (1997). Locus of control and affectivity by gender and occupational status: A 14 nation study. *Sex Roles, 36*(1–2), 51–77.

Snitow, A. B. (1995). Mass market ro-

mance: Pornography for women is different. In G. Dines & J. M. Humez (Eds.), *Gender, race, and class in media: A text reader* (pp. 190–201). Thousand Oaks, CA: Sage.

Snodgrass, S. E. (1985). Women's intuition: The effect of subordinate role on interpersonal sensitivity. *Journal of Personality & Social Psychology, 49*, 146–155.

Snodgrass, S. E. (1992). Further effects of role versus gender on interpersonal sensitivity. *Journal of Personality & Social Psychology, 62*, 154–158.

Snyder, R., & Hasbrouck, L. (1996). Feminist identity, gender traits, and symptoms of disturbed eating among college women. *Psychology of Women Quarterly, 20*, 593–598.

Sochting, I., Skoe, E. E., & Marcia, J. E. (1994). Care-oriented moral reasoning and prosocial behavior: A question of gender or sex-role orientation. *Sex Roles, 31*(3–4), 131–147.

Sommers, C. H. (2000). *The war against boys: How misguided feminism is harming our young sons.* New York: Simon & Schuster.

Sommers, S., & Kosmitzki, C. (1988). Emotion and social context: An American German comparison. *British Journal of Social Psychology, 27*, 35–49.

Sonnert, G., & Holton, G. (1995). *Gender differences in science careers: The project access study.* New Brunswick, NJ: Rutgers University Press.

Sontag, S. (1979). The double standard of aging. In J. H. Williams (Ed.), *Psychology of women: Selected readings.* New York: Norton.

Sookhoo, D. (1998). Coronary heart disease among Asians: Cultural and psychological considerations. *International Psychologist, 38*(1), 21–23.

Sorenson, G., Lewis, B., & Bishop, R. (1996). Gender, job factors and coronary heart disease risk. *American Journal of Health Behavior, 20*(1), 3–13.

South, S. J., & Spitze, G. (1994). Housework in marital and non-marital households. *American Sociological Review, 59*, 327–347.

Spence, J. T. (1985). Gender identification and its implications for masculinity and femininity. In T. B. Sonderegger (Ed.), *Nebraska symposium on motivation and achievement: Psychology and gender* (Vol. 32, pp. 59–95). Lincoln: University of Nebraska Press.

Spence, J. T., & Buckner, C. E. (2000). Instrumental and expressive traits, trait stereotypes and sexist attitudes: What do they signify? *Psychology of Women Quarterly, 24*(1), 44–62.

Spence, J. T., Helmreich, R., & Stapp, J. (1974). The Personal Attributes Questionnaire. A measure of sex-role stereotypes and masculinity–femininity. *JSAS Catalog of Selected Documents in Psychology, 4*, 43. (Ms. no. 617).

Sperry, L., & Mosak, H. H. (1993). Personality disorders. In L. Sperry & J. Carlson (Eds.), *Psychopathology and psychotherapy: From diagnosis to treatment* (pp. 269–368). Muncie, IN: Accelerated Development.

Spitzer, R. L., Gibbon, M., Skodol, A. E., Williams, J. B., & First, M. B. (Eds.). (1994). *DSM-IV case book* (pp. 363–365). Washington, DC: American Psychiatric Press.

Sprecher, S., & Felmlee, D. (1997). The balance of power in romantic heterosexual couples over time from "his" and "her" perspectives. *Sex Roles, 37*(5–6), 361–379.

Sprecher, S., & Regan, P. (1996). College virgins: How men and women perceive their sexual status. *Journal of Sex Research, 33*, 3–15.

Springer, S. P., & Deutsch, G. (1998). *Left brain, right brain* (5th ed.). New York: Freeman.

Sroufe, L. A., Bennett, C., England, M., & Urban, J. (1993). The significance of gender boundaries in preadolescence: Contemporary correlates and antecedents of boundary violation and maintenance. *Child Development, 64*, 455–466.

Stacey, J. (1996). *In the name of the family: Rethinking values in the postmodern age.* Boston: Beacon Press.

Stacey, J. (1998). Gay and lesbian families are here: All our families are queer: Let's get used to it. In S. Coontz, M. Parson, & G. Raley (Eds.), *American families: A multicultural reader* (pp. 372–405). New York: Routledge.

Stack, C. B. (1997). Different voices, different visions: Gender, culture, and moral reasoning. In M. Baca-Zinn, P. Hondagneu-Sotelo, & M. Messner (Eds.), *Through the prism of difference: Readings on sex and gender* (pp. 51–57). Boston: Allyn and Bacon.

Staggenborg, S. (1998). *Gender, family and social movements.* Thousand Oaks, CA: Sage.

Stake, J. E. (2000). When situations call for instrumentality and expressiveness: Resource appraisal , coping strategy choice and adjustment. *Sex Roles, 42*(9–10), 865–886.

Stam, H. (Ed.). (1998a). *The body and psychology.* London: Sage.

Stam, H. J. (1998b). The body's psychology and psychology's body. In H. J. Stam (Ed.), *The body and psychology* (pp. 1–12). Thousand Oaks, CA: Sage. Stanton, A. L. (1995). Psychology of women's health: Barriers and pathways to knowledge. In A. L. Stanton & J. Gallant (Eds.), *The psychology of women's health: Progress and challenges in research and application* (pp. 3–21). Washington, DC: American Psychological Association.

Stanton, A. L., & Gallant, S. J. (Eds.). (1995). *The psychology of women's health: Progress and challenges in research and application.* Washington, DC: American Psychological Association.

Staples, R., & Johnson, L. B. (1993). *Black families at the crossroads.* San Francisco: Jossey-Bass.

Steele, C. (1997). Race and the schooling of Black Americans. In L. A. Peplau & S. E. Taylor (Eds.), *Sociocultural perspectives in social psychology: Current readings* (pp. 359–371). Upper Saddle River, NJ: Prentice Hall.

Steele, J. R. (1999). Teenage sexuality and media practice: Factoring in the influences of family, friends, and school. *Journal of Sex Research, 36*(4), 331–341.

Steil, J. M. (1997). *Marital equity: Its relationship to the well-being of husbands and wives.* Thousand Oaks, CA: Sage.

Steil, J. M., & Hay, J. L. (1997). Social comparison in the workplace: A study of 60 dual-career couples. *Personality & Social Psychology, 23*(4), 427–438.

Stephens, M. A., & Franks, M. M. (1999). Parent care in the context of women's multiple roles. *Current Directions in Psychological Science, 8*(5), 149–152.

Steuve, A., & Link, B. G. (1998). Gender differences in the relationship between mental illness and violence: evidence from a community-based epidemiological study in Israel. *Social Psychiatry and Psychiatric Epidemiology, 33*(Suppl. 1), S61–S67.

Stevens, N. (1995). Gender and adaptation to widowhood in later life. *Aging and Society, 15*, 37–58.

Stewart, M. (1998). Gender issues in physics education. *Educational Research, 40*(3), 283–293.

Stice, E., Shaw, H., & Nemeroff, C. (1998). Dual pathway model of bulimia nervosa: Longitudinal support for dietary restraint and effect regulation mechanisms. *Journal of Social and Clinical Psychology, 17*, 129–149.

Stiegel-Moore, R. H., & Cachelin, F. M. (1999). Disordered body image concerns and disordered eating in adolescent girls: Real and protective factors. In N. G. Johnson, M. C. Roberts, & J. Worell (Eds.), *Beyond appearance: A new look at adolescent girls* (pp. 85–107). Washington, DC: American Psychological Association.

Stiehm, J. H. (Ed.). (1996). *It's our military too!* Philadelphia: Temple University Press.

Stillion, J. M. (1995). Premature death among males. In D. Sabo & D. F. Gordon (Eds.), *Men's health and illness: Gender, power and the body* (pp. 46–67). Thousand Oaks, CA: Sage.

Stock, W. E. (1997). Sex as commodity: Men and the sex industry. In R. F. Levant & G. R. Brooks (Eds.), *Men and sex: New psychological perspectives* (pp. 100–132). New York: Wiley.

Stockdale, M. S., Visio, M., & Batra, L. (1999). The sexual harassment of men: Evidence for a broader theory of sexual harassment and sex discrimination. *Psychology, Public Policy and Law, 5*(3), 630–664.

Stohs, J. H. (1995). Predictors of conflict over the household division of labor among women employed full time. *Sex Roles, 33*(3–4), 257–275.

Stoppard, J. M., & Gruchy, C. D. G. (1993). Gender context and expression of positive emotion. *Personality & Social Psychology Bulletin, 19*, 143–150.

Stoudemir A.e, (1998). *Human behavior: An introduction for medical students* (3rd ed.). Philadelphia: Lippincott-Raven.

Stowasser, B. (1998). Gender issues and contemporary Quran interpretation. In Y. Y. Haddad & J. L. Esposito (Eds.), *Islam, gender and social change* (pp. 30–44). New York: Oxford University Press.

Strauss, M. A. (1993). Identifying offenders in criminal justice research on domestic assault. *American Behavioral Scientist, 36*(5), 587–600.

Strauss, M., Gelles, R., & Steinmetz, S. (1980). *Behind closed doors: Violence in the American family*. Garden City, NJ: Anchor Books.

Strauss, R., & Goldberg, W. A. (1999). Self and possible selves during the transition to fatherhood. *Journal of Family Psychology, 13*(2), 244–259.

Strickland, B. (1995). Research on sexual orientation and human development. A commentary. *Developmental Psychology, 31*, 137–140.

Striegel-Moore, R. H., & Cachelin, F. M. (1999). Disordered body image concerns and disordered eating in adolescent girls: Real and projected factors. In N. G. Johnson, M. C. Roberts, & J. Worell (Eds.), *Beyond appearance: A new look at adolescent girls* (pp. 85–107). Washington, DC: American Psychological Association.

Strodtbeck, F. L. (1980). *A study of husband–wife interaction in three cultures*. New York: Arno Press.

Stroh, L. K., Brett, J. M., & Reilly, A. H. (1992). All the right stuff: A comparison of female and male managers career progression. *Journal of Applied Psychology, 77*, 251–260.

Stroh, L. K., Brett, J. M., & Reilly, A. H. (1996). Family structure, glass ceiling, and traditional explanations for the differential turnover of female and male managers. *Journal of Vocational Behavior, 49*, 99–118.

Stromquist, N. P. (1999). The impact of structural adjustment programmes in Africa and Latin America. In C. Heward & S. Bunwaree (Eds.), *Gender, education and development: Beyond access to empowerment* (pp. 17–32). London: Zed Books.

Stuart, S., & Bery, R. (1996). Powerful grassroots women communicators: Participatory video in Bangladesh. In D. Allen, R. R. Rush, & S. J. Kaufman (Eds.), *Women transforming communication* (pp. 303–312). Thousand Oaks, CA: Sage.

Stubbs, K. R. (1992). *Sacred orgasms*. Berkeley, CA: Secret Garden.

Stumpf, H., & Stanley, J. C. (1998). Stability and change in gender-related differences on the college board advanced placement and achievement tests. *Current Directions in Psychological Science, 7*(6), 192–196.

Stunkard, A., Sorenson, T., & Schulsinger, F. (1983). Use of the Danish adoption register for the study of obesity and thinness. In S. Kety, L. Rowland, R. Sidman, & S. Matthysse (Eds.), *Genetics of neurological and psychiatric disorders* (pp. 115–120). New York: Raven Press.

Subrahmanyam, K., & Greenfield, P. M. (1994). Effect of video game practice on spatial skills in girls and boys. *Journal of Applied Developmental Psychology, 15*, 13–32.

Subrahmanyam, K., & Greenfield, P. M. (1998). Computer games for girls: What makes them play? In J. Cassell & H. Jenkins (Eds.), *From Barbie to Mortal Kombat: Gender and computer games* (pp. 46–71). Cambridge, MA: MIT Press.

Sudarkasa, N. (1999). Interpreting the African heritage in Afro-American family organization. In S. Coontz, M. Parson, & G. Raley (Eds.), *American families: A multicultural reader* (pp. 59–73). New York: Routledge.

Sullivan, M. (1996). Rozzie and Harriet? Gender and family patterns of lesbian co-parents. *Gender & Society, 10*, 747–767.

Sullivan, P. F., Bulik, C. M., Fear, J. L., & Pickering, A. (1998). Outcome of anorexia nervosa: A case controlled study. *American Journal of Psychiatry, 155*(7), 939–946.

Sunday Times. (1999, October 10). Why blondes can't have more fun. Available online at http://www.suntimes.co.za/1999/10/10/insight/in10.htm. Retrieved April 21, 2002.

Sundstrom, G. (1994). Care by families: An overview of trends. In Organisation for Economic Co-operation and Development (OECD), *Caring for frail elderly people: New directions in care*. Social Policy Studies, 14. Paris: Organisation for Economic Co-operation and Development (OECD).

Suryakusuma, J. (1996). The state and sexuality in new order Indonesia. In L. Sears (Ed.), *Fantasizing the feminine in Indonesia* (pp. 92–119). Durham, NC: Duke University Press.

Susman, E. G., Worrall, B. K., Murowchick, E., Frobose, C. A., & Schwab, J. E. (1996). Experience and neuroendocrine parameters of development: Aggressive behavior and competencies. In D. M. Stoff & R. B. Cairns (Eds.), *Aggression and violence: Genetic, neurobiological & biosocial perspectives* (pp. 267–289). Mahwah, NJ: Erlbaum.

Sutker, P. B., Bugg, F., & West, J. A. (1993). Antisocial personality disorder. In P. B. Sutker & H. E. Adams (Eds.), *Comprehensive handbook of psychopathology* (pp. 337–369). New York: Plenum.

Suzuki, M. F. (1995). Women and television: Portrayal of women in the mass media. In K. Fujimura-Fanselow & A. Kameda (Eds.), *Japanese women: New feminist perspectives on the past, present and future* (pp. 75–90). New York: Feminist Press.

Svenska Institute. (2000). *Childcare in Sweden*. Available online at http://www.si.se.eng.esverige.childcar.html.

Swaab, D. F., & Hofman, M. A. (1990). An enlarged suprachiasmatic nucleus in homosexual men. *Brain Research, 537*, 141–148.

Swaab, D. F., & Hofman, M. A. (1995). Sexual differentiation of the human hypothalamus in relation to gender and sexual orientation. *Trends in Neurosciences, 18*, 264–270.

Swaab, D. F., Zhou, J., Fodos, M., & Hofman, M. A. (1997). Sexual differentiation of the human hypothalamus: Differences according to sex, sexual orientation and transsexuality. In L. Ellis & L. Ebertz (Eds.), *Sexual orientation: Toward biological understanding* (pp. 131–150). Westport, CT: Praeger.

Swain, S. O. (1992). Men's friendships with women. In P. M. Nardi (Ed.), *Men's friendships* (pp. 153–171). Newbury Park, CA: Sage.

Swillen, A., Fryns, J. P., Kleczkowska, A., Massa, G., Vanderschueren-Lodeweyckx, M., & Van den Berghe, H. (1993) Intelligence, behaviour and psychosocial development in Turner syndrome. A cross-sectional study of 50 pre-adolescent and adolescent girls (4–20 years). *Genetic Counseling, 4*(1), 7–18.

Swim, J., Borgida, E., Maruyama, G., & Myers, D. G. (1989). Joan McKay versus John McKay: Do gender stereotypes bias evaluations? *Psychological Bulletin, 105*, 409–429.

Swoboda, F. (1995, November 25). Law, education failing to break glass ceiling. *The Washington Post*, p. C2.

Tallerico, M. (1997). Gender and school administration. In J. Bank & P. Hall (Eds.), *Gender, equity and schooling: Policy and practice* (pp. 182–210). New York: Garland.

Tanaka-Matsumi, J., & Draguns, J. (1997). Culture and psychopathology. In J. W. Berry, M. H. Segall, & C. Kagitcibasi (Eds.), *Handbook of cross-cultural psychology. Vol. 3: Social behavior and applications* (pp. 449–491). Boston: Allyn and Bacon.

Tang, T., & McCollum, S. L. (1996). Sexual harassment in the workplace. *Public and Personnel Management, 25*(1), 53–58.

Tangri, S. S., & Hayes, S. M. (1997). Theories of sexual harassment. In W. O'Donohue (Ed.), *Sexual harassment: Theories, research and treatment* (pp. 112–128). Boston: Allyn and Bacon.

Tannen, D. (1990). *You just don't understand: Women and men in conversation.* New York: Ballantine Books.

Tanofsky, M. B., Wilfley, D. E., Spunnell, E. B., Welch, R., & Brownell, K. D. (1997). Comparison of men and women with binge eating disorder. *International Journal of Eating Disorders, 21*(1), 49–54.

Taris, T. W., & Bok, I. A. (1999). On gender specificity of person characteristics in personnel advertisements: A study among future applicants. *Journal of Psychology, 132*(6), 593–610.

Tasker, F. L., & Golombok, S. (1997). *Growing up in a lesbian family: Effects on child development.* New York: Guilford.

Tator, M. (1998). Violent delights in children's literature. In J. Goldstein (Ed.), *Why we watch* (pp. 69–87). New York: Oxford University Press.

Tavris, C. (1992). *The mismeasure of women.* New York: Simon & Schuster.

Terborgh, A. A. (1995). Family planning among indigenous populations in Latin America. *International Family Planning Perspectives, 21*(4), 143–149, 166.

Terman, L. M. (1925). *Genetic studies of genius. Vol. 1: Mental and physical traits of a thousand gifted children.* Stanford, CA: Stanford University Press.

Terwilliger, J. S., & Titus, J. C. (1995). Gender differences in attitude and attitude changes among mathematically talented youth. *Gifted Child Quarterly, 39,* 29–35.

Theodore, H., & Lloyd, B. F. (2000). Age and gender role conflict: A cross-sectional study of Australian men. *Sex Roles, 42*(11–12), 1027–1042.

Theriault, S. W., & Holmberg, D. (1998). The new old-fashioned girl: Effects of gender and social desirability on reported gender-role ideology. *Sex Roles, 39*(1–2), 97–112.

Theriot, N. (1996). Women's voices in nineteenth-century medical discourse: A step toward deconstructing science. In B. Laslett, S. G. Kohlstedt, H. Longino, & E. Hammonds (Eds.), *Gender and scientific authority* (pp. 124–154). Chicago: University of Chicago Press.

Thoits, P. A. (1994). Stressors and problem solving: The individual as psychological activist. *Journal of Health and Social Behavior, 35,* 143–159.

Thomas, A., & Sullen, S. (1974). *Racism and psychiatry.* Secaucus, NJ: Citadel.

Thomas, D. Q. (1994). In search of solutions: Women's police stations in Brazil. In M. Davies (Ed.), *Women and violence* (pp. 32–43). London: Zed Books.

Thomas, S. (1997). Why gender matters: The perceptions of women office holders. *Women and Politics, 17*(1), 27–53.

Thomas, S. (1998). Women and elective office: Past, present and future. In S. Thomas & C. Wilcox (Eds.), *Women and elective office* (pp. 1–14). New York: Oxford University Press.

Thompson, E. H., & Pleck, J. H. (1995). Masculinity ideologies: A review of research instrumentation on men and masculinities. In R. F. Levant & W. S. Pollack (Eds.), *A new psychology of men* (pp. 129–163). New York: Basic Books.

Thompson, M. S., & Keith, V. M. (2001). The blacker the berry: Gender skin tone, self-esteem and self-efficacy. *Gender & Society, 15*(3), 336–357.

Thompson, N. (1997). Masculinity and loss. In D. Field, J. Hockey, & N. Small (Eds.), *Death, gender and ethnicity* (pp. 76–88). New York: Routledge.

Thompson, S. (1995). *Going all the way: Teenage girls' tales of sex, romance and pregnancy.* New York: Hill and Wang.

Thompson, T. L., & Zerbinos, E. (1995). Gender roles in animated cartoons: Has the picture changed in 20 years? *Sex Roles, 32*(9/10), 651–672.

Thompson, T. L., & Zerbinos, E. Z. (1997). Television cartoons: Do children notice it's a boys' world? *Sex Roles, 37*(5–6), 415–432.

Thorne, A., & Michaelieu, Q. (1996). Situating adolescent gender and self-esteem with personal memories. *Child Development, 67*(4), 1374–1390.

Thorne, B. (1993). *Gender play: Girls & boys in school.* New Brunswick, NJ: Rutgers University Press.

Thurer, S. L. (1994). *The myths of motherhood.* New York: Penguin.

Thurman, S. (1997). "Dear love mother Eunice": Gender, motherhood and Shaker spirituality. *Church History, 6*(4), 750–761.

Tiano, S. (1994). *Patriarchy on the line.* Philadelphia: Temple University Press.

Tiefer, L. (1992). *Sex is not a natural act and other essays.* Boulder, CO: Westview Press.

Timmers, M., Fischer, A. H., & Manstead, A. S. R. (1998). Gender differences in motives for regulating emotions. *Personality and Social Psychology Bulletin, 24*(9), 974–985.

Tjaden, P., & Thoennes N. (2000). Prevalence and consequences of male to female and female to male intimate partner violence as measured by the National Violence Against Women Survey. *Violence Against Women, 6*(2), 142–161.

Tobacco smoke and women: A special vulnerability? (2000). *Harvard Women's Health Watch, 7*(9), 1–3.

Todd, H. (1996). *Women at the center: Grameen Bank borrowers after one decade.* Boulder, CO: Westview Press.

Toliver, S. D. (1998). *Black families in corporate America.* Thousand Oaks, CA: Sage.

Tolman, D. L. (1999). Object lessons: Romance, violation and female adolescent sexual desire. *Journal of Sex Education and Therapy, 25*(1), 70–79.

Tolman, D. L., & Brown, L. M. (2001). Adolescent girls voices: Resonating resistance in body and soul. In R. K. Unger (Ed.), *Handbook of the psychology of women and gender* (pp. 133–155). New York: Wiley.

Tom-Orme, L. (1995). Native American women's health concerns. In D. L. Adams (Ed.), *Health issues for women of color* (pp. 27–41). Newbury Park, CA: Sage.

Top, T. J. (1991). Sex bias in the evaluation of performance in the scientific, artistic, and literary professions: A review. *Sex Roles, 24*(1–2), 73–106.

Torgalsboen, A. (1999). Full recovery from schizophrenia: The prognostic role of premorbid adjustment symptoms at first admission, precipitating events and gender. *Psychiatry Research, 88* (2), 143–152.

Travis, C. B. (1988). *Women and health psychology: Biomedical issues*. Mahwah, NJ: Erlbaum.

Travis, C. B., Meginnis, K. L., & Bardari, K. M. (2000). Beauty, sexuality and identity: The social control of women. In C. B. Travis & J. W. White (Eds.), *Sexuality, society and feminism* (pp. 237–272). Washington, DC: American Psychological Association.

Travis, C. B., & White, J. W. (Eds.). (2000). *Sexuality, society and feminism*. Washington, DC: American Psychological Association.

Treffke, H., & Tiggemann, M., & Ross, M. (1992). The relationship between attitude, assertiveness, and condom use. *Psychology and Health, 6*, 45–52.

Trehub, S. E., Unyk, A. M., Kamenetsky, S. B., & Hill, D. S. (1997). Mothers and fathers singing to infants. *Developmental Psychology, 33*(3), 500–507.

Trentham, S., & Larwood, L. (1998). Gender discrimination and the workplace: An examination of rational bias theory. *Sex Roles, 38*(1–2), 1–28.

Trepagnier, B. (1994). The white and black bodies. *Feminism and Psychology, 4*(1), 199–205.

Triandis, H. C. (1994). *Culture and social behavior*. New York: McGraw-Hill.

Triandis, H. C. (1995). *Individualism and collectivism*. Boulder, CO: Westview Press.

Trobst, K. K., Collins, R. L., & Embree, J. M. (1994). The role of emotion in social support provision: Gender, empathy and expressions of distress. *Journal of Social and Personal Relationships, 11*(1), 15–62.

Truelove, M. (1996). Minding the baby in Canada. In K. England (Ed.), *Who will mind the baby?* (pp. 36–45). London: Routledge.

Tsui, L. (1998). The effects of gender, education, and personal skills self-confidence on income business management. *Sex Roles, 38*, 363–373.

Tucker, C. J., Barber, B. L., & Eccles, J. S. (1997). Advice about life plans and personal problems in late adolescent sibling relationships. *Journal of Youth & Adolescence, 26*(1), 63–76.

Tucker, J. S., Friedman, H. S., Schwartz, J. E., Criqui, M. H., Tomlinson-Keasey, C., Wingard, D. L., & Martin, L. R. (1997). Parental divorce: Effects on individual behavior and longevity. *Journal of Personality and Social Psychology, 73*(2), 381–391.

Twenge, J. M. (1997). "Mrs. his name": Women's preferences for married names. *Psychology of Women Quarterly, 21*, 417–429.

Uba, L. (1994). *Asian-American personality patterns, identity, and mental health*. New York: Guilford.

Umberson, D., Wortman, C. B., & Kessler, R. C. (1992). Widowhood and depression: Explaining long-term gender differences in vulnerability. *Journal of Health and Social Behavior, 33*, 10–24.

Unger, R. K. (1981). Sex as a social reality: Field and laboratory research. *Psychology of Women Quarterly, 5*, 645–653.

Unger, R. K. (1990). Imperfect reflections of reality: Psychology constructs gender. In R. T. Hare-Mustin & J. Marecek (Eds.), *Making a difference: Psychology and the construction of gender* (pp. 102–149). New Haven, CT: Yale University Press.

Unger, R. K. (1998). *Resisting gender: Twenty-five years of feminist psychology*. Thousand Oaks, CA: Sage.

Unger, R. K. (Ed.). (2000). *Handbook of the psychology of women and gender*. San Francisco: Jossey-Bass.

Unger, R. K., & Crawford, M. (1998a). Commentary: Sex and gender—the troubled relationship between terms and concepts. In D. L. Anselmi & A. L. Law (Eds.), *Questions of gender: Perspectives and paradoxes* (pp. 18–21). New York: McGraw-Hill.

Unger, R. K., & Crawford, M. (1998b). Sex and gender: The troubled relationship between terms and concepts. In D. L. Anselmi & A. L. Law (Eds.), *Questions of gender: Perspectives and paradoxes* (pp. 18–20). New York: McGraw-Hill.

UNICEF. (1997). The state of the world's children, *1997*. New York: United Nations Publications. Available on line at http://www.unicef.org/sowc97/sowcrite.htm.

United Nations. (1993). *Declaration on the elimination of all forms of violence against women*. New York: United Nations Publications.

United Nations. (1999a). *Women and health: Mainstreaming the gender perspective into the health sector*. New York: United Nations Publications.

United Nations. (1999b). *World survey on the role of women in development: Globalization, gender and work*. New York: United Nations Publications.

United States Bureau of Labor Statistics. (2000). Median weekly earnings of full-time wage and salary workers by detailed occupation and sex. *Employment and Earnings, 47*(1), 213–218.

United States Bureau of the Census. (1996, February). *How we're changing: Demographic state of the nation: 1996*. (Current Population Reports, Special Studies Series P-23-191). Washington, DC: U.S. Government Printing Office.

United States Bureau of the Census. (1998). *Statistical abstract of the United States* (118th ed.). Washington, DC: U.S. Government Printing Office.

United States Department of Labor. (2000). *Highlights of women's earnings*. Washington, DC: Bureau of Labor Statistics.

Unterhalter, E. (1999). The schooling of South African girls. In C. Heward & S. Bunwaree (Eds.), *Gender, education and development: Beyond access to empowerment* (pp. 49–64). London: Zed Books.

Usmaniani, S., & Daniluk, J. (1997). Mothers and their adolescent daughters: Relationship between self-esteem, gender-role identity and body image. *Journal of Youth & Adolescence, 26*(1), 45–62.

Vailliant, G. E. (1977). *Adaptation to life*. Boston: Little, Brown.

Vaillant, G. E. (1998). Where do we go from here? *Journal of Personality, 66*(2), 1147–1157.

Valian, V. (1998). *Why so slow? The advancement of women*. Cambridge, MA: MIT Press.

Van Howe, R. S. (1998). Circumcision and infectious diseases revisited. *Pediatric Infectious Diseases Journal, 17*(1), 1–6.

van Roosmalen, E., & McDaniel, S. A. (1998). Sexual harassment in academia: A hazard to women's health. *Women and Health, 28*(2), 33–54.

VanAllen, J. (1997). "Aba Riots" or "Igbo women's war"? Ideology, stratification and the invisibility of women. In C. B. Brettell & C. F. Sargent (Eds.), *Gender in cross-cultural perspectives* (pp. 488–503). Upper Saddle River, NJ: Prentice Hall.

Vance, E. B., & Wagner, N. W. (1976). Written descriptions of orgasms: A study of sex differences. *Archives of Sexual Behavior, 6*, 87–98.

Vandenberg, S. G. (1987). Sex differences in mental retardation and their implications for sex differences in abilities. In J. M. Reinisch, L. A. Rosenblum, & S. A.

Sanders (Eds.), *Masculinity/femininity: Basic perspectives* (pp. 157–171). New York: Oxford University Press.

Vanderecken, W., & Beumont, P. J. V. (Eds.). (1998). *Treating eating disorders: Ethical, legal and personal issues*. New York: New York University Press.

Vandewater, E. A., & Stewart, A. J. (1998). Making commitments, creating lives. *Psychology of Women Quarterly, 22,* 717–738.

Vannoy, D., Rimashevskaya, N., Cubbins, L., Malysheva, M., Meshterkina, E., & Pishlakova, M. (1999). *Marriage in Russia: Couples during the economic transition*. Westport, CT: Praeger.

Vanwesenbeeck, I., & Bekker, M., & van Lenning, A. (1998). Gender attitudes, sexual meanings and interactional patterns in heterosexual encounters among college students in the Netherlands. *Journal of Sex Research, 35*(9), 317–327.

Vasta, R., Knott, J. A., & Gaze, C. E. (1996). Can spatial training erase the gender differences on the water level task? *Psychology of Women Quarterly, 20,* 549–567.

Veniegas, R. C., & Conley, T. D. (2000). Biological research on women's sexual orientation: Evaluating the scientific evidence. *Journal of Social Issues, 56*(2), 267–282.

Veniegas, R. C., & Peplau, L. A. (1997). Power and the quality of same sex friendships. *Psychology of Women Quarterly, 21,* 279–297.

Verma, K. K., Khaitan, B. K., & Singh, O. P. (1998). The frequency of sexual dysfunction in patients attending a sextherapy clinic in north India. *Archives of Sexual Behavior, 27*(3), 309–312.

Vigorito, A. J., & Curry, T. J. (1998). Marketing masculinity: Gender identity and popular magazines. *Sex Roles, 38*(1–2), 135–152.

Visher, E. B., & Visher, J. S. (1993). Remarriage families and step parenting. In F. Walsh (Ed.), *Normal family processes* (2nd ed., pp. 235–253). New York: Guilford.

Vobejda, B. (1998). "Unwed Pairs Make Up 4 Million Households." Washington Post, July 27, p. A10.

Vogt, T. M., Hollis, J. F., Lichtenstein, E., Stevens, V. J., Glasgow, R., & Whitlock, E. (1998). The medical care system and prevention: The need for a new paradigm. *HMO Practice, 12*(1), 5–13.

Vonk, R., & Ashmore, R. D. (1993). The multifaceted self: Androgyny reassessed by open-ended self-descriptions. *Social Psychology Quarterly, 56*(4), 278–287.

Wajcman, J. (1998). *Managing like a man: Women and men in corporate management*. University Park: Pennsylvania State University Press.

Waldner, L. K., & Magruder, B. (1999). Coming out to parents: Perceptions of family relations, perceived resources, and identity disclosure for gay and lesbian adolescents. *Journal of Homosexuality, 37*(2), 83–100.

Walker, A. E. (1998). *The menstrual cycle*. New York: Routledge Press.

Walker, E. A., Gelfand, A., Katon, W. J., Koss, M. P., Von Korff, M., Bernstein, D., & Russo, J. (1999). Adult health status of women with histories of childhood abuse and neglect. *American Journal of Medicine, 107*(4), 332–339.

Walker, L. E. (1984). *The battered woman syndrome*. New York: Springer.

Walker, L. E. (1999). Psychology and domestic violence around the world. *American Psychologist, 54*(1), 21–29.

Walker, L. E., & Meloy, J. R. (1998). Stalking and domestic violence. In J. Reid & J. R. Meloy (Eds.), *The psychology of stalking: Clinical and forensic perspectives* (pp. 139–161). San Diego, CA: Academic Press.

Walker, L. J. (1984). Sex differences in the development of moral reasoning: A critical review. *Child Development, 55,* 677–691.

Walker, L. J. (1997). Is morality gendered in early parent–child relationships? A commentary on the Lollis, Ross and Leroux study. *Merrill-Palmer Quarterly, 43*(1), 148–159.

Walkerdine, V. (1997a). *Daddy's girl*. Cambridge, MA: Harvard University Press.

Walkerdine, V. (1997b). Femininity as performance. In M. M. Gergen & Davis (Eds.), *Toward a new psychology of gender* (pp. 171–184). New York: Routledge.

Walkup, J., & Gallagher, S. K. (1999). Schizophrenia and the life course: National findings on gender differences in disability and service use. *International Journal of Aging and Human Development, 49*(2), 79–105.

Wallerstein, J. (1998). Children of divorce: A society in search of policy. In M. M. Masson, A. Skolnich, & S. D. Sugarman

(Eds.), *All our families* (pp. 66–94). New York: Oxford University Press.

Wallin, K. L., Wiklund, F., Angstrom, T., Bergman, F., Stendahl, U., Wadell, G., Hallmans, G., & Dillner, J. (1999). Type-specific persistence of human papillomavirus DNA before the development of invasive cervical cancer. *New England Journal of Medicine, 341,* 1633–1638.

Walsh, B. T., & Devlin, M. J. (1998). Eating disorders: Progress and problems. *Science, 280,* 1387–1390.

Walsh, D. P., Rostosky, S. S., & Kawaguchi, M. C. (2000). A normative perspective of adolescent girls' developing sexuality. In C. B. Travis & J. W. White (Eds.), *Sexuality, society and feminism* (pp. 111–140). Washington, DC: American Psychological Association.

Walsh, M. R. (1977). *"Doctors wanted: No women need apply": Sexual barriers in the medical profession 1935–1975*. New Haven, CT: Yale University Press.

Walsh-Childers, K. (1996). Women as sex partners. In R. M. Lester (Ed.), *Images that injure* (pp. 81–85). Westport, CT: Praeger.

Walter, P. (1999). Defining literacy and its consequences in the developing world. *International Journal of Education, 18*(1), 31–48.

Walter, T., & Davie, G. (1998). The religiosity of women in the modern West. *British Journal of Sociology, 49*(4), 640–660.

Walters, V. (1993). Stress, anxiety, and depression: Women's accounts of their health problems. *Social Science and Medicine, 36*(4), 393–402.

Walzer, S. (1998). *Thinking about the baby*. Philadelphia: Temple University Press.

Ward, L. M., & Rivadeneyra, R. (1999). Contributions of entertainment television to adolescent sexual attitudes and expectations: The role of viewing versus viewer involvement. *Journal of Sex Research, 36*(3), 237–249.

Ward, T., Hudson, S. M., Johnston, L., & Marshall, W. L. (1997). Cognitive distortions in sex offenders: An integrative review. *Clinical Psychology Review, 17*(5), 479–507.

Wark, G. R., & Krebs, D. (1996). Gender and dilemma differences in real-life moral judgement. *Developmental Psychology, 32,* 220–230.

Warne, G. L. (1998). Advances and challenges with intersex disorders. *Reproductive, Fertility, Development, 10,* 79–85.

Warne, G. L., Zajac, J. D., & MacLeon, H. E. (1998). Androgen insensitivity syndrome in the era of molecular genetics and the Internet: A point of view. *Journal of Pediatric Endocrinology and Metabolism, 11,* 3–9.

Warne, M. M. (1998). Visual art as a factor in the quality of life for adults with cognitive disabilities. *Dissertations Abstracts International Section A: Humanities and Social Sciences, 59*(3-A): 0693.

Washington, P. A. (1999). Second assault of male survivors of sexual violence. *Journal of Interpersonal Violence, 14*(7), 713–730.

Watkins, E. S. (1998). *On the pill: A social history of oral contraceptives.* Baltimore, MD: Johns Hopkins University Press.

Watson, M. B., Stead, G. R., & de Jager, A. C. (1995). The career development of black and white South African university students. *International Journal for the Advancement of Counseling, 18*(1), 39–47.

Watson, M., Duvivier, V., Walsh, M. W., Ashley, S., Davidson, J., Papaikonomou, M., Murday, V., Sacks, N., & Eeles, R. (1998). Family history of breast cancer: What do women understand and recall about their genetic risk? *Journal of Medical Genetics, 35*(9), 731–738.

Watson, P. J., Biderman, J. D., & Sawyer, S. M. (1994). Empathy, sex role orientation and narcissism. *Sex Roles, 30,* 701–723.

Watts, J. (1999). When impotence leads contraception. *Lancet, 353*(9155), 819.

Way, N. (1995). "Can't you see the courage, the strength that I have?" Listening to urban adolescent girls speak about their relationships. *Psychology of Women Quarterly, 19*(1), 107–128.

Wear, D. (1997). *Privilege in the medical academy. A feminist examines gender, race, and power.* New York: Teachers College Press.

Weaver, J. B. (1994). Pornography and sexual callousness: The perceptual and behavioral consequences of exposure to pornography. In D. Zillman, J. Byrant, & A. C. Huston (Eds.), *Media, children and the family: Social, scientific, psychodynamic and clinical perspectives* (pp. 215–228). Mahwah, NJ: Erlbaum.

Webb, J. (1998). Sexual integration has harmed the military. In M. E. Williams, B. Stalcup, & K. L. Swisher (Eds.), *Working women: Opposing viewpoints* (pp. 137–146). San Diego, CA: Greenhaven Press.

Webb, R. E., & Daniluk, J. C. (1999). The end of the love: Infertile men's experiences of being unable to produce a child. *Men and Masculinities, 2*(1), 6–25.

Weber, L. (1998). A conceptual framework for understanding race, class, gender and sexuality. *Psychology of Women Quarterly, 22,* 13–32.

Websdale, N. (1998). *Rural woman battering and the justice system: An ethnography.* Thousand Oaks, CA: Sage.

Websdale, N., & Chesney-Lind, M. (1998). Doing violence to women. In L. H. Bowker (Ed.), *Masculinities and violence* (pp. 55–81). Thousand Oaks, CA: Sage.

Wechsberg, W. M., Craddock, G. G., & Hubbard, R. L. (1998). How are women who enter substance abuse treatment different from men? A gender comparison from DATOS. *Drugs and Society, 13*(1–2), 97–115.

Weinberg, M. S., Lottes, I. L., & Shaver, F. M. (1995). Swedish or American heterosexual college youth. Who is more permissive? *Archives of Sexual Behavior, 24*(4), 409–437.

Weinberg, M. S., Shaver, F. M., & Williams, C. J. (1999). Gendered sex work in the S.F. Tenderloin. *Archives of Sexual Behavior, 28*(6), 503–521.

Weinstock, L. S. (1999). Gender differences in the presentation and management of social anxiety disorder. *Journal of Clinical Psychiatry, 60*(Suppl. 9), 9–13.

Weis, D. L. (1998). The use of theory in sexuality research. *The Journal of Sex Research, 35*(1), 1–9.

Weisman, C. S. (1998). *Women's healthcare: Activist traditions and institutional change.* Baltimore: Johns Hopkins University Press, 1997.

Weisner, T. S. (1989a). Comparing sibling relationships across cultures. In P. G. Zukow (Ed.), *Sibling interaction across cultures: Theoretical and methodological issues* (pp. 11–25). NY: Springer.

Weisner, T. S. (1989b) Cultural and universal aspects of social support for children: Evidence from the Abuluyia of Kenya. In D. Belle (Ed.), *Children's social networks and social supports* (pp. 15–29). New York: Wiley.

Weiss, J. (1998). Making room for fathers. In L. McCall & D. Yacovone (Eds.), *A shared experience: Men, women and the history of gender* (pp. 349–365). New York: New York University Press.

Weissman, M. M., Bland, R., Joyce, P. R., Newman, S., Wells, J. E., & Wittchen, H. U. (1993). Sex differences in rates of depression: Cross-national perspectives. *Journal of Affective Disorders, 29,* 77–84.

Weisstein, N. (1977). "Kinde, Küche, Kirche" as scientific law: Psychology constructs the female. In R. Morgan (Ed.), *Sisterhood is powerful: An anthology of writings from the women's liberation movement* (pp. 228–245). New York: Vintage Books.

Weitz, R. (Ed.). (1998). *The politics of women's bodies.* New York: Oxford University Press.

Welch, D. P., Rostosky, S. S., & Kawaguchi, M. C. (2000). A normative perspective on adolescent girls developing sexuality. In C. B. Travis & J. W. White (Eds.), *Sexuality, society and feminism* (pp. 111–140). Washington, DC: American Psychological Association.

Welch-Ross, M. K., & Schmidt, C. R. (1996). Gender-schema development and children's constructive story memory. Evidence of a developmental model. *Child Development, 67,* 820–835.

Welter, B. (1978). The cult of true womanhood: 1820–1860. In M. Gordon (Ed.), *The American family in social-historical perspective* (2nd ed., pp. 313–333). New York: St. Martin's Press.

Wenger, N. K. (1998). Coronary heart disease in women: Evolution of our knowledge. In K. Orth-Gomer, M. Chesney, & N. K. Wegner (Eds.), *Women, stress and heart disease* (pp. 1–15). Mahwah, NJ: Erlbaum.

Werking, K. (1997). *We're just good friends: Women and men in nonromantic relationships.* New York: Guilford.

Wertham, F. (1954). *Seduction of the innocent.* New York: Rinehart.

West, C., & Fenstermaker, S. (1995). Doing difference. *Gender and Society, 9*(1), 8–37.

West, C., & Zimmerman, D. H. (1983). Small insults: A study of interruptions in cross-sex conversations between unacquainted persons. In B. Thorne, C. Kramarae, & N. Henley (Eds.), *Language, gender & society* (pp. 103–119). Rowley, MA: Newbury House.

West, C., & Zimmerman, D. H. (1985). Gender, language and discourse. In T. A. van Dijk (Ed.), *Handbook of discourse* analysis (Vol. 4, pp. 103–124). Orlando, FL: Academic Press.

West, C., & Zimmerman, D. H. (1987). Doing gender. Gender & Society, 1, 125–151.

Wetherell, M. (1997). Linguistic repertoires and literary criticism. New directions for a social psychology of gender. In M. M. Gergen & S. N. Davis (Eds.), Toward a new psychology of gender (pp. 149–165). New York: Routledge.

Wheeler, M. D. (1991). Physical changes of puberty. Endocrinology and Metabolism Clinics of North America, 20, 1–14.

White, J. W., & Koss, M. P. (1993). Adolescent sexual aggression within heterosexual relationships: Prevalence, characteristics, and causes. In H. E. Barbarbee, W. L. Marshall, & D. R. Laws (Eds.), The juvenile sexual offender (pp. 182–202). New York: Guilford Press.

White, J. W., & Kowalski, R. W. (1994). Deconstructing the myth of the nonaggressive woman: A feminist analysis. Psychology of Women Quarterly, 18, 487–508.

Whiteley, S. (1997). Sexing the groove: Popular music and gender. New York: Routledge.

Whiting, B. B., & Edwards, C. P. (1988). Children of different worlds: The formation of social behavior. Cambridge, MA: Harvard University Press.

Whitley, B. E. (1985). Sex-role orientation and psychological well-being: Two analyses. Sex Roles, 12, 207–225.

Whitley, B. E. (1997). Gender differences in computer related attitudes and behavior: A meta-analysis. Computers in Human Behavior, 13(1), 1–22.

Wickelgren, I. (1999). Discovery of "gay gene" questioned. Science, 284(5414), 571.

Widiger, T. A. (1998). Invited essay: Sex biases in the diagnosis of personality disorders. Journal of Personality Disorders, 12(2), 95–118.

Widmer, E. O., Treas, J., & Newcomb, R. (1998). Attitudes toward non-marital sex in 24 countries. Journal of Sex Research, 35(4), 349–358.

Wiederman, M. W. (1997). The truth must be in here somewhere: Examining the gender discrepancy in self-reported lifetime number of sex partners. Journal of Sex Research, 34, 375–386.

Wiederman, M. W., & Hurst, S. R. (1997). Physical attractiveness body image and women's sexual self-schema. Psychology of Women Quarterly, 21(4), 567–580.

Wiederman, M. W., & Hurst, S. R. (1998). Body size, physical attractiveness and body image among young adult women: Relationships to sexual experience and sexual esteem. Journal of Sex Research, 35(3), 272–281.

Wiederman, M., & Kendall, E. (1999). Evolution, sex and jealousy: Investigation with a sample from Sweden. Evolution and Human Behavior, 20(2), 121–128.

Wiest, W. M. (1977). Semantic differential profiles of orgasm and other experiences of men and women. Sex Roles, 3, 399–403.

Wilkie, C., Macdonald, S., & Hildahl, K. (1998). Community case study: Suicide clusters in a small Manitoba community. Canadian Journal of Psychiatry, 43(8), 823–828.

Willemsen, T. M. (1998). Widening the gender gap: Teenage magazines for girls and boys. Sex Roles, 38(9–10), 851–861.

Williams, C. L. (1995a). Gender differences at work. Berkeley: University of California Press.

Williams, C. L. (1995b). Still a man's world: Men who do women's work. Berkeley: University of California Press.

Williams, J. E., & Best, D. L. (1990). Measuring sex stereotypes: A multination study. Beverly Hills, CA: Sage.

Williams, J. E., & Best, D. L. (1994). Cross-cultural views of women and men. In W. J. Lonner & R. Malpass (Eds.), Psychology and culture (pp. 191–196). Boston: Allyn and Bacon.

Williams, M. E. (Ed.). (1998). Working women: Opposing viewpoints. San Diego: Greenhaven Press.

Wilsnack, S. C. (1995). Alcohol use and alcohol problems in women. In A. L. Stanton & S. J. Gallant (Eds.), The psychology of women's health: Progress and challenges in research and application (pp. 381–443). Washington, DC: American Psychological Association.

Wilson, J. D. (1999). The role of androgens in male gender role behavior. Endocrine Reviews, 20, 726-737.

Wilson, B. E., & Reiner, W. G. (1998). Management of intersex: A shifting paradigm. Journal of Clinical Ethics, 9(4), 360–370.

Wilson, K., & Gallois, C. (1993). Assertion and its social context. Oxford, England: Pergamon.

Wilson, M. H., Baker, S. P., Tenet, S. P., & Wilson, M. (1991). Saving children: A guide to injury prevention. New York: Oxford University Press.

Wilson, M., Daly, M., & Daniele, A. (1995). Familicide: The killing of spouse and children. Aggressive Behavior, 21, 275–291.

Wilson, R. (2000). Female scholars suggest slowing tenure clock. Chronicle of Higher Education, 47(18), A10.

Wingert, P., & Tesoriero, H. W. (2000, October 9). The abortion pill. Newsweek, pp. 26–30.

Wing-Foo, T., & Lee-Peng, K. (1995). Mental disorders in Singapore. In T. Lin, W. Tseng, & E. Yeh (Eds.), Chinese societies and mental health. Hong Kong: Oxford University Press.

Wingood, S., & Di Clemente, R. (1996). HIV sexual risk reduction: A review. American Journal of Preventive Medicine, 12, 209–217.

Winton, M. A. (2000). The medicalization of male sexual dysfunction: An analysis of sex therapy journals. Journal of Sex and Therapy, 25(4), 231–239.

Wisch, A. F., Mahalick, J. R., Hayes, J. A., & Nutt, E. A. (1995). The impact of gender role conflict and counseling technique on psychological help seeking in men. Sex Roles, 33, 77–89.

Witelson, S. F., Glezor, I. I. & Kigor, D. C. (1995). Women have greater density of neurons in posterior temporal cortex. Journal of Neuroscience, 15, 3418–3428.

Witkin, H. A., Lewis, H. B., Hertzman, M., Machover, K., Meissner, P. B., & Wapner, S. (1954). Personality through perception. New York: Harper & Row.

Witkin, H. A., Mednick, S. A., Schulsinger, F., Bakkstrom, E., Christiansen, K. O., Goodenough, D. R., Hirschhorn, K., Lundsteen, C., Owen, D. R., Philip, J., Rubin, D., & Stocking, M. (1976). Criminality in XYY and XXY men. Science, 193, 547–555.

Witt, S. D. (1996). Traditional or androgynous: An analysis to determine gender role orientation of basal readers. Child Study Journal, 26(4), 303–318.

Witt, Susan D. (2000). The influence of television on children's gender role socialization. Journal of Childhood Education: Infancy Through Adolescence, 76(5), 322–324.

Witzig, R. (1996). The medicalization of race: Scientific legitimization of a flawed social construct. *Annals of Internal Medicine, 125,* 675–679.

Wolf, M. (1972). *Women and the family in rural Taiwan.* Palo Alto, CA: Stanford University Press.

Wolf, N. (1991). *The beauty myth: How images of beauty are used against women.* New York: Morrow.

Wollstonecraft, M. (1929). *A vindication of the rights of woman.* New York: Dutton. Original work published 1792.

Womankind News. (1999, March 29). Move to save £millions of taxpayers money wasted overseas as a result of female circumcision. [Press release]. Available online at http://www.womankind.org.uk/9h%20news%2029.htm. Retrieved April 22, 2002.Wong, M. G. (1995). Chinese-Americans. In G. P. Min (Ed.), *Asian-Americans* (pp. 58–94). Thousand Oaks, CA: Sage.

Women smell better. (2002, March 13). Online at http://www.winetoday.co.za/pages/news/singlepage.asp?in=100. Retrieved April 21, 2002.

Wood, J. T. (1994). *Gendered lives: Communication, gender and culture.* Belmont, CA: Wadsworth.

Wood, J. T. (Ed.). (1996). *Gendered relationships.* Mountain View, CA: Mayfield.

Wood, W., Christensen, P. N., Hebl, M. R., & Rothgerber, H. (1997). Conformity to sex-typed norms, affect and the self-concept. *Journal of Personality & Social Psychology, 73,* 523–535.

World Health Organization. (1998). *The World Health Report 1998: Life in the 21st century—a vision for all.* Geneva: Author.

Worrell, J., & Etaugh, C. (1994). Transforming theory and research with women. Themes and variations. *Psychology of Women Quarterly, 18,* 443–450.

Wright, E. O., & Baxter, J. (1995). The gender gap in workplace authority: A cross-cultural study. *American Sociological Review, 60*(3), 407–435.

Wright, E. O., Baxter, J., & Birkelund, G. E. (1995). The gender gap in workplace authority: A cross-national study. *American Sociological Review, 60,* 407–435.

Wright, P. H. (1982). Men's friendships, women's friendships and the alleged inferiority of the latter. *Sex Roles, 8,* 1–20.

Wright, P. H. (1998). Toward an expanded orientation to the study of sex differences in friendship. In D. J. Canary & K. Dindia (Eds.), *Sex differences and similarities in communication* (pp. 41–63). Mahwah, NJ: Erlbaum.

Wright, R. A., Murray, J. B., Storey, P. L., & Williams, B. J. (1997). Ability analysis of gender relevance and sex differences in cardiovascular response to behavioral challenge. *Journal of Personality & Social Psychology, 73*(2), 405–417.

Wright, W. (1999). *Born that way: Genes, behavior, and personality.* New York: Routledge.

Wu, L. C. (1986). *Fundamentals of Chinese philosophy.* New York: Lanham.

Wu, Y., & Smith, D. E. (1997). Self-esteem in Taiwanese children. *Child Study Journal, 27*(1), 1–19.

Wulff, M. B., & Steitz, J. A. (1997). Curricular track, career choice, and androgyny among adolescent females. *Adolescence, 32*(125), 43–49.

Wurzburg, L. A., & Klonoff, R.H. (1997). Legal approaches to sex discrimination. In H. Landrine & E. A. Klonoff (Eds.), *Discrimination against women: Prevalence, consequences and remedies* (pp. 175–195). Thousand Oaks, CA: Sage.

Wyatt, G. E. (1994). The sociocultural relevance of sex research. Challenges for the 1990s and beyond. *American Psychologist, 49,* 748–754.

Wyke, S., Hunt, K., & Ford, G. (1998). Gender differences in consulting a general practitioner for common symptoms of minor illness. *Social Science & Medicine, 46*(7), 901–906.

Wynn, T. G., Tierson, F. D., & Palmer, C. T. (1996). Evolution of sex differences in spatial cognition. *Yearbook of Physical Anthropology, 39,* 11–42.

Xiao, H. (2000). Class, gender and parental values in the 1990's. *Gender and Society, 14*(6), 785–803.

Xiaohe, X., & Whyte, M. K. (1990). Love matches and arranged marriages: A Chinese replication. *Journal of Marriage & the Family, 52,* 709–722.

Yacobi, E., Tennant, C., Ferrante, J., Pal, N., & Roetzheim, R. (1999). University students' knowledge and awareness of HPV. *Preventive Medicine, 28*(6), 535–541.

Yamada, E. M., Tjosvold, D., & Draguns, J. G. (1987). Effects of sex-linked situations and sex composition on cooperation and style of interaction. *Sex Roles, 9,* 941–953.

Yang, B., Ollendick, T. H., Dong, Q., Xia, Y., & Lin, L. (1995). Only children and children with siblings in People's Republic of China: Levels of fear, anxiety and depression. *Child Development, 66*(5), 1301–1311.

Yap, P. M. (1967). Classification of the culture-bound reactive syndromes. *Australian and New Zealand Journal of Psychiatry, 1,* 172.

Yap, P. M. (1974). *Comparative psychiatry: A theoretical framework.* Toronto: University of Toronto.

Ybarra, M. J. (1999, December). Why won't women write code? *Sky Magazine,* pp. 40–42.

Yee, B. W. K., Huang, L. N., & Lew, A. (1998). Families: Life-span socialization in a cultural context. In L. C. Lee & N. W. S. Zane (Eds.), *Handbook of Asian American Psychology* (pp. 83–136). Thousand Oaks, CA: Sage.

Yee, J. L., & Schulz, R. (2000). Gender differences in psychiatric morbidity among family caregivers: A review and analysis. *The Gerontologist, 40,* 147–164.

Yelsma, P., & Athappilly, K. (1988). Marital satisfaction and communication practices: Comparisons among Indian and American couples. *Journal of Comparative Family Studies, 19,* 37–54.

Yildirim, A. (1997). Gender role influences on Turkish adolescents' self-identity. *Adolescence, 32*(125), 216–231.

Ying, Y., Lee, P. A., Tsui, J. L., Yeh, Y., & Huang, J. S. (2000). The conception of depression in Chinese-American college students. *Cultural Diversity and Ethnic Minority Psychology, 6*(2), 183–195.

Yoder, J. D., & Kahn, A. S. (1993). Working toward an inclusive psychology of women. *American Psychologist, 48,* 846–850.

Yoder, J. D., Schleicher, T. L., & McDonald, T. W. (1998). Empowering token women leaders: The importance of organizationally legitimated credibility. *Psychology of Women Quarterly, 22,* 209–222.

Young, E., & Korszun, A. (1999). Women stress and depression: Sex differences in hypothalamic-pituitary-adrenal axis regulation. In E. Leibenluft (Ed.), *Gender differences in mood and anxiety disorders* (pp. 31–48). Washington, DC: American Psychiatric Press.

Young, K. K. (1994). Introduction. In A. Sharma (Ed.), *Today's woman in world re-*

ligions (pp. 1–38). Albany: State University of New York (SUNY) Press.

Yu-huan, H., Ying-guan, Q., & Gui-qing, Z. (1990). Crossed aphasia in Chinese: A clinical survey. Brain and Language, 39, 347–356.

Yuksel, S., Kulaksizoglu, I. B., Turksoy, N., & Sahin, D. (2000). Group psychotherapy with female to male transsexuals in Turkey. Archives of Sexual Behavior, 29(3), 279–290.

Zang, E. A., & Winder, E. L. (1996). Differences in lung cancer risk between men and women: Examination of the evidence. Journal of the National Cancer Institute, 88, 183–192.

Zarit, S. H., Johansson, L., & Jarrott, S. E. (1998). Family caregiving: Stresses, social programs and cultural interventions. In I. H. Nordhus, G. R. VandenBos, S. Berg, & P. Fromholt (Eds.), Clinical geropsychology (pp. 345–360). Washington, DC: American Psychological Association.

Zemach, T., & Cohen, A. A. (1986). Perceptions of gender equality on television and in social reality. Journal of Broadcasting and Electronic Media, 30, 427–444.

Zhang, C. X., & Farley, J. E. (1995). Gender and the distribution of household work: A comparison of self-report by female college faculty in the US and Cuba. Journal of Comparative Family Studies, 26(2), 195–205.

Zhou, J., Hofman, M., Gooren, L., & Swaab, D. (1995). A sex difference in the human brain and its relation to transsexuality. Nature, 378, 68–70.

Zihlman, A. (1996). Reconstructions reconsidered: Chimpanzee models and human evolution. In W. C. McGrew, L. F. Marchant, & T. Nishida (Eds.), Great ape societies. Cambridge, England: Cambridge University Press.

Zilbergeld, B. (1992). The new male sexuality. New York: Bantam Books.

Zillman, D., & Bryant, J. (1989). Pornography: Research advances and policy considerations. Mahwah, NJ: Erlbaum.

Zillman, D., & Weaver, J. B., III. (1999). Effects of prolonged exposure to gratuitous media violence on provoked and unprovoked hostile behavior. Journal of Applied Social Psychology, 29, 145–165.

Zimbardo, P. G., Keough, K. A., & Boyd, J. N. (1997). Present time perspective as a predictor of risky driving. Personality and Individual Differences, 23(6), 1007-1023.

Zimmerman, M. K., & Hill, S. A. (1999). Health care as a gendered system. In J. S. Chavetz (Ed.), Handbook of the sociology of gender (pp. 483–518). New York: Kluwer Academic/Plenum.

Zita, J. (1998). Body talk: Philosophical reflections of sex and gender. New York: Columbia University Press.

Zlotnick, C., Hohlstein, L. A., Shea, M. T., Pearlstein, T., Recupero, P., & Bidadi, K. (1996). The relationship between sexual abuse and eating pathology. International Journal of Eating Disorders, 20, 129–134.

Zoch, L. M., & Turk, J. V. (1998). Women making news: Gender as a variable in source selection and use. Journalism and Mass Communication Quarterly, 75(4), 762–775.

Zucker, K. J., & Bradley, S. J. (1995). Gender identity disorder and psychosexual problems in children & adolescents. New York: Guilford.

Zucker, K. J., Bradley, S. J., & Sanikhani, M. (1997). Sex differences in referral rates of children with gender identity disorder: Some hypotheses. Journal of Abnormal Child Psychology, 25(3), 217–227.

Zucker, K. J., Wilson-Smith, D. N., Kurita, J. A., & Stern, A. (1995). Children's appraisals of sex typed behavior in their peers. Sex Roles, 33, 703–725.

Zuo, J. (1997). The effects of men's breadwinner status on their changing gender beliefs. Sex Roles, 37(9–10), 799–816.

Zweigenhaft, R. L., & Domhoff, G. W. (1998). Diversity in the power elite: Have women and minorities reached the top? New Haven, CT: Yale University Press.

Credits

This section constitutes an extension of the copyright page. We have made every effort to trace the ownership of all copyrighted material and to secure permission from copyright holders. In the event of any question arising as to the use of any material, we will be pleased to make the necessary corrections in future printings. Thanks are due to the following authors, publishers, and agents for permission to use the material indicated.

Box 1.3 Adapted from N. Dresser (1996), *Multicultural Manners* (New York: Wiley).
Figure 1.3 © The New Yorker Collection 1996, Ed Frascino from cartoonbank.com. All Rights Reserved.
Table 2.1 "Sex-Role Stereotypes: A Current Appraisal" by I. K. Broverman, S. R. Vogel, D. M. Broverman, F. E. Carlson, and P. S. Rosenkrantz, *Journal of Social Issues*, 1972, pp. 59–78. Copyright © 1972. Reprinted by permission.
Table 2.2 "Cross Cultural Views of Women and Men" by J. E. Williams and D. L. Best, in *Psychology and Culture*, edited by W. J. Lonner and R. Malpass. Published by Allyn and Bacon, Boston, MA. Copyright © 1994 by Pearson Education. Reprinted by permission of the publisher.
Table 3.2 E. Erikson (1985), *The Life Cycle Completed* (New York: Norton).
Figure 4.1 Drawings adapted from *Our Sexuality*, 8th Ed., by R. L. Crooks and K. Baur. Pacific Grove, CA: Wadsworth. Copyright © 2002. Reprinted with permission of Wadsworth, an imprint of the Wadsworth Group, a division of Thomson Learning. Fax 800/730-2215.
Table 4.1 "Sexual Differentiation of the Human Hypothalamus in Relation to Gender and Sexual Orientation" by D. F. Swaab and M. A. Hofman, *Trends in Neuroscience, 18,* 1995, pp. 264–270. Copyright © 1995. Reprinted by permission of Elsevier.
Table 4.2 From "Public Policy Implications of Sex Differences in Cognitive Abilities" by D. Halpern, in *Psychology, Public Policy and Law,* 1996, p. 564. Copyright © 1996 by American Psychological Association. Reprinted with permission.
Table 4.3 From "Gender Differences in Cognition: A Minefield of Research Issues" by T. MacIntyre, *Irish Journal of Psychology,* 1997,

18(4), p. 393. Reprinted by permission of Psychological Society of Ireland.
Table 4.4 From "Creating Gender Equality" by D. P. Baker and D. P. Jones, in *Sociology of Education*, 1993, p. 91. Copyright © 1993. Reprinted by permission of American Sociological Association.
Table 6.1 From "Young Singles Contemporary Dating Scripts" by S. Rose and I. H. Frieze in *Sex Roles, 28,* 1993, pp. 499–509. Copyright © 1993. Reprinted by permission of Kluwer Academic/Plenum Publishing.
Table 6.2 From "Gender Differences in Scripts for Different Types of Dates" by C. Alksnis, S. Desmarais, and E. Wood in *Sex Roles, 34*(5/6), 1996, p. 332. Copyright © 1996. Reprinted by permission of Kluwer Academic/Plenum Publishing.
Figure 6.1 Reprinted with special permission of King Features Syndicate.
Table 6.3 From *Engendering Motherhood: Identity and Self-Transformation in Women* by M. McMahon, pp. 197, 207. New York: Guilford. Copyright © 1995. Reprinted by permission of Guilford.
Box 6.2 "Meanings of Chocolate: Power and Gender in Valentine's Gift Giving" by Y. Ogasawara, *International Journal of Japanese Sociology, 5,* 1996, pp. 41–61.
Table 7.1 From J. E. Williams and D. L. Best, *Measuring Sex Stereotypes: A Multination Study.* Thousand Oaks, CA: Sage Publications. Copyright © 1990. Reprinted by permission of Sage Publications, Inc.
Figure 7.1 © The New Yorker Collection 1995, J. B. Handelsman from cartoonbank. com. All Rights Reserved.
Figure 7.2 STONE SOUP © 1999 Jan Eliot. Reprinted with permission of UNIVERSAL PRESS SYNDICATE. All rights reserved.
Table 7.2 From the *Bem Sex Role Inventory* by Sandra Bem. Reproduced by special permission of the Distributor, MIND GARDEN, Inc., 1690 Woodside Road #202, Redwood City, CA 94061 USA. www. mindgarden.com. Copyright 1978 by Consulting Psychologists Press, Inc. All rights reserved. Further reproduction is prohibited without the Distributor's written consent.
Figure 8.1 From *Our Sexuality*, 8th Ed., by R. L. Crooks and K. Baur. Pacific Grove, CA: Wadsworth. Copyright © 2002. Reprinted with permission of Wadsworth, an imprint of

the Wadsworth Group, a division of Thomson Learning. Fax 800/730-2215.
Figure 8.2 From *Our Sexuality*, 8th Ed., by R. L. Crooks and K. Baur. Pacific Grove, CA: Wadsworth. Copyright © 2002. Reprinted with permission of Wadsworth, an imprint of the Wadsworth Group, a division of Thomson Learning. Fax 800/730-2215.
Table 8.1 "Attitudes Toward Nonmarital Sex in 24 Countries" by E. D. Widmer, J. Treas, and R. Newcomb, *Journal of Sex Research, 35*(4), 1998, pp. 349–358. Copyright © 1998. Reprinted by permission of Society for the Scientific Study of Sexuality.
Table 8.2 From *JAMA, 281*(3), January 20, 1999, p. 276. Copyright © 1999. American Medical Association, Chicago, IL.
Figure 8.4 © The New Yorker Collection 1998, Robert Weber from cartoonbank.com. All Rights Reserved.
Figure 9.1 DILBERT © UFS. Reprinted by Permission.
Figure 9.2 (a and b) From *Scientific American,* May 1997. Copyright © 1997. Reprinted by permission.
Table 9.1 Adapted from *Fact File*, as published in *Chronicle of Higher Education,* January 18, 2000, 46(21): A50–51. Original source: *The American Freshman: National Norms for Fall 1999.* Published by American Council on Education and University of California at Los Angeles, Higher Education Research Institute.
Table 9.2 Adapted from *Fact File*, as published in *Chronicle of Higher Education,* January 18, 2000, 46(21): A50–51. Original source: *The American Freshman: National Norms for Fall 1999.* Published by American Council on Education and University of California at Los Angeles, Higher Education Research Institute.
Figure 9.4 From "Listening to Smaller Voices" by Victoria Johnson, Joanne Hill, and Edda Ivan-Smith, in *ActionAid*, London, 1995.
Table 10.1 From *Managing Like a Man* by J. Wajcman, p. 88. University Park: Penn State University Press. Copyright © 1998. Reprinted by permission of Penn State University Press.
Table 10.2 From *Where Women Stand* by N. Neft and A. D. Levine, pp. 55–56. New York: Random House. Copyright © 1997. Reprinted by permission of Random House, Inc.

Table 10.3 Adapted from Bureau of Labor Statistics (January, 2000), *Employment and Earnings, 47*(1), Table 39, pp. 213–218.

Figure 10.2 Adapted from C. B. Costello and B. K. Kringold (Eds.), *The American Woman 1996–1997*, p. 47. New York: W. W. Norton, 1998. Update (from 1994 to 1997) from Bureau of Labor Statistics (January, 2000), *Employment & Earnings, 47* (1), Table A-2, p. 11.

Figure 10.3 © The New Yorker Collection 1995, Kenneth Mahood from cartoonbank.com. All Rights Reserved.

Page 237 "We Real Cool" by Gwendolyn Brooks. Reprinted by permission of the estate of Gwendolyn Brooks.

Table 11.1 Association of American Medical Colleges (2002). Table B8, Women Enrollment and Graduates in U.S. Medical Schools. From DW: Student Section, 1992–93 to present. Information obtained from Collins Mikesell, Sr. Research Associate, Section for Student Services, Association of American Medical Colleges, 2501 M Street, NW, Washington, DC 20037, cmikesell@aamc.org.

Table 11.2 Association of American Medical Colleges (2002). Table B8, Women Enrollment and Graduates in U.S. Medical Schools. From DW: Student Section, 1992–93 to present. Information obtained from Collins Mikesell, Sr. Research Associate, Section for Student Services, Association of American Medical Colleges, 2501 M Street, NW, Washington, DC 20037, cmikesell@aamc.org.

Table 11.3 Population Reference Bureau (1999). World Population Data Sheet. Washington, DC: Author.

Table 11.4 Adapted from D. L. Hoyert, K. D. Kochanek, and S. L. Murphy, "Deaths: Final Data for 1997," *National Vital Statistics Report*, 1999, 47(19), 5.

Table 11.5 Adapted from W. H. Courtenay (2000a), "Behavioral Factors Associated With Male Disease, Injury, and Death: Evidence and Implications for Prevention," *Journal of Men's Studies*, 9(1), 81–142; and W. H. Courtenay (2000b), "Constructions of Masculinity and Their Influence on Men's Well-Being: A Theory of Gender and Health," *Social Science and Medicine*, 50(10), 1385–1401.

Figure 11.2 "Mapping the AIDS Epidemic's Hot Zone" from *Newsweek*, January 17, 2000, p. 37. Copyright © 2000 Newsweek, Inc. All rights reserved. Reprinted by permission.

Figure 11.3 © The New Yorker Collection 2000, Bruce Eric Kaplan from cartoonbank.com. All Rights Reserved.

Table 11.6 Source: K. D. Peters, M. A. Kochanek, S. L. Murphy (1998), "Report of Final Mortality Statistics, 1996." *National Vital Statistics Reports*, 47(9), 6.

Table 12.1 Adapted from C. M. Hartung and T. A. Widiger (1998), "Gender Differences in the Diagnosis of Mental Disorders: Conclusions and Controversies of the DSM-IV,"

Psychological Bulletin, 123(2), 260–278. Adapted from R. C. Kessler, K. A. McGonagle, K. A. Zhao, C. B. Nelson, et al. (1994), "Lifetime and 12-Month Prevalence of DSM-IIIR Psychiatric Disorders in the United States. Results from the National Co-morbidity Study." *Archive of General Psychiatry, 51*, 8–19.

Table 12.2 Adapted from C. M. Hartung and T. A. Widiger, (1998), "Gender Differences in the Diagnosis of Mental Disorders: Conclusions and Controversies of the DSM-IV," *Psychological Bulletin, 123*(2), 260–278.

Box 12.3 From *Sex and Gender: Student Projects and Exercises* by C. A. Rickabaugh, pp. 281–286. New York: McGraw-Hill. Copyright © 1998. Reprinted by permission of The McGraw-Hill Companies, Inc.

Figure 13.6 "Internet Pornography" from *Newsweek*, June 12, 2000. Copyright © 2000 Newsweek, Inc. All rights reserved. Reprinted by permission.

Table 14.1 From "Consent, Power, and Sexual Scripts" by S. B. Kurth, B. B. Spiller, and C. B. Travis, in C. B. Travis and J. W. White (Eds.), *Sexuality, Society and Feminism*, pp. 323–354. Copyright © 2000 by American Psychological Association. Reprinted by permission.

Table 14.2 "Prevalence and Consequences of Male-to-Female and Female-to-Male Intimate Partner Violence as Measured by the National Violence Against Women Survey" by P. Tjaden and N. Thoennes, in *Violence Against Women*, 6(2), pp. 142–161. Copyright © 2000. Reprinted by permission of Sage Publications, Inc.

Table 14.3 Adapted from *Equality Denied, The Status of Women in Policing, 1998*, copyright 1999, National Center for Women and Policing, a division of Feminist Majority Foundation, as cited in M. E. Gold (1999), *Top Cops*. Chicago, IL: Brittany Publications.

Table 14.4 "Introduction" from *Women and Elective Office* by S. Thomas and C. Wilcox, pp. 1–14. Copyright © 1998. Reprinted by permission of Oxford University Press.

Table 14.5 Adapted from B. L. Moore and S. C. Webb (2000), "Perceptions of Equal Opportunity Among Women and Minority Army Personnel," *Sociological Inquiry, 70* (2), 215–239; D. Priest (1998), "Sexual Integration Has Not Harmed the Military," in B. Leone (Ed.), *Working Women: Opposing Viewpoints* (pp. 129–139), San Diego: Greenhaven Press; J. Webb (1998), "Sexual Integration Has Harmed the Military," in B. Leone (Ed.), *Working Women: Opposing Viewpoints* (pp. 137–146), San Diego, CA: Greenhaven Press.

Figure 15.1 From "Living on a Fault Line" by Lisa Bennett, *Human Rights Campaign Quarterly*, Winter 2001, p. 11.

Figure 15.2 © The New Yorker Collection 2000, Davied Sipress from cartoonbank.com. All Rights Reserved.

Photo Credits

Figure 1.1 (left) Corbis; **Figure 1.1 (top right)** Rhonda Klevansky/Getty Images; **Figure 1.1 (bottom right)** HAGA Library/The Image Works.

Figure 2.2 (top) David R. Frazier/The Image Works; **Figure 2.2 (bottom)** Wayne Bilenduke/Getty Images.

Figure 3.1 (top left) Ken Usami/Getty Images; **Figure 3.1 (top right)** Michael K. Nichols/Getty Images; **Figure 3.1 (top middle)** Manoj Shah/Getty Images; **Figure 3.1 (bottom)** Kevin Schafer/Corbis.

Figure 4.3(a) Courtesy of *Chrysalis*; **Figure 4.3(b)** Courtesy of Intersex Society of North America; **Figure 4.3(c)** *Our Sexuality*, 8th Ed., by R. L. Crooks and K. Baur, Pacific Grove, CA: Wadsworth, 2002; **Figure 4.3(d)** From the collections of the Wangensteen Historical Library of Biology and Medicine, Bio-Medical Library, University of Minnesota.

Figure 5.1 Bob Daemmrich Photography, Inc./The Image Works.

Figure 8.3 David Young-Wolff/PhotoEdit.

Figure 9.3 (top) Corbis; **Figure 9.3 (bottom)** David & Peter Tumley/Corbis.

Figure 10.1 National Archives and Records Administration.

Figure 11.1 (top right) Michael Newman/PhotoEdit; **Figure 11.1 (bottom left)** Charles Thatcher/Getty Images.

Box 11.5 Khalil Senosi/AP Photo.

Figure 12.1 (left) Custom Medical Stock Photo; **Figure 12.1 (right)** Custom Medical Stock Photo.

Figure 12.2 (left) William Pugliano Photography, courtesy of Lynn Conway; **Figure 12.2 (right)** Kevin Bubriski/Beacon Press.

Figure 13.1 (left) Erich Lessing/Naturhistorisches Museum, Vienna, Austria/PhotoEdit; **Figure 13.1 (right)** Holton Collection/SuperStock.

Figure 13.2 Bill Aron/PhotoEdit.

Figure 13.3(a) Billy E. Barnes/PhotoEdit; **Figure 13.3(b)** Michael Newman/PhotoEdit; **Figure 13.3(c)** Bill Aron/PhotoEdit; **Figure 13.3(d)** Susan Van Etten/PhotoEdit.

Figure 13.4 (top) Davis Barber/PhotoEdit; **Figure 13.4 (bottom)** Michael Newman/PhotoEdit.

Figure 13.5 Bill Aron/PhotoEdit.

Figure 13.7 (top left) Corbis; **Figure 13.7 (top right)** EyeWire/Getty Images; **Figure 13.7 (bottom)** Corbis.

Figure 14.1 Corbis.

Figure 14.2 Michael Newman/PhotoEdit.

Figure 14.3 Eric Roxfelt/AP Photo.

Figure 14.4 Joe Marquette/AP Photo.

Figure 14.5 George Hall/Corbis.

Figure 14.6 Christine Osborne/Corbis.

Name Index

Subject Index

TO THE OWNER OF THIS BOOK:

We hope that you have found *Gender: Crossing Boundaries* useful. So that this book can be improved in a future edition, would you take the time to complete this sheet and return it? Thank you.

School and address: _____

Department: _____

Instructor's name: _____

1. What I like most about this book is: _____

_____

_____

2. What I like least about this book is: _____

_____

_____

3. My general reaction to this book is: _____

_____

4. The name of the course in which I used this book is: _____

_____

5. Were all of the chapters of the book assigned for you to read? _____

    If not, which ones weren't? _____

6. In the space below, or on a separate sheet of paper, please write specific suggestions for improving this book and anything else you'd care to share about your experience in using the book.

_____

_____

_____

_____

_____

Optional:

Your name: _____ Date: _____

May Wadsworth quote you, either in promotion for *Gender: Crossing Boundaries* or in future publishing ventures?

Yes: _____ No: _____

Sincerely,

Grace Galliano

FOLD HERE

BUSINESS REPLY MAIL

FIRST CLASS   PERMIT NO. 358   PACIFIC GROVE, CA

POSTAGE WILL BE PAID BY ADDRESSEE

ATT: Grace Galliano _____

Brooks/Cole Publishing Company
511 Forest Lodge Road
Pacific Grove, California 93950-9968

FOLD HERE

CPSIA information can be obtained
at www.ICGtesting.com
Printed in the USA
FFOW04n0056210714
6425FF